Fodor's

ESSENTIAL
ISRAEL

Welcome to Israel

Little did we realize that the emergence of a novel coronavirus in early 2020 would abruptly bring almost all travel to a halt. Although our Fodor's writers around the world have continued working to bring you, our readers, the best of the destinations they cover, we still anticipate that more than the usual number of businesses will close permanently in the coming months, perhaps with little advance notice. We don't expect that things will return to "normal" for some time. As you plan your upcoming travels to Israel, please reconfirm that places are still open and let us know when we need to make updates by writing to us at editors@fodors.com.

TOP REASONS TO GO

★ **Jerusalem:** This unique, golden-stone city is the crossroads of three faiths.

★ **Ancient Sites:** Masada, Megiddo, Caesarea, and others reveal millennia of history.

★ **Open-Air Markets:** Bustling crowds, fragrant foods, and colorful artisan gifts beckon.

★ **Desert Adventures:** Memorable camel treks, jeep rides, and hikes await in the Negev.

★ **Local Food:** Falafel, hummus, grilled fish, and Israeli wine tempt the palate.

★ **Biblical Landscapes:** Around the Galilee, scenes evoke New Testament scriptures.

Contents

Fodor's Features

MAPS

Chapter 1

EXPERIENCE ISRAEL

25 ULTIMATE EXPERIENCES

Israel offers terrific experiences that should be on every traveler's list. Here are Fodor's top picks for a memorable trip.

1 Float in the Dead Sea

Located at the lowest point on Earth, the Dead Sea is so named because its high salt content can support no aquatic life. It also means you'll float effortlessly in the water and soak up mineral-rich mud that famously heals everything from psoriasis to muscle aches. *(Ch. 4)*

2 Admire Ruins in Caesarea

Boasting some of Israel's most pristine beaches, this seaside town is also teeming with Roman, Byzantine, and Crusader ruins. *(Ch. 6)*

3 Eat an Israeli Breakfast

Offered in virtually every hotel and restaurant, the "Israeli breakfast" is a smorgasbord of veggies, fruits, cheeses, yogurts, smoked salmon, and eggs. *(Ch. 3, 5)*

4 See the Baha'i Shrine and Gardens

Haifa's stunning shrines and terraced gardens on the northern slope of the Carmel Mountain offer unparalleled views and a chance to learn more about the Baha'i faith. *(Ch. 6)*

5 Tour a Winery (or Three)

With more than 300 wineries, Israel has large-scale producers and small boutique wineries, some a few decades old and others a few centuries. Arguably the most famous is Golan Heights Winery. *(Ch. 6, 8)*

6 Stay in Boutique Hotels

Thanks to a tourism boom, a wave of small new hotels catering to every kind of tourist have cropped up, including the effortlessly luxurious Norman Hotel in Tel Aviv. *(Ch. 5)*

7 Sample Seafood

Israel's location on the Mediterranean coast means an abundance of seafood. Head to coastal towns like Akko for the best shrimp, calamari, sole, and more. *(Ch. 6)*

8 Wander Tel Aviv's Neighborhoods

Israel's cultural hub boasts at least 17 neighborhoods with plentiful culture, food, and history. Don't miss the small, colorful streets of Neve Tzedek. *(Ch. 5)*

9 Hike the Red Canyon

Take a day trip from Eilat and into the Negev to see this beautiful canyon, which was eroded by water and formed gradually over many years. *(Ch. 9)*

10 Sip Coffee at a Café

Israel's café culture is stronger than ever, its brews tasty enough to rival those in Rome or Vienna. People-watch over a *café hafuch*, or "upside-down latte" in Tel Aviv or Jerusalem. *(Ch. 3, 5)*

11 Explore the Sea of Galilee

It's believed that Jesus walked on water at Israel's largest freshwater lake, which is surrounded by a bevy of Christian sites and hiking paths. *(Ch. 7)*

12 Remember the Holocaust

Israel's official Holocaust memorial and museum, Yad Vashem, is home to powerful galleries including survivor testimonies, artifacts, photographs, and art installations. *(Ch. 3)*

13 Hop to Art Galleries

Of the many art galleries in Israel, highlights include Tel Aviv's Ilana Goor Museum, Florentin's progressive and makeshift art galleries, and the artists' colony in Tzfat. *(Ch. 5, 8)*

14 Soak Up History in Jerusalem

As the home to holy sites of all three monotheistic religions—Judaism, Islam, and Christianity—Jerusalem's Old City is a fascinating lesson in religion and history. *(Ch. 3)*

15 Make a Trip to Bethlehem

The "Little Town of Bethlehem" bustles with festivities during the Christmas and New Year's season, but it's a worthwhile and, at times, fraught destination year-round. *(Ch. 4)*

16 Party in Tel Aviv

The young, fervently secular city is home to seriously cool nightclubs, wine bars, and neighborhood pubs that feel a thousand miles from the politics of nearby Jerusalem. *(Ch. 5)*

17 Take a Dip in the Jordan River

The source of the Jordan River, the stream that led the Israelites to the Promised Land and which served the waters for Jesus's baptism, is one of Israel's most popular kayaking spots. *(Ch. 8)*

18 Try the Street Food

Colorful, bold, casual, and inevitably very messy, Israel's street food is everywhere—and it's a must. Add falafel and *sabich* (stuffed pita) to your list. *(Ch. 3–9)*

19 Visit Akko, the Ancient Seaport

Beloved for its centuries-old ruins and world-famous hummus, the UNESCO-heritage city has been shaped by the Crusaders, Romans, Ottomans, and Byzantines. *(Ch. 6)*

20 Take in Views From Masada

Hike or take a cable car up to the historic fortress for views of the Negev Desert and the Dead Sea and to reflect on its past as a final front between the Jews and Romans. *(Ch. 4)*

21 Venture into the Negev Desert

Craters, multicolor mountains, Bedouin villages, and rustic kibbutzim await adventure-seekers looking to bike, hike, or Jeep through the desert's breathtaking scenery. *(Ch. 9)*

22 Explore Nature Reserves

More than 400 nature reserves are home to Israel's stunning scenery, wildlife, and archaeological sites. Visit Tel Dan Nature Reserve for hiking paths weaving along streams. *(Ch. 8)*

23 Shop at Israeli Markets

Markets are Israeli cities' beating hearts. Browse Carmel Market in Tel Aviv and Machaneh Yehuda in Jerusalem for souvenirs, seasonal produce, and bites from food stalls. *(Ch. 3, 5)*

24 Make a Side Trip to Petra

Jordan's ancient city is a thrilling, easy side trip from Eilat, and its red ruins are perhaps even more majestic for having survived centuries of earthquakes and neglect. *(Ch. 10)*

25 Dive at Eilat's Beaches

Israel's southern city located on the dazzling shores of the Red Sea enjoys beach season virtually year-round. Take a diving class or snorkel at Coral Beach Nature Reserve. *(Ch. 9)*

WHAT'S WHERE

1 Jerusalem. The walls of the Old City embrace sites sacred to Judaism, Christianity, and Islam. Rub shoulders in the vibrant markets, sip coffee in a stone courtyard, and poke around the modern museums and tempting malls.

2 Around Jerusalem and the Dead Sea. Explore King Herod's mountaintop palace-citadel of Masada, float in the super-saline Dead Sea, or frolic under waterfalls in the Ein Gedi canyon. Bethlehem is another memorable option.

3 Tel Aviv. The "city that never sleeps" is Israel's cultural and entertainment center. Don't miss its beautiful beaches, lively seaside promenade, Bauhaus architecture, charming old neighborhoods, and first-class restaurants and nightlife.

4 Haifa and the Northern Coast. Although you're never far from a beach, take time to see the sights in Haifa, like the Baha'i Shrine and Gardens, and Akko's medieval Old City. South of Haifa are the ruins of Caesarea and the hills of Mount Carmel wine country.

5 Lower Galilee. Verdant valleys, rolling hills, and the freshwater Sea of Galilee are counterpoints to the historical riches in this region. Hike the Arbel cliffs, explore archaeology at Beit She'an and Zippori, and visit Nazareth.

6 Upper Galilee and the Golan. Historical treasures, quaint B&Bs, and the great outdoors draw visitors to Israel's northeast corner. The mountaintop city of Tzfat (Safed), cradle of Jewish mysticism, and Rosh Pina, a delightful restored village, are major draws, as well as Tel Dan Nature Reserve.

7 Eilat and the Negev. Visiting the Negev is about experiencing the desert's quiet vistas and remarkable geological treasures, and enjoying Eilat's gorgeous beaches and Red Sea coral reefs. The massive Makhtesh Ramon (Ramon Crater) and the developing city of Beersheva present different views of the area.

8 Petra. Take a side trip across the border to the remains of ancient Petra, in nearby Jordan, to see the magnificent temples and tombs carved out of red sandstone cliffs by the Nabatean people.

Israel's Natural Wonders

THE DEAD SEA

At the world's lowest point, the Dead Sea is actually a lake that is so high in salt content that it can support no aquatic life but enables visitors the unique experience of floating while soaking up its unique healing properties. Sadly, human activity has caused it to recede (Ch. 4).

MAKHTESH RAMON

Deep in the Negev Desert the multihue, heart-shape Makhtesh Ramon is one of Israel's most memorable sites. As the largest "erosion cirque," this unique geological formation was created not by meteor impact but by erosion. Take one of the many hiking trails to take in gorgeous desert views (Ch. 9).

EILAT'S RED CANYON AND TIMNA PARK

The stunning Red Canyon, accessible from Eilat by a daily shuttle, is particularly impressive in the early evening hours, when the descending sun makes the red-hued canyon walls glow. Farther north, you'll find another fantastic collection of desert hiking paths at Timna Park (Ch. 9).

EIN GEDI NATURE RESERVE

Between two canyons, in midst of the scorching Dead Sea Valley heat, you'll find this lush oasis, which boasts spectacular waterfalls, refreshingly cool springs, ancient ruins, and plenty of ibex, hyraxes, and other desert wildlife. This spot, which is the inspiration for the biblical passage *Song of Songs,* is the only place in the area to have water flowing year-round (Ch. 4).

CORAL BEACH NATURE RESERVE

Just south of Eilat, one of the most densely populated coral reefs in the world offers snorkelers and divers the chance to see more than 100 types of neon-color soft and hard coral reefs and 650 species of exotic Red Sea fish. You can rent gear on-site (Ch. 9).

NAHAL MEAROT NATURE RESERVE

If you're in the northern city of Haifa and looking for a day trip, head to the Nahal Me'arot Nature Reserve, a spectacular gathering of prehistoric caves that give insight into the ancient history of the Levant region. Its Camel Caves, so called because of their humplike shape, were recognized in 2012 as a UNESCO World Heritage site (Ch. 6).

TEL AVIV'S BEACHES

In addition to boasting vibrant food, arts, and culture scenes, Tel Aviv also has some truly fun beaches. They are almost all conveniently outfitted with

Ein Gedi Nature Reserve

restrooms, lockers, outdoor showers, and volleyball nets and other sports facilities. At the northern end, after the Tel Aviv port, Metzizim Beach, which has a sandbar that keeps the waves calm as well as a decent waterfront restaurant, is a hit with young families. Just a bit farther south, in front of the Hilton Hotel, is the Hilton Beach, which has the so-called Gay Beach, popular with the city's big LGBTQ+ community, as well as Dog Beach, where pups are free to play unrestricted (Ch. 5).

TEL DAN NATURE RESERVE
Spanning 120 acres and filled with fascinating ruins, the Galilee's gorgeous reserve is home to cool, babbling streams; wildlife that includes otters, mongoose, and hyrax; and archaeological ruins that tell the history of the Canaanite and Israelite civilizations that left their mark here (Ch. 8).

AVDAT NATIONAL PARK
Perched on a hilltop above the Zin Stream, the national park is home to unique desert flora, fauna, and wildlife. This site has a Roman burial cave and tower, as well as a bathhouse, and two impressive churches from the Byzantine era (Ch. 9).

YOTVATA HAI-BAR NATURE RESERVE
Spot rare desert wildlife mentioned in the Bible in this 3,000-acre refuge that aims to breed and acclimate endangered local wildlife. It successfully reintroduced the Asian wild ass into the the Negev (Ch. 9).

HERMON STREAM NATURE RESERVE
Also known as the Banias, this reserve has Israel's largest waterfall at 33 feet. Choose from three interconnected hiking paths, which weave through lush vegetation, Crusader-era ruins, caves, and Hellenistic and Roman temples (Ch. 8).

Israel's Most Historic Sights

TOMB OF KING DAVID, JERUSALEM
On Mount Zion outside of the Old City and with views of the nearby Temple Mount lies what is believed to be the burial site of the ancient Israeli King David. The ornately adorned tomb is located in the corner of a ground floor room of a supposed 5th-century AD synagogue where Jesus is also believed to have eaten his Last Supper (Ch. 3).

BAHA'I SHRINE AND GARDENS, HAIFA
The historic northern city of Haifa is the epicenter of the Baha'i religious group, and the community's gorgeous shrines and terraced gardens, on the northern slope of the Carmel Mountain, are open to visitors of all faiths (Ch. 6).

VIA DOLOROSA, JERUSALEM
The Via Dolorosa, or "Way of Sorrow," is the 40-minute path that winds through Jerusalem's Old City and which marks the journey that Jesus took, bearing his cross, from his place of trial and condemnation to his crucifixion and burial. It's marked by 14 stations, and the last five of them are located inside the Church of the Holy Sepulcher (Ch. 3).

WESTERN WALL, JERUSALEM
Known just as "the Wall," or Hakotel in Hebrew, the 2,000-year-old Western Wall is the holiest site of prayer in Judaism. Visitors from around the world flock to this controversial and politically charged white-stone structure and write hand-written wishes or prayers (Ch. 3).

CRUSADER RUINS OF AKKO
In the 12th century, the Crusaders made Akko their chief port city, valuing its strategic location as an entry point into the flourishing trade route of the greater Levant region. Some of the most fascinating ruins in this UNESCO World Heritage Site City are underground (Ch. 6).

CHURCH OF THE HOLY SEPULCHER, JERUSALEM

Built by the Crusaders in the 12th century, the Church of the Holy Sepulcher is the ornately adorned edifice where Jesus was believed to have been crucified, buried, and risen from the dead. Especially during Christmas season, pilgrims from around the world flock to the site by way of the Via Dolorosa (Ch. 3).

GARDEN OF GETHSEMANE, JERUSALEM

According to the New Testament, Jesus and his disciples walked from the Last Supper to the Garden of Gethsemane at the foot of the Mount of Olives. It is said that here he met his fate of betrayal. Today, the garden, dotted with 2,000-year-old olive trees, is a central pilgrimage site (Ch. 3).

DOME OF THE ROCK, JERUSALEM

The gold-plated, mosaic-laden Dome of the Rock on the Temple Mount has been historically revered by all three monotheistic religions and, in recent decades, the center of violent clashes in the Israeli-Palestinian conflict. However politcally loaded, it is still a top sight (Ch. 3).

BETHLEHEM

To get to the "little town of Bethlehem," the birthplace of Jesus, you'll need to cross the towering 26-foot concrete barrier that separates Israel from the Palestinian Territories. On this side of the Green Line, you'll find a modern, majority-Muslim city where the conflict is ever-present. However, the city also offers plenty of cultural and culinary treats (Ch. 4).

CAPERNAUM NATIONAL PARK, SEA OF GALILEE

The national park and remains of an ancient fishing village, the northern pilgrimage site is revered by both Christians and Jews. For Christians, it's the place where Jesus established his Galilee ministry. For Jews, it is the site of a Byzantine-era synagogue (Ch. 7).

What to Eat and Drink

HUMMUS

Beloved worldwide, this chickpea paste has a cultlike following among many Israelis and Palestinians alike, and is wonderful because it is hefty and silky at the same time. Everyone has their claim to the best hummus spot, but you really can't go wrong no matter which place you choose.

CAFÉ HAFUCH

The star of Israel's café culture is the "upside down" latte, which—as you might expect—has a layer of steamed milk on the bottom, topped with espresso and a layer of milk foam. It's reminiscent of a cappuccino yet still uniquely Israeli.

CHEESE

The world of Israeli cheese is vast and delicious, with a dizzying number of artisan options from boutique cheesemakers in the lush north and the arid south. Gvina levana, a soft white cheese, is a simple, lighter version of cream cheese, which, when spread on toast, expertly showcases veggies. Bulgarit is a firmer and sharper feta, while Tomme cheese, a semihard cheese that's like a zingy version of goat cheese, stands well on its own.

FALAFEL

The street food sandwich has been a staple since Israel was established in 1948, when European immigrants looked to adopt local foods as a means of building a new national identity. Part of the fun is stuffing as many extras on top of the deep-fried chickpea balls, from finely chopped salad to French fries to hummus, and tahini as well as a slew of options in the pickled vegetable variety.

ISRAELI BREAKFAST

Dubbed "the Jewish State's contribution to world cuisine," the richly colorful Israeli breakfast is a delightful, healthy way to start the day. While its particular dishes may vary, the meal is usually made up of a sampling of vibrant vegetables, eggs any style, a spread of breads and pastries, local dips and cheeses, as well as smoked salmon, herring, or other types of pickled fish.

SABICH

Sabich was a classic Saturday morning snack for the Jewish community of Iraq (its name is a take on "sabah," or "morning" in Arabic) and, when Iraqi Jews arrived to the country in the 1960s, was easily adapted into an all-day Israeli street food in the form of a pita stuffed with fried eggplant, hard boiled eggs, and nutty tahini sauce. Among the best spots is Sabich Tchernichovsky in Tel Aviv, where you can opt for a totally healthy version with a whole-wheat or gluten-free pita.

SALATIM

With Israel's nearly year-long sunshine and a health-obsessed culture, it's no surprise that you'll find a smorgasbord of salads, or salatim in Hebrew, at breakfast, lunch, and dinner. Easily a meal on its own, salatim are a great way to sample some of the country's vibrant produce as well as its diverse dips, like the nutty, silky sesame sauce known as tahini.

Shakshuka

SEAFOOD

For a country located on the Mediterranean Sea, many types of seafood are a surprisingly recent development in Israeli cuisine. That's because shellfish is not considered kosher and, for the first few decades of the country's existence, was barely allowed or wanted in many restaurants. But since the 1990s, when Israelis became thoroughly international, the seafood revolution arrived. Now you will find plenty of options, especially in coastal towns, including shrimp, sole, calamari, and caviar. A highlight, and longtime foodie pilgrimage site, is Uri Buri, a fish and seafood restaurant housed in a historic Ottoman building just on the shoreline in the northern city of Akko.

SHAKSHUKA

Another in Israel's long list of tasty culinary imports is shakshuka, a breakfast dish (but it's really good any time of day) of poached eggs and tomato-pepper sauce. It was brought to Israel by Jewish immigrants from Morocco and Tunisia. You can choose the classic or versions with hummus, chicken shawarma, or fried eggplant.

SHAWARMA

After a long day of exploring, there's nothing more satisfying than shawarma: a pita, or flatbread laffa, stuffed with meat that's roasted on a spit all day. Like the humble falafel, the shawarma is a casual affair, and your sandwich will come with often free sides like chopped salad, pickles, french fries, and an array of condiments.

WINE

While wine has been produced in Israel since the days of the Bible, only in the past few decades has the Israeli wine scene reclaimed its glory. The country has five wine-growing regions: the cool, high-elevation Galilee, home to the award-winning Golan Heights Winery; the Judean Hills around Jerusalem, where you'll find the boutique estate winery of Clos de Gat; Shimson, between the Judean Hills and the Coastal Plain; the Negev desert, where drip irrigation enables the excellent Rota Winery; and the Sharon, near Haifa.

WORLD CUISINE

In recent decades, Israeli cuisine has been infused with international influence. Israel's culture hub of Tel Aviv has an especially wide offering of establishments including Persian, Moroccan, French, Italian, and Thai. Bindella, on the picturesque Montefiore Street, is a classy choice for Italian, while the sleekly designed Taizu showcases the street foods of India, China, Thailand, Vietnam, and Cambodia.

Israel's Top Museums

UNDERWATER OBSERVATORY AND MARINE PARK
With more than 800 species of unique and vibrantly colored marine life (including some glow-in-the-dark fish), Eilat's Underwater Observatory and Marine Park is the largest public aquarium in the Middle East *(Ch. 9)*.

TIKOTIN MUSEUM OF JAPANESE ART
Haifa's Tikotin is the first and only Japanese art museum in the Middle East. Founded in 1957, the pavilion and extensive library, with 3,000 publications on Japanese culture, is located on Mount Carmel *(Ch. 6)*.

MUSEUM FOR ISLAMIC ART
Down the road from the prestigious Jerusalem Theater, this museum is an underrated gem. Founded in 1974, the collection includes rare pieces of Islamic art, pottery, textiles, jewelry, and cultural artifacts with provenances spanning from Spain to India *(Ch. 3)*.

DESIGN MUSEUM HOLON
Designed by Israeli architect Ron Arad, the two-story Design Museum Holon in the cultural section of the central Israeli city is the first such museum in the country. The building's bold facade, made up of metal spirals in hues of red and brown, has gained international acclaim and brought attention to this often-overlooked city less than half an hour outside of Tel Aviv *(Ch. 5)*.

HERZL MUSEUM
Next to the military cemetery on Mount Herzl you can find the interactive and engaging Herzl Museum, so named after the grandfather of the Zionist movement Theodor Herzl. The museum offers a multimedia-packed one-hour tour in various languages, chronicling Herzl's life. It details his life as a journalist in Paris, witnessing the Dreyfus Affair and the anti-Semitism that swept the city, to the World Zionist Conference in Basel and, ultimately, his successful efforts to create the Jewish State *(Ch. 3)*.

HOLOCAUST HISTORY MUSEUM
Israel's Holocaust History Museum is part of the greater Yad Vashem complex, named after the biblical phrase, "a memorial and a name." The powerful museum tells the story of the more than six million Jews who perished at the hands of the Nazis during World War II with galleries featuring survivor testimonies, artifacts, and art installations. Visitors

Tel Aviv Museum of Art

wind through the history of the Holocaust and end up in the Hall of Names, which features photos of those who died and a hole in the floor for those whose identity remains unknown. Visitors exit, into the light, onto a balcony that overlooks the peaceful Jerusalem Forest *(Ch. 3)*.

ILANA GOOR MUSEUM

The Ilana Goor Museum is the gallery space and residence of the Israeli artist who has long been a cultural staple of the port city of Jaffa. The dramatic white stone archways of this 18th-century building—once purposed as an inn for Jewish pilgrims planning to visit Jerusalem, then as an olive oil soap factory, then as a synagogue—elegantly frame Goor's eclectic collection of wood, stone, and metal sculptures *(Ch. 5)*.

ISRAEL AQUARIUM

Jerusalem's aquarium is a chance to learn about the habitats and marine life of Israel's four seas: the Mediterranean, the Dead Sea, the Red Sea, and the Sea of Galilee. It explores the ways climate change and human activity are endangering Israel's unique marine life *(Ch. 3)*.

TEL AVIV MUSEUM OF ART

In the heart of Tel Aviv, this impressive museum is identifiable by its modernist white envelope-shape facade. The collections include classical and contemporary Israeli and international art, including the works of iconic Jewish artists *(Ch. 5)*.

ISRAEL MUSEUM

The sleek and modernist museum in Jerusalem is the country's leading cultural institution. In addition to local archaeological artifacts and fine arts pieces, the museum's most unique attraction is its Dead Sea Scrolls, 900 of some of the world's oldest known manuscripts *(Ch. 3)*.

Israel Today

Israelis are at once warmly hospitable and assertive. The country's ethnic, religious, and political mix, endlessly fascinating, can be exasperating as well. But, with legendary resilience, Israelis thrive on complexity, and life between the headlines is astonishingly normal.

A VIBRANT ECONOMY

Israel's founding fathers were socialists and its early economy largely agrarian. That's history, though. Agriculture today is sophisticated and technology-based, but its share of the country's exports is less than 3%, as the economy has burgeoned and reinvented itself.

With few natural resources—beyond newly discovered natural gas—the human factor was always crucial. Diamond cutting, an early initiative of Jewish refugees from wartime Holland and Belgium, supplies some 40% of the world's cut and polished stones and 20% of all Israel's exports. Tourism is big, of course, with 3½ million visitors a year, mostly Holy Land pilgrims and Jewish "roots" travelers. The discovery of underwater gas fields off the coast of Haifa has Israel poised to become an energy exporter to Egypt and Jordan.

The real story of the last quarter century is high-tech. Israel is second only to the United States in the number of start-ups; computer systems, imaging, medical research, and biotech are leading specialties; and Israeli companies with attractive expertise are constantly being snapped up by big foreign corporations.

The country's financial environment, including vigilant bank regulation, has helped it weather global crises better than most. Although a member of the Organisation for Economic Co-operation and Development (OECD), the gap between the haves and have-nots is high, and one out of every five Israeli families lives below the poverty line.

THE PALESTINE CONUNDRUM

Relations between Israel and the Palestinians have always been fraught. There is mounting concern that time is running out for a "two-state solution," which envisages Israel and a viable sovereign Palestine state existing alongside each other. No other options have gotten widespread support on either side.

In 2012 the Palestinian Authority's president, Mahmoud Abbas, received a status upgrade at the United Nations to "nonmember observer state," which could indicate that the U.N. might eventually consider recognizing Palestinian statehood. The Palestinian Authority controls the West Bank, one of two Palestinian territories. It has virtually no sway in Gaza, which is run by Hamas, Fatah's Islamist rivals.

Hamas-controlled Gaza continues to have conflicts with Israel while the Palestinian Authority–controlled West Bank makes tiny steps at the grassroots level of cooperation between Israeli and Palestinian entrepreneurs, artists, and teachers.

BEYOND THE HEADLINES

Israel is so often a source of breaking news that its life beyond the headlines seems like a well-kept secret. The big cities are very cosmopolitan; a vigorous Israeli film industry has won kudos and awards at international festivals; and the nationwide Book Week is a major cultural event. Classical orchestras, ensembles, and solo artists perform in Israel and abroad. Athletes have enjoyed occasional bright moments on the Olympic podium—though Israeli Paralympians are always among the medalists—and in European club basketball. Israel is also a world-class chess nation.

Academia is strong. Twelve Israelis have been awarded Nobel Prizes since 1966. Innovative research in fields like nanotechnology and stem-cell treatment continue to make important biological and medical breakthroughs, at the conceptual, technological, and pharmacological levels, for the treatment of cancer and other diseases.

In the important business of Arab–Jewish relations (within Israel), much needs to be done; but there are joint business ventures, bilingual theater groups and bands, and interschool dialogue and collaborative projects.

GREENING ISRAEL

Israel's chronic water shortage has spurred the search for creative solutions. Drip irrigation is a clear winner; seawater desalination and wastewater treatment (an extraordinary 75% reclaimed) top up the reserves. Rooftop solar panels for domestic water heaters punctuate city skylines, and smaller, solar-energy plants operate in the Negev Desert. The Ashalim Power Station in the Negev, inaugurated in 2019, boasts the tallest solar power tower in the world. It receives reflected light from a field of 55,000 mirrors straddling 740 acres, and can be seen from dozens of miles away. Israel has embraced green concepts, developing and often exporting homegrown environmental products and technologies. Cities are widening their recycling programs, encouraging bikers, and improving public transportation.

JUDAISM IN ISRAEL TODAY

There's no firm separation of religion and state in Israel. Matters of personal status—marriage, divorce, adoption, and conversion—are the preserve of the religious authorities of the community concerned. For this reason there's no civil marriage; if one partner doesn't convert

to the faith of the other, the couple must marry abroad. Within the Jewish community, such functions fall under the supervision of the Orthodox chief rabbinate, much to the dismay of members of the tiny but growing Conservative and Reform movements and of the large number of nonobservant Jews.

Almost half of all Israeli Jews call themselves secular. The religiously observant—strict adherence to Sabbath laws and dietary laws, regular attendance at worship services, and so on—account for about 20%. At least another one-third of the Jewish population identify themselves as "traditional," meaning they observe some Jewish customs to some extent, often as a nod to Jewish heritage or a sense of family duty. Ultra-Orthodox (*haredi* in Hebrew) is the smaller of the two mainstreams that make up the Orthodox Jewish community; you can easily recognize the men by their black hats and garb. Their parallel universe embraces religion as a 24/7 lifestyle. Their independent school system, 80% government-funded, teaches only religious subjects. While some haredi men do go out to work, many have committed themselves to full-time study.

Israel: People, Religion, and State

"I could not conceive of a small country having so large a history," wrote Mark Twain after his visit to the Holy Land in 1867. The rich history certainly fascinates, as does the complex political situation despite, or because of, its constant sense of urgency. But beyond that are the people, a varied population of 8½ million, representing a startlingly wide array of ethnicities, nationalities, religious beliefs, and lifestyles. The diversity of Israel's population is one of the country's greatest strengths—and one of its essential challenges. It may explain, for example, why defining a national identity is still a work in progress, even after more than 70 years.

CREATING A NATION

Israel's founding generation saw the country as a modern reincarnation of the ancient Jewish nation-state. Israel was the "Promised Land" of Abraham and Moses, the Israelite kingdom of David and Solomon, and the home of Jesus of Nazareth and the Jewish Talmudic sages. Although the Jewish presence in the country has been unbroken for more than 3,000 years, several massive exiles—first by the Babylonians in 586 BC and then by the Romans in AD 70—created a Diaspora, a dispersion of the Jewish people throughout the world. The sense of historical roots still resonates for many, probably most, Jewish Israelis; and bringing their brethren home has been a national priority from the beginning.

The attachment to the ancient homeland, and a yearning for the restoration of "Zion and Jerusalem," weaves through the entire fabric of Jewish history and religious tradition. Over the centuries, many Jews trickled back to Eretz Yisrael (the Land of Israel), while others looked forward to fulfilling their dream of return in some future—many felt imminent— messianic age. Not all were prepared to

wait for divine intervention, however, and in the late 19th century, a variety of Jewish nationalist organizations emerged, bent on creating a home for their people in Israel (then the district of Palestine in the Ottoman Empire). Zionism was created as a political movement to give structure and impetus to that idea.

Some early Zionist leaders, like founding father Theodor Herzl, believed that the urgent priority was simply a Jewish haven that would be safe from persecution, wherever that haven might be. Argentina was suggested, and Great Britain offered Uganda. In light of Jewish historical and emotional links to the land of Israel, most Zionists rejected these "territorialist" proposals.

DIFFERING VIEWS

The establishment of the State of Israel did not, of course, meet with universal rejoicing. To the Arab world, it was anathema, an alien implant in a Muslim Middle East. Palestinian Arabs today mark Israel's independence as the *Nakba,* the Catastrophe, a moment in time when their own national aspirations were thwarted. For many ultra-Orthodox Jews, the founding of Israel was an arrogant preempting of God's divine plan; and to make matters worse, the newly minted state was blatantly secular, despite its many concessions to religious interests. This internal battle over the character of the Jewish state, and the implacable hostility of Israel's neighbors—which has resulted in more than six decades of unremitting conflict—have been the two main issues engaging the country since its birth.

THE ISRAELI PEOPLE

Roughly 6 million of Israel's citizens—a little more than 75%—are Jewish. Some trace their family roots back many generations on local soil; others are first- to fourth-generation *olim* (immigrants) from dozens of different countries. The first modern pioneers arrived from Russia in 1882, purchased land, and set about developing it with romantic zeal. A couple of decades later, inspired by the socialist ideas then current in Eastern Europe, a much larger wave founded the first kibbutzim—collective villages or communes. In time, these fiercely idealistic farmers became something of a moral elite, having little financial power but providing a greatly disproportionate percentage of the country's political leadership, military officer cadre, and intelligentsia.

Most of the immigrants before Israel's independence in 1948 were Ashkenazi Jews (of Central or Eastern European descent), but the biggest wave in the first decade of statehood came from the Arab lands of North Africa and the Middle East. Israel's Jewish population—600,000 at the time of independence—doubled within 3½ years and tripled within 10.

In the late 1980s and early '90s, a wave of about three-quarters of a million Jews moved to Israel from the former Soviet Union. The Russian influence is felt everywhere in Israel today, not least in the fields of technology and classical music. In the early 1980s, a smaller group of Jews from the long-isolated Ethiopian community trekked across Sudan, on their odyssey to the dreamed-of "Jerusalem." Many perished en route. Another 14,500 were airlifted into Israel over one weekend in 1991. Their challenge—and that of Israeli society—has been their integration into a modern technological society. Jews from France have moved to Israel in significant numbers: more than 16,500 arrived from 2015 to 2017.

The vast majority of Israel's 1.7 million Arabic-speaking citizens are Muslims (among them about 200,000 Bedouin), followed by 130,000 Druze (a separate religious group), and about 125,000 Christian Arabs. Most Israeli Arabs live in the mixed Jewish-Arab towns of Jaffa, Ramla, Lod, Haifa, and Akko; a number of good-size towns and villages on the eastern edge of the coastal plain; in Nazareth and throughout the Lower Galilee; and, in the case of the Bedouin, in the Negev Desert. The extent to which they're integrated with Israeli Jews often depends on location. In Haifa, for example, there's little tension between the two ethnic groups. On the other hand, Jerusalem's quarter-million Arab residents are Palestinian not Israeli, and the situation is more fraught. All Israeli Arabs are equal under the law and vote for and serve in the *Knesset,* the Israeli parliament.

However, social and economic gaps between the Arab and Jewish sectors do exist, and Arab complaints of government neglect and unequal allocation of resources have sometimes spilled into angry street demonstrations and other antiestablishment activity. The Muslims in Israel are mainstream Sunnis and regarded as both politically and religiously moderate by the standards of the region. Nevertheless, in recent years there has been some radicalization of the community's youth, who identify politically with the Palestinian liberation movement and/ or religiously with the Islamic revival that has swept the Middle East.

Israel with Kids

Your choices for keeping the kids busy in Israel are both abundant and varied. Let them expend energy exploring Crusader castles or caves in nature reserves. For fun on the water, try rafting on the Jordan River—and there are the beaches, of course. Check the Friday papers' entertainment guides (they have a children's section) or websites for up-to-date information on special activities.

EATING OUT

Restaurants are often happy to accommodate those seeking simple fare like pasta or chicken schnitzel and fries. Fast food is easily accessible and doesn't have to be junk. Falafel or shawarma, kebabs, and cheese- or potato-filled pastries called *bourekas* are very common, and pizza parlors abound.

NATURE (AND OLD STUFF, TOO)

Israel's nature reserves and national parks (⊕ *www.parks.org.il*) have plenty for the whole family to do. In the north, you can cycle around a part of the restored Hula Lake (at the site called Agmon Ha'Hula); laugh and learn at the fun 3-D movie about bird migrations at the **Hula Lake Nature Reserve**; kayak or raft the placid waters of the **Jordan River**; and bounce around some awesome landscapes in a Jeep or a 4x4 dune buggy. (In the south, the Negev Desert and Eilat Mountains have comparable off-road experiences.) Explore the medieval **Nimrod's Fortress** on the slopes of Mount Hermon, or the remains of mighty **Belvoir** overlooking the Upper Jordan Valley.

Standouts in the south are the oases and walking trails of **Ein Gedi Nature Reserve** (with a bonus of bathing under fresh waterfalls) and **Ein Avdat.** The wondrous **Masada,** Herod's mountaintop palace-fortress, is a real treat and can be reached by foot along the steep Snake Path (recommended for older kids), but there's always the cable car.

Walking is a lively and easy activity to do anywhere. Top in Jerusalem is the Old Testament–period **City of David,** south of the Old City. It's a maze of rock-hewn corridors, ending with a 30-minute wade in the spring water of Hezekiah's Tunnel. (There's a dry exit, too.) The **Ramparts Walk** on part of the city walls offers views of the Old City's residential quarters as well as of new Jerusalem outside the walls. Smaller kids can do part of it (with strict adult supervision).

In Tel Aviv, the **Tel Aviv Port** is great for coffee and a stroll—and even little kids can run around (with a bit of adult attention) while you enjoy iced drinks and the balmy weather. The city's beaches and beachfront promenade are also good for walking and using up energy.

MUSEUMS

A dirty word among kids? Maybe so, but the following museums might change some minds.

In West Jerusalem, the **Israel Museum's Youth Wing** has outdoor play areas as well as exhibitions, often interactive, and a "recycling room" where children can use their creative energy freely. Great rainy-day options include the **Bloomfield Science Museum** in Givat Ram.

The **Eretz Israel Museum** in Tel Aviv has a series of pavilions on its campus, each with a different theme: pottery, coins, glass, folklore, anthropology, and more. It also has a planetarium—complete with moon rocks. Nearby is the engaging **Museum of the Jewish People,** which tells the story of Jewish life outside Israel over the centuries.

Haifa's **National Museum of Science, Technology, and Space (MadaTech)** and the **National Maritime Museum** are geared to young and curious minds—of any age.

The **Israel Air Force Museum,** at the Hatzerim Air Force base (west of Beersheva), houses a huge collection of IAF airplanes and helicopters—from World War II Spitfires and Mustangs to contemporary F-16s and Cobras. Each exhibit has a story to tell. Guided tours in English can be arranged. This could be a stop on the way to or from Eilat, or a doable day trip from Jerusalem or Tel Aviv.

AT ONE WITH THE ANIMALS
In addition to the wonderful **Tisch Family Zoological Gardens** in Jerusalem, with its emphasis on fauna that feature in the Bible or are native to Israel, the small but delightful **Haifa Zoo** offers numerous options for time out with animals.

In the high Negev Desert, near Mitzpe Ramon, about as far as you can get from their native Andes mountains, gentle alpacas wait for you to hand-feed them. At the **Alpaca Farm** you can learn as well about the whole process of raising them and spinning their marvelously soft wool.

Horseback riding is an option pretty much throughout the country. In the Galilee, end a trail—of a few hours or a couple of days—with hot apple pie at **Vered Hagalil** or with a chunky steak at **Bat Ya'ar,** in the Biriya Forest near Tzfat (Safed). There are numerous outfits that do camel-hump trails in the Negev (near Beersheva and Arad) and near **Eilat.**

In the Upper Hula Valley, **Tel Dan Nature Reserve** is both beautiful and home to unusual wildlife; trails let you access different areas. Bird-watching isn't a casual activity, but if you have budding birders in the family, Israel provides excellent opportunities because it is on major migration routes. The **Hula Lake Nature Reserve** provides excellent viewing in season.

In Eilat the **Underwater Observatory and Marine Park,** with a large aquarium complex, gives visitors of all ages an excellent opportunity to observe colorful, rare fish and more.

BEACHES
You're never too far from a beach in Israel—but check for a lifeguard. This is a given at city beaches, but not at those off the beaten track.

For such a tiny country, the range of different beach experiences is amazing, from the Mediterranean to the Red Sea to the freshwater Sea of Galilee. **Tel Aviv** is right on the Mediterranean and has an enjoyable promenade and plenty of public beaches.

The **Dead Sea,** actually a hypersalty lake, draws people from all over the world to luxuriate in its waters, hot springs, and black medicinal mud. Kids (and adults) can float but not swim here. The southern shores—the lowest point on the surface of the planet—are filled with hotels that offer beach access.

AND MORE ...
The whole family enjoys getting their hands dirty at the three-hour **Dig for a Day** (⊕ *www.archesem.com*)—a chance to dig, sift, and examine artifacts.

Off the Tel Aviv–Jerusalem highway at Latrun is **Mini Israel**—hundreds of exact-replica models of the main sites around the country, historical, archaeological, and modern. It's great for an all-of-Israel orientation.

Israel and the Performing Arts

Israel has a wealth of cultural activity that reflects both its ethnic diversity and its cosmopolitanism. Innovation and experimentation cross-pollinate traditional forms, creating an exciting Israeli performing-arts scene infused by West and East. Look for listings in sections of the Friday *Haaretz* ("The Guide") and the *Jerusalem Post* ("Billboard"), available in many hotels. Online, ⊕ *www. timeout.com/israel* will give you the latest updates on things to do.

MUSIC

Israel's traditionally strong classical and opera scene was enhanced a generation ago by a wave of immigrant musicians from the former Soviet Union. Apart from the deep reservoir of local talent, a steady stream of visiting artists, ensembles, and even full operatic companies enrich the scene every year. The world-renowned **Israel Philharmonic Orchestra** (⊕ *www.ipo.co.il*) is based in Tel Aviv but plays concert series in Haifa and Jerusalem as well. Look for the **Jerusalem Symphony** (⊕ *www.jso.co.il*) and **Haifa Symphony** orchestras (⊕ *www.haifasymphony.co.il*) in their respective cities, but smaller orchestras and ensembles appear in other, often remote, venues, too. Chamber music listings are full and varied: check out intimate auditoriums like the **Felicja Blumental Center,** the **Israel Music Conservatory** (Stricker), and the **Tel Aviv Museum of Art** in Tel Aviv; the **Jerusalem Music Center** (Mishkenot), the **Eden-Tamir Center (Ein Kerem),** and various churches in the holy city; and the **Rappaport Hall** and **Tikotin (Japanese) Museum** in Haifa.

The **Israeli Opera** (⊕ *www.israel-opera. co.il*) stages up to 10 productions per season (November to July), including a crowd-pleasing extravaganza at the foot of Masada (near the Dead Sea) toward season's end. Its home base, the **Tel Aviv Performing Arts Center (TAPAC),** hosts smaller operatic and musical events as well.

Noteworthy annual festivals include the multidisciplinary **Israel Festival** (Jerusalem ⊕ *www.israel-festival.org.il*), the **Abu Gosh Vocal Festival** (near Jerusalem ⊕ *www. agfestival.co.il*), and three chamber music festivals: **Upper Galilee Voice of Music** (Kibbutz Kfar Blum), **Eilat** (Eilat ⊕ *www. eilat-festival.co.il*), and **Jerusalem International Chamber Music Festival** (Jerusalem ⊕ *www.jcmf.org.il*). Check websites for accurate dates for these events.

Popular Music: Israeli rock bands and balladeers fill radio playlists and venues around the country. Popular watering holes are Tel Aviv's **Zappa Club** and an ever-changing list of places in the Tel Aviv Port, a nightlife center. Big foreign acts like Elton John, Madonna, and The Rolling Stones take over the **Tel Aviv Performing Arts Center** or the outdoor **Yarkon Park.**

Jerusalem doesn't rock nearly as much as Tel Aviv, but look for cool gigs at **Zappa at the Lab** and **Yellow Submarine.** The weeklong midsummer Hutzot Hayotzer Arts and Crafts Festival in **Sultan's Pool,** just outside Jaffa Gate, has good Israeli acts nightly for no extra charge.

Jazz, Ethnic, and World Music have come of age at Eilat's **Red Sea Jazz Festival** (⊕ *en.redseajazz.co.il*), a twice-yearly jazz summit. The summer festival is a fixture on the international calendar, when local artists like trumpeter Avishai Cohen and his siblings return from the New York scene. The winter festival shines a light on home-grown talent. Tel Aviv's **Shablul Jazz** is the premier club, but pubs like **Mike's Place** can be hot as well. Middle Eastern influences are common in Israeli pop songs—that's a given—but even the quintessentially New World genre of jazz hasn't escaped fusion with Yemenite or Ethiopian sounds.

The **Jerusalem International Oud Festival** celebrates a musical tradition that extends from Spain to India (⊕ *www.confederationhouse.org*).

The Upper Galilee mountain town of Tzfat (Safed), home of 16th-century Jewish mysticism, is the setting for the annual **Klezmer Festival** (⊕ *www.safed.co.il*). Expect three summer days of fiddles, clarinets, and Eastern European schmaltz.

The veteran **Ein Gev Festival** in April, on the eastern shore of the Sea of Galilee, is devoted to Hebrew songs, many of them in a choral format.

DANCE

Israel owes its visibility on the world dance radar to modern, not ballet. Still, if tradition speaks to you, check the listings for the Tel Aviv–based **Israel Ballet** (⊕ *www.iballet.co.il*) or the more contemporary **Jerusalem Dance Theater** (⊕ *www.jdtcom.com*).

The center of Israeli modern dance is the finely restored **Suzanne Dellal Centre for Dance and Theatre** in Tel Aviv's historic Neve Tzedek neighborhood. Its four performance halls are home ground for the veteran and world-renowned **Batsheva Dance Company** (⊕ *www.batsheva.co.il*)—with legendary artistic director Ohad Naharin—and the **Inbal Pinto & Avshalom Pollak Dance Company** (⊕ *www.inbalpinto.com*). The center's season peaks with **Summer Dance,** a two-month feast of top local and international talent. **Tel Aviv Dance** is an autumn festival, while December brings the more intimate yet more intense **International Exposure.**

The field is much wider, however. The **Kibbutz Contemporary Dance Company** (⊕ *www.kcdc.co.il*)) has a fine reputation, and the Jerusalem-based **Vertigo Dance Company** (⊕ *www.vertigo.org.il*) takes the audience into new territory. (Ensembles are constantly on the road: regardless of their home base, they might be performing near you.) The **Israel Festival** brings top-class acts to Jerusalem, and the capital now enjoys its own dance festival, **Machol Shalem,** in winter.

THEATER

Theater in Israel is almost exclusively staged in Hebrew, with the exception of Tel Aviv's **Cameri Theatre,** which presents some of its popular productions with English subtitles.

The **Israel Festival** in Jerusalem is the place to take in an array of the best of the performing arts.

Language may not matter at Jerusalem's annual **International Festival of Puppet Theater** (⊕ *www.traintheater.co.il*) in summer.

FILM

Israel has a thriving film industry. The best movie meccas are the **Cinematheques** in Tel Aviv, Haifa, and Jerusalem. Most Israeli films have English subtitles. Real film buffs note the summer dates of the **Jerusalem International Film Festival.** The Haifa Cinematheque has a similar festival in fall (⊕ *www.haifaff.co.il*).

Tel Aviv celebrates **White Nights** in June— an all-night bash when most major museums, theaters, and clubs stay open.

What to Watch and Read

A TALE OF LOVE AND DARKNESS

This memoir by one of Israel's most prolific authors, Amos Oz, mourns both his mother's suicide and that of the early Zionist dream. The book was made into a movie by Jerusalem-born actress Natalie Portman and is a must for anyone looking to understand the multilayer narratives that went into the building of the Israeli identity.

THE BAND'S VISIT

The Band's Visit, the story of a touring Egyptian orchestra that mistakenly winds up in a remote desert town after a technical snafu, stars Ronit Elkabitz—sometimes dubbed the Israeli version of Meryl Streep—as a cynical local café owner who, in her brief but sincere connection with the Egyptian bandleader, reflects on her failed marriage and crushed hopes to escape her small town.

DANCING ARABS

Journalist, screenwriter, and novelist Sayed Kashua, arguably the most prominent Palestinian voice in Israeli pop culture, wrote *Dancing Arabs* as a semi-autobiographical knowledge, dealing with his own dilemmas around identity and isolation as a minority, with lots of heart and humor.

FOOTNOTE

A refreshingly nonpolitical Israeli film, "Footnote" chronicles the rivalry between a father and son toiling in an extremely narrow academic field of Talmud—the foundation of Jewish law and culture—at Hebrew University in Jerusalem.

GETT: THE TRIAL OF VIVIANE AMSELEM

A woman fights a seemingly interminable fight to break free from her marriage. To receive her "gett," or religious bill of divorce, Viviane needs the approval of a council of rabbis, who accusingly ask her why she allowed the marriage to fall apart, as well as her vengeful husband, who drags out the agonizing process.

KHIRBET HIZEH

Published in 1949, S. Yizhar's *Khirbet Hizeh* is the first piece of Israeli literature to deal with the moral quandary that was the mass expulsions of Palestinians in order to make way for Israel.

KNELLER'S HAPPY CAMPERS

Etgar Keret's novella is a darkly satiric twist on trauma. Set in a posthumous world populated with people who have all committed suicide, the story follows protagonist Haim after he takes his own life, gets a job in a pizzeria, and navigates an alternate reality.

TO THE END OF THE LAND

When his eldest son began his army service, David Grossman began writing the novel *To the End of the Land,* in which a mother fears her son has been killed at war and so escapes to hike half the length of the country along the Israel Trail. It was nearly completed when Grossman's younger son was killed in the Second Lebanon War.

WALTZ WITH BASHIR

Ari Folman's masterful, animated documentary is a nightmarish, near-hallucinatory film about the PTSD of Israeli soldiers returning from the 1982 Lebanon War. It's as much a fascinating piece of art as a history lesson in the atrocities of the Lebanon War.

ZERO MOTIVATION

It easy to forget that this darkly hilarious film about female soldiers in the Israeli army is actually about the army. The story follows two young soldiers–best friends who are primarily concerned with their cell phones and dating, but happen to be living on a boring desert army base, tied to meaningless desk jobs. It's a sharp criticism about sexism in the army.

ISRAEL
THROUGH THE AGES

Where else in the world can you find the living history of three major religions that have been intertwined for more than 1,000 years? Israel is the crossroads for Christianity, Islam, and Judaism, and many of the remarkable sites here help to tell this country's unique story. One of the best examples can be found in Jerusalem's Old City, where you can visit the Church of the Holy Sepulcher, the Dome of the Rock, and the Western Wall all within a short walk of each other.

TIMELINE

| 1800 BC Beginning of Patriarchal Age | 13th Century BC Israelite exodus from Egypt | 1000 BC David conquers Jerusalem. 950 BC Solomon builds the First Temple |

| 1800 BC | 1500 BC | 1200 BC | 900 BC |

(top left) The Bible—David playing the harp while bringing the Ark of the Covenant from Kirjath-Jearim with other musicians. (bottom) The goddess Asherah was worshipped by some in ancient Israel as the consort of El and in Judah as the consort of Yahweh (some Hebrews baked small cakes for her festival). (right) Artist's depiction of Solomon's court (Ingobertus, c. 880).

Prehistory
1.2 million BC

The land that is now Israel served as a land bridge for Homo Erectus on his epic journey out of Africa. The oldest human remains found outside that continent, 1.4 million years old, were unearthed at Ubediya near Lake Kinneret (Sea of Galilee). It was in the Carmel Caves in northern Israel that the only indication of direct contact between Neanderthal Man and Homo Sapiens, 40,000 years ago, has been found, lending credence to the theory that they lived contemporaneously.

Early Biblical Period
2000–1000 BC

The arrival of Abraham, Isaac, and Jacob marked the beginning of the Patriarchal Age, dated to around 1800 BC. The Israelite exodus from Egypt took place in the 13th century BC. It was at this time that Israel was divided into Canaanite city-kingdoms. As the Israelites established themselves in the hill country, the Philistines, originating in the Aegean, were landing on the coastal plain. Around 1150, the Philistines invaded. A place name deriving from their presence endures to this day—Palestine.

United Monarchy
1000–928 BC

David conquered Jerusalem around 1000 BC, united the Israelite tribes into one kingdom, and established his capital here. David's son, Solomon, became king in 968 BC. Around 950 BC, Solomon built the First Temple in Jerusalem, the religious center. Shortly after Solomon's death in 928 BC, the kingdom split in two—the northern tribes, which seceded and formed the Kingdom of Israel, and the southern tribes, now known as the Kingdom of Judah.

721 BC Assyrians conquer Israel	586 BC Babylonian rule	538 BC Cyrus the Great of Persia conquers Babylonia. Second Temple rebuilt	AD 27 Jesus's Galilean ministry takes place	AD 70 Romans destroy Second Temple. Masada falls in AD 73.

600 BC	300 BC	0	AD 300

In Focus | ISRAEL THROUGH THE AGES

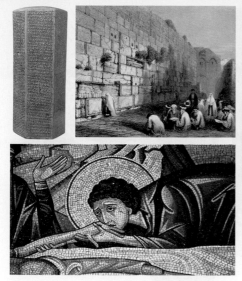

(top left) Hexagonal cylinder of King Sennacherib of Assyria inscribed with an account of his invasion of Palestine and the siege of Jerusalem in the reign of Hezekiah, King of Judah, dated 686 BC. (top center) 1860 engraving of the Western Wall. (top right) Masada. (bottom left) Mosaic in the Church of the Holy Sepulcher, Jerusalem.

928–587 BC

For 200 years, the Kingdom of Israel and the Kingdom of Judah coexisted, though relations were sometimes hostile. But in 721 BC, the Assyrian army, which dominated the region, conquered Israel and took its residents eastward into captivity. The fate of these "ten lost tribes" would be a subject of speculation by scholars thereafter. In 586 BC, the Assyrians were defeated by a new power, the Babylonians. Their king, Nebuchadnezzar, conquered Judah and destroyed Jerusalem and the temple. Those who survived were exiled to the "rivers of Babylon."

538 BC–AD 73

Second Temple Period

This exile ended after only 50 years when Cyrus the Great of Persia conquered Babylonia and permitted the exiles to return to Judah. Jerusalem was rebuilt and a new temple erected. The vast Persian Empire was defeated by Alexander the Great in 333 BC. Judah the Maccabee claimed victory over Hellenistic armies in 165 BC and rededicated the defiled Jewish temple. Judean independence brought the Hasmonean dynasty to power in 142 BC, which the Romans ended when they annexed the country in 63 BC.

Jesus was born in Bethlehem, and 26 years later began his ministry, teaching mostly around the Sea of Galilee. In AD 29, Jesus and his disciples celebrated Passover in Jerusalem; he was arrested, put on trial, and crucified by the Romans soon after.

In AD 66, the Jews rose up against Roman rule. Their fierce revolt failed and Jerusalem and the temple were destroyed in the process, in AD 70. A vestige of the temple compound, the Western Wall, is venerated by Jews to this day. The last Jewish stronghold, Masada, fell three years later.

| 325 Constantine makes Christianity the imperial religion | 622 Muhammad's hejira and the beginning of Islam | 1099 Crusaders conquer Jerusalem |

| 500 | 700 | 900 | 1100 |

(immediate left) Bar Kochba's coin: top, the Jewish Temple facade with the rising star; reverse: A lulav, the text that reads: "to the freedom of Jerusalem." (top left) Saladin, commander of Muslim forces, battles Christians in the 3rd Crusade. (top right) Richard the Lionheart In battle during the Crusades.

Late Roman & Byzantine Period

AD 73–640

In 132, the Roman emperor Hadrian threatened to rebuild Jerusalem as a pagan city and another Jewish revolt broke out, led by Bar-Kochba. In retribution, Hadrian leveled Jerusalem in 135 and changed the name of the country to Syria Palestina. Many of the remaining Jews were killed, enslaved, or exiled.

It wasn't until the 4th century AD that the Roman emperor Constantine made Christianity the imperial religion. This revived life in the Holy Land, making it a focus of pilgrimage and church construction that included the Church of the Nativity in Bethlehem. In spite of persecution, a vibrant Jewish community still existed.

Muhammad's *hejira* (flight) from Mecca to Medina in Arabia took place in 622, marking the beginning of Islam. This became Year One on the Muslim calendar. When Muhammad died in 632, his followers burst out of Arabia and created a Muslim empire that within a century would extend from India to Spain.

Medieval Period

640–1516

The Dome of the Rock was constructed in Jerusalem in 691 by Caliph Abd al-Malik. In 1099, the Crusaders conquered the city and massacred Jews and Muslims there. Cities like Akko (also called Acre) and castles like Belvoir were developed around 1100. Muslim reconquest of the land under the Mamluks began in 1265. In 1291 Akko fell, marking the end of the Crusades. An outstanding period of architecture followed, especially in Jerusalem's Temple Mount (Haram esh-Sharif) and in the Muslim Quarter.

| 1265 Muslim reconquest begins | Akko falls in 1291, marking the end of the Crusader kingdom | 1516 Mamluks defeated in Syria by the Ottoman Turks | 1897 First World Zionist Conference |

1300   1500   1700   1900

In Focus | ISRAEL THROUGH THE AGES

(top left) Jewish settlers known as Biluim, in Palestine, 1880s. The 38th Zionist congress, 1933. (bottom left) Palestine Post headline announcing declaration of independence in 1948.

Modern Period

1516–1917

In 1516, the Mamluks were defeated in Syria by the Ottoman Turks. Egyptian nationalists took control of Israel in 1832, but were expelled in 1840 with help from European nations. The country's population shifted in the 19th century, when the steamship made access easy.

The first World Zionist Conference, organized by Theodor Herzl, took place in 1897, fueling the idea of a Jewish homeland. In 1909, Tel Aviv was founded, and Degania, the first kibbutz, was established on the southern shore of the Sea of Galilee.

Creation of a Jewish State

1917–1948

The conquest of Palestine by the British in the First World War ushered in many critical changes. In 1917, the British government expressed support in the Balfour Declaration for creation of a Jewish homeland. Arab nationalism began to rise around 1920 in the post-Ottoman Middle East after Ottoman Turkey, which sided with Germany during the first World War, abandoned Palestine. This marked the point at which tension between Jews and Arabs began to increase, peaking in the massacre of Jews in 1920, 1929, and again in 1936. Various Jewish militias formed to counter the violence.

The British "White Paper" of 1939 restricted Jewish immigration and land purchase in Palestine. Tensions with Britain, and clashes between Arabs and Jews, peaked after World War II. The United Nations Partition Plan of 1947 envisioned two states in Palestine, one Jewish and one Arab. With the end of the British mandate in May 1948, David Ben-Gurion, the Palestinian Jewish leader who would later become Israel's first prime minister, declared Israel a Jewish state. In the following months, Israel survived invasions by the armies of several Arab nations.

| 1948 Creation of a Jewish State. David Ben-Gurion elected Israel's first prime minister | 1973 Yom Kippur War | 1994 Oslo Accord | 2000 2nd Intifada |
| | 1967 Six-Day War | 1987 Intifada begins | 2006 Hamas wins Palestinian elections |

1930 **1960** **1990** **2020**

(left) David Ben-Gurion in 1918. (top right) Knesset, Israeli parliament, Jerusalem. (bottom right) Israeli flag.

The First 50 Years

1948–1998

Fighting ended January, 1949, and a U.N.-supervised cease-fire agreement was signed. Transjordan annexed the West Bank and East Jerusalem; Egypt annexed the Gaza Strip. Palestinian Arabs who fled or were expelled settled in neighboring countries; those who stayed became Israeli citizens. The first elections to the Knesset took place, and David Ben-Gurion was elected prime minister. In 1950, the Knesset enacted the Law of Return, giving any Jew the right to Israeli citizenship.

Around 1964, the Palestine Liberation Organization (PLO) was founded, which sought an independent state for Palestinians and refused to recognize Israel as a state. In 1967, the Six-Day War broke out; Israel occupied territory including the Golan Heights. Egypt and Syria attacked Israel on Yom Kippur in 1973. The Lebanon War in 1982 met with unprecedented Israeli opposition. In 1987, the *intifada* (uprising) brought sustained Palestinian Arab unrest. The Oslo Accords, signed in 1994, involved mutual recognition of Israel and the PLO, as well as Palestinian autonomy in the Gaza Strip and parts of the West Bank.

Israel Today

1998–Present

After Ehud Barak was elected prime minister in 1999, Israel withdrew from Lebanon. The second *intifada* began in 2000 and subsided in 2005, costing more than 3,000 Israeli and Palestinian lives. When Israel withdrew from the Gaza Strip (2005), the Islamist Hamas took over and made it a base for rocket attacks against Israel. In November 2012, the Palestinian Authority won United Nations recognition of Palestine as a sovereign (but non-member) state. Despite this, tensions continue to flare periodically.

Chapter 2

TRAVEL SMART

Updated by
Shari Giddens

★ **CAPITAL:**
Jerusalem

🏛 **POPULATION:**
8,580,000

💬 **LANGUAGE:**
Hebrew and Arabic; English
is widely spoken

$ **CURRENCY:**
Israeli new shekel

☎ **COUNTRY CODE:**
972

⚠ **EMERGENCIES:**
100, 101, 102

🚗 **DRIVING:**
On the right

⚡ **ELECTRICITY:**
220v/50 cycles; plugs have
3 round or flat prongs in a
Y-shape

🕑 **TIME:**
Seven hours ahead of New
York

🌐 **WEBSITES:**
www.goisrael.com
www.timeout.com/israel
www.touristisrael.com
www.thinkisrael.com

LEBANON

SYRIA

*MEDITERRANEAN
SEA*

ISRAEL *West
Bank*

JERUSALEM ✪

Gaza

JORDAN

EGYPT

SAUDI
ARABIA

Know Before You Go

Is Israel safe? Are U.S. dollars accepted? Should you tip? Is everything closed on the weekend? You may have a few questions before you head out on vacation to Israel. Here are a few tips to make sure you're prepared and that your adventure runs as smoothly as possible.

IS ISRAEL A SAFE PLACE TO TRAVEL?

Israel is generally a safe place to travel, and violent crime against tourists is rare. More than three million people travel here each year, and few experience problems in popular tourist destinations like Jerusalem and Tel Aviv. However, you should still check with the U.S. Department of State for any travel warnings or advisories before your trip, especially if you plan to travel close to the border or West Bank. They sometimes advise exercising increased caution when traveling to these areas, though again, visitors rarely encounter problems if they only visit well-touristed areas.

EXPECT FREQUENT SECURITY CHECKS

Since its founding in 1948, Israel has been a country at war. That also means that, statistically in comparison to most major European countries, it is one of the safest countries due to its incredibly stringent system of security checks. You will certainly encounter a comprehensive check at Ben Gurion airport, and, if you're flying Israel's national carrier El Al, already at your departure city. You could be called aside for questioning at random, or if there is something in your travel documents that raises suspicion, such as having passport stamps to one of Israel's enemy countries like Lebanon or Syria. Expect also to open your bags for guards at shopping malls, cafés, and other crowded areas.

TOURISTS CAN VISIT PALESTINIAN TERRITORIES

While Israeli citizens are not allowed to visit Palestinian territories, like Jericho and Bethlehem, which are considered Area A (under total Palestinian control), tourists are able to visit. You can take an Arab cab that runs from just outside Jerusalem's Old City. Be sure to bring your passport with you, as you will be checked by soldiers when reentering Israel through the checkpoint.

CREDIT CARDS ARE WIDELY ACCEPTED

You shouldn't have any problem paying with a credit card in Israel, even in the smallest towns you plan to visit on your itinerary. While some places accept U.S. dollars or euros, it's generally best to pay in the local currency with an internationally recognized credit card that will do the exchange for you. Visa and MasterCard are the most commonly accepted, though American Express or Discover cards are usually accepted at ATMs.

TIP AT LEAST 12%

While 10% is usually the minimum at cafés and restaurants, it's generally expected to tip around 12% and up to 15% or 20% if the service was phenomenal. If you'd like to tip on your credit card, ask your server to do so before they swipe your card, as there's no option to add it on later; though it's usually better to tip in cash if you have it. There's no need to tip taxi drivers. In fact, some might rebuff you if you try.

ENGLISH IS COMMON

Many people in Israel speak at least one other language, in addition to Hebrew, and most speak English, especially in touristy cities like Jerusalem and Tel Aviv. At the same time, your traveling experience can be enriched by having at least a few words to contribute to the conversation or to use while touring and shopping, even at the local grocery store. Check out our Helpful Phrases section for some basic vocabulary.

BE AWARE OF CLOSINGS

While the weekend in Israel is generally from Friday to Saturday, and in some Christian communities from Saturday to Sunday, you'll need to check the opening hours of religious and historical sites. The Temple Mount, which is considered sacred to both Muslims and Jews, is generally closed to visitors on Friday and Saturday. Expect that much of the Jewish parts of West Jerusalem, including supermarkets and restaurants in religious and nonreligious neighborhoods, are closed from Friday night to Saturday night, during the Sabbath, during which no work is permitted. The same is true for Christian businesses on Sunday, the Christian day of rest, though religious sites like the Church of the Nativity in Bethlehem open partially to allow for visitors.

DRESS PROPERLY FOR RELIGIOUS SITES

While not all visitors to religious sites like the Western Wall, the Dome of the Rock, or the Church of the Holy Sepulcher are religious themselves, it is recommended to dress in conservative clothing out of respect for the local tradition. If you end up at the Western Wall without the appropriate clothing that covers your legs and arms, the guards can provide you with a shawl that you can use during your visit. It's a good idea to keep a scarf in your bag in case you want to visit a synagogue, mosque, or temple. And feel free to ask the local worshippers

what's acceptable, as norms can change from site to site.

RELIGIOUS ORTHODOX JEWS SEPARATE THE SEXES

Many ultra-Orthodox Jews maintain a tradition called "shomer negia," which means that members of the opposite sex who are not married or related cannot touch or speak with one another. While some men will break this rule so as not to embarrass a foreigner unfamiliar with the norms, it is also very possible that a woman will ask an ultra-Orthodox man for directions and he will look right past her. To avoid awkwardness as much as possible, dress modestly in those areas and try to find a person of the same sex to help you navigate out of the situation.

ISRAELIS ARE KNOWN TO BE DIRECT

A "sabra," or cactus, is the symbol of Israelis because they are prickly on the outside but soft on the inside. You'll sense this as soon as you get off the plane and into a taxi and your driver will ask personal questions about not just where you're from, but your religion, your family tree, and, most importantly, your opinion. To say that Israelis are direct is an understatement, but if you're able to embrace it, you'll pretty quickly find yourself in a house party of a guy who was a stranger just a few minutes ago, or with an invitation to that guy's distant cousin's wedding. In a country the size of New Jersey, and with decades of shared trauma under their

belt, virtually all Israelis seem to know each other— if not by one, then at most two or three degrees of separation—and see each other as one massive, extended family.

THERE ARE DIFFERING VIEWS ON ISRAEL'S CREATION

What sounds like a simple question—how was Israel created?—continues to be the center of hotly debated controversy that has only intensified as society has fractured with the years. For Israelis, the events of 1948 that led to the establishment of the Jewish State was known as the War of Independence, during which the British Mandate withdrew, and Jewish fighters successfully took control of the land previously known as Palestine. For Palestinians, it's known as the "nakba," or catastrophe, in which hundreds of thousands of people left or were forcibly expelled and made into refugees, and Palestine was conquered by a foreign power. If you want to discuss this essential question, be prepared for the emotional intensity that can come with an answer. The issue can be far more complex than you might imagine; come with an open mind.

Getting Here

Air

Flights to Israel tend to be least expensive from November through March, except for the holiday season at the end of December. Prices are higher during the Jewish High Holiday period (usually in September or October) and Passover (usually in April).

Flying time from New York to Israel is approximately 11 hours; from Los Angeles or San Francisco, it's about 14 hours nonstop, or 18 to 19 hours with the usual stopover in Europe or New York. International passengers are asked to arrive at the airport three hours prior to their flight time in order to allow for security checks.

From North America, the New York City area international airports have the highest number of nonstop flights, with El Al Airlines, United, and Delta providing nonstop service. Direct flights are also available on El Al from Los Angeles, Boston, Toronto, and Chicago (spring 2020), and on United from San Francisco. Major European carriers—including Aeroflot, Air France, Austrian Airways, British Airways, Brussels Airlines, Czech Airlines, Iberia, KLM, Lot, Lufthansa, Swissair, Turkish Airways, and Virgin Atlantic—have daily flights from the United States and on to Israel with stopovers in their domestic hub airports.

Because Israel is only slightly larger than New Jersey, it's more efficient to drive within the country than fly. The exception is the resort city of Eilat, which is about 360 km (224 miles) south of Tel Aviv on the Gulf of Aqaba. There are flights several times a day from Tel Aviv and Haifa.

Reconfirmation obligations differ from airline to airline (and change from time to time); be certain to check with your carrier for all legs of your journey.

AIRPORTS

Israel's main airport, Ben Gurion International Airport (TLV), is a 40-minute drive southeast of Tel Aviv. The airport has towering interior walls of Jerusalem stone adorned with 5th- and 6th-century Byzantine mosaics discovered throughout Israel. A soothing fountain is in the center of the departure hall, which has plenty of comfortable seating and cafés. Free Wi-Fi means you can stay connected while waiting for your flight. The spacious food court serves Middle Eastern cuisine and fast-food favorites. From Sde Dov Airport (SDV), about 4 km (2½ miles) north of Tel Aviv's center, domestic airlines fly to Eilat in the south and Haifa or Rosh Pina in the north.

From October to April, there are charter flights to the Red Sea resort town of Eilat from Moscow, St. Petersburg, Amsterdam, Copenhagen, Helsinki, and Tallinn. There are also charter flights to Eilat from Paris and London during the Jewish holiday months of September and October. Eilat is served by international Ramon Airport (⊕ www.iaa.gov.il), 19 km (12 miles) north of the city center.

GROUND TRANSPORTATION

The quickest and most convenient way to get to and from Ben Gurion International Airport is by taxi. Taxis are always available outside the arrivals hall and charge fixed prices. Fares, set by the government, are NIS 160 to Tel Aviv and NIS 295 to Jerusalem, plus NIS 4.50 per piece of luggage. Between 9 pm and 5:30 am, prices are NIS 185 to Tel Aviv and NIS 350 to Jerusalem.

From the airport, trains depart for Tel Aviv every half hour. They take you to the city in 15 minutes for NIS 13.50. Trains continue on to Herzliya, Netanya, Haifa, Akko, and Nahariya. For Jerusalem, change at Haganah Station in Tel Aviv, and expect a two-hour commute.

The Nesher shuttle service takes you to Jerusalem for NIS 64. The 10-passenger *sherut* taxis (minibuses) depart whenever they fill up. The main disadvantage is that there's no telling if you'll be the last passenger to be dropped off, so it can take an hour while the driver lets off the other passengers. To get to Ben Gurion International Airport from Jerusalem the same way, call Nesher a day in advance. Otherwise order a private cab from any taxi company, called a "special" taxi, for the fixed price of NIS 290, or NIS 340 after 9 pm nightly and on Saturday and holidays.

If you depart for the airport from central Tel Aviv by car or taxi at rush hour (7 to 9 am, 5 to 7 pm), note that the roads can get clogged. Allow 45 minutes for a trip that would otherwise take only about 20 minutes.

Taking the bus from Ben Gurion International Airport to Jerusalem is tedious. Board the Egged local shuttle (line 5, NIS 5.80) for the 10-minute ride to the El Al Junction, and wait there for a Jerusalem-bound bus (line 425 or 947, NIS 25). It runs to Jerusalem's Central Bus Station about every 30 minutes during the day, less frequently in the evening.

FLIGHTS

The national carrier, El Al Israel Airlines, is known for maintaining some of the world's strictest security standards. It's not necessarily the cheapest carrier, especially from the United States. United and Delta often have cheaper nonstop fares, and some European airlines have better prices if you don't mind a stopover in their hub cities. Within Israel, Arkia Israeli Airlines and Israir Airlines have flights from Tel Aviv to Eilat and Haifa. If you plan to travel in Jordan, Royal Jordanian is an option; it has flights from Ben Gurion International Airport.

🚲 Bicycle

Biking has taken off in Israel, with tens of thousands of avid cyclists hitting the trails every year. With mountains, deserts, and wooded hills, this small country is ideal for two-wheel adventures. Off-road tours take you to remote archaeological sites and other places not reachable by car. The Keren Kayemet LeIsrael (Jewish National Fund) has information about trails through some beautiful areas. Keep in mind that the going can get rough due to the summer's extreme heat, and there are winding and hilly roads with aggressive drivers. The weather is best from September to June.

Urban biking is also becoming popular. Tel Aviv has 120 km (75 miles) of designated bike lanes and a bike rental system. Look for the green Tel-O-Fun pay stations throughout the city. Use a credit card to pay the daily fee of NIS 17 (NIS 23 on Saturday and holidays) or weekly fee of NIS 70. If you need help, dial *6070 to talk to the call center.

In Jerusalem, there are a number of bicycle paths to ride, including the landscaped 5-km (3-mile) pedestrian and bike path that goes along the old train tracks, starting at the First Station, where you can rent bicycles. A new circular bike trail opened in Jerusalem's Metropolitan Park, and there are plans to expand it in coming years.

Bikes are welcome on intercity buses with luggage holds. Trains accept bikes Sunday through Thursday during nonpeak hours (between 9 and 3 and after 7) and anytime on Friday. Folding bicycles stored in carrying bags are always allowed.

Bike maps in English can be hard to find, but Israel Bike Trails has comprehensive trail information listing elevations and level of difficulty on its website.

Getting Here

👊 Boat

Many large cruise companies, including Costa, Holland America, Regent Seven Seas, and Seabourn have Mediterranean itineraries that include stops at the Israeli ports of Ashdod and Haifa. In addition, the Israeli company Mano sails from Haifa to many points in the Mediterranean between April and November.

🚌 Bus

Buses can take you almost anywhere in Israel. Most in Jerusalem are run by Egged and most buses in Tel Aviv are serviced by Dan, though other city bus companies also operate. Buses in Israel are clean, comfortable, air-conditioned, and some have Wi-Fi. Intercity bus fares vary according to distance traveled. During weekday rush hours, allow time for long lines at the obligatory security checks to enter most bus stations. Buses are often overcrowded on Saturday night as people return home after Shabbat and always packed on Sunday morning when it looks like the entire Israeli army is returning to base after a weekend at home.

The Central Bus Station in Tel Aviv resembles an M.C. Escher drawing: a jumble of staircases and escalators appearing to lead nowhere. The stark concrete building has multiple entrances and exits on several levels, endless corridors, and a dizzying array of platforms. It's all topped off by dozens of kiosks selling fast food and cheap merchandise, plus Asian minimarkets serving the local community of foreign workers. By contrast, Jerusalem's Central Bus Station is clean, well-organized, and easy to navigate. There's a pleasant enough food court, ATMs, information desk, and branches of some of the country's best-known stores.

Although buses resemble those in most other countries, there are a few quirks. When you're in Jerusalem, lines 1 and 3 primarily service ultra-Orthodox Jewish neighborhoods and end at the Western Wall area. On bus lines like these, it's generally accepted that women sit separately, in the back of the bus, and men in the front half. Although gender segregation is not compulsory by law, in ultra-Orthodox society it is the norm. If you're a woman and sit in an empty seat next to an ultra-Orthodox man, you shouldn't be surprised if he would rather stand than sit beside you. (In case you're wondering, ultra-Orthodox women generally accept this arrangement.)

Frequent bus service is available between Jerusalem and Tel Aviv. Egged Bus 405 runs from the Tel Aviv Central Bus Station every 15–20 minutes, and Bus 480 from the Arlozorov Street terminal (near the Savidor train station in Tel Aviv) leaves a bit more frequently, depending on the time of day (NIS 16 for each). There's a similar service to Jerusalem from most major cities, terminating at the Central Bus Station. The three small bus stations in East Jerusalem are for Palestinian-operated bus lines, with daily service to West Bank towns such as Bethlehem and Ramallah. The main bus depot is next to Damascus Gate light-rail stop.

FARES

For both local and long-distance travel, drivers accept payment in shekels. Drivers on long-distance buses grumble when they have to make change for a bill over NIS 100, so make sure to have smaller denominations. Unless you are running to catch a bus, it's almost always faster to buy your ticket at the office in the bus station. On city buses you don't need exact change. Children under age five ride free whether or not they occupy their own seat.

If you need a round-trip bus ticket, you have to buy an electronic Rav Kav card from the bus driver. It costs NIS 5 but you can load money on the card and use it for all tickets on all Israeli buses, trains, and Jerusalem's city tram.

The fare on most central city routes is NIS 5.90. If taking another bus within 90 minutes, ask for a free *ma'avar,* or transfer ticket.

Intercity fares are based on distance traveled. The one-hour trip between Tel Aviv and Jerusalem costs NIS 16, while the 2½-hour journey between Tel Aviv and Tiberias runs NIS 37.50. There are no advance reservations except to Eilat or the Dead Sea area.

SCHEDULES

Most major bus lines are available Sunday to Thursday from about 6 am to midnight. Keep in mind that public transportation in all cities except Haifa ceases to run on Jewish holidays and Shabbat, which lasts from sundown Friday afternoon to an hour after sundown Saturday evening. Be sure to give yourself extra time if traveling just before Shabbat.

Every large bus station has an information booth with schedule and platform information in English. The Egged website has an easy-to-use trip planner that includes timetables, routes, and fares.

⊜ Car

The Hebrew word for a native-born Israeli is *sabra,* which is the name of a prickly cactus that's sweet inside. You meet sweet Israelis if you get lost or have automotive difficulties—helping hands are quick to arrive—but behind the wheel, Israelis are aggressive and honk their horns far more than their Western counterparts.

Some travelers feel more comfortable hiring a driver, and there are plenty of ways to find someone reliable. Ask for recommendations at your hotel. Every hotel has taxi drivers who serve their guests, and most are familiar with all parts of the country and happy to quote you a daily rate.

Israel's highways are numbered, but most people still know them simply by the towns they connect: the Tiberias–Nazareth Road, for example. Intersections and turnoffs are similarly indicated, as in "the Tiberias Junction." Brown signs indicate tourist sites.

ADDRESSES

In Israel, streets are generally named after famous people or events, meaning that almost every community has a Herzl Street and a Ben Gurion Street. Don't worry about the "boulevard" or "alley" attached to many street names—Israelis just use the proper name. You don't find a Jabotinsky Street and a Jabotinsky Alley in the same city. What you likely encounter is a street that changes names after a couple of blocks. Street numbers follow the standard format, with odd numbers on one side and even numbers on the other.

If you know history, you'll have an easier time finding your way around Jerusalem's neighborhoods. In Baka a block of streets are named after biblical tribes, in Rehavia they're medieval Jewish scholars, and in Old Katamon, the brigades who fought in Israel's War of Independence.

Towns in Israel that have functioning Old Cities, some dating back to biblical times, include Jerusalem, Jaffa, Akko, and Tzfat. Streets and alleys in these areas have names, but sometimes it's hard to find numbers.

Getting Here

GASOLINE

Gas stations are found at regular intervals along the country's major highways, except in the Negev. On highways they're generally always open, while those in the city tend to close at midnight. Prices are standardized, so it doesn't matter which station you choose (though gas is cheaper in Eilat due to the Eilat tax-free zone). Most offer both full- and self-service pumps. If you go the full-service route, ask for a *kabbalah* (receipt). Attendants don't expect to be tipped. Most rental cars take unleaded gas, which at the time of this writing costs NIS 6.39 per liter. Most stations accept international credit cards.

PARKING

In Tel Aviv, Jerusalem, and Haifa, parking laws are stringently enforced. Expect a ticket of NIS 100 on your windshield if you've overstayed your welcome at a paid parking spot. Cars are towed if parked in a no-parking zone. Pay attention to the curb, as parking is forbidden where it's painted red. In downtown areas, parking is permitted only where there are blue and white stripes on the curb, meters, or pay stations.

Parking in Jerusalem costs NIS 5.70 per hour, and in central areas, pay stations print out small parking tickets to wedge at the top of the car window on the curb side. Parking in Tel Aviv costs NIS 6.20 an hour and you can only pay with a cell phone payment service like Pango. Read the signs carefully: in some areas free evening parking begins at 6, in others at 7 or 8.

Sound complicated? Stick to parking lots. Covered and open parking lots are plentiful in the major cities and can cost around NIS 15 per hour or NIS 70 per day.

RENTAL CARS

If you plan on heading north to the Golan or Upper Galilee, a rental car is a significant time-saver. If sticking to cities, a rental car is often more bother than boon. In Jerusalem, a combination of walking and taking cabs and the city tram is your best bet.

Familiar American car-rental companies operate in Israel, as do local ones such as Eldan. Rental rates in Israel start at around US$35 per day and US$200 per week for an economy car. Minivans and four-wheel-drive vehicles are very popular and should be reserved well in advance, especially during high season. Allow plenty of time to pick up and drop off your vehicle if renting from a city office.

Drivers must be at least 21. Your driver's license is acceptable in Israel.

RENTAL CARS IN THE WEST BANK

There are no restrictions on driving Israeli rental cars into West Bank areas under full Israeli control (known as Area C). However, your rental-car insurance coverage doesn't extend to West Bank areas under Palestinian control. If you rent from companies at the airport, in Tel Aviv, or in West Jerusalem, you are unable to drive the car to Bethlehem, Jericho, and other towns under the Palestinian Authority. If you plan on visiting these areas by car, use Dallah or one of the other Palestinian-operated car-rental companies in East Jerusalem. Have your passport with you to show Israeli guards at West Bank checkpoints if asked.

Even if you're using GPS, it's always a good idea to discuss possible routes with your car-rental company if you plan on passing through the West Bank.

ROAD CONDITIONS

Israel's highway system is very modern and has signs in English as well as Hebrew and Arabic. Route 6, the main north–south toll road, can save significant time on longer journeys. The highway starts at the Maahaz Junction, south of Kiryat Gat (south of Tel Aviv), and ends about 138 km (85 miles) north at the Ein Tut Junction near Yokneam (in the Lower Galilee). Electronic sensors read your license plate number and transmit the bill to your rental-car company. Car rental companies set their own rates for driving on Route 6, so be sure to ask what they charge. Expect to pay around NIS 60 to drive the length of the highway.

Route 1 is the chief route to Jerusalem from both the west (Tel Aviv, Ben Gurion International Airport, Mediterranean coast) and the east (Galilee via Jordan Valley, Dead Sea area, Eilat). The road from Tel Aviv is a divided highway that presents no problems except at morning rush hour (7 am to 9:30 am), when traffic backs up at the entrance to the city. For this reason, some drivers prefer Route 443—via Modi'in—which leaves Route 1 just east of the Ben Gurion Airport, and enters Jerusalem from the north (most convenient for East Jerusalem locations). Route 1, which enters Jerusalem under the Bridge of Strings, is more convenient for Givat Ram, West Jerusalem, and downtown.

Jerusalem, Haifa, and Tel Aviv are all clogged with traffic during the workday. In Jerusalem, the Old City and Jaffa Road are closed to private vehicles, with traffic routed around the periphery. Don't consider driving in Jerusalem if not comfortable negotiating narrow spaces or parking in tight spots.

If driving through the Negev, watch out for camels that can come loping out of the desert and onto the road. In the winter rainy season, sudden flash floods sometimes cascade through the desert *wadis* (streambeds that are usually dry) with little warning, washing out roads

and posing danger to motorists. It's best to postpone your desert trip if there's heavy rain in the forecast.

The desert can be unbelievably hot, sometimes even in the winter. It's a good idea to carry extra water—both for yourself and your car—while driving at any time of year.

ROADSIDE EMERGENCIES

In case of an accident or roadside emergency, call the police at 100. Should anything happen to your rental car, call your rental company for roadside repair or replacement of the vehicle.

RULES OF THE ROAD

By law, drivers and all passengers must wear seat belts at all times. Police crack down on drunk driving; the legal blood-alcohol limit is 0.05%. It's against the law to use a cell phone while driving.

Speed limits vary little across Israel: motorways (represented with blue signs) have speed limits of 110 kph (68 mph). Highways with green signs have speed limits of 80 or 90 kph (50 or 56 mph). Urban roads are 50 kph (31 mph).

Headlights must be turned on in daylight when driving on intercity roads from November 1 through March 31. A flashing green traffic light indicates that the red stoplight is about three seconds away and you should come to a halt.

Children under eight must be seated in age-appropriate car seats, and children under 13 aren't allowed in the front seat.

🚕 Taxi

Taxis are the most convenient way to get around cities. They're not cheap, but if you need to get somewhere fast or are unfamiliar with the area, a taxi (*monit* in Hebrew) is your best bet. Hail one on the

Getting Here

street or order by phone. Taxis are white sedans with a yellow sign on the roof. On the whole, drivers are knowledgeable, talkative, and like to practice their English with tourists. But be warned: some try to take advantage of tourists, charge hefty prices, or run up the meter.

According to law, taxi drivers must use the meter. Be firm when you request this (*moneh* is meter in Hebrew) and make sure the meter is running at the beginning of the ride. The exception is if you hire a driver for the day or a trip out of town, for which there are set rates. In those cases, agree on the price before you begin the journey and assume that the driver has built in a tip. In the event of a serious problem with the driver, report his cab number (on the illuminated plastic sign on the roof) or license plate number to the Ministry of Tourism or the Ministry of Transport. It is not customary to tip drivers.

Certain shared taxis or minivans have fixed rates and run set routes, such as from Tel Aviv to Haifa or from the airport to Jerusalem or Haifa; such a taxi is called a sherut (as opposed to a "special," the term used for a private cab). Some sheruts can be booked in advance.

Sheruts are an option if traveling between Jerusalem and Tel Aviv. They operate from the (grungy) side street alongside Tel Aviv's Central Bus Station seven days a week, departing when they fill up (NIS 24 on weekdays; NIS 35 on Saturday). They end their journey with stops near the Jerusalem Central Bus Station and 31 Haneviim Street, about a block from Zion Square. From Jerusalem, the sherut leaves from 31 Haneviim Street. A "special" cab on this route costs NIS 320, or about NIS 350 after 9 pm and on Saturday and holidays.

🚆 Train

Train travel between Jerusalem and Tel Aviv is more a pleasant and scenic excursion than an efficient way to travel. The journey currently takes nearly an hour and a half, compared to an hour by bus. It's a comfortable ride, and many just do it for the attractive scenery. The train, which departs every one to two hours, runs nonstop between Jerusalem's Malcha Station and Tel Aviv's Savidor Station. There are connections to Haifa and other destinations to the north. Service ends midafternoon on Friday and resumes about two hours after dark on Saturday. The fare to or from Tel Aviv is NIS 20 one way and NIS 32 round-trip.

Other cities—including Ashkelon, Beersheva, Beit Shemesh, Haifa, Herzliya, Akko, and Nahariya—are easily reachable by train from Tel Aviv. There are no different classes of service. All carriages are clean, spacious, and comfortable with well-upholstered seats. They're often crowded, however.

All train stations post up-to-date schedules in English. Complete schedules are also available on the website of the Israel Railway Authority. Tickets may be purchased at the ticket office in the station. Reserved seats are available Sunday to Thursday and may be bought up to a week in advance at the ticket office. Reserved seating is not available for the Jerusalem–Tel Aviv line and other short rides in metropolitan areas.

Jerusalem has a light-rail train, the country's first. It's a much more comfortable way to traverse the city than the bumpy roller-coaster rides on the city's buses. There's only one tram line, but it hits many points of interest. For information, see ⊕ *www.citypass.co.il*.

Essentials

🌐 Customs and Duties

For visitors with nothing to declare, clearing customs at Ben Gurion International Airport requires simply following the clearly marked green line to the baggage claims hall. There are generally no lines and customs inspectors rarely examine luggage. The red line for those with items to declare is next to the green line. Those over 17 may import into Israel duty-free: 250 grams of tobacco products; 2 liters of wine and 1 liter of spirits; ¼ liter of eau de cologne or perfume; and gifts totaling no more than US$200 in value. You may also import up to 3 kg of food products, but no fresh meat.

You may bring a pet if you bring a general health certificate in English issued by a government veterinary officer in your country of origin issued within 10 days prior to travel. The certificate must state that you've owned the pet for more than 90 days and that the animal has been vaccinated against rabies not more than a year and not less than one month prior to travel. Dogs and cats less than four months old won't be admitted. As soon as you receive the health certificate, but no less than 48 hours prior to arrival, pet owners must fax or email the veterinary department at Ben Gurion International Airport, including the name of the owner, veterinary health certificate, animal species, age, date of birth, breed, sex, identification number of electronic chip (for dogs), flight number, approximate arrival time, and your contact information.

⚠ Emergencies

Israel has an extremely sophisticated emergency response system and a high percentage of citizens who are trained medics. If you find yourself in any kind of medical or security emergency in a public place, the professional and citizen response is likely to be instantaneous.

To obtain police assistance at any time, dial 100. For emergency ambulance service, run by Magen David Adom, dial 101. To report a fire, dial 102. Emergency calls are free at public phones.

MEDICAL CENTERS

Emergency rooms in major hospitals are on duty 24 hours a day. Be sure to take your passport with you. There is a fee.

EILAT AND THE NEGEV

Three hospitals serve the Negev: Soroka in Beersheva, Barzilai in Ashkelon, and Yoseftal in Eilat. All have English speakers on staff and 24-hour emergency rooms (bring your insurance documents).

JERUSALEM

The privately run Terem Emergency Care Center in Jerusalem provides first aid and full medical attention, 24 hours a day, at its Romema and Bikur Holim clinics, and more limited hours at its third Jerusalem location.

The major hospitals in Jerusalem are Hadassah Ein Kerem, Shaare Zedek near Mount Herzl, and Hadassah Mount Scopus.

TEL AVIV

Tel Aviv Sourasky Medical Center (also known as Ichilov Hospital) is in north Tel Aviv, about a 10-minute drive (depending on traffic) from downtown. There's a 24-hour emergency room. Be sure to bring your passport with you. You are provided with all records in English for your insurance providers at home.

⊕ Health

No vaccinations are required to visit Israel. The country has one of the world's most advanced health-care systems.

Essentials

Most doctors at emergency clinics and hospitals in Israel speak English. Emergency and trauma care is among the best in the world.

It's safe to drink tap water and eat fresh produce after it's been washed as well as food from outdoor stands. Heat stroke and dehydration are real dangers if you're going to be outdoors for any length of time. A sun hat and sunblock are musts, as is plenty of bottled water (available even in the most remote places) to guard against dehydration. Take at least one liter per person for every hour you plan to be outside. Use sunscreen with SPF 30 or higher. Most supermarkets and pharmacies carry sunscreen in a range of SPFs, but it's much more expensive than in the United States.

U.S. brands of mosquito repellent with DEET are available in pharmacies and supermarkets. Wear light, long-sleeved clothing and long pants particularly at dusk, when mosquitoes are most likely to attack.

Yad Sarah is a nationwide voluntary organization that lends medical equipment and accessories such as wheelchairs, crutches, and canes. There's no charge, but a contribution is expected. In Jerusalem, it's open Sunday to Thursday 8:30 to 6:45 and Friday 8:30 to 11:45. Equipment can be returned elsewhere in the country.

OVER-THE-COUNTER REMEDIES

At the pharmacy (*beit mirkachat*), it's easy to find many of the same over-the-counter remedies as at home. Imodium (Rekamide) and Pepto-Bismol (the local version is Kal Beten) are available over the counter at every pharmacy. Everyday pain relievers such as Tylenol (called Acamol) and Advil are also widely available. You need a prescription for antibiotics. Medication can be obtained from pharmacies, which are plentiful. English is spoken in the majority of pharmacies. Locally produced medication is fairly inexpensive, but expect to pay more for drugs that are imported.

The municipal website of every city lists the pharmacies on duty at night, on Saturday, and holidays. This information is also available from Magen David Adom. In Jerusalem, Super-Pharm on the pedestrian mall is open Sunday to Thursday 8 am to 2 am, Friday 8:30 am to 4:30 pm, and Saturday one hour after the Sabbath ends until 2 am.

In Eilat, Michlin Pharmacy delivers to your hotel and is open Sunday to Thursday 8 am to 9 pm and Friday 8 to 3. Super-Pharm Mul Hayam is open Sunday to Thursday 9 am to 1 am, Friday 8:30 to midnight, and Saturday 9 am to 1 am. There are also pharmacies in this region in Arad, Beersheva, and Mitzpe Ramon.

⊗ Hours of Operation

Sunday is a regular workday in Israel. All government offices and most private offices and travel agencies are closed on Friday, Saturday, and all Jewish religious holidays. Businesses are generally open by 8:30 am.

Although hours can differ among banks, almost all open by 8:30 Sunday to Thursday. Most close around 12:30 and then reopen from 4 to 7 pm some evenings. Banks are closed on Saturday and Jewish religious holidays and have limited hours on Friday. In Muslim areas, banks are closed Friday. In Christian areas they're closed Sunday.

Museums don't have a fixed closing day, so although they are usually open 10 to 6 and on Saturday morning, confirm the schedule before you go.

Most local pharmacies close at 7 pm. Large chain stores, such as Super-Pharm and NewPharm, are usually open until at least 10 pm. In most cities a few drug-stores are open all night, on a rotating basis. Shops generally open at 9 or 9:30; neighborhood grocery stores usually open around 7. A few shops still close for a two- or three-hour siesta between 1 and 4. Most stores don't close before 7 pm; supermarkets are often open later, and in large cities, there are all-night supermarkets. Arab-owned stores usually open at 8 am and close in late afternoon. Mall hours are generally 9:30–9:30 Sunday to Thursday. In Jerusalem, malls shut down about two hours before sundown on Friday and reopen two hours after sunset on Saturday evening. Outside Jerusalem, some malls keep regular hours on Saturday, while others stay closed.

🧭 LGBTQ+ Travel

Israel has earned a reputation as a popular destination for LGBTQ+ travelers. The country recognizes same-sex marriages performed abroad, bans discrimination based on sexual orientation, and has long allowed gays to serve openly in the military. Most gays gravitate toward Tel Aviv, one of the most gay-friendly cities in the world. The city has a gay beach, a vibrant gay nightclub scene, an annual gay film festival, and a gay pride parade that attracts 100,000 participants every June. The Red Sea resort of Eilat is renowned for its pride festival in May.

🛏 Lodging

In Israel you can find every possible type of lodging, including luxury spa resorts, chic boutique hotels, country inns, and rural bed-and-breakfasts. There are also some more specialized offerings, including Christian guesthouses and kibbutz hotels (lodgings on the grounds of collective communities).

Some are utilitarian, but some recent trends are a rise in distinctive boutique hotels and in luxury properties, whether in the cities or the countryside. In contrast, options such as kibbutz hotels and bed-and-breakfasts (known as *zimmers* in Israel) offer a glimpse into local life and a more leisurely experience.

Israel has a one- to five-star ranking system for hotels similar to that used in many places in Europe, though only a limited number of hotels participate in the system. The Ministry of Tourism has already rated the country's 9,000 B&Bs. They're ranked A, B, or C, based on size and the facilities offered.

Non-Israeli citizens paying in foreign currency are exempt from the 17% V.A.T. on hotel rooms.

Throughout Israel, lodging prices often include breakfast. Prices in the reviews are the lowest cost of a standard double room in high season.

APARTMENT AND HOUSE RENTALS

Short-term rentals are popular, especially in Jerusalem and Tel Aviv and particularly for families who would otherwise be taking two or three hotel rooms. Options range from basic studios to mansions, and most are privately owned.

BED-AND-BREAKFASTS

Since the early 2000s, thousands of zimmers have sprung up, especially in the Galilee and the Golan. These are intimate cabins, usually featuring one or two bedrooms, a kitchenette, a hot tub, and an outdoor lounging area. Prices aren't necessarily lower than hotels, but if it's

Essentials

peace and quiet you're after, these may be just the thing.

Many zimmers are located in moshav-im—semicommunal rural communities. Private-home owners are also increasingly opening their doors to guests.

CHRISTIAN HOSPICES

Lodgings called Christian hospices (meaning hotels) provide accommodations and sometimes meals; these are mainly in and around Jerusalem and the Galilee. Some hospices are real bargains, while others are merely reasonable; facilities range from spare to luxurious. Those in rural settings are often tranquil retreats. Most give preference to pilgrimage groups, but many will accept individual travelers when space is available.

KIBBUTZ HOTELS

Around the country, kibbutz hotels offer a variety of accommodations in what are often lovely settings. Some kibbutz hotels are luxurious, while others are more basic. Most have large lawns, swimming pools, and athletic facilities. Some offer lectures about the history of kibbutzim and tours of the settlements and the surrounding areas. These kibbutz hotels are popular with tour groups.

$ Money

Israel is a country similarly priced to Western Europe for visitors, but more expensive than many of its Mediterranean neighbors. Prices tend to be cheaper in smaller towns. To save money, try the excellent prepared food from supermarkets, take public transportation, eat your main meal at lunch, eat inexpensive local foods such as falafel, and stay at hotels with kitchen facilities and guesthouses. Airfares are lowest November through March, except for the holiday season at the end of December.

Sample prices: cup of coffee, NIS 12; falafel, NIS 12; beer at a bar, from NIS 25; canned soft drink, NIS 14; hamburger at a fast-food restaurant, NIS 30; short taxi ride, about NIS 35 to NIS 45; museum admission, NIS 50; movie, NIS 38.

Prices throughout this guide are given for adults. Substantially reduced fees are almost always available for children, students, and senior citizens.

■TIP➔ Banks never have every foreign currency on hand, and it may take as long as a week to order. If planning to exchange funds before leaving home, don't wait until the last minute.

ATMS AND BANKS

ATMs—called *kaspomats* in Hebrew—are ubiquitous all over Israel. Look for machines that have stickers stating that they accept foreign credit cards or PLUS, NYCE, or CIRRUS signs. All have instructions in English. Almost all ATMs now have protective shields around the keypad to prevent anyone seeing your PIN.

With a debit card, the ATM gives you the desired amount of shekels and your home account is debited at the current exchange rate. Note that there may be a limit on how much money you are allowed to withdraw each day and that service charges are usually applied. Make sure you have enough cash in rural areas, villages, and small towns where ATMs may be harder to find.

The main branches of all the banks—Hapoalim, Leumi, Discount—are in Jerusalem's downtown area but are arguably the last resort for changing money. Several times a week they have morning hours only (different banks, different days) and give relatively low rates of exchange. It usually involves waiting in line and having the clerk fill out paperwork.

Your own bank probably charges a fee for using ATMs abroad, but some apply no foreign transaction fees. The foreign bank you use may also charge a fee. Nevertheless, you usually get a better rate of exchange at an ATM than in a bank. Extracting funds as you need is a safer option than carrying around a large amount of cash.

■TIP➔ PIN codes with more than four digits aren't recognized at ATMs in Israel. If yours has five or more, remember to change it before you leave.

CURRENCY AND EXCHANGE
Israel's monetary unit is the new Israeli shekel, abbreviated NIS. There are 100 agorot to the shekel. The silver 1-shekel coin is the size and shape of an American dime, but thicker. Smaller-value bronze coins are the half-shekel (50 agorot) and the 10-agorot coin (both of which are larger than the shekel). There's also a 2-shekel round coin (silver), a 5-shekel coin with 12 edges (silver), and a similar-size 10-shekel coin (bronze center, silver rim). Paper bills come in 20-, 50-, 100-, and 200-shekel denominations.

Dollars are widely accepted at hotels and shops, less so at restaurants. As of this writing, the exchange rate is about 3.5 shekels to the U.S. dollar.

In Israel, the best rates are at ATMs or at the myriad currency-exchange shops (typically marked "Change") in and around the central areas of the large cities. In Jerusalem, these are around Zion Square, the Ben Yehuda Street pedestrian mall, and a few strategic locations elsewhere in the city (Jerusalem Mall, German Colony neighborhood, Jewish Quarter).

🗋 Packing
Israel is a very casual country, and comfort comes first. For touring in the hot summer months, wear cool, easy-care clothing and sensible shoes for walking. If coming between May and September, you don't need a coat, but you should bring a sun hat that completely shades your face and neck. Take one light sweater for cool nights, particularly in hilly areas (including in and around Jerusalem) and the desert. Also take long pants to protect your legs and a spare pair of walking shoes for adventure travel or hiking shoes for more serious hiking. A raincoat with a zip-out lining is ideal for October to April, when the weather can get cold enough for snow (and is as likely to be warm enough in the south for outdoor swimming). Rain boots may also be a useful accessory in winter. Pack a bathing suit for all seasons.

Note that many religious sites forbid shorts and sleeveless shirts for both sexes, so a light scarf comes in handy to throw over the shoulders. You should bring modest dress for general touring in religious neighborhoods.

Along with a sun hat, take sunscreen, insect repellent, and sunglasses in summer. Essentials such as contact-lens solution and feminine hygiene supplies are available everywhere but are more costly than in North America.

🌐 Passport
Many Arab and Muslim countries in the Middle East, except Egypt and Jordan, have long refused to admit travelers whose passports carry any indication of having visited Israel. But that shouldn't be a problem now for tourists: Israel doesn't stamp passports anymore, only

Essentials

issues entry and exit permits on small slips of paper. Keep your entry permit paper in your passport during your visit.

📍 Restrooms

Public restrooms are plentiful in Israel and similar in facilities and cleanliness to those in the United States. At gas stations and some parks, toilet paper is sometimes in short supply, so you might want to carry some with you. Few public sinks, except those at hotels, have hot water, but most dispense liquid soap. Occasionally you may be asked to pay 1 shekel at some facilities.

➕ Safety

For the latest governmental travel advisories regarding travel to and within Israel, check with the U.S. State Department. The Israel Ministry of Tourism includes a section on its website with a nonalarmist perspective on visiting Israel during periods of unrest. For the latest local news, check the English-language papers *Haaretz,* the *Jerusalem Post,* or the *Times of Israel,* available online.

💲 Taxes

A value-added tax (V.A.T.) of 17% is charged on all purchases and transactions except tourists' hotel bills and car rentals paid in foreign currency (cash, traveler's checks, or foreign credit cards). Upon departure, you're entitled to a refund of tax on purchases made in foreign currency of more than NIS 400 (about US$100) on one invoice; but the refund isn't mandatory, and not all stores provide V.A.T. return forms. Stores so organized display "tax refund

for tourists" stickers, or you can inquire. Make sure you fill out the tax refund form.

Keep your receipts and the tax refund form, and ask for a cash refund at Ben Gurion Airport. Change Place Ltd. has a special desk for this purpose in the departures hall in Terminal 3. You also need to present the items you purchased.

💲 Tipping

There are no hard-and-fast rules for tipping in Israel. Locals do not tip taxi drivers. In other situations, a gratuity for good service is in order. If you've negotiated a price, assume the tip has been built in. If a restaurant bill doesn't include service, locals tend to tip 12% to 15%—round up if the service was particularly good, down if it was dismal. Hotel bellboys should be tipped a lump sum of NIS 10 to NIS 20, not per bag. Tipping is customary for tour guides, tour-bus drivers, and chauffeurs. Bus groups normally tip their guide NIS 30 to NIS 40 per person per day, and half that for the driver. Private guides normally get tipped NIS 100 to NIS 120 a day from the whole party. Both the person who washes your hair and the stylist expect a small tip—except if one of them owns the salon. Leave NIS 10 per day for your hotel's housekeeping staff, and the same for spa personnel.

🧭 Tours

If it's your first time in the Middle East and you're looking for a general overview of the main historic, religious, and natural sites, an escorted tour can be both efficient and cost effective. These trips are led by licensed tour guides and usually

Tipping Guidelines for Israel

Bartender	10%–15% per round, depending on the number of drinks.
Bellhop	NIS 10–20, not per bag.
Hotel Concierge	NIS 20 or more, if he or she performs a special service for you.
Hotel Doorman	NIS 10 if he helps you get a cab, but not necessary.
Hotel Maid	NIS 10 per day.
Hotel Room-Service Waiter	If service isn't already added to the bill, tip 10%–15%.
Taxi Driver	No tip expected.
Tour Guide	NIS 30–NIS 40 per day.
Waiter	If service isn't already added to the bill, tip 12%–15%. Tips in cash only, or ask if you can include in bill if paying by credit card.

include visits to Jerusalem, Tel Aviv, Masada, and the Dead Sea. It's not difficult to find itineraries tailored to your religious affiliation or areas of interest.

If an organized trip isn't for you, a private tour with a licensed guide is another option. However, all tours aren't equal, so be sure to check out the itinerary to make sure it matches your pace and whether the accommodations and restaurants are up to snuff.

SIGHTSEEING GUIDES

Licensed tour guides must undergo a rigorous two-year training program with annual continuing education required to maintain their credentials. Licensed guides can put together a complete customized itinerary for your group or take you on a private multiday tour. Many are native English speakers and have fascinating backgrounds they're happy to share with you.

Freelance guides may approach unaccompanied travelers near the Jaffa Gate in the Old City of Jerusalem and other places on the beaten path. Some of these guides aren't licensed, so it's impossible to know whether the tour they're offering is worthwhile or if they're planning on taking you to their best friend's souvenir stall. It's best to ignore them and walk on.

Modern, air-conditioned limousines and minibuses driven by expert, licensed guides are a great way to see the country for anyone whose budget can bear it. At this writing, the cost was US$500 to US$600 per day; add another US$100 for bigger vans. An additional US$150 to US$200 per night is charged for the driver's expenses if they sleep away from home. Half-day tours are also available, and you may hire a guide without a car.

Abboud Tours

EXCURSIONS | Haifa-based Abboud Tours, run by Israeli Christian Abboud Maroun, specializes in private minibus tours of Jerusalem and the Dead Sea, Nazareth and the Galilee, and the fascinating walled city of Akko. ☎ 04/852–5077 ⊕ www.abboudtours.com ✉ From $80 per person for day trip from Haifa to Jerusalem and the Dead Sea; price depends on size of group.

Consolidated Tour Operation

DRIVING TOURS | This experienced tour agency was founded by Moshe Eshed, a former president of the International Association of Tour Managers. The company arranges everything from day trips to Nazareth and the Galilee to a few

Essentials

days in Petra. ⊠ *Tel Aviv* ☎ *03/522–5253* ⊕ *www.highlightstoursofisrael.com* ✉ *From US$71 for a day tour of Jerusalem from Jerusalem or Tel Aviv.*

Superb Limousine Services

DRIVING TOURS | Getting around Israel can be daunting, so leave the driving to this experienced company. The company also arranges private tours for special interests such as archaeology or hiking, so prices vary widely. ☎ *03/973–1780* ⊕ *www.superb.co.il.*

GENERAL-INTEREST TOURS

Several major international tour companies run all-inclusive one- to two-week trips geared to the general traveler. On a smaller scale, two Israeli-based companies—Egged Tours and United Tours—offer shorter excursions. Prices start at around US$50 for half-day tours, US$100 per person for one-day tours, and US$300 per person for two-day tours. These tours are good options for solo travelers or people who don't want to be part of a tour for their entire trip.

Egged Tours

BUS TOURS | This well-regarded local company runs half-, one-, and two-day bus tours to many parts of Israel and the West Bank. There are also four-day tours that take you farther afield. ☎ *03/694–8888* ⊕ *www.eggedtours.com* ✉ *From $88 for day trip to Nazareth from Tel Aviv.*

Israel Discovery Tours

ADVENTURE TOURS | Perfect for first-time visitors to Israel, this company has tours that give you a general overview of the country. Tours last from 7 to 12 days and often include seldom-visited sights. ☎ *800/362–8882* ⊕ *israeldiscoverytours. com.*

United Tours

EXCURSIONS | If you want to explore mostly on your own, United Tours has great half- and full-day tours that give you the lay of the land. Several trips cover just Jerusalem, while others take you to Masada and the Dead Sea or the Roman ruins at Caesarea. ☎ *03/617–3333* ⊕ *www. unitedtours.co.il* ✉ *From $104 for a one-day trip including Caesarea, Haifa, Akko, and Rosh Hanikra.*

SPECIAL-INTEREST TOURS
ART
Israel My Way

SPECIAL-INTEREST | Haifa-based Israel My Way has exciting six-day "Art Lover" tours that include curator-guided tours of the latest exhibits at the country's top museums, studio visits with local artists, and a dinner in a chef's private home. They also offer other private tours tailored to your interests, such as architecture, diving, Israeli lifestyle, and other themes. ☎ *77/300–5717* ⊕ *www.israelmyway. co.il.*

BIKING
Tourist Israel

ADVENTURE TOURS | For a few half-day bike tours (or a bike-and-hike combination) throughout Israel, try Tourist Israel. ☎ *058/713–5678 Israel phone* ⊕ *www. touristisrael.com* ✉ *From $55 for a half-day bike tour in Tel Aviv.*

BIRD-WATCHING
Carmel Birding Tours

SPECIAL-INTEREST | The highly regarded Carmel Birding Tours is run by Dr. Carmel Zitronblat, an experienced birder whose single- and multiday tours for small groups include well-known birding destinations in the Beit She'an and Hula Valleys. ☎ *054/800–1212* ⊕ *www.carmel-birdingtours.com.*

Kibbutz Lotan Center for Birdwatching

SPECIAL-INTEREST | The center arranges bird-watching tours for small groups during the winter and spring around Eilat and Lotan. ☎ *08/635–6888* ⊕ *www. kibbutzlotan.com.*

HIKING
Israel Extreme
ADVENTURE TOURS | This company can create custom hiking itineraries for you in the Galilee and Golan, the Judean Desert, or around Eilat. You can also book kayaking tours and biking excursions. ☎ 052/647–8474 ⊕ www.israel-extreme. com.

Israel National Trail
ADVENTURE TOURS | Try a segment or two of the nearly 1,000-km (620-mile) Israel National Trail if you want to experience the diversity of the landscape. Note that this is a trail; it's not a hiking tour. ☎ 03/638–8719 ⊕ natureisrael.org/INT ✉ Trail is free.

Jesus Trail
ADVENTURE TOURS | For hiking the Galilee, the 65-km (36-mile) Jesus Trail combines rugged scenery with historic and religious sites. You can do the trail on your own, and the creators of the trail also offer tour packages of different lengths. ⊕ www.jesustrail.com.

Society for the Protection of Nature in Israel
SPECIAL-INTEREST | The Society for the Protection of Nature in Israel runs "field schools" across the country and conducts city walks and nature hikes with commentary in Hebrew. ☎ 03/638–8683 ⊕ www.natureisrael.org.

JEWISH EDUCATIONAL TOURS
Da'at Educational Expeditions
ADVENTURE TOURS | Providing in-depth explorations of the country and its history, Da'at Educational Expeditions is staffed by an experienced team of Jewish educators and guides. Another option is a tour with a private guide. The company offers Jewish-theme trips around the world. ☎ 888/811–2812 ⊕ www.daattravel.com.

Keshet
ADVENTURE TOURS | Offering customized guided tours, Keshet focuses on Judaism and Jewish history. ☎ 646/843–6221 ⊕ www.keshetisrael.co.il.

⦿ Trip Insurance

Comprehensive trip insurance is valuable if booking a very expensive or complicated trip (particularly to an isolated region) or booking far in advance. Comprehensive policies typically cover trip cancellation and interruption, letting you cancel or cut your trip short because of illness, or, in some cases, acts of terrorism. Such policies cover evacuation and medical care. Some also cover you for trip delays because of bad weather or mechanical problems as well as for lost or delayed luggage.

Another type of coverage to consider is financial default—that is, when your trip is disrupted because a tour operator, airline, or cruise line goes out of business. Generally you must buy this when you book your trip or shortly thereafter, and it's available to you only if your operator isn't on a list of excluded companies.

🛂 Visa

Israel issues three-month tourist visas free of charge at the point of entry when a valid passport is presented. Make sure your passport is valid for at least six months after your travel date or you won't be permitted entry. No health certificate or inoculations are required.

Israel's Major Holidays

If you're traveling to Israel during a religious holiday, you may find that businesses and sites are closed. Here's what to expect on major Jewish, Christian, and Muslim holidays.

JEWISH HOLIDAYS

In Israel Passover, Shavuot, and Sukkot/Simhat Torah are observed for seven, one, and eight days, respectively. All Jewish holidays begin at sundown the evening before the day of the holiday.

Shabbat (Sabbath). The Day of Rest in Israel is Saturday, the Jewish Sabbath, which begins at sundown Friday and ends at nightfall Saturday. Torah-observant Jews don't cook, travel, answer the telephone, or use money or writing materials during the Shabbat, hence the Sabbath ban on photography at Jewish holy sites like the Western Wall. In Jerusalem, the Downtown area clears out on Friday afternoon, and some religious neighborhoods are even closed to traffic.

Kosher restaurants close, except for the main hotel restaurants, where some menu restrictions apply. Outside Jerusalem you are scarcely affected.

There's no public intercity transportation on the Sabbath, although the private sherut taxis drive between the main cities. Urban buses operate only in Nazareth and, on a reduced schedule, in Haifa. Shabbat is also the busiest day for nature reserves and national parks. The highways toward the main cities can be choked with returning weekend traffic on Saturday afternoon.

Rosh Hashanah (Jewish New Year), September 18–20, 2020; September 6–8, 2021. This two-day holiday and Yom Kippur are collectively known as the High Holy Days. Rosh Hashanah traditionally begins a 10-day period of introspection and repentance. Observant Jews attend long synagogue services and eat festive meals. Nonobservant Jews may picnic or go to the beach.

Yom Kippur (Day of Atonement), September 27, 2020; September 15, 2021. Yom Kippur is the most solemn day of the Jewish year. Observant Jews fast, wear white clothing, avoid leather footwear, and abstain from pleasures of the flesh. Israeli radio and television stations shut down. By law, all sites, entertainment venues, and most restaurants must close. Much of the country comes to a halt, and in Jerusalem and other cities the roads are almost completely empty. It's considered a privilege to be invited to someone's house to "break the fast" as the holiday ends, at nightfall.

Sukkot (Feast of Tabernacles), October 2–9, 2020; September 20–27, 2021. Jews build open-roof huts or shelters called *sukkot* on porches and in backyards to remember the makeshift lodgings of the biblical Israelites as they wandered in the desert.

Simhat Torah, October 10, 2020; September 28, 2021. The last day of the Sukkot festival season, this holiday marks the end—and the immediate recommencement—of the annual cycle of the reading of the Torah, the Five Books of Moses. Services include singing, dancing, and carrying the Torah scrolls.

Hanukkah, December 10–18, 2020; November 28–December 6, 2021. A Jewish rebellion in the 2nd century BC renewed Jewish control of Jerusalem. In the rededicated Temple, the tradition tells, a vessel was found with enough oil to burn for a day. It miraculously burned for eight days, hence the eight-day holiday marked by the lighting of an increasing number of candles from night to night. Schools take a winter break. Shops, businesses, and services all remain open.

Purim, March 9, 2020; February 25, 2021 (one day later in Jerusalem). Children dress up in costumes leading up to Purim. In synagogues and on TV, devout Jews read the Scroll of Esther, the story of the valiant Jewish queen who prevented the massacre of her people in ancient Persia. On Purim day, it's customary to exchange gifts of foods with friends. Many towns hold street festivals.

Pesach (Passover), April 8–16, 2020; March 27–April 4, 2021. Dietary restrictions in force throughout. Passover is preceded by spring-cleaning to remove all traces of leavened bread from the home. During the seven days, no bread is sold in Jewish stores. On the first evening, families retell the story of exodus from Egyptian bondage and to eat a festive, symbolic meal called the seder (Hebrew for "order").

Yom Ha'atzma'ut (Independence Day), April 28, 2020; April 14, 2021. Israel declared independence on May 14, 1948, but the exact date of Yom Ha'atzma'ut every year follows the Hebrew calendar. Although there are gala events, fireworks, and military parades all over the country, most Israelis go picnicking or swimming. Stores are closed, but public transportation runs, and most sites are open.

Shavuot (Feast of Weeks), May 28–May 30, 2020; May 16–18, 2021. This holiday, seven weeks after Passover, marks the harvest of the first fruits and the day on which Moses received the Torah ("the Law") on Mount Sinai. It's customary to eat dairy products.

CHRISTIAN HOLIDAYS
Easter, April 12, 2020; April 4, 2021. This major festival celebrates the resurrection of Jesus. The nature and timing of its ceremonies are colorfully different in each Christian tradition represented in the Holy Land—Roman Catholic (Latin), Protestant, Greek Orthodox, Armenian Orthodox, Ethiopian, and so on. Western churches observe the date above.

Christmas. Except in towns with a large indigenous Christian population, such as Nazareth and Bethlehem, Christmas isn't a high-visibility holiday in Israel. The Christmas of the Catholic and Protestant traditions is celebrated on December 25. Christmas Eve (December 24) is the time for the international choir assembly in Bethlehem's Manger Square, followed by the Roman Catholic midnight mass.

MUSLIM HOLIDAYS
Muslims observe Friday as their holy day, but it's accompanied by none of the restrictions and far less of the solemnity of the Jewish Shabbat. The noontime prayer on Friday is the most important of the week and is typically preceded by a sermon, often broadcast from mosques' loudspeakers. The dates of Muslim holidays shift each year because of the lunar calendar. Holidays begin at sundown the evening before.

Ramadan, April 24–May 23, 2020; April 13–May 12, 2021. This monthlong fast commemorates the month in which the Koran was first revealed to Muhammad. Devout Muslims must abstain from food, drink, tobacco, and sex during daylight hours; the three-day festival of Eid el-Fitr marks its conclusion. The dates can change slightly at the very last moment. The Muslim holy sites on Jerusalem's Haram esh-Sharif (the Temple Mount) are only open a few morning hours and closed to tourists.

Eid al-Adha, July 31–August 3, 2020; July 20–23, 2021. This festival commemorating Abraham's willingness to sacrifice his son marks the end of the annual Haj, or pilgrimage to Mecca.

Helpful Hebrew Phrases

BASICS

Hello / good-bye / peace	Shalom	shah-**lohm**
Nice to meet you	Na'im me'od	nah-**eem** meh-**ohd**
Good morning	Boker tov	boh-ker **tohv**
Good evening	Erev tov	eh-rev **tohv**
Good night	Layla tov	lahy-lah tohv
How are you?	Ma shlomekh?	mah shloh-**maykh**
How are you? (to a man)	keif hhalak	kayf **hah**-luck
How are you? (woman speaking)	Ma shlomkha?	mah shlohm-**khah**
How are you?	Ma nishma?	mah-nee-**shmah**
Fine	Beseder	beh-**say-dehr**
Everything is fine	Hakol beseder	hah-kohl beh-**say-dehr**
Is everything okay?	Hakol beseder?	hah-kohl beh-**say-dehr**
Very well	Tov me'od	tohv-meh-**ohd**
Excellent/terrific	Metzuyan	meh-tzoo-**yahn**
Send regards!	Timsor dash	teem-sohr **dahsh**
Thank you	Toda	toh-**dah**
Thank you very much	Toda raba	toh-dah rah-**bah**
See you again	Lehitra'ot	leh-heet-rah-**oht**
Yes	Ken	kehn
No	Lo	lo
Maybe	Oolai	**oo**-ligh
Excuse me/Sorry	Slicha	slee-**khah**
Again/Could you repeat that?	Od pa'am	ohd pah-**ahm**

NUMBERS

1	Echad	eh-**khad**
2	Shtayim	shtah-**yeem**
3	Shalosh	shah-**lohsh**
4	Arba	ah-**rbah**
5	Chamesh	chah-**maysh**
6	Shesh	shehsh
7	Sheva	**sheh**-vah
8	Shmoneh	**shmoh**-neh
9	Teisha	**tay**-shah
10	Esser	**eh**-sehr
11	Achad esreh	ah-**chahd** eh-**sreh**
12	Shteim esreh	shtaym eh-**sreh**
20	Esrim	eh-**sreem**
50	Chamishim	khah-mee-**sheem**
100	Me'a	may-**ah**
200	Ma'tayim	mah-**tah-yeem**

DAYS

Today	Hayom	hah-**yohm**
Tomorrow	Machar	mah-**khahr**
Yesterday	Etmol	eht-**mohl**
Sunday	Yom Rishon	yohm ree-**shohn**
Monday	Yom Sheni	yohm sheh-**nee**
Tuesday	Yom Shlishi	yohm sh-**leeshee**
Wednesday	Yom Revi'i	yohm reh-**vee**
Thursday	Yom Chamishi	yohm kha-mee-**shee**
Friday	Shishi yohm	yohm shee-**shee**
Saturday	Sabbath Shabbat	yohm shah-**bat**

USEFUL PHRASES

Do you speak English?	Ata medaber anglit?	ah-ta meh-dah-ber ahng-**leet**
I don't understand (man)	Ani lo mevin	a-**nee** loh meh-**veen**
I don't understand (woman)	Ani lo m'vina	a-**nee** m'veena
I don't know (man)	Ani lo yodea	a-nee loh yoh-**day**-ah
I don't know (woman)	Ani lo yodaat	a-nee loh yoh-**dah**-aht
I am American (man)	Ani Amerika'i	ah-nee ah-mer-ee-**kah**-ee
I am British (man)	Ani Briti	ah-**nee** bree-tee
I am Canadian	Ani Canadi	ah-**nee** kah-**nah**-dee
What is the time?	Ma hasha'a?	mah hah-shah-**ah**
Just a minute	Rak rega	rahk **reh**-gah
Minute / Moment	Rega	reh-**gah**
Now	Achshav	ahkh-**shahv**
Not yet	Od lo	ohd loh
Later	Achar kach	ah-**khahr** kahkh
I would like	Hayiti mevakesh	hah-**yee**-tee m-vah-**kehsh**
Where is..?	Eifo..?	**ay**foh
The centra bus station	Hatachana hamerkazit	hah-tah-khah-**nah** hah-mehr-kah-**zeet**
The bus stop	Tachanat ha'autobus	tah-khah-**naht** hah-oh-toh-**boos**
The train station	Tachanat harakevet	tah-khah-**naht** hah-rah-**keh-veht**
The city center	Merkaz ha'ir	mehr kahz hah-**eer**
The post office	Hado'ar	hah-**doh**-ahr
A pharmacy	Beit mirkachat	bayt meer-**kah**-khaht

A public telephone	Telefon tziburi	teh-leh-**fohn** tzee-boo-**ree**
A good restaurant	Mis'ada tova	mee-sah-**dah** toh-**vah**
The rest rooms	Hasherutim	hah-shay-roo-**teem**
Right	Yemina	yeh-**mee**-nah
Left	Smola	s-**moh**-lah
Straight ahead	Yashar	yah-**shar**
Here	Kan	kahn
There	Sham	shahm
Do you have a (vacant) room?	Yesh lachem cheder (panui)?	yehsh lah-**chehm** **khedehr** (pah-**nooy**)
Is it possible to order a taxi?	Efshar lehazmin monit?	ehf-**shahr** leh-hahz **meen**moh-neet
Taxi	Monit	moh-**neet**
A little	k'tzat	keh-**tzaht**
A lot	harbe	hahr-beh
Enough	maspik	Mah-**speek**
I have a problem	Yesh li ba'aya	yehsh lee bah-**yah**
I don't feel well (man)	Ani lo margish tov	ah-**nee** loh mahr-**geesh** tohv
I don't feel well (woman)	Ani lo margisha tov	ah-**nee** loh mahr-**geeshah** tohv
I need a doctor (man)	Ani tzarich rofe	ah-**nee** tzah-**reech** roh-**feh**
I need a doctor (woman)	Ani tzricha rofe	ah-**nee** tzree-**khah** roh-**feh**
Help	Ezra	Eh-**zrah**
Fire	Dleika	duh-leh-**kah**

DINING OUT

I would like	Hayiti mevakesh	hah-**yee**-tee m-vah-**kehsh**
Some water, please	Mayim, bevakasha	mah-**yeem** beh-vah-kah-**shah**
Bread	Lechem	**leh**-khehm
Soup	Marak	mah-**rahk**
Meat	Bassar	bah-**ssahr**
Chicken	Off	ohf
Vegetables	Yerakot	yeh-rah-**koht**
Dessert	Kinuach	kee-**noo**-ahkh
Cake	Ooga	**oo**-gah
Fruit	Perot	peh-**roht**
Coffee	Cafe	kah-**feh**
Tea	Te	teh
Fork	Mazleg	mahz-**lehg**
Spoon	Kapit	kah-**peet**
Knife	Sakin	sah-**keen**
Plate	Tzalachat	tzah-**lah**-chaht
Food	Ochel	**oh**-khehl
Meal	Arucha	ah-roo-**khah**

Breakfast	Aruchat boker	ah-roo-**khaht** **boh**-ker
Lunch	Aruchat tzaharayim	ah-roo-khaht tzah-hah-**rah**-yeem
Dinner	Aruchat erev	Ahroo-**khaht** eh-rehv
Do you have a menu in English?	Yesh tafrit be'anglit?	yehsh tahf-**reet** beh- ahng-**leet**
A pita filled with falafel	Manat felafel	mah-naht feh-**lah**-fehl
Without hot sauce	Bli charif	blee khah-**reef**
It's tasty, delicious	Zeh ta'im	zeh tah-**eem**
I don't like the taste	Zeh lo ta'im li	zeh loh tah-**eem** lee
The check, please	Cheshbon, bevakasha	Khehsh-bohn beh-vah-kah-**shah**

SHOPPING

Do you have..?	Yesh lecha..?	yesh leh-khah
Milk	Chalav	khah-**lahv**
(Orange) Juice Mitz	(tapuzim) meetz	(tah-poo-zeem)
Butter	Chem'a	khem-**ah**
Cream cheese	Gevina levana	geh-vee-**nah** leh-vah-**nah**
Hard cheese	Gevina tzehuba	gevee-**nah** tzeh-**hoo**-bah
Sausage	Naknik	Nahk-**neek**
Jelly	Riba	**ree**-bah
Sugar	Sukar	**soo**-kahr
Ice cream	Glida	**glee**-da
Map	Mapa	**mah**-pa
Cigarettes	Sigariyot	see-gahr-ee-**yoht**
Telephone card (for public phones)	Telecart	teh-leh-**kahrt**
That one, please	Et zeh, bevakasha	eht zeh, beh-vah-kah-**shah**
May I see it?	Efshar lir'ot?	ehf-**shahr** leer-**oht**
How much does it cost?	Kama zeh oleh?	**kah**-ma zeh **ohleh**
That's expensive!	Yakar!	yah-**kahr**
No, it's too expensive	Lo, zeh yakar midai	loh, zeh yah-**kahr** meed-**igh**
Too big	Gadol midai	gah-dohl meed-**igh**
Too small	Katan midai	kah-tan meed-**igh**
Perhaps there's a discount?	Yesh hanacha oolai	Yehsh hah-na-**khah** oo-ligh oo-**ligh**
I'll take it	Ani ekach et zeh	ah-nee eh-**kakh** eht zeh

Helpful Palestinian Phrases

BASICS

Hello/ peace be upon you	Salamou alaikom	sah-**lah**-moo aah-**lay**-kom
(reply) Hello/ and peace be upon you	wa aalaikom essalaam	wah aah-**lay**-kom **ehss**-sah-**ahm**
Good-bye	maa issalameh	**maah** is-**ah-lah**-meh
Mr. / Sir	sayyed	**sigh**-yed
Mrs. / Madam	sayyida	**sigh**-yee-dah
Miss	anisseh	**ah**-niss-say
How are you? (man speaking)	keif hhalak	kayf **hah**-luck
How are you? (woman speaking)	keif hhalik	kayf **hah**-lik
Fine, thank you	bi kheir elhhamdilla	bee **khayr** el-**ham**-dihl-lah
Pleased to meet you	tsharrafna	tshahr-**ruhf**-nah
Please (man)	min fadlak	min **fahd**-lahk
Please (woman)	min fadlik	min **fahd**-lik
Thank you	shokran	shohk-rahn
God willing	Inshallah	ihn-**shahl-lah**
Yes	aah or naam	aah or naahm
No	la	lah
I'm Sorry (man)	mit assif	miht **ass**-sef
I'm Sorry (woman)	mit assfeh	miht **ass**-feh

NUMBERS

1	wahed	**wah**-hed
2	tinein	tee-**nayn**
3	talati	tah-**lah**-tee
4	arbaa	**ahr**-bah-aah
5	khamseh	**khahm**-seh
6	sitteh	**sit**-teh
7	sabaa	sub-**aah**
8	tamanyeh	tah-**mah**-nee-**yeh**
9	tisaa	**tiss**-aah
10	aashara	**aah**-shah-rah
11	ihhdaaesh	ihh-**dah**-ehsh
12	itnaaesh	it-**nah**-ehsh
20	ishreen	iish-**reen**
50	khamseen	khahm-**seen**
100	meyyeh	**may**-yeh
200	mitein	**mee**-tain

DAYS

Today	eliom	el-yohm
Tomorrow	bokra	bok-rah
Yesterday	embarehh	ehm-**bah**-rehh
Sunday	il ahhad	**il ah**-had
Monday	Ittinein	it-tee-**nayn**
Tuesday	ittalata	it-tah-**lah**-tah
Wednesday	il 'arbaa	il **ahr**-bah-**aah**
Thursday	il khamees	il khah-**mees**
Friday	iljumaa	il zhum-**aah**
Saturday	issabet	**iss-sah**-bet

USEFUL PHRASES

Do you speak English?	btihki inglizi?	btih-**kee** in-**glee**-zee?
I don't understand (man)	mish fahem	mish **fah**-him
I don't understand (woman)	mish fahmi	mish **fah**-meh
I don't know (man)	mish aarif	mish **aah**-ref
I don't know (woman)	mish aarfi	mish **aahr**-fee
I am American (man)	ana amriki	ah-nah ahm-**ree-kee**
I am American (woman)	ana amrikiyya	ah-nah ahm-**ree-key**-yah
I am British (man)	ana baritani	ah-nah bah-**ree-tah-nee**
I am British (woman)	ana baritaniya	ah-nah bah-**ree-tah-nay**-yah
What is this?	eish hada?	aysh **hah**-dah?
What time is it?	Addeish el wa'ed?	Ahd-**daysh**-el **wah**-ed
Where is?	wein?	wayn?
The train station	mahattit iltrain	mah-**huht-tit il-train**
The bus station	mahattit el buss	mah-**huht**-tit el **buhss**
The intracity bus station	mahattit el bus eddakheli	mah-**huht-tit el** buhss ed-dah-**khe-lee**
The taxi station	mujammaa el takasi	moo-**jam**-maah el tah-**kah**-see
The airport	el matar	el mah-**tahr**
The hotel	el oteil	el **ooh**-tayl
The cafe	el ahwi	el ah-**weh**
The restaurant	el mataam	el **matt-aahm**
The telephone	el tiliphon	el tih-lih-**fohn**
The hospital	el mostashfa	el moos-**tash**-fah
The post office	el bareed	el bah-**reed**
The rest room	el hammam	el huhm-**mahm**
The pharmacy	el saydaleyyeh	el sigh-dah-**lay-yeh**
The bank	el bank	el bahnk
The embassy	el safara	el sah-fah-**rah**
Right	yameen	yah-meen
Left	shmal	shmahl
Straight ahead	doughri	doo-ghree
I would like a room	beddi ghorfi	bed-dee **ghor-fih**

2

A little	shway or aleel	shway or ah-leel
A lot	kteer	kteer
Enough	bikaffi	bee-kaf-fee
I have a problem	aandi moshkili	aahn-dee **moosh**-keh-lee
I am ill	ana mareed	ah-nah mah-reed
I need a doctor	beddi daktor	bed-**dee** dac-**tor**
Help	saadoonee	**saah-doo**-nee
Fire	naar or harika	naahr or hah-**ree**-kah
Caution/ look out	entebeh or owaa	in-teh-beh or ohw-**aah**

DINING OUT

I would like	beddi	behd-dee
Water	mayy	muhyy
Bread	khobez	kho-bihz
Vegetables	khodra	khod-rah
Meat	lahhmi	**lahh**-meh
Fruits	fawakeh	fah-**wah**-keh
Cakes/ Sweets	helou/ halaweyyat	**heh**-loo/ hah-lah-**way-yaht**
Tea	shay	shahy
Coffee	ahwi	ah-weh
A fork	shokeh	show-keh
A spoon	maala a	**maah**-lah ah
A knife	sikkeen	sick-keen
A plate	sahin	sah-hin

SHOPPING

I would like to buy	beddi ashtri	bed-dee ahsh-tree
Cigarettes	sagayer or dokhkhan	sah-**gah**-yer or dokh-**khahn**
A city map	khareeta lal madeeni	khah-**ree**-tah lahl mah-**dee**-nee
A road map	khareeta lal tareek	khah-**ree**-tah lahl tah-**reek**
How much is it?	addaish ha o	**ad**-daysh **ha** oh
It's expensive	ghali	ghah-lee

Great Itineraries

Jerusalem, the Dead Sea, and the Galilee, 9 Days

Israel is a small but varied country. This itinerary lets you see the high points of Jerusalem and the northern half of the country in nine days; linger in Tel Aviv at its conclusion and the desert if you have another two to nine days.

JERUSALEM, DAYS 1 AND 2

You could spend a lifetime in Jerusalem, but two days is probably a good minimum to get a feel for the city. First, spend a day getting an overview of the holy sites of Judaism, Christianity, and Islam in the Old City. Start with the Western Wall, then go up to the Temple Mount (morning hours) to view the Muslim shrines. Follow the Via Dolorosa to the Church of the Holy Sepulcher. Stop for a Middle Eastern–style lunch in the Christian Quarter before walking down into the Jewish Quarter. (Note: The Temple Mount is closed Friday and Saturday, and some Jewish Quarter sites close early Friday and don't reopen until Sunday.) Explore the remarkable underworld of biblical (Old Testament) Jerusalem, at the City of David, or, if you have a car, pick up one or two of the panoramic views.

On your second day, venture farther afield in West Jerusalem. Many consider the Israel Museum and Yad Vashem, home to the Holocaust History Museum, essential if you're visiting Jerusalem. Mount Herzl National Memorial Park is also a meaningful excursion. A good plan is to avoid burnout by doing one of the big museums on Day 2, the other on Day 3. (Note: Yad Vashem and Mount Herzl are closed Saturday.) Add the Machaneh Yehuda produce market (closed Saturday) and the Knesset menorah.

AROUND THE DEAD SEA, DAYS 3 AND 4

After getting an early start in your rental car, head east through the stark Judean Desert to Qumran, where the Dead Sea Scrolls were discovered. You can spend an hour (max) touring the ruins and seeing the audiovisual presentation. About 45 minutes south of Qumran along the Dead Sea shore is Ein Gedi, where a leisurely hike to the waterfall and back should take about 1½ hours, including a dip in a freshwater pool. End the day with a float in the Dead Sea, and spend the night in one of the fine hotels at Ein Bokek, at the southern end of the lake. The spa treatments featuring the famously curative Dead Sea mud are a highlight for many.

In the morning, hike the Snake Path—or take the cable car—up Masada, site of Herod's winter palace. The gate to the trail opens before dawn so you can catch the sunrise at the top. Later, head back to Jerusalem to spend the night.

Note: If you don't have a car, one-day bus tours from Jerusalem let you see Masada and the Dead Sea. Or you can also drive to Qumran, Ein Gedi, the Dead Sea, and Masada for the day and return to Jerusalem: that's a full day, and you'd need to plan your time carefully.

THE GALILEE, DAYS 5–7

From Jerusalem, where you've spent the night, make an early start for a busy day. Retrace your steps down Route 1 East, stopping just north of the Dead Sea–Jerusalem highway at the oasis town of Jericho, the world's oldest city. It's almost worth a trip through this lush town—with its date palms, orange groves, banana plantations, bougainvillea, and papaya trees—just to be able to say "I was there," but Tel Jericho is also a significant

archaeological site. Sample the baklava and orange juice. Jericho is in the Palestinian Authority, so check ahead of time for any entry restrictions. Most car-rental agencies don't allow their cars into Palestinian areas. You must show your passport at the checkpoint.

Take the Jordan Valley route (Route 90) to the Galilee, stopping at the extensive Roman-Byzantine ruins at Beit She'an, where you can have lunch in town or take a sandwich to the site. The Crusader castle of Belvoir rounds out the day, and you can enjoy a lakeside fish dinner in Tiberias, where you spend the night.

The next day, spend an hour or two in the far north at the Tel Dan Nature Reserve, with its rushing water and biblical archaeology. Nearby Banias has Roman shrines, a fine walk, and the Suspended Trail overlooking a cauldron of seething white water. Depending on how you spend your day, you can also visit one of the many fine wineries on the Golan Heights, or do some hiking or bird-watching at Gamla. Stay overnight in Tiberias again, or better yet, farther north in a Hula Valley B&B.

On your third day, explore the treasures of Tzfat, with its beautiful vistas, old synagogues, and art and Judaica galleries. Spend the afternoon hiking or horseback riding at Bat Ya'ar (reserve if you want to go trail riding) or kayaking at Hagoshrim or Kfar Blum (seasonal, but no need to reserve). Stay overnight in Tiberias or at your Hula Valley B&B.

THE MEDITERRANEAN COAST, DAYS 8 AND 9

From Tiberias or your Hula Valley B&B, head west to the coast. Your first stop can be the cable-car ride to the sea grottoes of Rosh Hanikra. Then travel to Akko, with its Crusader halls and picturesque harbor. Akko is also an excellent place for a fish lunch. Then drive to Haifa for a view from the Dan Panorama Hotel at the top of Mount Carmel. Spend the night in Haifa.

The following day, visit Haifa's Baha'i Shrine and its magnificent gardens, then continue down the coast to visit the village of Zichron Ya'akov, home of the Carmel Winery and the Beit Aaronson Museum. Have lunch and then head to Tel Aviv, stopping at the Roman ruins of Caesarea on the way. In Tel Aviv, you can enjoy a night on the town, perhaps in Neve Tzedek or Jaffa. From Tel Aviv you can head to the airport if it's time to go home.

Great Itineraries

In the Footsteps of Jesus, 6 days

Visit the Holy Land, they say, and you'll never read the Bible the same way again; the landscapes and shrines that you'll see, and your encounters with local members of Christian communities at the landmarks of Jesus's life, will have a profound and lasting impact.

JERUSALEM AND BETHLEHEM, DAYS 1 AND 2

Spend your first day retracing the climax of the story of Jesus in Jerusalem, starting at the Mount of Olives. This is where Jesus taught and wept over the city (Luke 19:41), and the tear-shape Dominus Flevit church commemorates it. The walk down the Mount of Olives road, also known as the Palm Sunday road, leads to the ancient olive trees in the Garden of Gethsemane, where you can contemplate Jesus's "passion" and arrest.

Follow the Via Dolorosa, stopping at each Station of the Cross, to the Church of the Holy Sepulcher, where most Christians believe Jesus was crucified, buried, and resurrected. The Garden Tomb—the site of Calvary for many Protestants—offers an island of tranquility. Take your time contemplating the sites; this won't be a rushed day.

The next day, you can explore the Southern Wall excavations at the Jerusalem Archaeological Park and Davidson Center, adjacent to the Old City's Dung Gate. Scholars believe Jesus could have walked the stones of the ancient street here, and climbed the Southern Steps to the Temple. Down the hill is the City of David, the Old Testament heart of Jerusalem, including the excavated Area G and Warren's Shaft, and King Hezekiah's water tunnel. The steps of the pool of Siloam, where a blind man had his sight restored (John 9:7–11), were discovered only a few years ago. Add a visit to the Room of the Last Supper on Mount Zion, near Zion Gate, and then have lunch.

In the afternoon, you can visit Bethlehem, the birthplace of Jesus, to see the Church of the Nativity, one of the oldest churches in the world. Bethlehem is in the Palestinian Authority, so bring your passport. Most car-rental agencies don't allow their cars into Palestinian areas. It's best to take a taxi to the border crossing east of Jerusalem's Gilo neighborhood. The crossing for tourists is usually uncomplicated, and there are Palestinian taxis waiting on the other side to take you to the church. Or you can opt to spend the afternoon in Jerusalem.

ON THE WAY TO THE GALILEE, DAY 3

Making an early start, head east through the barren Judean Desert to Qumran, where the Dead Sea Scrolls were found. Some scholars believe John the Baptist may have passed through here, and a visit to the site—you can spend an hour here—is an opportunity to learn about the desert in which Jesus sought solitude, purity, and inspiration.

Then head up the Jordan Valley (Route 90), passing through or near Jericho (depending on political conditions). Jesus also healed a blind man here (Mark 10:46), and had a meal with the tax collector Zacchaeus (Luke 19:1–5). If the security situation isn't favorable, the Israeli soldiers at the checkpoint at Jericho don't allow you in (again, read a newspaper and use common sense). If you skip Jericho, Route 90 swings past it to the east. In Jericho, though, a visit to Tel Jericho, the first conquest of the Israelites in the Holy Land (Joshua 6), is a must. You can have lunch at the restaurant next to the tell or at a truck stop on the way north from Jericho.

Then it's on to the ruins at Beit She'an, including the ancient main street, a bathhouse, and mosaics. Not only is this an important Old Testament site, it was also the capital of the Decapolis, a league of 10 Roman cities, among which Jesus taught and healed (Mark 7:31).

Farther north, pilgrims go to Yardenit to be baptized in the Jordan River and remember the baptism of Jesus in these waters. Spend the night in Tiberias on the Sea of Galilee; enjoy a fish dinner.

SEA OF GALILEE, DAY 4

Start the day heading north to see the ancient wooden boat at Ginosar, which evokes Gospel descriptions of life on the lake—see, for example, Matthew 9:1. Then, after meditating on Jesus's famous sermon (Matthew 5) in the gardens of the Mount of Beatitudes and its chapel (off Route 90 north of the Sea of Galilee), descend to Tabgha to see the mosaics of the Church of the Multiplication of Loaves and Fishes. From a lakeshore perch at the nearby Church of the Primacy of St. Peter, where Jesus appeared to the disciples after the Resurrection (John 21), you can marvel at how Scripture and landscape blend before your eyes.

Farther east, the ruins of ancient Capernaum—the center of Jesus's local ministry—include a magnificent pillared synagogue (partially restored) and Peter's house.

An archaeological mound across the Jordan River, north of the Sea of Galilee, is ancient Bethsaida, where the Gospels say Jesus healed and taught (Luke 9:10, 10:13). To get there, continue east of Capernaum, cross the Jordan River north of the Sea of Galilee, turn left onto Route

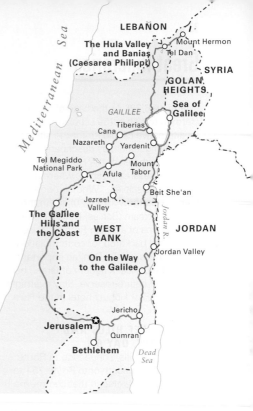

888, and a short distance thereafter turn left to Bethsaida in the Jordan River Park. From there, head back down to the lake and continue around its eastern shore to Kursi National Park and the ruins of a Byzantine church where, it's said, Jesus cast out demons into a herd of swine that stampeded into the water (Matthew 8:28–30).

A good idea for lunch is the fish restaurant at Kibbutz Ein Gev. Ask about a cruise on the lake after lunch (the kibbutz also has a boat company). Spend the night in Tiberias or at one of the kibbutz guesthouses or B&Bs in the Hula Valley.

THE HULA VALLEY AND BANIAS (CAESAREA PHILIPPI), DAY 5

The next day, drive through the Hula Valley; it's especially remarkable in the spring when the flowers bloom and bring alive Jesus's famous teaching from the Sermon on the Mount: "Consider the lilies of the field, how they grow"

Great Itineraries

(Matthew 6:28). At the base of Mount Hermon (which some scholars see as an alternative candidate for the site of the Transfiguration, as described in Mark 9:2–8), northeast of the Hula Valley, is Banias (Caesarea Philippi), where Jesus asked the disciples, "Who do people say I am?" (Matthew 16:13–20); it's in the Hermon Stream (Banias) Nature Reserve. The remains of a pagan Roman shrine are a powerful backdrop for contemplation of that message. Tel Dan, an important city in the biblical Kingdom of Israel, has a beautiful nature reserve. Stay overnight at your B&B or kibbutz hotel in the Hula Valley.

THE GALILEE HILLS AND THE COAST, DAY 6

Head for the hills, connecting to Route 77 and turning south onto Route 754 to Cana to see the church that commemorates Jesus's first miracle: changing water into wine (John 2:1–11). Continue to Nazareth, Jesus's childhood town. The massive modern Basilica of the Annunciation is built over a rock dwelling where Catholics believe the angel Gabriel appeared to Mary (Luke 1:26–38). The Greek Orthodox tradition is that the event took place at the village well, and their church is built over that site, some distance away. Nazareth's restaurants make tasty lunch stops.

A drive through the lush Jezreel Valley, via Route 60 and then north on Route 65 (the New Testament Valley of Armageddon), brings you to Mount Tabor, long identified as the Mount of Transfiguration. The valley is named Armageddon (Revelation 16:16), after the archaeological site of Tel Megiddo, now a national park south of Afula on Route 65. The drive back to Jerusalem from Tel Megiddo takes 1½ hours, using the Route 6 toll road, or you can spend the night in Haifa and return to Jerusalem the next day.

Tips

First and foremost, bring along a Bible if you have one; it gets a lot of use.

You don't need a car in Jerusalem, but you do need one for the rest of this itinerary. Your best bet is to pick up a car on the afternoon of the day before you head out of Jerusalem, so that you can make an early start the next day (remember that rental agencies are normally not open on Saturday). The agency provides you with a basic road map and advice.

Gas stations are numerous, many with convenience stores to stock up on snacks.

Contacts

📍 Visitor Information

Israel Government Tourist Office. ☎ 888/774–7723 in U.S. ⊕ israel.travel. **Israel Nature and Parks Authority.** ⊕ www.parks.org.il. **Times of Israel.** ⊕ timesofisrael. com. **U.S. Department of State.** ⊕ travel.state.gov.

🏛 Embassy

U.S. Embassy. ✉ 14 David Flusser, Jerusalem ☎ 02/630–4000 ⊕ il.usembassy.gov.

✈ Air

AIRPORTS Ben Gurion International Airport. ☎ 03/975–5555 ⊕ www. iaa.gov.il/rashat/en-US/ airports/bengurion. **Ramon Airport.** ✉ Timna Valley, Eilat ✛ 11 miles north of Eilat, next to Be'er Ora ☎ 03/972–3333 ⊕ www. iaa.gov.il.

AIRPORT TRANSFERS Egged. ☎ 03/694–8888 ⊕ www.egged.co.il. **Nesher.** ☎ 02/625–7227 ⊕ www.neshertours.co.il.

LOCAL AIRLINES Arkia Israeli Airlines. ☎ 03/690–2210 ⊕ www.arkia.com. **Israir Airlines.** ☎ 03/510–9589 ⊕ www.israirairlines. com.

🚲 Bicycle

Israel Bike Trails. ⊕ www. bikemap.net/en/l/294640 . **Israel Cycling.** ☎ 054/333–9543 ⊕ www.israelcycling. com. **Sovoo Jerusalem Electric Bike Rental.** ✉ First Station, 4 David Remez St., Jerusalem ☎ 02/648–0334 ⊕ www.gojerusa-lem.com. **Tel-O-Fun Bike Rental .** ⊕ www.tel-o-fun. co.il/en.

🚌 Bus

Dan. ☎ 03/639–4444 ⊕ www.dan.co.il/Eng. **East Jerusalem Bus Station.** ✉ Sultan Suleiman St., opposite Damascus Gate, East Jerusalem ☎ 02/627–2881. **Jerusalem Central Bus Station.** ✉ 224 Jaffa Rd., Romema ☎ 03/914–2237 ⊕ egged. co.il/eng. **National Bus Hotline.** ☎ *8787 ⊕ www. bus.co.il.

🚗 Car

LOCAL RENTAL AGENCIES Best. ☎ *8883 ⊕ www. best-car.co.il/en. **Green Peace Car Rental.** ✉ Mount of Olives Hotel, 53 Mount of Olives Rd., East Jerusalem ☎ 02/585–9756 ⊕ www.greenpeace.co.il.

🚕 Taxi

JERUSALEM TAXI CONTACTS Hapalmach. ☎ 02/679–3333. **Hapisgah.** ☎ 02/642–1111. **Rehavia.** ☎ 02/625–4444. **Smadar.** ☎ 02/566–4444.

EILAT TAXI CONTACTS Hacohanim. ☎ 08/631–6007. **Taba.** ☎ 08/633–3333.

🚆 Train

Israel Railways. ☎ 08/683–1222 ⊕ www.rail.co.il/EN.

🛏 Lodging

BED-AND-BREAKFASTS Home Accommodation Association of Jerusalem. ⊕ www.bnb.co.il. **Rural Tourism in Israel.** ⊕ www. zimmeril.com.

CHRISTIAN HOSPICES Travelujah. ☎ 052/744–4033 Israel phone number ⊕ www.travelujah. com/groups/category/ Christian-Guest-Houses.

⚠ Emergencies

Police. ☎ 100 ⊕ www. gov.il/en/departments/ israel_police.

Chapter 3

JERUSALEM

Updated by
Elianna Bar-El

Sights
★★★★★

Restaurants
★★★★★

Hotels
★★★★★

Shopping
★★★★★

Nightlife
★★★★★

WELCOME TO JERUSALEM

TOP REASONS TO GO

★ **City of David:** Plunge underground to explore Jerusalem's most ancient remains, and wade the 2,700-year-old water tunnel that once saved the besieged city—or exit dry.

★ **Israel Museum:** Renewed and revitalized, this museum is a winner, with the Dead Sea Scrolls, a huge outdoor model, and a stunning collection of fine art, archaeology, and Judaica.

★ **Machaneh Yehuda:** You can munch a falafel as you watch shoppers swirl and eddy through West Jerusalem's outstanding produce market.

★ **Mount of Olives:** This classic panorama puts the entire Old City, with the golden Dome of the Rock, squarely within your lens. The view is best with the morning sun behind you.

★ **The Old City:** For an astonishing montage of religions and cultures, the heart of Jerusalem—with the Holy Sepulcher, Arab bazaar, and Western Wall—has few equals anywhere in the world.

1 **The Old City.** With its narrow streets and hidden alleys, Jerusalem's legendary Old City is a labyrinth of memories and a bewitching kaleidoscope of colors and cultures.

2 **East Jerusalem.** Most visitors, particularly Christians, will identify with two or three particular sites—Mount of Olives, Gethsemane, and the Garden Tomb.

3 **West Jerusalem.** Within this extensive side of Jerusalem are several great but unrelated sights, some a few miles apart. Savor the extraordinary Israel Museum and the Yad Vashem Holocaust Museum.

4 **Center City.** West Jerusalem's Downtown areas have more subtle attractions than the postcard snapshots suggest. Check out the Yemin Moshe and Nahalat Shiva neighborhoods, Ben-Yehuda Street, and the Machaneh Yehuda market.

5 **German Colony and Baka.** Stone architecture, trendy restaurants, and great coffee shops offer a refreshing change of pace from the holy and historical.

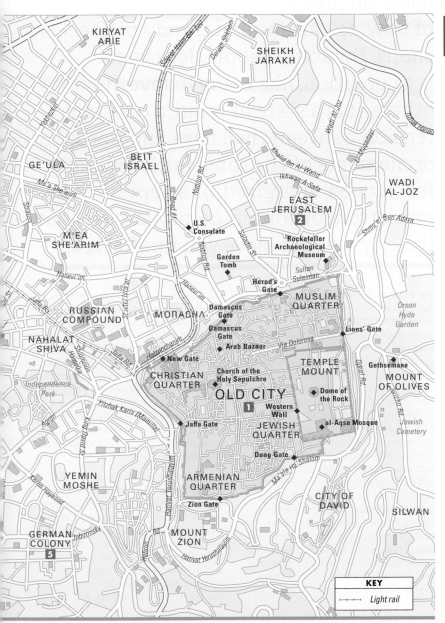

KIRYAT ARIE

SHEIKH JARAKH

GE'ULA

BEIT ISRAEL

WADI AL-JOZ

EAST JERUSALEM 2

M'EA SHE'ARIM

U.S. Consulate

Rockefeller Archaeological Museum

Garden Tomb

Sultan Suleiman

Herod's Gate

MUSLIM QUARTER

RUSSIAN COMPOUND

Damascus Gate

Orson Hyde Garden

Lions' Gate

NAHALAT SHIVA

Damascus Gate

Via Dolorosa

Arab Bazaar

Gethsemane

New Gate

TEMPLE MOUNT

MOUNT OF OLIVES

Independence Park

CHRISTIAN QUARTER

Church of the Holy Sepulchre

Dome of the Rock

OLD CITY 1

Western Wall

Jewish Cemetery

Jaffa Gate

JEWISH QUARTER

al-Aqsa Mosque

YEMIN MOSHE

Dung Gate

ARMENIAN QUARTER

CITY OF DAVID

SILWAN

Zion Gate

GERMAN COLONY 5

MOUNT ZION

KEY
⊢——⊢ Light rail

Jerusalem is a city suspended between heaven and earth, East and West, past and present—parallel universes of flowing caftans and trendy coffee shops. For some people, Jerusalem is a condition, like being in love; for others, it is a state of mind, a constant tension between rival flags and faiths, or members of the same faith. You may feel moved, energized, or swept into the maelstrom of contemporary issues—but the city will not leave you unaffected.

The word *unique* is easy to throw around, but Jerusalem has a real claim on it. The city is sacred to half the human race, and its iconic Old City walls embrace primary sites of the three great monotheistic religions. For Jews, Jerusalem has always been their spiritual focus and historical national center; the imposing Western Wall is the last remnant of the ancient Second Temple complex. For almost 2,000 years, Christians have venerated Jerusalem as the place where their faith was shaped—through the death, burial, and resurrection of Jesus of Nazareth—and the candlelit Church of the Holy Sepulcher is where the greater part of Christendom recognizes those events. Islamic tradition identifies Jerusalem as the *masjid al-aqsa,* the "farthermost place," from which Muhammad ascended to Heaven for his portentous meeting with God: the dazzling, gold-top Dome of the Rock marks the spot.

The Old City is far more than shrines, however. Its arches, hidden courtyards, and narrow cobblestone alleyways beckon you back in time. The streets are crowded with travelers, pilgrims, and vendors of everything from tourist trinkets and leather sandals to fresh produce and embroidered fabrics. Your senses are assaulted by intense colors and by the aromas of turmeric, fresh mint, wild sage, and cardamom-spiced coffee. The blare of Arabic music and the burble of languages fill the air.

Step outside the Old City and you'll be transported into the 21st century—well, at least the 20th: quaint neighborhoods, some restored, embody an earlier simplicity. West Jerusalem forms the bulk of a modern metropolis of 850,000, Israel's largest city. It's not as cosmopolitan as Tel Aviv, but it does have delicious and unexpected restaurants, fine hotels, vibrant markets, and upscale neighborhoods. The Downtown triangle of Jaffa Street, King George Street, and Ben-Yehuda Street, the elegant Mamilla Mall outside Jaffa Gate, and the restored First Station are natural gathering places.

The city prides itself on its historical continuity. A municipal bylaw dating back to 1918 makes it mandatory to face even high-rise commercial buildings with the honey-color "Jerusalem stone," the local limestone that has served Jerusalem's builders since, well, forever. Watch the stone walls glow at sunset—the source of the by-now clichéd but still compelling phrase "Jerusalem of Gold"—and understand the mystical hold Jerusalem has had on so many minds and hearts for so many thousands of years.

Planning

When to Go

Jerusalem, like Israel in general, is a year-round destination, but the very best months are late March through May, and late October through November, when prices are lower and the weather is good, even warm. Winter is colder than in Tel Aviv, but sunny days often follow gloomy ones. Jerusalem gets its own back in the hot, rainless summer months; the inland capital is dry and cools off toward evening. Avoid the main Jewish holidays, when hotels charge peak prices, and tourist attractions are way more crowded than usual.

Planning Your Time

Israel itineraries tend to favor Jerusalem. The Old City alone offers an absorbing two days. Beyond its religious shrines are ancient sites, panoramic walks, and museums. Allow time for poking around the Arab market and the stores of the Jewish Quarter. The immediate environs—the City of David, Mount of Olives, Mount Zion, and a few sites north of the Old City walls—can add another day. West Jerusalem's spread-out attractions take patience to explore. Add time for shopping and you're quickly up to a five- to six-day stay. Jerusalem is also a convenient base for day trips to Masada and the Dead Sea, and even Tel Aviv.

A few tips for maximizing your time: Make a list of must-see sights. Pay attention to opening times and plot out your day's destinations to minimize backtracking. Mix experiences each day, to avoid overdosing on museums, shrines, or archaeology. Above all, take time to let your senses absorb the city. Take time to walk around and sip a coffee at a sidewalk café. Jerusalem is as much about atmosphere as it is a checklist of world-class sights.

Travel Precautions

Violence against individuals is rare and tourists aren't specific targets. Nevertheless, avoid Muslim Quarter backstreets, and be cautious walking around the Old City at night (when almost everything is closed anyway). The important weekly Muslim prayers around midday Friday sometimes get passionate if there's a hot Palestinian-Israeli issue in the news. Emotions can spill into the streets of the Muslim Quarter as the crowds leave the al-Aqsa Mosque.

As in any major tourist destination, pickpockets can be a problem: keep purses closed and close to you, and wallets in less accessible pockets. Don't leave valuables in parked cars, and use hotel safes.

Getting Here and Around

AIR

A 40-minute drive from Jerusalem, Ben Gurion International Airport is the region's largest gateway and the point of entry for most travelers entering Israel. *For more information on air travel to Israel and airport transfer, see Getting Here and Around in Travel Smart.*

BUS

Taking the bus from Ben Gurion Airport to Jerusalem Central Station (or vice versa) is cheap but slow. The shuttle bus 485 runs every hour 6 days a week (excluding Shabbat on Saturday). The last service is at 2 pm on Friday afternoon and the first service after Shabbat is at 7 pm on Saturday evening. It stops at Jerusalem's Central Bus Station, and drops off close to the Light Railway, which provides easy access to hotels in the city center and runs to the edge of the Old City for easy access to hotels within the walls. Pickup is at Ben Gurion Airport on the arrivals concourse (arrivals level) of Terminal 3, which is the same level as the airport taxi stand. There is also a pickup from Terminal 1. Drop-off at Ben Gurion Airport is on the departures level at Terminal 3. There is also a drop-off at Terminal 1. The price is NIS 16 (Israeli Shekels) each way, and tickets may be purchased in cash on the bus directly.

Intercity buses travel all over the country from the Central Bus Station, with frequent departures on more popular routes. A few (like Eilat) require prebooking, which can be done online at ⊕ *www.egged.co.il. See Getting Here and Around in Travel Smart for more information.*

Egged also operates the extensive bus service within Jerusalem. The fare is NIS 5.90, and you don't need exact change. If you have several days in Jerusalem, consider a Rav Kav card, available at the Central Bus Station, which is good for travel on buses and the light-rail, and allows for transfers between them within a 90-minute period. Extra credit on the card can be bought from bus stations and any local kiosk.

CAR

By car, Route 1 is the chief route to Jerusalem. Route 443 is often quicker, although it passes through a quiet part of the West Bank and, though unlikely, you may be stopped very briefly at an Israeli army checkpoint.

In the city, walking and hailing or ordering a taxi or van as needed is a better idea than a rental car: traffic, navigation, and parking may be more than your schedule and disposition can bear.

LIGHT RAIL

Jerusalem's single light-rail line is useful (if it's going your way) and pleasant (if it's not rush hour). It runs from Pisgat Ze'ev in the far northeast of the city, via French Hill, Damascus Gate, Jaffa Street, the Central Bus Station, over the Bridge of Strings, to Mount Herzl in the southwest. The trains operate Sunday to Thursday between 5:30 am and midnight. On Friday and Jewish holiday eves, the last train leaves from either terminus about two hours before sunset, and service resumes on Saturday about an hour after dark. Route details and updated schedules are available online in English. Single tickets (NIS 5.90) can be purchased from machines at each station platform using cash shekels or a credit card, but the process is a bit cumbersome. Validation in the train of the ticket or Rav Kav card *(see Bus Travel, above)* must be done immediately on boarding.

INFORMATION Jerusalem Light Rail. ☎ *073/210–0601* ⊕ *www.citypass.co.il/en.*

TAXI

The fare for taxis to and from the airport is NIS 180 during the day and NIS 250 after 9 pm.

Jerusalem Through the Ages

The first known mention of Jerusalem is in Egyptian "hate texts" of the 20th century BC, but many archaeologists give the city a considerably earlier founding date. Abraham and the biblical Joshua may have been here, but it was King David, circa 1004 BC, who captured the city and made it his capital, thus propelling it onto the center stage of history.

First and Second Temples

King David's son Solomon built the "First" Temple, giving the city a preeminence it enjoyed until its destruction by the Babylonians, and the exile of its population, in 586 BC. Jews returned 50 years later, rebuilt the Temple (the "Second"), and began the slow process of revival. By the 2nd century BC, Jerusalem was again a vibrant Jewish capital, albeit one with a good dose of Hellenistic cultural influence. Herod the Great (who reigned 37 BC–4 BC) revamped the Temple on a magnificent scale and expanded the city into a cosmopolis of world renown.

This was the Jerusalem Jesus knew, a city of monumental architecture, teeming—especially during the Jewish pilgrim festivals—with tens of thousands of visitors. It was here that the Romans crucified Jesus (circa AD 29), and here, too, that the Great Jewish Revolt against Rome erupted, ending in AD 70 with the destruction (once again) of the city and the Temple.

From the Romans to the British

The Roman emperor Hadrian built a redesigned Jerusalem as the pagan polis of Aelia Capitolina (AD 135), an urban plan that became the basis for the Old City of today. The Byzantines made it a Christian center, with a massive wave of church building (4th–6th centuries AD), until the Arab conquest of AD 638 brought the holy city under Muslim sway. Except during the golden age of the Ummayad Dynasty, in the late 7th and early 8th centuries, Jerusalem was no more than a provincial town under the Muslim regimes of the early Middle Ages. The Crusaders stormed it in 1099 and made it the capital of their Latin Kingdom. With the reconquest of Jerusalem by the Muslims, the city again lapsed into a languid provincialism for 700 years under the Mamluk and Ottoman empires. The British conquest in 1917 thrust the city back into the world limelight as rising Jewish and Arab nationalisms vied to possess it.

Divided and Reunited

Jerusalem was divided by the 1948 war: the larger Jewish western sector became the capital of the new State of Israel, while Jordan annexed the smaller, predominantly Arab eastern sector, which included the Old City. The Six-Day War of 1967 reunited the city under Israeli rule, but the concept of an Arab "East" Jerusalem and a Jewish "West" Jerusalem remains, even though new Jewish neighborhoods in the northeastern and southeastern parts of town have made the distinction oversimplified.

The holy city continues to engage the attention of devotees of Christianity, Judaism, and Islam. Between Jews and Arabs it remains a source of hot dispute and occasional violence as rival visions clash for possession of the city's past and control of its future.

Taxis can be flagged on the street, reserved by phone, or picked up at major hotels. The law requires taxi drivers to use their meters.

TRAIN

Trains run from Jerusalem's Malcha Train Station to Tel Aviv. There is no service on the Sabbath or Jewish religious holidays. The last train on Friday or holiday eves departs from either city about two hours before sunset. Service resumes late Saturday night (🌐 www.rail.co.il for updated schedules). The trip takes about 85 minutes and costs NIS 20 one way, NIS 32 return. It's a fun family excursion.

Sights

Immerse yourself in Jerusalem. Of course, you can see the primary sights in a couple of days—some visitors claim to have done it in less—but don't short-change yourself if you can help it. Take time to wander where the spirit takes you, to linger longer over a snack and people-watch, to follow the late Hebrew poet, Yehuda Amichai, "in the evening into the Old City / and … emerge from it pockets stuffed with images / and metaphors and well-constructed parables. …" The poet struggled for breath in an atmosphere "saturated with prayers and dreams"; but the city's baggage of history and religion doesn't have to weigh you down. Decompress in the markets and eateries of the Old City, and the jewelry and art stores, coffee shops, and pubs of the New.

The city is built on a series of hills, part of the country's north–south watershed. To the east, the Judean Desert tumbles down to the Dead Sea, the lowest point on Earth, less than an hour's drive away. The main highway to the west winds down through the pine-covered Judean Hills toward the international airport and Tel Aviv. North and south of the city—Samaria and Judea, respectively—is

what is known today as the West Bank. Since 1967, this contested area has been administered largely by Israel, though the major concentrations of Arab population are currently under autonomous Palestinian control.

Restaurants

Jerusalem's dining scene is smaller and more modest than Tel Aviv's, but is steeped in 4,000 years of culinary traditions. Among Jewish residents, more than a century of immigration has infused the local fare with the best of Kurdish, Moroccan, French, Polish, Yemenite, and Italian flavors. On the Palestinian side, most restaurants rely on a rich heritage of family cooking. On both sides, an elite class of chefs has begun combining the best of local ingredients with advanced cooking techniques and imaginative serving styles.

All this is to say that when you're in Jerusalem you can enjoy the best of both worlds: hole-in-the-wall eateries brimming with aromatic stews and garlicky hummus or high-end dining rooms serving inspired and elegant riffs on the city's flavors and produce.

Some cuisine designations are self-explanatory, but other terms may be confusing. A restaurant billing itself as "dairy" will serve meals without meat; many such places do serve fish, in addition to pasta, soup, and salads. "Oriental" usually means Middle Eastern (in contrast to Western), often meaning hummus, kebabs, and stews.

The term kosher doesn't imply a particular style of cooking, only that the cooks followed Jewish dietary law in selecting and preparing the food. In Jerusalem, where there are many kosher standards from which to choose, the selection can be dizzying. But unless specific kosher standards govern your eating habits, don't worry. Jerusalem is home to dozens of kosher restaurants preparing excellent food. Remember that most kosher restaurants are closed for Friday dinner and Saturday lunch in observation of the Jewish Sabbath. A generous handful of nonkosher cafés, bars, and restaurants remain open all weekend.

What It Costs			
$	$$	$$$	$$$$
RESTAURANTS			
Under NIS 50	NIS 50–NIS 75	NIS 76–NIS 100	over NIS 100

Hotels

Some travelers insist on a hotel in a central location; others prefer to retreat to a haven at the end of the day, with atmosphere more important than accessibility. Jerusalem has more of the first kind than the second, and many hotels once considered remote are really no more than 10 minutes by cab or train from the city center. Most hotels are contemporary and modern, but a few have retained an old-world allure. There are also guesthouses, B&Bs, and other lodgings that offer more of the local charm coupled with often-cheaper prices.

Defining high season is not an exact science. Some hotels may talk about peak periods in addition to or instead of high season, typically the weeklong Jewish holiday of Passover (March or April), and a similar period around the Jewish High Holidays including Rosh Hashanah, Yom Kippur, and Sukkot (September or October). Because of variations in hotel policy, and because the dates of Jewish holidays shift annually in accordance with the Hebrew calendar, the difference in room rates can be significant.

Almost all West Jerusalem hotels are kosher.

Hotel reviews have been shortened. For more information, visit Fodors.com.

What It Costs			
$	$$	$$$	$$$$
HOTELS			
Under $200	$200–$300	$301–$400	over $400

Nightlife

Although Jerusalem can't compete with Tel Aviv in terms of the number of nightlife attractions, what the city lacks in quantity it more than makes up for in quality. Pubs, bars, and nightclubs in Jerusalem tend to be more relaxed than those in Tel Aviv—they're friendlier, more informal, and often less expensive. As in Tel Aviv, the nightlife scene in Jerusalem starts very late: some places only begin to fill up after midnight, and most pubs are open until the early hours of the morning. Given the university presence in the city, there's often a younger crowd at many places.

Performing Arts

Classical music is the capital's strong suit. Artists in other musical genres pass through from time to time, but Jerusalem is seldom their main focus. For English-language schedules of performances and other cultural events, consult the Friday weekend section of the *Jerusalem Post* and its insert "In Jerusalem," Friday's "The Guide" of *Haaretz*'s English edition, and the free weekly and monthly booklets available at hotels and information bureaus. Ticket prices typically range from NIS 75 to NIS 350, depending on venue size and artist.

Festivals

★ Hutzot Hayotzer Arts and Crafts Festival

ARTS FESTIVALS | FAMILY | The fine crafts and lively concerts presented at this festival are a highlight of August. Located in the Sultan's Pool, an ancient reservoir in the Hinnom Valley beneath the walls of the Old City, the two-week event showcases crafts by Israeli and international artisans and features open-air concerts by top Israeli rock and pop performers. Arrive early for the best seats. ⊠ *Hativat Yerushalayim, Center City* ✛ *Hutzot Hayotzer, Mitchell Parks & Gardens, and Merrill Hassenfeld Amphitheater at Sultan's Pool* ☎ *02/623–7000* ⊕ *artfair-jer. com/english.*

International Festival of Puppet Theater

FESTIVALS | FAMILY | Each August, puppeteers from around the globe bring their productions to venues around the city in a festival organized by Jerusalem's Train Theater. The shows are generally geared toward youngsters, although some are entertaining for the whole family. Many shows are in English or without words. ⊠ *Liberty Bell Park (Gan Hapa'amon), Center City* ✛ *Jabotinsky St. and King David St.* ☎ *02/561–8514* ⊕ *traintheater. co.il/en.*

★ Israel Festival

ARTS FESTIVALS | Top national and international orchestras, theater companies, choirs, dance troupes, and street entertainers participate in this dynamic annual festival, usually held for three weeks in late May or early June. Styles range from classical to avant-garde. The Jerusalem Theatre is the main venue, but a dozen secondary locations around the city get some of the smaller acts. ⊠ *Jerusalem* ☎ *02/563–1544* ⊕ *israel-festival.org/en.*

★ Jerusalem Film Festival

FILM FESTIVALS | Held in July each year, this festival attracts large crowds for screenings of Israeli and international films. Some screenings and the awards ceremony are held at the Cinematheque, while other screenings are at a number of venues throughout the city. Reserve tickets in advance. ⊠ *11 Hebron Rd., Center City* ☎ *02/565–4333* ⊕ *www.jff. org.il* ☞ *From NIS 46 for screenings.*

Jerusalem International Chamber Music Festival

MUSIC | The 600-seat YMCA Concert Hall is the main venue for the much-acclaimed Jerusalem International Chamber Music Festival, held over 10 days each year in late August or early September. Tickets for single concerts are NIS 170. ⊠ *YMCA Three Arches Hotel, 26 King David St., Center City* ☎ *02/625–0444* ⊕ *jcmf.org.il.*

Jerusalem International Oud Festival

ARTS FESTIVALS | This festival paying homage to the Arabic lute presents a range of ethnic music from Turkey, Iraq, India, and a host of other cultures, often including Israeli rock. Performances are held at various concert halls around town in November and also include literature and poetry readings. ⊠ *Confederation House, 12 Emile Botta St., Center City* ☎ *02/624–5206* ⊕ *www.confederation-house.org.*

★ Jerusalem Season of Culture

ARTS FESTIVALS | Held for three weeks in September, this diverse selection of events highlights local and international artists, musicians, dancers, and other types of performers. Many of the offerings are delightfully offbeat. ⊠ *Hutzot Hayotzer, Center City* ☎ *02/653–5880* ⊕ *en.mekudeshet.com.*

Jerusalem Wine Festival

FESTIVALS | Held annually in late summer, this festival presents the latest vintages from 200 national and international wineries while often hosting local musicians. It takes place in the Art Garden of the Israel Museum. ⊠ *Israel Museum, Ruppin Blvd., Givat Ram* ☎ *02/625–9703*

⊕ www.imj.org.il/en/events 🕮 NIS 95 for unlimited tastings.

Palestine Festival of Literature

ARTS FESTIVALS | The weeklong festival brings together local and international artists to read prose and poetry related to Arab culture. Free events take place in East Jerusalem and the Old City during the spring season, and the festival travels to other cities in Israel, the West Bank, and Gaza. ⊠ Shimon Hatsadik St., East Jerusalem ⊕ www.palfest.org.

Shopping

Jerusalem offers distinctive gifts from modern jewelry to traditional crafts to religious icons. The top shopping spots are the Downtown area, the Old City, and the Mamilla outdoor mall. The Hutzot Hayotzer artists' collective just outside the Old City walls is another popular and particularly beautiful spot, where during the August Arts and Crafts Festival you can visit the studios of resident artists and enjoy open-air music performances at night.

Prices are generally fixed in the Center City and the Jewish Quarter of the Old City, although you can sometimes negotiate for significant discounts on expensive art and jewelry. However, bargaining is common practice in the Old City's colorful Arab bazaar, or souk (pronounced "shook" in Hebrew—rhymes with "book"); it's fascinating but can be a trap for the unwary.

Young fashion designers, often graduates of Jerusalem's Bezalel Academy of Arts and Design, have opened a stream of shops and boutiques. They're scattered throughout the city. Several galleries representing Israeli artists are close to the hotels on King David Street.

Stores generally open by 8:30 am or 9 am, and some close between 1 pm and 4 pm. A few still close on Tuesday afternoon, a traditional but less and less observed half day. Jewish-owned stores (that is, all of West Jerusalem and the Old City's Jewish Quarter) close on Friday afternoon by 2 pm or 3 pm, depending on the season and the kind of store (food and souvenir shops tend to stay open later), and reopen on Sunday morning. Some stores geared to the tourist trade, particularly Downtown, reopen on Saturday night after the Jewish Sabbath ends, especially in summer. Arab-owned stores in the Old City and East Jerusalem are busiest on Saturday and quietest on Sunday, when many (but not all) Christian storekeepers close for the day.

Tours

BIKE TOURS

Bike Jerusalem

BICYCLE TOURS | You should be fairly skilled to join Bike Jerusalem's day tours through the city, but the night tours can accommodate less-experienced bikers. The company prides itself on its broad range of biking excursions throughout the country and its English-speaking guides. The four-hour tours can include up to six participants. ⊠ Jaffa Gate ☎ 02/579–6353, 052/320–1273 ⊕ www.bikejerusalem.com 🕮 NIS 1290 for group of 6, NIS 215 for each additional person.

Jerusalem Midnight Biking

BICYCLE TOURS | This company offers its nighttime rides through the alleyways of the Old City, as well as daytime rides through other parts of Jerusalem. Private tours from 2½ to 3 hours allow more flexibility with what you do and see. The cost includes bike and helmet rentals. Tours are led by English-speaking guides and are limited to riders age 12 and over. Tours meet on Kariv Street, just outside Jaffa Gate. ⊠ Jerusalem ☎ 02/566–1441 ⊕ www.jerusalembiking.com 🕮 From NIS 230 per person.

ORIENTATION TOURS
Bein Harim Tours
GUIDED TOURS | Half-day Jerusalem orientation tours include a panoramic view of the Old City and a close-up view of the highlights. Except for Saturday, full-day tours usually add the Holocaust museum at Yad Vashem (although many visitors prefer to do this museum on their own so they can see it at their own pace). The price includes pickup from major Jerusalem hotels (additional charge for pickup in Tel Aviv and coast). ⊠ *Tel Aviv* ☎ *03/542–2000* ⊕ *www.beinharimtours. com* ⌧ *From $49*.

PRIVATE GUIDES
The daily rate for a guide-driven car or limo-van, up to seven passengers, is in the range of US$700; tourists paying in foreign currency are exempt from V.A.T. (Value-Added Tax). Entrance fees are not included and over-mileage charges apply. Many guides will offer their services without a car for US$250 to US$350 per day. For a private tour, approach Kedma Israel Travel, GUY Tours, or Genesis Boutique Travel.

Genesis Boutique Travel
PERSONAL GUIDES | This intimate operation provides guide-driven vehicles and customized ground services throughout the Jerusalem area and the rest of the country. ⊠ *Jerusalem* ☎ *02/676–5868, 052/286–2650* ⊕ *www.genesis-boutique-travel.com*.

GUY Tours
PERSONAL GUIDES | In business for more than 55 years, GUY Tours is the country's largest private tour company. It offers guided tours both in and around Jerusalem, as well as the rest of the country. They can pick you up from your hotel. ⊠ *Jerusalem* ☎ *02/538–3318* ⊕ *guy-tours. com*.

Kedma Israel Travel
PERSONAL GUIDES | This boutique agency prides itself on its personal touch in handling everything for your tailor-made trip. Guide-driven tours are its strong suit. ☎ *08/970–4139, 054/345–1808* ⊕ *www. kedmatravel.com*.

WALKING TOURS
★ Sandeman's New Europe
WALKING TOURS | This European company offers free two-hour tours of the most famous sights, led by licensed guides, as well as longer, in-depth routes in and around the Old City (the latter for payment). ⊠ *Jerusalem* ⊕ *www. newjerusalemtours.com* ⌧ *From NIS 100 (tip-based)*.

Visitor Information

Christian Information Centre
Run by the Franciscans (Roman Catholic), the CIC is a source of information about Christian holy sites, and the times, places, and language of Catholic masses and Protestant services. It is closed Sunday. ⊠ *Omar ibn el-Khatab Sq., Jaffa Gate* ⌖ *Just inside Jaffa Gate* ☎ *02/627–2692* ⊕ *www.cicts.org*.

Jerusalem Tourist Information Center
Open daily and run by the Israel Ministry of Tourism, the center is a useful stopping point for orientation information and more. ⊠ *Omar Ibn Hatab Sq., Jaffa Gate* ⌖ *Just inside Jaffa Gate* ☎ *02/627–1422* ⊕ *israel.travel*.

The Old City

The city's primary religious sites in the Christian and Muslim quarters, and at the Western Wall, are the very essence of historical Jerusalem: explore and touch the different cultures that share it. The Old City's 36,000 inhabitants jostle in the cobblestone lanes. Devout Jews in black and white scurry from their neighborhoods north and west of the Old City, through Damascus Gate and the Muslim Quarter, toward the Western Wall. Arab women in long, embroidered dresses flow across the Western Wall plaza to Dung Gate and the village of Silwan beyond it. It's not unusual to stand at the Western Wall, surrounded by the sounds of devotions, and hear the piercing call to prayer of the Muslim *muezzin* above you, with the more distant bells of the Christian Quarter providing a counterpoint.

Sites such as the Western Wall, Calvary, and the Haram esh-Sharif bring a thrill of recognition to ancient history. The devout can't fail to be moved by the holy city, and its special, if sometimes dissonant, moods and modes of devotion tend to fascinate the nonbeliever as well.

GETTING HERE AND AROUND
To explore the key sites in one day, keep in mind opening times and geography, and plan accordingly. Beat the security line for the Temple Mount (Muslim shrines) with a really early start; the only entrance is above the Western Wall and visiting times are limited. Exit the northern end of the mount to the Via Dolorosa and Holy Sepulcher. Entering the Old City via Jaffa Gate will take you right to the Holy Sepulcher and on to the Western Wall. Lions' Gate is best for beginning with St. Anne's Church and the Via Dolorosa. Damascus Gate plunges you into the bazaar, and thence to whatever sequence of sights you prefer. Of course, you can spread your visit over more than one day.

TIMING AND PRECAUTIONS
Avoid the Muslim Quarter, and thus the first six stations of the Via Dolorosa, between noon and 2 pm Friday, the time of important weekly Muslim prayers. All the holy places demand modest dress: no shorts or short capris, no sleeveless tops, no low necklines.

Jewish Quarter

This is at once the Old City's oldest quarter and its newest neighborhood. Abandoned for a generation after the War of Independence, the quarter was restored and resettled after the Six-Day War of 1967. The subsequent archaeological excavations exposed artifacts and structures that date back 27 centuries and more. If you have a photographer's eye, get off the main streets and stroll at random. The limestone houses and alleys—often counterpointed with a shock of bougainvillea or palm fronds and ficus trees—offer pleasing compositions.

If you like to people-watch, find a shaded café table and sip a good latte while the world jitterbugs by. The population of the Jewish Quarter is almost entirely religious, roughly split between "modern" Orthodox (devout, but integrated into contemporary Israeli society at every level) and the more traditional ultra-Orthodox (men in black frock coats and black hats, in many ways a community apart). The locals tend to dress very conservatively. Several religious-study institutions attract a transient population of young students, many of them from abroad. If you see a big group of Israeli soldiers, don't assume the worst. The army maintains a center for its educational tours here, and the recruits are more likely than not boisterously kidding around with each other as they follow their guide. Shopping is good here—especially jewelry and Judaica—and there are decent fast-food options.

A renewed landmark of the quarter is the high, white-domed Hurva Synagogue. It was built and soon destroyed in the 18th century, rebuilt in the 19th, and blown up when the Jordanian Arab Legion captured the area in the 1948 war. The current building, rededicated in spring 2010, is a faithful reconstruction of its predecessor.

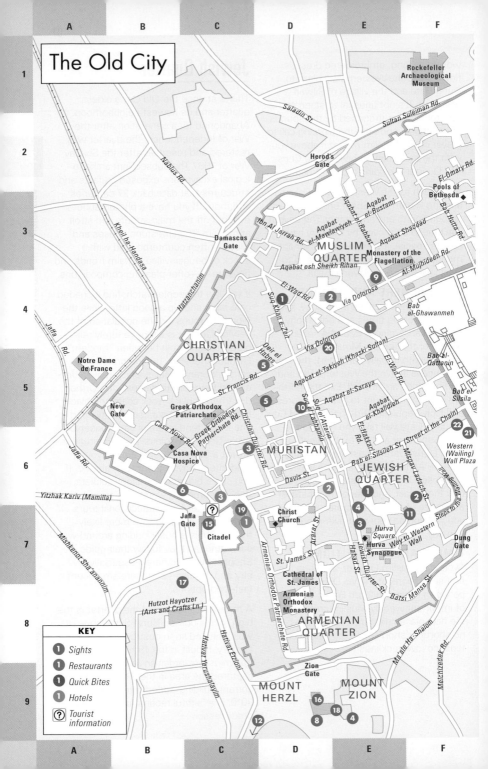

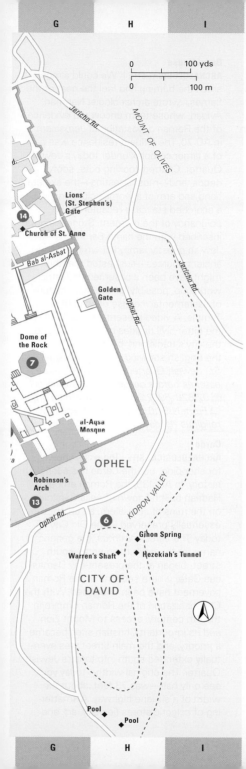

Sights ▼
1 Broad Wall **E6**
2 Burnt House **F6**
3 Cardo **E7**
4 Chamber of the Holocaust **E9**
5 Church of the Holy Sepulcher **D5**
6 City of David **H7**
7 Dome of the Rock and Haram esh-Sharif (Temple Mount) **G5**
8 Dormition Abbey **D9**
9 Ecce Homo Convent of the Sisters of Zion **E4**
10 Ethiopian Monastery ... **D5**
11 Herodian Quarter/ Wohl Archaeological Museum **F7**
12 Hinnom Valley **D9**
13 Jerusalem Archaeological Park and Davidson Center **G6**
14 Pools of Bethesda and Church of St. Anne **G3**
15 Ramparts Walk **C7**
16 Room of the Last Supper **D9**
17 Teddy Park **B7**
18 Tomb of David **E9**
19 Tower of David Museum **C7**
20 Via Dolorosa **D4**
21 Western Wall **F6**
22 Western Wall Tunnel **F5**

Restaurants ▼
1 Abu Shukri **E4**
2 Austrian Hospice Café **E4**
3 Costa **C6**
4 Holy Cafe **E7**
5 Hummus Lina **D5**
6 Nafoura **C6**

Quick Bites ▼
1 Jaffar Sweets **D4**

Hotels ▼
1 Christ Church Guest House **C7**
2 Lutheran Guesthouse **D6**
3 New Imperial Hotel **C6**

GETTING HERE AND AROUND

It's best to approach the Jewish Quarter on foot. From Jaffa Gate, you can plunge directly ahead into the Arab bazaar and follow David Street until it becomes a T-junction: the right turn becomes Jewish Quarter Street. Alternatively, after you enter Jaffa Gate, follow the vehicle road to the right and through a small tunnel, then turn left (on foot) onto St. James Street and down to the quarter. A third idea is to begin your tour on Mount Zion, and then continue to the Jewish Quarter through Zion Gate.

TIMING AND PRECAUTIONS

Allow at least two hours to explore the Jewish Quarter, not counting shopping and eating. If you're pressed for time, absorb the scene over the rim of a glass or mug, and take time to visit the Herodian Quarter. Avoid visiting on Saturday, when everything is closed, and some religious locals may resent you taking pictures on their Sabbath. Sites with entrance fees close by midday Friday.

◉ Sights

Broad Wall

ARCHAEOLOGICAL SITE | The discovery in the 1970s of the massive 23-foot-thick foundations of an Old Testament city wall was hailed as one of the most important archaeological finds in the Jewish Quarter. Hezekiah, King of Judah and a contemporary of the prophet Isaiah, built the wall in 701 BC to protect the city against an impending Assyrian invasion. The unearthing of the Broad Wall—a biblical name—resolved a long-running scholarly debate about the size of Old Testament Jerusalem: a large on-site map shows that the ancient city was far more extensive than was once thought. ⊠ Plugat Hakotel St., off Jewish Quarter St., Jewish Quarter ⊕ www.rova-yehudi. org.il ⊠ Free.

Burnt House

ARCHAEOLOGICAL SITE | "We could almost smell the burning and feel the heat of the flames," wrote archaeologist Nahman Avigad, whose team uncovered evidence of the Roman devastation of Jerusalem in AD 70. The affluent residence was part of a larger complex under today's Jewish Quarter. Charred cooking pots, sooty debris, and—most arresting—the skeletal hand and arm of a woman clutching a scorched staircase recaptured the poignancy of the moment. Stone weights inscribed with the name Bar Katros—a Jewish priestly family known from ancient sources—suggested that this might have been a basement industrial workshop, possibly for the manufacture of sacramental incense used in the Temple. A video presentation re-creates the bitter civil rivalries of the period and the city's tragic end; book online for the English showing. ⊠ 2 Tiferet Israel St., Jewish Quarter ✛ At end of line of eateries before descent to Western Wall ☎ 02/626–5922 ⊕ www.rova-yehudi.org.il ⊠ From NIS 10 ⊗ Closed Sat. and Jewish religious holidays.

Cardo

ARCHAEOLOGICAL SITE | Today it's known for shopping, but the Cardo has a long history. In AD 135, the Roman emperor Hadrian built his town of Aelia Capitolina on the ruins of Jerusalem, an urban plan essentially preserved in the Old City of today. The cardo maximus, the generic name for the city's main north–south street, began at the present-day Damascus Gate, where sections of the Roman pavement have been unearthed. With the Christianization of the Roman Empire in the 4th century, access to Mount Zion and its important Christian sites became a priority, and the main street was eventually extended south into today's Jewish Quarter. The original width—today you see only half—was 73 feet, about the width of a six-lane highway. A smattering of eclectic stores (jewelry, art, and

With its cobblestone streets and limestone houses, the Jewish Quarter of the Old City is charming.

Judaica) occupies the Cardo's medieval reincarnation. ⊠ *Jewish Quarter St., Jewish Quarter* ⊕ *www.rova-yehudi.org. il* ⊠ *Free.*

★ Herodian Quarter/Wohl Archaeological Museum

ARCHAEOLOGICAL SITE | Excavations in the 1970s exposed the Jewish Quarter's most visually interesting site: the remains of sumptuous mansions from the late Second Temple period. Preserved in the basement of a modern Jewish seminary—but entered separately—the geometrically patterned mosaic floors, still-vibrant frescoes, and costly glassware and ceramics provide a peek into the life of the wealthy in the days of Herod and Jesus. Several small plastered cisterns, with broad steps descending into them, have been identified as private *mikvahs* (Jewish ritual baths); holograms depict their use. Large stone water jars are just like those described in the New Testament story of the wedding at Cana (John 2). Rare stone tables resemble the dining-room furniture depicted in Roman stone reliefs found in Europe.

On the last of the site's three distinct levels is a mansion with an estimated original floor area of some 6,000 square feet. None of the upper stories has survived, but the fine, fashionable stucco work and the quality of the artifacts found here indicate an exceptional standard of living, leading some scholars to suggest this may have been the long-sought palace of the high priest. The charred ceiling beams and scorched mosaic floor and fresco at the southern end of the reception hall bear witness to the Roman torching of the neighborhood in the late summer of AD 70, exactly one month after the Temple itself had been destroyed. Allow about 45 minutes to explore the site. ⊠ *1 Hakara'im Rd., Jewish Quarter* ⊕ *Entrance a few steps east of Hurva Sq.* ☎ *02/626–5922* ⊕ *www. rova-yehudi.org.il* ⊠ *NIS 20* ⊗ *Closed Sat. and Jewish religious holidays.*

★ **Jerusalem Archaeological Park and Davidson Center**

ARCHAEOLOGICAL SITE | FAMILY | Though strictly speaking outside the Jewish Quarter, this site is related to it historically, and is often visited at the same time. A gold mine for Israeli archaeologists, its most dramatic and monumental finds were from the Herodian period, the late 1st century BC. The low-rise, air-conditioned **Davidson Center** (on your right as you enter the site) offers visual aids, some artifacts, two interesting videos (which alternate between English and Hebrew), and modern restrooms. Allow 30 minutes for the center and another 40 minutes for the site.

The best place to start a tour is the high corner, off to the left as you enter the site. King Herod the Great rebuilt the Second Temple on the exact site of its predecessor, more or less where the Dome of the Rock now stands. He expanded the sacred enclosure by constructing a massive, shoebox-shaped retaining wall on the slopes of the hill, the biblical Mount Moriah. The inside was filled with thousands of tons of rubble to level off the hill and create the huge platform, the size of 27 football fields, known today as the Temple Mount. The stones near the corner, with their signature precision-cut borders, are not held together with mortar; their sheer weight gives the structure its stability. The original wall is thought to have been a third higher than it is today.

To the left of the corner is the white pavement of an impressive main street and commercial area from the Second Temple period. The protrusion high above your head is known as **Robinson's Arch,** named for a 19th-century American explorer. It is a remnant of a monumental bridge to the Temple Mount that was reached by a staircase from the street where you now stand: look for the ancient steps. The square-cut building stones heaped on the street came from the top of the original wall, dramatic evidence of the Roman destruction of AD 70. A piece of Hebrew scriptural graffiti (Isaiah 66:14) was etched into a stone, possibly by a Jewish pilgrim, some 15 centuries ago.

Climb the wooden steps and turn left through the shaded square. A modern spiral staircase descends below present ground level to a partially reconstructed labyrinth of Byzantine dwellings and mosaics; from here you reemerge outside the present city walls. Alternatively, stay at ground level and continue east through a small arched gate. The broad, impressive **Southern Steps** on your left, a good part of them original, once brought hordes of Jewish pilgrims through the now-blocked southern gates of the Temple Mount. The rock-hewn ritual baths near the bottom of the steps were used for the purification rites once demanded of Jews before they entered the sacred temple precincts. This section of the site, directly below the al-Aqsa Mosque, closes at 11 am on Friday, before the Muslim prayer time. ⊠ *Inside Dung Gate, Jewish Quarter ✛ South of Western Wall* ☎ *02/626–8700* ⊕ *www.cityofdavid.org. il/en* ☒ *NIS 65* ⊙ *Closed Sat. and Jewish religious holidays.*

★ **Western Wall**

ARCHAEOLOGICAL SITE | The 2,000-year-old Western Wall is in a class of its own. Its status as the most important existing Jewish shrine derives from its connection with the ancient Temple, the House of God. It was not itself part of the Temple edifice, but of the massive retaining wall King Herod built to create the vast platform now known as the Temple Mount.

After the destruction of Jerusalem by the Romans in AD 70, and especially after the dedication of a pagan town in its place 65 years later, the city was off-limits to Jews for generations. The

Jews in the Old City

The history of Jewish life in the Old City has been marked by the trials of conflict and the joys of creating and rebuilding community. Here are some highlights from the medieval period on.

1099. Crusaders conquer Jerusalem and massacre much of its population. Jews lived at the time in today's Muslim Quarter.

1267. Spanish rabbi Nachmanides ("Ramban") reestablishes Jewish community. (His synagogue is on Jewish Quarter Street.)

1517. Ottoman Turks conquer Palestine and allow Sephardic Jews (expelled from Spain a generation earlier) to resettle the country. A cluster of four interlinked synagogues gradually emerges in the quarter.

1700. A large group of Ashkenazi Jews from Eastern Europe settles in Jerusalem.

1860. The first neighborhood is established outside the walls (Mishkenot Sha'ananim). Initially, very few Old City Jews had the courage to move out.

1948. Israel's War of Independence. The Jewish Quarter surrenders to Jordanian forces and is abandoned. By then, the residents of the quarter represent only a tiny percentage of Jerusalem's Jewish population.

1967. Six-Day War. The Jewish Quarter, much of it ruined, is recaptured. Archaeological excavations and restoration work begin side by side.

1980s to present. The Jewish Quarter becomes revitalized, with the conservation and construction of housing, educational institutions, synagogues, and stores, and the opening of new archaeological sites.

memory of the precise location of the Temple—in the vicinity of today's Dome of the Rock—was lost. Even when access was eventually regained, Jews avoided entering the Temple Mount for fear of unwittingly trespassing on the most sacred, and thus forbidden, areas of the long-gone ancient sanctuary. With time, the closest remnant of the period took on the aura of the Temple itself, making the Western Wall a kind of holy place by proxy.

Jewish visitors often just refer to the site as "the Wall" (*Kotel* in Hebrew); the "Wailing Wall" is a Gentile appellation, describing the sight—more common once—of devout Jews grieving for God's House. It is a telling point that, for many Jews, the ancient Temple was as much a national site as a religious one, and its destruction as much a national trauma as a religious cataclysm.

The Western Wall is in the southeast corner of the Old City, accessible from the Dung Gate, the Jewish Quarter, and the Muslim Quarter's El-Wad Road and the Street of the Chain. It functions under the aegis of the Orthodox rabbinic authorities, with all the trappings of an Orthodox synagogue. ■**TIP→ Modest dress is required: for women, this means no shorts or bare shoulders. Men must cover their heads in the prayer area.** There is segregation of men and women in prayer, and smoking and photography on the Sabbath and religious holidays are prohibited. The cracks between the massive stones are stuffed with slips of paper bearing prayers and petitions. (These are collected several times a year and buried in a Jewish cemetery.) The swaying and praying of the devout reveal the powerful hold this place still has on the hearts and minds of many Jews.

The Wall is often crowded, but many people find that it's only when the crowds have gone (the Wall is floodlit at night and always open), and you share the warm, prayer-drenched stones with just a handful of bearded stalwarts or kerchiefed women, that the true spirituality of the Western Wall is palpable. (Expect a routine security check at all four entrances to the modern plaza, including a magnetic gate—visitors with pacemakers can avoid this—and examination of bags.) *For more information about this sight, see the "Jerusalem: Keeping the Faith" feature in this chapter.* ✉ *Near Dung Gate, Jewish Quarter* 🌐 *english.thekotel.org* 🎫 *Free.*

★ Western Wall Tunnel

ARCHAEOLOGICAL SITE | The long tunnel beyond the men's side of the Western Wall is not a rediscovered ancient thoroughfare, but was deliberately dug in recent years with the purpose of exposing a strip of the 2,000-year-old Western Wall along its entire length. The massive construction, part of the retaining wall of King Herod's Temple Mount, includes two building stones estimated to weigh an incredible 400 tons and 570 tons, respectively. Local guided tours in English are available and are recommended—you can visit the site only as part of an organized tour—but the times change from week to week (some include evening hours). The tour takes about 75 minutes and includes computer-generated graphics of how the area might have looked in its heyday. During daylight hours, tours end at the beginning of the Via Dolorosa, in the Muslim Quarter. After dark, that exit is closed, and the tour retraces its steps through the tunnel. The ticket office is under the arches at the northern end of the Western Wall plaza, but advance booking online is essential. ✉ *North of Western Wall, Jewish Quarter* ☎ *02/627–1333* 🌐 *english.thekotel.org* 🎫 *NIS 35* 🕒 *Closed Sat. and Jewish religious holidays.*

🍴 Restaurants

Holy Cafe

$$ | ISRAELI | FAMILY | With wooden tables in the tile-floored dining room and under the trees in the nearby square, this is one of the few full-service restaurants in the Jewish Quarter of the Old City. The modest menu ranges from fresh salads to salmon burgers, and there is beer and wine. **Known for:** light dairy and vegetarian dishes; welcoming staff; charming outdoor seating. [$] *Average main: NIS 50* ✉ *2 Tiferet Israel St., Jewish Quarter* ☎ *050/352–5400* 🕒 *Closed Sat. No dinner Fri.*

🛍 Shopping

Blue and White Art Gallery

ART GALLERIES | Udi Merioz, the artist and owner of this gallery, does "soft painting," a special appliqué technique that uses synthetic fibers on canvas. The gallery is the largest exporter of artwork from Israel and specializes in lithographs and Judaica prints. ✉ *1 Cardo St., Jewish Quarter* ☎ *02/628–8464* 🌐 *www.blueandwhiteart.com* 🕒 *Closed Fri. and Sat.*

Cardo

SPECIALTY STORES | In the Old City's Jewish Quarter, the Cardo began life as the main thoroughfare of Byzantine Jerusalem. It was a commercial street during the Crusader era, and has now been converted into an attractive shopping area. Beyond souvenirs and Judaica, you'll find beautifully crafted jewelry and artwork, although at quite high prices. ✉ *Jewish Quarter St., Jewish Quarter* ✣ *From Damascus Gate to David St.*

Stores along the narrow streets of the souk in the Old City tempt passersby with food, fabrics, and ceramics.

Christian and Muslim Quarters

Fragmented into a dozen denominational domains, the Christian Quarter is capped by the great gray dome of the Church of the Holy Sepulcher. (The struggle for visibility in the holy city seems to be as much about dominating the skyline as about controlling real estate.) The numerous churches and religious institutions in this quarter, which is west of the Muslim Quarter, make for low population density.

The Muslim Quarter, located between Damascus Gate and the Western Wall, and west of Lions' Gate, is by far the largest in both area and population. The famous Via Dolorosa (Way of the Cross) that begins in and winds through this quarter on its way to the Holy Sepulcher is lined with stores displaying Christian souvenirs and artifacts. It's a facade: the side streets, with their little grocery stores, neighborhood mosques, and stenciled pictures of Mecca, bespeak the real character of this residential area. Short dead-end alleys give tantalizing glimpses of the enormous gold Dome of the Rock on the Haram esh-Sharif (aka the Temple Mount).

👁 Sights

★ Church of the Holy Sepulcher

HISTORIC SITE | This church, which was built by the Crusaders in the 12th century (the fourth to be built on this site), is believed to be the place where Jesus was crucified by the Romans, was buried, and rose from the dead. The site was officially consecrated, and the first church built here, following the visit in AD 326 by Helena, mother of the Byzantine emperor Constantine the Great. It and the adjacent Via Dolorosa encompass the stations of the cross.

Steep steps take you up from the church to **Golgotha,** or Calvary, as the site of the crucifixion is described in the New

Testament. At the foot of the hill, opposite the main entrance, is the rectangular pink **Stone of Unction,** where, it is said, the body of Jesus was cleansed and prepared for burial. The **tomb of Jesus,** encased in a pink marble edifice, is in the rotunda to the left of the main entrance of the church.

The church is shared, albeit unequally and uncomfortably, by six Christian denominations: Roman Catholic, Greek Orthodox, Armenian Orthodox, Syrian Orthodox, Egyptian Coptic, and Ethiopian, under an agreement imposed by the Ottoman Turkish authorities in 1852. Each section is guarded by its own denomination.

If you visit in the late afternoon (the time changes with the seasons), you can watch the groups in turn—Greek Orthodox, Latins (as Roman Catholics are known in the Holy Land), Armenian Orthodox, and Egyptian Copts—in procession from Calvary to the tomb. A modern agreement among the Greeks, the Latins, and the Armenians on the interior restoration of the great dome was hailed as an almost miraculous breakthrough in ecumenical relations. *For information about the church, see the feature "Jerusalem: Keeping the Faith" in this chapter.* ⊠ *Between Suq Khan e-Zeit and Christian Quarter Rd., Christian Quarter* ☎ *02/626–6561* ⊕ *www.custodia.org/en* ⊠ *Free.*

★ Dome of the Rock and Haram esh-Sharif (Temple Mount)

RELIGIOUS SITE | The magnificent golden **Dome of the Rock** dominates the vast 35-acre Temple Mount, the area known to Muslims as *Haram esh-Sharif* (the Noble Sanctuary). At its southern end, immediately in front of you as you enter the area from the Western Wall plaza (the only gate for non-Muslims), is the large, black-domed **al-Aqsa Mosque,** the third in holiness for Muslims everywhere.

Herod the Great built the Temple Mount in the late 1st century BC, and included on the center of the plaza was the Second Temple, the one Jesus knew.

Jewish tradition identifies the great **rock** at the summit of the hill—now under the gold dome—as the foundation stone of the world, and the place where Abraham bound and almost sacrificed his son Isaac (Genesis 22). With greater probability, this was where the biblical King David made a repentance offering to the Lord (II Samuel 22), and where his son Solomon built "God's House," the so-called First Temple. The Second Temple stood on the identical spot, but the memory of its precise location was lost after the Roman destruction and the banning of Jews from Jerusalem.

The Haram today is a Muslim preserve, and tradition has it that Muhammad rose to heaven from this spot in Jerusalem to meet God face-to-face, received the teachings of Islam, and returned to Mecca the same night, and the great rock was the very spot from which the Prophet ascended.

The Muslim shrines are closed to non-Muslims to leave the faithful alone to enjoy the wondrous interiors of stained-glass windows, granite columns, green-and-gold mosaics, arabesques, and superb medieval masonry. Even if you can't get inside, the vast plaza is both visually and historically arresting and worth a visit. Take a look at the bright exterior tiles of the Dome of the Rock and the remarkable jigsaws of fitted red, white, and black stone in the 14th- and 15th-century Mamluk buildings that line the western edge of the plaza.

Security check lines to enter the area are often long; it's best to come early. Note that the gate near the Western Wall is for entrance only. You can exit through any of the other eight gates on the site. The Muslim attendants are very strict about modest dress, and prohibit Bibles in the area. *For information about these sites, see the feature "Jerusalem: Keeping the Faith" in this chapter.* ✉ *Access between Western Wall and Dung Gate, Muslim Quarter* ☎ *02/595–5820* ⊕ *www. noblesanctuary.com* 🎫 *Free* ☉ *Closed Fri. and Sat.*

Ecce Homo Convent of the Sisters of Zion

ARCHAEOLOGICAL SITE | The arch that crosses the Via Dolorosa, just beyond Station II, and continues into the chapel of the adjacent convent, was once thought to have been the gate of Herod's Antonia fortress, perhaps the spot where the Roman governor Pontius Pilate presented Jesus to the crowd with the words "*Ecce homo!*" ("Behold, the man!"). Recent scholarship has determined otherwise: it was a triumphal arch built by the Roman emperor Hadrian in the 2nd century AD after his suppression of the second Jewish revolt and the dedication of a new Roman town, Aelia Capitolina, in place of Jerusalem.

The basement of the convent has several points of interest: an impressive reservoir with a barrel-vault roof, apparently built by Hadrian in the moat of Herod's older Antonia fortress; a tiny but attractive collection of ancient artifacts found on-site; and the famous *lithostratos,* or stone pavement, etched with games played by Roman legionnaires. The origin of one such diversion—the notorious Game of the King—called for the execution of a mock king, a sequence tantalizingly reminiscent of the New Testament description of the treatment of Jesus by the Roman soldiers. Contrary to tradition, however, the pavement of large, footworn brown flagstones is apparently not from Jesus's day, but was laid down a century or two later. Allow 30 minutes for the visit. ✉ *41 Via Dolorosa, Muslim Quarter* ☎ *02/627–7292* ⊕ *www.eccehomopilgrimhouse.com.*

Ethiopian Monastery

HISTORIC SITE | Stand in the monastery's courtyard beneath the medieval bulge of the Church of the Holy Sepulcher, and you have a cross-section of Christendom. The adjacent Egyptian Coptic monastery peeks through the entrance gate, and a Russian Orthodox gable, a Lutheran bell tower, and the crosses of Greek Orthodox, Armenian Orthodox, and Roman Catholic churches break the skyline.

The robed Ethiopian monks live in tiny cells in the rooftop monastery. One of the modern paintings in their small, dark chapel depicts the visit of the Queen of Sheba to King Solomon, as described in the Bible (I Kings 10). Ethiopian tradition holds that more passed between the two than the Bible is telling—she came to "prove" his wisdom "with hard questions"—and that their supposed union produced an heir to both royal houses. In Solomon's court, the prince was met with hostility by the king's legitimate offspring, says the legend, and the young man was sent home—with the precious Ark of the Covenant as a gift. To this day (say the Ethiopians), it remains in a sealed crypt in their homeland. The script in the paintings is Ge'ez, the ecclesiastical language of the Ethiopian church. Taking in the rooftop view and the chapel will occupy about 15 minutes. The exit, via a short stairway to another, lower-level chapel, deposits you in the courtyard of the Church of the Holy Sepulcher. ✉ *Off Suq Khan e-Zeit, near the Church of the Holy Sepulcher, Christian Quarter* 🎫 *Free.*

Pools of Bethesda and Church of St. Anne

ARCHAEOLOGICAL SITE | The transition is sudden and complete, from the raucous cobbled streets and persistent vendors to the pepper trees, flower beds, and birdsong of this serene Catholic monastery of the amiable White Fathers. The Romanesque **Church of St. Anne** was built by the Crusaders in 1140, and restored

The Via Dolorosa often teems with pilgrims but can sometimes offer a quiet path.

in the 19th century. Its austere and unadorned stone interior and extraordinarily reverberant acoustics make it one of the finest examples of medieval architecture in the country. According to local tradition, the Virgin Mary was born in the grotto over which the church is built, and the church is supposedly named after her mother (although "Anne" is never mentioned in the Gospels). In the same compound are the excavated **Pools of Bethesda,** a large public reservoir in use during the 1st century BC and 1st century AD. The New Testament speaks of Jesus miraculously curing a lame man by "a pool, which is called in the Hebrew tongue Bethesda" (John 5). The actual bathing pools were probably the small ones, east of the reservoir, but it was over the big pools that both the Byzantines and the Crusaders built churches, now ruined, to commemorate the miracle. A visit to both sites takes no more than 30 minutes. The good bathrooms here are a welcome addition.
■ TIP➜ Wait for one or two pilgrim groups

who often test the acoustics in the church with some hymn-singing. ✉ Al-Mujahideen Rd., Muslim Quarter ✛ Just inside Lions' Gate ☎ 02/628–3285 ☜ NIS 10.

★ **Via Dolorosa**
HISTORIC SITE | Commonly called "the Way of the Cross" in English, the Latin Via Dolorosa literally translates as "the Way of Sorrow." It's venerated as the route Jesus walked, carrying his cross, from the place of his trial and condemnation by the Roman governor Pontius Pilate to the site of his crucifixion and burial. (Stations I and II are where the Antonia fortress once stood, widely regarded as the site of the "praetorium" referred to in the Gospels.) The present tradition jelled no earlier than the 18th century, but it draws on much older beliefs. Some of the incidents represented by the 14 Stations of the Cross are scriptural; others (III, IV, VI, VII, and IX) are not. Tiny chapels mark a few of the stations; the last five are inside the Church of the Holy Sepulcher. Catholic pilgrim groups, or the

Franciscan-led Friday afternoon procession, take about 45 minutes to wind their way through the busy market streets of the Muslim and Christian quarters, with prayers and chants at each station of the almost-mile-long route.

Here are the 14 stations on the Via Dolorosa that mark the route that Jesus took, from trial and condemnation to crucifixion and burial.

Station I. Jesus is tried and condemned by Pontius Pilate.

Station II. Jesus is scourged and given the cross.

Station III. Jesus falls for the first time. (Soldiers of the Free Polish Forces built the chapel here after World War II.)

Station IV. Mary embraces Jesus.

Station V. Simon of Cyrene picks up the cross.

Station VI. A woman wipes the face of Jesus, whose image remains on the cloth. (She is remembered as Veronica, apparently derived from the Latin word *vera* and the Greek word *icon,* meaning "true image.")

Station VII. Jesus falls for the second time. (The chapel contains one of the columns of the Byzantine Cardo, the main street of 6th-century Jerusalem.)

Station VIII. Jesus addresses the women in the crowd.

Station IX. Jesus falls for the third time.

Station X. Jesus is stripped of his garments.

Station XI. Jesus is nailed to the cross.

Station XII. Jesus dies on the cross.

Station XIII. Jesus is taken down from the cross.

Station XIV. Jesus is buried. ✉ *Christian Quarter* ✣ *Winds east to west, ending in Church of the Holy Sepulcher* 🎫 *Free.*

🍴 Restaurants

The walled Old City pretty much shuts down at night, so most watering holes cater to the lunch customer. There are several outstanding hummus and shawarma places in the Christian Quarter and a broader range of options in and around the Jewish Quarter's Hurva Square and on the route to the Western Wall.

Abu Shukri

$ | **MIDDLE EASTERN** | In the heart of the Old City, this place has some of the best hummus in town, served fast to locals crammed around rickety tables under fluorescent lights. Enjoy the excellent falafel, eggplant salad, and *labaneh* (a slightly tart yogurt served with olive oil and spices). **Known for:** being light on the wallet; colorful salads; family-style dining. [$] *Average main: NIS 25* ✉ *63 El-Wad Rd., Muslim Quarter* ✣ *Next to the 6th station of Via Dolorosa* ☎ *02/627–1538* 💳 *No credit cards* 🕒 *No dinner.*

★ Austrian Hospice Café

$ | **AUSTRIAN** | This Viennese-style second-floor garden café in a guesthouse for pilgrims is a refined retreat from the chaos of the Old City markets down below. Lunch and dinner are available, and the deep burgundy walls, wooden tables, and classical music make this a lovely wintertime spot for light fare or dessert. **Known for:** the famous apple strudel, Sachertorte; a frothy coffee for a reboot while touring; views of the Old City from the roof. [$] *Average main: NIS 40* ✉ *37 Via Dolorosa, Muslim Quarter* ☎ *02/626–5800* 🌐 *www.austrianhospice.com.*

Costa

$ | **MIDDLE EASTERN** | Steps from the Church of the Holy Sepulcher, Palestinians crowd into this tiny, barebones spot to tuck into *hammam mehshi,* or stuffed pigeon. It's a delicately flavored specialty served with salads and rice. **Known for:**

A Walk on the Via Dolorosa

The Old City's main Jewish and Muslim sites can be visited individually, but the primary Christian shrines—the **Via Dolorosa** (or Way of the Cross) and the Holy Sepulcher—are best experienced in sequence. This walk will keep you oriented in the confusing marketplace through which the Via Dolorosa winds its way. (Beware of slick pickpockets.) The route takes a leisurely 40 minutes; plan additional time if you want to linger at specific sites. About 200 yards up the road from St. Anne's Church (near Lions' Gate), look for a ramp on your left leading to the dark metal door of a school. This is the site of the ancient Antonia fortress. On Friday afternoons at 4 (April to September; at 3 from October to March), the brown-robed Franciscans begin their procession of the Via Dolorosa outside the metal door. This is Station I; Station II is across the street. Just beyond it, on the right, is the entrance to the **Ecce Homo Convent of the Sisters of Zion**, with a Roman arch in the chapel. The continuation of the arch crosses the street outside; just beyond it, a small vestibule on the right has a view of the chapel's interior.

The Via Dolorosa runs down into El-Wad Road, one of the Old City's most important thoroughfares. To the right, the street climbs toward the Damascus Gate, and beyond it to East Jerusalem. To the left, it passes through the heart of the Muslim Quarter and reaches the Western Wall. Black-hatted Hasidic Jews hurry on divine missions, nimble local Arab kids in T-shirts and jeans play in the street, and Christian pilgrims pace out ancient footsteps.

As you turn left onto El-Wad Road, Station III is on your left. Right next to it is Station IV and, on the next corner, 50 yards farther, Station V. There the Via Dolorosa turns right and begins its ascent toward Calvary. Halfway up the street, a brown wooden door on your left marks Station VI.

Facing you at the top of the stepped street, on the busy Suq Khan e-Zeit, is Station VII. The little chapel preserves one of the columns of the Byzantine Cardo (main street). Step to the left, and walk 30 yards up the street facing you to Station VIII, marked by nothing more than an inscribed stone in the wall opposite a souvenir store. Return to the main street and turn right. (If you skip Station VIII, turn left as you reach Station VII from the stepped street.) About 100 yards along Suq Khan e-Zeit from Station VII, turn onto the ramp on your right that ascends parallel to the street and becomes a lane. (Stay alert: the clutter of market merchandise makes it easy to miss.) At the end of the lane is a column that represents Station IX.

Step through the open door to the left of the column into the courtyard of the **Ethiopian Monastery** known as Deir es-Sultan. From the monastery's upper chapel, descend through a lower one and out a small wooden door to the court of the **Church of the Holy Sepulcher.** Most Christians venerate this site as that of the death, burial, and resurrection of Jesus—you'll find Stations X, XI, XII, XIII, and XIV within the church. A good time to be here is in the late afternoon, after 4 pm, when the different denominations in turn chant their way between Calvary and the tomb.

local spot for delicious delicacies; fair prices; friendly service. $ *Average main: NIS 45* ⊠ *28 Hakoptim St., Christian Quarter* ☎ *02/627–4480* ▭ *No credit cards.*

Hummus Lina
$ | **MIDDLE EASTERN** | With an upstairs dining area, Lina offers a respite from the hubbub of the Old City. Hand-ground hummus is the main event here, and you can order it topped with chickpeas, fava beans, or pine nuts. **Known for:** freshly made masabacha hummus; perfectly sweet baklava; family-run business. $ *Average main: NIS 20* ⊠ *42 Al Khanka St., Christian Quarter* ☎ *02/627–7230* ⊗ *No dinner.*

Nafoura
$$ | **MIDDLE EASTERN** | **FAMILY** | Just inside the Jaffa Gate, Nafoura offers a tranquil courtyard for alfresco lunchtime dining. Your table might even lean against the Old City wall. **Known for:** local and Armenian specialties; grilled meat; bucolic setting. $ *Average main: NIS 75* ⊠ *26 Latin Patriarch Rd., Christian Quarter* ☎ *02/626–0034* ⊕ *nafoura-rest.com* ⊗ *Closed Sun.*

☕ Coffee and Quick Bites

★ Jaffar Sweets
$ | **MIDDLE EASTERN** | Jaffar specializes in *kunafe,* the Nablus sweet made of goat cheese topped with syrupy semolina crumbles. You may be tempted to split your first plate, but the treat soon grows addictive. Jaffar also makes sheets of golden baklava topped with nuts. **Known for:** massive portions; addictive desserts; value for money. $ *Average main: NIS 20* ⊠ *Khan A-Zeit St., Muslim Quarter* ☎ *02/628–3582* ▭ *No credit cards.*

🛍 Shopping

★ Bilal Abu Khalaf
TEXTILES/SEWING | The family of Bilal Abu Khalaf has been trading in fine fabrics for Jerusalem's elite for three generations. The shop is a treasure trove of Damascene silks woven with golden thread, Moroccan brocade set with semiprecious stones, and the finest fabrics from Kashmir. Phone ahead to arrange a riveting 20-minute presentation of the shop's most beautiful treasures, and an explanation of the Crusader church visible through the glass floor. ⊠ *164 Suq Aftimus, Muristan, Christian Quarter* ☎ *02/626–1718.*

★ Elia Photo Service
SPECIALTY STORES | **FAMILY** | Kevork Kahvedjian's collection of 3,500 photographic prints of Jerusalem and the Holy Land dating back to 1860 provides a window into a vanished world. Many of them have been published in history books and adorn the walls of local hotels and restaurants. All are available as high-quality prints in various sizes, mounted and ready for framing. ⊠ *14 Al-Khanka St., Christian Quarter* ☎ *02/628–2074* ⊕ *www.eliaphoto.com* ⊗ *Closed Sun.*

★ Jerusalem Pottery
SPECIALTY STORES | **FAMILY** | Meticulously crafted Armenian tiles and pottery can be found in this family-run store of two fine local artisans, Stefan Karakashian and his son Hagop. Their particularly high-quality work includes plates, bowls, tiles, and plaques painted with peacocks and flowers and can be shipped all over the world. ⊠ *3 Greek Orthodox Patriarchate St., Old City* ☎ *02/626–1587* ⊕ *www.jerusalempottery.biz* ⊗ *Closed Sun.*

★ Sandrouni
CERAMICS/GLASSWARE | This shop just inside the New Gate stocks intricately hand-painted ceramic tiles in any shape or size, from small decorative tiles to elaborate tiled mirrors, tables, and trays.

Continued on page 118

Jerusalem THE OLD CITY

3

JERUSALEM: KEEPING THE FAITH

✡ ✝ ☪

Unforgotten and unforgettable, the city of Jerusalem is holy ground for the three great monotheistic religions, whose numbers embrace half the world's population. Its Old City is home to some of the most sacred sites of Judaism, Christianity, and Islam: the Western Wall, the Temple Mount/Haram esh-Sharif, the Church of the Holy Sepulcher, and the Dome of the Rock and al-Aqsa Mosque. Some travelers visit them to find their soul, others to seek a sense of communion with ancient epochs. Whether pilgrim or tourist, you'll discover that history, faith, and culture commingle here as perhaps nowhere else on earth.

By Mike Rogoff

(right) The Western Wall, (opposite left) Dome of the Church of the Holy Sepulcher, (opposite right) The Dome of the Rock

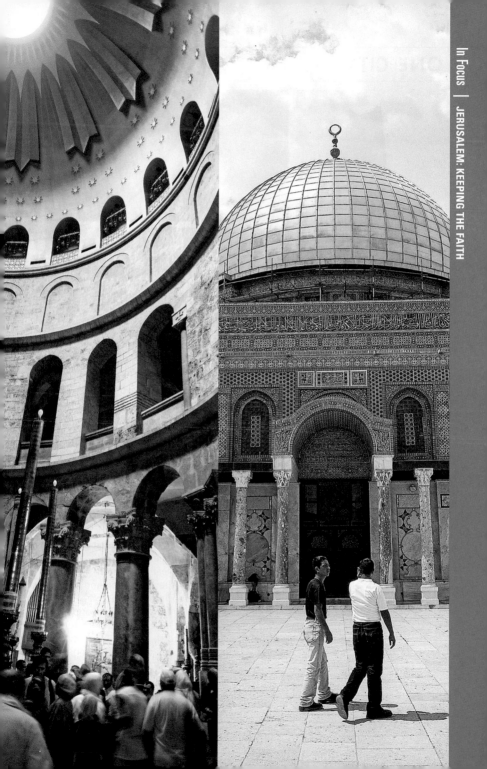

ONE CITY UNDER GOD

Jerusalem is a composite of three faith-civilizations: Jewish, Christian, and Muslim. They cohabit the Old City uneasily, burdened by centuries of struggle with each other for rights and real estate. But at the level of day-to-day routine, each draws its adherents to, respectively, the Western Wall, the Church of the Holy Sepulcher, and the al-Aqsa Mosque. To the visitor, the collage of spiritual traditions is often bewildering, sometimes alien, always fascinating. The intricate choreographies of devotion have been known to move nonbelievers as well as the devout.

HISTORY AND HOLY STONES

Wander the cobblestone lanes of historical Jerusalem and you can hear in your mind's ear the echoes of King David's harp, trace the revered footsteps of Jesus of Nazareth, and sense the presence of the Prophet Muhammad. In the

(left) Woman praying, (top right) Miracle of Holy Fire, Church of the Holy Sepulcher, (bottom right) Men praying near the Dome of the Rock

space of just a few hours, you can visit Golgotha and the tomb of Jesus, gaze at the shrine that caps "the farthermost place" from which Islam's founder rose to heaven, and stand before the only extant remnant of the Second Temple compound. Not without reason do some visitors imagine their fold-out atlases to be road maps leading to heaven itself.

Great dramas played out on these stones—occasionally, it is claimed, on the very same stone. The rock capped by the gold dome is the summit of Mount Moriah, identified in Jewish tradition with the biblical site where Abraham erected an altar and prepared to sacrifice his son Isaac. It was here on the Temple Mount that the "First" and "Second" Jewish Temples stood for a total of one thousand years. In the same rock, devout Muslims point to the imprint of a foot, regarded as that of Muhammad himself, as evidence that it was here that the Prophet ascended to heaven for his meeting with God. The Dome of the

Rock and the nearby al-Aqsa Mosque enshrine that tradition.

On the one hand, Jerusalem is a layer-cake of time, each period leaving distinct strata. The biblical kings David and Solomon transformed a small and already-ancient Jebusite town into an important metropolis. The march of history proceeded through destruction and the Babylonian captivity, Hellenization, Roman rule and another destruction, Byzantine Christianity, the Muslim invasions, the 12th-century Crusades, the Muslim reconquest, European rediscovery of the Holy Land and British control, and down to Jerusalem's contemporary status as the capital (though some dispute it) of the State of Israel.

At another level—change the metaphor—Jerusalem is a complex tangle, a Gordian knot of related but competing faith traditions, historical narratives, and national dreams. The knot seems fated to be around for a while yet, with no hero in sight to slice it through with one bold stroke.

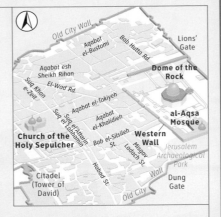

Israelites enslaved during the Babylonian Captivity after the fall of Jerusalem in 586 BC

FINDING YOUR FEET

Each of the three religious sites is infused with its own unique tradition. Making a connection between these stone structures of the past and the wellsprings of religious faith or cultural identity can be uplifting. Many pilgrims focus on their own shrines; some take the time to explore the others so close at hand. The Western Wall is just steps from the Jerusalem Archaeological Park, where excavations turned up remnants of King Herod the Great's grand structures that Jesus almost certainly knew. The bridge between the Western Wall and the park leads up to the vast plaza—the Temple Mount or Haram esh-Sharif—now dominated by the Muslim shrines. Any of the gates at its far northern end will deposit you on the Via Dolorosa. A twenty-minute stroll through the bustling bazaar brings you to the Church of the Holy Sepulcher, revered as the site of Jesus's death and burial.

Whichever site you start with (this feature lists them in historical order: Wall, Church, Dome), a tour of all three unfailingly provokes a powerful appreciation of Jerusalem as an epicenter of faith.

THE WESTERN WALL

No Jewish shrine is holier than the Western Wall, the remains of the ancient Second Temple compound, whose stones are saturated with centuries of prayers and tears.

The status of the Western Wall as the most important existing Jewish shrine derives from its connection with the ancient Temple, the House of God. The 2,000-year-old Wall was not itself part of the Temple edifice, but of the massive retaining wall King Herod built to create the vast plaza now known as the Temple Mount.

After the destruction of Jerusalem by the Romans in AD 70, and especially after the dedication of a pagan town in its place 65 years later, the city became off-limits to Jews for generations. The precise location of the Temple—in the vicinity of today's Dome of the Rock—was lost.

Even when access was regained, Jews avoided entering the Temple Mount out of fear of trespassing on the most sacred, and thus forbidden, areas of the ancient sanctuary. With time, the closest remnant of the period took on the aura of the Temple itself, making the Western Wall a kind of holy place by proxy.

Jewish visitors often just refer to the site as "the Wall" (*Kotel* in Hebrew); "Wailing Wall" is a Gentile term, describing the sight—once more common—of devout Jews grieving for God's House. For many Jews, the ancient Temple was as much a national site as a religious one, and its destruction as much a national trauma as a religious cataclysm.

(top) Jewish man praying at the Western Wall,
(right) Western Wall

VISITING THE WALL

The swaying and praying of the devout reveal the powerful hold this place has on the hearts and minds of many Jews.

On Monday and Thursday mornings, the Wall bubbles with colorful bar-mitzvah ceremonies, when Jewish families celebrate the coming of age of their 13-year-old sons. The excitement is still greater on Friday evenings just after sunset, when the young men of a nearby yeshiva, a Jewish seminary, often come dancing and singing down to the Wall to welcome in the "Sabbath bride." The fervor reaches its highest point three times a year during the three Jewish pilgrimage festivals—Passover, Shavuot (Feast of Weeks), and Sukkot (Feast of Tabernacies), when many Jews come to pray. But many people find that it's only when the crowds have gone (the Wall is floodlit at night and always open), and you share the warm, prayer-drenched stones with just a handful of bearded stalwarts or kerchiefed women, that the true spirituality of the Western Wall is palpable.

The Wall precinct functions under the aegis of the rabbinic authorities, with all the trappings of an Orthodox synagogue. Modest dress is required (men must cover their heads in the prayer area), there is segregation of men and women in prayer, and smoking and photography on the Sabbath and religious holidays are prohibited. Expect a routine check of your bags.

NOTES IN THE WALL

The cracks between the massive stones of the Western Wall are stuffed with slips of paper bearing prayers and petitions. "They reach their destination more quickly than the Israeli postal service," it has been said, with a mixture of serious faith and light cynicism. The cracks are cleared several times a year, but the slips are never simply dumped. Since they often contain God's name, and are written from the heart, the slips are collected in a sack and buried with reverence in a Jewish cemetery.

THE TEMPLE MOUNT, OR HARAM ESH-SHARIF

The size of 27 football fields, the Temple Mount is the vast plaza constructed around the Second Temple in the late 1st century BC by King Herod the Great.

In order to rebuild the Temple on a grand scale, and significantly expand the courts around it, Herod leveled off the top of Mt. Moriah with thousands of tons of rubble. The massive retaining walls include some of the largest building stones known. Structurally, the famous Western Wall is simply the western side of the huge shoebox-like project.

Some scholars regard the Temple Mount as perhaps the greatest religious enclosure of the ancient world, and the splendid Temple, the one Jesus knew, as

an architectural wonder of its day. The Romans reduced the building to smoldering ruins in the summer of AD 70, in the last stages of the Great Revolt of the Jews (AD 66–73). Many of its treasures, including the gold menorah, were carried off to Rome as booty.

Jewish tradition identifies the great rock at the summit of the hill—now under the golden Dome of the Rock—as the foundation stone of the world, and the place where Abraham bound and almost sacrificed his son Isaac (Genesis 22). With greater probability, this was where the biblical King David made a repentance offering to the Lord (II Samuel 22), and where his son Solomon built "God's

(top) Aerial view of the Jewish Quarter and the Temple Mount, (top left) al-Aqsa Mosque, (top right) Drawing of a reconstruction of the First Temple

House," the so-called First Temple. The Second Temple stood on the identical spot, but the precise location of its innermost holy of holies is a question that engages religious Jews and archaeologists to this day.

Christian tradition adds the New Testament dimension. Here Jesus disputed points of law with other Jewish teachers, angrily overturned the tables of money changers, and, looking down at the Temple precinct from the Mount of Olives, predicted its destruction. The Byzantines seem to have neglected the place (perhaps believing it cursed); the medieval Templars took their name from the area in which they set up their headquarters.

Muslims identify it as "the farthermost place," from which Muhammad rose to heaven, and call this area Haram esh-Sharif, the Noble Sanctuary.

JERUSALEM ARCHAEOLOGICAL PARK

Immediately south of the Western Wall, in the shadow of the Temple Mount, is an important archaeological site, still popularly known as the Western and Southern Wall excavations. The dominant monumental structures were the work of King Herod the Great, some 2,000 years ago, though there are Byzantine and early Arab buildings of interest. Robinson's Arch, named for a 19th-century American explorer, once supported a monumental stairway leading up to the Temple Mount. Also discovered were numerous "mikva'ot" (singular "mikveh," a Jewish ritual bath) and a Herodian street, once lined with shops. In the southern part of the site is the low-rise Davidson Center; its exhibits range from ancient artifacts to computer-animated recreations of the Second Temple. *For complete information, see the separate entry for Jerusalem Archaeological Park in this chapter.*

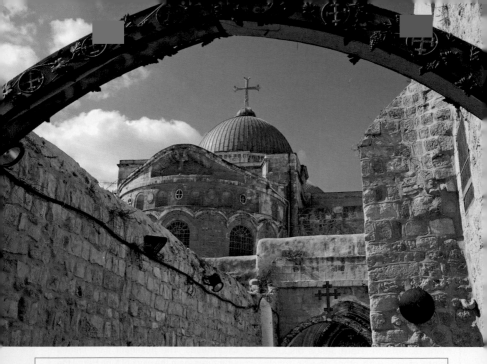

THE CHURCH OF THE HOLY SEPULCHER

Follow the footsteps of Jesus along the Via Dolorosa to the hallowed church that enshrines Golgotha—the hillside of Jesus's crucifixion, burial, and resurrection.

Vast numbers of Christians, especially adherents of the older "mainline" churches, believe that this church marks the place where Jesus was crucified by the Romans and buried by his followers, and where he rose from the dead three days later. Some claim that the antiquity of the Holy Sepulcher tradition argues in favor of its authenticity, since the fervent early Christian community would have striven to preserve the memory of such an important site. The church is outside the city walls of *Jesus's day*—a vital point, for no executions or burials took place within Jerusalem's sacred precincts.

The site was officially consecrated, and the first church built here, following the visit in AD 326 by Helena, mother of the Byzantine emperor Constantine the Great. The present imposing structure, the fourth church on the site, was built by the Crusaders in the 12th century. Interior additions over the years have distorted the Gothic plan, but look for the Norman-style vault at the far end of the Greek Orthodox basilica (facing the tomb), and the ceiling of the dim corridor leading to the adjacent Catholic chapel. After a fire in 1808, much of the church was rebuilt in 19th-century style.

(top) Church of the Holy Sepulcher, (top right) Greek Orthodox chapel, Calvary, (bottom right) Monk kissing the Stone of Unction

HOLIEST LANDMARKS

On the floor just inside the entrance of the church is the rectangular pink **Stone of Unction**, where, it is said, the body of Jesus was cleansed and prepared for burial. Pilgrims often rub fabric or religious trinkets on the stone to absorb its sanctity, and take them home as mementos. Nearby steep steps take you up to **Golgotha**, or Calvary, meaning "the place of the skull," as the site is described in the New Testament. Up the steps, the chapel on the right is Roman Catholic: a window looks out at Station X of the Via Dolorosa, a wall mosaic at the front of the chapel depicts Jesus being nailed to the cross (Station XI), and a bust of Mary in a cabinet to the left of it represents Station XIII where Jesus was taken off the cross. The central chapel—all candlelight, oil lamps, and icons—is Greek Orthodox. Under the altar, and capping the rocky hillock on which you stand, is a silver disc with a hole, purportedly the place—Station XII—where the cross actually stood.

The **tomb** itself (Station XIV), encased in a pink marble edifice, is in the rotunda to the left of the main entrance of the church, under the great dome that dominates the Christian Quarter. The only hint of what the tomb must have been like 2,000 years ago is the ledge in the inner chamber (now covered with marble) on which Jesus's body would have been laid. You can see a more pristine example of an upscale Jewish tomb of the period in the gloomy Chapel of St. Nicodemus, opposite the Coptic chapel in the back of the sepulcher.

SHARING THE CHURCH

An astonishing peculiarity of the Holy Sepulcher is that it is shared, albeit unequally and uncomfortably, by six Christian denominations. Centuries of sometimes-violent competition for control of key Christian

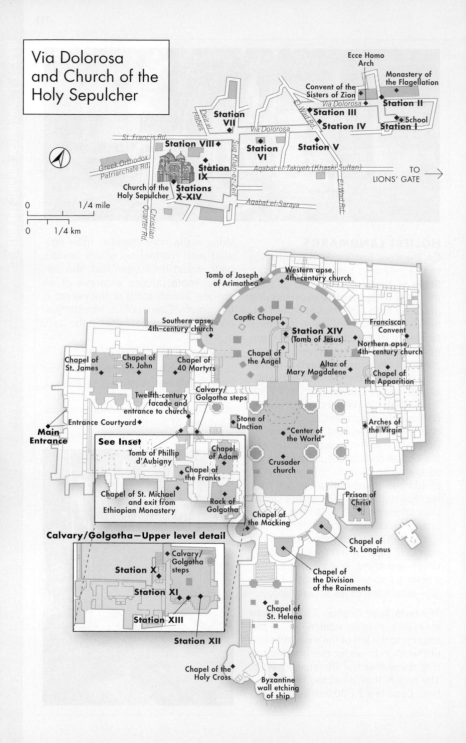

Via Dolorosa and Church of the Holy Sepulcher

Ecce Homo Arch

Monastery of the Flagellation

Convent of the Sisters of Zion

Via Dolorosa

Station II

Station III

School

Station IV

Station I

Station VII

Via Dolorosa

Del el Hadea

St. Francis Rd.

Station V

Station VIII

Station VI

Greek Orthodox Patriarchate Rd.

Suq Khan-ez-Zeil

Aqabat el-Takiyeh (Khaski Sultan)

TO LIONS' GATE

Station IX

Church of the Holy Sepulcher

Stations X–XIV

El-Wad Rd.

Aqabat el-Saraya

Christian Quarter Rd.

0 — 1/4 mile

0 — 1/4 km

Tomb of Joseph of Arimathea

Western apse, 4th-century church

Southern apse, 4th-century church

Coptic Chapel

Station XIV (Tomb of Jesus)

Franciscan Convent

Chapel of St. James

Chapel of St. John

Chapel of 40 Martyrs

Chapel of the Angel

Northern apse, 4th-century church

Chapel of Mary Magdalene

Altar of Mary Magdalene

Chapel of the Apparition

Twelfth-century facade and entrance to church

Calvary/ Golgotha steps

Entrance Courtyard

Stone of Unction

"Center of the World"

Arches of the Virgin

Main Entrance

See Inset

Tomb of Phillip d'Aubigny

Chapel of Adam

Chapel of the Franks

Crusader church

Chapel of St. Michael and exit from Ethiopian Monastery

Rock of Golgotha

Prison of Christ

Chapel of the Mocking

Chapel of St. Longinus

Calvary/Golgotha—Upper level detail

Station X

Calvary/ Golgotha steps

Chapel of the Division of the Rainments

Station XI

Station XIII

Chapel of St. Helena

Station XII

Chapel of the Holy Cross

Byzantine wall etching of ship

Mosaic of Jesus near the Stone of Unction

sites culminated in the Status Quo Agreement of 1852. Under the pressure of Orthodox Russia, the Ottoman Turks recognized the precedence of the Greek Orthodox as on-the-ground representatives of the Eastern Rite churches.

Each denomination guards its assigned privileges, and minor infringements by one of its neighbors can flare up into open hostility. At the same time, the phenomenon gives the place much of its color. Try visiting in the late afternoon (the exact time changes with the seasons), and watch the groups in turn—Greek Orthodox, Latins (as Roman Catholics are known in the Holy Land), Armenian Orthodox, and Egyptian Copts—in procession from Calvary to the tomb. The candlelight and swinging censers are passingly similar; the robes and lusty hymn-singing are different.

A modern agreement among the Greeks, the Latins, and the Armenians on the interior restoration of the great dome was hailed as a breakthrough in ecumenical relations, and it was rededicated in January 1997 in an unprecedented interdenominational service.

SUGGESTIONS FOR YOUR VISIT

While the first nine Stations of the Cross are to be found along the Way of the Cross—the Via Dolorosa—the final and most holy ones are within the Church of the Holy Sepulcher itself. The best time to visit may be around 4pm when many denominations are found worshipping. *For more information, see the separate entry for the Via Dolorosa elsewhere in this chapter.*

As in many religious sites, modest dress and discreet behavior are required here, but it's difficult for the clergy of any particular community to assert authority. Come early or late to avoid the worst crowds; be patient, too. A small flashlight or some candles will help you explore the small tomb of St. Nicodemus, an authentic Jewish tomb of the period.

Entrance of the Church of the Holy Sepulcher

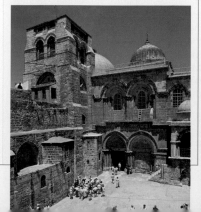

THE DOME OF THE ROCK AND AL-AQSA MOSQUE

The focal point of these sanctuaries, whose interiors are currently open only to Muslims, is the Rock—the place from which Muhammad is believed to have ascended to heaven to be given the divine precepts of Islam.

The magnificent golden **Dome of the Rock** dominates the vast 35-acre Temple Mount, the area known to Muslims as Haram esh-Sharif (the Noble Sanctuary). This is the original octagonal building, completed in AD 691. It enshrines the great rock—the summit of Mount Moriah—from which the prophet Muhammad is said to have risen to heaven. Jerusalem is not mentioned in the Qur an, but Muhammad's "Night

(top) Eight *qanatirs* (arcades) stand by sets of steps leading to the Dome of the Rock, (top right) The rock, the Dome's central shrine

Ride" is. Awakened by the archangel Gabriel, he was taken on the fabulous winged horse el-Burak to the *masjid al-aqsa*, the "farthermost place." From there he rose to heaven, met God face to face, received the teachings of Islam, and returned to Mecca the same night. Tradition has it that the *masjid al-aqsa* was none other than Jerusalem, and the great rock the very spot from which the prophet ascended.

To be sure, Muhammad's triumphant successors venerated Jerusalem's biblical sanctity; but some modern scholars suggest they did not like the feeling of being Johnnies-come-lately in the holy city of rival faiths. The impressive Dome

of the Rock, built by the Ummayad caliph Abd el-Malik, was almost certainly intended to proclaim the ascendancy of the "true faith."

A SPLENDID SHRINE

Considering the original builders and craftsmen adopted the artistic traditions of their Byzantine predecessors, it's hardly surprising that the plan of the shrine resembles those of its Christian contemporaries, like the Byzantine Church of San Vitale in Ravenna, Italy. Take a close look at the bright exterior tiles in variegated shades of blue. The marvelous gold dome was restored in the 1990s, with 176 pounds of 24-carat gold electroplated on copper.

At the time of this writing, non-Muslims were denied entry to the interior of the building, with its beautiful granite columns supporting arches, some of which bear the original green-and-gold mosaics set in arabesque motifs. In obedience to Islamic religious tradition, no human or animal forms appear in the artwork. The mosaics were restored in 1027, but preserved much of the original work.

All this splendor was designed to emphasize the importance of the rock itself, directly under the great dome. The faithful reach out and touch an indentation which, they believe, was nothing less than the Prophet's footprint, left there as he ascended to heaven.

THE THIRD-HOLIEST OF ALL

At the southern end of the Haram, immediately in front of you as you enter the area from the Western Wall plaza (the only gate for non-Muslims), is the large, black-domed **Al-Aqsa Mosque**. The Dome of the Rock is a shrine, the place where a hallowed event is believed to have taken place. Individuals go there

THE DOME'S MOSAICS

Some of the Arabic inscriptions in the mosaics are quotations from the Qur an, others are dedications. One of the latter originally lauded Abd el-Malik, caliph of the Damascus-based Ummayad dynasty, who built the shrine. Some 140 years later, the caliph of a rival dynasty removed el-Malik's name and replaced it with his own, but he neglected to change the date.

to pray, but al-Aqsa is a true mosque, attracting thousands of worshippers on Fridays and Muslim holidays. It is third in holiness for Muslims everywhere, after the great mosques of Mecca and Medina, both in Saudi Arabia.

Built by the Ummayad dynasty in the early 8th century AD, it has been destroyed and restored several times. In the 12th century, the al-Aqsa Mosque became the headquarters of the Templars, a Crusader monastic order that took its name from the ancient temple that once stood nearby. The spot has been the setting for more recent dramas, most importantly the assassination of King Abdullah I of Jordan (the present king's great-grandfather) in 1951.

EXPLORING THE HARAM

The Haram today is a Muslim preserve, a legacy that dates back to AD 638, when the Arab caliph Omar Ibn-Khatib seized Jerusalem from the Byzantines. At the time of this writing, the Muslim shrines were closed to non-Muslims indefinitely, leaving the faithful alone to enjoy their wondrous interiors.

Even if you can't get inside, the vast plaza is visually and historically arresting, and worth a visit. Fifteenth-century Mamluk buildings line the western edge. Overlooking the plaza at its northwestern corner is a long building, today an elementary school, built on the artificial scarp that protected Herod's Antonia fortress. Christian tradition, very possibly accurate, identifies the site as the praetorium where Jesus was tried.

Security check lines to enter the Haram esh-Sharif are often long; it's best to come early. Note that the Muslim attendants prohibit Bibles in the area.

(top) Parts of columns on the Haram, (right) Mosaics and arches grace the Dome's interior

Jerusalem's Cafés

Sitting down for coffee and cake in one of Jerusalem's fine cafés is something of a tradition. Yeast cakes and strudels recall the past, but today's palate craves flaky brioches and savory tarts. Italian coffee machines have driven a rise in quality and a demand for the perfect *hafuch*, the strong Israeli version of a cappuccino.

In Jerusalem, the open-air mall of Ben-Yehuda Street has several venerable hangouts, but the newer cafés along the bars and restaurants of Shlomzion Hamalka Street offer more sophisticated menus—and better coffee. The upscale Mamilla Mall, outside Jaffa Gate, is known for its coffee places, but don't overlook Emek Refa'im Street in the German Colony or Bethlehem Road in Baka.

Most popular coffee spots serve decent light, affordable meals for lunch and dinner as well, and courtyard seating gets full in fine weather and on summer evenings. Coffee and a pastry are about NIS 30 to NIS 40; sandwiches, salads, quiche, and pasta will cost NIS 30 to NIS 60. If you're not a coffee drinker, consider trying a *gazoz*, a fizzy drink made of soda water and syrup.

From the Jaffa Gate, take the first left onto Latin Patriarch Road. ⊠ *New Gate Rd., Christian Quarter* ☎ *02/626–3744* ⊕ *www.sandrouni.com.*

★ Souk

OUTDOOR/FLEA/GREEN MARKETS | Jerusalem's main market is the souk in the Old City, spread over a warren of intersecting streets. This is where much of Arab Jerusalem shops. It's awash with color and redolent with the clashing scents of exotic spices. Baskets of produce vie for attention with hanging shanks of lamb, fresh fish on ice, and fresh-baked delicacies. Food stalls are interspersed with purveyors of fabrics and shoes. The baubles and trinkets of the tourist trade often seem secondary, except along the well-trodden paths of the Via Dolorosa, David Street, and Christian Quarter Road.

Haggling with merchants in the Arab market—a time-honored tradition—is not for everyone. If you know what you want and what you are willing to pay, it can be fun to try to knock the price down; if not, seek out shops with set prices, either in the Old City or outside its walls. ⊠ *Muslim Quarter.*

Jaffa Gate

Jaffa Gate got its name from its westerly orientation, toward the Mediterranean harbor of Jaffa, now part of Tel Aviv. Its Arabic name of Bab el-Khalil, "Gate of the Beloved," points you south, toward the city of Hebron (in the West Bank of today) where the biblical Abraham, the "Beloved of God" in Muslim tradition, is buried. The old pedestrian gate, like most of the Old City wall itself, was built by the Ottoman Turkish sultan, Suleiman the Magnificent, in the 16th century. The vehicle road is a newer, grand entrance created in 1898 for the royal visit of the German emperor, Kaiser Wilhelm II. The British general, Sir Edmund Allenby, took a different approach when he seized the city from the Turks in December 1917: eschewing pomp and ceremony, he and his staff officers dismounted from their horses to enter the holy city on foot with the humility befitting pilgrims. Outside the walls is the deep Hinnom Valley, the natural western defense of the ancient city.

Behind the railings just inside the imposing gate are, traditionally, the graves of the two Muslim architects who built Suleiman's city walls. According to legend, they were executed by order of the Sultan, either (says one version) because they angered Suleiman by not including Mount Zion and the venerated Tomb of David within the walls, or (relates another) because the satisfied Sultan wanted to make sure they would never build anything grander for anyone else.

Directly ahead is the souk (bazaar), engaging in itself, but also a convenient route to the Christian and Jewish quarters.

The huge stone tower on the right as you enter Jaffa Gate is the last survivor of the strategic fortress built by King Herod 2,000 years ago to secure the city's weak point: the saddle between the deep Hinnom Valley to the west and the shallow valley to the north (today's bazaar). The massive Citadel, as it's still often known, houses the Tower of David Museum—well worth your time as a springboard for exploring this part of the historical city. Opposite the museum entrance (once a drawbridge) is the Gothic-style Christ Church (Anglican), built in 1849 as the first Protestant church in the Middle East.

The vehicle road continues through the Armenian Quarter, the Old City's smallest neighborhood. Its closed enclave perpetuates the life and faith of a far-off land, the first to embrace Christianity. A short walk beyond it brings you to Zion Gate (and through it, Mount Zion) and to the Jewish Quarter.

GETTING HERE AND AROUND

Jaffa Gate, a logical entry point for visits to the Old City, is an easy walk from the Downtown or King David Street areas. Many Downtown bus stops are within striking distance as well.

TIMING AND PRECAUTIONS

Jaffa Gate is always open, though within the Old City itself some sites have limited hours or are closed Friday, Saturday, or Sunday.

◉ Sights

★ Ramparts Walk

ARCHAEOLOGICAL SITE | The narrow stone catwalks of the Old City walls provide great panoramic views and interesting perspectives of this intriguing city. But they also offer an innocent bit of voyeurism as you look down into gardens and courtyards and become, for a moment, a more intimate partner in the secret domestic life of the different quarters you pass. Across the rooftops, the domes and spires of the three religions that call Jerusalem holy compete for the skyline, just as their adherents jealously guard their territory down below. Peer through the shooting niches, just as watchmen and snipers did in the not-so-distant past. The hotels and high-rises of the new city dominate the skyline to the west; Mount Zion is immediately to the south; the bustle of East Jerusalem is almost tangible to the north; and the churches and cemeteries quietly cling to the Mount of Olives to the east. ■TIP➔ **There are many high steps on this route; the railings are secure, but small children should not walk alone; good footwear, a hat, and water are recommended.**

The two sections of the walk are separated by Jaffa Gate, though the same ticket covers both (available from the commercial tourist services office just inside Jaffa Gate and at the entrance to the southern route). The shorter southern section is accessible only from the end of the seemingly dead-end terrace outside Jaffa Gate at the exit of the Tower of David Museum. Descent is at Zion Gate or just before Dung Gate. The longer and more varied walk begins at Jaffa Gate (up the stairs immediately on the left as you enter the Old City), with descent at New, Damascus, Herod's, or Lions' Gates. Allow 30 to 40 minutes for the shorter section to Zion Gate, adding 10 to 15 minutes to get to Dung Gate. For the longer section, it takes 20 minutes to walk north-northeast to the New Gate, another 20 minutes east to Damascus Gate, 15 minutes from there to Herod's Gate, and about 20 minutes more to Lions' Gate. ■TIP→ Since much of the long northern route passes through or above Palestinian areas, it's advisable to end your walk at the New Gate during times of tension. ⊠ Entry near Jaffa Gate, Jaffa Gate ☎ 02/625–4403 ⊕ www.pami.co.il/en ☜ NIS 20 ⊙ Northern route closed Fri.

Teddy Park

AMUSEMENT PARK/WATER PARK | FAMILY | Set just west of Jaffa Gate next to Hutzot Hayotzer Artist Colony compound is Teddy Park, named for Teddy Kollek, the popular mayor of Jerusalem from 1965 to 1993. On the park's upper terrace, a small mirrorlike globe is designed as a jigsaw of the continents. Entering the globe through the "oceans," you encounter a floor engraving of a famous Renaissance map that shows Jerusalem as the center of the world. The middle terrace boasts an intriguingly innovative sundial that not only tells time, but also tracks the solstices, equinoxes, and a few memorable dates. In the summer, a large square platform on the lower terrace becomes a cool children's playground when multiple water jets spurt unpredictably into the air for 20 minutes, four times daily. At night, the fountain plays to an orchestration of light and music. ⊠ Outside Old City walls, below Jaffa Gate, Jaffa Gate ⊕ www.tod.org.il/en/museum/teddy-park ☜ Free.

★ Tower of David Museum

ARCHAEOLOGICAL SITE | FAMILY | Many visitors find this museum invaluable in mapping Jerusalem's often-confusing historical byways. Housed in a series of medieval halls, known locally as the Citadel (Hametzuda in Hebrew), the museum tells the city's four-millennium story through models, maps, holograms, and videos. The galleries are organized by historical period around the Citadel's central courtyard, where the old stone walls and arches add an appropriately antique atmosphere. Walking on the Citadel ramparts provides unexpected panoramas: don't miss the wonderful view from the top of the big tower. The basement has a model of 19th-century Jerusalem, constructed for the Ottoman pavilion at the Vienna World Fair in 1873. Guided tours in English are offered weekdays at 11. You'll need 90 minutes to do justice to this museum.

The outdoor "Night Spectacular" is a stunning 45-minute sound-and-light pageant of historical images played onto the ancient stone walls and towers. The event runs throughout the year, but days and times change with the seasons. Reserve in advance. ⊠ Armenian Orthodox Patriarchate Rd., Jaffa Gate ✛ On vehicle road, just inside Jaffa Gate ☎ 02/626–5333 ⊕ www.towerofdavid.org.il ☜ From NIS 40.

🛏 Hotels

The Old City, the historic walled heart of Jerusalem, includes the Armenian Quarter, the Christian Quarter, the Jewish Quarter, and the Muslim Quarter. Lodging options here are limited, and you'll trade luxurious amenities for the ability to step out of your room and into the ancient cobbled streets.

Christ Church Guest House

$ | B&B/INN | Inside the Jaffa Gate, this guesthouse is part of the oldest Protestant church in the Middle East. **Pros:** tranquil haven; free parking; excellent for sightseeing. **Cons:** not always comfortable for non-Christian guests; rooms and beds are small; inconsistent service.

$ *Rooms from: $170* ✉ *55 Armenian Orthodox Patriarchate Rd., Armenian Quarter* ☎ *02/627–7727* 🌐 *cmj-israel.org* 🛏 *32 rooms* 🍴 *Free Breakfast.*

Lutheran Guesthouse

$ | B&B/INN | Tucked into an alleyway behind the souk in the Armenian Quarter, this guesthouse is a maze of stone buildings and tranquil gardens. **Pros:** hospitable service; leaf-framed panoramas; rooftop terrace. **Cons:** not all rooms have a/c; spotty Wi-Fi in some rooms; can be loud. $ *Rooms from: $115* ✉ *9 Saint Mark St., Armenian Quarter* ☎ *02/626–6888* 🌐 *www.luth-guesthouse-jerusalem.com* 🛏 *36 rooms* 🍴 *Free Breakfast.*

New Imperial Hotel

$ | HOTEL | Tiny iron balconies overlooking Jaffa Gate make this century-old hotel a solid choice for a historic—if humble—night near the Old City walls. **Pros:** great location; authentic feel; budget-friendly rates. **Cons:** can be noisy; outdated decor; spotty Wi-Fi access. $ *Rooms from: $125* ✉ *Omar Ibn El-Khattib St., Jaffa Gate* ☎ *02/628–2261* 🌐 *www.newimperial.com* 🛏 *50 rooms* 🍴 *Free Breakfast.*

Shopping

Antreassian's Ceramics

CERAMICS/GLASSWARE | The standouts in Armenian Hagop Antreassian's studio are his wonderful large bowls. They won't fit in your carry-ons, but the owner is happy to ship your orders. You can often find him painting or firing his clay creations in his studio just inside Zion Gate. ✉ *13 Zion Gate St., opposite Zion Gate, Armenian Quarter* ☎ *02/626–3871* 🌐 *www.antreassian.com.*

Mount Zion

Thousands of years ago, Mount Zion lay within the compass of the city walls, protected in the west and south by the virtually unassailable slopes of the Hinnom Valley. No more. The 16th-century Turkish wall slashes across Mount Zion, leaving it outside the Old City, connected to it by the narrow Zion Gate. The faiths that call Jerusalem holy cross paths on this hilltop. For Judaism—and, by extension, Islam—this is where King David was buried 30 centuries ago: his supposed tomb is venerated to this day. Christianity identifies the area with key scriptural events, and churches, monasteries, institutions, and graveyards are visible landmarks. There are few must-see sites here; but if you enjoy less compulsive sightseeing, Mount Zion is worth an hour or two of your time.

GETTING HERE AND AROUND

Get to Mount Zion on foot from Jaffa Gate. Most interesting is taking the southern Ramparts Walk (coming down at Zion Gate), or strolling the path that skirts the outside of the Old City wall: both offer fine views across the Hinnom Valley. Or share the road through the Armenian Quarter with the cabs and minivans.

TIMING AND PRECAUTIONS

Modest dress is de rigueur for David's Tomb and the churches. Pay attention to opening times on Friday and Saturday (for the tomb) and Sunday (for the churches).

Sights

Chamber of the Holocaust (*Martef Hasho'ah*)

MEMORIAL | This small museum is dedicated to the memory of the 6 million European Jews annihilated by the Nazis in the Second World War. Among the artifacts salvaged from the Holocaust are items that the Nazis forced Jews to make out of sacred Torah scrolls. One Jewish tailor fashioned a vest for his Nazi "customer" out of the inscribed parchment, but with grim humor he chose sections that contained the worst of the biblical curses. Plaques commemorate many of the 5,000 European Jewish communities destroyed from 1939 to 1945. ⊠ *Ma'ale Shazakh, Mount Zion* ⊹ *On east side of Tomb of David* ☎ *02/671–5105* ⌧ *Free (donation expected)* ⊗ *Closed Fri., Sat., and Jewish religious holidays.*

Dormition Abbey

RELIGIOUS SITE | The large, round Roman Catholic church, with its distinctive cone-shaped roof, ornamented turrets, and landmark clock tower, is a Jerusalem landmark. It was built on land bought by the German emperor Kaiser Wilhelm II when he visited Jerusalem in 1898. The German Benedictines dedicated the echoing main church, with its Byzantine-style apse and mosaic floors, in 1910. The lower-level crypt houses a cenotaph with a carved-stone figure of Mary in repose (*dormitio*), reflecting the tradition that she fell into eternal sleep. Among the adjacent little chapels is one donated by the Ivory Coast, with wooden figures and motifs inlaid with ivory. The premises include a bookstore and a coffee shop. A visit takes about 25 minutes. ⊠ *Off Har Tsiyon St., near Room of the Last Supper, Mount Zion* ☎ *02/565–5330* ⊕ *www.dormitio.net* ⌧ *Free.*

Hinnom Valley

ARCHAEOLOGICAL SITE | A few minutes from the Jaffa Gate is the deep Hinnom Valley, which offers some fine views of Mount Zion and the Old City walls. The area achieved notoriety in the 7th century BC during the long reign of the Israelite king Menasseh (697–640 BC). He was not merely an idolater, the Bible relates, but supported a cult of child sacrifice by fire in the Valley of the Son of Hinnom. Over time, the biblical Hebrew name of the valley—*Gei Ben Hinnom,* contracted to *Gehennom* or *Gehenna*—became a synonym for a hellish place of burning, in both Hebrew and New Testament Greek.

In the late 1970s, Israeli archaeologist Gabriel Barkai discovered a series of Old Testament–period rock tombs at the bend in the valley, below the fortresslike St. Andrew's Scots Church. The most spectacular finds were two tiny rolled strips of silver, designed to be worn as amulets around the neck. The painstaking opening of the little cylinders revealed the biblical "priestly benediction" (Nos. 6), inscribed in the ancient Hebrew script. This 7th-century-BC sample, beginning "The Lord bless you and keep you," is the oldest biblical passage ever found. The tombs are an open site, accessed through the Menachem Begin Heritage Center during its visiting hours. ⊠ *6 Nachon St., Mount Zion* ⊹ *Below St. Andrew's Scots Church* ☎ *02/565–2020* ⊕ *www.begincenter.org.il/en* ⌧ *NIS 25* ⊗ *Tomb site closed Sat.*

Room of the Last Supper

HISTORIC SITE | Tradition has enshrined this spare, 14th-century second-story room as the location of the New Testament "upper room," where Jesus and his disciples celebrated the ceremonial Passover meal that would become known in popular parlance as the Last Supper (Mark 14). At that time, archaeologists tell us, the site was inside the city walls. Formally known as the Cenacle or the Coenaculum (dining room), the room is also associated with a second New Testament tradition (Acts 2) as the place where the disciples gathered on Pentecost, seven weeks after Jesus's death, and were "filled with the Holy Spirit."

A little incongruously, the chamber has the trappings of a mosque as well: restored stained-glass Arabic inscriptions in the Gothic windows, an ornate *mihrab* (an alcove indicating the Muslim direction of prayer, toward Mecca), and two Arabic plaques in the wall. The Muslims were not concerned with the site's Christian traditions but with the supposed Tomb of King David—the "Prophet" David in their belief—on the level below. Allow 10 minutes to fully soak in the atmosphere. ⊠ *Off Ma'ale HaShalom, Mount Zion* ⊹ *Above David's Tomb, by means of outside staircase* ⌧ *Free.*

The City of David, just south of the Temple Mount, is one of the oldest parts of Jerusalem.

Tomb of David

HISTORIC SITE | According to the Hebrew Bible, King David, the great Israelite king of the 10th century BC, was buried in "the City of David"—the Bible's dynastic name for his capital, Jerusalem. Archaeologists have identified and excavated that site, on a low ridge to the east; but medieval Jewish pilgrims erroneously placed the ancient city on this hill, where they sought—and supposedly found—the royal tomb. Its authenticity may be questionable, but a millennium of tears and prayers has sanctified the place.

The tomb is capped by a cenotaph, a massive stone marker draped with a velvet cloth embroidered with symbols and Hebrew texts traditionally associated with David. Ultra-Orthodox religious authorities have divided the shrine, already cramped, into two tiny prayer areas to separate men and women. Modest dress is required, and men must cover their heads. There's no photography on the Sabbath and Jewish religious holidays. ⊠ *Off Ma'ale HaShalom, Mount Zion* ⊕ *Just beyond Dormition Abbey when coming from Zion Gate, beneath the Room of the Last Supper* ☎ *02/581–1911* 🎟 *Free.*

City of David

If you thrill to the thought of standing where the ancients once stood, you'll be in your element in this city of memories, from Old Testament walls and water systems to Second Temple streets and stones.

GETTING HERE AND AROUND
Parking is nonexistent: come by cab, or walk down from the Old City by way of Dung Gate.

TIMING AND PRECAUTIONS
Allow 2½ to 3 hours for a full unhurried tour of the City of David (though you can cover a lot of ground in less time). The site is in the heart of the predominantly Arab Silwan neighborhood, with

occasional tension between Palestinians and Jewish settlers, but the layout of the enclosure and the security arrangements should dispel concerns.

Sights

★ City of David

ARCHAEOLOGICAL SITE | FAMILY | Lying just south of today's Old City walls, the City of David was the very core of Old Testament Jerusalem, built more than four millennia ago on a 15-acre spur over the vital Gihon Spring. It was given its royal Israelite sobriquet 1,000 years later, when the legendary King David conquered the city and made it his capital (II Samuel 5). Begin with the great rooftop observation point above the visitor center. Consider the 15-minute 3-D movie, despite its ideological bias; it's a good historical introduction to the site, especially for kids (call ahead for English-language show times). Below the floorboards of the center are the excavated remains of a large building of the 10th century BC, identified by some archaeologists as King David's fortified palace; others demur. A few flights of steps down from the center is Area G, dominated by a sloping structure of the same period, possibly a support ramp for the "palace" above. The most intriguing artifacts found here were 51 *bullae*, clay seal impressions no bigger than a fingernail, used for sealing documents or official correspondence. Some were inscribed, in ancient Hebrew, with the names of personages mentioned in the biblical book of Jeremiah. There is strong circumstantial evidence to suggest that the bullae were baked into permanent pottery by the Babylonian burning of Jerusalem in 586 BC.

Take the steps about a third of the way down the hillside: a small sign on the right directs you to Warren's Shaft and the descent to the spring. Charles Warren, a British army engineer, discovered the spacious, sloping access

tunnel—note the ancient chisel marks and rough-cut steps—in 1867. The deep vertical shaft that drops into the Gihon Spring may not have been the actual biblical "gutter" or "water-shaft" through which David's warriors penetrated the city 3,000 years ago—it was apparently hewn in a later era—but an alternative access to the spring has kept the biblical story alive. Three centuries later, King Hezekiah of Judah had a horizontal tunnel dug through solid rock to bring the spring water safely into a new inner-city reservoir.

The tunnel—variously called Siloam, Shilo'ach, or Hezekiah's Tunnel—can be waded today. You will need water shoes or sandals, a flashlight (cheap LED ones are on sale at the visitor center), and appropriate clothing: the water is thigh-deep for the first few minutes, and then below the knees for almost the entire length of the tunnel (a 30-minute walk). The visitor center has lockers for your gear. In this very conservative neighborhood, it's advisable to wear covering over swimsuits when walking outside. The wade is not recommended for very small children or for claustrophobes of any age.

If you don't fancy getting wet, you can still view the spring, and then continue through the dry Canaanite tunnel to emerge above ground.

The tunnel ends in the Pool of Siloam, mentioned in the New Testament as the place where a blind man had his sight restored (John 9); the current pool is its Byzantine successor. From the exit, modern wooden steps take you down and over the large flagstones of a 1st-century-BC commercial street to the edge of an ancient pool unearthed in 2004 by city workers repairing a sewage pipe. Archaeologists exposed finely cut steps and two corners of the pool, apparently a large public mikvah, or Jewish ritual bath, for pilgrims who flocked here 2,000 years ago—and arguably the very pool of the

Gospel miracle. Hezekiah's original pool remains hidden.

An underground Roman-period drainage ditch is the adventurous route back up the hill. For an additional fee you can continue still further north through the ditch (bypassing the visitor center), to the Jerusalem Archaeological Park inside the city walls. ■TIP→ There is a shuttle van (NIS 5) from the pool up the steep hill back to the visitor center, but currently not from the dry exit. ⊠ Off Ophel Rd., Silwan ⊹ South of Old City walls, 200 yards down from Dung Gate ☎ 02/626–8700 ⊕ www.cityofdavid.org.il ⊠ City of David NIS 29; guided tour including admission NIS 62 ⊘ Closed Sat. and Jewish religious holidays, limited entry Fri.

East Jerusalem

Loosely speaking, East Jerusalem refers to the Arab neighborhoods controlled by Jordan in the years when the city was divided (1948–67). That includes the Mount of Olives, and the areas north and southeast of the Old City.

The sights in this area are for the most part distinctly Christian. A few are a little off the beaten path, and the best way to explore them—if you're energetic enough—is on foot. If you're driving, however, you can sometimes find free parking at the Seven Arches Hotel on the Mount of Olives and paid parking at the cluster of large hotels near the American Colony; or take a cab.

GETTING HERE AND AROUND
If you enjoy a bit of a walk and the weather is fine, it's no more than a 25-minute walk from Hebrew University's Mount Scopus campus (served by West Jerusalem bus routes 19, 34, and 68) across to the Mount of Olives. The panoramic view of the Judean Desert to the east is a bonus. A cab ride is an alternative, but if you skip the top of the mountain, the rest

of the sights are accessible by foot from the Old City.

TIMING AND PRECAUTIONS
Morning views are best from the Mount of Olives. Some of the sites are closed on Sunday. Watch out for pickpockets on the Mount of Olives, on the road down to Gethsemane, and on Nablus Road outside the Garden Tomb.

◉ Sights

Church of Mary Magdalene
HISTORIC SITE | With its sculpted white turrets and gold onion domes, this Russian Orthodox church looks like something out of a fairy tale. It was dedicated in 1888, when the competition among European powers for influence in this part of the world was at its height. Princess Alice, the mother of Prince Philip, Duke of Edinburgh, is buried here, near her aunt, Elizabeth, the Russian grand duchess–turned-nun, who was murdered by the Bolsheviks in 1918. The church has limited hours, but its icon-studded interior and tranquil garden are well worth a visit if your plans bring you to the area at the right time. ⊠ Palm Sunday Rd., off El-Mansuriya Rd., Mount of Olives ⊹ Above the Garden of Gethsemane ☎ 02/628–4371 ⊕ www.jerusalem-mission.org/convent_magdalene.html ⊠ Free ⊘ Closed Fri.–Mon. and Wed., and Tues. and Thurs. afternoon.

Dominus Flevit
RELIGIOUS SITE | Designed by Antonio Barluzzi in the 1950s, the tear-shape church—its name means "The Lord Wept"—preserves the New Testament story of Jesus's sorrowful prediction of the destruction of Jerusalem (Luke 19). The remarkable feature of its simple interior is a picture window facing west, the iron cross on the altar silhouetted against a superb view of the Old City. Many archaeological items were unearthed here, including a group of ancient stone

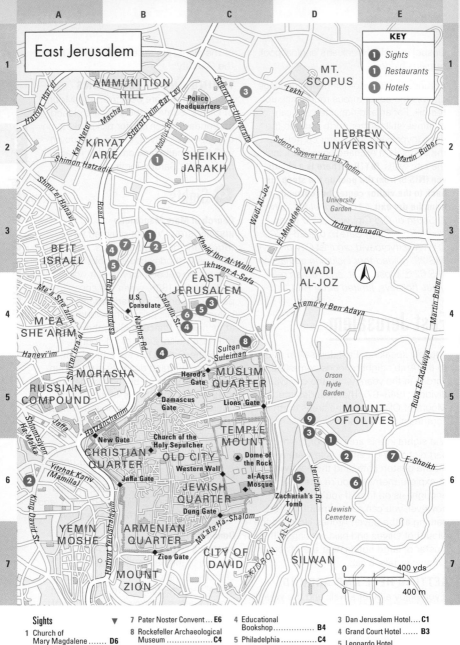

East Jerusalem

KEY
- ① Sights
- ① Restaurants
- ① Hotels

AMMUNITION HILL

MT. SCOPUS

Police Headquarters

HEBREW UNIVERSITY

KIRYAT ARIE

SHEIKH JARAKH

University Garden

BEIT ISRAEL

EAST JERUSALEM

WADI AL-JOZ

U.S. Consulate

M'EA SHE'ARIM

MORASHA

RUSSIAN COMPOUND

Sultan Suleiman

Herod's Gate

MUSLIM QUARTER

Orson Hyde Garden

MOUNT OF OLIVES

Damascus Gate

Lions' Gate

New Gate

Church of the Holy Sepulcher

CHRISTIAN QUARTER

TEMPLE MOUNT

OLD CITY

Dome of the Rock

Western Wall

al-Aqsa Mosque

Zachariah's Tomb

Jewish Cemetery

Jaffa Gate

JEWISH QUARTER

Dung Gate

YEMIN MOSHE

ARMENIAN QUARTER

Ma'ale Ha-Shalom

CITY OF DAVID

SILWAN

Zion Gate

MOUNT ZION

0   400 yds

0   400 m

ossuaries, or bone boxes, preserved in a grotto on the right as you enter the site. The courtyard is a good place to enjoy the view in peace between waves of pilgrim groups. (Equally worthy of mention are the restrooms, rare in this area.) The church is about one-third of the way down the steep road that descends to Gethsemane from the Mount of Olives observation point. ⚠ **Beware of pickpockets on the street outside.** ✉ *Palm Sunday Rd., Mount of Olives ✟ Below Mount of Olives Observation Point* ☎ *02/626–6561* 🖃 *Free.*

Garden of Gethsemane

HISTORIC SITE | After the Last Supper, the New Testament relates, Jesus and his disciples walked to the Mount of Olives, to a place called Gethsemane, where he was betrayed and arrested. Gethsemane derives from the Aramaic or Hebrew word for "oil press," referring to the precious olive that has always flourished here. The enormous, gnarled, and still-productive olive trees on the site may be older than Christianity itself, according to some botanists. They make a fine picture, but a fence prevents pilgrims from taking home sprigs as a more tangible souvenir.

The **Church of All Nations,** with its brilliantly colorful, landmark mosaic facade, was completed in 1924 on the scanty remains of its Byzantine predecessor. The prolific architect, Antonio Barluzzi, filled the church's interior domes with mosaic symbols of the Catholic communities that contributed to its construction. The windows are glazed with translucent alabaster in somber browns and purples, creating a mystical feeling in the dim interior. At the altar is the so-called Rock of the Agony, where Jesus is said to have endured his Passion; this is the source of the older name of the church, the **Basilica of the Agony.**

A popular approach to Gethsemane is walking down the steep road from the top of the Mount of Olives—identified by pilgrims as the Palm Sunday Road—perhaps stopping in on the way at the Dominus Flevit church where, tradition has it, Jesus wept as he foretold the destruction of the city (Luke 19). The entrance to the well-tended garden at the foot of the hill is marked by a small platoon of vendors outside. ✉ *Jericho Rd., corner of El-Mansuriya Rd., Kidron Valley ✟ Foot of Mount of Olives and its Palm Sunday Rd.* ☎ *02/628–3264* ⊕ *www.gethsemane-en.custodia.org* 🖃 *Free.*

Garden Tomb

ARCHAEOLOGICAL SITE | A beautifully tended English-style country garden makes this an island of tranquility in bustling East Jerusalem. What Christian pilgrims come for, however, is an empty ancient tomb, and a moving opportunity to ponder the Gospel account of the death and resurrection of Jesus. It is a favorite site for the many Protestant visitors who respond less or not at all to the ornamentation and ritual of the Holy Sepulcher.

In 1883, British general Charles Gordon spent several months in Jerusalem. From his window looking out over the Old City walls, he was struck by the skull-like features of a cliff face north of the Damascus Gate. He was convinced that this, rather than the Church of the Holy Sepulcher, was "the place of the skull" (Mark 15) where Jesus was crucified. An ancient rock-cut tomb had already been uncovered there, and subsequent excavations exposed cisterns and a wine press, features typical of an ancient garden.

According to the New Testament, Jesus was buried in the fresh tomb of the wealthy Joseph of Arimathea, in a garden close to the execution site, and some archaeologists identified the tomb as an upper-class Jewish burial place of the Second Temple period. Recent research, however, indicates that this tomb is apparently from the Old Testament period, making it too old to have been that of

Jesus. In general, the gentle guardians of the Garden Tomb do not insist on the identification of the site as that of Calvary and the tomb of Christ, but are keen to provide a contemplative setting for the pilgrim, in a place that just might have been historically significant. ✉ *Conrad Schick St., off Nablus Rd., East Jerusalem* ☎ *02/539–8100* ⊕ *www.gardentomb.com* ✆ *Free* ☾ *Closed Sun.*

Kidron Valley

ARCHAEOLOGICAL SITE | This deep valley separates the Old City and the City of David from the high ridge of the Mount of Olives and the Arab neighborhood of Silwan. In the cliff face below the neighborhood are the symmetrical openings of tombs from both the First Temple (Old Testament) and Second Temple (Hellenistic-Roman) periods. You can view the impressive group of 2,200-year-old funerary monuments from the lookout terrace at the southeast corner of the Old City wall, down and to your left, or wander down into the valley itself and see them close up. The huge, square, stone structure with the conical roof is known as **Absalom's Pillar.** The one crowned by a pyramidal roof, a solid block of stone cut out of the mountain, is called **Zachariah's Tomb.** The association with those Old Testament personalities was a medieval mistake, and the structures more probably mark the tombs of wealthy Jerusalemites of the Second Temple period who wished to await the coming of the Messiah and the resurrection to follow in the style to which they were accustomed. ✉ *Jericho Rd., between Mount of Olives and the Old City, Kidron Valley* ✆ *Free.*

★ Mount of Olives Observation Point

LOCAL INTEREST | The Old City, with its landmark domes and towers, is squarely within your lens in this classic, picture-postcard panoramic view. It's best in the early morning, with the sun at your back, or at sunset on days with some clouds, when the golden glow and sunbeams more than compensate for the glare.

The magnificent, gold Dome of the Rock and the black-domed al-Aqsa Mosque to the left of it dominate the skyline; but look behind them for the large gray dome of the Holy Sepulcher and (farther left) the white one of the Jewish Quarter's Hurva Synagogue for a hint of the long-running visibility contest among faiths and nations. To the left of the Old City, the cone-roof Dormition Abbey and its adjacent clock tower crown Mount Zion, today outside the walls but within the city of the Second Temple period.

The Mount of Olives has been bathed in sanctity for millennia. On the slope beneath you, and off to your left, is the vast Jewish cemetery, reputedly the oldest still in use anywhere in the world. For more than 2,000 years, Jews have been buried here to await the coming of the Messiah and the resurrection to follow. The raised structures over the graves are merely tomb markers, not crypts; burial is belowground.

✉ *E-Sheikh St., in front of Seven Arches Hotel, Mount of Olives.*

Pater Noster Convent

RELIGIOUS SITE | The church built here in the 4th century AD by Constantine the Great became known as the Eleona (olive), and was associated back then with the ascension of Jesus to heaven. By the Middle Ages, tradition had firmly settled on a small grotto—the focal point of the site—as the place where Jesus taught his disciples the Lord's Prayer: "Our Father [Pater Noster]..." (Matthew 6). The land was purchased by the Princesse de la Tour d'Auvergne of France in 1868, and the Carmelite convent stands on the site of the earlier Byzantine and Crusader structures. An ambitious basilica, begun in the 1920s, was designed to follow the lines of the 4th-century church, but was never

The Church of All Nations stands at the base of the Mount of Olives, next to the Garden of Gethsemane.

completed: its aisles, open to the sky, are now lined with pine trees. The real attractions of the site, however, are the many large ceramic plaques adorning the cloister walls and the small church, with the Lord's Prayer in more than 100 different languages. (Look for the high wall, metal door, and French flag on a bend 200 yards before the Mount of Olives Observation Point.) ⊠ *E-Sheikh St. at Rub'a el-Adawiya, Mount of Olives* ☎ *02/628–3143* ⌘ *NIS 10* ⊙ *Closed Sun.*

Rockefeller Archaeological Museum
BUILDING | Built in the 1930s, and now a branch of the Israel Museum, the museum has echoing stone halls and somewhat old-fashioned displays that recall the period of the British Mandate. Among the most important exhibits are stucco and other decorations from the 8th-century AD Hisham's Palace (Umayyad dynasty) just north of Jericho, the doors of the original al-Aqsa Mosque (also 8th century), and gold Canaanite jewelry. Stone bas-reliefs by Eric Gill,

representing different ancient cultures, overlook the pool in the inner courtyard. The museum's octagonal white stone tower is an East Jerusalem landmark. Parking is only available on Saturday. ■ **TIP→ For winter visitors, note that the buildings have no heating.** ⊠ *27 Sultan Suleiman St., East Jerusalem* ✛ *Opposite Herod's Gate (northeastern corner of Old City)* ☎ *02/628–2251* ⊕ *www.imj.org.il/ en/wings/archaeology/rockefeller-archae- ological-museum* ⌘ *Free* ⊙ *Closed Tues., Fri., and Jewish holiday eves.*

Tomb of the Virgin
HISTORIC SITE | The Gothic facade of the underground Church of the Assumption, which contains this shrine, clearly dates it to the Crusader era (12th century). Tradition has it that this is where the Virgin Mary was interred and then "assumed" into heaven, hence the more common name, the Tomb of the Virgin. In an otherwise gloomy church—hung with age-darkened icons and brass lamps— the marble sarcophagus, apparently

Did You Know?

Many graves in the Jewish cemetery on the slope of the Mount of Olives have small stones placed on the marker by visitors (burial is below-ground). The ancient custom is a way of paying your respects to the deceased.

medieval, remains illuminated. The 1852 Status Quo Agreement in force in the Church of the Holy Sepulcher and Bethlehem's Church of the Nativity pertains here, too: the Greek Orthodox, Armenian Orthodox, and even the Muslims control different parts of the property. The Roman Catholic Franciscans were expelled in 1757, a loss of privilege that rankles to this day. ✉ *Jericho Rd., Kidron Valley* ✥ *A few steps away from Garden of Gethsemane* 🎟 *Free* ⏲ *Closed Sun.*

🍴 Restaurants

The heart of East Jerusalem runs through Salah A-Din Street, lined with hummus joints, colorful vegetable shops, fresh juice stands, and a few modest coffee spots. Palestinian students and foreign journalists and aid workers gravitate toward the more upscale eateries.

★ American Colony Hotel
$$ | CAFÉ | This upscale hotel is an elegant 19th-century limestone building with cane furniture, Armenian ceramic tiles, and a delightful courtyard. The food is very good, and a light lunch or afternoon tea in the cool lobby lounge, at the poolside restaurant, or on the patio under the trees makes for a well-earned break. **Known for:** charming location; local cuisine; welcoming staff. [$] *Average main: NIS 50* ✉ *1 Louis Vincent St., American Colony, at Nablus Rd., East Jerusalem* ☎ *02/627–9777* 🌐 *www.americancolony.com* 💳 *No credit cards.*

Askadinya
$$ | ECLECTIC | At this East Jerusalem bistro, the stone walls are hung with local art and antique musical instruments. In summer, you can enjoy your meal on a lovely patio. **Known for:** authentic tabbouleh; open on Friday night; hidden gem. [$] *Average main: NIS 75* ✉ *11 Shimon Hatzadik, East Jerusalem* ☎ *02/532–4590.*

★ Azzahra
$$ | MIDDLE EASTERN | FAMILY | On a quiet alley off the main East Jerusalem thoroughfare, this white-tablecloth restaurant in a hotel by the same name has long been popular with journalists, NGO workers, and local families, who flock here for pizzas from the olive-wood-burning brick oven and Palestinian favorites. High wooden ceilings, stone walls, and a simple outdoor garden create a lovely setting perfect for groups of any size. **Known for:** beautiful 100-year-old building; delicious maklubeh dish; outdoor seating. [$] *Average main: NIS 65* ✉ *13 Azzahra St., East Jerusalem* ☎ *02/628–2447.*

Educational Bookshop
$ | MIDDLE EASTERN | Part coffee shop, part bookstore, this spot has an endless trove of literature exploring the Arab-Israeli conflict from a Palestinian perspective. Take a volume upstairs and peruse it over a lunch of a savory *manaqeesh* bread topped with thyme and olive oil, freshly made labaneh cheese, or salmon sandwiches. **Known for:** engaging atmosphere; hospitality; special events and book launches. [$] *Average main: NIS 20* ✉ *19 Salah A-Din St., East Jerusalem* ☎ *02/627–5858* 🌐 *educationalbookshop.com.*

Philadelphia
$$$ | MIDDLE EASTERN | FAMILY | Steps from the Old City, this East Jerusalem landmark has been in business for decades—a thank-you note from President Jimmy Carter proves it. Traditional fare like stuffed carrots and onions, or *musakhan* chicken cooked in sumac and onions, show Palestinian home cooking at its finest. **Known for:** welcoming owner; regional wines; familial atmosphere. [$] *Average main: NIS 100* ✉ *9 AlZahra St., East Jerusalem* ☎ *02/532–2626* 🌐 *thephiladelphiarestaurant.com.*

★ Sarwa Street Kitchen
$ | ECLECTIC | Brothers Mo and Mick Tahhan opened this cheery café in the space

that was once their father's travel agency with the vision of creating a gathering spot as comfy and as fun as your living room at home. Staff often joins patrons for a chat on the bright blue couches and encourages them to add or take from the in-house library stocked with a selection of English-language books. **Known for:** Palestinian beer; maqloubeh, a Palestinian rice and chicken dish; laidback atmosphere. [$] *Average main: NIS 40* ✉ *42 Salah A-Din St., East Jerusalem* ☎ *02/627–4626* 🕓 *Closed Fri.*

Hotels

The cluster of hotels here, some Israeli run, some Palestinian, are within yards of each other. They are on the old "seam" (as it's sometimes called) that once divided Jerusalem into East and West. At some levels, the old divisions remain, but the seam area itself has become a comfortable middle ground.

Ambassador Hotel
$ | **HOTEL** | One of East Jerusalem's longtime favorites, the Ambassador has been tastefully renovated with loads of Jerusalem stone. **Pros:** outdoor dining; lovely views; comfortable rooms. **Cons:** 15-minute walk from attractions; area dead at night; understaffed. [$] *Rooms from: $180* ✉ *5 Nablus Rd., East Jerusalem* ☎ *02/560–9302* 🌐 *ambassadorhotel.com-israel.com/en* 🛏 *118 rooms* 🍴 *Free Breakfast.*

★ American Colony Hotel
$$$ | **HOTEL** | Once a pasha's palace, this cool limestone oasis with its flower-filled inner courtyard and gorgeous garden is in a class of its own—no wonder it's a favored haunt of statesmen and celebrities. **Pros:** atmospheric cellar bar in winter, lovely garden bar in summer; good English bookstore and gift shop; beautiful pool. **Cons:** quiet neighborhood at night; a cab or light-rail ride from most attractions; hotel staff could be friendlier. [$] *Rooms from: $310* ✉ *1 Louis Vincent St., East Jerusalem* ☎ *02/627–9777* 🌐 *www.americancolony.com* 🛏 *92 rooms* 🍴 *Free Breakfast.*

Dan Jerusalem Hotel
$$ | **HOTEL** | Cascading down Mount Scopus, the sprawling Dan Jerusalem has spectacular views, an oasis-like pool, and a bold design. **Pros:** impressive architecture; spacious lounge/lobby; impressive spa and Turkish bath. **Cons:** remote location; a bit overpriced; outdated decor. [$] *Rooms from: $200* ✉ *32 Lehi St., East Jerusalem* ☎ *02/533–1234* 🌐 *www.danhotels.com* 🛏 *505 rooms* 🍴 *Free Breakfast.*

Grand Court Hotel
$ | **HOTEL** | **FAMILY** | This huge hotel is a celebration of light and space: from the large, airy lobby, with its limestone walls and marble arches, to the well-lit, comfortable guest rooms, with their soft decor and bright bathrooms. **Pros:** 10-minute walk from Damascus Gate; close to light-rail; gym and pool on-site. **Cons:** neighborhood dead at night; overcrowded dining area; spotty Wi-Fi. [$] *Rooms from: $171* ✉ *15 Saint George St., East Jerusalem* ☎ *02/591–7777* 🌐 *www.grandhotels-israel.com* 🛏 *442 rooms* 🍴 *Free Breakfast.*

Leonardo Hotel Jerusalem
$ | **HOTEL** | **FAMILY** | A huge circular skylight in the middle of the lobby gives this hotel a sense of light and space. **Pros:** comfortable rooms; close to lesser known attractions like Museum on the Seam and The Palestinian Heritage Museum; 10-minute walk from Damascus Gate. **Cons:** neighborhood dead at night; no distinctive character; inconsistent service staff. [$] *Rooms from: $160* ✉ *9 Saint George St., East Jerusalem* ☎ *02/532–0000* 🌐 *www.leonardo-hotels.com* 🛏 *397 rooms* 🍴 *Free Breakfast.*

National Hotel

$ | **HOTEL** | Five minutes from the Old City, this historic hotel puts you in close proximity to Jerusalem's great sights. **Pros:** free parking; reasonable rates; great service. **Cons:** a bit out of the way; no pool; outdated decor/furniture. [$] *Rooms from: $120* ✉ *4 Al Zahra St., East Jerusalem* ☎ *02/627–8880* 🛏 *100 rooms* 🍴 *Free Breakfast.*

Olive Tree Hotel

$$ | **HOTEL** | The stone arches, lacey latticework, and bronze ornaments in the reception area help create a distinctly regional atmosphere, as do the old flagstones in the skylit atrium and polished floorboards in the comfortable lounge. **Pros:** 10-minute walk from Damascus Gate; superior sports facilities; elegant atmosphere. **Cons:** smallish rooms; neighborhood is dead at night; busy. [$] *Rooms from: $250* ✉ *23 Saint George St., East Jerusalem* ☎ *02/541–0410* 🌐 *www.olivetreehotel.co.il* 🛏 *304 rooms* 🍴 *Free Breakfast.*

🍸 Nightlife

Borderline

BARS/PUBS | Borderline has a delightful summer garden and a huge screen for watching soccer games. In winter, seats are plentiful inside the century-old building. This Palestinian place is a great spot to try anise-flavored arak from Ramallah. Borderline is connected to Pasha's, a reliable source for great Middle Eastern cooking. ✉ *13 Shimon Hatzadik, East Jerusalem* ☎ *02/532–8342.*

★ Cellar Bar

BARS/PUBS | Set within the American Colony Hotel, this in-the-know place has the feel of an intimate wine cellar, with small tables, quiet corners, and a mix of languages that makes you feel far away from all the political problems of the day. It's open only during the winter months, but from June to October you can enjoy the same well-made cocktails at the outdoor Summer Bar. ✉ *American Colony Hotel, 1 Louis Vincent St., at Nablus Rd., East Jerusalem* ☎ *02/627–9777* 🌐 *www.americancolony.com.*

West Jerusalem

Visitors tend to focus, naturally enough, on the historical and religious sights in the Old City, on the eastern side of town; but West Jerusalem houses the nation's institutions, is the repository for its collective memory, and—together with Downtown—gives more insight into contemporary life in Israel's largest city. The world-class Israel Museum and the Yad Vashem Holocaust museum are located here, as well as poignant Mount Herzl and the picturesque neighborhood of Ein Kerem. These attractions, which are spread out over a number of West Jerusalem neighborhoods, are most easily accessed by car or by a combination of buses, light-rail, and short cab rides.

GETTING HERE AND AROUND

There are good city bus services and the single-line light-rail in this part of town (ask at each site how to get to the next), but a few cab rides will be a much better use of limited time.

TIMING AND PRECAUTIONS

Pay attention to the closing times of sites: several aren't open on Saturday and close early on Friday. Some museums have evening hours on particular days—a time-efficient option. Avoid burnout by staggering visits to the museums and combining them on any given day with other kinds of experiences.

👁 Sights

Bible Lands Museum

MEMORIAL | **FAMILY** | Most archaeological museums group artifacts according to their place of origin, but the curators here

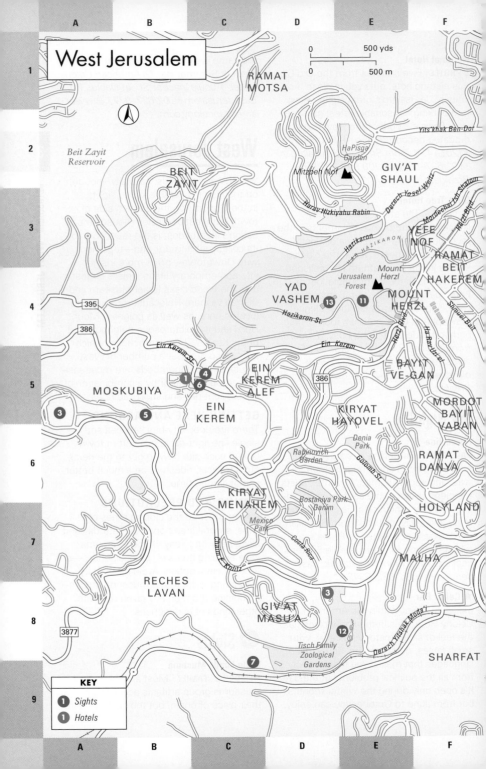

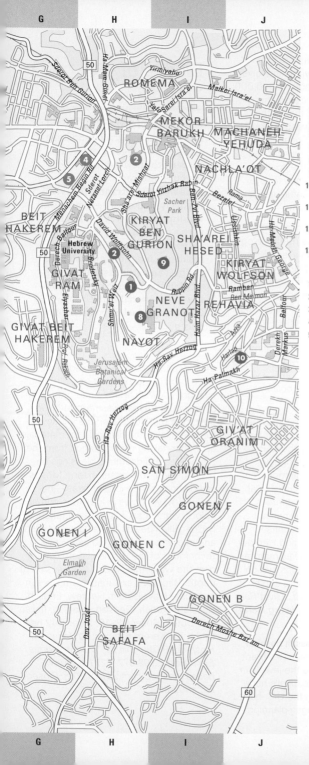

Sights ▼

1 Bible Lands Museum.............. **H4**
2 Bloomfield Science Museum **H3**
3 Chagall Windows and
  Hadassah Hospital **A5**
4 Church of St. John the Baptist **C5**
5 Church of the Visitation **B5**
6 Ein Kerem...........................**C5**
7 Israel Aquarium.....................**C9**
8 Israel Museum.....................**H4**
9 Knesset **I3**
10 L.A. Mayer Museum
  for Islamic Art......................**J5**
11 Mount Herzl National
  Memorial Park **E4**
12 The Tisch Family
  Zoological Gardens.................**E8**
13 Yad Vashem **D4**

Hotels ▼

1 Alegra Boutique Hotel **B5**
2 Crowne Plaza Jerusalem......... **H2**
3 Hotel Yehuda **D8**
4 Prima Park Hotel................... **H2**
5 Ramada Jerusalem............... **G2**

3

Jerusalem WEST JERUSALEM

favor a chronological display, seeking cross-cultural influences within any given era. The exhibits cover a more than 6,000 years—from the prehistoric Neolithic period (Late Stone Age) to that of the Byzantine Empire—and sweep geographically from Afghanistan to Sudan. Rare clay vessels, fertility idols, cylinder seals, ivories, and sarcophagi fill the soaring, naturally lighted galleries. Look for the ancient Egyptian wooden coffin, in a stunning state of preservation.

The concept of the museum is intriguing, but some have criticized its methodology. A concept was imposed on a largely pre-existing collection, rather than a collection being created item by selected item to illustrate a concept. Plan on an hour to see the permanent exhibition—a guided tour will enhance the experience—and check out the temporary exhibitions downstairs. ⊠ Museum Row, 21 Shmuel Stefan Wise St., Givat Ram ✛ Adjacent to Israel Museum ☎ 02/561–1066 ⊕ www. blmj.org ≅ NIS 44 ⊗ Closed holidays.

Bloomfield Science Museum

MUSEUM | FAMILY | For kids, this may be the city's best rainy-day option, but don't wait for a rainy day to enjoy the museum. Along with a range of intriguing, please-touch interactive equipment that demonstrates scientific principles in an engagingly fun environment, there is a lot of innovation and creativity—not least of all in the changing exhibits. Explanations are in English, and Hebrew University science students, as many as 20 at a time on busy weekends, are on hand to explain exhibit displays and host workshops. ⊠ Museum Blvd., Givat Ram ☎ 02/654–4888 ⊕ www.mada.org.il/en ≅ NIS 45 ⊗ Closed Sun.

Chagall Windows and Hadassah Hospital

HOSPITAL—SIGHT | Marc Chagall's vibrant stained-glass windows are the jewels in the crown of Hadassah Hospital's huge Ein Kerem campus. When the U.S.-based Hadassah organization began planning

Bridge of Strings 👁

The "Bridge of Strings" (or "Chords Bridge") was designed by Spanish architect Santiago Calatrava to suspend the new light-rail over the busy intersection at Jerusalem's western entrance (Tel Aviv Highway, Route 1). The commission was intended to provide the city with a contemporary icon. "What do we need it for?" complained some residents. Judge for yourself from the best angle: not as you enter the city but from the sidewalk outside the International Convention Center (*Binyanei Ha'ooma, Zalman Shazar Blvd.*).

this hospital on the western edge of town back in the 1950s, it asked the Russian-born Jewish artist to adorn the small synagogue. Chagall was reportedly so delighted that he created the windows for free: Hadassah only paid for materials and labor. Taking his inspiration from the Bible—Jacob's deathbed blessings on his sons and, to a lesser extent, Moses's valediction to the tribes of Israel—he created 12 windows in luminous primary colors, with an ark-full of characteristically Chagallian beasts and a bag of Jewish and esoteric symbols. The innovative techniques of the Reims glassmakers give the wafer-thin windows an illusion of depth. Recorded explanations in the synagogue are available in Hebrew, English, Russian, French, German, Spanish, Italian and Dutch. Buses 12, 19, 27, and 42 head to the Ein Kerem campus. ⊠ Hadassah Hospital, 8 Churchill St., Mount Scopus, Ein Kerem ☎ 02/677–6271 ⊕ www. hadassah-med.com ≅ NIS 20 ⊗ Closed Fri. and Sat.

Church of St. John the Baptist

RELIGIOUS SITE | The village of Ein Kerem is not mentioned by name in the New Testament, but its identification as the birthplace of John the Baptist is a tradition that apparently goes back to the Byzantine period (5th century AD). The grotto associated with that event is enshrined in the large, late-17th-century Franciscan church that bears his name, its orange tile roof a prominent landmark in the heart of Ein Kerem. The walls of the sanctuary are covered in age-darkened paintings and glazed tiles. ⊠ *Homat Ha Tsalafim St., Ein Kerem* ☎ *02/632–3000* 🖭 *Free.*

Church of the Visitation

RELIGIOUS SITE | Built over what is thought to have been the home of John the Baptist's parents, Zechariah and Elizabeth, this church sits high up the hillside in Ein Kerem, with a wonderful view of the valley and the surrounding wooded hills. It is a short but stiff walk up from the spring at the center of the village. When Mary, pregnant with Jesus, came to visit her cousin, the aging Elizabeth, who was also with child, "the babe leaped in [Elizabeth's] womb" with joy at recognizing the unborn Jesus. Mary thereupon pronounced the paean to God known as the Magnificat ("My soul doth magnify the Lord" [Luke 1]). One wall of the church courtyard is covered with ceramic tiles quoting the Magnificat in 41 languages. The upper church is adorned with large wall paintings depicting the mantles with which Mary has been endowed—Mother of God, Refuge of Sinners, Dispenser of All Grace, Help of Christians—as well as the Immaculate Conception. Other frescoes depict Hebrew women of the Bible also known for their "hymns and canticles," as the Franciscan guide puts it. Ring the bell for entry on Saturday. ⊠ *Madreigot Habikur, Ein Kerem* ✥ *At end of Hama'ayan St., beyond spring* ☎ *02/641–7291* 🖭 *Free.*

★ Ein Kerem

HISTORIC SITE | The neighborhood of Ein Kerem still retains much of its old village character. Tree-framed stone houses spill across its hillsides with a pleasing Mediterranean nonchalance. Artists and professionals who have joined the older working-class population over the last 40 or 50 years have marvelously renovated many homes and made an effort to keep developers at bay. Back alleys provide an off-the-beaten-path feel, and occasionally a serendipitous art or craft studio.

Tradition identifies Ein Kerem as the birthplace of John the Baptist, and its most prominent landmarks are the orange-roofed Church of St. John the Baptist in the heart of the village, the Church of the Visitation up the hillside above the Spring of the Virgin—both Roman Catholic—and the gold-domed Russian church above that along the road to Hadassah Hospital. The neighborhood is served by city Bus 28 from Mount Herzl. There is free underground parking in the neighborhood center. Ein Kerem is less than five minutes from Mount Herzl by bus or taxi, and about 15 minutes by taxi from Downtown. ⊠ *Ein Kerem.*

↗ Israel Aquarium

Officially the Gottesman Family Israel Aquarium Jerusalem, this new spot is the first public aquarium in Israel. You can combine a visit with the Tisch Family Zoological Gardens next door and see all kinds of aquatic life from the Mediterranean Sea to the Red Sea's coral reefs and beyond. The museum is dedicated to the conservation of Israel's marine habitats, and its modern exhibits have high-tech digital displays. A devoted and knowledgeable staff guides visitors through the experience. Public transportation reaches as far as the Zoo's main entrance. ⊠ *3 Derekh Aharon Shulov* ☎ *073/339–9000* ⊕ *www.israel-aquarium.org.il/english* 🖭 *NIS 54, must be purchased online in advance.*

★ Israel Museum

MUSEUM VILLAGE | FAMILY | This world-class museum shines after a massive makeover that brought with it modern exhibits and state-of-the-art technology. The **Dead Sea Scrolls** are certainly the museum's most famous—and most important—collection. A Bedouin boy discovered the first of the 2,000-year-old parchments in 1947 in a Judean Desert cave, overlooking the Dead Sea. Of the nine main scrolls and bags full of small fragments that surfaced over the years, many of the most important and most complete are preserved here; the Antiquities Authority holds the rest of the parchments, and a unique copper scroll is in Jordan. The white dome of the Shrine of the Book, the separate pavilion in which the scrolls are housed, was inspired by the lids of the clay jars in which the first ones were found.

The scrolls were written in the Second Temple period by a fiercely zealous, separatist, and monastic Jewish sect, widely identified as the Essenes, a group described by contemporary historians. Archaeological, laboratory, and textual evidence dates the earliest of the scrolls to the 2nd century BC; none could have been written later than AD 68, the year in which their home community, known today as Qumran, was destroyed by the Romans. The parchments, still in an extraordinary state of preservation because of the dryness of the Dead Sea region, contain the oldest Hebrew manuscripts of the Old Testament ever found, authenticating the almost identical Hebrew texts still in use today. The sectarian literature provides an insight into this esoteric community. The early-medieval Aleppo Codex, on display in the small lower gallery under the white dome, is considered the most authoritative text of the Hebrew Bible in existence.

The quarter-acre outdoor **1:50 scale model,** adjacent to the Shrine of the Book, represents Jerusalem as it was on the eve of the Great Revolt against Rome (AD 66). Designed in the mid-1960s by the late Professor Michael Avi-Yonah, it stood on the grounds of the Holyland Hotel in West Jerusalem until 2006, when new (and controversial) urban development brought it here. Avi-Yonah relied on considerable data gleaned from Roman-period historians, important Jewish texts, and even the New Testament, and based some of his generic reconstructions (villas, a theater, markets, etc.) on Roman structures that have survived across the ancient empire. Later archaeological excavations have sometimes confirmed and sometimes challenged Avi-Yonah's sharp intuition, and the model has been updated occasionally to incorporate new knowledge. The available audio guide is a worthwhile aid in deciphering the site.

Taken together, the Dead Sea Scrolls, the huge model, and Roman-period exhibits in the Archaeology Wing evoke the turbulent and historically momentous Second Temple period. That was the era from which Christianity emerged; when the Romans razed the Temple in Jerusalem, it compelled a slow revolution in Jewish life and religious practice that has defined Judaism to this day.

The **Archaeology Wing** has been reorganized to highlight particular treasures in galleries that follow a historical sequence. If you know a bit of Bible, many artifacts in the Canaanite, Israelite, and Hellenistic-Roman sections offer evocative illustrations of familiar texts. Don't miss the small side rooms devoted to glass, coins, and the Hebrew script.

Jewish Art and Life is the name for the wing made up mostly of finely wrought Jewish ceremonial objects (Judaica) from widely disparate communities. The "synagogue route" includes reconstructed old synagogues from India, Germany, Italy, and Suriname.

The Shrine of the Book at the Israel Museum dramatically displays fragile sections of the Dead Sea Scrolls.

The **Art Wing** is a slightly confusing maze spread over different levels, but if you have patience and time, the payoff is great. Older European art rubs shoulders with modern works, contemporary Israeli art, design, and photography. The flyer available at the museum entrance lists new and temporary exhibitions. Landscape architect Isamu Noguchi designed the open-air **Art Garden.** Crunch over the gravel amid works by Daumier, Rodin, Moore, Picasso, and less-legendary local luminaries.

The **Youth Wing** mounts one major new exhibition a year, interactive and often adult-friendly, designed to encourage children to appreciate the arts and the world around them, or to be creative in a crafts workshop. Parents with younger kids will also be grateful for the outdoor play areas.

The vegetarian/dairy café, Mansfeld, is a great place for a light meal or coffee. The more expensive Modern has tempting meat and fish combinations and remains open beyond museum hours. The lockers and ATM in the museum's entrance hall are useful. Large bags or packs have to be checked. Photography (without flash) is allowed everywhere except in the Shrine of the Book. Check the website for summer days with longer hours and free entrance for kids. ✉ *11 Ruppin Rd., Givat Ram* ✛ *Near Knesset* ☎ *02/670–8811* ⊕ *www.imj.org.il/en* 🎟 *NIS 54.*

Knesset

GOVERNMENT BUILDING | Both the name of Israel's one-chamber parliament and its number of seats (120) were taken from *Haknesset Hagedolah,* the Great Assembly of the Second Temple period, some 2,000 years ago. The free hour-long public tour, offered Sunday and Thursday, includes the session hall and three enormous, brilliantly colored tapestries designed by Marc Chagall on the subjects of the Creation, the Exodus, and Jerusalem. Arrive at least 30 minutes before the tour (especially in summer, when the lines are longer), and be sure to bring your passport. Bags and cameras have to be deposited with security. On other days, when in session, Knesset proceedings (conducted in Hebrew) are open to the public—call ahead to verify. There are a wide range of other in-depth tours available to the public Sunday through Thursday.

Across the road from the Knesset main gate is a 14-foot-high, 4-ton bronze menorah, based on the one that once stood within the sanctuary of the ancient temple in Jerusalem. The seven-branch candelabrum was adopted soon after independence as the official symbol of the modern State of Israel. This one, designed by sculptor Benno Elkan, and given as a gift by British parliamentarians to the Knesset in 1956, is decorated with bas-relief depictions of events and personages in Jewish history, from biblical times to the modern day. Behind the menorah is the Wohl Rose Garden, which has hundreds of varieties of roses, many lawns for children to romp on, and adult-friendly nooks in its upper section (entry from outside the Knesset complex). ✉ *Kiryat Ben-Gurion, Givat Ram* ✢ *Near Israel Museum* ☎ *02/675–3337* ⊕ *www.knesset.gov.il* 💲 *Free.*

L.A. Mayer Museum for Islamic Art

MUSEUM | The considerable and diverse artistic achievements of Islamic culture are what this small museum is all about. Its rich collections—ceramics, glass, carpets, fabrics, jewelry, metalwork, and painting—reflect a creativity that spanned half a hemisphere, from Spain to India, and from the 7th century to the 19th. Unconnected to the main theme is a unique and stunning collection of rare (some priceless) antique European clocks and watches, the pride of the founder's family: this alone is worth the visit. ✉ *2 Hapalmach St., Katamon* Tel ☎ *02/566– 1291* ⊕ *www.islamicart.co.il* 💲 *NIS 44* ☾ *Closed Sun.*

Mount Herzl National Memorial Park

CEMETERY | Cedars of Lebanon and native pine and cypress trees surround the entrance to Mount Herzl National Memorial Park, the last resting place of Zionist visionary Theodor Herzl and many Israeli leaders.

In 1894, the Budapest-born Herzl was the Paris correspondent for a Vienna newspaper, covering the controversial treason trial of Alfred Dreyfus, a Jewish officer in the French army. Dreyfus was later exonerated, but Herzl was shocked by the anti-Semitic outbursts that accompanied the trial. He devoted himself to the need for a Jewish state, convening the first World Zionist Congress, in Basel, Switzerland, in 1897. Herzl wrote in his diary that year: "If not in five years, then in 50 [a Jewish state] will become reality." True to his prediction, the United Nations approved the idea exactly 50 years later, in November 1947. Herzl died in 1904, and his remains were brought to Israel in 1949. His simple tombstone, inscribed in Hebrew with just his last name, caps the hill.

To the left (west) of his tomb, a gravel path leads down to a section containing the graves of Israeli national leaders— among them prime ministers Golda Meir and Yitzhak Rabin, and presidents Zalman Shazar, Chaim Herzog, and Shimon Peres—and the country's main military cemetery. Note that officers and privates are buried alongside one another—they are mourned equally, regardless of rank.

The Herzl Center (on the left as you enter the park) presents an engaging, multimedia introduction to the life, times, and legacy of Israel's spiritual forebear, Theodor Herzl. The program takes 50 minutes and costs NIS 25. Call ahead for English time slots. ✉ *Herzl Blvd., Mount Herzl* ☎ *02/632–1515* ⊕ *www.wzo.org.il/ mount-herzl-site* 💲 *Free* ☾ *Closed Sat.*

In Yad Vashem's Holocaust History Museum, the Hall of Names includes 600 photos of Jews who perished.

↗ Tisch Family Zoological Gardens

Spread over a scenic 62-acre ridge among Jerusalem's hilly southern neighborhoods, this zoo has many of the usual species that delight zoo visitors everywhere: monkeys and elephants, snakes and birds, and all the rest. But it goes much further, focusing on two groups of wildlife. The first is creatures mentioned in the Bible that have become locally extinct, some as late as the 20th century. Among these are Asian lions, bears, cheetahs, the Nile crocodile, and the Persian fallow deer. The second focus is on endangered species worldwide, among them the Asian elephant and rare macaws.

This is a wonderful place to let kids expend some energy—there are lawns and playground equipment—and allow adults some downtime from touring. Early morning and late afternoon are the best hours in summer; budget 2½ hours to see (almost) everything. A wagon train does the rounds of the zoo, at a nominal fee of NIS 2 (not on Saturday and Jewish holidays). The Noah's Ark Visitors Center has a movie and computer programs. The zoo is served by city routes 26A (from Central Bus Station) and 33 (from Mount Herzl). The ride is about 30 minutes; a cab would take 15 minutes from Downtown hotels. ✉ *1 Derech Aharon Shulov, near Jerusalem Malcha Mall, Malcha* ☎ *02/675–0111* ⊕ *www.jerusalemzoo.org. il* 🎫 *NIS 59.*

★ Yad Vashem

MEMORIAL | The experience of the Holocaust—the annihilation of 6 million Jews by the Nazis during World War II—is so deeply seared into the Jewish national psyche that understanding it goes a long way toward understanding Israelis themselves. Yad Vashem was created in 1953 by an act of the Knesset, and charged with preserving a record of those times. The multifaceted campus includes a museum, an archive and research facility, an energetic education department, art galleries, and numerous monuments.

(The name Yad Vashem—"a memorial and a name"—comes from the biblical book of Isaiah [56:5].) The Israeli government has made a tradition of bringing almost all high-ranking official foreign guests to visit the place.

The riveting **Holocaust History Museum**—a well-lit, 200-yard-long triangular concrete "prism"—is the centerpiece of the site. Powerful visual and audiovisual techniques in a series of galleries document Jewish life in Europe before the catastrophe and follow the escalation of persecution and internment to the hideous climax of the Nazi's "Final Solution." Video interviews and personal artifacts individualize the experience. ■**TIP→ Note that children under 10 are not admitted, photography is not allowed in the exhibition areas, and large bags have to be checked.**

The small **Children's Memorial** is dedicated to the 1½ million Jewish children murdered by the Nazis. Architect Moshe Safdie wanted to convey the enormity of the crime without numbing the visitor's emotions or losing sight of the victims' individuality. The result is a single dark room, lit by just a few candles infinitely reflected in hundreds of mirrors. Recorded narrators intone the names, ages, and countries of origin of known victims. The effect is electrifying. Also focusing on children is a poignant exhibition called "No Child's Play," about children's activities during the Holocaust. It's in an art museum beyond the exit of the Holocaust History Museum.

The **Avenue of the Righteous** encircles Yad Vashem with thousands of trees marked with the names of Gentiles in Europe who risked and sometimes lost their lives trying to save Jews from the Nazis. Raoul Wallenberg, King Christian X of Denmark, Corrie ten Boom, Oskar Schindler, and American journalist Varian Fry are among the more famous honorees. The **Hall of Remembrance** is a heavy basalt-and-concrete building that houses an eternal flame, with the names of the death camps and main concentration camps in relief on the floor.

A detour takes you to the **Valley of the Communities** at the bottom of the hill, where large, rough-hewn limestone boulders divide the site into a series of small, man-made canyons. Each clearing represents a region of Nazi Europe, laid out geographically. The names of some 5,000 destroyed Jewish communities are inscribed in the stone walls, with larger letters highlighting those that were particularly important in prewar Europe.

There is an information booth (be sure to buy the inexpensive map of the site), a bookstore, and a cafeteria at the entrance to Yad Vashem.

Allow about two hours to see the Holocaust History Museum, more if you rent an audio guide. If your time is short, be sure to see the Children's Memorial and the Avenue of the Righteous. To avoid the biggest crowds, come first thing in the morning or around noon. The site is an easy 10-minute walk or a quick free shuttle from the Mount Herzl intersection, which in turn is served by many city bus lines and the light-rail. ⊠ *Hazikaron St., Mount Herzl* ✛ *Near Herzl Blvd.* ☎ *02/644–3400* ⊕ *www.yadvashem.org* 🎟 *Free* 🕒 *Closed Sat.*

🛏 Hotels

This cluster of hotels in Givat Ram and Romema is near the point where the Tel Aviv Highway (Route 1) enters Jerusalem. Some properties are near the Central Bus Station, others closer to the Israel Museum and the Knesset. Many hotels lie along the light-rail line that connects the western and eastern parts of the city. Ein Kerem, a leafy enclave, is included here, too, along with Mount Herzl and Givat Massuah, close to the Malcha Mall. Downtown is some distance away, the Old City even farther—a long walk, but 10 to 15 minutes by cab or bus, and bus lines are plentiful. If you're after hotel deals or if other places in town are booked, this area makes a great option.

★ Alegra Boutique Hotel

$$$ | **B&B/INN** | In the picturesque village of Ein Kerem, this boutique hotel occupies a century-old house famous for the true-life-Romeo-and-Juliet story of a Jewish-Arab couple. **Pros:** modern design; gorgeous rooms; delicious culinary options. **Cons:** far from attractions; not for families; brusque staff. $ *Rooms from: $333* ⊠ *13 Derech HaAchayot, Ein Kerem* ☎ *02/650–0506* ⊕ *www.hotelalegra.com* ⮑ *13 suites* ⦿ *Free Breakfast.*

Crowne Plaza Jerusalem

$ | **HOTEL** | Although this gleaming white tower with sweeping city views is a classic business hotel, it's also a comfortable option when you're on vacation. **Pros:** away from city noise; nice spa, tennis, and pool facilities; close to light-rail. **Cons:** business-oriented; limited parking; inconsistent service. $ *Rooms from: $108* ⊠ *1 HaAliyah St., Givat Ram* ☎ *02/658–8888* ⊕ *www.ihg.com/crowneplaza* ⮑ *397 rooms* ⦿ *Free Breakfast.*

Hotel Yehuda

$ | **HOTEL** | **FAMILY** | This popular hotel makes a practical—if a bit remote—base for families, since rooms are reasonably priced and there's plenty of space for kids to run around. **Pros:** large swimming pool; great views of Jerusalem; lovely spa. **Cons:** remote location; dining hall feels institutional; two-night minimum stays over weekends. $ *Rooms from: $117* ⊠ *11 Haim Kulitz St., Malcha* ☎ *02/632–2777* ⊕ *www.byh.co.il* ⮑ *129 rooms* ⦿ *Free Breakfast.*

Prima Park Hotel

$ | **HOTEL** | This West Jerusalem hotel right on the light-rail line has a good reputation thanks to its pretty stone courtyard, reasonable prices, and tastefully decorated rooms. **Pros:** friendly staff; intimate atmosphere; close to light-rail. **Cons:** far from Downtown; area dead at night; limited parking. $ *Rooms from: $108* ⊠ *2 Vilnai St., Givat Ram* ☎ *02/658–2222* ⊕ *www.prima-hotels-israel.com* ⮑ *217 rooms* ⦿ *Free Breakfast.*

Ramada Jerusalem

$ | **HOTEL** | **FAMILY** | This massive hotel's marble lobby, with its reflective ceiling, clubby leather chairs, and frilly potted palms, has a feeling of grandeur. **Pros:** close to the light-rail; well-equipped gym; wonderful for families. **Cons:** dated furnishings; expensive rates; staff are not always informative. $ *Rooms from: $175* ⊠ *Ruppin Bridge at Herzl Blvd., Givat Ram* ☎ *02/659–9999* ⊕ *jerusalemramadahotel.com/en* ⮑ *360 rooms* ⦿ *Free Breakfast.*

▼ Nightlife

★ Yellow Submarine

MUSIC CLUBS | A not-for-profit music center, Yellow Submarine offers free jazz concerts once a week, as well as popular sing-along evenings and performances by major Israeli and international rock and pop artists A decent bar also serves salads and other light fare. ⊠ *13 HaRechavim St., East Talpiot* ☎ *02/679–4040* ⊕ *www.yellowsubmarine.org.il.*

● Performing Arts

Classical music abounds in Jerusalem, with Israeli orchestras and chamber ensembles performing year-round and a trickle of international artists passing through.

★ Israel Philharmonic Orchestra

CULTURAL FESTIVALS | **FAMILY** | This world-renowned orchestra, which is based in Tel Aviv, performs locally at the International Convention Center, opposite the Central Bus Station. The venue also hosts traveling art exhibits and musicians from around the world. ⊠ *1 Zalman Shazar Blvd., Givat Ram* ☎ *02/655–8558* ⊕ *www.ipo.co.il/en.*

🛍 Shopping

Klein

CRAFTS | Israeli prime ministers have been shopping for gifts here since 1951. This is the factory showroom, and it stocks everything from high-quality olive-wood cutting boards to attractive trays decorated with Armenian pottery tiles. ⊠ *3 Ziv St., at Bar Ilan St., Tel Arza* ☎ *02/538–9992* ⊕ *www.aklein.co.il.*

Malcha Mall

SHOPPING CENTERS/MALLS | **FAMILY** | Known locally as Kenyon Malcha, this sprawling mix of shops covers 500,000 square feet and is one of the largest malls in the Middle East. It includes a department store, a supermarket, and almost 200 shops and eateries, all near the train station to Tel Aviv. Expect brands like Mango, Zara, and H&M. On Friday morning there is a range of home-cooked food, breads, cakes and more on offer before Shabbat. ⊠ *1 Agudat Sport Maccabi St., Malcha* ☎ *02/679–1333* ⊕ *www.azrielimalls.co.il.*

Ruth Havilio

CRAFTS | Artist Ruth Havilio makes hand-painted tiles that can make your table shine, give your floors a shot of Middle Eastern color, or brighten up a child's room. You can have your tiles personalized, but keep in mind that this can't be done on the spot. To get there, take the alley to the left of St. John's Church. Part of the charm of the gallery is its evocative courtyard setting. ⊠ *18 Ein Kerem St., Ein Kerem* ☎ *02/641–7912.*

Center City

West Jerusalem's Downtown and near-Downtown areas, just west of the Old City, are a mix of old neighborhoods, new limestone edifices, monuments, and markets. There are plenty of hotels and restaurants here, too. Few of the attractions appear on a Jerusalem don't-miss checklist, but you'll rub shoulders with the locals in the vibrant Machaneh Yehuda produce market, breathe the atmosphere of day-to-day life on Ben-Yehuda and Jaffa Streets, get a feel for the city's more recent history in Nahalat Shiva and Yemin Moshe—in short, for a few brief hours you can be a bit less of a tourist.

GETTING HERE AND AROUND

There's paid parking in the Center City, but you're better off walking, grabbing a cab, or riding the light-rail. The area is served by many bus lines from the Central Bus Station; 34 and 77 from the German Colony and Talbieh; and 7 and 9 from the Knesset and the Israel Museum.

TIMING AND PRECAUTIONS

Jaffa Street, Ben-Yehuda Street, and Machaneh Yehuda are ghostly quiet from Friday afternoon until after dark Saturday because of the Jewish Sabbath. Friday morning through early afternoon is the most bustling, as Jerusalemites meet friends for coffee or lunch, and do their weekend shopping.

👁 Sights

Ben-Yehuda Street

NEIGHBORHOOD | **FAMILY** | Most of the street is an open-air pedestrian mall, in the heart of Downtown, forming a triangle with King George Street and Jaffa Street. It is known locally as the **Midrachov,** a term concocted from two Hebrew words: *midracha* (sidewalk) and *rechov* (street). The street is named after the brilliant linguist Eliezer Ben-Yehuda, who in the late 19th century almost single-handedly revived Hebrew as a modern spoken language; he would have liked the clever new word. Cafés have tables out on the cobblestones, and buskers are usually around in good weather, playing tunes old and new. It's a great place to sip coffee or munch falafel and watch the passing crowd. On Saturday and Jewish holidays, only a few restaurants and convenience stores are open, but after nightfall (especially in warm weather) the area comes back to life. ⊠ *Ben-Yehuda St., Center City* ⊕ *Between King George St. and Zion Sq.*

Independence Park

CITY PARK | This is a great area for lounging around, throwing Frisbees, or eating a picnic lunch in warm weather. Some of the Muslim graves at the bottom of the park date from the 13th century. The large defunct reservoir nearby, known as the Mamilla Pool, is probably late medieval, though it may have much earlier Roman origins. ⊠ *Between Agron and Hillel Sts., Center City* ⊠ *Free.*

Jerusalem YMCA

BUILDING | FAMILY | The YMCA exudes old-world charm: its high-domed landmark bell tower thrusts out of a palatial white-limestone facade, full of carved arcane symbols and ancient scripts. The complex boasts the usual YMCA fitness facilities, a hotel, a concert hall, a restaurant, and a bilingual preschool. For NIS 20 you can ride the small elevator (they insist on two people minimum) to tiny balconies, with breathtaking views of the city in all directions. A bit of trivia: the building, dedicated in 1933, was designed by Arthur Loomis Harmon, one of the architects of New York City's Empire State Building. ⊠ *26 King David St., Center City* ⊕ *Opposite King David Hotel* ☎ *02/569–2692* ⊕ *ymca.org.il* ⊠ *Tower NIS 20.*

★ Machaneh Yehuda

MARKET | For a unique local experience, head to this two-block-long covered lane and its adjacent alleys, filled with the brilliant colors of the city's best-quality produce, cheeses, and baked goods. It's fun to elbow your way through this decidedly unslick market anytime, but it's riotously busy on Friday, when Jewish Jerusalem does its last-minute shopping for the Sabbath. Its traditional Mediterranean-Middle Eastern character, going back generations, still dominates; but

a liberal sprinkling of stall-size Western eateries, wine shops, and bars, and a few arts-and-crafts or souvenir shops, have given Machaneh Yehuda a more cosmopolitan feel. By night, the market has become a happening nightlife hotspot, with converted stalls serving as bars and lounge areas. The market links Jaffa Street and Agrippas Street, parallel to and just a five-minute walk up from King George Street. Many of the Downtown bus lines stop on King George, and several on Agrippas itself, while the light-rail runs the length of Jaffa Street (which is otherwise closed to traffic). There is some paid parking close to the market, but it is most easily approached on foot. ⊠ *Etz Hayim St., at Agrippas St., Center City* ⊙ *Closed Sat.*

Montefiore's Windmill

HISTORIC SITE | This limestone, wind-driven flour mill was built by Sir Moses Montefiore in 1857 to provide a source of income for his planned neighborhood of Mishkenot Sha'ananim, the first outside the city walls. Its usefulness was cut short when steam mills made their appearance; but in 2012, with Dutch and English expertise, the landmark windmill was restored to working order.

Montefiore was a prominent figure in the financial circles of mid-19th-century London—a rare phenomenon for a Jew at the time. He married into the legendary Rothschild family, becoming the stockbroker of its London branch, and retired early. The larger-than-life philanthropist—he stood a remarkable 6 feet 3 inches tall—devoted much of his long life, and his wealth, to aiding fellow Jews in distress, wherever they might be. To this end he visited Palestine, as this district of the Ottoman Empire was then known, seven times. A replica of the carriage that conveyed him around the country is behind thick glass: vandals torched its predecessor. ⊠ *Yemin Moshe St., Center City* ⊠ *Free.*

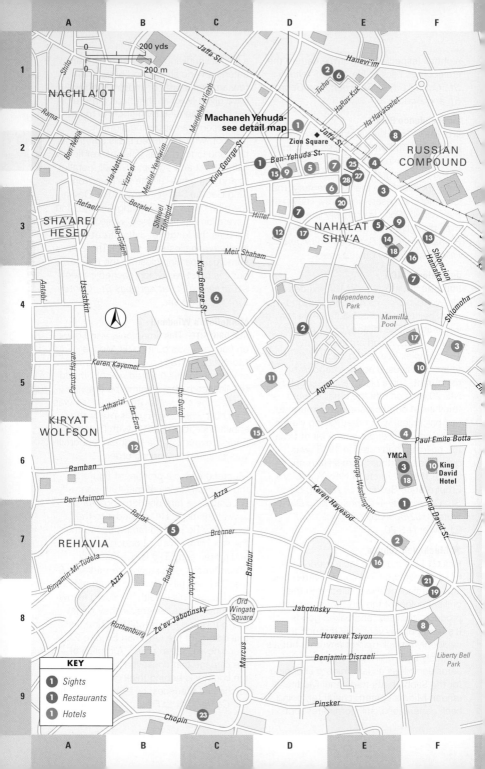

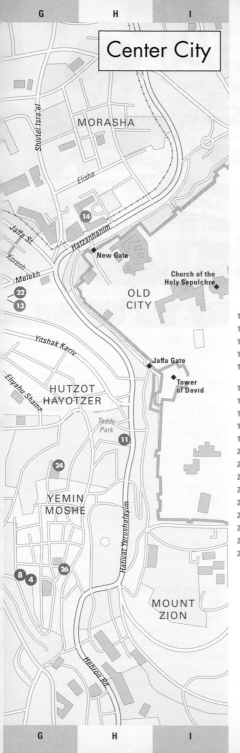

Center City

3

Jerusalem CENTER CITY

The Machaneh Yehuda Covered Market offers a unique traditional shopping experience.

★ Nahalat Shiva

HISTORIC SITE | This small neighborhood has a funky feel, with worn flagstones, wrought-iron banisters, and defunct water cisterns. Its name translates roughly as "the Estate of the Seven," so called by the seven Jewish families that founded the quarter in 1869. The alleys and courtyards have been refashioned as a pedestrian district, offering equal opportunities for photographers, shoppers, and gastronomes. An eclectic variety of eateries, from Israeli to Italian, Asian to Arabic, tempt you to take a break from the jewelry and ceramics. ⊠ *Bordered by Salomon, Rivlin, Jaffa, and Hillel Sts., Center City* ✛ *Near Zion Sq.*

Ticho House (*Beit Ticho*)

BUILDING | Operated as part of the Israel Museum, this handsome, two-story, 19th-century building is worth a visit for its selection of artist Anna Ticho's works, and changing, intimate exhibitions of contemporary Israeli art. It was the home of Dr. A. A. Ticho, a renowned Jewish ophthalmologist, and his wife, Anna. He moved from Vienna to Jerusalem in 1912, and his cousin, Anna, followed soon after, to assist him in his pioneering struggle against the endemic scourge of trachoma. They were soon married, and in 1924 they bought and renovated this stone house. Anna's artistic talent gradually earned her a reputation as a brilliant chronicler—in charcoal, pen, and brush—of the landscape around Jerusalem. The upper level houses a fantastic Italian café called Anna. ⊠ *10 Harav Agan St., Center City* ☎ *02/645–3746* ⊕ *www.imj.org.il/en/wings/arts/ticho-house* ⊠ *Free* ◷ *Closed Sat.*

Umberto Nahon Museum of Italian Jewish Art

MUSEUM | A little-known gem, the museum shares its classic old stone building with a cultural center (ask to see the frescoes in the ground-floor hall). The second-floor galleries include the interior of an ornate Italian synagogue from 1701; illustrated manuscripts; and ritual

A Good Walk in Center City

Jerusalem is a good city to stroll. The limestone buildings, shaded courtyards, and colorful peoplescapes of the Center City make for an absorbing experience. The first part of the walk—up to the YMCA—is good anytime; avoid the rest of it late Friday and on Saturday, when the Downtown area shuts down for the Jewish Sabbath. The route will take 1½ hours to walk, not counting stops.

Montefiore's Windmill to the YMCA

Begin at the landmark **Montefiore's Windmill,** across the valley from Mount Zion. Immediately below the adjacent patio is the long, crenellated roof of Mishkenot Sha'ananim, the first neighborhood outside the walls of Jerusalem, built by Sir Moses (Moshe) Montefiore in 1860.

Separating you from Mount Zion and the Old City is the deep **Hinnom Valley,** the biblical border between the Israelite tribes of Judah (to the south) and Benjamin (to the north). A few hundred yards off to your right is the fortresslike St. Andrew's Scots Church, right above the bend in the valley known as Ketef Hinnom (the Hinnom Shoulder). An excavation in the late 1970s on the rock scarp below the church uncovered hewn-out Old Testament–period tombs and a treasure trove of archaeological finds.

Stroll through the attractive cobblestone streets of the **Yemin Moshe** neighborhood, abutting the windmill, and up through the small park that separates it from King David Street. The landmark King David Hotel is a handsome, rectangular limestone building with a back terrace overlooking the Old City walls. Drinks and desserts aren't cheap, but the location and Hollywood echoes (Paul Newman and Eva Marie Saint in *Exodus*) count for something. Across the street is the **Jerusalem YMCA**: its tower has stunning panoramas.

Independence Park to Machaneh Yehuda

Turn onto Abraham Lincoln Street, alongside the YMCA and opposite the gas station. From the intersection 70 yards beyond it, a pedestrian lane (George Eliot Street) continues in the same direction, emerging at Agron Street, next to the U.S. Consulate General. Cross Agron and walk over the lawns of **Independence Park.** The park's crossroad, 50 yards to your right, emerges at Hillel Street, where there are excellent coffee shops.

Across Hillel is Yoel Salomon Street, and to the right and parallel to it is Yosef Rivlin Street, named after two of the seven founders of **Nahalat Shiva,** the second neighborhood built outside the city walls, in 1869. Hidden courtyards, funky stores, and eateries make this a fun time-out option. At the other end of Salomon Street is Zion Square, where Jaffa Street, Jerusalem's main thoroughfare, meets **Ben-Yehuda Street,** a pedestrian-only commercial street.

At the top of Ben-Yehuda Street, cross King George Street, turn right, and take your first left onto Agrippas Street. (The corner falafel stand is your landmark.) A short walk up the street, on your right, is the entrance to the colorful **Machaneh Yehuda** produce market. It extends for two city blocks, to Jaffa Street. *For more information on the sights in bold type, see the listings in Center City.*

Me'a She'arim

👁

The name of this neighborhood just north of Downtown is the biblical "hundredfold," describing the bountiful blessing God gave Isaac (Genesis 26). The appearance of that verse in the cyclical Torah reading the very week the neighborhood was founded, in 1874, was regarded as a good omen. This is a stronghold of 24/7 ultra-Orthodox Judaism, mostly of the charismatic Hasidic variety. The community is insular and uncompromising and clings to an old-world lifestyle: residents have no TVs; many reject the legitimacy of modern secular Israel; and Yiddish rather than the "sacred" Hebrew tongue is the conversational language of choice.

Modesty in dress and behavior is imperative for anyone entering the neighborhood. Visitors (best in tiny groups) must avoid male-female contact; women should wear long skirts, long sleeves, and nothing exposed below the neck. Sternly worded street banners (in English) emphasize the public norms, and some discourage casual tourists altogether. It's a voyeuristic experience, to be sure; but if you do choose to go, avoid the Sabbath and photograph very discreetly at other times.

Me'a She'arim is traversed by Me'a She'arim Street, and most of the historic neighborhood is on the slope above it (in the direction of Hanevi'im Street and the Downtown area). To the west it's bounded by Strauss Street; to the east it almost touches Road No. 1.

artifacts in metal, wood, and embroidered fabric from the Italian Renaissance to modern times. The attention to detail characteristic of the best Italian art was adopted and adapted by skilled Jewish craftspeople. The result is a feast for the eyes, even if the spiritual significance of some exhibits may be less familiar to some visitors. ✉ *25 Hillel St., Center City* 📞 *02/580–1144* 🌐 *www.ijamuseum.org* 💲 *NIS 25* ⊘ *Closed Fri. and Sat.*

Yemin Moshe

NEIGHBORHOOD | Attractive old stone buildings, bursts of greenery and bougainvillea, and well-kept cobblestone streets distinguish a now-affluent neighborhood that grew up a century ago alongside the older Mishkenot Sha'ananim, and was named for that project's founder, Sir Moses (*Moshe* in Hebrew) Montefiore. In the 1950s and '60s, the area overlooked the armistice line that gashed through the city, and was dangerously exposed to Jordanian sniper positions on the nearby Old City walls. Most families sought safer lodgings elsewhere, leaving only those who couldn't afford to move, and the neighborhood ran to seed. The reunification of Jerusalem under Israeli rule after the Six-Day War in 1967 changed all that. Developers bought up the area, renovated old buildings, and built new and spacious homes in a compatible style. Yemin Moshe is now a place to wander at random, offering joy to photographers and quiet nooks for meditation. ✉ *Between King David St. and Emile Botta St., Center City.*

🍴 Restaurants

The area extends from the Machaneh Yehuda market and Nachla'ot neighborhood, through the central Downtown triangle, to King David Street. The range is vast, from funky budget or takeaway joints to upscale fine-dining specialists, from Middle Eastern food to

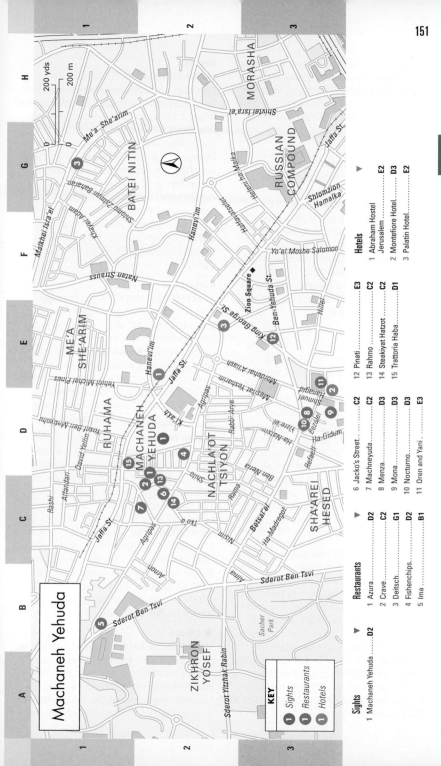

Map: Machaneh Yehuda

KEY

- Sights
- Restaurants
- Hotels

European cuisine, and several surprises in between. Nonkosher restaurants do a roaring trade on Friday night, after the Sabbath begins, when their kosher counterparts are closed and the city streets quiet.

Angelica

$$$$ | MODERN ISRAELI | This popular eatery with a geometric mirrored ceiling is steps from the King David Street hotel district. The desserts are among the city's finest, including the dark-chocolate mousse and the fresh fruit over tapioca pudding. **Known for:** inventive combinations; Israeli ingredients; unusual Israeli vintage wines. $ Average main: NIS 140 ⊠ 4 George Washington St., Center City ☎ 02/623–0056 ⊕ angelicarest.com ⊗ Closed Fri. and Sat.

★ Anna

$$ | ITALIAN | This stunning 200-year-old stone building called Beit Ticho (Ticho House) was once the home of artist Anna Ticho, whose evocative drawings of Jerusalem adorn its walls. Anna has a number of hit dishes for moderate prices, but the pizzas and fish dishes like the whole sea bream baked with lemony herb potatoes are especially popular. **Known for:** brunch on the patio; beautiful art; rustic Italian dishes. $ Average main: NIS 74 ⊠ Ticho House, 10 Harav Agan St., Center City ☎ 02/543–4144 ⊕ annarest.co.il ⊗ No dinner Fri. Closed Sat.

★ Azura

$$ | MIDDLE EASTERN | Jerusalem is famous for its Kurdish kubbeh soup, made with softball-size meat-and-semolina dumplings, and Azura is the perfect place to try this classic dish. Tucked away in a plaza off the Machaneh Yehuda market, the cavelike kitchen is packed with massive pots simmering on kerosene burners. **Known for:** comforting Israeli home cooking; beet kubbeh soup; outdoor dining. $ Average main: NIS 55 ⊠ 4 Haeshkol St., Center City ☎ 02/623–5204 ⊗ Closed Sat. No dinner.

Barood

$$$ | MIDDLE EASTERN | Jerusalemite Daniella Lerer combines her family's Sephardic culinary traditions with modern Israeli cooking techniques and personal favorites from two decades in the business. Reservations are a must for dinner Friday night and on Saturday, when there are often live performances outside. **Known for:** tucked-away location in a hidden alley; sufrito (braised dumplings with Jerusalem artichokes); homemade citrus schnapps. $ Average main: NIS 88 ⊠ Feingold Courtyard, 31 Jaffa St., Center City ☎ 02/625–9081 ⊗ Closed Sun.

Burgers Bar

$ | FAST FOOD | FAMILY | At this popular kosher chain, the hamburgers are more like cakes than patties. They come with your choice of tasty sauces, and all are made to order. **Known for:** kosher burgers; lamb, chicken, and beef options; vegetarian portobello burger. $ Average main: NIS 43 ⊠ 12 Shammai St., Center City ☎ 02/622–1555 ⊕ www.burgersbar.co.il/en ⊗ No dinner Fri. No lunch Sat.

★ Café Yehoshua

$$ | AMERICAN | FAMILY | One of the restaurants that locals flock to for breakfast, lunch, or dinner, Café Yehoshua offers an Israeli take on American diner food. The menu includes everything from tahini pancakes to spaghetti tossed with shrimp. **Known for:** rooftop dining in one of Jerusalem's quaintest neighborhoods; laid-back yet vibrant atmosphere; quality people-watching. $ Average main: NIS 55 ⊠ 17 Azza St., Center City ☎ 02/563–2898 ⊕ www.cafeyehoshua.com ⊗ No dinner Fri. No lunch Sat.

★ Chakra

$$$$ | MODERN ISRAELI | Despite being one of the city's best-known restaurants, Chakra still feigns anonymity: its name is nowhere in sight. It draws a lively thirtysomething crowd of hip Jerusalemites who appreciate the tasty fare from

the open kitchen. **Known for:** indulgent tasting menu; patio with a park view; well-stocked bar. $ *Average main: NIS 120* ⊠ *41 King George St., Center City* ☎ *02/625–2733* ⊕ *www.chakra-rest.com* ☺ *No lunch Sun.–Fri.*

★ Cielo

$$$$ | ITALIAN | Personable chef Adi Cohen has been serving the same classic dishes from his family's native northern Italy for a couple of decades—and they are still fantastic. The decor is understated and cheery, with bright green tablecloths, warm brick floors, and flowers in the windows. **Known for:** traditional dishes like ravioli; veal and beef; homemade limoncello. $ *Average main: NIS 105* ⊠ *18 Ben Sira St., Center City* ☎ *02/625–1132* ⊕ *www.cielo.co.il* ☺ *No lunch Fri.*

★ Crave

$$ | AMERICAN | FAMILY | Locals rejoiced big time when this casual kosher spot opened, bringing with it a menu of creative street food (not to mention Jerusalem's best artisan bread and meat purveyors). It's all complemented by craft Israeli beers and signature cocktails in a vibrant and loud "America in Israel" atmosphere. **Known for:** gourmet street food; lively atmosphere; duck fries, sliders, and a "taco bar". $ *Average main: NIS 65* ⊠ *Machaneh Yehuda Market, 1 Hashikma St., Jerusalem* ☎ *02/627–2830* ☺ *No dinner Fri.; no lunch Sat.*

★ Darna

$$$$ | MOROCCAN | A vaulted tunnel sets you down in a corner of Morocco, complete with imported tiles, inlaid chairs, and a delightful outdoor garden. Don't miss the *harira* soup of veal, chickpeas, and lentils flavored with cumin or any of the stews cooked in clay pots and flavored with olives or sweet dried fruit. **Known for:** Moroccan home-cooking; roast lamb shoulder; wine cellar with 1,000 bottles. $ *Average main: NIS 115* ⊠ *3 Horkanos St., Center City* ☎ *02/624–5406* ⊕ *www.darna.co.il* ☺ *Closed Fri.; no lunch Sat.*

Deitsch

$ | POLISH | *Cholent* is a dish that evolved from necessity: Jewish law forbids cooking on the Sabbath, and so observant Jews often start a stew on Friday that will be ready the following afternoon. Every Jewish community has its own recipe, but in Jerusalem the best place to try cholent is in the ultra-Orthodox quarter of Mea Shearim, where on Thursday nights locals crowd into Deitsch for a plate straight out of Poland. **Known for:** authentic cholent; age-old tradition; ultra-Orthodox local spot. $ *Average main: NIS 40* ⊠ *32 Mea Shearim St., Center City* ☎ *02/582–9529* ▭ *No credit cards* ☺ *Closed Sat. No dinner Fri.*

Dolphin Yam

$$$ | SEAFOOD | FAMILY | Hebrew for "Sea Dolphin," this lively eatery serves some of the city's best seafood. The decor is pleasant enough—pale yellow stucco walls, recessed wine racks, arched windows, and an outdoor patio—but it's not a place for intimacy. **Known for:** seafood platter; family-friendly; shrimp in mushroom cream sauce. $ *Average main: NIS 95* ⊠ *9 Ben Shetach St., Center City* ☎ *02/623–2272* ⊕ *seadolphin.co.il.*

★ 1868

$$$$ | MODERN ISRAELI | In an old stone house with a delightful back garden, 1868 is Jerusalem's most innovative, exacting kosher restaurant, on par with the city's best. Jerusalemite chef Yankele Turjeman combines the flavors of the city with high-quality ingredients and exquisite cooking techniques to create an unforgettable dining experience. Most of the fruits and vegetables are organic, and the menu changes monthly to incorporate the best of the season. **Known for:** modern Israeli cooking; seasonal ingredients; changing menu that may include duck or veal sweetbreads. $ *Average main: NIS 110* ⊠ *10 King David St., Center City* ☎ *02/622–2312* ⊕ *1868.co.il* ☺ *Closed Fri. No lunch Sat.*

3

Jerusalem CENTER CITY

★ Eucalyptus

$$$$ | **MIDDLE EASTERN** | Chef Moshe Basson, repeated winner of international couscous contests, has mined the kitchens of older Jewish and Arab women to revive nearly forgotten recipes and ingredients. Grab a seat on the outside porch, adjacent to the Old City walls on one side and overlooking the picturesque Hutzot Hayotzer artists colony on the other. **Known for:** one of the most acclaimed restaurants in Jerusalem; traditional makloubeh with chicken and rice; tasting menu. $ *Average main: NIS 110* ⊠ *14 Hativat Jerusalem St., Center City* ⊹ *Felt Alley (between 14 Hativat Jerusalem St. and Dror Eliel St.)* ☎ *02/624–4331* ⊕ *www.the-eucalyptus.com* ⊙ *Closed Fri. No lunch Sat.*

Fishenchips

$ | **BRITISH** | **FAMILY** | Brothers Aviram and Shlomi Ohana's tiny fish-and-chips emporium in the heart of the Machaneh Yehuda market offers fresh selections direct from their father Haim's seafood stall down the alley. Everything is garnished with a range of tasty dressings and accompanied by great fries. **Known for:** cheap and delicious; classic British-style battered cod; beers on tap. $ *Average main: NIS 37* ⊠ *Machaneh Yehuda Market, 12 HaEgoz St., Center City* ☎ *02/624–9503* ⊙ *Closed Sat. No dinner Fri.*

Focaccia Bar

$$ | **ITALIAN** | This popular haunt has been baking fluffy focaccias for 20 years. There are many toppings (don't miss the black-olive spread), and some tasty starters (try the mushrooms stuffed with goat cheese or the fried calamari). **Known for:** one of the few spots to flout Passover restrictions on eating leavened dough; a host of vegan and gluten-free options; sirloin strip sandwich. $ *Average main: NIS 63* ⊠ *4 Rabbi Akiva St., Center City* ☎ *02/625–6428* ⊕ *bar.focaccia.co.*

Fast Foods to Try 🍴

Falafel and hummus are ubiquitous in Jerusalem, as is the **sabich**, a pita stuffed with deep-fried eggplant and a hard-boiled egg. Tasty **shawarma** is grilled lamb or turkey, also served in pita bread. Try the stands in the Ben-Yehuda Street open-air mall.

If you crave meat, the **me'orav Yerushalmi** (Jerusalem-style mixed grill) is a specialty of the eateries on Agrippas Street, near the Machaneh Yehuda market. It's a deliciously seasoned meal of stuffed pitas.

Hamarakia

$ | **ISRAELI** | Share a long wooden table with university students at this restaurant named for a soup pot and enjoy an ever-changing menu of hearty soups and stews served with white bread, butter, and pesto. *Shakshuka* (a tangy dish of eggs, tomatoes, garlic, and onions), interesting salads, and other vegetarian and vegan options complete the menu. There's a piano in the corner, a box of old records, and a chandelier made of spoons. **Known for:** comforting soups and shakshuka; live jazz on Wednesday in winter; student favorite. $ *Average main: NIS 30* ⊠ *4 Koresh St., Center City* ☎ *02/625–7797* ⊟ *No credit cards* ⊙ *Closed Fri. No lunch Sat.*

Harvey's Smokehouse

$$$$ | **AMERICAN** | **FAMILY** | Run by Canadian immigrant Harvey Sandler, this hotspot (once called Gabriel's) has become a landmark in the city for American smokehouse barbecue. It serves smoked meats, home-style sides like yam fries, hand-crafted onion rings, and lamb bacon in Bourbon sauce, plus a smattering of

southern-inspired cocktails and refreshing craft beers. **Known for:** jovial atmosphere; good old American barbecue; southern-inspired cocktails. [$] *Average main: NIS 129* ✉ *7 Ben Shatakh St., Center City* ☎ *02/624–6444* 🌐 *harveys.co.il* 🕒 *Closed Fri. and Sat.*

Hasabichiya

$ | ISRAELI | The sign is only in Hebrew at this hole-in-the-wall stand, which features what many say is the best *sabich* in the city. The Middle Eastern street food staple has thin slices of fried eggplant combined with hard-boiled egg and your choice of greens, wrapped in a *laffa* (flatbread) or stuffed into a pita, then topped with tehina and/or amba, a tangy, pickled mango sauce. **Known for:** traditional street food; the place to try sabich (fried eggplant and egg in pita); open until the eggplant runs out. [$] *Average main: NIS 22* ✉ *9 Shamai St., Center City* ☎ *050/368–8705* 🕒 *Closed Fri. and Sat.*

Hummus Ben Sira

$ | MIDDLE EASTERN | All walks of life share elbow space at this casual eatery's long bar inlaid with Armenian painted tiles. The hummus here is especially tasty and is served from morning until well after midnight. **Known for:** fresh hummus for breakfast or the after party; open late; casual atmosphere. [$] *Average main: NIS 30* ✉ *3 Ben Sira St., Center City* ☎ *02/625–3893* 💳 *No credit cards* 🕒 *No dinner Fri. No lunch Sat.*

Ima

$$ | MIDDLE EASTERN | FAMILY | With a name that means "Mom," Ima honors the owner's Kurdish-Jewish mother, who inspired many of the excellent traditional Middle Eastern offerings served in this century-old stone house just a few minutes from the Machaneh Yehuda market. This is a great place to try Kurdish kubbeh soups, made with beets or pumpkin and blessed with softball-sized meat-and-semolina dumplings. **Known for:** hearty, homemade dishes; filling portions; Kurdish kubbeh soups and kibbeh (meat deep-fried in a wheat jacket). [$] *Average main: NIS 70* ✉ *189 Agripas St., Center City* ☎ *02/624–6860* 🕒 *No dinner Fri. Closed Sat.*

★ Iwo's

$$ | FAST FOOD | Consistently ranked among the country's best burger places, Iwo's was founded by a butcher and serves expertly grilled patties on pillowy rolls. Black-and-white-tiled walls evoke American diner traditions, but this is a sleeves-up, self-service destination. **Known for:** rich burger toppings like truffle butter and smoked goose breast; diner vibes; beer. [$] *Average main: NIS 55* ✉ *28 Hillel St., Center City* ☎ *02/622–2513* 🌐 *www.iwos.co.il.*

★ Jacko's Street

$$$ | ISRAELI | This is where Jerusalemites go to have a loud, raucous good time and eat great Israeli food all in one fell swoop. Be sure to check out the hidden bar, Jacko's Son, behind the "fridge of Tequila bottles." It is tough to score a reservation, so call way in advance. **Known for:** dry-aged meats; lively atmosphere; delicious cocktails. [$] *Average main: NIS 85* ✉ *74 Agripas St.* ☎ *02/581–7178* 🌐 *jackos.rol.co.il/english* 🕒 *Closed Fri.*

★ Machneyuda

$$$$ | ISRAELI | On the edge of its namesake market, this restaurant is considered one of the best in Jerusalem, possibly the country. Celebrity-chef Assaf Granit grew up in Jerusalem and pays homage to the city's colors and cacophony in his elegant dishes. **Known for:** top restaurant in Jerusalem; exuberant chefs; changing menu that may include chamshuka, a fusion of meat and hummus. [$] *Average main: NIS 140* ✉ *10 Beit Yaakov St., Center City* ☎ *02/533–3442* 🌐 *www.machneyuda.co.il* 🕒 *No dinner Fri. No lunch Sat.*

★ **Menza**

$$$ | MODERN ISRAELI | Sink into one of Menza's retro-style banquettes or take a seat around a robust wooden table for a deliciously prepared meal in this lovely café between downtown and Machaneh Yehuda market. Israeli breakfast or brunch dishes like croque monsieur are served as late as 1 pm, but be sure to stop by again in the evening to try the creative versions of bistro classics such as seared tuna nicoise salad. **Known for:** one of the city's best burgers; bistro classics; brunch. $ Average main: NIS 84 ✉ 10 Bezalel St., City Center ☎ 02/625–5222 ⊕ www.menza.today.

★ **Mona**

$$$$ | MODERN ISRAELI | Nestled into a stone-walled garden, Mona has a work-ing fireplace and a tree growing through the indoor section, creating a rustic set-ting for eminently modern Israeli cooking. Start your night with the light red tuna sashimi with chili or the award-winning crab bisque. **Known for:** beautiful location; equally stunning food; decadent brunch. $ Average main: NIS 108 ✉ 12 Shmuel Hanagid, Center City ☎ 02/622–2283 ⊕ monarest.co.il ⊗ No lunch Sun.–Thurs.

★ **Nadi**

$$ | ISRAELI | FAMILY | Nadi has great food all day but shines in the morning, when the breakfast plates come crowded with mouthwatering spreads of sun-dried tomato, olive tapenade, local chees-es, tuna, and tahini, all meant to be slathered on fabulous sourdough bread. Other offerings are delicious, colorful salads; earthy asparagus and spinach pasta; shakshuka made out of tomatoes, spinach, or beets; croissant sandwich-es; quiches; or fresh coffee. **Known for:** fresh, healthy, colorful breakfast spreads; shakshuka; coffee. $ Average main: NIS 50 ✉ 10 Shatz St., Center City ☎ 02/625–1737 ⊕ naadicafe.com ⊗ Closed Sat. No dinner Fri.

Nocturno

$ | CAFÉ | Part of a workshop space for local artists, this landmark café has a fun and funky atmosphere. The menu is rich with sandwiches filled with delectable ingredients like avocado, feta cheese, or grilled vegetables, and they all come with side salads drizzled with a delightful basil dressing. **Known for:** live music; hipster hangout at night; sandwiches. $ Average main: NIS 41 ✉ 7 Bezalel St., Center City ☎ 077/700–8510 ⊕ www.nocturno.co.il ⊗ No dinner Fri. No lunch Sat.

Olive & Fish

$$$ | MODERN ISRAELI | FAMILY | Its location near many of the major hotels is part of the appeal, but Olive & Fish also pleases locals with its dependable contemporary Israeli dishes. For starters, try the tasty grilled eggplant with tahini, or great fish options like whole grilled trout or St. Peter's fish on a bed of pasta with zuc-chini, sun-dried tomatoes, garlic, mint, and lemon. **Known for:** convenient, central location; helpful with large groups; half duck cooked in pears. $ Average main: NIS 95 ✉ 2 Jabotinsky St., Center City ☎ 02/566–5020 ⊕ oliveandfish.rest.co.il ⊗ Closed Fri. No lunch Sat.

Oren and Yani

$ | DELI | Locals swear by this deli's inexpensive sandwiches, which come piled high with smoked meats, exotic cheeses, or pickled herring. Meat and dairy are prepared in separate kitchens, so you have an unusually wide range of choices for a kosher eatery. **Known for:** best sandwiches in town; wide range of kosher options; street-side tables. $ Average main: NIS 25 ✉ 8 Schatz St., Center City ☎ 02/579–7378 ⊗ Closed Sat. No dinner Fri.

Piccolino

$$ | ITALIAN | FAMILY | Inside an atmos-pheric old building, this kosher Italian restaurant has stone walls, graceful arches, and a sunny courtyard. The house salad, made with seasonal fruit and drizzled with a mustard-orange dressing, is delicious. **Known for:** peaceful spot to dine outside with wine and some tunes; part of the "Music Square" complex; pappardelle. [$] *Average main: NIS 70* ✉ *12 Yoel Solomon St., Center City* ☎ *02/624–4186* 🌐 *piccolino.co.il* 🕑 *No dinner Fri. No lunch Sat.*

★ Pinati

$ | MIDDLE EASTERN | When aficionados of local standards like garlicky hummus, skewered shish kebabs, fried chicken schnitzel, and bean soup argue hotly about the merits of *their* favorite eateries, Pinati—which means "corner" in Hebrew—comes up as a leading contender. It's now a chain, but this simple downtown spot remains a convenient place to rub shoulders with locals while eating expertly prepared food. **Known for:** being the locals' spot; hummus; convenient. [$] *Average main: NIS 40* ✉ *13 King George St., Center City* ☎ *02/625–4540* 🕑 *Closed Sat. No dinner Fri.*

P2 Pizza

$$ | ITALIAN | Grab a seat at the bar and sip a Peroni while you watch the young, friendly staff roll out extra-thin pizza dough in this narrow temple to Italian fast food. Toppings are tasty combinations of cheese, vegetables, and meats. **Known for:** specialty slices; fettuccine; wine. [$] *Average main: NIS 55* ✉ *36 Keren Hayesod St., Center City* ☎ *02/563–5555* 🕑 *Closed Fri.*

Rahmo

$$ | ISRAELI | You'll probably smell this eatery long before you see it: rich stews of eggplant, potatoes, and meat cook all day on kerosene burners, and the aromas waft into the Machaneh Yehuda market, taunting passersby. Try the stuffed grape leaves, scoop up hummus with freshly baked pitas, or order beef heaped over rice for a meal that will stick to your ribs. **Known for:** down-to-earth cooking; homemade stew; amazing aromas. [$] *Average main: NIS 55* ✉ *5 Haeshkol St., Machaneh Yehuda* ☎ *02/623–4595* 🌐 *www.rachmo.rol.co.il* 🕑 *Closed Sat. No dinner Fri.*

★ Rooftop

$$$$ | MODERN ISRAELI | On the top of the Mamilla Hotel, this open-air restaurant lays claim to one of the best views of Jerusalem, and you can enjoy it from a cushioned chair as you sip spiked iced tea and dine on seared sea bass or grilled lamb chops with Swiss chard. The extensive wine list features more than 20 local boutique labels. **Known for:** one-of-a-kind alfresco dining; unbeatable views; salads and fish. [$] *Average main: NIS 125* ✉ *Mamilla Hotel, 11 King Solomon St., Center City* ☎ *02/548–2230* 🌐 *www.mamillahotel.com/rooftop* 🕑 *No lunch Sun.–Thurs.*

Steakiyat Hatzot

$$$ | MIDDLE EASTERN | FAMILY | Down the block from the Machaneh Yehuda produce market, Agrippas Street has some of Jerusalem's best-known greasy spoons. Loyalists claim that Steakiyat Hatzot, which means "Midnight Grill," actually pioneered the local favorite known as Me'orav Yerushalmi. Jerusalem mixed grill is a substantial and delicious meal-in-a-pita of cumin-flavored bits of chicken hearts, livers, and other organ meats. **Known for:** mixed grill pita; stand-up eating; local favorite. [$] *Average main: NIS 77* ✉ *121 Agrippas St., Center City* ☎ *073/758–4204* 🌐 *www.hatzot.co.il* 🕑 *No dinner Fri. No lunch Sat.*

★ Talbiye

$$$$ | FRENCH | Just under the Jerusalem Theatre, Talbiye is a cozy neighborhood restaurant and wine bar specializing in French-Israeli cuisine. The soundtrack of classical music during the day and jazz at night, as well as the rustic-chic decor, provide a sophisticated atmosphere for a solid clientele of politicians, judges, and Jerusalemite intelligentsia. **Known for:** cream of the crop clientele; fine dining; moules frites. [$] *Average main: NIS 102*

✉ 5 Chopin St., Center City ✣ Under Jerusalem Theater ☎ 02/581–1927 🌐 www.talbiye.com.

Te'enim

$$ | VEGETARIAN | In the classic limestone Confederation House—with stone arches, flagstone floors, and tantalizing views of the Old City walls—Te'enim finds a delicate balance between traditional and innovative in its vegetarian fare. Great choices include the spinach salad with baked ricotta or the endive salad with Roquefort and arugula. **Known for:** standout vegetarian food; maharajah majadra, with bulgur, lentils, onions, ginger chutney, and yogurt; homemade sorbet. *[$] Average main: NIS 54 ✉ 12 Emile Botta St., Center City ✣ Close to King David Hotel ☎ 02/625–1967 ⏲ Closed Fri. and Sat.*

★ Tmol Shilshom

$$ | ISRAELI | FAMILY | The name—a Hebrew literary phrase that translates roughly as "yesteryear"—is a clue to the character of the place. A tiny passageway leads to a rear courtyard and an iron stairway, which takes you up to this funky restaurant and bookstore in two separate rooms on the top floor of a 19th-century house. **Known for:** cozy, go-to nook for great food and community; poetry readings and book parties; salads, pasta, and fish. *[$] Average main: NIS 54 ✉ 5 Yoel Salomon St., Nahalat Shiva ☎ 02/623–2758 🌐 www.tmol-shilshom.co.il/en ⏲ No dinner Fri. No lunch Sat.*

★ Touro

$$$$ | MODERN ISRAELI | On a hillside opposite Jerusalem's Old City, this is one of the best spots to dine when the stone walls reflect the golden sunset. The menu is heavy on meat and draws from Mediterranean influences. **Known for:** views of Hinom Valley and Mt. Zion; gorgeous 150-year-old building; shpondra, or thin rib, cooked for seven hours. *[$] Average main: NIS 120 ✉ 2 Nachon St., Center City ☎ 02/570–2189 🌐 www.touro.co.il ⏲ Closed Fri. No lunch Sat.*

Trattoria Haba

$$ | MODERN ISRAELI | FAMILY | The son of a prominent family of Iraqi bakers founded this airy, spacious bistro featuring fresh breads, pastries, and pastas. It's considered a top spot for brunch as well as Italian-style aperitivo in the evening, and the large wooden communal table is the perfect way to share a light meal with strangers. **Known for:** perfect stop coming or going to Machaneh Yehuda market; ricotta gnocchi; Israeli wines. *[$] Average main: NIS 69 ✉ 119 Jaffa St., Center City ☎ 02/623–3379 ⏲ No dinner Fri. Sat Closed.*

Village Green

$ | VEGETARIAN | This airy vegetarian restaurant prides itself on the quality of its soups, salads, and quiches. Many ingredients are organic, and the options for vegans are abundant. **Known for:** being the first kosher vegan restaurant in Jerusalem; hot buffet and cold salad bar; eating home-baked cake at a table on the shaded sidewalk. *[$] Average main: NIS 42 ✉ 5 Yoel Salomon St., Center City ☎ 02/645–7676 🌐 villagegreen.co.il ⏲ Closed Sat. No dinner Fri.*

★ Zuni

$$$ | AMERICAN | FAMILY | In this elegantly clubby version of the 24-hour diner, you can enjoy a wide variety of breakfast options, from the traditional English breakfast of bacon, sausage, baked beans, and a sunny-side-up egg to the classic Israeli breakfast of eggs, cheeses, and fresh vegetables. Later on you can sample the house-made pumpkin tortellini or the famous French toast. **Known for:** jovial atmosphere; diner food 24/7; famous French toast. *[$] Average main: NIS 93 ✉ 15 Yoel Salomon St., Center City ☎ 02/625–7776 🌐 www.zuni.rest-e.co.il.*

Hotels

This vast area is more about central locations than leafy retreats. Parking is at a premium: this is discouraging territory for those with rental cars. However, you'll enjoy feeling the pulse of West Jerusalem, watching locals as they hang laundry, walk dogs, and sip coffee.

★ Abraham Hostel Jerusalem
$ | B&B/INN | FAMILY | If a luxury Jerusalem hotel is not on your must-have list, Abraham Hostel ticks all the other boxes when it comes to location, service, value, and extra amenities. **Pros:** welcoming staff; unique tours available; special weekly events that add local flavor. **Cons:** basic rooms; amenities are all communal; shared rooms and bathrooms, unless specified. [$] *Rooms from: $45 ✉ 67 Haneviim St., Davidka Sq. ☎ 02/650–2200 🌐 abrahamhostels.com/jerusalem 🛏 75 rooms 🍴 Free Breakfast.*

★ Arthur Hotel
$ | HOTEL | In this stylish boutique lodging, named after Arthur Balfour of the famed Balfour Declaration that promised the Jews a state, an abundant breakfast is served in the charming lobby with wooden furniture or outside in a small garden. **Pros:** excellent service; central location; friendly staff. **Cons:** none of the amenities of larger hotels; cramped; can be noisy. [$] *Rooms from: $175 ✉ 13 Dorot Rishonim St., Center City ☎ 02/623–9999 🌐 www.atlas.co.il/arthur-jerusalem 🛏 54 rooms 🍴 Free Breakfast.*

Dan Panorama Jerusalem
$$ | HOTEL | The guest rooms at this 11-story landmark in the middle of the hotel district are a bit compact, but thoughtful lighting, well-placed furnishings, and interesting artwork make a difference. **Pros:** excellent location; pleasant staff; thoughtful renovations. **Cons:** a bit overpriced; pool is small; feels corporate. [$] *Rooms from: $215 ✉ 39 Keren Hayesod St., Center City ☎ 02/569–5695 🌐 www.danhotels.com 🛏 292 rooms 🍴 Free Breakfast.*

★ David Citadel
$$$$ | HOTEL | FAMILY | Talk about a great first impression—this hotel's lobby, by noted Italian architect Piero Lissoni, is modern and welcoming, illuminated by the natural sunlight streaming in from the arched glass roof. **Pros:** impeccable service; year-round outdoor pool; fantastic breakfast. **Cons:** rooms have little character; expensive rates; some may not like the buttoned-up atmosphere. [$] *Rooms from: $432 ✉ 7 King David St., Center City ☎ 02/621–1111 🌐 thedavidcitadel.com 🛏 385 rooms 🍴 Free Breakfast.*

Eldan Hotel
$ | HOTEL | The address in the heart of a prestigious hotel district—just a five-minute walk from Downtown or from Jaffa Gate—is a major draw here. **Pros:** prime location; cheerful rooms; some nice views. **Cons:** few frills; no pool; limited parking. [$] *Rooms from: $180 ✉ 24 King David St., Center City ☎ 02/567–9777 🌐 www.eldanhotel.com 🛏 75 rooms 🍴 Free Breakfast.*

Eyal Hotel
$ | HOTEL | An unbeatable location and lovely rooftop terrace make this a welcome addition to the neighborhood's growing list of boutique hotels. **Pros:** great location; pleasant balconies; USB outlets in every room. **Cons:** small standard rooms face an external wall; can get noisy at night; entrance is a bit cheap looking. [$] *Rooms from: $145 ✉ 21 Shamai St., Center City ☎ 072/256-6967 🌐 eyalhotel.co.il 🛏 68 rooms 🍴 Free Breakfast.*

★ Harmony Hotel
$$ | HOTEL | A combination of stellar service and delightful rooms heralded this first of many boutique hotels in the historic Nahalat Shiva neighborhood, in the heart of downtown Jerusalem.

Pros: perfect location; daily happy hour; free leaflets for self-guided tours. **Cons:** downtown noise when you open windows; small rooms; very basic amenities. $ *Rooms from: $275* ✉ *6 Yoel Salomon St., Center City* ☎ *02/621–9999* ⊕ *www.atlas.co.il/harmony-hotel-jerusalem* ⇨ *50 rooms* ¶◎¶ *Free Breakfast.*

★ Herbert Samuel Hotel Jerusalem

$$ | HOTEL | Named after the British-Jewish politician who governed Israel during the Mandate, Herbert Samuel is a widely celebrated hotel in the downtown area. **Pros:** gorgeous heated pool; beautiful design; great location. **Cons:** service can be slow; street noise is loud when the windows are open. $ *Rooms from: $285* ✉ *25 Shamai St., Center City* ☎ *02/560–0600* ⊕ *www.herbertsamuel.com* ⇨ *137 rooms* ¶◎¶ *Free Breakfast.*

★ Inbal Jerusalem Hotel

$$$ | HOTEL | FAMILY | Jerusalem stone lends a warm glow to this low-slung hotel, which is wrapped around a central courtyard and atrium. **Pros:** excellent location; free parking; top-tier in-house restaurant, 02. **Cons:** city noise; beds are made up of 2 twins pushed together; pricey. $ *Rooms from: $400* ✉ *3 Jabotinsky St., Center City* ☎ *02/675–6666* ⊕ *www.inbalhotel.com* ⇨ *335 rooms* ¶◎¶ *Free Breakfast.*

Jerusalem Tower Hotel

$ | HOTEL | Steps from the Old City, this hotel's prime location makes it a great option if you want to be close to the action. **Pros:** good value; in the heart of things; free Wi-Fi access. **Cons:** not many amenities; no room to spread out; parking for a fee. $ *Rooms from: $105* ✉ *23 Hillel St., Center City* ☎ *02/620–9209* ⊕ *www.jerusalemtowerhotel.com* ⇨ *120 rooms* ¶◎¶ *Free Breakfast.*

★ King David

$$$$ | HOTEL | This grande dame of Israeli luxury hotels opened in 1931 and it has successfully defended its title ever since, adding modern amenities like a well-appointed gym and luxuries like a French-style restaurant called La Régence. **Pros:** outstanding pool and garden; terrific location and views; historic building with stunning decoration. **Cons:** limited parking; older rooms are quite small and shabby; expensive. $ *Rooms from: $560* ✉ *23 King David St., Center City* ☎ *02/620–8888* ⊕ *www.danhotels.com* ⇨ *233 rooms* ¶◎¶ *Free Breakfast.*

Leonardo Plaza Hotel Jerusalem

$$$ | HOTEL | Overlooking Independence Park, the 22-story Leonardo Plaza is a Jerusalem landmark with terrific views, especially from upper floors. **Pros:** 10-minute walk from the Old City; good restaurants; up-to-date gym. **Cons:** business hotel feel; pay parking; pricey rates. $ *Rooms from: $375* ✉ *47 King George St., Center City* ☎ *02/629–8666* ⊕ *www.leonardo-hotels.com* ⇨ *270 rooms* ¶◎¶ *Free Breakfast.*

Little House in Rechavia

$ | B&B/INN | The small hotel makes no pretensions about being a full-service facility, but it is comfortably furnished, a good value, and within walking distance of the Old City. **Pros:** neighborhood feel; reasonable rates; rooftop terrace. **Cons:** no restaurant; no pool; no parking. $ *Rooms from: $168* ✉ *20 Ibn Ezra St., Center City* ☎ *02/563–3344* ⊕ *www.jerusalem-hotel.co.il* ⇨ *28 rooms* ¶◎¶ *Free Breakfast.*

★ Mamilla Hotel

$$$$ | HOTEL | With clever and soaring architectural flourishes by starchitect Moshe Safdie and a restrained yet luxurious modern interior design by Piero Lissoni, the Mamilla is a sleek and comfortable haven with bars and restaurants that appeal to locals and travelers alike. **Pros:** stunning, contemporary design; central location; pristine service. **Cons:** Happy Fish restaurant is uncharacteristically mediocre; street noise; Akasha Spa is across the street, not part of the hotel.

Ⓢ Rooms from: $600 ✉ 11 King Solomon St., Center City ☎ 02/548–2222 ⊕ www.mamillahotel.com ⇌ 194 rooms ⑩ Free Breakfast.

Montefiore Hotel

$ | HOTEL | The side-street location in the center of town—on a pedestrian-only block with shops and restaurants just outside the front door—adds to the serenity of this reasonably priced hotel. **Pros:** 10-minute walk from Old City; interesting shops and cafés nearby; free Wi-Fi access. **Cons:** a bit old-fashioned; paid parking; elevator is loud and stops on every floor on the Sabbath. Ⓢ Rooms from: $175 ✉ 7 Shatz St., Center City ☎ 02/656–6967 ⊕ smarthotels.co.il/en/our-hotels/montefiore ⇌ 48 rooms ⑩ Free Breakfast.

Notre Dame Guest House

$$ | B&B/INN | Pilgrim tour groups have long been drawn to the modest rooms and stellar location (a 10-minute walk from the Church of the Holy Sepulcher in the Old City) of this gorgeous stone castlelike building owned by the Vatican and dating back to the 1880s. **Pros:** free parking; a short walk to the Old City; amazing historic architecture. **Cons:** few room amenities; overbooked rooms; no TVs in rooms. Ⓢ Rooms from: $270 ✉ 3 HaTsanhanim Rd., Center City ☎ 02/376–0451 ⊕ notredamecenter.org ⇌ 142 rooms ⑩ Free Breakfast.

Palatin Hotel

$ | HOTEL | Proprietor Tody Warshavsky's grandfather built the Palatin Hotel in 1936, and members of the Knesset, which used to be just up the road, stayed here when parliament was in session. **Pros:** central location; multilingual staff; free coffee all day. **Cons:** no elevator; can get noisy; no parking. Ⓢ Rooms from: $100 ✉ 4 Agrippas St., Center City ☎ 02/623–1141 ⊕ palatinhotel.com ⇌ 28 rooms ⑩ Free Breakfast.

Prima Kings Hotel

$ | HOTEL | FAMILY | "The Kings"—the name by which it's still known—sits on a busy intersection, less than a 10-minute walk from Downtown and the Old City. **Pros:** near the Great Synagogue and Machaneh Yehuda market; adjacent late-night supermarket; thoughtful customer service. **Cons:** a bit overpriced; rooms need an update; basic. Ⓢ Rooms from: $153 ✉ 60 King George St., Center City ☎ 02/620–1201 ⊕ www.prima-hotels-israel.com ⇌ 213 rooms ⑩ Free Breakfast.

Prima Royale Hotel

$ | HOTEL | The centerpiece of this centrally located boutique hotel is a spectacular rooftop deck where you can sip cocktails, listen to classical or jazz music on summer evenings, or gaze through telescopes at the 360-degree panorama. **Pros:** live music; tasteful decor; quiet location. **Cons:** no pool; limited parking; small accommodations. Ⓢ Rooms from: $170 ✉ 3 Mendele St., Center City ☎ 02/560–7111 ⊕ www.prima-hotels-israel.com ⇌ 133 rooms ⑩ Free Breakfast.

Waldorf Astoria Jerusalem

$$$$ | HOTEL | Designed by award-winning Turkish architect Sinan Kafadar, this former treasury building has been transformed into a luxurious lodging wrapping around a four-story courtyard flooded with natural light and sparkling with greenery. **Pros:** unmitigated luxury; beautiful courtyard; breakfast includes Champagne and the work of an in-house French bakery. **Cons:** limited outdoor space; few rooms have view of Old City; expensive rates. Ⓢ Rooms from: $575 ✉ 26 Agron St., Center City ☎ 02/542–3333 ⊕ waldorfastoria.com ⇌ 226 rooms ⑩ Free Breakfast.

YMCA Three Arches Hotel

$ | HOTEL | FAMILY | Built in 1933, this limestone building with its famous domed bell tower has long been a Jerusalem landmark, and its basic guest rooms have fabulous Old City views. **Pros:** great location; complimentary sports facilities; affordable rates. **Cons:** dated decor; smallish rooms; needs some maintenance. [$] *Rooms from: $144* ✉ *26 King David St., Center City* ☎ *02/374–1225* 🌐 *ymca3arches.com* 🛏 *54 rooms* 🍴 *Free Breakfast.*

Nightlife

BARS AND PUBS

★ Casino de Paris

BARS/PUBS | Owned by Israeli rock star Shaanan Streett, this bar in the heart of the vegetable market occupies what was once a British Army brothel. It serves a fine selection of original cocktails and beers from local microbreweries, along with stellar cured fish platters. ✉ *Georgian Market, 3 Machaneh Yehuda St., Center City* ☎ *02/650–4235.*

Gatsby

BARS/PUBS | An unmarked door opens to a library with bookshelves that slide apart to reveal a bar inspired by the Roaring '20s. Eager young bartenders mix classic cocktails and drinks of their own creation, accented by crushed star anise, arak liquor, absinthe, or honey syrup. ✉ *18 Hillel St., Center City* ☎ *054/814–7143.*

Hashchena

BARS/PUBS | Hebrew for "Neighbor," Hashchena is a youthful bar steps from the Mahaneh Yehuda market that greets you with hanging laundry and a wall of beer cans from around the world. There are plenty of local and imported brews along with a satisfying food menu. ✉ *11 Beit Yaacov St., Center City* ☎ *02/537–5916* 🕓 *Closed Fri. night and Sat. until 8 pm.*

HaTaklit

BARS/PUBS | The name means "The Record," a nostalgic tribute by the three young, musically inclined owners. This is a great place for beer, especially during happy hour. There's live music, occasional dance parties, and a back room where international soccer games are screened. ✉ *7 Heleni Hamalka St., Center City* ☎ *02/624–4073.*

★ Mirror Bar

BARS/PUBS | This chic bar in Jerusalem's elegant Mamilla Hotel appeals to a cross section of locals, travelers, and expats. The intimate space (and yes, there are plenty of mirrors) is perfect for a nightcap or a table of excellent tapas. ✉ *Mamilla Hotel, 11 King Solomon St., Center City* ☎ *02/548–2230* 🌐 *www.mamillahotel.com/mirrorbar.*

★ Notre Dame Cheese and Wine Restaurant

WINE BARS—NIGHTLIFE | Across from the New Gate of the Old City, this rooftop eatery offers an unrivaled vista of Old Jerusalem and the hills beyond. Take it all in while nibbling on some of the 45 local and imported cheeses and sipping one of the 85 wines. There's also a rather pricey menu, but the best reasons to come here are the drinks and the view. ✉ *Notre Dame Guest House, 3 HaTsanhanim Rd., Center City* ☎ *02/627–9177* 🌐 *notredamecenter.org.*

★ Yudaleh

BARS/PUBS | Owned, operated, and across the street from the well-regarded Machneyuda restaurant, this vibrant bar serves smaller versions of the classics served there. It's good for a drink before dinner or before hitting the town. It is definitely worth trying your luck here if getting a reservation at Machneyuda doesn't work out. ✉ *11 Beit Yaacov St., Center City* ☎ *02/533–3442.*

DANCE CLUBS

★ The Distillery (*Hamazkeka*)

DANCE CLUBS | This austere open space in the center of town once served as a cistern and a storage area, but today the Distillery is the center of Jerusalem's art and alternative music scene. During the day it's an artists' workspace, and at night this spot is a performance space where you can get Palestinian beer on tap and dance alongside throngs of art students. Try to make it when local DJ mini-celebrities Tali Ben Itzhak or Markey Funk are on the lineup. ⊠ *3 Shoshan St., Center City* ☎ *02/582–2090* ⊕ *www. mazkeka.com.*

★ Sira

DANCE CLUBS | A great watering hole with a gritty edge, Sira features a variety of music spun by DJs. Open until the wee hours, it's one of the most fun places in the city to dance. Here you'll find a hodgepodge of students and young professionals who gather on weekend afternoons. ⊠ *4 Ben-Sira St., Center City* ☎ *02/623–4366.*

Toy Bar

DANCE CLUBS | Named for a beloved toy store that previously occupied this space, Toy Bar is a multilevel club with cozy couches for conversation, a great selection of local DJs, and massive flat-screen TVs for live performances and keeping an eye on the game. ⊠ *6 Dhu Nuwas St., Downtown* ☎ *02/623–6666.*

🎬 Performing Arts

TICKETS

Bimot

TICKETS | This is the main ticket agency for performances in Jerusalem. ⊠ *8 Shammai St., Center City* ☎ *02/624–4535* ⊕ *www.bimot.co.il.*

ARTS CENTERS

★ Art Cube Artist's Studios

ARTS CENTERS | This space houses various rotating exhibits, workshops, and lectures. It also serves as a home base for the annual Manofim Jerusalem Contemporary Art Festival. ⊠ *26 HaOman St., 3rd fl., Talpiot* ☎ *02/679–7508* ⊕ *www. artiststudiosjlm.org* ☞ *Closed Tues. and weekends.*

Beit Avi Chai

FILM | This 270-seat auditorium hosts lectures, concerts, and theater in Hebrew and English throughout the year, often on topics related to Jewish culture and history. ⊠ *44 King George St., Center City* ☎ *02/621–5300* ⊕ *www.bac.org.il/ENG.*

Beit Shmuel

MUSIC | Musical and theatrical performances fill the season at this theater. Most of the plays are in Hebrew, but some are in English. Beit Shmuel also offers themed walking tours around Jerusalem. ⊠ *6 Eliyahu Shama'a St., Center City* ☎ *02/620–3555* ⊕ *www.beitshmuel. co.il.*

Jerusalem Theatre

ARTS FESTIVALS | **FAMILY** | Also known as the Jerusalem Centre for the Performing Arts, this venue hosts some of the city's best plays, music, dance, and film screenings. The 760-seat Henry Crown Auditorium is the home of the Jerusalem Symphony Orchestra. The Israeli Camerata Orchestra plays occasional concerts here at 11 am on Friday. Some of the Hebrew plays have English subtitles. Check the website for updated schedules and performances. ⊠ *20 Marcus St., Center City* ☎ *02/560–5755* ⊕ *www. jerusalem-theatre.co.il.*

DANCE

★ Gerard Behar Center

ARTS CENTERS | **FAMILY** | This historical arts center is home base for two excellent local contemporary dance companies, Vertigo and Kolben. Additionally, the complex hosts an annual roster of independent theater, dance, musical productions, children's shows, art exhibitions, artist workshops, and festivals. Historically, it's known as the venue where Nazi officer Adolph Eichmann was put on trial in 1961, convicted of crimes against humanity, and sentenced to the death penalty. ⊠ *11 Bezalel St., Center City* ☎ *02/545–6868.*

FILM

Israeli films have been garnering international praise in recent years; they and other non-English-speaking movies are almost always subtitled in English.

★ HaMiffal "The Factory"

CULTURAL FESTIVALS | Run by a local collective of 50 multidisciplinary artists, this meeting place is housed in a 140-year-old abandoned estate that has been renovated into a cultural and artistic center. The factory produces and hosts exhibitions, concerts, parties, concept events, culinary events, and workshops. ⊠ 3 HaMa'aravim St. ⊕ hamiffal.com ✆ Closed Fri. and Sat.

★ Jerusalem Cinematheque

ARTS CENTERS | Specializing in old, rare, and art films, this complex has four theaters, a café, and splendid views of the Old City and the Hinnom Valley from the terrace. Its monthly programs focus on specific directors, actors, or subjects. The annual Jerusalem Film Festival, held in July, attracts large crowds, as does December's Jewish Film Festival. ⊠ 11 Hebron Rd., Center City ✆ 02/565–4333 ⊕ www.jer-cin.org.il.

🛍 Shopping

ART

Motke Blum Studio

ART GALLERIES | On Arts and Crafts Lane, Holocaust survivor Motke Blum works in everything from soft-color oil paintings of abstract shapes to vivid cityscapes of Jerusalem. Visits are by appointment only. ⊠ 20 Hutzot Hayotzer, Center City ✆ 02/623–4002 ⊕ www.motke-blum. com.

BEAUTY

Ahava Center

PERFUME/COSMETICS | This store stocks all the global company's products using minerals from the Dead Sea, but at less attractive prices than elsewhere. ⊠ 5 Ben-Yehuda St., Center City ✆ 02/625–2592 ⊕ www.ahava.co.il.

Laline

PERFUME/COSMETICS | This shop is known for its trademark white-and-black setting for luxe creams and soaps, all made in Israel. Additional branches are in the Malcha Mall and on Ben Yehuda Street. ⊠ Alrov Mamilla Ave., Center City ✆ 054/334–5032 ⊕ www.laline.co.il.

CLOTHING

Adi Kilav

SHOES/LUGGAGE/LEATHER GOODS | This shop sells striking handmade leather shoes that you definitely won't find back home. Adi Kilav's classic lines reflect his training in architecture. ⊠ 6 Shatz St., Center City ✆ 02/563–3701 ⊕ www.adikilav.com.

Best Line

CLOTHING | Head here for a good selection of T-shirts ready for custom decoration. ⊠ 5 Ben-Yehuda St., Center City ✆ 02/624–9269 ⊕ www.jerusalemtshirts. com.

★ Daniella Lehavi

SHOES/LUGGAGE/LEATHER GOODS | Local designer Daniella Lehavi makes distinctive, well-crafted leather bags, shoes, and accessories. ⊠ Mamilla Ave., Center City ✆ 02/624–3791 ⊕ daniellalehavi. com.

Him with the Shirts

CLOTHING | Here's where to find a great array of T-shirts with clever slogans and designs, primarily in Hebrew. ⊠ 3 Ben Sira St., Center City ✆ 077/783–3499 ⊕ www.h-i-h.co.il.

Naama Bezalel

CLOTHING | Naama Bezalel specializes in decidedly feminine lines for a range of ages, as well as a selection of distinctly beautiful bridal dresses. ⊠ 27 King George St., Center City ✆ 02/625–5611 ⊕ naamabezalel.com.

Poenta

CLOTHING | This store offers a distinctive selection of Israeli designer clothing, bags, and jewelry. ⊠ 5 Shlomzion Hamalka St., Center City ☎ 02/628–7258.

★ **Ronen Chen**

CLOTHING | Simple, classic styles in very comfortable fabrics are this well-known Israeli clothing designer's hallmark. ⊠ 6 Yitzhak Kariv St., Center City ☎ 02/930–9463 ⊕ www.ronenchen.com.

Shoofra

SHOES/LUGGAGE/LEATHER GOODS | Hip shoes from Europe, Israel, and the United States are the specialty at this shop, including mod boots and loafers from brands like Jeffrey Cambell, Irregular Choice, Trippen, A.S. 98 and more. There's a second branch in the Malcha Mall. ⊠ 18 Shlomzion Hamalka St., Center City ☎ 02/623–3414 ⊕ www.shoofra.co.il.

Sofia

CLOTHING | Owner Miri Ashur Zuta offers a well-honed selection of Israeli designer clothing and accessories. ⊠ 2 Bezalel St., Center City ☎ 02/625–2765.

Tashtari

CLOTHING | This exclusive boutique features owner Amos Sadan's outstanding "wearable art"—much of which is influenced by Japanese aesthetics—predominantly as elaborately beaded or woven headbands, scarves, and belts. ⊠ 25 King George St., Center City ☎ 02/625–3282.

CRAFTS

Cadim

CERAMICS/GLASSWARE | A decidedly contemporary selection of ceramics is on view at this shop showcasing the works of 15 artists. ⊠ 4 Yoel Salomon St., Center City ☎ 02/623–4869.

★ **Charlotte Artefacts**

CRAFTS | This 80-year-old shop carries colorful Persian, Bedouin, and Armenian pottery and ceramics, weavings, painted silks, and jewelry. ⊠ 4 Koresh St., Center City ☎ 02/625–1632.

★ **Danny Azoulay**

LOCAL SPECIALTIES | These delicate items in fine porcelain are all hand-painted in rich shades of blue, red, and gold. Traditional Jewish ritual objects include fine papercuts and a range of ornamental ketubot (wedding contracts). Less expensive items include napkin rings and bottle stoppers. ⊠ 5 Yoel Salomon St., Center City ☎ 02/992–4202 ⊕ www.ketubahazoulayart.com.

★ **Darian Armenian Gallery and Ceramics**

CERAMICS/GLASSWARE | Arman Darian's exacting painting can be seen in prestigious buildings around Israel and the world. Besides ceramic pieces with Jewish themes, the shop carries hand-painted tables and mirrors and has a plentiful selection of bargain-priced seconds. You can often catch Darian and his staff working on new designs. ⊠ 12 Shlomzion Hamalka St., Center City ☎ 02/623–4802, 053/470–2582 ⊕ armandarian.com.

★ **Guild of Ceramicists**

CERAMICS/GLASSWARE | This shop beckons with its delightfully colorful tiled steps. The functional and ornamental pottery is made by a dozen Israeli artists, and many pieces are bright and cheerful. ⊠ 27 Yoel Salomon St., Center City ☎ 02/624–4065.

★ **Judaicut**

LOCAL SPECIALTIES | This shop sells traditional and affordable papercuts, a well-established Jewish art form. These pieces make unusual gifts—to say nothing of being both light and easy to pack. They can be customized with your name. ⊠ 21 Yoel Salomon St., Center City ☎ 02/623–3634 ⊕ www.judaicut.co.il.

Salomon

CRAFTS | This is the Jerusalem outpost for art works by David Gerstein, who creates brightly painted metal cutouts of bikers, flowers, butterflies, and streetscapes. There's also a wide selection of handmade jewelry. ⊠ *6 Yoel Salomon St., Center City* ☎ *02/623–6031.*

Sari Srulovitch

LOCAL SPECIALTIES | The shop's award-winning hand-crafted silver tableware and Jewish ceremonial objects combine traditional and modern themes in distinctive designs with a clean, contemporary feel. ⊠ *7 Hutzot Hayotzer, opposite Jaffa Gate, Center City* ☎ *02/628–6699* ⊕ *www.sarisrulovitch.com.*

HOME FURNISHINGS

A.B.C.

GIFTS/SOUVENIRS | A.B.C. is a homegrown label selling well-made gifts and accessories for the home. Their wooden boxes and apothecary bottles wrapped in bamboo make unique gifts. ⊠ *25 King George St., Center City* ☎ *02/624–2549* ⊕ *mygiftshop.co.il.*

JEWELRY

Dan Alsberg

JEWELRY/ACCESSORIES | Jeweler Dan Alsberg has crafted outstanding modern gold and silver pieces for more than 40 years. ⊠ *15 Hutzot Hayotzer, outside Jaffa Gate, Center City* ☎ *02/627–1430* ⊕ *www.studioalsberg.com.*

H. Stern

JEWELRY/ACCESSORIES | The Jerusalem flagship store of this international company offers high-quality pieces. ⊠ *Alrov Mamilla Ave., Center City* ☎ *02/624–2855* ⊕ *www.hstern.co.il.*

Hedya

JEWELRY/ACCESSORIES | This boutique carries the collections of owners Ze'ev and Sharon Tammuz, as well as other local artists. Necklaces and earrings are made from antique gold, silver, amber, and other materials that retain a feel of the past. ⊠ *23 Hillel St., Center City* ☎ *02/622–1151, 054/424–7452.*

Idit

JEWELRY/ACCESSORIES | Offering an intriguing range of in-house designs, this family jewelry business is run by the children of the founder, craftsman Chaim Paz. ⊠ *23 King George St., Center City* ☎ *02/622–1911* ⊕ *www.idit-jewelry.myshopify.com.*

Turquoise

JEWELRY/ACCESSORIES | Itzik Sasson has been creating chunky jewelry from pounded gold since 1989. He also has an intriguing collection of baubles made with aqua-color Roman glass from Caesarea. ⊠ *8 Yoel Salomon St., Center City* ☎ *02/624–1192.*

MALLS AND SHOPPING CENTERS

★ Arts and Crafts Lane

SHOPPING NEIGHBORHOODS | **FAMILY** | Outside Jaffa Gate, Hutzot Hayotzer is home to goldsmiths and silversmiths specializing in jewelry, fine art, and Judaica, generally done in a modern, minimalist style. The work is of extremely high quality and priced accordingly. ⊠ *Hutzot Hayotzer, Center City.*

★ Designers in the City

SPECIALTY STORES | **FAMILY** | More than 20 Israeli jewelry designers, leather workers, clothing makers, and ceramics artists have studios here, where you can watch them work and buy original items. ⊠ *7 Bezalel St, Center City.*

King David Street

SHOPPING NEIGHBORHOODS | Prestigious stores and galleries, most with an emphasis on art, antiquities, jewelry, and Jewish ritual objects, line this avenue. ⊠ *King David St., Center City.*

★ Mamilla Mall

SHOPPING NEIGHBORHOODS | **FAMILY** | Bordered by Old City's Jaffa Gate on one end and the Mamilla Hotel on the other, this open-air shopping center features such familiar clothing chains as Topshop, Urban Outfitters, Mango, and Zara. There's also a growing number of independent Israeli fashion and jewelry designers. The restaurants and cafés all have spectacular views, and the street is lined by Israeli-designed sculptures. ✉ *Alrov Mamilla Ave., Center City.*

★ Midrachov
SHOPPING NEIGHBORHOODS | FAMILY |
This pedestrian-only strip of Ben-Yehuda Street makes for a fun shopping experience. Street musicians serenade passersby and those seated at the many outdoor cafés. Summer evenings are lively, as the mall fills with peddlers of cheap jewelry and crafts. Some of the city's best restaurants are tucked into the nearby alleys. ✉ *Ben-Yehuda St., Center City.*

★ Yoel Moshe Salomon Street
SHOPPING NEIGHBORHOODS | FAMILY | In the old neighborhood of Nahalat Shiva, just off Zion Square, is the pedestrian-only Yoel Moshe Salomon Street. Between the restaurants on the main drag and in the adjacent alleys and courtyards, you'll find several crafts galleries, unique ceramics stores, and artsy jewelry and clothing shops. ✉ *Yoel Moshe Salomon St., Center City.*

MARKETS
★ Bezalel Arts Fair
OUTDOOR/FLEA/GREEN MARKETS | FAMILY |
Every Friday, local artists and craftspeople hawk handmade jewelry and bags, whimsical puppets, hefty wooden cutting boards, and other pieces at this art market in central Jerusalem. The pace is relaxed and friendly. Stalls run from the pedestrian section of Bezalel Street and continue onto Shatz Street to the small Schieber Park. ✉ *Bezalel St., Center City.*

TOYS
★ Gaya
TOYS | FAMILY | Well-crafted wooden toys and games fill the shelves of this vaulted underground shop. Kids are welcome to try out many of them. Gaya also has a branch at the First Station. ✉ *7 Yoel Salomon St., Center City* ☎ *02/625–1515* ⊕ *gaya-game.co.il.*

German Colony and Baka

The German Colony got its name from a group of breakaway Lutherans known as the Templers (not the medieval ones: these are spelled with an *"e"*). They established half a dozen communities around the country in the 1860s and '70s in the belief that their presence in the Holy Land would hasten the Second Coming. Feelings of German patriotism ran high among the Templers in World War I, and many were interned as enemy aliens by the victorious British forces in 1918. Pro-Nazi sentiments and symbols surfaced in the 1930s, and the British deported most of the group en masse when World War II broke out. Look for the row of private stone houses towards the northern end of Emek Refa'im, many with German inscriptions and dates over the doorways.

Israelis have discovered the old-world charms of "the Moshava" (the German Colony) and its environs, and so should you. This isn't the place for headline sights, but take in the good eateries and cafés, some memorable restaurants and pubs in the First Station and Colony compounds, and a sprinkling of little stores, particularly along Emek Refa'im Street. Relax with the residents, especially daytime Friday or on warm summer evenings (except Friday), when the area is at its liveliest.

The Baka neighborhood, just across the old train tracks east of the German Colony, has its busy thoroughfares, stores, and coffee shops, to be sure, but its true character lies in a maze of eucalyptus-shaded backstreets and century-old homes built in the Jerusalem style with honey-color limestone. Many have been preserved or restored, while others have given way to (mercifully) low-rise modernization.

◉ Sights

★ First Station

MARKET | FAMILY | This was once the terminus of the old Jaffa–Jerusalem railroad, inaugurated in 1892. It survived two world wars and two regime changes until the suspension of rail service in 1998. Despite being boarded up, the handsome building's limestone facade, gabled roof, and arched doorways stood as a reminder of its glory days. A creative renovation has won accolades, especially from Jerusalemites. In a city not known for its contemporary attractions, First Station made a splash with its cafés and restaurants, shaded crafts stalls, and play equipment for the kids (and sometimes balloon artists or puppeteers). Evening performances and other cultural events have become popular, especially in the warmer months. The compound is open on Saturday, but only really comes alive in the evening. ⊠ *4 David Remez St., German Colony ✛ Entrance also from Derech Beit Lehem (Bethlehem Rd.)* ☎ *02/653–5239* ⊕ *firststation.co.il/en* ⊡ *Free.*

↗ Haas Promenade

Get your bearings in Jerusalem by taking in the panorama from the Haas Promenade, an attractive 1-km (½-mile) promenade along one of the city's highest ridges. Hidden behind a grove of trees to the east (your right as you pan the view) is a turreted limestone building, the residence of the British High Commissioner for Palestine in the 1930s and 1940s. In Hebrew, the whole ridge is known as Armon Hanatziv, the Commissioner's Palace. In 1949, the building became the headquarters of the U.N. Truce Supervision Organization (UNTSO), charged with monitoring the armistice line that divided the city. It remained a neutral enclave between Israeli West Jerusalem and Jordanian-controlled East Jerusalem until the reunification of the city in the Six-Day War of 1967. You can reach the promenade by car from Hebron Road—consult a map, and look for signs to East Talpiot and the Haas Promenade—by Bus 78 from the Central Bus Station, Downtown, and the First Station; Bus 12 from Hadassah Ein Kerem and Malkha Mall; or by cab. If the traffic flows well, it's a 10-minute drive from Downtown, five minutes from the German Colony. There are restrooms just off the sidewalk at the "city" end of the ridge, before the promenade dips down into the valley. ⊠ *Daniel Yanovsky St., East Talpiot* ⊡ *Free.*

Train Track Park

NATIONAL/STATE PARK | This park separates the picturesque neighborhoods of Baka and the German Colony, to your left and right respectively as you leave the First Station. It was a swath of stones and weeds after the trains stopped running, but residents could see its potential, and (for once) successfully fought the city and the developers. The old train tracks now bracket a boardwalk and are flanked by pedestrian and bike paths, lovely greenery, and conveniently placed benches. A charming series of signs along the route relates the story of the railway, illustrated by photos and anecdotes. The path is about 7 km (4½ miles) long, but the most popular section for visitors is the first kilometer (roughly a half mile) as you walk south from the First Station. ⊠ *David Remez St., Baka ✛ Behind First Station, then south toward Katamon* ⊡ *Free.*

🍴 Restaurants

South of Downtown, the German Colony is a hot spot for eateries, cafés, and little shops. It's a fun, if crowded, spot to pass a morning, afternoon, or evening. The First Station compound is home to nearly a dozen restaurants. Nearby Baka has its own set of quirky cafés and delis. It's worth the 10-minute walk.

Adom

$$$$ | **MODERN ISRAELI** | **FAMILY** | The name means "red" in Hebrew, referring to the 150 kinds of wine that decorate every wall in this large yet cozy restaurant. The menu has roots in Mediterranean kitchens, and includes loads of meat and seafood options. **Known for:** fresh seafood; open on the weekend; Jerusalem mixed grill. [$] *Average main: NIS 115* ✉ *First Station, 4 David Remez St., German Colony* ☎ *02/624–6242* 🌐 *www.adom.rest.*

Caffit

$$ | **CAFÉ** | **FAMILY** | Even though this German Colony institution is part of a chain, it's still quaint with welcoming service. It's well-known for its sweet potato soup and juicy salmon skewers. **Known for:** multiple branches in great locations; local favorite; sweet potato soup. [$] *Average main: NIS 66* ✉ *36 Emek Refa'im St., German Colony* ☎ *02/563–5284* 🌐 *www.caffit-jr.co.il* 🕒 *No dinner Fri. No lunch Sat.*

Focaccia Moshava

$$$ | **ITALIAN** | **FAMILY** | This kosher cousin of the popular Downtown restaurant welcomes you with a large display of fresh vegetables and an open *taboon* oven where the focaccias are baked. The inventive menu offers eight different focaccias, including an excellent roast beef variety. **Known for:** roast beef focaccia; kosher preparation; enjoying starters at the bar. [$] *Average main: NIS 76* ✉ *35 Emek Refaim St., German Colony* ☎ *02/538–7182* 🌐 *m.focaccia.co* 🕒 *No dinner Fri. No lunch Sat.*

Hamiznon Kitchen Station

$$ | **MODERN ISRAELI** | In the former cafeteria of Jerusalem's train station, this casual eatery prints its menus on newspaper broadsheet and has maintained more than a century of peeling paint on the walls. Come in as late as 2 pm on weekdays for generous European-inspired breakfasts. **Known for:** rustic, old-fashioned setting; "Barcelona" frittata; breakfast until 2 pm. [$] *Average main: NIS 64* ✉ *6 David Remez St., German Colony* ☎ *02/561–1497* 🌐 *www.hamiznon.co.il* 🕒 *No dinner Fri. No lunch Sat.*

★ **Hasandwich Shel Rachel**

$$ | **MIDDLE EASTERN** | **FAMILY** | This Tunisian hole-in-the-wall offers pillowy hand-rolled couscous, slow-cooked stews, and zingy tuna and egg sandwiches, served outside on tiny tables or packed up to go. There is no menu, just whatever owner Motti Hadad is cooking in the closet-size kitchen. **Known for:** quick bites; no menu; Tunisian favorites. [$] *Average main: NIS 52* ✉ *17 Beit Lechem St., Baka* ☎ *02/671–3918* 💳 *No credit cards* 🕒 *Closed Sat. No dinner Fri.*

★ **Roza**

$$ | **ITALIAN** | **FAMILY** | The varied menu, generous portions, and reasonable prices have made this kosher restaurant a hit with locals in the German Colony. Decorated with cobalt blue tiles, the dining room is friendly and informal. **Known for:** nine types of focaccia, including roast beef and goose breast; fettuccine with chicken and cilantro; tasty tortilla wraps. [$] *Average main: NIS 50* ✉ *2 Rachel Imenu St., German Colony* ☎ *02/563–8000* 🕒 *No dinner Fri. No lunch Sat.*

🛏 Hotels

This area lies in Jerusalem's southwest quadrant, due south of Jaffa Gate. Baka is some distance away, but all other listed properties are a fairly easy walk from the Old City. The German Colony is an excellent place for people-watching, or for a relaxed afternoon of boutique shopping. The addition of Isrotel's luxurious Orient Hotel has been an elegant addition to the German Colony.

The Colony Hotel

$ | **B&B/INN** | On a quiet street, this small inn was built by the original settlers of the German Colony, and the creaking wooden floors attest to its European roots. **Pros:** quiet and intimate feel; shops and eateries nearby; a bargain in Jerusalem, plus free parking. **Cons:** basic amenities; no elevator; some bathrooms are minuscule. [$] *Rooms from: $120* ✉ *4a Lloyd George St., German Colony* ☎ *02/566–2424* 🌐 *www.jerusalem-hotel.co.il* 🛏 *23 rooms* 🍴 *Free Breakfast.*

Dan Boutique Jerusalem
$$ | **HOTEL** | A lovely sundeck, deluxe rooms with delightful views, and a funky lobby lounge give this hotel a contemporary appeal. **Pros:** great design; inviting public area; close to First Station dining and shopping complex. **Cons:** limited free parking; no pool; some rooms need updates. [$] *Rooms from: $200* ✉ *31 Hebron Rd., German Colony* ☎ *02/568–9999* 🌐 *www.danhotels.com* 🛏 *160 rooms* 🍴 *Free Breakfast.*

Little House in Bakah
$ | **B&B/INN** | This handsome Ottoman-style mansion with dramatic arched windows sits on the edge of a residential neighborhood dotted with many shops and restaurants. **Pros:** intimate vibe; good value; near public transportation. **Cons:** no extra facilities and a bit dowdy; no elevator; traffic noise. [$] *Rooms from: $100* ✉ *1 Yehuda St., corner of Hebron Rd., Baka* ☎ *02/673–7944* 🌐 *www.jerusalem-hotel.co.il* 🛏 *33 rooms* 🍴 *Free Breakfast.*

★ **Mount Zion Hotel**
$$$$ | **HOTEL** | Arched doorways and windows in golden-hue Jerusalem stone frame this hotel's ethereal views of the Hinnom Valley. **Pros:** wonderful mix of old and new; inviting pool area; easy walk to Old City, First Station, and German Colony. **Cons:** staff could be cheerier; some dated decor; low-level gym facilities. [$] *Rooms from: $420* ✉ *17 Hebron Rd., German Colony* ☎ *02/568–9555* 🌐 *www.mountzion.co.il* 🛏 *137 rooms* 🍴 *Free Breakfast.*

Orient Isrotel Exclusive Collection
$$$$ | **RESORT** | Situated at the tip of Jerusalem's German Colony, this exclusive luxury hotel by the Isrotel chain initiated somewhat of a renaissance in Jerusalem's hotel industry. **Pros:** rooftop pool with Turkish bath; on-point customer service; the Carmel Forest Spa features more than 70 beauty and body treatments. **Cons:** 30-minute walking distance from Jerusalem's city center; parking is available at an extra cost; pricey. [$] *Rooms from: $430* ✉ *3 Emek Refaim St.* ☎ *02/569–9090* 🌐 *www.isrotel.co.il* 🛏 *243 rooms* 🍴 *Free Breakfast.*

Rafael Residence
$ | **HOTEL** | **FAMILY** | In the heart of leafy Baka, this apartment hotel offers mostly two-room suites with well-equipped kitchenettes and extra space for the kids. **Pros:** great value for families; modern vibe; underground parking. **Cons:** far from Downtown; breakfast costs extra; very basic rooms. [$] *Rooms from: $150* ✉ *70 Bethlehem Rd., Baka* ☎ *077/777–2222* 🌐 *www.rafael-residence.com* 🛏 *34 suites* 🍴 *No meals.*

🍸 Nightlife

★ **Hasadna Culinary Workshop**
TAPAS BARS | Helmed by the geniuses behind Machneyuda restaurant and housed in an old factory, this is a temple to the craft of cocktails on the outskirts of Jerusalem's First Station shopping and dining complex. The drinks—mixed with outstanding homemade syrups and juices—change frequently, but if it's on the menu try a celery daiquiri. Tapas-style dishes emphasize expertly prepared seafood and include a sea-bass bruschetta, seafood curry, and smoked octopus. ✉ *28 Hebron Rd., German Colony* ☎ *053/934–4990* 🌐 *www.hasadna.rest-e.co.il.*

🎭 Performing Arts

★ Khan Theater

CULTURAL FESTIVALS | Set in a former stable, this intimate venue offers some special events in English. There's a beautiful courtyard and a charming coffee shop and bar. ✉ *2 David Remez Sq., German Colony* ☎ *02/630–3600* ⊕ *www. khan.co.il.*

Lev Smadar

CULTURAL FESTIVALS | **FAMILY** | In the German Colony, this venue is a bit of a throwback to yesteryear's movie atmosphere. It's a single-screen cinema with a snack bar in an older building on a narrow lane. Its local following watches independent films, as well as the occasional blockbuster. Films are screened in their original language with Hebrew subtitles. ✉ *4 Lloyd George St., German Colony* ☎ *02/566–0954* ⊕ *www.lev.co.il* ✉ *NIS 39.*

★ Zappa at the Lab

CONCERTS | This popular music venue hosts the country's top jazz, rock, and pop performers. Small and intimate, it's a great place to see Israel's best musicians close up. Dinner and drinks are usually available. Posters around town announce upcoming concerts. ✉ *28 Hebron Rd., German Colony* ☎ *03/762–6666* ⊕ *www. zappa-club.co.il.*

🛍 Shopping

BEAUTY

★ Sabon

PERFUME/COSMETICS | Sabon—Hebrew for soap—sells its aromatic herb-infused soaps, creams, and lotions all around the world. The ritual hand washing in the shop is a delight. There's another branch in the Malcha Mall. ✉ *35 Emek Refa'im St., German Colony* ☎ *02/650–6644* ⊕ *www.sabon.co.il/en.*

CLOTHING

Osfa

CLOTHING | Carrying well-chosen pieces by local designers, this small but well-stocked boutique has a friendly staff that knows its wares. ✉ *53 Bethlehem Rd., Baka* ☎ *02/672–8815* ⊕ *www.osfacollect. com.*

Pashmina

CLOTHING | Here you'll find a wonderful selection of Israeli-designed clothing, jewelry, shoes, belts, and bags. Let the owner, Michal, or her skilled assistants advise you; they know their inventory and are helpful without being pushy. ✉ *4 HaMelitz St., German Colony* ☎ *02/561–0567.*

CRAFTS

Barbara Shaw

CRAFTS | Australian immigrant Barbara Shaw has put her colorful, contemporary stamp on a selection of household gifts, from crisp dish towels and whimsical aprons to soft pillows and roomy tote bags. ✉ *26 Emek Refa'im St., German Colony* ☎ *02/579–9621* ⊕ *www.barbarashawgifts.com.*

Hoshen

CRAFTS | Jewelry and attractive items in wood, ceramics, and fabric are available at Hoshen. ✉ *32 Emek Refa'im St., German Colony* ☎ *02/563–0966.*

★ Jerusalem House of Quality

CRAFTS | Here you'll discover the work of 20 excellent Israeli craftspeople working in ceramics, glass, jewelry, sculpture, and wood. You can join them for a crafts workshop in their studios on the second floor. The store offers guided tours in English on the history of art in Jerusalem as well as on the building itself, which served as a hospital during the British Mandate. ✉ *12 Hebron Rd., German Colony* ☎ *02/671–7430* ⊕ *www.art-jerusalem.co.il.*

Nisha

CRAFTS | This shop displays an ample selection of reasonably priced Israeli crafts, from FIMO clay jewelry to whimsical pottery. ⊠ *43 Emek Refa'im St., German Colony* ☎ *02/674–6060* ⊕ *www. nishagifts.co.il.*

Set Gifts

CRAFTS | Solve your gift problems here with an array of different objects, from jewelry to art pieces, dishes to handbags, in both traditional and modern styles. ⊠ *Alrov Mamilla Ave., Mamilla* ☎ *02/624–3954* ⊕ *www.set-gifts.com.*

JEWELRY

Keo

JEWELRY/ACCESSORIES | Handmade jewelry in delicate, modern designs is the specialty of this shop. ⊠ *23 Emek Refa'im St., German Colony* ☎ *02/563–7026.*

Sheshet

JEWELRY/ACCESSORIES | The shop carries a solid selection of contemporary Israeli gold and silver jewelry, as well as locally designed leather bags, belts, and wallets. ⊠ *34 Emek Refa'im St., German Colony* ☎ *02/566–2261.*

Stav

JEWELRY/ACCESSORIES | Exquisite, and exquisitely priced, pieces in gold or silver show a graceful mix of modern and traditional influences. ⊠ *40 Emek Refa'im St., German Colony* ☎ *02/563–7059* ⊕ *www. stavjewelry.com.*

MALLS AND SHOPPING CENTERS
Emek Refa'im Street

SHOPPING NEIGHBORHOODS | This area is a great destination for shopping and people-watching from early morning to late at night. Jewelry is easy to find in a rainbow of styles and tastes. Food choices can be limited, so check out the options at First Station. ⊠ *Emek Refa'im St., German Colony.*

Chapter 4

AROUND JERUSALEM AND THE DEAD SEA

WITH MASADA AND BETHLEHEM

Updated by
Sara Toth Stub

⊙ Sights	🍴 Restaurants	🛏 Hotels	🛍 Shopping	▼ Nightlife
★★★★★	★★★☆☆	★★★☆☆	★★☆☆☆	★☆☆☆☆

WELCOME TO AROUND JERUSALEM AND THE DEAD SEA

TOP REASONS TO GO

★ **Bethlehem:** Follow in the footsteps of Jesus from the Church of the Nativity to the grotto where Mary nursed him.

★ **Dead Sea:** At the lowest point on Earth, float effortlessly on one of the world's saltiest bodies of water, renowned for its therapeutic qualities. In Ein Bokek, cover yourself with the mud and check in to a resort.

★ **Ein Gedi:** This oasis rich in flora, fauna, and archaeology—praised in the Bible for its beauty and today one of Israel's most impressive national parks—offers spectacular hiking near waterfalls and canyons.

★ **Judean Hills wineries:** Close to Jerusalem, this area is home to more than two dozen wineries that produce some excellent and highly prized wines.

★ **Masada:** The awe-inspiring remains of this mountaintop palace overlooking the Dead Sea recall its history as a retreat for Herod the Great and as the last stand of the Jewish rebels against Rome in AD 73.

1 Good Samaritan Museum. See the mosaic and cultural exhibits at the site renowned for a famous New Testament story.

2 Jericho. Ancient city featuring archaeological sites, monasteries, and relaxed modern life.

3 Qumran National Park. Archaeological site near caves where the famous Dead Sea scrolls were found.

4 Ein Gedi Nature Reserve. Lush desert oasis filled with waterfalls, ancient ruins, Biblical lore, and hiking trails.

5 Masada. Historic 2,000-year-old clifftop estate with views of the Dead Sea.

6 Arad. Vibrant desert town filled with artists; a good base for hiking trips.

7 Ein Bokek. Hotels, beaches, and a walking path line the Dead Sea.

8 Abu Gosh. A laid-back hilly village.

9 Latrun. Site of a military museum, a towering monastery, and sweeping views.

10 Beit Shemesh. Caves, wineries, and historic sites surround this modern suburban town.

11 Ella Valley. Green expanse of agricultural communities and Beit Guvrin National Park.

12 Bethlehem. The birthplace of Jesus is today marked by the Church of the Nativity on Manger Square.

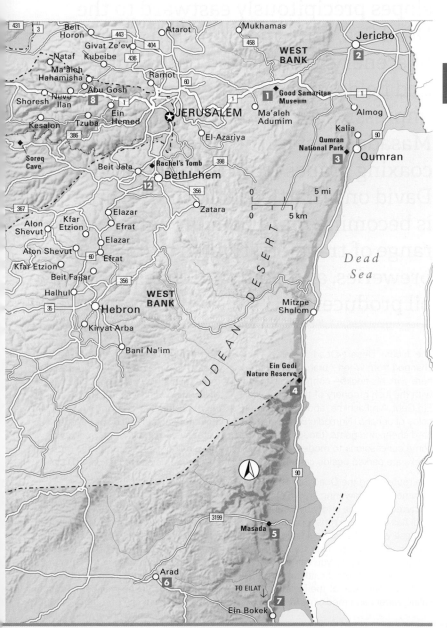

The Judean Hills that encircle Jerusalem, together with the wilderness that slopes precipitously eastward to the Dead Sea, host an astonishing range of scenery: springs and oases, forests and fields, caves, hiking trails, and impressive archaeological sites such as Masada. West of the city, farmers are coaxing grapes from the valley where David once battled Goliath. The area is becoming more popular with a wide range of travelers, thanks to its wineries, breweries, and boutique cheese and olive oil producers.

The Judean Desert–Dead Sea area—little changed from when Abraham wandered here with his flocks—contrasts sharply with the lush greenery of the oases of Ein Gedi, Ain Fashkha, and the verdant fields of Jericho. Nomadic Bedouin still herd sheep and goats, though you notice some concessions to modernity: pickup trucks are parked beside camels.

The route along the Dead Sea shore is hemmed in by towering brown cliffs fractured by *wadis,* or dry riverbeds. Ein Gedi has two of the most spectacular of these wadis, Nahal David and Nahal Arugot. In Ein Bokek, near the southern end of the Dead Sea, you can settle into one of the numerous health and beauty spas that make use of the Dead Sea's saline waters and medicinal mud.

North of Ein Bokek is Masada, Herod the Great's mountaintop palace-fortress built more than 2,000 years ago, which is a UNESCO World Heritage Site. Overlooking the Dead Sea, the king's extravagant architectural feat still displays ingenious water systems, elaborate frescoes, mosaic floors, and bathhouses. Add the human drama of the last Jewish stand against Rome during the Great Revolt, and it's easy to understand why this is one of the most visited sights in Israel.

Just south of Jerusalem, Bethlehem is a major site of Christian pilgrimage. The Church of the Nativity, the oldest church in the country, erected in the 4th century, is built over the grotto where Christian tradition holds Jesus was born. The West Bank Palestinian city of roughly 30,000 sits on the ancient highway through the rocky Judean Hills. Farmers tend century-old terraces of olives, figs, and grapes all around the ancient city.

Planning

Major Regions

The 4,000-foot descent from Jerusalem to **the Dead Sea** is only 24 km (15 miles) but takes you on a journey from one climate to another. Annual precipitation plummets from 22 inches in Jerusalem to 2 inches at the Dead Sea. Still, the desert's proximity has always made it part of that city's consciousness. Refugees fled here, hermits sought its solitude; and when the Temple stood, on the Day of Atonement a scapegoat bearing the sins of the Jewish people was symbolically driven off its stark precipices. Ein Gedi or Ein Bokek, both near the Dead Sea, offer unforgettable desert adventures. They're best combined with a trip to **Masada,** famous for being where hundreds of Jews committed suicide rather than surrender to Rome. Hike (or take the cable car) to the top of the plateau for sunrise over the Dead Sea. Afterward, take a relaxing dip in this saltiest of all lakes.

The rugged Judean Hills tumble down **West of Jerusalem,** eventually easing into the gentler terrain of the coastal lowlands (known in Hebrew as the *Shfela*). This is a region of forests, springs, monasteries, battlefields, national parks, and archaeological treasures. It's the fastest-growing wine-producing area in the country, encompassing more than two-dozen vineyards. A number of locals also produce goat and sheep cheese, as well as craft beers. For Jerusalemites, the Judean Hills are a place to hike and picnic. For many visitors, this sparsely populated region with its ancient terraced hills evokes the landscape of the Bible with none of the distractions of a big

city. Pack a picnic and take the winding road to visit Soreq Cave and Beit Guvrin National Park.

A few miles south of Jerusalem in the West Bank is **Bethlehem,** known for being the birthplace of Jesus.

When to Go

The Dead Sea region is pleasant between October and April but suffers from searing dry heat during the summer. Beginning the day with a tour of Masada can help beat the heat and the crowds. Ein Bokek, with its unique hotels and spas by the Dead Sea, attracts visitors even in broiling hot summer. Bethlehem is best early or late in the day if you want to avoid the crowds. Before you set out, check the hours for the Church of the Nativity. The area to the west of Jerusalem is agreeable any time of the year.

Some advance planning pays off if you want to visit this region during a religious holiday, since transportation can be difficult during Jewish holidays like Yom Kippur and the Muslim observance of Ramadan. On Passover, Israelis tend to mob the Dead Sea. Similarly, Christmas is celebrated three times in Jerusalem and Bethlehem, according to the Western, Orthodox, and Armenian rites. Visit Bethlehem's Manger Square on Christmas Eve for an unforgettable holiday, but book hotels far in advance.

Planning Your Time

The Dead Sea can be a great day trip from Jerusalem, but you have a richer experience if you spend a few nights in Ein Bokek or other hotels in the area. An ideal itinerary might be: On the first morning, climb Masada and marvel at the views, then head to your Ein Bokek hotel for an afternoon at the Dead Sea; watch the hills of Jordan redden as the sun sets. On the second day, drive to Ein

Gedi (a half hour north of Ein Bokek) for the waterfalls and a dip in the pools. On the third day, stop in Jericho on the way back to Jerusalem.

When traveling to Bethlehem, Jericho, and other areas under Palestinian control, you need to present your passport at the checkpoint. This usually just takes a minute if you're traveling by car. There can be traffic crossing back from Bethlehem to Jerusalem, so allow extra time. Be aware that some of the Dead Sea beaches and the Ahava factory store mentioned in this section are actually in the West Bank, though under Israeli control.

Getting Here and Around

BUS

Egged buses are modern, air-conditioned, and reasonably priced. Service is dependable on main routes but infrequent to outlying rural districts. Egged buses don't run from sunset Friday to sunset Saturday.

From the Beersheva Central Bus Station, buses depart four times a day for Arad, Ein Bokek, and other southern points. For Ein Bokek, there's also a daily 8:40 am bus from Tel Aviv's Arlozorov Bus Station (a three-hour ride) and several buses, departing on the hour, from Jerusalem (a two-hour journey). There is a bus line that drops passengers at the front door of the Ein Gedi Hotel. Buses can be crowded, especially on Friday and Sunday. You can't buy tickets or reserve seats by phone for the above routes; go to the bus station early and be aware that buses often are off schedule.

Buses to Bethlehem and Beit Jala run from the Palestinian bus station at Damascus Gate in Jerusalem's Old City. Expect to be stopped and checked by Israeli troops on the way back to Jerusalem.

CAR

Driving is preferable to relying on public transportation here, as some sights are on secondary roads where bus service is scarce. Highway conditions are good, and most destinations are signposted in both Hebrew and English. The steep road between Arad and Ein Bokek has one hairpin turn after another. Unless otherwise posted, stick to the intercity speed of 90 kph (56 mph). Budget extra time for leaving Jerusalem during rush hours. Gas stations are plentiful; some are open 24 hours, but play it safe and keep the tank at least half full.

If you plan to drive to areas controlled by the Palestinian Authority, several East Jerusalem car-rental companies have insurance for the West Bank. Always check whether there's political unrest that could make roads unsafe. Throw a *keffiyeh,* the traditional checkered headscarf, onto your dashboard for extra security.

SHERUT

Sheruts, or shared taxis seating up to 10 passengers, run set routes (usually along major bus routes) and charge a nominally more expensive fare. These run on Saturday between Tel Aviv and Jerusalem. Known in Arabic as *serveeses,* they run to Bethlehem and Jericho from East Jerusalem's Damascus Gate, though an Arab taxi may be delayed at military checkpoints.

TRAIN

Israel Railways runs a high-speed train line connecting Jerusalem's centrally-located Yitzhak Navon station to Ben Gurion Airport. The journey takes about 20 minutes, with trains leaving Jerusalem and Ben Gurion every 30 minutes. The Ben Gurion station offers connecting trains to all parts of Israel, including to Tel Aviv and Beit Shemesh. There is also a regular—but slow—train service between Jerusalem and Tel Aviv, departing every two hours from 7 am to 7 pm, from the southern neighborhood of Malcha; there are occasional departures from the Jerusalem Biblical Zoo. The beautiful one-hour and 40-minute ride through forested hills to the Judean lowlands is spectacular for the scenery alone and includes a stop at Beit Shemesh.

Restaurants

Some Judean Hills wineries serve fancy meals along with their tastings, but these should be reserved in advance. Abu Gosh, on the way to Latrun, is known for its hummus and kebab restaurants. There are also some passable cafeterias west of Jerusalem and a handful of excellent restaurants set in the hills. An alternative is to take a packed lunch or have a picnic west of Jerusalem with wine and cheese. At the Dead Sea, it's always a good idea to make reservations in Ein Bokek restaurants, especially on Friday and Saturday night.

Hotels

Visitors, national and international, who come to "take the waters" and enjoy the serene desert scenery, heavily use the lodgings in the Dead Sea region. On the northern shore, facilities range from youth hostels to kibbutz inns. Although they might conjure up visions of spartan plainness, the kibbutz inns are surprisingly comfortable. They also give you a chance to see life on the communal settlements firsthand.

Along the southern shore, hotels in sunny Ein Bokek run from family-style simplicity to huge resorts, many of which were once hailed as the country's finest but have in recent years been subject to some neglect. Shuttle buses link hotels with each other and the center of town. A beautiful and luxurious spa with a wide range of facilities is an important feature of each large hotel and many smaller hotels as well. The high seasons are

mid-March to mid-June, and mid-September to the end of November.

Since visitors typically explore the area west of Jerusalem on a day trip, lodgings are few and far between. The exceptions are some fine bed-and-breakfast–style guesthouses known as *zimmers* and some larger guesthouses on the cooperative moshavim and kibbutzim.

Hotel reviews have been shortened. For more information, visit Fodors.com.

What It Costs			
$	$$	$$$	$$$$
RESTAURANTS			
Under NIS 50	NIS 50–NIS 75	NIS 76–NIS 100	over NIS 100
HOTELS			
Under $200	$200–$300	$301–$400	over $400

Tours

Bus tours pick you up and return you to your hotel in Jerusalem: very convenient. Egged and United have full-day tours of Masada, the Dead Sea, and Ein Gedi daily for about $100 per person from Jerusalem. *For more information see Tours in Travel Smart.*

★ Abraham Tours

This well-regarded company offers a variety of packages to Masada and the Dead Sea, as well as the West Bank. Several specialized tours focus on themes like hiking, food, and the Israeli-Palestinian conflict, and involve meeting local residents. ☎ 02/566–0045 ⊕ www.abraham-tours.com.

Bein Harim Tourism Services

GUIDED TOURS | This full-service company offers single- and multiday tours all around Israel and the West Bank, including Bethlehem and Jericho. The company also provides airport transfers, including directly to the Dead Sea area. ☎ *03/542–2000* 🌐 *www.beinharimtours.com.*

Tour Adumim

PERSONAL GUIDES | FAMILY | This locally run company arranges private and group tours in the area between Jerusalem and the Dead Sea. In addition to arranging visits to the archaeological, religious, and cultural sites, the company also sets up home visits and workshops. They also arrange visits to local art studios, factories, and Bedouin villages. ✉ *Maaleh Adumim* ☎ *054/527–5404* 🌐 *www.touradumim.com.*

Masada and the Dead Sea

Good Samaritan Museum

20 km (13 miles) east of Jerusalem on Rte. 1 and 500 yards east of the junction with Rte. 458.

A popular spot for many tours, this site just east of Jerusalem is steeped in New Testament lore.

GETTING HERE AND AROUND

Follow Route 1 east from Jerusalem for 20 km (13 miles). The site is clearly signposted on the south side of the road. You need your own car, as buses do not stop here.

Sights

Genesis Land

TOUR—SIGHT | FAMILY | On the scrubby mountains where Abraham likely walked, ride camels with actors dressed up as the patriarch and his manservant Eliezer. Young children find the reenactment of biblical stories enchanting, especially when they can enjoy making pita bread or eating lunch in a Bedouin-style tent overlooking the desert. Older children roll their eyes at the actors wearing simple robes over jeans and sneakers. ✉ *Off Rte. 458* ☎ *02/997–4477* 🌐 *www.genesisland.co.il* 🎟 *NIS 105* 🕓 *Closed Sat.*

Good Samaritan Museum

MUSEUM | About 2,000 years ago, thieves ambushed a man traveling the Jerusalem–Jericho road, and only one passing Samaritan bothered to help him, dragging him to a nearby inn (Luke 10). Today, on what may be the same spot, is this museum, housed in a restored Ottoman inn. It's an extensive collection of intricate mosaics scraped off the floors of churches, synagogues, and Samaritan houses of worship in Gaza and the West Bank. When you visit, ask to see the silent film about the parable dating from the 1920s, filmed on the very same arid hills that stretch for miles from the museum. Audio guides for the museum are available in English. The staff here has plenty of information and maps about nearby sites and trails as well. The museum is 8 km (5 miles) east of Maaleh Adumim. ✉ *Rte. 1, Maaleh Adumim* ☎ *02/633–8230* 🌐 *www.parks.org.il* 🎟 *NIS 22.*

Jericho

35 km (22 miles) east of Jerusalem.

The sleepy oasis of Jericho—full of date palms, orange groves, banana plantations, bougainvillea bushes, and papaya trees—is aptly called *Ariha,* or "fragrant," in Arabic. This oldest continuously inhabited city in the world is immortalized as the place where "the walls came tumblin' down" at the sound of Joshua's trumpets. Those ramparts haven't been found, but the ruins of Hisham's Palace give you an idea of the devastating power of an earthquake at a time when cities were built of mud, wood, and stone.

The Palestinian population of about 25,000 is mostly Muslim, but the tiny Christian minority is well represented by a number of landmark churches and monasteries. These biblical and archaeological sites are what draw most tourists today.

GETTING HERE AND AROUND

Follow Route 1 east from Jerusalem for 35 km (21 miles), then turn north on Old Route 90. Jericho is clearly signposted. Egged bus drivers drop you off at the side of Route 1, but it's still 5 km (3 miles) to Jericho. Arab serveeses from Damascus Gate go to Azariya (Abu Dis); another shared taxi goes from there to Jericho. Serveeses also travel from Bethlehem to Jericho.

TIMING

Jericho is very pleasant during the winter months but swelteringly hot in the summer.

SAFETY AND PRECAUTIONS

As always, it's wise to check on the political situation before venturing into the Palestinian Authority. There are seldom problems in Jericho, however. Although there are no restrictions on tourists in private cars visiting the town, you need to present your foreign passport to reenter Israeli-controlled territory. Only Palestinian car-rental companies have insurance for driving in the West Bank. Another option is to hire a driver or visit with a tour group.

 Sights

Auja Eco Center

LOCAL INTEREST | **FAMILY** | This tiny Palestinian village north of Jericho has turned an acute water shortage into an ecotourism opportunity at this center. Established by Friends of the Earth Middle East, it brings together Palestinian, Israeli, and Jordanian environmentalists. The knowledgeable staff leads hikes in the surrounding areas, including a moonlit trek in the stark desert and visits to nearby Bedouin communities that are also suffering from diminished water supplies. A rooftop restaurant offers traditional food with

lovely views of the area. Younger children can enjoy the playground. There's an 11-room B&B should you wish to sleep over. ☒ *Rte. 90 ⊹ 13 km (9 miles) north of Jericho* ☎ *02/231–0424, 059/884–4006* ⊕ *www.aujaecocenter.org* ☒ *NIS 1000 for group hike (6–18 people), including lunch; NIS 400 for group tour and visit to Bedouin village.*

Hisham's Palace

ARCHAEOLOGICAL SITE | Known as Khirbet al-Mafjar in Arabic, this restored palace has exquisite stonework and a spectacular mosaic floor. Hisham was a scion of the Umayyad dynasty, which built the Dome of the Rock and al-Aqsa Mosque in Jerusalem. Although the palace was severely damaged by the great earthquake of AD 749 while still under construction, the surviving mosaics and stone and plaster reliefs are evidence of its splendor. A small gatehouse leads into a wide courtyard dominated by a star-shape stone window that once graced an upper floor. Several sections of the fine geometric mosaics have been left exposed; others are covered by sand. The most impressive part of the complex is the reception room, off the plaza. Its intricate mosaic floor, depicting a lion hunting gazelles, is one of the most beautiful in the country. (At the time of this writing, a carpet covered the floor during renovation work.) The balustrade of an ornamental pool reflects the artistic influences of both East and West. Fragments of ornate stucco reliefs are still visible on some of the walls.

To get here go north from the traffic circle that constitutes downtown Jericho, follow Hisham's Palace Road for 4 km (2½ miles), turn right at the sign to Hisham's Palace after the Police Intelligence Building, and then take an immediate left down a 1-km (½-mile) access road. ☒ *Hisham's Palace Rd.* ☎ *02/232–2522* ☒ *NIS 10.*

★ Jericho Cable Car

TRANSPORTATION SITE (AIRPORT/BUS/FERRY/ TRAIN) | To the west of Tel Jericho is the Mount of Temptation, identified by tradition as the "exceedingly high mountain" from which Satan tempted Jesus with dominion over "all the kingdoms of the world" (Matthew 4). Departing from a ticket booth facing Tel Jericho, a cable car (locals know it by the French: "Téléphérique") brings riders up and down the mountain. You can see all of Jericho and parts of Jordan from the restaurant at the cable car's upper station. Halfway down the mountain sits the remarkable Greek Orthodox monastery of Qarantal, the name being a corruption of *quarantena*—a period of 40 days (the source of the English word *quarantine*)—the period of Jesus's temptation. Built into the cliff face in 1895 on Byzantine and Crusader remains, it is flanked by caves that once housed hermits. ⊠ *Ain as-Sultan St.* ☎ *02/232–1590* ⊕ *www.jericho-cablecar. com* 🎫 *NIS 60 round-trip.*

★ Monastery of St. George

ARCHAEOLOGICAL SITE | Reached by a 20-minute hike, this ancient Greek Orthodox monastery is built into the cliffs overlooking Wadi Qelt, a desert stream bed that fills with the winter rains. The monastery was one of many established in the desert outside Jerusalem in the fourth century, and has drawn devoted monks and pilgrims ever since. With several previous versions destroyed in various wars and earthquakes, most of the current building stems from an extensive renovation project in the 19th century, but some sections are much older. There are mosaics from the sixth century, elaborate wooden doors from the 12th century, and a chapel inside a cave where some believe the prophet Elijah once took refuge. The monks living here offer visitors coffee, tea and cold water, and are happy to answer questions about their lifestyle. Modest dress is required, including long skirts for women. Both

Israeli- and Palestinian-plated cars are allowed here. ⊠ *Wadi Qelt* ✛ *Coming from Jerusalem on Hwy 1, turn left near Mitzpe Jericho, where there is a brown sign labeled St. George's Monastery* ☎ *054/730–6557* ⊙ *Closed Sun. and Sat. after 1 pm.*

★ Nabi Musa

MEMORIAL | This expansive domed mosque complex was built in the 13th century on the site that Muslims believe to be the tomb of Moses. Wander the halls and courtyards to admire the well-preserved Islamic architecture, and peek into the shrine dedicated to Moses. The second floor offers stunning views of the surrounding desert landscape. The complex's hospice, which once hosted local pilgrims and those on their way to Mecca, is currently being turned into a guesthouse. There is also a small tent built in the shade of some olive trees where local Bedouin offer visitors tea, cold drinks, and snacks. Modest dress is required, including long skirts for women. Both Israeli- and Palestinian-plated cars are allowed here. ✛ *From Hwy. 1, about 14 miles outside of Jerusalem, turn right at brown sign labeled Nabi Musa, and drive a few minutes down dirt road to find parking lot next to mosque* ☎ *052/244–8715.*

Qasr Al Yahud

RELIGIOUS SITE | Just outside Jericho, this is the site where Jesus is said to have been baptized (Matthew 3:13–17), and where the Israelites crossed the Jordan River to enter the Promised Land (Joshua 3). Back then, the Jordan was a mighty, roaring river; today, it is little more than a silty creek which environmentalists say is polluted, but the Israel Nature and Parks Authority, which runs the site, says is certifiably clean. Facilities include a wooden deck, picnic tables, changing rooms, a coffee shop, and an inexpensive gift shop. You can almost shake hands with the Jordanian soldier guarding the

Continued on page 186

THE DEAD SEA
A NATURAL WONDER

The Dead Sea at Ein Bokek

Taking a dip in the Dead Sea is a must-do experience in Israel. This unique body of water—the shores of which are the lowest point of dry land on Earth—was a resort for King Herod in the 1st century BC and the site of Queen Cleopatra's cosmetics empire.

Today, though, the Dead Sea is slowly dying. A combination of less rainfall in the region and Israeli and Jordanian diversion of the Jordan river for irrigation has caused its waters to recede at a rapid rate, threatening the area's ecology.

Israel started developing the Dead Sea as a tourist destination in the 1950s. Today, more than a dozen hotels in the area take advantage of the Dead Sea's mineral-rich mud and waters, known for nourishing, cleansing, and stimulating the skin, as well as for therapeutic bene-

fits for treating medical conditions. Spas offer an array of services: body wraps, mud massages, facial peels, and the like, in addition to general amenities such as Jacuzzis and saunas.

It's an easy day-trip from Jerusalem, but spending the night allows you to watch the sun rise over Jordan. After a day on the beach, you can head back to your hotel for lunch and a spa treatment, followed by a Turkish bath or a dip in a warm sulfur pool.

THE DEAD SEA: PAST AND PRESENT

The stark, beautiful shores of the Dead Sea are literally the lowest point of dry land on Earth, at 1,373 feet below sea level. It's called the Dead Sea because virtually nothing can live in it; with a salt concentration of about 32%, the water is almost 9 times saltier than the ocean.

WHY IS THE DEAD SEA SALTY?

The Dead Sea is salty because water flows in from the Jordan River and other sources, but has no way of flowing out. Evaporation leaves a massive amount of salt behind. Beaches here aren't sandy—they're caked with hardened crystals of salt. The consistently dry air surrounding the Dead Sea has a high oxygen content, low pollution and allergen levels, and weakened ultraviolet radiation.

HOW DID THE DEAD SEA FORM?

The high mesas of the Judean desert nearby, also below sea level, bear testimony to the millions of years of geological changes that created this unique place. The Dead Sea was formed by fault lines shifting in the Earth's crust, a process that began about 15 million years ago and created the basin where the Dead Sea is now located.

WHY IS THE DEAD SEA IN DANGER?

Since it receives a maximum of 2 to 4 inches of rain per year, the Dead Sea's main source of water is the Jordan River, and by extension, the Sea of Galilee to the north.

The Dead Sea's water levels have fluctuated greatly over the last 10,000 years. However, its shores have significantly receded in the past few decades—about one meter per year—due to the lack of rainfall in Israel's north and human activity. Israel, Jordan, and Syria all divert water away from the Jordan River for drinking and irrigation. Less than 7% of the river's original flow reaches the Dead Sea.

WHAT'S BEING DONE TO STOP IT?

Israel and Jordan have been in talks for years to seek a solution to this pressing environmental problem. Currently the countries hope to build a canal to pump water into the Dead Sea from the Red Sea. Environmentalists are concerned about the possible negative impacts of such a canal both on the Dead Sea and on the Arava region. No firm plans to move forward have been announced. To find out more, visit www.ecopeaceme.org.

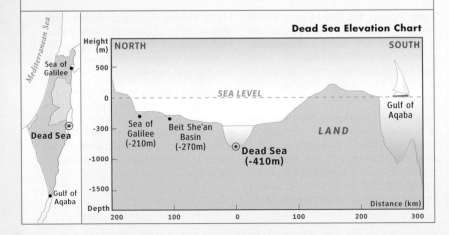

Dead Sea Elevation Chart

EXPERIENCING THE SPAS AND BEACHES

Before booking at a hotel or spa, carefully check what services it offers and whether any particular areas are closed for the season or for repairs. Quality of treatments at the spas can vary widely.

ENJOYING THE WATER

When entering the Dead Sea, wear flip flops or waterproof sandals, as the sea's floor has a rough, rock salt surface. Before getting in the water, check for the nearest source of fresh water, in case you get painful salt water in your eyes. Lean back slowly and rise gently, and be careful not to splash water toward yourself or others.

Small wounds such as scratches will burn for a few moments, but avoid getting salt water in any deep or open wounds. Don't stay in the Dead Sea (or in the spas' warmed mineral pools) for more than 15 minutes at a time, and drink plenty of water afterward.

GETTING MUDDY

It can be surprisingly difficult to find free Dead Sea mud. Some hotels pump the mud to their grounds, or provide vats of it at their beach. You can also purchase more refined mud in packets and apply it at the beach for your photos.

(top) People sunbathing on the shores of the Dead Sea. (bottom) Covered in Dead Sea mud

Bring a friend to the mudbaths so that you can help each other slather the dark goo on every inch of exposed skin. Cake it on evenly but thinly, so that it will dry within 15–20 minutes in the sun. You might need a third person to take pictures, unless you want mud on your camera!

Dead Sea products, including salts and mud, make great gifts and are available at all the spas, but note that similar items may be available at your local health food store at home.

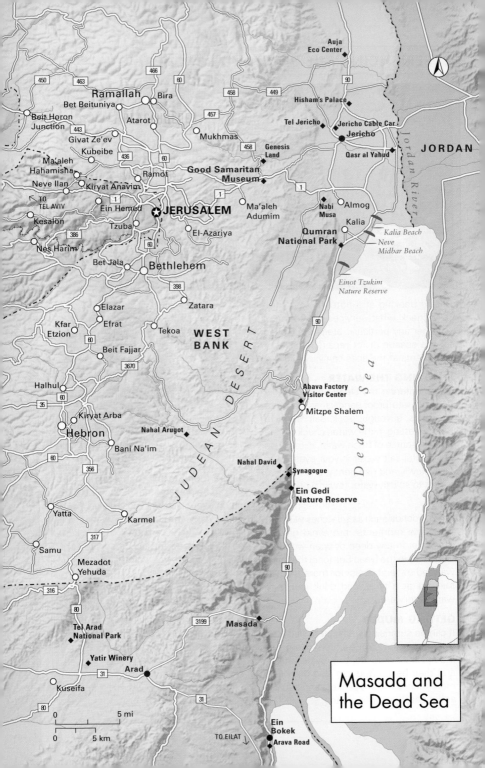

Masada and
the Dead Sea

opposite bank. A project to clear the area of landmines, expected to be complete in mid-2020, will once again allow access to dozens of old churches and monasteries, now blocked off by barbed wire. If you plan to go in the water, you must go in with modest clothing, or a white gown, which can be purchased on site for 27 shekels. Swim suits are not allowed. ✉ *Off Rte. 90* ☎ *02/650–4844* 🌐 *www.parks.org.il* 🎟 *Free.*

Russian Museum

HISTORIC SITE | Russian funding has given a glorious status to the gnarled sycamore that tradition identifies as the Tree of Zacchaeus, which the chief tax collector climbed to get a better look at Jesus (Luke 19:1–4). The Russian Museum was built as a Greek-style palace just behind the tree and houses an extensive collection of Palestinian artifacts and archaeological finds. Behind the museum is a sprawling garden complex with lush green lawns and towering palm trees. ✉ *Medvedev St.* ✥ *As you reach Jericho via Rte. 1, take left fork at traffic island. When road swings to left, look for museum on right* ☎ *02/231–3004* 🎟 *NIS 20.*

Tel Jericho

ARCHAEOLOGICAL SITE | Also called Tel es-Sultan (Sultan's Hill), the archaeological site of Tel Jericho covers the legendary ancient city. Nearly 200 years of excavations have still not uncovered the walls that fell when Joshua stormed the city in the mid-13th century BC. The most impressive ruins unearthed are a massive tower and wall, remains of the world's oldest walled city. Little is known about these early urbanites, who lived here in the Neolithic period between 7800 and 6500 BC, or why they needed such fortifications thousands of years before they became common in the region. Across the road is Ain as-Sultan, or the Sultan's Spring. The name comes from the prophet Elijah's miracle of sweetening the water with a bowl of salt (II Kings 2:19–22). The waters are still eminently drinkable if you wish to refill your bottles. To the east in Jordan are the mountains of the biblical kingdoms of Ammon and Moab, among them the peak of Mount Nebo, from which Moses viewed the Promised Land before dying at the ripe old age of 120.

To get to Tel Jericho by car, drive along Old Route 90, the main road through Jericho, and turn left at the traffic circle onto Ain as-Sultan Street. The parking lot is about 2 km (1 mile) down the road. ✉ *Ain as-Sultan St.* ☎ *02/232–4815* 🎟 *NIS 10.*

🍴 Restaurants

Abu Omar Shaabi Restaurant

$$ | **MIDDLE EASTERN** | Sheets of golden baklava line the walls of this bakery, steps from Jericho's main square. The *bourma*, a sugary rope of angel-hair-like dough wrapped around whole pistachios, is the ideal complement to strong, black Arabic coffee. **Known for:** central location; local crowd; grilled meat at the attached restaurant. [$] *Average main: NIS 50* ✉ *Arrasheed St.* ✥ *Off main square* ☎ *02/232–3429* 💳 *No credit cards.*

Chance Inn

$$ | **MIDDLE EASTERN** | **FAMILY** | On the main highway just outside Jericho, this family-run roadside restaurant specializes in meat dishes like chicken schnitzel and pastries filled with spicy ground beef. There is also a large breakfast menu, featuring shakshuka with tomato, spices, and egg, and potato-filled pastries, as well as quicker bites, like hummus and salads. **Known for:** meat-stuffed dates; local crowd; convenient highway location. [$] *Average main: NIS 55* ✉ *Almog Junction, Hwy. 1* ☎ *050/352–5035.*

HaCanaanite Restaurant

$$ | **MEDITERRANEAN** | **FAMILY** | This modern kosher bistro serves burgers, grilled meats, and Mediterranean-inspired dishes in an expansive and airy indoor dining area, as well as at tables outside offering sweeping views of the desert. The restaurant is also the base for Canaan Tours, which offers jeep tours, ATV treks, rappelling, and other activities. **Known for:** post-hike dinners; healthy children's menu; convenient roadside location. [$] *Average main: NIS 75* ✉ *Kfar Adumim, Hwy. 1, Maaleh Adumim* ✥ *Coming from Jerusalem on Hwy. 1, turn left onto Rte. 458 at Sonol Gas Station; turn into gas station to access parking lot* ☎ *02/535–3840* 🌐 *hacnaanit.rest.co.il* 🕒 *Closed on Fri., no lunch.*

★ Limonah

$$ | MIDDLE EASTERN | FAMILY | Sun-dappled tables under green palm leaves and passion-fruit plants provide a delightful setting for Palestinian basics done right on Jericho's main restaurant street. The minty lemonade is a revelation after a hot day. **Known for:** Middle Eastern mezze salads; on-site playground; grilled fish. [$] *Average main: NIS 70* ✉ *1 Muntazahat St.* ☎ *02/231–2977.*

Sultan

$$ | MIDDLE EASTERN | FAMILY | Reached by the Jericho Cable Car, this restaurant is the only cup of coffee (and the only place selling lunch) near the Qarantal monastery. Tables are scattered on terraces built into the mountainside. **Known for:** great views; lunch service; hummus. [$] *Average main: NIS 50* ✉ *Qarantal St.* ☎ *02/232–1590* 🌐 *jericho-cablecar.com.*

Temptation

$$ | MIDDLE EASTERN | The closest restaurant to Tel Jericho (they share a parking lot), this touristy spot serves standard versions of grilled meat and chicken, Palestinian standards like hummus and salads, and a wide range of mezzes (Middle Eastern salads). Buffet lunches are a good value, though some customers note inattentive service and unclean facilities. **Known for:** buffet lunches; catering to tour groups; slow service at busy times. [$] *Average main: NIS 50* ✉ *Ain as-Sultan St.* ☎ *02/232–2614* 🌐 *www.temptationcenter.com/restaurants.html.*

🛏 Hotels

Oasis Hotel

$$$$ | RESORT | A Moorish-inspired lobby decorated with soaring stone arches lets you know that you've arrived at a sumptuous desert resort, as do the pools that sparkle in the arid valley. **Pros:** lovely pools; plenty of amenities; great value. **Cons:** smoking allowed in some public areas; not within walking distance of downtown. [$] *Rooms from: NIS 550* ✉ *Jerusalem–Jericho Rd.* ☎ *02/231–1200* 🌐 *oasis-jericho.ps* 🛏 *179 rooms* 🍴 *Breakfast.*

Qumran National Park

13 km (8 miles) south of the Almog Junction on Rte. 90, 20 km (13 miles) south of Jericho, 50 km (31 miles) east of Jerusalem.

If you're interested in archaeology, Qumran definitely should be on your itinerary. This is where the famous Dead Sea Scrolls were unearthed, and the museum here recounts the amazing story of how they were discovered and how they contributed to our understanding of the world.

GETTING HERE AND AROUND

Follow Route 1 east from Jerusalem for 50 km (31 miles), turning south on Route 90. Qumran is on the right. Not far from Qumran are some Dead Sea beaches worth a stop if you have a car. Qumran is in the West Bank, but cars are routinely waved through the checkpoints.

SAFETY AND PRECAUTIONS

Check the weather forecast before hiking in the winter. On rare occasions, flash floods cause closures on Route 90.

The dryness of Qumran helped preserve the Dead Sea Scrolls stored in caves in the sculpted rock.

👁 Sights

⭐ Qumran National Park

ARCHAEOLOGICAL SITE | The sandy caves in the cliffs north of the Dead Sea yielded the most significant archaeological find ever made in Israel: the Dead Sea Scrolls. These biblical, apocryphal, and sectarian religious texts were found under extraordinary circumstances in 1947 when a young Bedouin goatherd stumbled on a cave containing scrolls in earthen jars. Because the scrolls were made from animal hide, he first went to a shoemaker to turn them into sandals. The shoemaker alerted a local antiquities dealer, who brought them to the attention of Professor Eliezer Sukenik of the Hebrew University of Jerusalem. Six other major scrolls and hundreds of fragments have since been discovered in 11 of the caves, and some are on display in Jerusalem's Israel Museum.

Most scholars believe that the Essenes, a Jewish separatist sect that set up a monastic community here in the late 2nd century BC, wrote the scrolls. During the Jewish revolt against Rome (AD 66–73), they apparently hid their precious scrolls in the caves before the site was destroyed in AD 68. Others contend the texts were brought from libraries in Jerusalem, possibly even the library of the Jewish Temple.

Almost all books of the Hebrew Bible were discovered here, many of them virtually identical to the texts still used in Jewish communities today. Sectarian texts were also found, including the constitution or "Community Rule," a description of an end-of-days battle ("The War of the Sons of Light Against the Sons of Darkness"), and the "Thanksgiving Scroll," containing hymns reminiscent of biblical psalms.

A short film at the visitor center introduces the mysterious sect that once lived here. Climb the tower for a good view, and note the elaborate system of channels and cisterns that gathered precious floodwater from the cliffs. Just below the tower is a long room some scholars have identified as the scriptorium. A plaster writing table and bronze and ceramic inkwells found here suggest that this may have been where the scrolls were written. You shouldn't need more than an hour to tour the basics of this site, but there are also hiking trails starting from here, including one that stops at the caves where some of the scrolls were discovered. There is also a large and clean cafeteria offering simple food, such as falafel, chicken schnitzel, and salads, and large windows with panoramic views of the Dead Sea and surrounding desert. A new visitors center is under construction, and expected to be completed in late 2020. ⊠ *Rte. 90 ✛ 13 km (8 miles) south of Almog Junction* ☎ *02/994–2235* ⊕ *www.parks.org.il* ⧖ *NIS 29.*

🏖 Beaches

Qumran is conveniently located near some beaches on the Dead Sea. You can't actually swim in the briny water; you take a leisurely float in its incredible salinity, about 10 times that of the ocean. Anyone can enjoy the benefits of the mineral concentration in the Dead Sea water and mud, and the oxygen-rich atmosphere at the lowest point on Earth. Beach shoes or rubber sandals are a must, as the salt in the hypersaturated water builds up into sharp ridges that are hard to walk on. Any open cuts on your body sting when they encounter the briny water, so avoid shaving the day you go to the sea.

Einot Tzukim Nature Reserve

BEACH—SIGHT | **FAMILY** | Known for its freshwater springs, Einot Tzukim (also called Ein Fashkha) is a nature reserve with many species of trees and reeds not often found in the arid Judean Desert. You can swim in three shallow spring-fed pools, peek at the receding Dead Sea water, and visit an archaeological site that contains ruins of a perfume factory and a Roman-style manor house from the Second Temple period. A fourth deeper

pool is open on weekends during spring and summer. There are free English tours on Friday and Sunday at 11 am and 1 pm, but not during July and August, when the heat is extreme. A small stand sells ice cream, snacks, and cold drinks. A visitor center, which will contain a small museum about the Dead Sea, is currently under construction, and expected to be completed in late 2020. Last entry is an hour before closure. **Amenities:** food and drink; lifeguards; parking (free); showers; toilets. **Best for:** walking; swimming. ⊠ *Rte. 90 ✛ 3 km (2 miles) south of Qumran* ☎ *02/994–2355* ⊕ *www.parks. org.il* ⧖ *NIS 29.*

★ Kalia Beach

BEACH—SIGHT | On the Dead Sea, Kalia Beach (the name derives from *kalium*, the Latin name for potassium, found in abundance here) is the place to go for a free mud bath. Slather your whole body with the mineral-rich black mud and let it dry before showering or rinsing off in the Dead Sea. A bar built on a wooden deck overlooking the water plays lively music and serves a wide variety of beer, wine, and cocktails along with burgers, pizza, falafel, and ice cream. Plenty of beach chairs, sun shades, and the bar's free library of books makes this a place where you can spend a whole morning or afternoon. Shops sell Dead Sea cosmetics, hats, and swimwear, along with locally made products like dates, wine, and spices. There is also a juice bar. While the winding path down to the Dead Sea shore is well-kept and not too difficult to navigate, there are also regular free shuttles. An on-site spa offers massages and other treatments in relaxing and modern rooms, but it is best to reserve ahead. Towel rentals are also available. **Amenities:** food and drink; lifeguards; parking (free); showers; toilets. **Best for:** swimming; walking. ⊠ *Off Rte. 90, 3 km (2 miles) north of Qumran* ☎ *02/994–2391* ⊕ *kaliabeach.com/en* ⧖ *NIS 59.*

Neve Midbar Beach

BEACH—SIGHT | FAMILY | Just south of Biankini Beach, Neve Midbar Beach is well-kept, offering a large swimming pool, a wading pool with a fountain, and several food venues. A modern glass-enclosed restaurant serves Middle Eastern fare, and a bar offers a large drink menu along with snacks and ice cream. Access the beach by a set of winding stairs, or with the free shuttle. There's ample black mud and plenty of shade from beach umbrellas. The beach stays open all night for camping and sometimes weddings, although swimming is allowed during daylight hours only. **Amenities:** food and drink; lifeguards; parking (free); showers; toilets. **Best for:** families; sunset; swimming. ⊠ *Rte. 90, 3 km (2 miles) north of Qumran* ☎ *02/994–2781* ⊕ *www.nevemidbar-beach.com* ⊠ *NIS 50 Sun.–Thurs.; NIS 60 Fri. and Sat.*

↗ **Ahava Factory Visitors Center**
Ahava manufactures its excellent skin- and hair-care products based on (but not smelling like) Dead Sea minerals at a factory on Kibbutz Mitzpe Shalem. The outlet here, about 20 km (12½ miles) south of Qumran, sells a wide variety of the products. A new factory is being built nearby in Ein Gedi, but is not expected to be completed until late 2020. ⊠ *Rte. 90* ☎ *02/994–5123* ⊕ *www.ahavaus.com.*

🛏 Hotels

Kalia Kibbutz Hotel

$$$$ | HOTEL | FAMILY | Offering basic accommodations in a tranquil environment, this casual hotel consists of clusters of rooms, each with its own patio, arranged along pathways on a green lawn. **Pros:** great views; quiet; nice pool. **Cons:** some facilities are old; need a shuttle to reach Dead Sea; breakfast is in kibbutz dining hall. $ *Rooms from: NIS 490* ⊠ *Kibbutz Kalia, Ein Gedi* ☎ *02/993–6333* ⊕ *www.kaliahotel.co.il* ↪ *64 rooms* ⊚⊙ *Free Breakfast.*

🏃 Activities

Dead Sea Graffiti Tours

SPECIAL-INTEREST | FAMILY | Israeli photographer Yael Aisenthal leads tours that explore abandoned military and industrial buildings near the Dead Sea that have recently been decorated with street art and graffiti. Most of the colorful graffiti explores the environmental crisis that is causing the Dead Sea to shrink. Customized tours can also include scavenger hunts, puzzles, and the opportunity to create your own graffiti. Yael meets tour participants at nearby Kalia Beach. ⊠ *Kalia Beach* ✛ *From Rd. 90, turn off on road toward Kalia Beach and continue to parking lot* ☎ *52/682–0538* ⊕ *www.creative-yael.com* ⊠ *Tours from 180 shekels per person for group of 10.*

★ Salty Landscapes Dead Sea Boat and Kayak Tours

BOATING | Jacky Ben Zaken runs the only boat tours on the Dead Sea. Departing from the shore near Kibbutz Mitzpe Shalem, the 12-passenger boat explores salt islands and hidden beaches, focusing on the natural landscape around the Dead Sea and the effects of its receding water levels. The company also offers kayak tours that paddle along the shore, stopping to admire salt formations and dig for so-called salt diamonds in the black mud. Tours must be reserved in advance. They last 1½ hours, or three hours, and are suitable for children ages four and up. ⊠ *Kibbutz Mitzpe Shalem* ✛ *Ben Zaken meets clients in parking area across Hwy. 1 from entrance to kibbutz* ☎ *052/433–3050* ⊠ *Boat tours from 180 shekels per person.*

Ein Gedi Nature Reserve

33 km (21 miles) south of Qumran, 20 km (12½ miles) north of Masada, 83 km (52 miles) southeast of Jerusalem.

After miles of burned brown and beige desert rock, the green lushness of the

Waterfalls, pools, and desert landscapes await hikers in Ein Gedi's nature reserve.

Ein Gedi oasis leaps out in vivid and unexpected contrast. This nature reserve is one of the most beautiful places in Israel—with everything from hiking trails to ancient ruins. Settled for thousands of years, it inspired the writer of the *Song of Songs* to describe his beloved "as a cluster of henna in the vineyards of Ein Gedi." Loads of waterfalls and gurgling springs make this an option for summer hiking, too.

GETTING HERE AND AROUND
Follow Route 1 east from Jerusalem for 50 km (31 miles), turning south on Route 90. Ein Gedi is on the right. Egged bus drivers drop you off at the side of Route 90. From there, it's a short walk to the gate of the nature reserve.

SAFETY AND PRECAUTIONS
Check the weather forecast before hiking in the winter. Flash floods are an occasional danger.

Sights

★ Ein Gedi Nature Reserve
NATURE PRESERVE | FAMILY | This beautiful nature reserve has a number of well-marked trails to explore, all of which are off the main entrance. It is home to Nahal David (David's Stream), and the cave at Nahal David is believed to be the place where David hid while Saul hunted him down 3,000 years ago (I Samuel 24:1–22). Walkers can also visit the canyon of Nahal Arugot and the remains of an ancient synagogue and village. Get a map from the admission booth and you can spend anywhere from an hour to a day here, depending on your interest in nature and hiking. Reaching Ein Gedi from the north, the first turnoff to the right is the parking lot at the entrance to the reserve.

The clearly marked trail to Nahal David rises past several pools and small waterfalls to the upper waterfall. There are many steps, but it's not too daunting. Allow at least 1¼ hours to include a dip under one of the lower waterfalls. Look out for ibex (wild goats), especially in the afternoon, and for the small, furry hyrax, often seen on tree branches. Leopards here face extinction because of breeding problems and are seldom seen nowadays.

If you're a serious hiker, don't miss the trail that breaks off to the right 50 yards down the return path from the top waterfall. It passes the remains of Byzantine irrigation systems and has breathtaking views of the Dead Sea. The trail doubles back on itself toward the source of Nahal David. Near the top, a short side path climbs to the remains of a 4th-millennium-BC Chalcolithic temple, the treasures of which can be seen in Jerusalem's Israel Museum. The main path leads on to the streambed, again turns east, and reaches Dudim Cave, formed by boulders and filled with crystal clear spring water. Swimming in "Lover's Cave" is one of the most refreshing and romantic experiences in Israel. Since this trail involves a considerable climb (and hikers invariably take time to bathe in the "cave"), access to the trail is permitted only up to 3½ hours before closing time.

Although not as lush as Nahal David, the deep canyon of Nahal Arugot is perhaps more spectacular. Enormous boulders and slabs of stone on the opposite cliff face seem poised in midcataclysm. The hour-long hike to the Hidden Waterfall (not too difficult) passes by spots where the stream bubbles over rock shelves and shallow pools give relief from the heat. If you're adventurous and have water shoes, you can return through the greenery of the streambed. Experienced hikers can ascend the Tsafit Trail to Mapal Hachalon (translated as "window waterfall"), where there are stunning views over the Dead Sea.

A Jewish community lived in Ein Gedi for more than 1,200 years, beginning in the 7th century BC. In the 3rd century AD, they built a synagogue between Nahal David and Nahal Arugot with a beautiful mosaic floor. The mosaic includes an inscription in Hebrew and Aramaic invoking the wrath of heaven on troublemakers including "whoever reveals the secret of the town." The secret is believed to refer to a method of cultivating balsam plants, which were used to make the prized perfume for which Ein Gedi was once famous. These famous plants, brought back to the area in the last decade after disappearing hundreds of years ago, can be seen in the botanical garden of the nearby Kibbutz Ein Gedi. ✉ *Rte. 90, Ein Gedi* ☎ *08/658–4285* 🌐 *www.parks.org.il* 🎟 *NIS 28, NIS 14 synagogue only.*

🍴 Restaurants

Baobar

$$ | **ISRAELI** | The café at the Ein Gedi Hotel is a great option in the area for fresh salads, pastas, and coffee after a hike at the nearby Ein Gedi Nature Reserve. Sit on the outdoor deck amid the baobob trees and landscaped gardens and enjoy the gorgeous views and the aromatic botanical gardens. **Known for:** evening drinks; kosher fare; open on Saturday. [$] *Average main: NIS 53* ✉ *Ein Gedi Hotel, Rte. 90, Ein Gedi* ☎ *08/659–4220.*

🛏 Hotels

Ein Gedi Camp Lodge

$$ | **B&B/INN** | Set on the side of a cliff overlooking the Dead Sea, this whimsical and friendly lodge includes 16 air-conditioned wood-framed tents that come with mattresses and bedding. **Pros:** magnificent views and starry night skies; 24-hour restaurant and bar at reception; 50-shekel shuttle to Masada. **Cons:** noise from the outdoor bar can make sleeping difficult; no a/c in the bar and restaurant area; bathrooms and showers are modern but can get crowded. [$] *Rooms from: NIS 240* ✉ *Kibbutz Ein Gedi, Ein*

Gedi ✥ From Rte. 90, turn onto road for Kibbutz Ein Gedi; the lodge is on your left ☎ 52/370–9830 🌐 www.facebook.com/eingedicamplodge 🛏 16 tents 🍴 No meals.

Ein Gedi Field School

$$$ | HOTEL | On top of a mountain overlooking the Dead Sea, this facility run by the Society for the Protection of Nature in Israel, offers basic and clean (though aging) accommodations and breakfast. **Pros:** great views; helpful staff; good value. **Cons:** aging; limited breakfast selection; no entertainment or recreation facilities. [$] *Rooms from: NIS 377 ✉ Ein Gedi Nature Reserve, Rte. 90, Ein Gedi ✥ From Rte. 90, turn onto road to the Ein Gedi Nature Reserve and continue up steep hill to gate. Ring buzzer for entrance ☎ 08/658–4288 🛏 33 rooms 🍴 Free Breakfast.*

★ Ein Gedi Hostel

$$$$ | HOTEL | FAMILY | This hotel-like hostel next to the Ein Gedi Nature Reserve offers comfortable air-conditioned private rooms, all equipped with televisions, refrigerators, and a hot water kettle; many have balconies facing the Dead Sea or surrounding desert. **Pros:** great views; accessible by public transportation; guests receive discount on admission to Ein Gedi Nature Reserve. **Cons:** no pool, common areas in need of renovation, breakfast only served until 9:30 am. [$] *Rooms from: NIS 419 ✉ Ein Gedi Nature Reserve, Rte. 90, Ein Gedi ✥ From Rte. 90, turn onto road to Ein Gedi Nature Reserve; entrance is on your right ☎ 02/594–5681 🌐 www.hihostels.com/hostels/ein-gedi 🛏 87 rooms 🍴 Free Breakfast.*

★ Ein Gedi Hotel

$ | HOTEL | FAMILY | Desert ibexes, kibbutz members, and tourists share the footpaths of this hotel, surrounded by majestic baobab trees, aromatic herbs, and hundreds of species of tropical flora. **Pros:** serene oasis atmosphere; fantastic spa; grounds and activities great for families. **Cons:** some dingy rooms; limited hours at the beach; dining hall and pool get crowded and loud when hotel is full. [$] *Rooms from: $190 ✉ Rte. 90, Ein Gedi ☎ 08/659–4220 🌐 www.ein-gedi.co.il/en 🛏 166 rooms 🍴 Breakfast.*

Activities

★ Synergy Spa

SPA—SIGHT | At the Ein Gedi Hotel's impressive spa, you can float in an indoor pool rich in sulfur, magnesium, and potassium as you enjoy the stunning view of mountains on one side and the Dead Sea on the other. Treatment rooms, like the rest of the spa, are elegantly simple, decorated in soft hues that showcase the surrounding oasis. Try the Turkish hammam, and get a smoothie from the bar and lounge beside the freshwater pool. Body peels use materials like myrrh and frankincense; the cost is NIS 295 for 40 minutes. The spa's tranquillity and superior services make it a better option than the hectic Ein Gedi Spa nearby. Hotel guests have free access to pools and saunas, and receive a discount on treatments. Nonguests should call at least a day in advance to make reservations. One day entrance to the spa for nonguests is 130 shekels, and includes access to the main swimming pool, the mineral and salt pools, the Turkish hammam, and dry sauna. *✉ Ein Gedi Hotel, Rte. 90, Ein Gedi, Ein Gedi ☎ 08/659–4058 🌐 www.ein-gedi.co.il/en 🎫 NIS 415 for day package with 40-min massage and breakfast.*

Masada

19 km (12 miles) south of Ein Gedi on Rte. 90, 103 km (64 miles) east and south of Jerusalem, 20 km (12½ miles) north of Ein Bokek.

The isolated flattop rock of Masada commands the surrounding desert, its ancient remains bearing witness to long-ago power and conflict. One of Israel's most stunning archaeological sites, Masada earned fame and a place in history first as one of King Herod's palace-fortresses and later as the site of the last stand of Jewish rebels against the legions of Rome, almost 2,000 years ago.

⊙ Sights

★ Masada

ARCHAEOLOGICAL SITE | A symbol of the ancient kingdom of Israel, Masada (Hebrew for "fortress") towers majestically over the western shore of the Dead Sea. Its unusual natural form—a plateau set off on all sides by towering cliffs—attracted Herod the Great, who built an opulent desert palace here in the 1st century AD. Masada became the last refuge of the Jews in AD 73 to 74, during their final fight against Rome. The historian Flavius Josephus wrote that the rebels (almost 1,000 people) chose to commit suicide rather than surrender, although no one can be sure what happened at the end. In recognition of its historical significance, this was the first site in Israel to be added to the UNESCO World Heritage List in 2001.

To reach the top, most visitors make use of the speedy cable car (NIS 74 round-trip). More intrepid visitors climb the eastern Snake Path (at least 45 minutes of steep walking), some even starting before dawn to watch the sunrise. Others take the less arduous western Roman Ramp path, accessible only from the road that descends from Arad. ■TIP→ Water fountains (but no other refreshments) are available on Masada itself, so save bottles for refilling. Allow no less than 1½ hours to explore the site. The most popular route heads counterclockwise. If time allows, be sure to visit the southern area as well (especially the huge cistern and echo wall). Maps, a detailed brochure, and a very useful audio guide are available at the top entrance.

The entire mountaintop—less than 20 acres—is surrounded by a 4,250-foot-long casemate, a double wall that included living quarters and guardrooms. Most of the important buildings are concentrated in the high northern area.

The Northern Palace, Masada's most impressive structure, is an extraordinary three-tiered structure that seems to hang off the highest and most northerly point of the mountain. The panoramic effect is awesome: baked brown precipices and bleached valleys shimmer in the midday glare.

Clearly visible from the upper terrace are the Roman camps—the remains of the most complete Roman siege system in the world—and "runner's path" (used for communication between the camps).

The synagogue, one of only four that have been uncovered from the Second Temple period, can be seen in the western casemate. The building's orientation toward Jerusalem suggested its function, but the stone benches (synagogue means "place of assembly") and the man made pit for damaged scrolls (a genizah) confirmed it.

At an opening in the walls on the western edge, you can stand where the Roman legionnaires breached Masada's defenses. The original wedge-shape ramp is below, though its upper part has since collapsed. The Western Gate leads to a modern trail down this side of the mountain (access via Arad only).

Adjoining the lower cable-car station is the Masada Museum, with hundreds of artifacts from the site. Especially moving is a set of 12 pottery shards, each bearing a single name. Archaeologists believe these might have been lots drawn to decide the order in which the last remaining rebels would die. All the artifacts are placed within scenes of daily life.

Continued on page 201

MASADA: DESERT FORTRESS

The isolated flattop rock of Masada commands the surrounding desert, its ancient remains bearing witness to long-ago power and conflict. One of Israel's most stunning archaeological sites, Masada earned fame and a place in history first as one of King Herod's opulent palace-fortresses and later as the site of the last stand of Jewish rebels against the legions of Rome, almost 2,000 years ago.

A KING'S PALACE

Surrounded by steep cliffs and with spectacular views of the Dead Sea and the desert, the Masada plateau offers nearly impregnable natural protection.

Herod the Great, the brilliant builder and paranoid leader who reigned over Israel as king of the Jews by the grace of the Roman Empire in the 1st century BC, developed the 18-acre site. Both for his relaxation and as a possible refuge from his enemies (including Cleopatra) and hostile subjects, Herod built atop Masada a fantastic, state-of-the-art complex of palaces, storehouses, and water systems.

THE REVOLT OF THE JEWS

Herod died around 4 BC, and the Jews rebelled against Rome in AD 66. By AD 70, the Roman Empire had destroyed Jerusalem and crushed the Jewish revolt there. Around AD 72, the last Jewish rebels took refuge at Masada. For at least a year, 960 Israelite men, women, and children lived here, protected from thousands of Roman soldiers by cliffs more than 1,400 feet high.

The Roman general and governor Flavius Silva, determined to end the rebellion, built eight legionnaire camps around the mountain. Silva's forces gradually erected an assault ramp on Masada's western side.

THE REBELS' "TERRIBLE RESOLVE"

According to a few survivors who related the story to the 1st-century historian Flavius Josephus, the night before the Romans reached Masada's walls, the rebel leader Elazar Ben-Yair gave a rallying speech. He reminded his community that they had resolved "neither to serve the Romans nor any other save God." After discussion, the Jews agreed to commit suicide rather than be taken captive.

The men drew lots to choose the ten who would kill the others. Those ten, having carried out "their terrible resolve," Josephus wrote, drew additional lots to select the one who would kill the other nine and then himself. When the Romans breached the walls the next morning, they found hundreds of corpses. The zealots' final action made the Roman victory at Masada a hollow one.

Although Josephus' physical description of Masada is accurate, some historians doubt his narrative. Several artifacts, including pottery shards bearing names (the lots, perhaps?), support the accuracy of Josephus' text, but no one can be sure what happened at the end. Masada continues to inspire debate.

TOURING MASADA'S TOP SIGHTS

Ride the cable car up Masada, hike the Snake Path, or walk the easier Ramp Path. Take in these highlights of Herod's buildings and the Jewish rebels' presence—and awesome desert views.

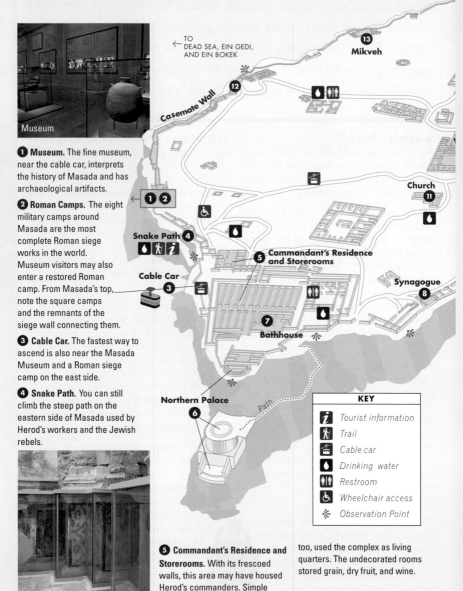

Museum

1 Museum. The fine museum, near the cable car, interprets the history of Masada and has archaeological artifacts.

2 Roman Camps. The eight military camps around Masada are the most complete Roman siege works in the world. Museum visitors may also enter a restored Roman camp. From Masada's top, note the square camps and the remnants of the siege wall connecting them.

3 Cable Car. The fastest way to ascend is also near the Masada Museum and a Roman siege camp on the east side.

4 Snake Path. You can still climb the steep path on the eastern side of Masada used by Herod's workers and the Jewish rebels.

Frescoed walls

TO DEAD SEA, EIN GEDI, AND EIN BOKEK

13 Mikveh

12

Casemate Wall

11 Church

Snake Path 4

5 Commandant's Residence and Storerooms

Cable Car

3

Synagogue 8

7

Bathhouse

Northern Palace

6

Path

KEY

𝑖	Tourist information
🚶	Trail
🚠	Cable car
💧	Drinking water
🚻	Restroom
♿	Wheelchair access
⚶	Observation Point

5 Commandant's Residence and Storerooms. With its frescoed walls, this area may have housed Herod's commanders. Simple ovens here indicate that the Jews, too, used the complex as living quarters. The undecorated rooms stored grain, dry fruit, and wine.

Water Cistern ⑭

Casemate Wall ⑫

Western Palace ⑩

Western gate ◆

Ramp path

⑨ **Roman Ramp**

Casemate Wall ⑫

TO ARAD →

Inauguration of the synagogue: blowing the shofar (2005)

Bathhouse

Roman Ramp on the western slopes of Masada

❼ **Bathhouse.** This spa on a desert cliff demonstrates Herod's grandiosity, his dedication to Roman culture, and the success of Masada's water systems. The building has cold and lukewarm baths, a sauna, frescoes, and tile work. Jewish rebels incorporated a ritual bath.

❽ **Synagogue.** Built into the wall, the synagogue is oddly shaped, but its benches and geniza (burial for damaged scrolls) indicate its function. Here, perhaps, the rebels agreed to die at their own hands. Today the synagogue is used for bar and bat mitzvahs.

❾ **Roman Ramp.** You can stand on the western edge where Romans breached Masada's defenses. The original ramp is below, as well as a modern path for walkers.

❿ **Western Palace.** Believed to have been an administrative base and a guest house, this palace retains frescoed walls and mosaics in Greek style; unusual for Herodian mosaics, one has a fruit motif.

⓫ **Church.** During the 5th to 7th centuries, monks lived at Masada, choosing it for its isolation. This 5th-century chapel is Byzantine in design, with mosaic floors.

⓬ **Casemate Wall.** Despite Masada's strategic advantages, Herod built a casemate (double-layered) wall around the oblong flattop rock, including offices and storerooms. The Jewish rebels used these rooms as dwellings.

⓭ **Mikveh.** In Jewish culture, the mikveh, or ritual bath, is a symbol of life and purity. Two found on Masada were built in accordance with Jewish laws still followed today. The presence of mikvehs indicates the rebels' religious piety.

⓮ **Water Cistern.** Like other cisterns at Masada, the southern cistern—into which you may descend—was built underground to prevent evaporation. Also make your way to see the spectacular canyon view to the south, and test the echoes.

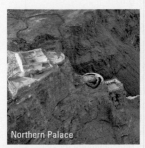

Northern Palace

❻ **Northern Palace.** Herod's personal living quarters is an extraordinary three-tiered structure that seems to hang from the cliffs. The amazing, terraced buildings feature colorful frescoes, Greek-inspired architecture, and Herod's personal bathhouse.

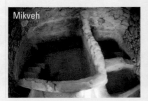

Mikveh

MAKING THE MOST OF YOUR VISIT

WHEN TO VISIT
The weather at Masada is fairly consistent year-round; it's hot during the day. Visit in the early morning or late afternoon, when the sun is weakest. ■TIP→ **It's popular to hike up before dawn via the Snake or Ramp Path, and watch the sun rise from behind Jordan and the Dead Sea. After 9 or 10 am, extreme heat may dictate that you use the cable car.**

WHAT TO WEAR AND BRING
Layered clothing is recommended, as cool early-morning temperatures rise to uncomfortable heat. Good walking shoes and hats or bandanas are musts. Free drinking water is available at Masada, but bring plenty to start with. Food is not sold atop the site. The museum cafeteria sells lunch after 11 am, Sunscreen and a camera are essential.

TIMING AND HIGHLIGHTS
Visiting Masada, a UNESCO World Heritage Site, can take three to seven hours, depending on your interest. The museum takes about an hour. Going up can take from three minutes (cable car) to sixty minutes (Snake Path). Your tour at the top might take ninety minutes or up to three hours.

The **Masada Museum**, near the cable car, offers an excellent combination of life-size scenes depicting the history of Masada; archaeological artifacts; and audio guide (available in English). Watch the short English-language film near the cable-car entrance. Atop Masada, many highlights

Cable car heading down from Masada

such as Herod's **Northern Palace** and the **bathhouse** are toward the site's northern end. On the sparser southern side, the views and echo point near the southern **water cistern** are notable.

OTHER THINGS TO DO
If you're traveling or staying overnight on the Dead Sea side, combine your excursion with a hike in **Ein Gedi** or a visit to a spa in **Ein Bokek**. You'll find plenty of hotels in Ein Bokek and its beaches are good for a float in the Dead Sea. Masada's western side has a seasonal sound-and-light show. For information, see www.parks.org.il.

THREE WAYS TO GET UP AND DOWN MASADA

On Masada's east side, the cable car takes only three minutes. The quickest way up, the **cable car** is convenient to the Masada Museum and a restored Roman siege camp. The long, steep Snake Path up the east side is an arduous but rewarding one-hour hike, recommended for visitors who are fit or determined to ascend Masada the same way the Jewish rebels did. Accessible from Arad on the west side, the **Ramp Path** is less grueling and takes fifteen to thirty minutes to ascend; it's equivalent to climbing about twenty flights of stairs.

Cooking pots at Masada

A fine summer-night diversion is the sound-and-light show at Masada's western base. The show runs every Tuesday and Thursday from March to October and costs NIS 45. ✉ *Off Rte. 3199, Ein Gedi* ☎ *08/658–4207/8* 🌐 *www.parks.org.il* 🎟 *NIS 31, entrance and round-trip cable car NIS 77, museum NIS 20.*

Hotels

Masada Hostel
$ | **B&B/INN** | This moderately priced hostel at the foot of Masada is the most convenient lodging for those intent on watching the spectacular sunrise over the Dead Sea; it has single, double, and family rooms, each with private bath. **Pros:** convenient to Masada; swimming pool; air-conditioned rooms. **Cons:** rowdy teenage groups; no evening entertainment; minimalist twin beds; plain decor. [$] *Rooms from: NIS 462* ✉ *Off Rte. 90, Ein Gedi* ✥ *At entrance to Masada* ☎ *08/995–3222* 🌐 *en.iyha.org.il* 🛏 *88 rooms* 🍴 *Breakfast.*

Arad

64 km (40 miles) south of Ein Gedi, 20 km (12½ miles) west of Masada, 25 km (15½ miles) west of Ein Bokek and the Dead Sea, 45 km (28 miles) east of Beersheva.

Breathe deeply: Arad sits 2,000 feet above sea level and is famous for its dry, pollution-free air and mild climate, ideal for asthma sufferers. The modern town was established by ex-kibbutzniks as a planned community in 1962 and today hosts a growing alternative music and art scene. Its population of nearly 25,000 now includes immigrants from Russia and Ethiopia, and until recently, Arad was home to acclaimed Israeli writer Amos Oz, who passed away in 2018.

Arad is often used as a base for excursions to sites in the Dead Sea area. It has an archaeological site and is near Yatir, one of the country's finest desert wineries. You can also take a stroll through the galleries and workshops of Eshet Lot, the artists' quarter.

GETTING HERE AND AROUND

Arad is accessible by Route 31; the city is 45 km (28 miles) east of Beersheva. From Ein Gedi, the trip is around an hour, starting from Route 90 south and continuing onto Route 31. Driving from Jerusalem by Route 40 takes about 2½ hours; avoid Route 60 and Hebron in the West Bank. Egged bus lines run to Arad from Beersheva, Tel Aviv, and Jerusalem.

VISITOR INFORMATION

CONTACTS Arad Tourism Department. ✉ *34 Chen St., inside Arad municipality* ☎ *08/995–1871* 🌐 *www.travelarad.com/en.*

Sights

Artists Quarter
LOCAL INTEREST | A handful of artist studios and other venues, including a brewery and a winery, fill what was once an industrial area on the outskirts of Arad. Explore glass-making at Heli Studio and soap-making at Yonat BaMidbar. Stop at Studio Coffee, on the ground floor of Zvi's Gallery, for a cup of coffee roasted on-site, a fresh smoothie, and a variety of creative sandwiches. On weekends, Casa Paniz offers homemade Middle Eastern food inside a wood-working studio. In addition, the Midbar winery offers tours and tastings for 50 shekels, while the Sheeta Brewery serves homemade beer and bar food. This area is more lively on the weekends, as many of the businesses are closed or have limited hours during the week. It is best to call ahead. ✉ *Artists Quarter, Sadan St.* ☎ *058/627–5976 Studio Coffee, 052/530–7616 Yonat BaMidbar, 08/899–2100 Midbar Winery, 052/665–0380 Sheeta Brewery, 050/665-2961 Heli Studio, 054/465–0629 Cafe Paniz.*

Tel Arad National Park
ARCHAEOLOGICAL SITE | FAMILY | The 250-acre site of the biblical city of Arad (to the northwest of the modern city) contains the remains of a major metropolis from the Bronze Age and the Israelite period. The lower city, with its meticulously planned streets and plazas, was inhabited in the Early Bronze Age (3150–2200 BC), when it was one of the largest cities in this region. Here you can walk around a walled urban community and enter the carefully reconstructed dwellings, whose style became known as the "Arad house."

After the Early Bronze Age, Arad was abandoned. The book of Numbers (21:1–3) relates that the Canaanite king of Arad battled the Israelites during the exodus from Egypt but that his cities were "utterly destroyed." The upper city was first settled in the Israelite period (1200 BC). It's worth the trek up the somewhat steep path to see the Israelite temple, a miniature version of Solomon's Temple in Jerusalem.

At the entrance, pick up a free pamphlet explaining the ongoing excavations and purchase a map of the Canaanite city of Arad, with its recommended walking route and diagrams of a typical Arad house. Tel Arad is 8 km (5 miles) west of Arad. At the Tel Arad Junction on Route 31, turn north on Route 80 for 3 km (2 miles). ✉ *Rte. 80* ☎ *08/699–2444* 🌐 *www.parks.org.il* 🎟 *NIS 14.*

Yatir Winery
WINERY/DISTILLERY | Near ancient Tel Arad, this boutique vineyard, now a subsidiary of Carmel Wines, was established in 2000. Yatir Forest (a Cabernet Sauvignon blend) is the premier label. The adjacent Yatir Forest, after which the winery is named, is the largest planted forest in Israel. A new visitor center offers views of the nearby desert vineyards and a larger area for tastings. Call ahead and speak to Smadar to arrange an appointment for a visit and tasting. ✉ *Rte. 80* ☎ *054/645–8725, 054/645–8871 Smadar, for tours* 🌐 *yatirwinery.com/en* 🎟 *NIS 45* 🕒 *Closed Sat.*

🍴 Restaurants

Aradika
$$ | ECLECTIC | Located in a complex that houses a youth center and technology college, this cozy restaurant and bar serves a variety of tasty food, from pizza to Pad Thai to burgers. It is popular with students as well as locals, and is one of the few places open late at night. **Known for:** evening local bar scene; outdoor courtyard seating; cool vibe. [$] *Average main: NIS 60* ✉ *16 Yoshiyahu St.* ☎ *08/615–1545.*

Kaparuchka
$ | ITALIAN | FAMILY | A neighborhood spot, this unpretentious pizzeria makes everything from scratch. The simple Italian fare is lovingly prepared by the owner-chefs, a young couple who made the trek back home from Tel Aviv. **Known for:** dill-and-ricotta calzones; local lunch crowds; evening beers. [$] *Average main: NIS 49* ✉ *Akhva 19* ☎ *08/860–6615* 🕒 *Closed Sat.*

Muza
$$ | MIDDLE EASTERN | Every inch of wall, ceiling, and bar real estate is plastered with the scarves of worldwide soccer teams at this beloved, more than 30-year-old roadside eatery on Route 31 at the entrance to Arad. Burgers are best here, served with spicy potato wedges and washed down with a large selection of Israeli and imported beers. **Known for:** friendly staff; cozy atmosphere; TV always showing soccer. [$] *Average main: NIS 55* ✉ *Rte. 31* ✥ *Near Alon gas station* ☎ *08/997–5555* 🌐 *www.muza-arad.co.il.*

🛏 Hotels

Desert Bird Guesthouse
$ | B&B/INN | FAMILY | Located in a residential neighborhood, this friendly

guesthouse has a large yard filled with giant cacti and palm trees, along with plenty of patio chairs and hammocks for lounging. **Pros:** friendly staff; relaxing atmosphere; beautiful grounds. **Cons:** no meals; small pool; books up quickly. [$] *Rooms from: NIS 300* ✉ *28 Bareket* ☎ *052/595–8833* 🌐 *www.desertbird.co.il* 🛏 *4 rooms* 🍴 *No meals.*

Kfar HaNokdim
$$$$ | RESORT | FAMILY | This expansive educational resort located in a desert valley outside Arad includes stand-alone stone rooms, luxurious tents, simple group tents, and the option to set up your own tent. **Pros:** scenery; quiet; interesting guided tours and activities. **Cons:** no public transportation; can get hot in the summer and cold in the winter; no pool. [$] *Rooms from: NIS 970* ✉ *Rte. 3199* ✥ *Follow Moab St. out of Arad, turn left on Odem St., then left on Tsor St., which turns into Rte 3199. Kfar HaNokdim is on your left in about 15 min.* ☎ *08/995–0097* 🌐 *kfarhanokdim.co.il* 🛏 *60 rooms* 🍴 *All-inclusive.*

★ Yehelim Boutique Hotel
$$ | B&B/INN | The main terrace and every room of this luxurious, award-winning small hotel face the desert. **Pros:** lovely views; friendly staff; delicious breakfast. **Cons:** books up fast; no pool; no spa. [$] *Rooms from: $230* ✉ *72 Moav St.* ☎ *052/652–2718* 🌐 *www.yehelim.com* 🛏 *12 rooms* 🍴 *Free Breakfast.*

Shopping

Adi Miraro Jewelry
JEWELRY/ACCESSORIES | Local artist Adi Miraro makes necklaces, earrings, watches, and other jewelry from gold and silver, often intricately decorated with colorful beads and semiprecious gem stones. Adi, who began making jewelry from string as a young girl, also makes custom-designed items and is usually at the store to help you pick out the perfect gift or treat for yourself. ✉ *19 Achva St.* ☎ *52/408–5577* 🌐 *www.adimirarojewelry.com* 🕒 *Closed Sat.*

Activities

★ Windows to the Desert
ART GALLERIES—ARTS | Dozens of local artists, chefs, and other makers in Arad open their homes to visitors for meals, performances, and workshops. Among those offering activities in English are Amos and Ronit Redlich, whose house includes an art gallery. Amos, a sculptor, and Ronit, an author of children's books, talk about how the desert and the city of Arad provide inspiration for their work. There are also light refreshments. **■ TIP→ Visiting local families requires making arrangements in advance. Contact Amos to arrange a visit to his home or with other participants with Windows to the Desert.** ✉ *Arad* ☎ *053/773–7562 Amos Redlich* 🌐 *www.facebook.com/windowstothedesert.*

Ein Bokek

40 km (25 miles) east of Arad, 8 km (5 miles) north of Zohar–Arad Junction on Rte. 90.

The sudden and startling sight, in this bare landscape, of gleaming, ultramodern hotels surrounded by waving palm trees signals your arrival at the spa-resort area of Ein Bokek, near the southern tip of the Dead Sea. According to the Bible, it was along these shores that the Lord rained fire and brimstone on the people of Sodom and Gomorrah (Genesis 19:24) and turned Lot's wife into a pillar of salt (Genesis 26). Here, at the lowest point on Earth, the hot, sulfur-pungent air hangs heavy, and a haze often shimmers over the water. You can float, but you can't sink, in the warm, salty water.

Once upon a time, Ein Bokek comprised a handful of hotels, each with a small "spa," and a pebbly beach out front. Today, it's a collection of large resorts with curvy pools, rooftop solariums, and landscaped outdoor areas. While the downsides of many hotels are the outdated decor and buffet-style dining options, the pools and state-of-the-art spas are a welcome relief from the often sweltering heat on the rocky Dead Sea beaches. There are no full-service restaurants outside the hotels, although a few casual eating places are along the beach and in two tiny shopping centers. The central cluster of hotels is linked by a promenade to two hotels at the southern end of the area.

GETTING HERE AND AROUND
To drive to Ein Bokek from Jerusalem, take Route 1 eastbound, marked Jericho–Dead Sea. At the Dead Sea, take Route 90 south, passing Qumran, Ein Gedi, and Masada, until you reach Ein Bokek. From Arad, head southeast on Route 31 and continue onto Route 90 north. Egged buses run between Jerusalem and Ein Bokek several times a day. The trip is 1½ hours.

Sights

Arava Road
SCENIC DRIVE | Traversing the Arava Valley from Ein Bokek to Eilat, the 177-km (111-mile) Route 90 parallels the Israel-Jordan border, almost touching it at some points. To the east rise the spiky, red-brown mountains of Moab, in Jordan. The road follows an ancient route mentioned in biblical descriptions of the journeys of the Children of Israel.

The *Arava* (meaning "wilderness") is part of the Great Rift Valley, the deep fissure in the earth stretching from Turkey to East Africa, the result of an ancient shift of landmasses. Just south of Ein Bokek, you pass signs for the communities Neot HaKikar and Ein Tamar (home to many metalwork and jewelry artists), whose date palms draw water from underground springs rather than irrigation.

With the Edom Mountains rising in the east, the road continues along the southern Dead Sea valley, where you cross one of the largest dry riverbeds in the Negev, Nahal Zin, and pass several sprawling date orchards that belong to neighboring kibbutzim. ⊠ *Ein Bokek.*

Hotels

Daniel Dead Sea Hotel
$$ | RESORT | At this upscale lodging, an undulating front wall swirls around a huge flower-shape pool. **Pros:** lovely pool; all-inclusive option; video games for kids. **Cons:** outdated decor; staff can be brusque. Ⓢ *Rooms from: $219* ⊠ *Off Rte. 90* ☎ *08/668–9999* ⊕ *www.tamareshotels.com/daniel_dead_sea* ➴ *300 rooms* ⦿ *Free Breakfast.*

David Dead Sea Resort and Spa
$$ | RESORT | Reached via a trail of baby palm trees, Ein Bokek's largest hotel stands out for its cavernous lobby, wonderful views, delightful spa, and endless swimming pool. **Pros:** lovely rooms; pretty grounds; option to include all meals in the price. **Cons:** up a steep hill; can seem immense and impersonal; inconsistent service. Ⓢ *Rooms from: $236* ⊠ *Off Rte. 90* ☎ *08/659–1234* ⊕ *www.david-deadsea.com* ➴ *600 rooms* ⦿ *Free Breakfast.*

★ Herods Dead Sea
$$ | RESORT | On the Dead Sea beach is this palatial hotel, decorated in relaxing blues, teals, and grays to echo the natural landscape. **Pros:** on the beach; gleaming furnishings; good food. **Cons:** pricey. Ⓢ *Rooms from: $236* ⊠ *Off Rte. 90* ☎ *08/659–1591* ⊕ *www.fattal-hotels.com* ➴ *223 rooms* ⦿ *Free Breakfast.*

★ Isrotel Dead Sea Resort and Spa
$$$ | RESORT | Walk into the nine-story Isrotel and look to your left at the gorgeous wooden wall carved with date palms and fruit; this hotel puts an emphasis on being a part of the natural world. **Pros:** sparkling pool; beer on tap for dinner; good business lounge. **Cons:**

across the sometimes blisteringly hot street from the Dead Sea; in summer, can be overrun with kids; service can be brusque. $ *Rooms from: $373* ⊠ *Off Rte. 90* ☎ *08/668–9666* ⊕ *www.isrotel.com* ⇆ *296 rooms* ⎟⊙⎟ *Free Breakfast.*

Isrotel Ganim

$$ | RESORT | Compared to some of the palatial resorts of Ein Bokek, Isrotel Ganim is a smaller and less expensive property distinguished by a lobby of vintage furniture and loads of large windows overlooking the Dead Sea. Rooms are average in size, and some of the third-floor ones have balconies. **Pros:** spa; every room faces the Dead Sea; two Dead Sea–water pools at different temperatures; meal plans include one for all meals. **Cons:** small gym; private Dead Sea beach across the street requires golf cart on hot days; room decor is uninspired. $ *Rooms from: $220* ⊠ *Off Rte. 90* ☎ *08/668–9090* ⊕ *www.isrotel. com/isrotel-ganim* ⇆ *200 rooms* ⎟⊙⎟ *Free Breakfast.*

Leonardo Club Dead Sea

$$ | RESORT | FAMILY | Bring the whole family to this all-inclusive property, where adults can enjoy a midnight supper or the spa and kids can cool off with ice pops around the clock. **Pros:** the area's only all-inclusive hotel; excellent kids' programs; nice views; on the beach. **Cons:** small rooms; drab entry; noisy lobby; many children. $ *Rooms from: $203* ⊠ *Off Rte. 90* ☎ *08/668–9444* ⊕ *www.fattal-hotels.com* ⇆ *388 rooms* ⎟⊙⎟ *All-inclusive.*

The Royal Hotel

$$ | RESORT | FAMILY | Within walking distance of the newly revamped public beach, promenade, and shopping mall, this sleek and modern hotel offers a great spa and comfortable rooms with views of the Dead Sea and surrounding desert. **Pros:** great location; beautiful outdoor pool; balconies with views in all rooms. **Cons:** outdoor pool closed in winter; no private beach; dining area

can get crowded. $ *Rooms from: $238* ⊠ *Off Rte. 90* ☎ *08/668–8555* ⊕ *royal. deadseahotel.co.il* ⇆ *400 rooms* ⎟⊙⎟ *Free Breakfast.*

🛍 Shopping

Several companies manufacture excellent Dead Sea skin and beauty products made from mud, salts, and minerals; the actual mud is sold in squishy, leak-proof packages. Ahava and Jericho are popular brands sold at the shopping centers of Ein Bokek and shops in most hotels.

Dead Sea Diamond Center

JEWELRY/ACCESSORIES | Unique, handcrafted jewelry by Israeli designers is sold at this establishment just outside the David Dead Sea Resort and Spa. Call for a free shuttle to pick you up. ⊠ *Rte. 90* ☎ *08/995–8777.*

🏃 Activities

The beaches of Ein Bokek have recently been renovated, and feature modern and clean facilities, including numerous restrooms, changing rooms, showers, playgrounds, and drinking fountains. Most also have lifeguards. Some have free shaded areas under pavilions and umbrellas, but many beaches require a small charge for using a lounge chair and umbrella. A new promenade connects the beaches as well as the two main hotel areas of Ein Bokek and Neve Zohar. The promenade, which also includes many shaded seating areas, is a great place for walking, running, or cycling while taking in the views of the Dead Sea and surrounding mountains. It is also well-lit at night, which is the best time for a walk during the scorching summer season.

Dead Sea Divers

DIVING/SNORKELING | In the sea where everyone floats, diving requires lots of weights just to keep you below the surface. Under the sea is another world of rocky, white salt crystals. A day's training and diving costs NIS 2,400. Avi Bresler picks you up from your hotel in Ein Bokek. ✉ *Ein Bokek* ☎ *077/710–9100* ⊕ *deadseadivers.com.*

Abu Gosh

11 km (7 miles) west of Jerusalem on Rte. 1.

The Arab village of Abu Gosh is said to be the biblical site of Kiryat Yearim, where the Ark of the Covenant rested for 20 years, out of the reach of the Israelites (1 Samuel 7:2). In modern times, Abu Gosh is better known as the national capital of hummus, that lemony chickpea spread ubiquitous around the Middle East. Jerusalem's secular Jews flock to Abu Gosh on weekends to escape the religious Sabbath with hummus and water pipes. But it's not all escapism: Abu Gosh retains a spiritual quality, with Crusader-era churches and a recently built mega-mosque bankrolled by the Islamic Republic of Chechnya. These religious buildings provide an evocative background for the village's annual summer music festival.

GETTING HERE AND AROUND

Coming from Jerusalem, Abu Gosh is easily accessible via Route 1. There are no good public transportation options.

◉ Sights

Our Lady of the Ark of the Covenant Church

RELIGIOUS SITE | Built in 1924, this church is said to be on the site where the Ark of the Covenant remained for 20 years in the ancient town of Kiryat Yearim. A statue of Mary holding Jesus in her arms towers above the church and can be seen across the village. The Byzantines built a church on the same site in the 5th century, and pieces of floor mosaic and other telltale leftovers give this church a patina far richer than its age. The church

is located on the property of the Notre Dame Arche D'Alliance monastery and is surrounded by gardens offering views of the village below. There is a gift shop selling rosaries, olive-wood carvings of Mary, and other religious objects. You need to ring the bell at the main gate of the monastery complex to enter, even during visiting hours. ✉ *1 Notre Dame St.* ☎ *02/534–2818* ⏱ *Closed Sun. Closed daily between 11:30 am and 2:30 pm.*

St. Mary of the Resurrection Benedictine Abbey

RELIGIOUS SITE | The Crusaders believed that Abu Gosh was the site where Jesus revealed himself after his resurrection, and in the 12th century they built this Benedictine monastery to commemorate the event. Parts of it still stand today, with magnificent frescoes covering the walls and a small stream bubbling out of the underground crypt. Here you can see some of the best-preserved Crusader architecture in the country. There is still a religious community here: try to visit during prayers, which are recited in Gregorian chant. ✉ *3 Mahmoud Rashid St.* ☎ *02/534–2798* ⏱ *Closed Sun. except for services. Closed daily between 11 am and 2:30 pm.*

🍴 Restaurants

Abu Ghosh Restaurant

$$ | MIDDLE EASTERN | Jawdat Ibrahim won the Illinois state lottery in 1991 and plowed his earnings back into his village, creating a local restaurant as well as a scholarship fund for Arab and Jewish students. Jawdat was the driving force behind Israel's Guinness World Record for the largest plate of hummus, served on a satellite dish; taste the hummus yourself at his restaurant, along with freshly cut salads, tasty bean soup, stuffed vine leaves, and juicy meat skewers. There are stunning views of the village from large windows or outdoor seating on the balcony. **Known for:** stuffed grape leaves; stunning views;

homemade sweets. $ *Average main: NIS 65* ✉ *Hashalom 65* ☎ *02/533–2019.*

Efrat Bakery

$$ | **CAFÉ** | **FAMILY** | This cute bakery in Kibbutz Kiryat Anavim near Abu Gosh serves sandwiches, salads, and breakfast along with a wide variety of breads, cakes, and cookies, all baked on-site. There is seating in a large, chic concrete-floored dining area with glass walls offering views of the surrounding gardens and hills. **Known for:** picnic provisions; garden seating; local family hangout. $ *Average main: NIS 50* ✉ *Kiryat Anavim, Kiryat Anavim* ☎ *02/673–5529* ⊗ *Closed Sat.*

Hummus Abu Shukri

$ | **MIDDLE EASTERN** | This popular hummus joint is also the village's oldest, and started out as two tables in Samir Abu Shukri's home in 1965 (now his grandson, Fadi, is the restaurant's third-generation manager). Grab a table by the large windows and look out at the towering mosque minarets in the village while enjoying big plates of hummus served with fresh pita. **Known for:** meat-topped hummus; great views; relaxed atmosphere. $ *Average main: NIS 30* ✉ *63 Derech Hashalom* ☎ *052/233–0399.*

Naji Restaurant

$$ | **MIDDLE EASTERN** | **FAMILY** | People from near and far seek out this casual eatery for its excellent kebabs, made from ground beef and lamb, along with plenty of parsley. Opened in 1936, the family-owned restaurant also offers a large menu of grilled meats, salads, and desserts made in its nearby bakery. **Known for:** sweeping views; quality service; local lunch crowd. $ *Average main: NIS 60* ✉ *4 Mahmud Rashid* ☎ *02/533–6520.*

Naya Asian Mountain Restaurant

$$$ | **ASIAN** | Located inside Moshav Beit Nekofa outside Abu Gosh, this large modern restaurant is a great place for a leisurely lunch or indulgent dinner after a day of hiking on nearby trails or exploring archaeological ruins. The main dining area includes an open kitchen, plenty of high windows, and pots full of orchids. **Known for:** sushi; ginger lemonade; sleek interior design. $ *Average main: NIS 85* ✉ *Shvil Halulim* ☎ *02/990–0070* ⊕ *na-ya. com* ⊗ *Closed Fri. and before sundown on Sat.*

🛏 Hotels

There are some very good kibbutz guesthouses in the wooded enclaves of the Judean Hills, a 15- to 20-minute drive west of Jerusalem. All have commanding hilltop views, quiet surroundings, very comfortable if not luxurious accommodations, and good swimming pools.

C Hotel Neve Ilan

$ | **HOTEL** | **FAMILY** | A cut above its neighbors, this hotel has spacious, nicely furnished rooms, a sparkling heated pool, and a well-equipped exercise room. **Pros:** panoramic views; children's activities; choice of meal plans. **Cons:** gym and pool are at nearby sports facility; inattentive staff; gets crowded on weekends. $ *Rooms from: NIS 700* ✉ *North of Rte. 1, Neve Ilan* ✛ *15 km (10 miles) west of Jerusalem* ☎ *03/919–0669* ⊕ *www.c-hotels.co.il* ⇥ *174 rooms* ⦿ *Free Breakfast.*

★ Cramim Spa & Wine Hotel

$$$ | **HOTEL** | The name of this hotel, part of the Isrotel chain, translates to "vineyards," and grapes are the inspiration for every facet of this spa hotel set in the beautiful Jerusalem hills. **Pros:** serene, gorgeous setting; fantastic spa treatments; great food. **Cons:** books up months in advance; small swimming pools; staff can be brusque. $ *Rooms from: $324* ✉ *Off Rte. 425, Kiryat Anavim* ☎ *02/548–9800* ⊕ *www.isrotel.com* ⇥ *156 rooms* ⦿ *Free Breakfast.*

Hotel Tzuba

$ | **HOTEL** | **FAMILY** | Great views, delicious brunches, and a nearby Galita chocolate factory offering children's workshops make this hotel a great choice for families. **Pros:** great place for young children; interesting tours; panoramic views. **Cons:** no evening entertainment; meals eaten in the kibbutz dining hall; minimum stays during holiday seasons and August. [$] *Rooms from: $179* ✉ *Rte. 39, Tzuba* ✣ *12 km (7½ miles) west of Jerusalem* ☎ *02/534–7000* 🌐 *www.tzubahotel.co.il/en* 🛏 *65 rooms* 🍴 *Free Breakfast.*

Ye'arim Hotel

$$ | **HOTEL** | This large guesthouse, spread over beautifully landscaped gardens, is ideal for nature lovers and families. **Pros:** panoramic views and parklike setting; sunlit indoor pool; free calls to the United States from lobby. **Cons:** can get crowded with tour groups or families; older wings are in dire need of renovation; some small rooms. [$] *Rooms from: $205* ✉ *Rte. 1, Maaleh Hahamisha* ✣ *14 km (9 miles) west of Jerusalem* ☎ *02/533–1331* 🌐 *eng.yearimhotel.com* 🛏 *230 rooms* 🍴 *Free Breakfast.*

Shopping

Ikar Haaretz

FOOD/CANDY | Three siblings from Moshav Beit Nekofa have turned an old chicken coop into a store selling products from the surrounding countryside, along with a café serving sandwiches, salads, pasta, and other dishes made with local ingredients. Stop here to buy locally made wine, beer, cheeses, baked goods, jars of honey, and produce from many of the farms in the Judean Hills. Enjoy breakfast, lunch, or dinner here, complete with live music on Thursday night. Or, pick up lunch or picnic provisions to take the nearby Ein Hemed or Castel national parks. ✉ *3 Shvil Halulim, Beit Nekofa, Kiryat Anavim* ☎ *02/545–3397* ⏲ *Closed Sat.*

Latrun

14 km (8 miles) west of Abu Gosh, 25 km (16 miles) west of Jerusalem on Rte. 1.

Latrun is the ridge that projects into and dominates the western side of the Ayalon Valley. A natural passage between the coastal plain and the Judean Hills, the strategic valley has served as a battleground throughout history, from the conquests of the biblical Israelite leader Joshua in the 13th century BC, through the Hasmonean campaigns of the 2nd century BC, to the bloody defeat of the newly established Israel Defense Force by Jordan's Arab Legion in 1948. Today, the Trappist monastery is known for its olive oil and wine, and Mini Israel is a favorite for children of all ages.

GETTING HERE AND AROUND

Coming from Jerusalem on Route 1, exit onto Route 3 (the Modi'in and Ashkelon–Beersheva road), about 5 km (3 miles) west of the Sha'ar Hagai gas station. At the T-junction, turn left for the Trappist Abbey of Latrun, the Latrun Armored Corps Museum, and Mini Israel. There are no good public transportation options.

Sights

Domaine du Castel

WINERY/DISTILLERY | This vineyard consistently produces some of the country's best wines. The small winery, with its exquisite cellar, runs tours and tastings of wine and cheese. ✉ *Rte. 4115, Yad Hashmona* ☎ *02/535–8555* 🌐 *www.castel.co.il* 🎟 *Tour and tasting NIS 130* ⏲ *Closed Fri. afternoon and Sat. By appointment only.*

Latrun Armored Corps Museum

MUSEUM | **FAMILY** | The name Latrun is thought to derive from "La Toron de Chevaliers" (the Tower of the Knights), the French name of the Crusader castle that occupied the crest of the hill in the 12th century. Eight centuries later, in 1940, the British erected the concrete

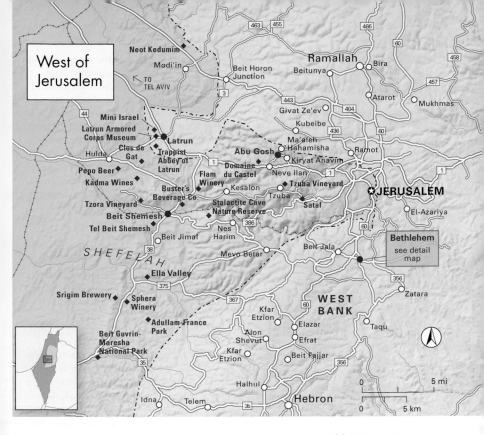

West of Jerusalem

fortress that today holds the museum. In the 1948 War of Independence, Israeli forces attempted five times to capture the fortress from Jordanian soldiers. The names of 142 Israeli soldiers who fell in these unsuccessful attempts are engraved on the walls. There are more than 100 assorted antique and modern tanks on which children love to climb. ⊠ *Rte. 3 ✛ 1 km (½ mile) south of Rte. 1* ☎ *08/630–7400* ⊕ *www.yadlashiryon. com* ⌚ *NIS 30.*

★ Mini Israel

AMUSEMENT PARK/WATER PARK | FAMILY |
One of the most popular attractions in Israel, this theme park spreads over 13 acres and contains nearly 400 models of the most important historical, national, religious, and natural sites in the country, all scaled down to 1:25. Worth at least an hour's visit, it is especially fun for children. About 25,000 miniature "residents" have been meticulously created to present not just the physical, but also the cultural, religious, and social aspects of contemporary Israel. A walk through the park—along with a 3-D film about Israel—lets you see and hear the people of different faiths and cultures that make up the country's human landscape. ⊠ *Rte. 424* ☎ *700/559–559* ⊕ *www. minisrael.co.il/en* ⌚ *NIS 69.*

↗ Neot Kedumim

At Israel's only Biblical Landscape Reserve, paved paths wind around ancient olive terraces, bushes of sage and hyssop, and millennia-old winepresses. The name of the site means "Oases of Antiquity." Show yourself around well-planned trails with the help of the available English map, or take a guided tour, available only to groups of 20 people or more, to fully appreciate the threshing floors, the Dale of the Song of Songs, and the Valley of Milk and Honey. Tours focus on Jewish, Christian, or interfaith themes. Ask about Biblical meals as well. Allow two hours minimum for the visit. ⊠ *Rte. 443 ✛ 20 km (12 miles) north of Latrun* ☎ *08/977–0777* ⊕ *www.neot-kedumim.org.il* ✉ *NIS 25* ⊙ *Closed Sat.*

Pepo Beer

WINERY/DISTILLERY | Moti Bohadana named his brewery for his father and the eight beers for all the women in his life. Elisheva, named after his grandmother, is a bitter, hoppy IPA. Tamara is a red, flowery ale and Tirza is an Irish stout. There's also hard apple and cherry cider. Call ahead about visits and occasional music events held Thursday nights, or to reserve a table at unlimited Friday brunch for NIS 60 per person. To get here from Latrun, take Route 3 toward Ashkelon and turn left on Route 44. Follow signs for the Navot Winery. ⊠ *49 Hate'ena St., Tzlafon* ☎ *054/530–4576, 02/999–2291* ⊕ *tour-yehuda.org.il/1216/* ⊙ *Closed Sat.*

★ Sataf

FARM/RANCH | **FAMILY** | Just outside Jerusalem, Sataf was one of many Arab villages that were abandoned in the 1948 War of Independence. You can hike here on well-marked trails amid ancient terraces shaded with pine, fig, and almond trees. Hikes last two or four hours and pass springs where you can get your feet wet. On weekends, follow the pictures of goats to get to Shai Seltzer, who raises goats in the forest and ages unique and delicious cheese in an old Byzantine cave. You can walk to Sataf from Ein Kerem in about an hour. ⊠ *Sataf Junction, Intersection of Rtes. 395 and 3965, Sataf* ☎ *054/440–3762 Seltzer farm* ⊕ *www.goat-cheese.co.il* ✉ *Free.*

Trappist Abbey of Latrun

RELIGIOUS SITE | Trappist monks have been producing wine here since the 1890s. The interior of the 19th-century abbey is an odd mix of round neo-Byzantine

arches and apses and the soaring ceiling that seems Gothic in inspiration. Survivors of the Cistercian Order suppressed in the French Revolution, the Trappists keep a vow of silence. But the staff of the shop, which sells wine, olive oil, and other items made on-site, chats with you in English, French, Hebrew, or Arabic, and offers wine-tastings. The setting in the foothills is lovely. ⊠ *Rte. 3 ✛ 2 km (1 mile) off Rte. 1* ☎ *08/922–0065* ⊕ *www.holy-wine.com* ✉ *Free* ⊙ *Closed Sun.*

🍴 Restaurants

Elvis Inn

$$ | **DINER** | **FAMILY** | At the edge of the gas station by Neve Ilan, this American-style diner has the largest collection of Elvis memorabilia this side of Graceland, including 1,700 photos, two statues that tower outside, and three inside. Grab some classic American food like burgers and fries, or stay local and order hummus. **Known for:** burgers; Elvis impersonators; Americana souvenir shop. $ *Average main: NIS 55* ⊠ *Rte. 4115, Neve Ilan* ☎ *02/534–1275* ⊙ *No dinner Fri. and Sat.*

★ Rama's Kitchen

$$$ | **ISRAELI** | Chef Rama Ben Zvi combines local cheeses and vegetables with wild herbs gathered from as far away as the Dead Sea for a meal that could easily last hours amid the gorgeous Judean Hills. The menu changes at this spot open only a couple of days a week, but the beet hummus is outstanding, and grilled lamb ribs served on bulgur wheat with tomato chutney are delightful. **Known for:** coriander cocktails; seasonal menu; weekend hangout. $ *Average main: NIS 95* ⊠ *Off Rte. 1, Nataf* ☎ *02/570–0954* ⊕ *ramakitchen.co.il* ⊙ *Closed Sun.–Wed.*

Shvilim

$$$ | **MEDITERRANEAN** | **FAMILY** | Located in the cooperative agricultural community of Tal Shahar, this restaurant offers a vegetarian menu, including fish, pasta, salads,

Wineries in the Judean Hills

For years, good Israeli wine was an oxymoron, but the days of producing only sweet sacramental wines are long gone. In the past few decades, a viniculture revolution has yielded an abundance of wines that easily compete against those from older vineyards. The Judean Hills area is now home to more than two dozen vineyards, the majority of them close to Route 38, north and south of Beit Shemesh. Since most vineyards are "boutique"—producing fewer than 100,000 bottles per year—few have visitor centers that encourage drop-in visits or have regularly scheduled tours, so be sure to call ahead if you want to visit. The wineries are convenient to Tel Aviv (40 minutes away) as well as Jerusalem (about 20 minutes) so you can easily make a day trip. Every October, the area's more than 20 wineries sponsor a wine festival; the venue usually changes.

and sandwiches. The indoor seating area is spacious with high ceilings and rustic wooden rafters, and the tables on the large outdoor deck offer views of the surrounding rolling hills, vineyards, olive groves, and horses. **Known for:** scrumptious breakfast; goat cheese; popular wedding venue. $ *Average main: NIS 90* ✉ *Tal Shahar* ✢ *From Latrun Junction, continue west on Rte. 3, then make left into Moshav Tal Shahar, near Dor Alon gas station; make left into parking lot* ☎ *077/360–9060* ⊙ *Closed Sat.*

Yad Hashmona Restaurant
$$$ | EUROPEAN | Finnish Christians built this moshav, a kind of cooperative farm, outside Jerusalem with pine beams imported from home, lending a Scandinavian setting to the famously abundant Friday brunch of salads, cheeses, quiche, and fish (NIS 110 per person). The moshav is called Yad Hashmona, or "memorial to the eight," to atone for the Finnish government's turning over of eight Jewish fellow countrymen to the Nazis. **Known for:** Holocaust history; fresh focaccia bread; Bible-inspired gardens. $ *Average main: NIS 80* ✉ *Off Rte. 1, Yad Hashmona* ☎ *02/594–2004* ⊕ *www. yadha8.co.il* ⊙ *Closed Sat.–Thurs. No dinner Fri.*

Beit Shemesh

16 km (10 miles) south of Latrun, 35 km (22 miles) west of Jerusalem.

The modern town of Beit Shemesh, Hebrew for "House of the Sun," takes its name from an ancient city now entombed by the tell on a rise on Route 38, 2 km (1 mile) south of the main entrance. Nearby are a number of wineries and breweries worth exploring.

This is Samson country. Samson, one of the judges of Old Testament Israel, is better known for his physical prowess and lust for Philistine women than for his shining spiritual qualities, but it was here, "between Tzorah and Eshta'ol," that "the Spirit of the Lord began to stir him" (Judges 13). Today, Eshta'ol is a moshav (a cooperative settlement composed of individual farms) a few minutes' drive north, and Tzora is the wine-producing kibbutz immediately to the west.

GETTING HERE AND AROUND
Follow Route 1 west from Jerusalem, then head south on Route 38 to Beit Shemesh. Israel Railways provides regular train service between Jerusalem and Tel Aviv via Beit Shemesh every two hours from 7 am to 7 pm.

⊙ Sights

Buster's Beverage Co.

WINERY/DISTILLERY | Californian Denny Neilson and his son, Matthew, brew beer, alcoholic apple cider, and hard lemonade in Beit Shemesh. The brewery is named for the family dog; the cider—dry or sweet—is crisp and delicious. The visitor center offers tastings, and sells the bottled beverages along with home-brewing equipment. Free factory tours are offered at 11, noon, and 1 pm on Friday, but require advance booking online. Group tours are also available during the week, by appointment. ⊠ Nacham Industrial Park ⊕ Off Rte. 38 ☎ 054/638–1103 ⊕ www.busters. co.il ⌦ Tasting flights are 30 shekels ⊙ Closed Sat.–Mon.

★ Clos de Gat

WINERY/DISTILLERY | Winemaker Eyal Rotem puts a premium on quality at this boutique estate winery that produces 90,000 bottles a year. While it's not kosher, the winery prides itself on its participation in ancient and modern Jewish history: it houses a 3,000-year-old-winepress and during the 1948 war served as the base for Itzhak Rabin and his Har'el Brigades. Many Clos de Gat wines age beautifully, including the Sycra series, which has garnered international accolades. The tour and tasting fee is deductible with the purchase of six bottles. ⊠ Har'el Vineyards, Rte. 44 ☎ 02/999–3505 ⊕ closdegat.com ⌦ Tours and tastings NIS 100 ⊙ Closed Sat. Other days, by appointment only.

★ Flam Winery

WINERY/DISTILLERY | Family-owned, this well-regarded winery sources grapes from the Judean Hills and the Upper Galilee. Many of its bottles, including the Bordeaux blend called The Noble, have garnered international praise for their complexity. Wine-and-cheese tastings are held by appointment only at an elegantly rustic communal table indoors, or outside on a wooden deck overlooking the vineyards that are surrounded by pine forests. ⊠ Yaar Hakodshim, Eshtaol, Rte. 38 ☎ 02/992–9923, 054/211–3324 Mireia (for appointments) ⊕ flamwinery.com ⌦ Tasting from NIS 70, by appointment only ⊙ Closed Sat.

Kadma Wines

WINERY/DISTILLERY | Born in the Republic of Georgia, former software engineer Lina Slutzkin remembers how wine was once made there in egg-shape clay casks. At Kadma Wines, she uses these unusual vessels to produce a range of red wines. Tours run every hour from 11 to 2 on Friday and Saturday, but fill up fast, so a reservation is recommended. Tastings are also available during these hours, or on other days by appointment only. There is a small food menu of cheeses, smoked fish, roasted vegetables and other dishes to go along with the wine tastings. ⊠ Rte. 44, 14½ km (9 miles) northwest of Beit Shemesh, Kfar Uriya ☎ 02/992–7894, 054/919–5156 ⊕ www.kadma-wine.co.il ⌦ Tastings are NIS 45 or 75 shekels; reservation required.

Stalactite Cave Nature Reserve

CAVE | FAMILY | On the western slopes of the Judean Hills, the Stalactite Cave, also called Soreq Cave, contains a wondrous variety of stalactites and stalagmites. The 300,000-year-old cave was discovered in 1968 when a routine blast in the nearby Har-Tuv quarry tore away the rock face, revealing a subterranean wonderland.

Lights are used to highlight the natural whites and honey browns of the stones. Local guides have given the stalactite forms nicknames like "macaroni," "curtains," and "sombreros." Despite the high humidity, the temperature in the cave is comfortable year-round.

There are 150 steps down to the cave, but special arrangements can be made for those with mobility concerns to enter by a nearby road, avoiding the steps.

Entry is only with a 45-minute guided tour, which leaves at least every 30 minutes. Photography is allowed only at the discretion of the guides. English language tours are offered daily at 11 am and one hour before closing; it is recommended to arrive at least 20 minutes before the English tour. There are no English tours on weekends or holidays. An English-language video explains how the cave was formed. ⊠ *Rte. 3866, Avshalom Nature Reserve* ☎ *02/991–1117* ⊕ *www. parks.org.il* ✉ *NIS 28.*

Tel Beit Shemesh

ARCHAEOLOGICAL SITE | This low-profile archaeological site has fine views of the fields of Nahal Soreq, where Samson dallied with Delilah (Judges 16). When the Philistines captured the Israelite Ark of the Covenant in battle (11th century BC), they found that their prize brought divine retribution with it, destroying their idol Dagon and afflicting their bodies with tumors and cities with rats (I Samuel 5). The Philistines rid themselves of the jinxed ark by sending it back to the Israelites at Beit Shemesh. The stone ruins of the tell—including the oldest iron workshop in the world—are hard to interpret without an archaeologist on hand. ⊠ *Rte. 38, 2 km (1 mile) from Tzora turnoff* ✉ *Free.*

Tzora Vineyard

WINERY/DISTILLERY | Overlooking the Soreq Valley, this kibbutz winery sells and serves reds and whites, including their Shoresh red blend of single-vineyard Cabernet Sauvignon, Syrah, and Merlot. Tastings, which must be booked in advance, include sampling of several kinds of wine, as well as local bread, cheese, and olives. The winemaker also explains the unique soil of the area and the history of the winery. Those who purchase five bottles get an additional one free. ⊠ *Rte. 3835* ☎ *02/990–8261* ⊕ *www.tzorawines. com* ✉ *Tasting NIS 75* ⊗ *Closed Sat.*

Tzuba Vineyard

WINERY/DISTILLERY | Part of the eponymous kibbutz, this winery produces excellent Cabernet Sauvignon, Syrah, and Chardonnay. Call winemaker Paul Dubb to coordinate a visit for a tasting or a tour, and make sure to order a platter of local cheeses to go along with your wine-tasting when making a reservation Tours also explore the nearby vineyards and ancient winepresses that dot the area. The visitor center is open daily, except for Saturday, and it is also possible to drop in for a wine-tasting, but reservations are recommended. ⊠ *Rte. 395, Tzuba ✛ 12 km (7½ miles) west of Jerusalem* ☎ *02/534– 7000, 054/563–7788 Paul Dubb* ⊕ *www. tzubawinery.co.il* ✉ *Tours are 55 shekels, and include tastings* ⊗ *Closed Sat.*

🍴 Restaurants

Bar Behar

$$ | MEDITERRANEAN | Fresh Mediterranean cuisine including homemade pastas, tabun-baked pizzas, and Israeli favorites like shakshuka are served on a stone patio overlooking the Judean Hills. This casual and relaxing restaurant is perfect for breakfast and lunch, and popular with local residents from the surrounding communal *moshavim* and kibbutzim, as well as with hikers and cyclists, who often stop here for morning coffee and fresh pastries. **Known for:** cauliflower-stuffed calzones; posthike lunches; hiking maps and advice. Ⓢ *Average main: NIS 50* ⊠ *Nahal Katlav Parking Lot, Rd. 3866, Bar Giora ✛ From Beit Shemesh, take Rte. 3866 E; the restaurant will be on your left after 15 min.* ☎ *02/533–3889.*

Derech Hagefen

$$ | MEDITERRANEAN | Just outside Jerusalem, a leafy garden interspersed by lily pad–filled streams makes a rustic setting for delicious takes on new Israeli cooking. Try the brioche French toast with raspberry sauce for a hearty breakfast, or Beit Zayit salad with mushrooms, cherry tomatoes, and asparagus. **Known**

for: impeccable service; on-site plant nursery; big salads. $ *Average main: NIS 70* ✉ *Derech Hagefen 1, Beit Zayit* ☎ *02/650–2044* ⊕ *www.d-hagefen.co.il* ⊙ *Closed Sat. and Jewish holidays. No dinner Fri.*

Majda

$$$ | **MIDDLE EASTERN** | An earnest Jewish-Arab couple makes fresh food straight from their garden in this picturesque spot a few miles west of Jerusalem. Yakub Barhum built the outdoor deck and pergola overhead. **Known for:** diverse crowds; fig salad; weekend hangout. $ *Average main: NIS 97* ✉ *Off Rte. 3975, Ein Rafah* ☎ *02/579–7108* ⊙ *Closed Sun.–Thurs.*

Ella Valley

10 km (6 miles) south of Beit Shemesh, 42 km (26 miles) west of Jerusalem.

The Ella Valley is one of those delightful places—not uncommon in Israel—where you can relate the scenery to a specific biblical text and confirm the maxim that once you've visited this country, you'll never read the Bible in quite the same way again. Beyond the junction of Route 38 with Route 383, and up to the right above the pinewood slopes of Park Britannia, is a distinctively bald flattop hill, **Tel Azekah,** the site of an ancient Israelite town. The hills are especially delightful in March and April when the wildflowers are out; hiking paths are plentiful.

In the Ella Valley, the southernmost of the great valleys that cut from the Judean highlands toward the coast, Route 38 crosses a usually dry streambed; 200 yards beyond is a place to pull off and park. If you have a Bible, open it to I Samuel 17 and read about the dramatic duel between the Israelite shepherd David and the Philistine champion Goliath. The battle probably took place close to where you're standing:

And Saul and the men of Israel were gathered, and encamped in the valley of Ella, and drew up in line of battle against the Philistines. And the Philistines stood on the mountain on the one side, and Israel stood on the mountain on the other side, with a valley between them.

Look east up the valley to the mountains of Judah in the distance and the road from Bethlehem—the same road by which David reached the battlefield. The white northern ridge, a spur of the mountains of Judah, may have been the camp of the Israelite army. The southern ridge (where the gas station is today) is where the Philistines gathered. The creek, the only one in the valley, is where David "chose five smooth stones." The rest, as they say, is history: Goliath was slain, the Philistines were routed, and David went on to become the darling of the nation and eventually its king.

GETTING HERE AND AROUND

Follow Route 1 west from Jerusalem, then head south on Route 38, passing Beit Shemesh on your left.

◉ Sights

Adullam-France Park

NATURE PRESERVE | This lush green park has paths and lookouts over the Ella Valley as well as archaeological sites. The historical sites here include an ancient synagogue and village, and numerous caves that historians say Jewish rebels used for hiding, storing goods, and burials during the second century Bar Kokhba revolt against the ruling Roman empire. In addition to walking trails, there are also off-road vehicle trails and bicycle trails. ✉ *Off Rte. 3544, Tzafririm* ☎ *800/350–550* ⊕ *kkl-jnf.org.*

★ Beit Guvrin–Maresha National Park

ARCHAEOLOGICAL SITE | **FAMILY** | This national park encompasses some 1,250 acres of rolling hills in the Judean lowlands, where for thousands of years people dug quarries, burial caves, storerooms,

Beit Guvrin-Maresha National Park preserves ancient caves used for storage, industry, and tombs.

hideouts, and dovecotes in a subterranean labyrinth of unparalleled complexity. In the Second Temple period, millions of pilgrims ascended to Jerusalem to offer animal sacrifices. At Beit Guvrin, doves were raised on a vast scale to supply the pilgrims' need. Unlike many ruins, this national park allows you to readily envision life 2,000 years ago, both above- and underground.

The antiquities sprawl around the kibbutz of Beit Guvrin, just beyond the junction of Routes 38 and 35. These are bits and pieces of the 2nd- to 3rd-century AD Beit Guvrin, renamed (around the year 200) *Eleuthropolis,* "the city of free men." The amphitheater—an arena for Roman blood sports and mock sea battles—is one of only a few discovered in Israel.

After entering the park, drive south toward the flattop mound of ancient Maresha, known today as Tel Maresha. King Rehoboam of Judah fortified it, but it was during the Hellenistic period (4th to 2nd centuries BC) that the city reached its height and the endless

complexes of chalk caves were dug. Maresha was finally destroyed by the Parthians in 40 BC and replaced by the nearby Roman city of Beit Guvrin. The view from the tell is worth the short climb.

Ancient Mareshans excavated thousands of underground chambers to extract soft chalk bricks, with which they built their homes above-ground. Residents then turned their "basement" quarries into industrial complexes, with water cisterns, olive-oil presses, and columbaria (derived from the Latin word *columba,* meaning dove or pigeon). The birds were used in ritual sacrifice and as food, producers of fertilizer, and message carriers.

The most interesting and extensive cave system is just off the road on the opposite side of the tell (the trail begins at a parking lot). It includes water cisterns, storerooms, and a restored ancient olive press. The excitement of exploration makes this site a must for kids (with close parental supervision, though the safety features are good), but the many steps are physically demanding.

The great "bell caves" of Beit Guvrin date from the late Roman, Byzantine, and early Arab periods (2nd to 7th century AD), when the locals created a quarry to extract lime for cement. At the top of each bell-shape space is a hole through the 4-foot-thick stone crust of the ground. When the ancient diggers reached the soft chalk below, they began reaming out their quarry in the structurally secure bell shape, each bell eventually cutting into the one adjacent to it. Although not built to be inhabited, the caves may have been used as refuges by early Christians. In the North Cave, a cross high on the wall, at the same level as an Arabic inscription, suggests a degree of coexistence even after the Arab conquest of the area in AD 636. More recently, Beit Guvrin was an Arab village, depopulated in 1948.

After leaving this system, continue walking down the hill to visit the Sidonian Burial Caves. These magnificent 3rd- to 2nd-century BC tombs—adorned with colorful, restored frescoes and inscriptions—have important archaeological evidence as to the nature of the town's ancient Phoenician colonists.

The undeveloped complexes of caves near the tell are off-limits to visitors. Keep to the marked sites only. The brochure at the entrance has a good map of the site. ⌧ Off Rte. 35, Beit Shemesh ⊹ 21 km (13 miles) south of Beit Shemesh ☎ 08/681–1020 ⊕ www.parks. org.il ⌧ NIS 28.

★ Dig for a Day

ARCHAEOLOGICAL SITE | Archaeological Seminars, in Jerusalem, runs this program at Beit Guvrin-Maresha National Park. The three-hour activity includes supervised digging in a real excavation site inside a cave, into which local inhabitants dumped earth and artifacts 21 centuries ago. Participants then sift

Microbreweries in Israel Ⓨ

In the last decade, microbreweries have taken off in Israel. Importers are bringing in more exotic varieties of barley and hops, and well-traveled Israelis are re-creating favorites they sipped in Belgium, Germany, England, and the United States. The area around the Ella Valley, Beit Shemesh, and Latrun is especially easy to tour because most breweries are a short distance from each other. It's worth calling in advance, as the hours change frequently.

the buckets of dirt they have hauled out of the cave, looking for finds. Some museum-quality artifacts of the 3rd to 2nd centuries BC (Hellenistic period) have been uncovered here. (No, you can't take home what you find!) You are then led on a fun 30-minute exploration through caves not yet open to the public. This involves some crawling, because some spaces are too tight or too low for walking upright. The tour ends with a short talk in the pottery shed about how clay vessels are reconstructed. You must reserve ahead. ⌧ Beit Shemesh ☎ 02/586–2011 ⊕ www.digforaday.com ⌧ 110 shekels plus park entrance fee.

Sphera Winery

WINERY/DISTILLERY | Founded in 2012, this family-owned winery on Moshav Givat Yeshayahu specializes in white wines made from grapes grown in local vineyards. The winery takes advantage of its location in the Ella Valley, where the low altitude brings plunging nighttime temperatures despite the hot and dry days, ideal conditions for growing grapes with a robust taste spectrum. Tours and tastings are offered daily by appointment only, and include a generous platter of local cheeses and bread from a nearby bakery. The tasting room has large windows, giving panoramic views of the green land around the moshav. ✉ *Moshav Givat Yeshayahu, Givat Yeshayahu* ☎ *02/993–8577* 🌐 *spherawinery.com* 🎫 *Tasting including bread and cheese is 80 shekels per person.*

Srigim Brewery
WINERY/DISTILLERY | Ohad Eilon and Ofer Ronen fell in love with European and American beers while traveling for work in the Israeli high-tech industry, and they quit their jobs to found this award-winning brewery. The two take great care when crafting their fantastic Bavarian-style wheat beer, dark ale, and India pale ale, which you can sip while overlooking the Ella Valley. Call ahead for guided tours with a minimum group size of 10 Sunday to Thursday, or stop by for beer and pub fare served at wooden picnic tables in the brewery's outdoor beer garden Thursday nights, and during the day on Friday and Saturday. ✉ *Rte. 353, Srigim* ☎ *052/622–7679, 052/593–8287* 🌐 *www.srigim-beer.co.il* 🎫 *Tour NIS 27.*

🍴 Restaurants

★ Hans Sternbach Vineyards
$$ | **MODERN ISRAELI** | **FAMILY** | It's worth the drive here to sample the rustic and delicious creations by vintner Gadi Sternbach, who makes nearly everything on the menu, from the bread to the ricotta and the outstanding cured beef, tuna, and salmon. The succulent beef stew and unforgettable glazed onions are cooked in a sauce that uses the winery's own red wines. **Known for:** winery tours; history lessons from its owner; beef stew. [$] *Average main: NIS 75* ✉ *Farm 83, Rte. 3544, Givat Yeshayahu* ☎ *02/999–0162* 🌐 *www.hsw.co.il* 🕒 *Closed Sun.–Thurs. except for groups with prior arrangements.*

En Route 👁

Instead of the Tel Aviv–Jerusalem expressway, an attractive alternative route back to Jerusalem is Route 375 through the Ella Valley, past Israel's main satellite communications receiver, and up through wooded hill country to Tzur Hadassah (look out for the rock-hewn Roman road on the right). Route 386 heads off to the left and runs north to Jerusalem through rugged mountain scenery, emerging in the Ein Kerem neighborhood on the city's western edge.

🛍 Shopping

★ Kakadu Art Gallery
HOUSEHOLD ITEMS/FURNITURE | **FAMILY** | This gallery is filled with bright and colorful hand-painted wooden dishes, furniture, and other housewares and decorative objects. The pieces feature geometric desings and Israeli motifs, including pomegranates, grapes, and birds. In addition to shopping for Kakadu art, visitors can chat with the owners while sipping tea or coffee on comfortable couches overlooking the lush Ella Valley. Workshops, by appointment only, allow visitors of all ages to create their own colorful wooden art pieces. The gallery ships globally. ✉ *Moshav Tzafririm, 29 Tzafririm* ☎ *02/999–8921, 052/862–5271 for workshops* 🌐 *kakadu.co.il.*

🏃 Activities

★ Nekudat Motsa Bike Rentals and Tours
BICYCLING | **FAMILY** | This bike and tour company located in the cooperative agricultural community of Moshav Tzafririm offers both independent bicycle rentals as well as guided bike tours of the Ella Valley Region. In addition to road and mountain bikes, the outfit also rents

Christmas in Bethlehem includes a colorful Greek Orthodox procession in Manger Square.

helmets and bike trailers for children. There's a small selection of ice cream and cold drinks for sale at the rental site. It is best to make reservations in advance. ✉ *27 Tzafririm, Tzafririm* ☎ *02/579–9268* ⊕ *www.nekudat-motsa. co.il/en/home* 🚲 *Mountain bike is 70 shekels for 2 hrs, and guided bike tours are 160 shekels per person with a minimum of 8 participants.*

Bethlehem

8 km (5 miles) south of Jerusalem.

Even from a distance, it's easy to identify the minarets and steeples that symbolically vie for control of the skyline of Bethlehem, home to one of the oldest Christian communities in the world. Although a few decades ago most residents were Christians, today the great majority of greater Bethlehem's 30,000 residents are Muslim, as elsewhere in the West Bank.

For Christians the world over, the city is synonymous with the birth of Jesus and the many shrines that celebrate that event. Bethlehem is also the site of the Tomb of Rachel, Jacob's wife, who died in childbirth here. Rachel's Tomb today lies in Israeli-controlled territory, immediately to the north of the wall that divides the area.

GETTING HERE AND AROUND

The birthplace of Jesus is 15 minutes south of Jerusalem, although the ride seldom goes so quickly. This is because Bethlehem is part of the Palestinian Authority and set off from Jerusalem by the controversial security barrier that snakes roughly along the border with the West Bank. The wall is especially intimidating around the Bethlehem border crossing, as it stands taller than most of the surrounding buildings and is constructed of solid concrete. Graffiti artists have covered the Bethlehem side with demands for rights for Palestinians. British artist Banksy also left his mark, inspiring a falafel stand and souvenir stand named after him. As daunting as it seems, tourists with a foreign passport have no difficulty visiting Bethlehem. Simply show the cover of your passport and be whisked through, usually without a single question.

TIMING
Allow at least two hours for a visit to the Church of the Nativity and Manger Square.

SAFETY AND PRECAUTIONS
Tourists are unlikely to be bothered in Bethlehem, but check travel advisories before your trip. You can also ask your hotel concierge if there have been any recent issues.

TOURS
In recent years Bethlehem has made a concerted effort to woo tourists. Several companies like the Alternative Tourism Group organize people-to-people meetings and unusual hiking trips through farming villages.

Alternative Tourism Group
GUIDED TOURS | This West Bank–based organization offers everything from day trips to overnight visits to Bethlehem and other spots in the West Bank. Tours of Bethlehem and Hebron, as well as culinary workshops, run daily according to demand. ☎ 02/277–2151 ⊕ www.atg. ps ✉ NIS 335.

Green Olive Tours
GUIDED TOURS | Local guides lead half-day tours of Bethlehem on Tuesday and Friday. On Monday and Saturday, there is a half-day tour focusing on Banksy's work and other art in Bethlehem for 295 shekels, including transportation from Jerusalem. ✉ King David St., Jerusalem ☎ 03/721–9540 ⊕ www.toursinenglish. com ✉ 305 shekels, including transportation from Jerusalem.

VISITOR INFORMATION
CONTACTS Bethlehem Tourist Information Office. ✉ Peace Center, Manger Sq. ☎ 02/277–6832 ⊕ www.travelpalestine.

ps. **Visitor Information Center.** ✉ Manger Sq. ☎ 02/275–4235 ⊕ vicbethlehem. wordpress.com.

◉ Sights

Church of St. Catherine
RELIGIOUS SITE | Built by Franciscans in 1882, Bethlehem's Roman Catholic parish church incorporates remnants of its 12th-century Crusader predecessor. Note the bronze doors with reliefs of St. Jerome, St. Paula, and St. Eustochium. From this church, the midnight Catholic Christmas mass is broadcast around the world. Steps descend from within the church to a series of dim grottoes, clearly once used as living quarters. Chapels here are dedicated to Joseph, the Innocents killed by Herod the Great, and to the 4th-century St. Jerome, who wrote the Vulgate—the Latin translation of the Bible—supposedly right here. St. Catherine is adjacent to the Church of the Nativity, and accessible by a passage from its Armenian chapel. Next to the church is a lovely cloister, restored in 1949. A small wooden door (kept locked) connects the complex with the Grotto of the Nativity. Call ahead to check hours, as they change frequently. ✉ Manger Sq. ☎ 02/274–2425 ⊕ www.custodia.org/en/ sanctuaries/bethlehem.

★ Church of the Nativity
RELIGIOUS SITE | At this church marking the traditional site of the birth of Jesus, the stone exterior is crowned by the crosses of the three denominations sharing it: the Greek Orthodox, Latins (Roman Catholic, represented by the Franciscan order), and Armenian Orthodox. The blocked, square entranceway dates from the time of the Byzantine emperor Justinian (6th century); the arched entrance (also blocked) within the Byzantine one is 12th-century Crusader; and the current low entrance was designed in the 16th century to protect the worshippers from attack by hostile Muslim neighbors.

The church interior is vast and gloomy. In the central nave, a large wooden trapdoor reveals a remnant of a striking mosaic floor from the original basilica, built in the 4th century by Helena, mother of Constantine the Great, the Roman emperor who first embraced Christianity. Emperor Justinian's rebuilding two centuries later enlarged the church, creating its present-day plan and structure, including the 44 red-stone columns with Corinthian capitals that run the length of the nave in two paired lines.

This is the oldest standing church in the country. When the Persians invaded in 614, they destroyed every Christian church and monastery in the land except this one. Legend holds that the church was adorned with a wall painting depicting the Nativity, including the visit to the infant Jesus by the Three Wise Men of the East. For the local artist, "east" meant Persia, and he dressed his wise men in Persian garb. The Persian conquerors did not understand the picture's significance, but "recognized" themselves in the painting and so spared the church. In the 8th century, the church was pillaged by the Muslims and was later renovated by the Crusaders. Patches of 12th-century mosaics high on the walls, the medieval oak ceiling beams, and figures of saints on the Corinthian pillars hint at its medieval splendor.

The elaborately ornamented front of the church serves as the parish church of Bethlehem's Greek Orthodox community. The right transept is theirs, too, but the left transept belongs to the Armenian Orthodox. The altar in the left transept is known as the altar of the kings, because tradition holds this to be the place where the three magi dismounted. For centuries, all three "shareholders" in the church have vied for control of the holiest Christian sites in the Holy Land. The 19th-century Status Quo Agreement that froze their respective rights and privileges in Jerusalem's Church of the Holy Sepulcher and the Tomb of the Virgin pertains here, too: ownership, the timing of ceremonies, number of oil lamps, and so on are all clearly defined.

From the right transept at the front of the church, descend to the Grotto of the Nativity, encased in white marble. Long lines can form at the entrance to the grotto, making the suggestion of spending just an hour to see the church an impossibility. Once a cave—precisely the kind of place that might have been used as a barn—the grotto has been reamed, plastered, and decorated beyond recognition. Immediately on the right is a small altar, and on the floor below it is the focal point of the entire site: a 14-point silver star with the Latin inscription "*hic de virgine maria jesus christus natus est*" (Here of the Virgin Mary, Jesus Christ was born). The Latins placed the original star here in 1717 but lost control of the altar 40 years later to the more influential Greek Orthodox. In 1847 the star mysteriously disappeared, and pressure from the Turkish sultan compelled the Greeks to allow the present Latin replacement to be installed in 1853. The Franciscan guardians do have possession, however, of the little alcove a few steps down on the left at the entrance to the grotto, said to be the manger where the infant Jesus was laid. ⊠ *Manger Sq.* ⊕ *www. bethlehem.custodia.org* ⊠ *Free* ⊙ *Grotto closed Sun. morning.*

Manger Square

HISTORIC SITE | Bethlehem's central plaza and the site of the Church of the Nativity, Manger Square is built over the grotto thought to be the birthplace of Jesus. The end of the square opposite the church is the Mosque of Omar, the city's largest Muslim house of worship. The square occupies the center of Bethlehem's Old City and has a tourist information office, several good souvenir shops, and restaurants where you can drink a coffee while people-watching. On Christmas, it is filled with lights, music tents, Palestinian

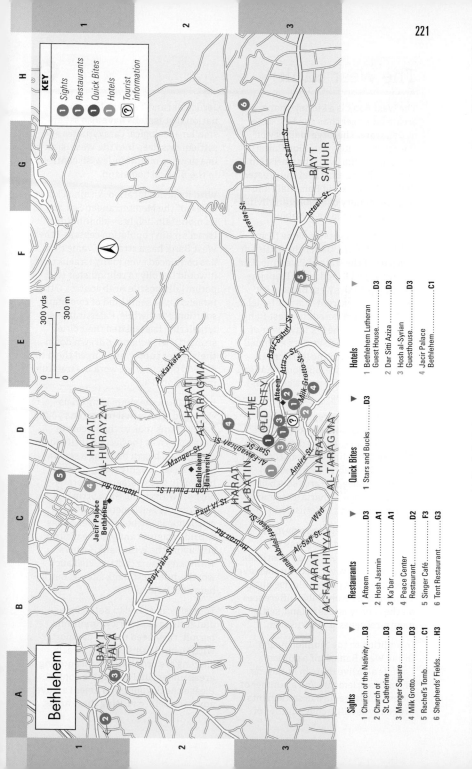

Bethlehem

KEY

- ● Sights
- ● Restaurants
- ● Quick Bites
- ● Hotels
- ⑦ Tourist information

0 ___ 300 yds
0 ___ 300 m

BAYT JALA

HARAT AL-HURAYZAT

HARAT AL-TARAGMA

THE OLD CITY

HARAT AL-BATIN

HARAT AL-TARAG VIA

HARAT AL-FARAHIYYA

BAYT SAHUR

Jacir Palace Bethlehem

Bethlehem University

Al-Karkafa St.
Manger St.
John Paul II St.
Paul VI St.
Hebron Rd.
Jamal Abdel Nasser St.
Bayt Jala St.
Hebron Rd.
Al-Saff St.
Wad
Anaira St.
Star St.
Al-Fawaghreh St.
Attarn St.
Bayt Sahul St.
Milk Grotto St.
Arafat St.
Ash Suhni St.
Isteeh St.
Afteem

Sights ▶

1. Church of the Nativity....**D3**
2. Church of St. Catherine............**D3**
3. Manger Square...........**D3**
4. Milk Grotto............**D3**
5. Rachel's Tomb............**C1**
6. Shepherds' Fields........**H3**

Restaurants ▶

1. Afteem...................**D3**
2. Hosh Jasmin.............**A1**
3. Ka'bar..................**A1**
4. Peace Center Restaurant...........**D2**
5. Singer Café.............**F3**
6. Tent Restaurant.........**G3**

Quick Bites ▶

1. Stars and Bucks.........**D3**

Hotels ▶

1. Bethlehem Lutheran Guest House........**D3**
2. Dar Sitti Aziza.........**D3**
3. Hosh al-Syrian Guesthouse..........**D3**
4. Jacir Palace Bethlehem...........**C1**

The West Bank

The West Bank is a kidney-shape area, a bit larger than the U.S. state of Delaware. The large majority of the approximately 2 million Palestinians are Muslim, with the Christian minority living mostly in the greater Bethlehem area and Ramallah, and a tiny community of Samaritans living on Mount Gerizim near Nablus.

The West Bank gets its name from the Jordan River. Under the British, it was part of the state of Palestine. The newly formed Kingdom of Transjordan occupied the West Bank in its war with the nascent State of Israel in 1948. Israel conquered the West Bank from Jordan in the Six Days' War of 1967. At first, Israeli leaders assumed they would return the territory in exchange for peace, but soon changed tack and saw it as a resource of land, water, and heritage.

In Israel itself, the region is often referred to as "the territories," "over the Green Line" (a term denoting the 1949 armistice line between the West Bank and Israel), or by its biblical names of Judea (the area south of Jerusalem) and Samaria (the much larger area north of Jerusalem).

Following the Oslo Accords in 1993, much of the West Bank was, on paper, turned over to the Palestinian Authority. However, a comprehensive agreement has proven elusive due to seemingly irreconcilable differences on the thorny issues of land, settlements, refugees, and Jerusalem.

In addition to the 2 million Arabs in the West Bank, half a million Israelis also live there in hundreds of small settlements and a number of cities. The larger urban settlements are really satellite communities of Jerusalem and Tel Aviv; however, nationalist Israelis have also set up smaller, ideological caravan sites and settlements deep into the West Bank in a drive to maintain Jewish control in the Biblical homeland.

With its prime location within 14 km (9 miles) of the Mediterranean Sea, and its mountain heights—dominating Israel's main population centers—the West Bank has a strategic value that has convinced even many Israelis that it would be folly to relinquish it to potentially hostile Arab control. Other Israelis favor some kind of two-state solution. Meanwhile, Palestinians say Israeli rule has isolated their cities, stunted their economy, drawn down their water supply, and forced them to depend on low-wage work in Israel and international aid.

In late 2000, the simmering crisis exploded with lethal ferocity as young Palestinians took to the streets in riots known as the Second Intifada. In 2002, Israel began building a separation barrier roughly along the 1967 border. In 2005, Israel unilaterally withdrew from the Gaza Strip and four remote settlements in northern Samaria. Although violence has subsided significantly, some visitors still avoid the West Bank. Others, while exercising caution, visit such worthwhile West Bank sites as Bethlehem and Jericho.

Tourists can travel to Bethlehem and Jericho as security conditions permit; they need to take passports with them. At this writing, Israeli citizens are prohibited from entering areas under full Palestinian control. Please check your government's travel advisory before visiting these areas.

children's marching bands, and merry-makers in Santa hats.

★ Milk Grotto

RELIGIOUS SITE | Legend has it that when Mary stopped here to nurse the baby Jesus, a drop of milk fell on the floor in this cavelike grotto and the walls turned white. The grotto and the church above are beautiful, especially just before sunset when the light catches the stained-glass windows. ✉ *Milk Grotto St.* ☎ *02/274–6680* 🌐 *www.custodia.org/en/sanctuaries/bethlehem* 🎫 *Free* 🕒 *Closed Sun. Apr.–Sept.*

Rachel's Tomb

MEMORIAL | The Bible relates that the matriarch Rachel, second and favorite wife of Jacob, died in childbirth on the outskirts of Bethlehem, "and Jacob set up a pillar upon her grave" (Genesis 35:19–20). There is no trace of that pillar, but observant Jews for centuries have hallowed the velvet-draped cenotaph inside the building as the site of Rachel's tomb. People come to pray here for good health, fertility, and a safe birth. Some pilgrims wind a red thread seven times around the tomb, and give away snippets of it as talismans to cure all ills. Today, Rachel's Tomb is an Israeli enclave in the Palestinian area of Bethlehem.

Islam as well venerates Rachel. Next to the tomb is a Muslim cemetery, reflecting the Middle Eastern tradition that it is a special privilege to be buried near a great personage. Note that men and women are separated here and have different entrances. Egged Bus 163 runs from Jerusalem to the tomb. The site is surrounded by a concrete barrier, so for access from Bethlehem you must return to Jerusalem. ✉ *Rte. 60* ☎ *02/580–0863* 🌐 *www.keverrachel.com* 🎫 *Free* 🕒 *Closed Sat. and holidays.*

★ Shepherds' Fields

RELIGIOUS SITE | Just east of Bethlehem is the town of Beit Sahour, famous in Christian tradition for the Shepherds' Fields, where herdsmen received the "tidings of great joy" that Jesus was born in Bethlehem (Luke 2). The same fields are also said to be where the biblical Ruth the Moabite, daughter-in-law of Naomi, "gleaned in the field" (Ruth 2:2). Local Christians disagree about where the real Shepherds' Fields are, and two chapels and gardens give rival interpretations, complete with rival Byzantine relics. Entrance is free to both.

The Greek Orthodox Der El Rawat Chapel is a small white building with a charming red dome; inside, bright paintings of the Stations of the Cross cover the walls and soaring ceilings. A mosaic dating to a 5th-century Byzantine church lies just outside. A Catholic church—Shepherds' Field of the Franciscan Custody of the Holy Land—is a short walk away. This tiny, minimalist chapel built over a cave is tucked away in a lush garden, with walking paths surrounded by soaring pines and bright aloe plants. Outside are a number of souvenir stores and coffee shops. ✉ *Beit Sahour* 🌐 *www.bethlehem.custodia.org* 🎫 *Free* 🕒 *Greek Orthodox chapel closed Sun.*

🍴 Restaurants

★ Afteem

$ | MIDDLE EASTERN | Just off Manger Square, Afteem draws locals and tourists alike for its falafel, hummus, and chicken platters. Enjoy them sitting inside a stone cave or standing on the steps outside. **Known for:** local beer; great prices; fresh ingredients. [$] *Average main: NIS 20* ✉ *Manger Sq.* ☎ *02/274–7940.*

★ Hosh Jasmin

$$ | MIDDLE EASTERN | FAMILY | Filmmaker Mazen Saadeh learned organic farming techniques in Oregon and returned to his native West Bank to cook what he grows on the rocky terraces outside Bethlehem. Sit at a table, order rabbit cooked in a *zarb,* or underground oven, wash it down with freshly distilled arak

Christmas in Bethlehem

Perhaps unsurprisingly, Christmas is the most popular time of year for travelers to visit Bethlehem, the town where Jesus is said to have been born. In fact, the holiday celebration draws more than 1 million tourists annually. In Bethlehem, Christmas is celebrated three times: December 25 by the Roman Catholics and Protestants; January 6 by the Greek, Coptic, and Russian Orthodox; and January 19 by the Armenian Orthodox. For nearly a month, Manger Square is brilliantly illuminated with lights and bursting with life and joyous celebration. On December 24, choirs from around the world perform carols and sacred music in the square between 8:30 pm and 11:30 pm, and at midnight at the Franciscan Church of St. Catherine. That service is relayed on closed-circuit television onto a large screen in Manger Square and, via satellite, to all parts of the globe.

liquor or red wine made on-site, and gaze at olive trees that have been growing here for centuries. **Known for:** homemade wine; rabbit cooked in an underground oven; friendly owner. $ *Average main: NIS 55* ✉ *Al Makhrour, Beit Jala* ☎ *059/986–8914.*

★ Ka'bar

$ | **MIDDLE EASTERN** | Just west of Bethlehem in Beit Jala, this fluorescent-lit hole-in-the-wall has perfected the art of grilled chicken—a good thing, since it's the only item on the menu. The birds are butterflied and charred on a six-foot-long grill outside. **Known for:** addictive olive oil-garlic tapenade; attracting politicians and other notables; half or whole grilled chicken. $ *Average main: NIS 40* ✉ *Near Beit Jala Municipality Bldg., Beit Jala* ☎ *02/274–1419* ⊟ *No credit cards* ⊘ *Closed Sun.*

Peace Center Restaurant

$ | **MIDDLE EASTERN** | Palestinian classics are the main draw at this eatery steps from the Church of the Nativity. Try the *maqloubeh,* a spiced and baked chicken leg served with a colorful pilaf of yellow rice and eggplant, cauliflower, and carrots. **Known for:** tour groups; chicken and onion baked in sumac sauce; fresh desserts. $ *Average main: NIS 35* ✉ *20 Manger Sq.* ☎ *02/276–6677.*

Singer Café

$ | **CAFÉ** | Reflecting the backgrounds of the Dutch-Palestinian couple that founded this coffee shop for the literati of Bethlehem, old Singer sewing machines are the tables and portraits of Palestinian poet laureate Mahmoud Darwish dot the walls. Besides good coffee, you can enjoy fresh juice or lighter fare like sandwiches and salads. **Known for:** book readings and local events; sandwiches and salad; friendly owners. $ *Average main: NIS 25* ✉ *Near Beit Sahour municipality, Beit Sahour* ☎ *059/992–9989.*

Tent Restaurant

$$ | **MIDDLE EASTERN** | Slip into a bright red chair, order a water pipe, and wait for waiters in white shirts and black vests to bring out well-spiced grilled meats, hummus, and salads. This massive restaurant with wide windows is a great way to end a day of sightseeing; it's in Beit Sahour. **Known for:** huge picture windows; Middle Eastern hospitality; chicken liver cooked in pomegranate molasses. $ *Average main: NIS 70* ✉ *Shepherd's Field St., Beit Sahour* ☎ *02/277–3875* ⊕ *tent.ps.*

Coffee and Quick Bites

Stars and Bucks

$ | **CAFÉ** | Come to this Palestinian-owned chain for the freshly pressed orange and pomegranate juices or a potent cup of thick Arabic coffee. Take home a souvenir mug printed with a green circle that looks strikingly like one from a certain U.S. coffee behemoth. **Known for:** great selfie place; souvenir mugs; fast service. [$] *Average main: NIS 12* ✉ *Manger St.* ☎ *02/275–8787.*

Hotels

Bethlehem Lutheran Guest House (*Abu Jubran*)

$ | **B&B/INN** | Rooms are named for nearby villages in this stone-walled, clean, and modest guesthouse that overlooks a busy market street a few steps from Manger Square. **Pros:** inexpensive; central location; charming. **Cons:** can get noisy; bathrooms are quite basic. [$] *Rooms from: $102* ✉ *Dar Annadwa, Paul IV St. 109* ☎ *02/277–0047* 🌐 *www.diyar.ps* 🛏 *13 rooms* 🍴 *Free Breakfast.*

Dar Sitti Aziza

$ | **B&B/INN** | Scientist Nabil Rishmawi renovated his grandmother's house and created Bethlehem's first heritage hotel, with each room named for its original function: the wine room, olive room, and horse room, and so on. **Pros:** unique restoration property; personal service; great location near all the major sites. **Cons:** basic rooms and bathroom; a bit overpriced. [$] *Rooms from: $160* ✉ *Anatra St.* ☎ *02/274–4848* 🌐 *www.darsittiaziza.ps/en* 🛏 *9 rooms* 🍴 *Free Breakfast.*

★ **Hosh al-Syrian Guesthouse**

$ | **B&B/INN** | This charming guesthouse, in the quarter formerly home to city's once-vibrant Assyrian community (some of whom still remain), has great rooftop views and thoughtfully designed stone-walled rooms with Palestinian soaps from Nablus and vintage portraits of local Bethlehem families. **Pros:** walking distance to all the sites; sophisticated ambience; reasonable rates. **Cons:** none of the amenities of larger hotels; some rooms without air conditioning. [$] *Rooms from: $80* ✉ *Assyrian Quarter, Children St.* ☎ *02/274–7529* 🌐 *www.hoshalsyrian.com* 🛏 *12 rooms* 🍴 *Free Breakfast.*

★ **Jacir Palace Bethlehem**

$ | **HOTEL** | Bethlehem's most luxurious accommodation is in a century-old mansion, and the stunning stone building and five-star service make you feel like a sultan. **Pros:** amazing atmosphere; excellent service; swimming pool. **Cons:** navigating the hallways can be tough; long walk to main Bethlehem sites. [$] *Rooms from: $140* ✉ *Jerusalem–Hebron Rd.* ☎ *02/276–6777* 🌐 *www.jacirpalace.ps* 🛏 *250 rooms* 🍴 *Free Breakfast.*

Shopping

In the city's 300 workshops, Bethlehem craftspeople make carved olive-wood and mother-of-pearl objects, mostly of a religious nature, but many stores along the tourist route in town sell jewelry and trinkets. For quality and reliability, most of the large establishments on Manger Street are worth investigating, but some of the merchants near the Church of the Nativity, on Manger Square, have good-quality items as well.

Christmas House

SPECIALTY STORES | **FAMILY** | At this olive-wood factory, the gracious owner is happy to show you how the well-known souvenirs are made—by a small army of Palestinian craftsmen whittling away the local wood. Ask to go up to the roof, which has a great view of Manger Square. The shop ships worldwide. Don't forget to bargain. ✉ *74 Milk Grotto St.* ☎ *02/275–7233* 🌐 *mychristmashouse.com.*

Chapter 5

TEL AVIV

Updated by
Isabelle Kliger

👁 **Sights**
★★★★★

🍽 **Restaurants**
★★★★★

🛏 **Hotels**
★★★★☆

💼 **Shopping**
★★★★☆

🌙 **Nightlife**
★★★★★

WELCOME TO TEL AVIV

TOP REASONS TO GO

★ **Bauhaus architecture:** Tel Aviv is also known as "The White City" because it is home to the largest concentration of Bauhaus architecture in the world. Explore it on a walking tour.

★ **Israel's best modern cuisine:** Inventive chefs have put the city on the gastronomic map—all good news for the hungry traveling foodie.

★ **Lively neighborhoods:** Check out Neve Tzedek's pastel-color homes and boutiques, Jaffa's jumble of a flea market, Tel Aviv Port's undulating boardwalk, and Florentin's urban hipster feel.

★ **Mediterranean beaches:** Hit the sand, walk along the promenade, or watch the sun dip into the Mediterranean with the locals in the evening.

★ **Nahalat Binyamin Pedestrian Mall:** Stalls of this twice-weekly street fair offer a range of handmade crafts from pottery to jewelry at reasonable prices.

Tel Aviv's compact size and flat landscape make it easy to get around on foot. The city's main north–south thoroughfares of Hayarkon, Ben Yehuda (which becomes Allenby), Dizengoff, and Ibn Gvirol streets run more or less parallel to the Mediterranean shoreline. Closest to the water is Hayarkon and the beachfront Tayelet. At the northern end of Hayarkon is the Tel Aviv Port. Most large hotels can be found on the beachfront along Hayarkon, while a variety of smaller boutique hotels have recently opened in the Jaffa and Neve Tzedek neighborhoods and in the city center, around Rothschild Boulevard.

1 Center City. Most of Tel Aviv's major sites can be found in this warren of small side streets and hidden parks. Look for Rothschild Boulevard brimming with Bauhaus buildings, Carmel Market, and the Nahalat Binyamin Pedestrian Mall.

2 Neve Tzedek. Restoration has meant a renaissance for this neighborhood of narrow roads lined with boutiques, galleries, and cafés. The Suzanne Dellal Centre for Dance and Theatre, with its orange tree-studded square, is magical.

3 Florentin. Those seeking reasonable rents have brought a youthful, hipster vibe to this rough-around-the-edges part of town south of Neve Tzedek. Bars and restaurants make it lively at night.

4 Jaffa. This port— where a certain whale is said to have swallowed Jonah—is one of the oldest in the world. Here you'll find a flea market crammed with antique furniture and a growing number of trendy boutiques and restaurants.

5 North Tel Aviv. The abandoned warehouses of the Tel Aviv Port have been transformed into upscale restaurants, cafés, and clubs. Cyclists and strolling families pack the undulating boardwalk.

6 Herzliya Pituach. A seaside suburb north of Tel Aviv, this affluent neighborhood has beautiful beaches and restaurants and great views.

STREET FOOD IN ISRAEL

0 .5 mi

0 .5 km

KOKHAV HA TSAFON

TEL AVIV PORT

Rokach

Yarkon River

6

GIVAT AMAL BET

Haifa Rd.

Yehuda Hamaccabi St.

NORTH TEL AVIV

5

Ussishkin

Yeshayahu

Ibn Gvirol St.

Pinkas

Nordau

Renner

Weizmann

Lipski

Mediterranean Sea

Hilton Beach

Ben Yehuda

Dizengoff St.

Basel

Jabotinsky

KIKAR HAMEDINA

Central Railway Station

Hayarkon

Arlosoroff

Dr. Gvirol

Bloth

Weizmann

Arlosoroff

Ben-Gurion Blvd.

Rabin Square

David Hamelech

Sha'ar Hamelech

Derech Hasi

Gordon Beach

Gordon

Dizengoff

Frishman

Cheln

Ibn Gvirol

Kaplan

Netivei Ayalon

Derech Namir

Yigal Allon

Mapu

KIKAR DIZENGOFF

Zamenhoff

CENTER CITY

1

Dizengoff

BITSARON

Frishman Beach

Mendele

Bograshov

Gan Meir

Ben Zion

King George

Ha'arba'a St.

Hahashmonaim

Herbert Samuel Esplanade

Allenby

Bialik

Rashi

Rothschild Blvd.

Jerusalem Beach

Geula

Rav Kook

KIKAR MAGEN DAVID

Ahad Ha'am

Yehuda Halevi

Lincoln

Carmel Market

Sheinkin

Hayarkon

Allenby

Balfour

Maze

Yitzhak Sade

Banana Beach

Nahalat Binyamin Pedestrian Mall

King Albert Square

Nachmani

Petah Tikva Rd.

Montefiore

Yigal Allon

Suzanne Dellal Centre for Dance and Theatre

Kaufman

Neveh Tzedek

V-Harari

Lilienblum

AHUZAT BAYIT

Harakevet

LaGuardia

YAD ELIYAHU

Alma Beach

NEVE TZEDEK

2

Eilat

Herzl

Aliya

Levinski

Shalom

Levanda

Israel Misrlani

Hagana Rd.

Ha'etzel

Emek Yezreel

Florentin

Central Bus Station

Eilat

Elifelet

Poriyya

Marzouk Veazar

FLORENTIN

3

Sderot Har Zion

SHAPIRA

Derech Hacharash

Lehi

JAFFA

4

Yefet

Olei Zion

Jerusalem Blvd.

Shabazi

Kibbutz Galuyo

Nemal Yafo

Yehuda Hayamit

Ben Zvi Rd.

Sha arei

Nicanor

STREET FOOD IN ISRAEL

Fast, faster, fastest! If you're hungry right now, the streets of the Holy Land await your eating pleasure. Israel has a refined culture of noshing on the run, because everyone is always in a hurry and apparently hungry most of the time. Put food and drink in hand and join the locals.

To find the goods from falafel to papayas, look for the food stalls and kiosks that line Israel's main streets and shopping areas. Fruit and vegetable markets, notably Carmel Market in Tel Aviv and Machaneh Yehuda in Jerusalem, offer snack opportunities. In Tel Aviv, Rothschild Boulevard and Ben-Gurion Boulevard have popular food kiosks offering made-to-order sandwiches and fresh-squeezed juices. In Jerusalem, try the Old City's hummus spots or home-style restaurants. Most fast-food stalls serve lunch only. The outdoor markets in Tel Aviv and Jerusalem close in late afternoon and on Shabbat. In Jerusalem, no food stalls open on Shabbat, but in the Old City (except the Jewish Quarter) hummus and falafel joints do business.

GRAB IT AND GO

Some street fare is substantial, whether it's falafel or the sandwiches on five-nut artisanal breads that are edging out traditional favorites in Tel Aviv. Other choices are lighter. Sold in markets, in bakeries, and on street stands are sweet pastries called *rugelach*: these two-bite-size twists are rolled up with cinnamon or oozing with chocolate. Just-roasted nuts or sunflower seeds are a quick pick-me-up; or sip fresh-squeezed juices. In winter, try a cup of warming, hot custardlike *sahlab*.

FALAFEL

The region's ultimate fast-food snack consists of deep-fried chickpea balls—the best are crispy outside with soft centers. "Falafel" also refers to the whole production of the balls served in pita pockets with an array of chopped vegetable salads plus hummus, tahini, and pickles that you add yourself and then eat (watch for drips!) with a waxed paper napkin for further refinement. Vendors compete with extra touches such as free salads. It's filling, nutritious, and cheap.

HUMMUS

Ubiquitous in the Middle East, hummus is a creamy paste made from mashed chickpeas, olive oil, garlic, and tahini, a sesame sauce. You eat it in a pita or scoop it up from a plate with the same. In Hebrew, there's a verb for this action specifically related to hummus: *lenagev,* which means "to wipe." Heartfelt arguments prevail among Israelis over where to find the best hummus, but you should try it at a Middle Eastern specialty place; some of the best are on market alleys and side streets—even at gas stations.

SHAWARMA

For this fast-food favorite, marinated lamb or turkey slices are stacked and grilled on a vertical spit, then sliced off and stuffed into a pita. Accompaniments are usually the same as for falafel, though onion rings and french fries are other extras. Jerusalem mixed grill (*me'orav Yerushalmi*) is unique to the holy city; look for it on Agrippas Street, alongside the outdoor fruit and vegetable market. It's a well-seasoned meal of grilled chicken hearts and other organ meats eaten in a pita with grilled onions.

TAHINI

Silky in texture, this sauce with a nutty, slightly sweet taste is made from ground sesame seeds, fresh lemon juice, and sometimes garlic. The tasty green variety has parsley chopped in. Tahini is used as a sauce and is the main ingredient in halvah, the famous Middle Eastern sweet. A popular dessert—among those not watching their calories—is a dish of vanilla ice cream topped with tahini and crumbled halvah and flooded with date syrup.

BOUREKAS

From the Balkans comes Israel's favorite snack: flaky, crispy, golden-brown *bourekas.* Best eaten warm, these pastry triangles, squares, or crescents are deliciously filled with tangy cheese or mashed potato or creamy spinach and sometimes mushrooms.

—By Judy Stacey Goldman

BAUHAUS STYLE IN TEL AVIV

Classic Bauhaus style at 17 Emile Zola Street

Viewing Bauhaus, the defining architectural style of Tel Aviv, is a great way to explore and understand the city. The geometric forms and pastel colors of this modern design ethos, transplanted in the 1930s by Jewish architects fleeing Europe, fit both the landscape and Zionist notions of a socialist Utopia.

The so-called White City, the central part of Tel Aviv that is home to the largest concentration of Bauhaus buildings, was named a World Cultural Heritage Site by UNESCO in 2003. Bauhaus-inspired architecture, more accurately referred to as the Modern or International Style, was based on the idea that art should serve society and that form should also have function. For example, balconies were not designed to be merely decorative but to serve as a source of shade, fresh air, and a place from which to interact with neighbors. Today conservation efforts are making headway, but many classic buildings need repair, their beauty lost under peeling paint and cracked concrete. It's a work in progress as the city offers incentives to owners to restore their properties.

STYLE ELEMENTS

Bauhaus is all about function over design. Signature **vertical staircases** often offset horizontal lines and are recognizable by the steel-frame windows that provide light. **Roof gardens**, identifiable by pergolas of beams and columns, were designed with the expectation that neighbors would socialize on their rooftops. **Balconies** of Bauhaus buildings can be curved or square or rectangular in shape, and are often overhung with ledges that provide shade. Colors are usually white, gray, or beige.

A BAUHAUS WALK

The city's Bauhaus bounty is best discovered by foot. A good place to stroll is along Rothschild Boulevard and its side streets, which also have pleasant cafés and restaurants. A walking tour can begin at **90 Rothschild Boulevard,** at the corner of Balfour Street. Here a three-story, mustard-color building, with the clean lines that are a trademark of the style, stands in contrast to the highly decorated building next door. Note the front door with horizontal strips of wood inlaid in the glass. Its wooden shutters aren't necessarily an element that would be seen in European Bauhaus examples, but here became a necessity because of the sun. Walk to **89 and 91 Rothschild Boulevard,** twin buildings in need of renovation, and see the small vertical windows indicating the placement of a central staircase and the two main styles of balcony, rounded and rectangular.

Walk back across the boulevard and look for Engel Street, a pedestrian-friendly lane lined with Bauhaus buildings. **7 Engel Street** features horizontal bands of balconies and windows. The front door has an asymmetrical overhang and canopy. For an example of the city's restoration efforts, look up to its top floor, which continues the horizontal theme.

Returning to Rothschild Boulevard, walk to **113 and 115 Rothschild Boulevard.** Here again you can see the "thermometer" staircase and its small, elegant windows.

SEEING MORE

Check the city tourist office for free Bauhaus walking tours. The **Bauhaus Center** at 99 Dizengoff Street sells books and more, and offers excellent walking tours. Another resource is the **Bauhaus Foundation Museum** at 21 Bialik Street, open Wednesday and Friday. Bialik Street has many attractive older buildings.

Exploring on your own? Here are a few key buildings around the city.

9 Gordon Street. Take in this 1935 building's elegant cube-within-a-cube design, wooden shutters, and rooftop pergola.

Haaretz Print Works, 56 Mazeh Street. The 1934 building where *Haaretz* newspaper was once printed has steel-framed glass windows and balconies with rounded railings and cantilevered roofs.

25 Idelson Street. Designed in 1931, this family villa has interesting balconies, an asymmetric form, and a mix of small horizontal and vertical windows.

Tel Aviv, Israel's ever-growing metropolis, would be unrecognizable to its founders, a small group of Jewish immigrant families in what was then Ottoman-ruled Palestine. A skyline of shimmering skyscrapers has replaced the towering sand dunes of just over a century ago. The city is now known for its boxy Bauhaus apartment buildings, theaters, and concert halls, as well as its legions of sidewalk cafés that host overflowing crowds every night of the week.

The city manages to pull off the seemingly impossible task of being both hip and homey: witness the happy mix of wine bars, clothing boutiques, hardware shops, and greengrocers—often on the same block. High-end restaurants mingle with old-school eateries where elderly men hold noisy court about the issues of the day over black coffee and apple turnovers.

Sometimes described as an urban village, Tel Aviv is made for walking (or biking, now that it has an extensive network of more than 100 km [62 miles] of bike paths and a bike-share system). From most parts of the city, the sea is never more than a 20-minute walk. In this combination beach town, business center, and arts mecca, people spend Friday afternoon bumping into friends, wandering from café to café, and pausing to hear live jazz trios, all the while strolling with their dogs down boulevards lined with 1940s-era newspaper kiosks

that have been transformed into gourmet sandwich stands.

Tel Aviv isn't the most beautiful of cities, although its charms have a way of making you forgive its aesthetic shortcomings. It was declared a UNESCO World Cultural Heritage Site in 2003 because its collection of International Style architecture, known more commonly as Bauhaus, is the largest in the world. Although restoration efforts are moving along, many of these buildings are in need of a face-lift. It might take an hour or two of wandering on the tree-lined side streets for you to appreciate their graceful lines and subtle architectural flourishes.

There's a spirit of freedom in Tel Aviv, where it's possible to escape from the difficult political realities that are closer to the surface in places like Jerusalem. After all, the city's nickname among Israelis is "the Bubble." Residents tend to be politically and socially liberal. The LGBTQ+ scene is thriving, as are the arts and music communities. It's an exciting city, one that newcomers, returning visitors, and longtime residents all find captivating.

Planning

When to Go

Tel Aviv's mild Mediterranean climate means that any time is a good time to visit. Nevertheless, midday summer temperatures in the 90s may mean choosing museums and other air-conditioned sites until the sun dips and the sea breeze stirs. Weekends (in Israel this means Thursday night, Friday, and Saturday) are the busiest times, but also the most fun in terms of people-watching and special events.

Planning Your Time

With two to four days, you can explore most of Tel Aviv and still have time for the beach. Although it's not a huge area to cover, see the city in geographical order. Start with Old Jaffa in the south, and amble through the art galleries, flea market, and fishing port. Jaffa can also be a good choice in the evening for strolling, low-key restaurants, and wine bars. From here, it's a short walk north to Neve Tzedek. Shop, dine, check out the well-restored buildings, and catch an evening dance performance at the Suzanne Dellal Centre. In the center of town, don't miss the Bauhaus buildings of the White City, bustling Carmel Market, or the Nahalat Binyamin market (on Tuesday or Friday). If you have more time, head to the Museum of the Jewish People, the Palmach Museum, and the Eretz Israel Museum, as well as Hayarkon Park for boating or cycling. Tel Aviv Port is a good place for trendy dining and nightlife.

Getting Here and Around

AIR

Ben Gurion International Airport, a few miles southeast of Tel Aviv, is the country's main airport and has both international and domestic flights.

For full information about air travel and transfers, see Getting Here and Around in Travel Smart Israel.

BICYCLE

Tel Aviv has more than 100 km (62 miles) of designated bike lanes and a user-friendly bike rental system called Tel-O-Fun. Look for the bright green bike stands throughout the city. The basic access fee is NIS 17 Sunday through Friday and NIS 23 on Saturday and on holidays. There's even a weekly basic access fee of NIS 70. Beyond the access fee, you pay an extra fee based on how long you keep the bike: NIS 12 for up to 90 minutes or NIS 72 for 3½ hours, for example.

BUS

Bus fare is a fixed NIS 5.90 within the city center, and you buy your tickets onboard. There's a small discount for a 10-ride card. Combined train-and-bus tickets are also available. Privately run minibuses, called "service taxis," run along two of the major lines: Bus 4 (Ben Yehuda and Allenby Streets) and Bus 5 (Dizengoff Street and Rothschild Boulevard). You can flag these down and ask to get off at any point along their routes; the fare is the same as on regular buses. Minibuses also run on Saturday, when regular buses don't.

From Tel Aviv's Central Bus Station, Jerusalem-bound buses depart every 15 minutes.

CAR

Driving in Tel Aviv isn't for the fainthearted; Israeli drivers are aggressive, and motorbikes weave in and out of traffic. Major highways lead in and out of Tel

Aviv: Route 1 from Jerusalem, Route 4 from the northern coast, and Route 5 from the east. Take advantage of Tel Aviv's belt road, the Ayalon Freeway, to access various parts of the city. The city has started work on a light-rail system, causing some street closures that change frequently.

TAXI

The fastest and easiest way into the city from Ben Gurion International Airport is by taxi, and costs NIS 110–NIS 190. During rush hour, allow 45 minutes for a trip that would otherwise be 20 minutes.

Taxis can be any car model or color and have lighted signs on top. They're plentiful, even in bad weather; drivers honk to catch your attention, even if you're not trying to catch theirs. If traveling within the metropolitan area, make sure the driver turns the meter on when you get in. Rates are NIS 13.10 for the first 18 seconds and 30 *agorot* in increments thereafter. *Sherut* taxis consist mainly of a fleet of vans at the Central Bus Station that run the same routes as the buses, at comparable one-way prices. They run on Saturday at a higher charge. Extra charges apply for luggage at nighttime.

TRAIN

From Ben Gurion International Airport, the train is a money- and time-saver for NIS 15 and takes about 20 minutes. There are taxis waiting outside each train station to get you to your final destination.

The train is an excellent way to travel between Tel Aviv and cities and towns to the north, such as Netanya, Hadera, Haifa, and Nahariya. A high-speed train line between Tel Aviv and Jerusalem is currently under construction. At present it runs between Jerusalem and Ben Gurion. Northbound trains depart from the Central Railway Station (Savidor/Mercaz) and the Azrieli Station. Trains run roughly every hour on weekdays from between 5 am and 6 am to between 10 pm and 11

pm depending on the destination; there are fewer trains on Friday and Jewish holiday eves and no service on Saturday or on holidays. There's also a line to Beersheva. The information office is open Sunday to Thursday 6 am to 11 pm and Friday 6 to 3.

TRAIN CONTACTS Tel Aviv Savidor Center (Central Railway Station). ⊠ *Arlozoroff St.* ☎ *08/683–1222* ⊕ *www.rail.co.il/en.*

Sights

From the city center, it's easy to head south to Jaffa and its ancient port and lively flea market—to get there the scenic way, saunter along the seaside promenade overlooking the beach—and the other southern neighborhoods like the gentrified Neve Tzedek and the more rough-edged Florentin.

Farther north, at the edge of Tel Aviv proper, lies the sprawling green lung of Tel Aviv, Hayarkon Park. You'll also discover the city's renovated port area, an ideal setting for a seaside breakfast or a toast at sunset with which to usher in Tel Aviv's famous inexhaustible nightlife.

Beaches

Tel Aviv's western border, an idyllic stretch of Mediterranean sand, has miles of beaches and a beachfront promenade. Just after dawn, it's the territory of joggers, cyclists, and yoga enthusiasts. As the sun rises, so does the number of beachgoers, some playing the ever-popular (and noisy) ball-and-paddle game called *matkot*. Sunsets here are spectacular.

The city beaches have many of the same amenities: restrooms, changing areas, towel and umbrella rentals, and restaurants or cafés. Beaches are generally named after something nearby—a street or a hotel, for example. They're hugely popular, especially on weekends. If you'd rather not battle the crowds, you'll find fewer people during the week. The lapping of gentle waves offers respite and relaxation for most of the year. There's a strong undertow on these beaches, so exercise caution.

Restaurants

Tel Aviv is very much a café society. Locals of all ages love their morning, afternoon, and evening coffee time—so much so that it's often hard to get a seat. The city's cosmopolitan character is reflected in its restaurants, which offer cuisines from around the world. Still occupying many street corners are stands selling delicious Middle Eastern fast food—such as falafel (patties made from chickpeas) and shawarma (spit-grilled meat).

The city's cosmopolitan character is happily represented in its food, although stands selling the Middle Eastern fast food for which this part of the world is famous—such as falafel and shawarma—still occupy countless street corners. You'll find restaurants serving everything from American-style burgers to sushi and chili con carne. In contrast to Jerusalem, diners who keep kosher have to search for a kosher restaurant, aside from those in the hotels. A spate of new kosher establishments caters to a significant slice of the discerning dining market, but with the fairly rapid turnover of some Tel Aviv eateries, the concierge is still the best person to ask about the latest in kosher restaurants.

Most Tel Aviv restaurants, except those that keep kosher, are open seven days a week. Many serve business lunches at reasonable prices, making them less-expensive options than the price categories suggest. As elsewhere in the Mediterranean, Israelis dine late; chances are there will be no trouble getting a table at 7 pm, whereas past 10, diners may face a long

line. Casual attire is always acceptable in Tel Aviv.

Israelis love to eat at all hours and you will never have to walk far to find food. However, Tel Aviv's restaurants are especially concentrated around Shenkin and Rothschild streets, in Basel, Ibn Gvirol Street, in the Floretin area and around Jaffa Flea Market, and Tel Aviv Port.

What It Costs

$	$$	$$$	$$$$
RESTAURANTS			
Under NIS 50	NIS 50–NIS 75	NIS 76–NIS 100	over NIS 100

Hotels

Nothing stands between Tel Aviv's luxury hotels and the Mediterranean Sea except the golden beach and a promenade outfitted with chairs and gazebos. Traditionally, Tel Aviv's hotel row has been on Hayarkon Street, which becomes Herbert Samuel Esplanade as you proceed south between the Tel Aviv Port area and Jaffa. The international chain hotels along Hayarkon Street are right on the Tayelet next to the beach. Across the street from the luxury hotels are a number of more economical ones. Staying at a boutique hotel in a restored historic building adds a wonderful accent to the Tel Aviv experience; these have been proliferating, especially around Jaffa, Neve Tzedek, and in the city center area around Rothschild Boulevard. Stay in one of these and you'll never be far from the trendy shops of Ben Yahuda and Dizengoff streets or the buzzy restaurants and bars of Rothschild Boulevard. Tel Aviv is small and easily walkable and most of the city's hotels are only a short distance from its major attractions.

Hotel reservations are essential during all Jewish holidays and are advised throughout the year. Some hotels have parking lots, but a few rely on public lots that can be at least a short walk away.

Hotel reviews have been shortened. For more information, visit Fodors.com.

What It Costs			
$	$$	$$$	$$$$
HOTELS			
Under $200	$200–$300	$301–$400	over $400

Nightlife

"When do they sleep?" That's what visitors tend to ask about Tel Avivians because they always seem to be out and about, coming or going from a bar, restaurant, or a performance. Tel Aviv's reputation for having some of the world's best nightlife is well deserved, and the city is also Israel's cultural center.

On Lilienblum and Allenby streets, and in Florentin, where many of the pubs and bars are clustered, things don't really get started until at least 10 pm, especially on Friday night. Most places stay open "until the last customer," which means it's at least 3 am when things finally begin to wind down, although some places are still crowded at 5 am.

For those who want to start and finish the evening early, some nightspots—particularly wine bars—open before the night owls descend. Happy hours are becoming more and more popular.

Performing Arts

Tel Aviv is Israel's cultural capital, and it fulfills this role with relish. The Tel Aviv Museum of Art, the city's major artistic venue (for concerts and lectures as well as the fine arts), is complemented by a host of galleries, especially along Gordon Street. Tel Aviv is also home to a dynamic performing arts scene, including the iconic Batsheva Dance Company and the Israel Philharmonic Orchestra led by Zubin Mehta.

The Friday editions of the English-language *Jerusalem Post* and *Haaretz* contain extensive entertainment listings for the entire country. There are a handful of mostly online ticket agencies for performances in Tel Aviv.

■ **TIP →** **While there are a few exceptions, theater performances are almost always in Hebrew, so inquire before booking.**

Most of Israel's dance groups, including the contemporary Batsheva Dance Company and Inbal Pinto, perform in the Suzanne Dellal Centre for Dance and Theatre (⊕ *www.suzannedellal.org.il*) in Neve Tzedek. The complex itself is an example of new Israeli architectural styles used to restore some of the oldest buildings in Tel Aviv.

TICKETS Hadran. ☎ *03/521–5200* ⊕ *www.hadran.co.il.* **Leaan.** ☎ *03/524–7373* ⊕ *www.leaan.co.il.*

Shopping

The Tel Aviv shopping scene is the most varied in the country. It's Israel's fashion capital, and you'll find styles quite different from what you might see back home in terms of design and color. The real pleasure of shopping in Tel Aviv is access to the exciting creations of its cadre of young designers who have made waves around the world. Dizengoff Street, north of Arlozoroff Street, is where you'll find the shops of many of Israel's best-known designers.

If it's crafts and jewelry you're shopping for, Neve Tzedek is the place to go, especially along the main drag of Shabazi Street. Local crafts and jewelry also star in the Tuesday and Friday Nahalat Binyamin Pedestrian Mall, where prices can be lower than at regular stores and you can almost always meet the artist who made them. As for Judaica, there are a number of stores on Ben Yehuda and Dizengoff streets.

Tours

The Tel Aviv–Jaffa Municipality has laid out a series of free walking tours: an Old Jaffa tour, beginning at the clock tower at various times throughout the week; an urban sustainability tour starting at 50 Dizengoff Street on Thursday at 4 pm; a Sarona Colony tour beginning at 11 Alluf Mandler Street on Tuesday and Friday at 11 am; a tour of historic Neve Tzedek leaving from 11 Rothshild Boulevard on Thursday at 10 am; and the Bauhaus White City, Saturday at 11 am, beginning at 46 Rothschild Boulevard. Personal guides can also be arranged through most hotels.

Bauhaus Center Tour

GUIDED TOURS | FAMILY | Expert guides lead the center's popular introductory walking tours of Tel Aviv's Bauhaus district. After a 25-minute presentation on historical background, the tour visits a variety of prominent Bauhaus buildings. A two-hour tour in English departs every Friday at 10 am from the Bauhaus Center; groups may be as large as 50 people, and each participant is provided with a wireless audio receiver. No reservations are required. ⊠ 77 Dizengoff St., Center City ☎ 03/522–0249 ⊕ www.bauhaus-center. com ⊠ NIS 80 for 2-hr tour.

★ Delicious Israel

GUIDED TOURS | An ideal way to learn the history of a city is through the lens of food. This culinary tour company offers seven guided tasting tours in Tel Aviv (and two in Jerusalem) that visit the backstreets of the cities' markets and foodie neighborhoods, a Night Bites food and alcohol tour, a "Shuk + Cook" workshop that includes a visit to the market followed by preparing an Israeli meal with a chef, and a popular Sustainable

Food Scene tour. Tours range from two to five hours in length, and customized food journeys are an option for those wanting a deeper dive into the culinary scene. ⊠ Tel Aviv ☎ 052/569–9499 ⊕ www. deliciousisrael.com ⊠ From $90 for group walking tour (2½ or 4½ hrs); $150 for group Shuk + Cook (4 hrs).

Pomegranate Travel

PERSONAL GUIDES | Israel experts with excellent tours and outstanding guides, Pomegranate Travel makes this complex and fascinating country come alive. They specialize in multiday tours, which cover the highlights, in addition to specialized food and market, geopolitical, desert, and adventure experiences. They also offer single-day tours in the Old City of Jerusalem, and in Tel Aviv-Jaffa. Some of their most popular offerings include culinary tours and off-road jeep rides in the Golan and Negev. ⊠ Tel Aviv ☎ 058/771–6061, 646/688–2964 U.S. number ⊕ www. pomegranate-travel.com ⊠ Specialist tours start from $500; full-day tours from $600.

Visitor Information

The Israeli Government Tourist Office operates a 24-hour information desk in the arrivals hall at Ben Gurion International Airport that will make same-day reservations. The city tourist office, on the oceanfront promenade, stocks maps of walking tours around the city and is open Sunday to Thursday 9:30 to 5:30, Friday 9 to 1. It is closed on Saturday.

CONTACTS Israel Government Tourist Office. ☎ 050/900–0400 ⊕ info.goisrael. com/en. Tel Aviv Tourist Information Office. ⊠ 46 Herbert Samuel St., Center City ☎ 03/516–6188 ⊕ www.visit-tel-aviv.com.

Center City

Think of downtown Tel Aviv as a cat's cradle of boulevards and side streets leading to all of the city's great sights. These few square miles are the heart and soul of the city; they also hold the thousands of Bauhaus buildings, known as the White City, that have been named a UNESCO World Cultural Heritage Site. As you explore, you might see surfers heading up from the beach, film crews shooting commercials, and couples walking their dogs along leafy boulevards.

GETTING HERE AND AROUND

Most of the main bus lines travel through the center of the city, but two in particular are of interest to travelers: Bus 4 on Ben Yehuda Street and Bus 5 on Dizengoff Street. Both run at frequent intervals. Both of these thoroughfares also have minibuses that can be hailed like taxis and are often an even faster option for getting around. The flat landscape makes strolling along streets like Dizengoff, King George, Rothschild, and Ibn Gvirol very easy.

TIMING

Give yourself the better part of a day to savor some highlights of this part of the city, as there is a lot to see. It's well lighted at night and safe for evening strolls.

◉ Sights

Azrieli Towers

VIEWPOINT | A spectacular 360-degree view of Tel Aviv and beyond awaits on the 49th-floor observation deck of the circular building in this office complex, which consists of one triangular, one circular, and one square tower. Call ahead, as the observation deck sometimes closes early for special events. ⊠ Azrieli Towers, 132 Menachem Begin Rd., Center City ☎ 03/608–1990 ⊕ www.mitzpe49. co.il/home ⊠ NIS 22 for observatory ⊘ Closed Sat.

Bauhaus Foundation Museum

MUSEUM | A good stop for those who love architecture, this one-room museum on historic Bialik Street occupies the ground floor of an original Bauhaus building, built in 1934. You'll discover that the pristine lines and basic geometric forms typical of the Bauhaus school extend to everyday objects as well, from furniture to light fixtures to glazed stoneware. There's even a door handle designed by Walter Gropius (1883–1969), founder and first director of the Bauhaus in Germany. ⊠ 21 Bialik St., Center City ☎ 03/620–4664 ⊕ www.bauhaus.org.il ⊠ Free ⊘ Closed Sat.–Tues., Thurs.

Beit Bialik (Bialik House)

HOUSE | Bold colors and many original furnishings enhance the charming two-story home of Chaim Nachman Bialik (1873–1934), considered the father of Hebrew poetry. An exhibit explores the significance of his writings and cultural activity. Bialik was already a respected poet and publisher by the time he moved to Tel Aviv from Russia in 1924; in the remaining 10 years of his life, his house, built in 1927, became the intellectual center of Tel Aviv. It's said that when Bialik lived here, the street was closed to traffic in the afternoon in order to let him write in peace and quiet. English-language tours can be arranged in advance. ⊠ 22 Bialik St., Center City ☎ 03/525–4530 ⊕ beithair.org/en/bialik_house ⊘ Closed Sun.

★ Beit Ha'ir

MUSEUM | Catch up on Tel Aviv's remarkable history at this historical museum in the original 1924 municipal building, an architectural masterpiece that has been lovingly restored. Among the exhibits highlighting the progress of the last century is a brief film tracing the city's development from huts in the sand to gleaming apartment towers. There's also a pretty patchwork floor made up of colorful tiles typical of vintage buildings and the restored office of the city's first

Dizengoff Street is a favorite nighttime destination for its many bars, restaurants, and cafés.

mayor, Meir Dizengoff, with the original map of Tel Aviv hanging on a wall. ✉ *27 Bialik St., Center City* ☎ *03/724–0311* ⊕ *www.beithair.org* ✉ *NIS 20* ☉ *Closed Sun.*

Ben-Gurion House

HISTORIC SITE | To learn more about the history of the state of Israel, visit the modest house where its first Prime Minister, David Ben-Gurion, lived from 1931 to 1953. Historical material and curious snippets of information give insight into both his personal and public life. Don't miss the statue of him doing a headstand in a pair of blue briefs on Frishman Beach. It turns out this hardened political strategist was also an early adopter of yoga, and rumor has it he could often be spotted standing on his head in his garden or on the beach—even during his time as Prime Minister. ✉ *17 Ben-Gurion Blvd., Center City* ☎ *03/522–1010* ⊕ *www.bg-house.org* ☉ *Closed afternoons.*

Bialik Street

NEIGHBORHOOD | This area has been more successful than many other Tel Aviv neighborhoods in maintaining its older buildings. Bialik has long been a popular address with many of the city's artists and literati, so it's not surprising that some of the houses have been converted into small museums, including Beit Ha'ir, Beit Bialik, the Rubin Museum, and the Bauhaus Foundation Museum. ✉ *Bialik St., Center City.*

★ Carmel Market

MARKET | The northern half of the Carmel Market (commonly referred to as the *shuk*) consists of cheap clothing and housewares, but continue farther down to the fruit and vegetable section, where the real show begins. Vendors loudly hawk their fresh produce, and the crowded aisles reveal Israel's incredible ethnic mix. Don't pass by the small side streets filled with unusual treats. The market is busiest on Tuesday and Friday, when it can be combined with a visit to the Nahalat Binyamin Pedestrian Mall's crafts

The former city hall on Bialik Square is now the Beit Ha'ir, a museum about Tel Aviv's history.

fair. If you don't like crowds, though, avoid Friday, when shoppers preparing for Shabbat pack the market. ⊠ *Along HaCarmel St., Center City* ⊹ *Enter from intersection of Allenby, Nahalat Binyamin, Sheinkin, and King George Sts.* ⊗ *Closed Sat.*

Founders' Monument and Fountain

FOUNTAIN | Dedicated in 1949, the Founders' Monument honors those who founded Tel Aviv. This large slab of stone also encapsulates the city's past in three copper bas-relief panels representing the earliest pioneer days of planting and building as well as modern architecture. ⊠ *Rothschild Blvd., at Nahalat Binyamin St., Center City* ⊠ *Free.*

Gan Meir (*Meir Park*)

CITY PARK | **FAMILY** | In the midst of crowded, noisy King George Street, you can wander through Meir Park and relax on benches shaded by beautiful old trees. The first trees were planted in 1936 when the city offered to name the park after its first mayor, Meir Dizengoff, in honor of his 70th birthday. The feisty

Dizengoff objected, so the park only got its official name in 1944, years after he passed away. There's a large playground that's extremely popular with local kids. ⊠ *King George and Hashmonim Sts., Center City* ⊹ *Near Dizengoff Center* ⊠ *Free.*

Habima Square

PLAZA | **FAMILY** | Here you'll find a number of cultural institutions, including the Habima Theatre, the Charles Bronfman Auditorium, and the Helena Rubinstein Pavilion for Contemporary Art. A great place for kids to run around, the square also has a relaxation garden with music wafting from the ecologically designed seating. ⊠ *Rothschild Blvd. at Marmorek St., Center City* ⊠ *Free.*

Helena Rubinstein Pavilion

MUSEUM | This annex of the Tel Aviv Museum of Art houses changing contemporary art exhibits in an intimate space that's perfect for one-person shows. It's also a great escape from the midday sun. ⊠ *6 Tarsat St., Center City* ☎ *03/528–7196*

🌐 *www.tamuseum.org.il* ✉ *NIS50*
🕙 *Closed Sun.*

Independence Hall Museum

MUSEUM | This impressive building was originally the home of the city's first mayor, Meir Dizengoff. The country's leaders assembled here on May 14, 1948, to announce to the world the establishment of the State of Israel. Today the museum's **Hall of Declaration** stands as it did on that dramatic day, with the original microphones on the long table where the dignitaries sat. Behind the table is a portrait of the Zionist leader Theodor Herzl. Tours are available on-site, while an evening walking tour on the independence trail is held every Sunday. Call ahead to reserve a tour. ✉ *16 Rothschild Blvd., Center City* ☎ *03/517–3942* 🌐 *eng.ihi.org.il* ✉ *NIS 24* 🕙 *Closed Sat.*

Kikar Magen David

NEIGHBORHOOD | This meeting point of six streets is named for the six-point Magen David, or Star of David. Faded historic buildings flank it on one side, shops and eateries on the other. It's the gateway to the Carmel Market, the open-air fruit and vegetable market. Musicians and street performers find their way to the open area in the middle of the hustle and bustle. ✉ *King George and Allenby Sts., Center City.*

King Albert Square

PLAZA | Named after the Belgian monarch who was a personal friend of Mayor Meir Dizengoff, this prominent square is surrounded by some interesting monuments. The Bauhaus-style Pagoda House, now luxuriously restored as a private home, was built in 1924. The rooftop ornament gives the building its name. Inside the elegant stairwell of Shifrin House, at 2 Melchett Street, are crumbling remnants of frescoes of the Western Wall and Rachel's Tomb. ✉ *Nahmani and Montefiore Sts., Center City.*

★ Nahalat Binyamin Pedestrian Mall

MARKET | Everything from plastic trinkets to handmade silver jewelry can be found at this bustling artisans street market, open on Tuesday and Friday along this pedestrian mall. A profusion of buskers compete to entertain you. For a finishing touch of local color, cafés serving cakes and light meals line the street. At the end of the market is a large Bedouin tent, where you can treat yourself to a *laffa* with *labaneh* and *za'atar* (large pita bread with tangy sour cream, sprinkled with hyssop, an oregano-like herb). ✉ *Nahalat Binyamin St., off Allenby St., Center City* ✉ *Free* 🕙 *Closed Sat.–Mon., Wed., and Thurs.*

Rabin Square

PLAZA | The square was renamed for Prime Minister Yitzhak Rabin after he was assassinated here on November 4, 1995. Passersby often pause at the small monument of black stones, rippled and uneven as if after an earthquake. This quiet memorial is the work of Israeli artist Danny Karavan. The southeast corner of the square is a great place to grab a coffee, reflect, and people-watch. ✉ *Ibn Gvirol St. and Frishman St., Center City.*

★ Rothschild Boulevard

NEIGHBORHOOD | Half a century ago, this magnificent tree-lined boulevard was one of the most exclusive streets in the city. Today it's once again what visionaries at the beginning of the 20th century meant it to be—a place for people to meet, stroll, and relax. Along the street are some of the city's best restaurants and bars, and many Bauhaus gems are on or just off the street. ✉ *Center City* ✚ *Runs for 1½ km (1 mile) from Herzl St. to Marmorek St./Habima Sq.*

Rubin Museum

MUSEUM | Recognized as one of Israel's major painters, Reuven Rubin (1893–1974) bequeathed his house to Tel Aviv along with 45 of his works, which make up the permanent collection here. The house, built in 1930, is now an art gallery,

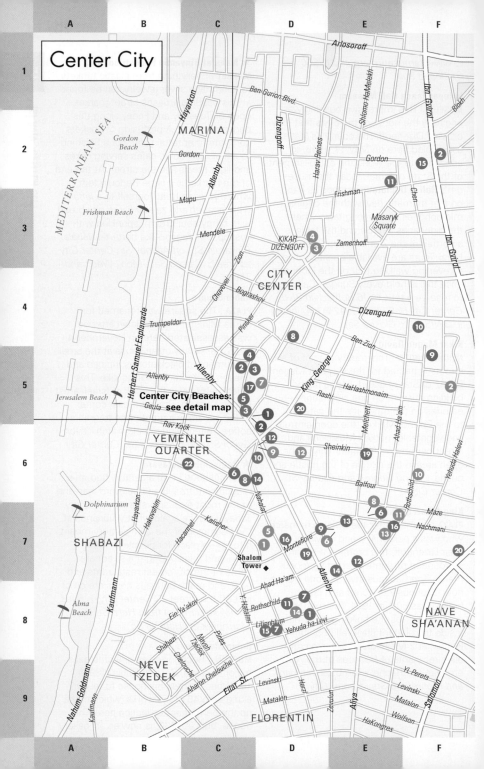

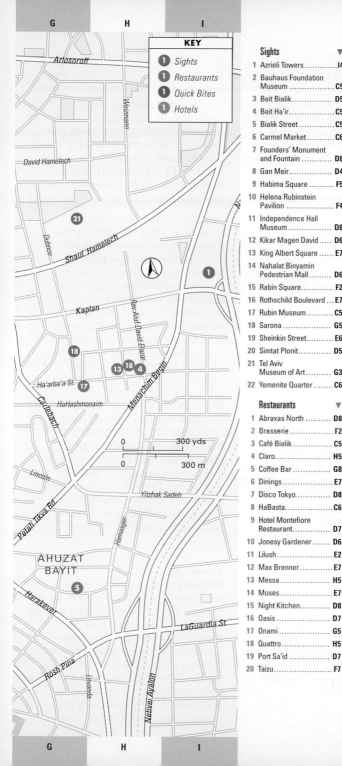

KEY

1 Sights
1 Restaurants
1 Quick Bites
1 Hotels

Sights ▼

1 Azrieli Towers **I4**
2 Bauhaus Foundation
Museum **C5**
3 Beit Bialik................**D5**
4 Beit Ha'ir.................**C5**
5 Bialik Street **C5**
6 Carmel Market...........**C6**
7 Founders' Monument
and Fountain **D8**
8 Gan Meir.................**D4**
9 Habima Square **F5**
10 Helena Rubinstein
Pavilion **F4**
11 Independence Hall
Museum **D8**
12 Kikar Magen David **D6**
13 King Albert Square **E7**
14 Nahalat Binyamin
Pedestrian Mall.........**D6**
15 Rabin Square.............**F2**
16 Rothschild Boulevard ...**E7**
17 Rubin Museum...........**C5**
18 Sarona **G5**
19 Sheinkin Street..........**E6**
20 Simtat Plonit.............**D5**
21 Tel Aviv
Museum of Art **G3**
22 Yemenite Quarter **C6**

Restaurants ▼

1 Abraxas North **D8**
2 Brasserie **F2**
3 Café Bialik **C5**
4 Claro......................**H5**
5 Coffee Bar **G8**
6 Dinings....................**E7**
7 Disco Tokyo..............**D8**
8 HaBasta...................**C6**
9 Hotel Montefiore
Restaurant...............**D7**
10 Jonesy Gardener **D6**
11 Lilush **E2**
12 Max Brenner.............**E7**
13 Messa.....................**H5**
14 Moses.....................**E7**
15 Night Kitchen............**D8**
16 Oasis **D7**
17 Onami **G5**
18 Quattro...................**H5**
19 Port Sa'id **D7**
20 Taizu......................**F7**

Quick Bites ▼

1 Falafel Benin Johnny... **D5**
2 Sabich
Tchernikovsky...........**D6**

Hotels ▼

1 Brown TLV...............**D7**
2 Hotel B
Berdichevsky............**F5**
3 Center Chic Hotel
Tel Aviv...................**D3**
4 Cinema Hotel
Tel Aviv...................**D3**
5 Fabric Hotel **D7**
6 Hotel Montefiore........**D7**
7 Hotel Saul................**D5**
8 The Norman Hotel.......**E6**
9 Poli House **D6**
10 The Rothschild Hotel **F6**
11 The Rothschild 71........**E7**
12 Shenkin Hotel **D6**
13 65 Hotel Rothschild
Tel Aviv...................**E7**
14 The Vera Hotel **D8**

The Origins of Tel Aviv

Having risen from desolate sand dunes starting in the late 19th century, Tel Aviv lacks the ancient aura of Jerusalem (which some say is part of its attraction). Still, the city's southern border, the port of Jaffa, is as old as they come: Jonah set sail from here for what turned out to be his journey to the belly of a whale. The cedars of Lebanon used to build Solomon's Temple arrived in Jaffa before being transported to Jerusalem.

Jaffa was founded in the Middle Canaanite period, around 1600 BC. For the next 1,000 years, one ancient people after another—Egyptians, Philistines, Israelites, Phoenicians, and Greeks—dominated it. After being taken by Crusaders twice, in the 11th and 12th centuries, it was recaptured by the Muslims and remained largely under Arab control until the 20th century.

In the second half of the 19th century, Jewish pioneers began immigrating here in numbers that strained the small port's capacity. By the late 1880s, a group of Jewish families moved from the overcrowded city to the empty sands north of Jaffa to found Neve Tzedek, now a beautifully restored shopping, cultural, and residential area. The next move was to Ahuzat Bayit (literally, "housing estate"), an area to the north of Neve Tzedek that became the precursor of Tel Aviv. The city was named Tel Aviv in 1909; Arab riots in Jaffa in the 1920s then drove more Jews to Ahuzat Bayit, spurring further growth.

Immigrants from Europe joined these Jews. These new, urban arrivals—unlike the pioneers from earlier immigrant waves—brought with them an appreciation for the arts and a penchant for sidewalk cafés, and left a strong social and cultural mark on Tel Aviv. The wave of immigration included some of the world's leading architects of the time, who saw their new home as virtually a blank slate on which they could realize their innovative and exciting ideas about urban planning. Scottish urban planner Patrick Geddes developed the 1929 plan for a functionalist, humanistic Garden City, and architects from Germany's Bauhaus School designed and built modern buildings for the growing city. Today Tel Aviv's many Bauhaus-style buildings, now protected as a UNESCO World Cultural Heritage Site, are a major attraction for architecture lovers.

with changing exhibits by Israeli artists. Upstairs is a small but well-stocked library where you can pore over press clippings and browse through books. A moving audiovisual presentation tells the story of Rubin's life, and his original studio can still be seen on the third floor. ⊠ 14 Bialik St., Center City ☎ 03/525–5961 ⊕ www.rubinmuseum.org.il/en ▦ NIS 20 ⊗ Closed Sun.

Sarona

HISTORIC SITE | Shaded by leafy trees, this area was formerly an agricultural colony established by German Templers in 1871. The picturesque houses have been transformed into a bustling complex with a visitor center, restaurants, bars, boutiques, and cultural institutions. The Sarona Market's 90 food stalls and shops showcase some of Israel's top chefs and bakeries, as well as locally produced wine and craft beer. Pick up some

If you're looking for a "bird's-eye" view of the city, it doesn't get better than from the top of Azrieli Towers.

essentials at the Friday morning Farmers' Market for a picnic in one of Sarona's grassy open areas. ⊠ *Kaplan St., near Begin Rd., Center City* 🕾 *03/609–9028* ⊕ *www.saronatlv.co.il* 🖅 *Free.*

Sheinkin Street
NEIGHBORHOOD | This popular thoroughfare off Allenby Street has plenty of cafés and restaurants where you can watch passersby. This is where young people shop for the latest fashions: the sizes are tiny, the favored color is black, and some of the boutiques are so minuscule you'll think you walked straight into the dressing room. ⊠ *Sheinkin St., Center City.*

Simtat Plonit
NEIGHBORHOOD | Wander down this alley to see old Tel Aviv decorative architecture at its best. Two plaster obelisks at the entrance mark the city's first "gated" community. Note the stucco lion in front of **Number 7,** which used to have glowing eyes fitted with lightbulbs. The original apartment house is painted pale yellow with garish orange trim. An outspoken builder named Meir Getzel

Shapira bought Simtat Plonit in the 1920s and insisted that this pint-size street be named after him. Tel Aviv's first mayor, Meir Dizengoff, argued that another street already had that name. The mayor emerged victorious and named it Simtat Plonit, meaning "John Doe Street." ⊠ *Simtat Plonit, Center City* ✥ *Off King George St., near HaAvoda St.*

★ Tel Aviv Museum of Art
MUSEUM | This museum houses a fine collection of Israeli and international art, including changing exhibits as well as a permanent section with works by prominent Jewish artists like Marc Chagall and Roy Lichtenstein. There's also an impressive French impressionist collection and many sculptures by Aleksandr Archipenko. The Herta and Paul Amir Building, designed by Preston Scott Cohen, is a dramatic, light-filled modern addition to the 1971 main building. The gift shop sells unique pieces of jewelry and other items that make memorable souvenirs. Visiting on Saturday is a great option, as many other places are closed for the

The relaxation garden in Habima Square is surrounded by major cultural institutions like the Habima Theatre.

Sabbath. ✉ *27 Shaul Hamelech Blvd., Center City* ☎ *03/607–7020* ⊕ *www. tamuseum.org.il* ✆ *NIS 50* ⊙ *Closed Sun.*

Yemenite Quarter

NEIGHBORHOOD | FAMILY | Bordering the Carmel Market, this small area hides several cheap and satisfying third-generation eateries owned by Yemenite families whose traditional foods have been passed down since their arrival to the neighborhood in the 1920s and '30s. Wash your meal down with a beer as you gaze out onto the warren of cobblestone lanes. Some streets that are nice to stroll include Nahliel and Haim Havshush, lined with restaurants serving tasty hummus and flatbread. This is a soothing place for a stroll on a Friday afternoon, as the neighborhood hushes to a close for the Sabbath. Though the Yemenite Quarter was once a haven to families who could not afford living in central Tel Aviv, the historic buildings are slowly being renovated by foreign investors as vacation rental properties. ✉ *Around Kehilat Eden St. and Yishkon St., Center City.*

🔁 Beaches

Dolphinarium Beach

BEACH—SIGHT | At the southern end of Hayarkon Street, Dolphinarium Beach (sometimes known as Aviv Beach) has a festive atmosphere, especially on Friday around sunset. Young Israelis, many of whom have returned from postarmy trips to Asia or South America, gather for drumming circles and other group activities. It's also a popular spot for music festivals and concerts. **Amenities:** food and drink; lifeguards; showers; toilets; water sports. **Best for:** partiers; sunset. ✉ *Shlomo Lahat Promenade, Center City* ⊹ *Facing InterContinental David Tel Aviv* ✆ *Free.*

Frishman Beach

BEACH—SIGHT | Facing a strip of restaurants and cafés on the seaside promenade, Frishman Beach is across from many of the larger hotels and gets its fair share of tourists. The shallow water makes it popular with families. Saturday morning it attracts Israeli dancing circles. Lounge chairs are available for a fee, but there's not much quiet because of the lifeguards constantly screeching over the loudspeaker. **Amenities:** food and drink; lifeguards; showers; toilets. **Best for:** sunset. ✉ *Frishman St. and Hayarkon St., Center City* 🎟 *Free.*

Gordon Beach

BEACH—SIGHT | **FAMILY** | At the end of Gordon Street, this wide beach is popular with local families because of its calm water and tidal pool. Weekends you'll find both sunbathing travelers and youngsters lining the beach with sand castles. Gordon Pool, just north of the beach, is a saltwater pool that's good for swimming laps. **Amenities:** food and drink; lifeguards; toilets. **Good for:** swimming; walking. ✉ *Gordon St., at Hayarkon St., Center City* 🎟 *Free.*

★ Hilton Beach

BEACH—SIGHT | In front of the hotel of the same name, Hilton Beach is very popular, especially with enthusiastic matkot players. The northern end of the beach is a gay-friendly area known as Gay Beach, which can get packed on sunny summer afternoons, especially during Tel Aviv Pride. Here you'll also find Dog Beach, which got its name because pampered pooches are let off their leashes to play. There is no car access, so walk or bike down the promenade to reach this stretch of sand. **Amenities:** food and drink; lifeguards; showers; toilets; water sports. **Best for:** surfing; swimming; walking; windsurfing. ✉ *Shlomo Lahat Promenade, north of Tel Aviv Marina, Center City* 🎟 *Free.*

Jerusalem Beach

BEACH—SIGHT | At the bottom of Allenby Road, Jerusalem Beach is known for its beachside café featuring Brazilian bands that get the crowd dancing. **Amenities:** food and drink; showers; toilets; water sports. **Best for:** partiers. ✉ *Allenby Rd., at Herbert Samuel St., Center City* 🎟 *Free.*

🍴 Restaurants

Home of the historic White City, the center of town is chock-full of cafés and restaurants that run the gamut from simple storefront eateries to chic dining rooms run by celebrity chefs. When you just want a quick bite, the boulevards are lined with food kiosks.

North Abraxass

$$$ | **ISRAELI** | For one of the best meals in the city, take your place at one of the tables spilling out onto the sidewalk or alongside the small, chic bar. The menu changes daily, depending on what Eyal Shani, its celebrity chef, finds to be the freshest produce or catch of the day. **Known for:** lively outdoor terrace; celebrity chef; food served in paper bags or directly on tablecloth. [$] *Average main: NIS 80* ✉ *40 Lilienblum St., Center City* ☎ *03/516–6660* 🌐 *www.facebook.com/northabraxass.*

Allora

$$ | **ITALIAN** | The well-stocked wooden bar is the centerpiece of this tiny eatery, where the roaring brick oven and pizza-dough kneaders are in full view. The focaccia makes a great starter, served with a variety of dips including Clemente-olive spread, garlic confit, and, for Middle Eastern good measure, labaneh (yogurt cheese). **Known for:** pizza and focaccia; wood-fired oven; cozy terrace right on busy Rothschild Boulevard. [$] *Average main: NIS 70* ✉ *60 Rothschild Blvd., Center City* ☎ *03/566–5655* 🌐 *allora.co.il.*

★ Bar 51

$$ | **MEDITERRANEAN** | Part of the ultra-chic Renoma boutique hotel, Bar 51 has become one of the hottest spots on the Tel Aviv food scene since opening in 2019. Everything here is on trend, from the hip, laid-back staff to the postindustrial design and the small plates of

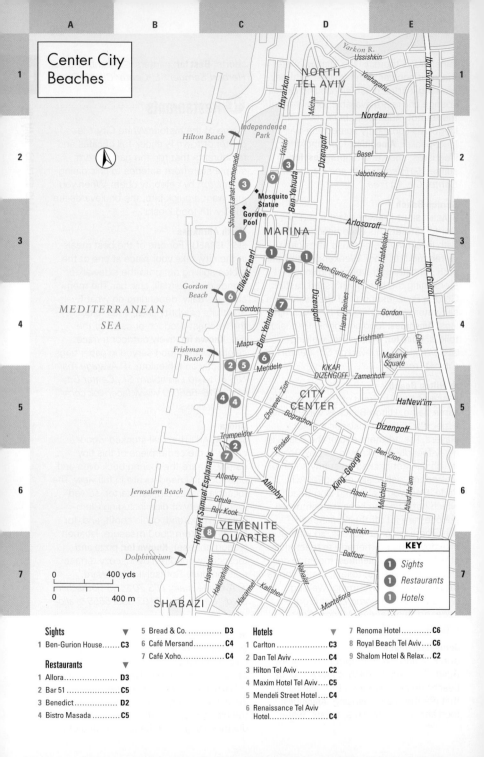

Center City Beaches

A   **B**   **C**   **D**   **E**

1   Yarkon R.   Ussishkin   **1**

NORTH
TEL AVIV

Hilton Beach   Independence
Park

2   Nordau   **2**

Basel
Jabotinsky

Shlomo Lahat-Promenade

Mosquito
Statue

Gordon
Pool

MARINA   Arlosoroff

3   **3**

Gordon
Beach

Eliezer Pearl

Ben-Gurion Blvd.

Gordon

4   MEDITERRANEAN
SEA   Mapu   Frishman   **4**

Frishman
Beach

Mendele   Masaryk
Square

KIKAR
DIZENGOFF   Zamenhoff

HaNevi'im

5   CITY
CENTER   Dizengoff   **5**

Trumpeldor   Bograshov   Ben Zion

Herbert Samuel Esplanade

Allenby   Pinsker   King George   Rashi

6   Jerusalem Beach   Geula
Rav Kook   Melchett   **6**

YEMENITE
QUARTER   Sheinkin

Balfour

Dolphinarium

7   0   400 yds   Nahalat   **7**

0   400 m

SHABAZI

KEY
- Sights
- Restaurants
- Hotels

Sights ▼

1 Ben-Gurion House **C3**

Restaurants ▼

1 Allora **D3**
2 Bar 51 .... **C5**
3 Benedict **D2**
4 Bistro Masada **C5**

5 Bread & Co. **D3**
6 Café Mersand **C4**
7 Café Xoho **C4**

Hotels ▼

1 Carlton **C3**
2 Dan Tel Aviv **C4**
3 Hilton Tel Aviv **C2**
4 Maxim Hotel Tel Aviv **C5**
5 Mendeli Street Hotel **C4**
6 Renaissance Tel Aviv
   Hotel **C4**

7 Renoma Hotel **C6**
8 Royal Beach Tel Aviv **C6**
9 Shalom Hotel & Relax ... **C2**

creative, contemporary Mediterranean cuisine made for sharing. **Known for:** the signature lemon-infused roasted kohlrabi; bar seating to watch the kitchen at work; wine pairing. [$] *Average main: NIS 70* ✉ *59 Hayarkon St., Center City* ☎ *03/540–6680* 🌐 *www.bar51tlv.com* 🕑 *No lunch Mon.–Thurs. Closed Sun. night.*

Benedict
$$ | CAFÉ | FAMILY | Celebrating the love that Israelis have for breakfast, this restaurant with simple and sunny decor features many variations on the morning meal, served around the clock, seven days a week. Choose the classic Israeli breakfast with all the trimmings, the Mexican egg scramble, or several different styles of eggs Benedict. **Known for:** 24-hour breakfast; international dishes; the best eggs Benedict in town. [$] *Average main: NIS 67* ✉ *29 Rothschild Blvd., Center City* ☎ *03/686–8657* 🌐 *www.benedict.co.il.*

Bistro Masada
$$ | CAFÉ | A varied but simple menu—including steak, salads, sandwiches, and pasta—makes this a good place to recharge after a day at the beach or a nice spot to relax with a glass of wine at sunset. The highlight of this café is not the food but the indoor or outdoor seating with fabulous Mediterranean views. **Known for:** patio with seaviews; sunset hangout; breakfast. [$] *Average main: NIS 70* ✉ *83 Hayarkon St., Center City* ☎ *03/510–3353* 🌐 *bistromasada.rest.co.il.*

Brasserie
$$ | FRENCH | The dark upholstery, mustard-color walls, and menu in French (as well as Hebrew and English) are all meant to recall Paris, and the wide selection of excellently prepared food is a credit to French cuisine. It's open around the clock, and always seems to have a crowd. **Known for:** open 24 hours; always packed with locals; classic French dishes like steak tartare and moules frites. [$] *Average main: NIS 65* ✉ *70 Ibn Gvirol St., Center City* ☎ *03/696–7111* 🌐 *www.brasserie.co.il.*

Bread & Co.
$$ | BAKERY | FAMILY | The aromas emanating from this street-corner bakery and café make it well worth the visit. Choose from the savory or sweet section of French-style baked goods, made throughout the day by chefs trained in Paris. **Known for:** Israeli breakfast; freshly baked French-style pastries; breakfast until 5 pm. [$] *Average main: NIS 55* ✉ *128 Ben Yehuda St., Center City* ☎ *03/624–7100* 🌐 *www.facebook.com/breadandco.tlv* 🕑 *Closed Fri. and Sun. night.*

Café Bialik
$ | CAFÉ | FAMILY | This veteran of Tel Aviv café culture is the perfect complement to a stroll down historic Bialik Street. Plenty of restaurants serve more or less the same menu as Café Bialik but it's the neighborhood-hangout feel and the old-fashioned chrome bar stools and wooden tables that make this place stand out. **Known for:** charming old-school café; classic Israeli breakfast; popular local hangout on the patio. [$] *Average main: NIS 49* ✉ *2 Bialik St., Center City* ☎ *03/620–0832* 🌐 *www.cafebialik.co.il.*

Café Mersand
$ | CAFÉ | For a taste of the local hipster scene, score a table on this eatery's sunny sidewalk. The older customers, some of whom have been coming since the place opened its doors in 1955, mingle unusually well with the younger crowd. **Known for:** classic Tel Aviv café; popular sidewalk patio; superb Israeli and Middle Eastern breakfast selection. [$] *Average main: NIS 40* ✉ *18 Frishman St., Center City* ☎ *03/523–4318.*

Café Xoho
$ | CAFÉ | FAMILY | Doubling as an art-and-music haven for locals, this inviting neighborhood café will make you feel as if you're in someone's fun and relaxing living room. The service is personal, the patrons are friendly (you will most likely

end up in a conversation with many of them), and the extensive menu has options for everyone. **Known for:** friendly, international crowd; all-day breakfast; plenty of vegan and gluten-free options. Ⓢ *Average main: NIS 45 ✉ 17 Gordon St., Center City* ☎ *072/249–5497* ⊕ *www. cafexoho.com* ⊗ *Closed Mon. No dinner.*

★ Claro

$$$$ | **MEDITERRANEAN** | Helmed by one of Israel's most highly regarded veteran chefs, Ran Shmueli, Claro is one of those spots that has it all. The farm-to-table Mediterranean menu changes daily, featuring only the freshest seasonal, locally sourced produce, and the building, originally constructed by the German Templers in 1886, makes the experience unforgettable. **Known for:** modern Israeli cuisine; breathtaking historic setting; outstanding service. Ⓢ *Average main: NIS 140 ✉ 23 HaArba'a St., Center City* ⊕ *Corner of 30 Rav Aluf David Elazar, next to Sarona Market* ☎ *03/601–7777* ⊕ *www.clarotlv.com.*

Coffee Bar

$$$ | **MEDITERRANEAN** | **FAMILY** | A Tel Aviv classic that has stood the test of time, Coffee Bar is neither a coffee shop nor a bar—in fact, it is a rather elegant bistro. The service is excellent, the menu is fresh and contemporary, and the design is on point. **Known for:** popularity with locals; contemporary Mediterranean food; industrial, slightly gritty neighborhood. Ⓢ *Average main: NIS 95 ✉ 13 Yad Harutzim St., Center City* ⊕ *Between Hamasger St. and Menachem Begin Rd.* ☎ *03/688–9696* ⊕ *www.coffeebar.co.il/ en.*

Dinings

$$$ | **JAPANESE** | The Tel Aviv outpost of this world-renowned Japanese brand is on the third floor of one of Israel's most exclusive hotels, The Norman. And while Tel Aviv may be home to more than its fair share of Japanese eateries, Dinings stands out not only for its quality, but also for its impeccable service and stunning setting. **Known for:** excellent Japanese cuisine; enviable setting in The Norman hotel; superb service. Ⓢ *Average main: NIS 80 ✉ 23–25 Nachmani St., Center City* ⊕ *3rd fl., The Norman hotel* ☎ *03/543–5444* ⊕ *www.thenorman.com* ⊗ *No lunch Sun.–Thurs.*

Disco Tokyo

$$$ | **ASIAN FUSION** | Part of the achingly hip Herzl 16 complex, Disco Tokyo delivers creative Pan-Asian-Israeli fusion dishes served with tunes from the in-house DJ. The vibe is hip, dynamic and as Tel Avivian as it gets. **Known for:** Japanese-Israeli fusion; food, cocktails and DJs; young, cool vibe. Ⓢ *Average main: NIS 95 ✉ 16 Herzl St., Center City* ⊕ *Entrance via the Herzl 16 complex* ☎ *03/554–4300* ⊗ *No lunch Fri. and Sat.*

★ HaBasta

$$$$ | **MEDITERRANEAN** | This tiny restaurant and wine bar, just a clutch of round tables on an alley just off Carmel Market, draws its inspiration from the market's fresh offerings (the name is Hebrew for "market stall.") The choices change daily, and the kitchen is well-known for dishing out organ meats you might not see much back home. For the less adventurous, the seafood and pork options are sure to be fresh and aesthetically appealing. **Known for:** creative Israeli cuisine; market-fresh produce; informal sidewalk tables. Ⓢ *Average main: NIS 120 ✉ 4 HaShomer St., Center City* ☎ *03/516–9234* ⊕ *www. facebook.com/Habasta.*

★ Hotel Montefiore Restaurant

$$$ | **FRENCH** | The restaurant at this boutique hotel serves modern brasserie fare, throwing in a few unexpected Asian twists along the way. The seasonal menu changes regularly but you can always find impressive Mediterranean-Asian fusion dishes like sea bream fillet with lemongrass cream. The dining room is in a lovingly restored home on Montefiore Street in the heart of historic Tel Aviv. **Known for:** one of the best meals in Tel Aviv; old-world atmosphere; the place to

Shop for local foods in the Sarona Market.

see and be seen. $ *Average main: NIS 100* ✉ *Hotel Montefiore, 36 Montefiore St., Center City* ☎ *03/564–6100* ⊕ *www. hotelmontefiore.co.il/the-resturant.*

Jonesy Gardener
$$ | ISRAELI | FAMILY | In the midst of the buzzing Nachalat Binyamin Art Fair, the secret garden at Jonesy Gardener is an oasis of calm. To escape the madness, sit on Jonesy's green leafy patio, where you can enjoy a great cup of coffee or try local specialities like *shakshuka* or *sabich*. **Known for:** charming interior patio; breakfast and lunch; great coffee. $ *Average main: NIS 52* ✉ *Nahalat Binyamin St. 3, Center City* ☎ *03/516–4412* ⊕ *www. facebook.com/JonesyGardener* ☾ *Closed Fri. and Sat. night.*

Lilush
$ | MEDITERRANEAN | FAMILY | At this cozy neighborhood bistro, the portions are generous, the prices extremely reasonable, and the atmosphere a friendly hubbub of clattering dishes and animated conversations. Tables are packed close together, both in the small dining room and on the sidewalk. **Known for:** popular local hangout; laid-back vibes; great panini and hearty soup in winter. $ *Average main: NIS 45* ✉ *73 Frishman St., Center City* ☎ *03/529–1852* ⊕ *facebook. com/lilushbistro.*

Max Brenner
$ | ECLECTIC | FAMILY | Chocolate lovers should run, not walk, to this eatery for a mouthwatering, *Charlie and the Chocolate Factory* experience. Beneath pipes of imaginary chocolate crisscrossing the ceiling, children of all ages can order the likes of chocolate pizza—topped with chocolate chips, of course—or chocolate fondue for dipping toasted marshmallows and fruit like melon, dates, and bananas. **Known for:** chocolatey treats galore; appealing to chocolate lovers of all ages; service is hit and miss. $ *Average main: NIS 49* ✉ *45 Rothschild Blvd., Center City* ☎ *03/560–4570* ⊕ *www. max-brenner.co.il.*

Messa
$$$$ | MODERN ISRAELI | Chef Aviv Moshe serves traditional dishes like the

shredded-wheat type of pastry called *kadaif,* but his method of preparation is in a class of its own. This Mediterranean–Middle Eastern haute cuisine is enlivened with French and Italian touches. **Known for:** award-winning design; fine dining from one of Israel's top chefs; outstanding dessert menu. Ⓢ *Average main: NIS 154* ✉ *19 Ha'arbaa St., Center City* ☎ *03/685–6859* ⊕ *www.messa.co.il.*

Moses

$$ | **AMERICAN** | **FAMILY** | This bar and grill is part retro lounge, part bistro. Best known for its burgers, the place has an extensive menu that includes everything from shish kebabs to calamari and quesadillas. **Known for:** outstanding burgers; homey ambience; open late (until 2 am; 4 am on weekends). Ⓢ *Average main: NIS 70* ✉ *35 Rothschild Blvd., Center City* ☎ *03/566–4949* ⊕ *www.mosesrest.co.il.*

Night Kitchen (*Mitbach Layla*)

$$ | **MEDITERRANEAN** | As the name suggests, this popular eatery is geared toward the city's night owls, open every night until midnight. Using local ingredients and highlighting modern takes on traditional Israeli cuisine, the menu items are meant to be shared like tapas. **Known for:** dishes made for sharing; cozy, intimate ambience; tomato carpaccio with za'atar leaves. Ⓢ *Average main: NIS 70* ✉ *43 Lilienblum St., Center City* ☎ *03/566–0481* ⊕ *www.nightkitchen.co.il.*

Oasis

$$$$ | **CONTEMPORARY** | Chef Rima Olivera's 30 years of experience in the world's best kitchens and her principles of cooking set this eatery apart from the rest in the Tel Aviv food scene. The menu changes constantly based on the choicest seasonal ingredients, including those that are locally grown and those that are hand-picked from abroad. **Known for:** unpretentious fine dining; California-born chef with flair; open kitchen. Ⓢ *Average main: NIS 145* ✉ *17 Montefiore St.,*

Center City ☎ *03/620–6022* ⊕ *www.oasistlv.co.il* ⊘ *Closed Sat.*

Onami

$$$ | **JAPANESE** | This distinguished Japanese restaurant is consistently ranked among the best in a city with no shortage of sushi. The expansive bar is the restaurant's centerpiece, and the surrounding tables are filled with all sorts of locals, from extended families enjoying an early meal to young people who arrive in clusters later in the evening. **Known for:** top-notch sushi and sashimi; agedashi tofu; opened in 1999 and still going strong. Ⓢ *Average main: NIS 78* ✉ *18 Ha'arba'a St., Center City* ☎ *03/562–1172* ⊕ *www.onami.co.il.*

Quattro

$$$$ | **ITALIAN** | Acclaimed Israeli chef Aviv Moshe turns his plating charm on high at the Italian-Mediterranean Quattro. A playfully colorful chandelier centerpiece contrasts with the stark black-and-white walls also found in Moshe's sister restaurant, Messa. **Known for:** photo-friendly Italian dishes; sceney vibes; leafy patio. Ⓢ *Average main: NIS 120* ✉ *Platinum Bldg., 21 HaArba'a St., Center City* ☎ *03/919–1555* ⊕ *www.facebook.com/Quattro.Rest.*

Port Sa'id

$ | **ISRAELI** | This laid-back sidewalk restaurant set in the shadow of The Great Synagogue of Tel Aviv is always packed with a lively young crowd smoking cigarettes and engaging in animated conversation. They come here for the buzzing atmosphere and celebrity Chef Eyal Shani's delicious take on Israeli specialties such as grilled eggplant, chicken liver, *freekeh,* and *malabi* for dessert. **Known for:** lively tables lining the sidewalk; modern Israeli cuisine; hipster favorite. Ⓢ *Average main: NIS 48* ✉ *5 Har Sinai St., Center City* ✛ *next to The Great Synagogue of Tel Aviv* ☎ *03/620–7436* ⊕ *www.facebook.com/theportsaid* ⊘ *Closed Fri. night.*

Taizu

$$$$ | ASIAN FUSION | Part of the city's influx of Asian restaurants, the "Asia-ter-ranean" kitchen of Taizu is a nod to the street food of India, China, Thailand, Vietnam, and Cambodia. The interior design is based on the five elements of Chinese philosophy: water, wood, fire, earth, and metal, each of which is also represented in the style of food. **Known for:** pan-Asian delights; seafood dump-lings and Indian curry; reservations can be hard to score. $ *Average main: NIS 108* ✉ *23 Menachem Begin St., Center City* ☎ *03/522–5005* ⊕ *www.taizu.co.il* ⊘ *Closed at lunch Sun.–Wed.*

☕ Coffee and Quick Bites

Falafel Benin Johnny

$ | MIDDLE EASTERN | Passed down from father to son, this local landmark has been serving some of the best falafel for more than 50 years. For a few shekels, you'll get a pita filled with plentiful, perfectly prepared falafel balls, fried pota-toes (called "chips" here) and just the right amount of salad. **Known for:** classic street food joint; some of the best falafel in town; busy and very informal. $ *Aver-age main: NIS 16* ✉ *2 Tchernichovsky St., Center City* ▭ *No credit cards* ⊘ *Closed Sat. and evenings from 7:30 pm.*

Sabich Tchernichovsky

$ | ISRAELI | This food stand is one of the best spots to sample the classic Iraqi-Is-raeli street food called *sabich*. The Zen-like concentration of the owner results in a hearty and thoughtful dish consisting of fried eggplant, hard-boiled eggs, potatoes, tahini, and spice (if you say you can handle it)—a perfect combination of flavors. Here you have the rare options of a whole-wheat or gluten-free pita. **Known for:** Tel Aviv's most famous sabich stand; ramshackle street food joint; minimal seating space and no restrooms. $ *Aver-age main: NIS 23* ✉ *2 Tchernichovsky St., Center City* ☎ *50/530-6654* ▭ *No credit cards* ⊘ *Closed Sat.*

🛏 Hotels

For convenience, the center of the city is the ideal place to rest after long days of sightseeing. These hotels put you within walking or biking distance of just about anywhere you'll want to visit in Tel Aviv.

Brown TLV

$$ | HOTEL | As hip as the city around it, this fun boutique hotel offers good-qual-ity accommodation in an unbeatable location at a reasonable price (at least by Tel Aviv standards), making it a great find. **Pros:** warm and attentive service; included breakfast at local eateries; walk to the beach. **Cons:** small rooms; no breakfast on-site; interior spaces are on the dark side. $ *Rooms from: $230* ✉ *25 Kalisher St., Center City* ☎ *03/717–0200* ⊕ *brownhotels.com/tlv* ⤳ *30 rooms* ❍ *Free Breakfast.*

Hotel B Berdichevsky

$$ | HOTEL | Tucked away down an unas-suming side street just off Rothschild Boulevard, Hotel B Berdichevsky is one of the most under-the-radar boutique hotels in the city and probably more famous as the home of the superb Bell-boy cocktail bar. **Pros:** shares an address with one of Tel Aviv's top cocktail bars; friendly, personalized service; affordable. **Cons:** cozy but small rooms; interior is on the dark side; no breakfast served on site. $ *Rooms from: $210* ✉ *14 Berdi-chevsky St., Center City* ☎ *03/744–8888* ⊕ *www.hotelbtlv.co.il* ⤳ *22 rooms* ❍ *Free Breakfast.*

Carlton

$$$ | HOTEL | This classic five-star hotel on the Tel Aviv beachfront has held up better than many of its nearby neigh-bors, and its friendly service and casual atmosphere make it a favorite with tour groups. **Pros:** homey feel; great service and amenities; close to public beach. **Cons:** location near Atarim Square, which is rather shabby; slightly dated but feels more modern than most beachfront hotels; attracts big groups. $ *Rooms* *from: $400 ✉ 10 Eliezer Peri St., Center City ☎ 03/520–1818 🌐 www.carlton.co.il 🛏 280 rooms 🍴 Free Breakfast.*

Center Chic Hotel Tel Aviv

$$ | HOTEL | This member of the Atlas chain of boutique hotels has a cozy lobby filled with books about Tel Aviv and a lounge area that screens vintage black-and-white films about Israel. **Pros:** free bicycles for guests; trendy Bauhaus design; charming balconies and rooftop view. **Cons:** small rooms; no on-site restaurant; location can get noisy at night. [$] *Rooms from: $250 ✉ 2 Zamenhoff St., Center City ☎ 03/542–5555 🌐 www.atlas.co.il/center-hotel-tel-aviv 🛏 56 rooms 🍴 Free Breakfast.*

Cinema Hotel Tel Aviv

$$ | HOTEL | In the 1930s this was the Esther Cinema, one of the first movie theaters in Tel Aviv. **Pros:** a sense of history and style; careful renovation; daily happy hour on the rooftop. **Cons:** no pool; small rooms; no lunch or dinner service. [$] *Rooms from: $250 ✉ 1 Zamenhoff St., Center City ☎ 03/520–7100 🌐 www.atlas.co.il/cinema-hotel-tel-aviv-israel 🛏 82 rooms 🍴 Free Breakfast.*

Dan Tel Aviv

$$$$ | HOTEL | Return visitors say they love the sense of history at the Dan, built in 1953 and billed as Tel Aviv's very first hotel. **Pros:** historic premises; close to the beach; large outdoor pool. **Cons:** guest lounge bans children; historic, but somewhat dated hotel; expensive for what you get. [$] *Rooms from: $405 ✉ 99 Hayarkon St., Center City ☎ 03/520–2525 🌐 www.danhotels.com 🛏 329 rooms 🍴 Free Breakfast.*

Hilton Tel Aviv

$$$$ | HOTEL | FAMILY | Perched on a cliff, this sprawling hotel is buffered on three sides by Independence Park and has direct access to the beach and a large saltwater swimming pool. **Pros:** fantastic beachfront location; quiet; separate shower stalls in many rooms. **Cons:** at the end of the hotel strip, somewhat detached from the city; slightly dated property; pricey. [$] *Rooms from: $580 ✉ Hayarkon St., at Independence Park, Center City ☎ 03/520–2222 🌐 www3.hilton.com 🛏 584 rooms 🍴 Free Breakfast.*

Fabric Hotel

$$ | HOTEL | With its postindustrial design and cozy rooftop terrace, Fabric is a hip option for those seeking a comfortable, affordable, and well-designed boutique hotel in the city center. **Pros:** trendy boutique hotel; popular restaurant downstairs; free yoga on the rooftop terrace. **Cons:** noisy location; smallish rooms; no facilities for extra beds in rooms. [$] *Rooms from: $250 ✉ 28 Nahalat Binyamin St., Center City ☎ 03/567–8000 🌐 www.atlas.co.il/fabric-hotel-tel-aviv 🛏 43 rooms 🍴 Free Breakfast.*

★ Hotel Montefiore

$$$$ | HOTEL | It doesn't get much trendier than this stunning boutique hotel, which showcases what restoration can bring to the historic buildings of Tel Aviv. **Pros:** great service; historic building; exceptional on-site restaurant. **Cons:** front entrance is not wheelchair accessible; rather pricey; restaurant and bar get packed every night. [$] *Rooms from: $450 ✉ 36 Montefiore St., Center City ☎ 03/564–6100 🌐 www.hotelmontefiore.co.il 🛏 12 rooms 🍴 Free Breakfast.*

Hotel Saul

$$ | HOTEL | Set in a laid-back residential neighborhood within easy walking distance of all the downtown action, Hotel Saul reflects the young, funky, and dynamic city that surrounds it. **Pros:** helpful, friendly staff; affordable accommodation in a good location; rooftop sundeck with self-serve ice cream. **Cons:** rooms are on the small side; basic bathroom; no pool or fitness center. [$] *Rooms from: $220 ✉ 17 Tchernichovsky St., Center City ☎ 03/527–7700 🌐 www.hotelsaul.com 🛏 34 rooms 🍴 No meals.*

Maxim Hotel Tel Aviv

$ | HOTEL | Located across from the beach, Maxim has simply decorated rooms, many with sea views. **Pros:** affordable; free parking; nice location near the ocean. **Cons:** small rooms; very basic; patchy Wi-Fi. $ *Rooms from: $180* ✉ *86 Hayarkon St., Center City* ☎ *03/517–3721* ⊕ *www.telavivmaxim.com* ⊋ *71 rooms* ⦿ *Free Breakfast.*

Mendeli Street Hotel

$ | HOTEL | A location on a side street between Hayarkon Street and Ben Yehuda means this amiable five-story hotel is a short walk from the beach and a growing crop of cafés and restaurants. **Pros:** excellent breakfast; modern renovations; close to the beach. **Cons:** no sea views; limited parking; small rooms. $ *Rooms from: $195* ✉ *5 Mendeli St., Center City* ☎ *03/520–2700* ⊕ *www.mendelistreethotel.com* ⊋ *66 rooms* ⦿ *Free Breakfast.*

★ The Norman Hotel

$$$$ | HOTEL | Two immaculately restored historic buildings in central Tel Aviv make up this contemporary urban hot spot that evokes Bauhaus-era elegance and old world charm. **Pros:** spacious rooms and stunning design; some of the comfiest beds ever; rooftop infinity pool. **Cons:** extremely pricey; pool can get busy; you have to go outside to move between buildings. $ *Rooms from: $515* ✉ *23–25 Nachmani St., Center City* ☎ *03/543–5555* ⊕ *www.thenorman.com* ⊋ *50 rooms* ⦿ *Free Breakfast.*

Poli House

$$ | HOTEL | Star designer Karim Rashid chose the iconic Polishuk House, a Bauhaus building, for his first venture into Tel Aviv's boutique hotel scene. **Pros:** heated rooftop infinity pool; central location; trendy bar. **Cons:** design tends to overlook practicality; very busy location, can get noisy; no loungers on the rooftop. $ *Rooms from: $270* ✉ *1 Nahalat Binyamin St., Center City* ⊹ *Entrance accessible from pedestrian street*

☎ *03/710–5000* ⊕ *brownhotels.com/poli* ⊋ *40 rooms* ⦿ *Free Breakfast.*

Renaissance Tel Aviv Hotel

$$ | HOTEL | FAMILY | All the rooms and suites have spectacular sea-facing balconies at this comfortable luxury hotel with a geometric facade. **Pros:** pretty sundecks; beautiful indoor pool; direct access to beach. **Cons:** business lounge closes at midnight; rooms that have not been recently renovated are a bit tired; no outdoor pool. $ *Rooms from: $280* ✉ *121 Hayarkon St., Center City* ☎ *03/521–5555* ⊕ *www.marriott.com* ⊋ *346 rooms* ⦿ *Free Breakfast.*

★ Renoma Hotel

$$$$ | HOTEL | One of the only upscale boutique properties on the Tel Aviv beachfront, Renoma offers stunning individually designed suites in a beautifully restored 1930s building, as well as a number of serviced apartments in the modern mini-tower next door. **Pros:** exceptional, highly personal service; thoughtful touches like gym passes, beach bags and bike rental; dreamy location right on the beach. **Cons:** limited breakfast options; set on a heavily trafficked street; no budget rooms in this all-suite hotel. $ *Rooms from: $500* ✉ *59 HaYarkon St., Center City* ☎ *077/614–0400* ⊕ *www.renomahotel.com* ⊋ *21 suites* ⦿ *No meals.*

The Rothschild Hotel

$$ | HOTEL | On Rothschild Boulevard, this boutique hotel has a color scheme and design aesthetic intended to evoke the Tel Aviv of days gone by. **Pros:** free on-site parking available; top-notch restaurant with excellent breakfast; nespresso machine in each room. **Cons:** on a busy street; on-site restaurant only serves breakfast; rooms on the small side. $ *Rooms from: $285* ✉ *96 Rothschild Blvd., Center City* ☎ *03/957–8888* ⊕ *www.the-rothschild-hotel.com* ⊋ *29 rooms* ⦿ *Free Breakfast.*

The Rothschild 71

$$ | **HOTEL** | When you enter this nicely renovated International Style building you'll feel right at home, thanks to a living-room-style lobby where you can enjoy coffee and tea. **Pros:** personal service; espresso machine in each room; good value for the area. **Cons:** included breakfast is at underwhelming restaurant; pricey, though it's still a good value; on a noisy street. $ *Rooms from: $250* ✉ *71 Rothschild Blvd., Center City* ☎ *03/629–0555* ⊕ *www.the-rothschild. com* ⤳ *30 rooms* ¶◯¶ *Free Breakfast.*

Royal Beach Tel Aviv

$$$$ | **HOTEL** | One of many five-star properties linked to large hotel chains along the Tel Aviv promenade, Royal Beach Tel Aviv offers an outdoor pool, an à la carte restaurant, and a spa and wellness area. **Pros:** infinity pool overlooking the sea; fantastic kosher restaurant in hotel; beachfront location. **Cons:** additional cost for spa and wellness area; overpriced, especially in high season; service is hit and miss. $ *Rooms from: $405* ✉ *19 Hayarkon St., Center City* ☎ *03/740–5000* ⊕ *www.isrotel.com* ⤳ *230 rooms* ¶◯¶ *Free Breakfast.*

Shalom Hotel & Relax

$$ | **HOTEL** | At this boutique hotel, the attentive staff, always friendly and accommodating, greets you with a cold beverage and a chocolate treat, and the daily happy hour includes snacks and complimentary alcoholic beverages—a great way to wind down after a day of sun, sea, and sightseeing. **Pros:** rooftop lounge with sea view; outstanding breakfast; free use of bikes. **Cons:** no pool; parking around here is tricky; on a noisy street. $ *Rooms from: $295* ✉ *216 Hayarkon St., Center City* ☎ *03/762–5400* ⊕ *www.atlas.co.il/shalom-hotel-tel-aviv* ⤳ *51 rooms* ¶◯¶ *Free Breakfast.*

Shenkin Hotel

$ | **HOTEL** | The Shenkin Hotel is a small, friendly boutique hotel situated close to some of Tel Aviv's busiest tourist attractions, including Shenkin Street, Carmel Market, and the Nachalat Binyamin Art Fair. **Pros:** affordable accommodation in central location; cozy rooftop terrace; plenty of generous extra touches. **Cons:** no pool; quite far from the beach; blackout curtains not very effective. $ *Rooms from: $175* ✉ *21 Brenner St., Center City* ☎ *03/600–9400* ⊕ *www.shenkinhotel. com* ⤳ *30 rooms* ¶◯¶ *No meals.*

★ 65 Hotel Rothschild Tel Aviv

$$ | **HOTEL** | This sophisticated, beautifully designed hotel harmonizes with the central business location in the heart of Rothschild Boulevard. **Pros:** daily happy hour with drinks and snacks; excellent breakfast offering both buffet and à la carte options; ideal location for business travelers. **Cons:** no pool or gym; smallish rooms; location can get noisy. $ *Rooms from: $275* ✉ *65 Rothschild Blvd., Center City* ☎ *03/767–7677* ⊕ *www.atlas. co.il/65-hotel-tel-aviv* ⤳ *74 rooms* ¶◯¶ *Free Breakfast.*

★ The Vera Hotel

$ | **HOTEL** | Of all the stylish boutique hotels to have opened in Tel Aviv in recent years, none is hipper or more on trend than The Vera Hotel, an eco-conscious option with a breezy, two-story rooftop terrace exclusively for hotel guests. **Pros:** ultratrendy; gorgeous two-tier rooftop; complimentary extras like yoga, breakfast, and wine. **Cons:** no pool or fitness center; rooms are minimalist; no meat or fish served. $ *Rooms from: $195* ✉ *27 Lilienblum St., Center City* ☎ *03/77–3800* ⊕ *theverahotel.com* ⤳ *39 rooms* ¶◯¶ *Free Breakfast.*

🅨 Nightlife

BARS AND CLUBS

Aria Lounge Bar

PIANO BARS/LOUNGES | This Manhattan-style lounge bar offers the rare combination of classy food, cocktails, and dancing in the same space. Seats in the lounge circle the DJ booth, where top

Tel Aviv is a music lover's paradise, and it's not hard to find live performances in bars, restaurants, or even on the street.

local and international DJs, and occasional live-music performers, hold forth. A full dinner menu is available from the upstairs fine-dining restaurant, along with craft cocktails like Say Hello 2 Heaven, a fresh, citrusy concoction of champagne, gin, black mint, lemon juice, and fresh basil. ⊠ *66 Nahalat Binyamin St., Center City* ☎ *03/529–6054* ⊕ *www.ariatlv.co.il.*

Bar Barbunia

BARS/PUBS | Aptly named for a small fish that's a staple of the city's old-time restaurants, Bar Barbunia draws a mixed crowd that ranges from fishermen to financial planners. It manages to be both smoky and cheerful, and the music tends toward classics from the '70s. The bar is small and can get extremely busy so don't be surprised if the party spills out onto the street. ⊠ *163 Ben Yehuda St., Center City* ☎ *03/524–0961* ⊕ *barbunya. co.il.*

★ Bellboy

BARS/PUBS | Many of the cocktails here are lit up with a fiery uproar, and some come with garnishes straight out of a

toy shop. It's definitely worth watching the skilled bartenders do their stuff in a room that takes you straight back to the 1920s. Small dishes are served with a bit less drama and include beef tartare, crispy calamari, and house-made fried kale chips (hard to find in Israel). In true speakeasy fashion, the bar is expertly hidden inside a small boutique hotel, on a side street near the northern end of Rothschild Boulevard. ⊠ *14 Berdichevsky St., Center City* ☎ *03/728–9213* ⊕ *www. bellboybar.com.*

Bushwick

BARS/PUBS | Paying homage to a certain neighborhood in Brooklyn, Bushwick is known for its lively atmosphere and excellent cocktail menu. The bar is situated on the ground floor of the trendy new Fabric Hotel and, apart from serving breakfast to hotel guests, is also a popular spot for sipping a morning coffee or chilling over afternoon drinks. Don't miss the Rhubarbara Streisand or the wild and smoky Here Comes the Tiger. They're brought to you by the team of mixology maestros behind the immensely popular Imperial Craft Cocktail Bar. ⊠ *28 Nahalat Binyamin St., Center City* ☎ *03/567–8006* ⊕ *www.bushwicktlv.com.*

Café Europa

CAFES—NIGHTLIFE | At this place to see and be seen, especially in summer evenings, the sparkling cocktails and creative small plates draw attractive customers to a packed outdoor patio. Be adventurous and taste one of the cocktails made with a local product, such as the anise-flavored arak. ⊠ *9B Rothschild Blvd., Center City* ☎ *03/525–9987* ⊕ *cafeeuropa.co.il/en.*

HaMaoz

BARS/PUBS | The quirky interior of this bar geared toward the twenty- and thirty-something crowd resembles someone's apartment, down to the black-and-white family photos on the walls. There's even a refrigerator in the kitchen and a working shower in the bathroom. It's always crowded in the living room, where there's a flat-screen TV. ⊠ *32 King George St., Center City* ☎ *03/620–9458.*

HaMinzar

BARS/PUBS | One of the oldest bars in Tel Aviv, the Monastery is a gritty, down-to-earth pub that's popular with a slightly older after-work crowd, as well as with students later in the evening and on weekends. The kitchen serves up some fine food, too. ⊠ *60 Allenby St., Center City* ☎ *03/517–3015* ⊕ *www.facebook.com/minzarbar.*

Hashoftim

BARS/PUBS | At this neighborhood tavern rich with history, the regulars tend to be older and mellower. Groups of friends congregate outside in the beer garden or inside at the small bar while enjoying jazz or blues. ⊠ *39 Ibn Gvirol St., at Hashoftim St., Center City* ☎ *03/695–1153.*

★ Imperial Craft Cocktail Bar

BARS/PUBS | Head to the hidden back entrance of a somewhat lackluster hotel lobby and discover this colonial-British-themed playground run by five of Tel Aviv's top mixologists. Nightly specials enhance the standard menu of 150 precisely concocted cocktails. Drop in for happy hour, every night from 6 to 8 pm, when the "special price" cocktails are particularly appealing, or reserve for late night, when you may be sitting next to the city's top chefs. ⊠ *Imperial Hotel, 66 Hayarkon St., Center City* ☎ *073/264–9464* ⊕ *www.imperialtlv.com.*

Kuli Alma

BARS/PUBS | A two-level subterranean courtyard adorned by local graffiti artists draws bohemian music addicts and casual partiers for alternative music, not to mention fresh baked pizza and mojito slushies. Any night of the week you can find a relaxed crowd enjoying either a live band or an international DJ playing hip-hop, soul, or electronic music. ⊠ *10 Mikveh Israel St., Center City* ☎ *03/656–5155.*

Levontin 7

BARS/PUBS | This is a vibrant spot to experience the local music scene. Live music is on offer almost every night, featuring the widest possible mix of musical offerings, from solo singers to bands blasting indie rock in Arabic. There's a cozy bar upstairs. ⊠ *7 Levontin St., Center City* ☎ *03/560–5084* ⊕ *www.levontin7.com.*

Library Bar

WINE BARS—NIGHTLIFE | In the lobby of the elegant Norman Hotel, the stately 1940s colonial-style Library Bar is ideal for refreshment at any time of day. Open from 10 am to 1 am, this posh refuge serves a traditional English high tea by day and pours wines from one of Tel Aviv's most luxurious wine lists throughout the evening. Aperitifs with complimentary snacks are served during happy hour, Monday to Thursday from 6 pm to 8 pm. Look out for the bar's art and fashion evenings, which bring together the city's tastemakers for cultural conversation. ⊠ *The Norman Hotel, 23–25 Nachmani*

St., Center City ☎ 03/543–5400 ⊕ www.
thenorman.com.

Lima Lima

DANCE CLUBS | This fun, laid-back nightclub
has an indoor dance floor and an outdoor
garden area. Every night of the week
has a different theme, including gay,
mainstream, hip hop and reggaeton.
Lima Lima is especially popular for its
LGBTQ+-theme nights, which include
Monday's Hip Hop nights, and the Sunday night Eurovision party. The latter is a
must for fans of the mega-camp European pop extravaganza that is the Eurovision Song Contest. ⊠ 42 Lilienblum St.,
Center City ☎ 054/246–7906 ⊕ www.
facebook.com/LimaLimaBar.

Mike's Place

BARS/PUBS | This well-stocked bar with
multiple locations throughout the city
appeals mainly to the over-thirty crowd.
Live sports on TV, live music, and its primary location, on the promenade facing
the beach, make it popular with tourists.
⊠ 86 Herbert Samuel St., Center City
☎ 03/510–6392 ⊕ www.mikesplacebars.
com.

Molly Bloom

BARS/PUBS | The country's most authen-
tic Irish pub is—no surprise—run by an
Irishman, Robert Segal. Live music rever-
berates on Monday and Friday afternoon.
There's a full menu, including such Emerald Isle favorites as shepherd's pie and
beef stew. ⊠ 100 Hayarkon St., corner of
Mendeli St., Center City ☎ 52/233–0202
⊕ www.molly-blooms.com.

Nanuchka

BARS/PUBS | This ornate bistro and bar
occupies a courtyard and a large interior
space adorned with tapestries and paintings. The dancing gets going around 10
pm every night. Drinks include specialties
of the house—a selection of sweet but
light wines from the country of Geor-
gia. The vegan menu is delicious and is
surprising considering Georgian food is
generally rich with meat. ⊠ 30 Lilienblum

St., Center City ☎ 03/516–2254 ⊕ www.
nanuchka.co.il.

★ Tasting Room

WINE BARS—NIGHTLIFE | Showcasing Israeli
vintages is the name of the game at this
beautifully designed underground wine
bar in the Sarona complex. An innovative
automated pouring system allows you
to taste 40 different wines from Israel
and further afield using a prepaid smart
card. Tastings are available by the sip,
half glass, or full glass. If you particularly
enjoy a certain wine, you can purchase
a full bottle. The kosher menu features
expertly prepared modern Mediterranean
dishes. ⊠ Sarona, 36 Kaplan St., Center
City ☎ 03/533–3213 ⊕ www.tastingroom.
co.il.

223

BARS/PUBS | This stylish neighborhood bar
has the feel of Prohibition-era New York
City. The suspender-wearing bartenders
specialize in excellent mixed drinks.
Order a spicy apple martini to go alongside the expertly crafted bar food. ⊠ 223
Dizengoff St., Center City ☎ 03/544–6537
⊕ www.223.co.il.

Whiskey Bar & Museum

BARS/PUBS | With an impressive selec-
tion of whiskey from every corner of
the globe, Whiskey Bar & Museum (bar,
museum, and restaurant, actually) showcases more than 1,000 different bottles,
all of which you can sample and buy.
Set in one of the historic tunnels built
under the Sarona district by the German
Templers in the 19th century, the space
is steeped in history, having previously
been a local winery and, more recently, home to the Israeli secret service,
Mossad. The menu features a selection
of kosher dishes designed to pair well
with whiskey, including charcuterie and
desserts. ⊠ Sarona, 27 David Elazar St.,
Center City ☎ 03/955–1105 ⊕ whiskey-
bm.co.il.

Zizi

DANCE CLUBS | This hot club's focus is on dancing, but some secluded corners can be found for quiet conversation. Bartenders wave their hands in the air to the beat of the music, adding to the feel of escapist abandon. Check the schedule for gay party nights. ⊠ *7 Carlebach St., Center City* ☎ *03/561–1597.*

🎭 Performing Arts

★ Cameri Theatre of Tel Aviv

THEATER | Founded in 1944, this long-standing Hebrew performance theater, located in the Tel Aviv Performing Arts Center, offers a useful "See it in Hebrew, Read it in English" program every Tuesday, in which the performance is simultaneously translated into English. Shows range from classic plays to international dramas, comedies, and local pieces. ⊠ *19 Shaul Hamelech St., Center City* ☎ *03/606–1900* ⊕ *www.cameri.co.il.*

★ Charles Bronfman Auditorium

MUSIC | Israel's largest concert hall is the home of the Israel Philharmonic Orchestra, led by maestro Zubin Mehta. The low-slung gray building was among the most architecturally sophisticated cultural buildings in the country when it was completed in 1957. It has excellent acoustics and a seating capacity of 3,000 people. The hall also hosts pop and rock concerts. ⊠ *1 Huberman St., Center City* ☎ *03/543–0777* ⊕ *www.ipo.co.il.*

Enav Cultural Center

MUSIC | Run by the city, the Enav Cultural Center is a 300-seat venue offering eclectic music and theater, ranging from Israeli music to classical, opera, jazz, and blues. ⊠ *71 Ibn Gvirol St., Center City* ☎ *03/521–7763.*

Habima National Theater

THEATER | This troupe is rooted in the Russian Revolution, when a group of young Jewish artists established a theater company that performed in Hebrew—this at a time when Hebrew was barely a living language. Subsequent tours through Europe and the United States in the 1920s won wide acclaim. Many of the group's members moved to Israel and helped establish a theater company that now inhabits multiple spaces, including a nicely renovated complex at Habima Square. Even though the vast majority of productions are in Hebrew, many are also simultaneously translated into English. ⊠ *Habima Sq., end of Rothschild Blvd., Center City* ☎ *03/629–5555, 03/629–5555* ⊕ *www.habima.co.il.*

Tel Aviv Performing Arts Center

DANCE | The Tel Aviv Performing Arts Center is home to the Israeli Opera, as well as the Israel Ballet and the Cameri Theatre. It's possible to book a behind-the-scenes tour 75 minutes prior to the performance. ⊠ *19 Shaul Hamelech St., Center City* ☎ *03/692–7777* ⊕ *www.israel-opera.co.il.*

🛍 Shopping

CLOTHING

Couple Of

SHOES/LUGGAGE/LEATHER GOODS | This shop is known for making beautiful and comfortable shoes for hard-to-fit feet. Whether vintage or modern in style, the carefully crafted footwear is "handmade for walking." ⊠ *207 Dizengoff St., Center City* ☎ *03/604–4451* ⊕ *www.couple-of.com.*

Kisim

JEWELRY/ACCESSORIES | This designer is influenced by Japanese origami, which you'll notice in the handbags, clutches, and wallets. The designer's informal style has an elegant twist. One of the bags was famously used by Sarah Jessica Parker in *Sex and the City.* ⊠ *8 HaHashmal St., Center City* ☎ *03/560–4890* ⊕ *www.kisim.com.*

Continued on page 267

TEL AVIV AFTER DARK

Settling in at your hotel after dinner isn't an option if you want to truly experience Tel Aviv like a local. In this city famous for its nightlife, dusk is the catalyst that propels the day's steady buzz of activity into high gear. Restaurants fill to max capacity, bars become packed, and people rush to dance and musical performances. Generally speaking, southern Tel Aviv—where you'll find Florentin and Jaffa—has a mellow, low-key vibe with a bohemian flavor. Areas farther north, along Rothschild Boulevard and the Tel Aviv Port, tend to have pricier places frequented by movers and shakers. In the middle is newly hip Neve Tzedek, where everyone mixes.

JAFFA

Jaffa at night

A winding, cobblestone street in Jaffa

An ancient port, mentioned in the Bible, this is one of the few examples of Jewish and Arab citizens living side-by-side. Like the Old City in Jerusalem, this area of winding stone alleyways retains its historic feel, and is today a serene spot perched on a hill in the southern end of Tel Aviv with promenades that afford alluring nighttime views of the twinkling coastline.

THE SCENE

With its tranquil vibe, Jaffa is the city's least fast-paced night spot. It's preeminently a romantic place to spend the evening to stroll, eat, and shop, where you'll find a relatively mature crowd of tourists and locals alike.

LOCATION LOWDOWN

Amble along the streets of the artist's quarter to Kedumim Plaza, and you'll find yourself at the top of the hill in the heart of Jaffa. There's live music offered here on Saturday evenings. Or catch a classical quartet at the Franciscan Church of St. Peter, a 17th-century building where Napoleon stayed after capturing the city.

NEIGHBORHOOD KNOW-HOW

If you're in the mood to learn something before going out, the Association for Tourism–Tel-Aviv-Jaffa (☎ 03/516–6188 ⊕ www.visit-TLV.co.il) offers free evening walking tours every Wednesday at 9:30 PM.

TOP PICKS

Try the romantic **Kalamata** (10 Kedumim Sq., ☎ 03/681–7998) in the center of Old Jaffa.

Shaffa Bar (Yeffet 30, ☎ 050/214-1444) draws an older, sophisticated clientele.

Saloona (Tirza 17, in the Noga Compound, ☎ 03/518–1719) is Jaffa's sexiest lounge-bar with a hip, artistic feel.

Roam the **Jaffa Flea Market** (Olei Zion St.) and around Rabbi Yohanan Street. Have a drink in one of many great bars.

NEVE TZEDEK

The Mann Auditorium

After many years of neglect, Neve Tzedek has been rediscovered, becoming Tel Aviv's most popular neighborhood day or night. It brims with laid-back wine bars, galleries, boutiques, and restored two-storey houses painted in warm pastels.

THE SCENE
The first Jewish neighborhood outside of Jaffa was once home to Israeli artists and writers, and still attracts a trendy, avant-garde crowd mixed with nouveau-riche locals.

LOCATION LOWDOWN
The most scenic way to reach Neve Tzedek is to walk the Shlush Bridge. Neve Tzedek centers around the Suzanne Dellal Center, Tel Aviv's modern dance hub and headquarters of internationally acclaimed dance companies such as Bat-Sheva, Inbal, and Vertigo.

NEIGHBORHOOD KNOW-HOW
After watching a contemporary dance performance, walk through the Dellal Center's beautiful piazza, with its burbling fountains and orange trees, to the neighborhood's main thoroughfare, Shabazi Street, which intersects Neve Tzedek's charming smaller lanes.

TOP PICKS

A trendy spot with an outdoor bodega vibe in the Hatachana 'Old Train Station' complex, **Vicky Cristina** (☎ 03/736-7272), or on the terrace at **Suzana** (Shabazi 9).

Neve Tzedek also happens to be a short walk from **Manta Ray** (☎ 03/517–4773, ⊕ www. mantaray.co.il), the quintessential Tel Aviv restaurant, and the perfect place to sip an aperitif on the curving terrace overlooking Alma Beach.

TEL AVIV PORT

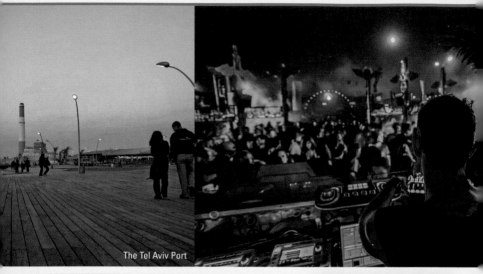

The Tel Aviv Port

Tel Aviv's hottest, loudest, most throbbing nightlife spot is the Tel Aviv Port (in Hebrew, the Namal) in the city's northern reaches (www.namal.co.il). With its cutting edge music, DJ-spun grooves, and raucous crowds, the Port has contributed in no small measure to Tel Aviv's newly-acquired fame as a major player in the clubbing world.

THE SCENE

Luckily for some, clubs here come alive only on weekends, when they house churning thickets of stylish club crawlers. During the week, it's all about trying the latest trendy restaurant.

LOCATION LOWDOWN

Restaurants and clubs here were built above a small, artificial harbor which stands beside the Yarkon River's estuary. Over the last decade, the port was transformed into a chic waterfront area that includes a wooden boardwalk, the largest in Israel, its undulating shape inspired by the sand dunes of Tel Aviv's early days.

NEIGHBORHOOD KNOW-HOW

Long, disorganized lines form at club entrances, so do your best to catch the doorman's eye. Speaking English sometimes helps. The Port's clubs only warm up at 2 AM, so fortify yourself with a disco nap. And most clubs won't take plastic for cover charges or drinks.

TOP PICKS

Two of the Port's most flamboyant clubs are the **Light House** (☎ 052/245-8600), with its massive dance floor featuring top international DJs and fashionable **Shalvata beach club** (☎ 03/544-1279), guaranteed to be a hit during summer months.

If clubs aren't your scene, satisfy your musical appetite and catch a trio at the first-rate **Shablul Jazz Club** (⊕ www.shabluljazz.com), housed in spacious quarters at the Port's Hangar 13.

Maya Bash

CLOTHING | These designer clothing collections made from wearable cottons and other light materials are great for the Tel Aviv climate. The unique cuts and comfortable materials are making Maya Bash a hit in Germany and Japan as well. ⊠ *5 Barzilay St., Center City* ☎ *03/560–0305* ⊕ *www.mayabash.com.*

CRAFTS
Raphael

CRAFTS | One of the most pleasant shopping experiences in Tel Aviv, this shop carries a large selection of Judaica, jewelry, and handicrafts by some of the best Israeli artists. ⊠ *94 Ben Yehuda St., Center City* ☎ *03/527–3619* ⊕ *www. raphaels.co.il.*

JEWELRY
Hagar Satat

JEWELRY/ACCESSORIES | Weaving together leather with gold and silver, Hagar Satat's jewelry is great for special occasions or everyday wear. Pick up bargain-priced pieces from the outlet store in the trendy Gan HaHashmal fashion neighborhood. ⊠ *8 HaHashmal St., Center City* ☎ *77/560–7300* ⊕ *www.hagar-satat.com.*

JUDAICA
Miller

LOCAL SPECIALTIES | Specializing in Judaica, Miller has a particularly wide selection of silver items, including a jewelry collection. ⊠ *Azrieli Center, 132 Derech Menachem Begin, Center City* ☎ *03/608–1118* ⊕ *www.miller.co.il.*

LOCAL SPECIALTIES
Bauhaus Center

LOCAL SPECIALTIES | The attractive displays of books, maps, posters, furnishings, dishes, and even Judaica, all inspired by Bauhaus design, are a reminder that this school of design embraced more than buildings. There's a gallery of changing exhibits related to Bauhaus style and history, and the center organizes both group and private Bauhaus (and other) walking tours. ⊠ *77 Dizengoff St., Center City* ☎ *03/522–0249* ⊕ *www.bauhaus-center. com.*

★ **Zalmania** (*The PhotoHouse*)
GIFTS/SOUVENIRS | Established in 1940, the Zalmania PhotoHouse is the oldest photography shop in Israel and has been family owned and operated for generations. With more than a million negatives documenting Israel's history, this nostalgic shop sells historical photographs, books, postcards, posters, and gifts, many of which are only found in this shop. ⊠ *5 Tchernichovsky St., Center City* ☎ *03/517–7916* ⊕ *www.thephotohouse. co.il.*

🏃 Activities

BIKING
Tel-O-Fun

BICYCLING | Tel Aviv runs this convenient bike-sharing system—pick up a bike at one station and return it there or at any other station around the city. The fees (starting at NIS 17 daily, plus an additional hourly fee when more than ½ hour) can either be paid by credit card at the pickup bike station or online via the Tel-O-Fun website. The bikes are quite heavy and are useful for getting from point to point throughout the city or for riding along the seafront promenade. ⊠ *Center City* ☎ **6070* ⊕ *www.tel-o-fun.co.il/en.*

BOATING
Ganei Yehoshua Boating (*Hayarkon Park*)

BOATING | **FAMILY** | In the northern part of the city, at the lake in Hayarkon Park (Ganei Yehoshua), you can rent pedal boats, rowboats, and motorboats. ⊠ *Rokach Blvd., Center City* ☎ *03/642–0541* ⊕ *park.co.il/en/activites/the-park-lake* 💲 *From NIS 95 per hr.*

SAILING
Ofek Yachts

SAILING | Charter a weeklong yacht journey with a skipper or a day party boat for up to 22 people at Ofek Yachts at the Tel

Aviv Marina. ⊠ *Tel Aviv Marina, 14 Eliezer Peri St., Center City* ☎ *03/529–9988* ⊕ *www.ofek-yachts.co.il.*

Sea Tel Aviv

BOATING | You can charter a variety of boats here for daytime excursions or romantic sunset sails leaving from Tel Aviv Marina. It's also possible to arrange scuba diving, snorkeling, and other activities. ⊠ *Tel Aviv Marina, 10 Eliezer Peri St., Center City* ☎ *052/869–8080* ⊕ *www. seatelaviv.co.il.*

SWIMMING

Gordon Pool

SWIMMING | **FAMILY** | This outdoor complex includes an Olympic-size swimming pool with a separate section for kids. There are also dressing rooms and lounge chairs. ⊠ *14 Eliezer Peri St., Center City* ☎ *03/762–3300* ⊕ *www.gordon-pool.co.il* 🎫 *NIS 69.*

Neve Tzedek

Made up of about a dozen tiny streets crammed with one- and two-story dwellings in various stages of renovation, Neve Tzedek is rich with history. This is where the saga of Tel Aviv began, when a small group of Jewish families from Jaffa laid the cornerstone for their new neighborhood, naming it Neve Tzedek (Oasis of Justice). When Tel Aviv was busy expanding to the north and the east in the early days of the state, Neve Tzedek was allowed to deteriorate. But in recent years the beautiful old buildings were rediscovered, and the lovingly restored homes here are now among the most prestigious addresses in the city.

Full of restaurants and cafés, Neve Tzedek is where you'll find the fantastic dance and theater complex, the Suzanne Dellal Centre for Dance and Theatre, as well as a growing number of trendy galleries and boutiques. Though bordered on three sides by major thoroughfares (Eilat Road to the south, Herzl Street to the east, and Kaufman Street along the sea), this quarter is very tranquil.

GETTING HERE AND AROUND

The spine of Neve Tzedek is Shabazi Street, which runs the length of the neighborhood. Most shops and restaurants are either on or near Shabazi Street. The roads here are notoriously narrow, and pedestrians have the right-of-way.

TIMING

Neve Tzedek is the perfect place to spend a few leisurely hours exploring the interesting shops and tasty eateries. The neighborhood can get pretty crowded on weekends, and most of the action is in the bars and restaurants along and around Shabazi Street.

◉ Sights

Gutman Museum

MUSEUM | In the 1920s, a number of Tel Aviv's most famous writers lived in this building, whose renovations have somewhat obscured its original look. One of the first houses in Neve Tzedek, the building now displays the art of Nahum Gutman, colorful chronicler of early Tel Aviv. Tours in English are available by appointment. ⊠ *21 Rokach St., Neve Tzedek* ☎ *03/516–1970* ⊕ *www.gutman-museum.co.il* 🎫 *NIS 24* 🕙 *Closed Sun.*

HaTachana

LOCAL INTEREST | On the edge of Neve Tzedek, this Turkish-era train station is where travelers once embarked to Jerusalem on the first piece of railroad in the Middle East. Even Theodor Herzl, founder of modern Zionism, passed through here. Dubbed HaTachana, Hebrew for "The Station," the 49-acre complex includes 22 different buildings, among them the former station that now houses art exhibits. A pair of restored train cars tells the story of the station's days as a major travel hub in the region. You'll also find restaurants, cafés, and boutiques peddling handcrafted jewelry and homegrown designer clothes. At the entrance is a

Neve Tzedek and Florentin

Sights

1 Gutman Museum **D2**
2 HaTachana **C3**
3 Levinsky Market **F2**
4 Rokach House **E2**
5 Suzanne Dellal Centre for
   Dance and Theatre **D2**

Restaurants

1 Dallal **C2**
2 Disco Tokyo **E2**
3 Hatraklin **E2**
4 Meshek Barzilay **E1**
5 Mezcal **E3**
6 NG **E1**
7 Opa **F2**
8 Popina **E1**
9 Suzana **C2**

Hotels

1 Dan Panorama
   Tel Aviv **C1**
2 InterContinental David
   Tel Aviv **C1**
3 The Levee **E2**

KEY

1 Sights
1 Restaurants
1 Hotels

tourist information stand. Thursday night is "Unique" night, when up-and-coming Israeli designers, artists, and creatives showcase their work, accompanied by live music and DJs. The space also plays host to an urban organic market on Friday mornings. ✉ *Koifman and Ha'Mered Sts., Neve Tzedek* 🌐 *www.hatachana.co.il* 🎫 *Free.*

Rokach House

HOUSE | Built in 1887, the home of Neve Tzedek founder Shimon Rokach had fallen into disrepair and was slated for demolition before being reclaimed and restored in the 1980s by his granddaughter, artist Leah Majaro-Mintz. It now houses an exhibit of items from the quarter's early days, as well as pieces of her own art. Guided tours in English are available by calling ahead. A cabaret-style performance (in Hebrew) showcasing Neve Tzedek's history, preceded by samples of the period's cuisine, is offered for groups on Thursday and Friday evening at 8:30 pm. ✉ *36 Rokach St., Neve Tzedek* ☎ *03/516–8042* 🌐 *www.rokach-house.co.il* 🎫 *NIS 10* 🕒 *Closed Sun.–Wed.*

★ Suzanne Dellal Centre for Dance and Theatre

ARTS VENUE | A pair of whitewashed buildings—one built in 1892, the other in 1908—make up this attractive complex. The square, designed by noted landscape architect Shlomo Aronson, has hints of a medieval Middle Eastern courtyard in its scattering of orange trees connected by water channels. One side of the square is decorated with a tile triptych that illustrates the neighborhood's history and famous people who lived here in the early years, including S. Y. Agnon, who went on to win the Nobel Prize in Literature. There's a café-bar on the premises and a number of great restaurants nearby for pre- or postperformance meals. It's worth a stroll here even if you aren't seeing a performance. ✉ *5 Yehieli St., near Shabazi St., Neve Tzedek* ☎ *03/510–5656* 🌐 *www.suzannedellal.org.il.*

🍴 Restaurants

Elegant wine bars and contemporary dining rooms are what you will find in historic Neve Tzedek. As the home of the Suzanne Dellal Centre for Dance and Theatre, this neighborhood is the ideal place for a pre- or postperformance meal.

Dallal

$$$$ | **MEDITERRANEAN** | Inside a beautifully restored historic building, this bistro has a rarefied atmosphere and an on-the-premises bakery that turns out a luscious array of French-style pastries. The breakfast menu highlights some of the baked delights, including smoked-salmon croissants and the indulgent French toast sandwich with fruit, ricotta cheese, and maple syrup. **Known for:** superb baked goods; a well-heeled crowd; delightful patio. [$] *Average main: NIS 170* ✉ *10 Shabazi St., Neve Tzedek* ☎ *03/510–9292* 🌐 *www.dallal.co.il.*

Hatraklin

$$$$ | **STEAKHOUSE** | At this bistro in the heart of Neve Tzedek, the warm environment, hearty food, fine wine, and excellent service will leave you feeling satisfied. The wine menu boasts more than 160 Israeli boutique wines, and the friendly owner-sommelier, Yossi Ben Odis, will let you know exactly which wine pairs well with your meal. **Known for:** cook-yourself seared sirloin; extensive selection of Israeli wines; cozy outdoor patio. [$] *Average main: NIS 120* ✉ *4 Heichal Hatalmud St., Neve Tzedek* ☎ *03/566–0013* 🌐 *www.hatraklin.co.il* 🕒 *Closed Tues. No lunch Sun.–Fri.*

Meshek Barzilay

$$ | **VEGETARIAN** | **FAMILY** | Israel has the highest population of vegans per capita, so it's impressive that Meshek Barzilay started blazing the plant-based trail long before farm-to-table eating became trendy. Tucked away on a quiet, secluded street in Neve Tzedek, the restaurant serves only locally sourced, organic, plant-based ingredients. **Known for:** local, organic, seasonal vegan food; veggie burger and beetroot gnocchi; leafy patio in charming Neve Tzedek. $ Average main: NIS 65 ⊠ 6 Ahad Ha'Am St., Neve Tzedek ☎ 03/516–6329 ⊕ www.meshek-barzilay.co.il.

NG

$$$$ | CONTEMPORARY | Tucked away in a quiet corner of the city, this small, elegant bistro specializes in fine cuts of expertly prepared meat. It's purported to be the only place in Israel where you can enjoy a real porterhouse steak. **Known for:** one of the best steak houses in Tel Aviv; historic building with contemporary decor; porterhouse steak. $ Average main: NIS 150 ⊠ 6 Ahad Ha'am St., Neve Tzedek ☎ 03/516–7888 ⊕ www.ngrestaurant.co.il ⊗ Closed Tues. No lunch Sun. and Mon. or Wed.–Fri.

Popina

$$$$ | MEDITERRANEAN | Few restaurants have made a splash on the Tel Aviv dining scene as big as Popina, Chef Orel Kimchi's trendy Neve Tzedek eatery. The menu is divided into cooking techniques: cured, steamed, baked, roasted, and slow-cooked and uses innovative flavor combinations, like the pumpkin jam ravioli with amaretto, foie gras, roasted almonds, and truffle foam, the shrimp burger with yuzu aioli, or the raw fish tartare with gin and tonic jelly. **Known for:** creative cuisine from a top chef; exceptional tasting menu; open kitchen. $ Average main: NIS 110 ⊠ 3 Ahad Ha'Am St., Neve Tzedek ☎ 03/575–7477 ⊕ www.popina.co.il ⊗ No lunch except Sat.

Suzana

$$ | MEDITERRANEAN | FAMILY | In a century-old building near the Suzanne Dellal Centre for Dance and Theatre, this popular eatery bustles day and night. Sample the Kurdish *kubbeh* (meat-filled semolina dumplings) and pumpkin soup, the okra in tomato sauce, the red peppers stuffed with meat and rice, or the Moroccan *harira*, a thick soup with chickpeas, veal, and coriander. **Known for:**

unbeatable setting on a charming patio; Middle Eastern-Israeli menu; good stop pre- or postperformance at Suzanne Dellal Center. $ Average main: NIS 69 ⊠ 9 Shabazi St., Neve Tzedek ☎ 03/517–7580 ⊕ www.suzana.rest-e.co.il.

🛏 Hotels

Historic Neve Tzedek has a few modern lodgings with a convenient location a short distance from the sea.

Dan Panorama Tel Aviv

$$$ | HOTEL | At the southern end of the beach, this high-rise is a short walk from Jaffa and Neve Tzedek. **Pros:** across the street from the beach; handy location; all rooms have balconies, many with sea views. **Cons:** staid atmosphere; feels more business hotel than luxury vacation spot; slightly tired. $ Rooms from: $310 ⊠ 10 Koifman St., Neve Tzedek ☎ 03/519–0190 ⊕ www.danhotels.com ⤳ 500 rooms ⦿ Free Breakfast.

InterContinental David Tel Aviv

$$$ | HOTEL | FAMILY | At the southern end of the beachfront promenade, this luxurious hotel has suites that are often reserved by visiting celebrities—and with the jaw-dropping views of the sea and the Tel Aviv skyline, it's easy to understand why. **Pros:** ocean and city views; huge breakfast selection; close to the beach and the city center. **Cons:** no balconies; massive and slightly impersonal; some parts of the hotel feel a bit dated. $ Rooms from: $395 ⊠ 12 Kaufman St., Neve Tzedek ☎ 03/795–1111 ⊕ www.ihg.com ⤳ 555 rooms ⦿ Free Breakfast.

The Levee

$$$$ | HOTEL | FAMILY | Offering eight exclusive, serviced apartments that were beautifully renovated from a 1913 villa, The Levee is a one-of-a-kind luxury accommodation in Tel Aviv's prettiest neighborhood. **Pros:** fully equipped, exclusive serviced apartment; private, secure parking on site; stunning renovation, state-of-the-art equipment. **Cons:** no

24-hour service on site; no restaurant on site; no gym or pool on site. $ *Rooms from: $650* ⊠ *16 Yehuda Halevi St., Neve Tzedek* ☎ *03/771–4421* ⊕ *www.leveetlv. com* ⤳ *8 apartments* ❍❘ *Free Breakfast.*

▼ Nightlife

After many years of neglect, Neve Tzedek has been rediscovered, becoming one of Tel Aviv's most popular neighborhoods by day and night. It brims with laid-back wine bars and other places perfect for an afternoon drink or a night on the town.

BARS AND CLUBS

Vicky Cristina

TAPAS BARS | Part of the trendy HaTachana train station compound, this tapas bar evokes a Latin atmosphere with its sultry mood music. Sangria and other Spanish-style beverages are the theme of the large outdoor bar, where you may be lucky enough to catch some live music. ⊠ *HaTachana, 1 Koifman St., Neve Tzedek* ☎ *03/736–7272* ⊕ *en.vicky-cristi-na.co.il.*

📋 Shopping

CRAFTS

Chomer Tov Ceramics Gallery

CERAMICS/GLASSWARE | A cooperative of 15 local artists, potters, and jewelry designers, this ceramics gallery is on Neve Tzedek's main drag. The gallery showcases everything from decorative art to Judaica and jewelry. Keep an eye on the events calendar for special exhibitions and festive happenings. ⊠ *27 Shabazi St., Neve Tzedek* ☎ *03/516–6229* ⊕ *www.chomertov.co.il.*

Shlush Shloshim Ceramics Gallery

CERAMICS/GLASSWARE | Established as a cooperative in 1992, this gallery showcases the work of 11 local ceramic artists who display a pleasingly eclectic mix of both decorative and practical items in a variety of colors, shapes, and textures. The artists are deeply involved in the day-to-day running of the cooperative and can often be found in the shop guiding customers to the perfect purchase. ⊠ *31 Shabazi St., Neve Tzedek* ☎ *03/510–6067* ⊕ *www.shlushshloshim.com.*

JEWELRY

Ayala Bar

JEWELRY/ACCESSORIES | Israeli designer Ayala Bar's sparkling, multicolor bracelets, earrings, and necklaces, now famous around the world, can be seen from time to time in shops throughout the country, but the best selection is at this flagship store. ⊠ *36 Shabazi St., Neve Tzedek* ☎ *03/510–0082* ⊕ *www. ayalabar.com.*

LOCAL SPECIALTIES

SOHO Design Center

GIFTS/SOUVENIRS | Carrying pieces by Israeli and international designers, this store is filled to the brim with interesting items, from kitchen accessories to handbags to children's toys. ⊠ *HaTachana, Koifman and Ha'Mered Sts., Hangar 12, Neve Tzedek* ☎ *03/716–7010* ⊕ *www. sohocenter.co.il.*

Florentin

A gritty section of town that once served as a base to Greek and Turkish Jewish immigrants in the '20s and '30s is experiencing a slow and steady hipster renaissance. Moving away from the high rental costs of central Tel Aviv, musicians, artists, and students adopted the neighborhood and are bringing a youthful vibe that's felt in the street art, vegan eateries, and plant-filled green balconies. Spend an afternoon exploring the Levinsky Market and the evening in the colorful bohemian bars. The neighborhood is bounded by Eilat Street to the north, Salame Street to the south, Elifelet Street to the west, and HaAliya Street to the east.

GETTING HERE AND AROUND

The neighborhood is an easy 10- or 15-minute walk from Rothschild Boulevard or a 10- or 15-minute cab from most hotels. Shared taxis drop you off near the Central Bus Station area; walk south and west toward Florentin Street.

TIMING AND PRECAUTIONS

Since there are no real sights, our best advice is to just wander around. If you're heading here for bars and clubs, stick to the area around the intersection of Florentin and Vital Streets, as a block or two in most directions will leave you in a less interesting residential part of the neighborhood.

Sights

Levinsky Market

MARKET | The heart of this edgy, bohemian part of Tel Aviv is Levinsky Market, known as a spice-and-herb market and also a great place to sample wonderful Mediterranean delicacies. Nearby you'll find good Persian eateries. Once considered off the beaten path, the Levinsky Market is now a popular destination. ✉ *43 Levinsky St., Florentine* ⏲ *Closed Sat.*

Restaurants

Bordering Neve Tzedek, the up-and-coming Florentin neighborhood has a well-earned reputation as a foodie favorite. The crowd here is young and hip, and so are the eateries. Restaurants here tend to come and go quickly, so take a stroll and see which places are drawing the crowds.

Mezcal

$ | MEXICAN | This lively neighborhood restaurant and bar hits the spot with refreshing margaritas and authentic, tasty Mexican fare. Kick things off with the refreshing Peruvian Tiradito with spicy yellow pepper salsa before ordering barbacoa tacos and green enchiladas. **Known for:** fun, boisterous energy; large portions and affordable prices; happy hour at 5 pm. [$] *Average main: NIS 48* ✉ *2 Vital St., Florentine* ☎ *03/518–7925* 🌐 *mezcaltlv.co.il.*

★ Opa

$$ | VEGETARIAN | All of Tel Aviv is raving about Opa, a vegan hot spot in Florentin that has garnered the kind of universal approval that few—if any—vegan restaurants have achieved before. Although the entire menu is plant-based, the food is so delicious, so fresh, and so packed with flavor, that it appeals to vegans and nonvegans alike. **Known for:** exceptional vegan dinner and dessert; plant-based tasting menu; colorful, organic, seasonal vegetables. [$] *Average main: NIS 55* ✉ *8 Ha-Khalutzim St., Florentine* ☎ *052/583–8245* 🌐 *www.opatlv.co.il/en* ⏲ *Closed Sat. No lunch.*

Nightlife

Ranked internationally as a top hipster living spot, Florentin has bohemian nightlife that is filled with youthful, creative energy.

BARS AND CLUBS

Hoodna

BARS/PUBS | This place mainly attracts students and an eclectic crowd of young, bohemian, and open-minded people. The bar is split in two, with an alley down the middle that's ideal for kicking back and enjoying a pint. Order a burger and fries, or try some of the excellent homemade hummus. ✉ *13 Abarbanel St., Florentine* ☎ *03/518–4558* 🌐 *www.facebook.com/hoodnabar.*

Norma Jean

BARS/PUBS | With an attractive brick facade, this bistro and bar on the edge of Florentin serves more than 200 kinds of whiskey, said to be one of the biggest collections in the country. The kitchen serves full meals, ranging from burgers to steak, fish-and-chips, and vegetarian options. ✉ *23 Elifelet St., Florentine* ☎ *03/683–7383* 🌐 *www.normajean.co.il.*

Jaffa

Part of the sprawling municipality of Tel Aviv, the ancient port city of Jaffa is home to a mixture of faiths: Judaism, Christianity, and Islam. It's an ideal place for strolling down cobblestone streets and for dining at one of the no-frills fish restaurants that line the quay. Don't miss the Old City, where art galleries and shops occupy the centuries-old buildings along the narrow roads. At the Jaffa Flea Market, you can be part of the trading and bargaining for treasures—real and perceived—that are a hallmark of the Middle East.

The streets around Clock Tower Square bustle on weekday afternoons, when school children stop by the open-air eateries for flaky pastries, and weekend evenings, when the bars empty out and their patrons go in search of a late-night bite. An oceanfront promenade connects Tel Aviv with Jaffa. The sprawling park that runs parallel to the promenade was once a landfill, but is now one of the city's greenest areas. Kids love the playgrounds and vast stretches of grass.

South of Jaffa are two worthwhile excursions. Design Museum Holon, in the suburb of that name, is an exciting contemporary art museum. Even farther south, in Rehovot, is the Weizmann Institute of Science.

Some historians claim that Jaffa was named after its founder, Japhet, son of Noah; others think its name is from the Hebrew *yafeh* (beautiful). What's certain is its status as one of the world's oldest ports—perhaps the oldest. The Bible says the cedars used in the construction of the Holy Temple passed through Jaffa on their way to Jerusalem; the prophet Jonah set off from Jaffa before being swallowed by the whale; and St. Peter raised Tabitha from the dead here. Napoléon was but one of a succession of invaders who brought the city walls down; these walls were rebuilt for the last time in the early 19th century by the Turks and torn down yet again as recently as 1879.

GETTING HERE AND AROUND

From central Tel Aviv, Dan Buses 18 and 10 take you to Jaffa. You can also walk or bike along the seafront promenade to get here. A cab ride costing about 50 shekels will also get you to Jaffa.

TIMING

A few hours is enough time to soak up the atmosphere in Jaffa. Some less-traveled streets in Jaffa can feel deserted at night. Although the flea market and the port area are safe, at night you should stay away from dark streets and avoid walking alone.

◉ Sights

Andromeda's Rock

NATURE SITE | From Kedumim Square, a number of large boulders can be seen out at sea not far from shore. Greek mythology says one of these (pick your own, everyone does) is where the people of Jaffa tied the virgin Andromeda in sacrifice to a sea monster to appease Poseidon, god of the sea. But the hero Perseus, riding the winged horse Pegasus, soared down from the sky to behead the monster, rescue Andromeda, and promptly marry her. ⊠ *Jaffa*.

Clock Tower Square

CLOCK | Completed in 1906, in time to mark the 30th anniversary of the reign of Sultan Abdul Hamid II, this eye-catching limestone spire marks the entrance of Jaffa and is a city landmark. The stained-glass windows from 1965 depict events in Jaffa's history. The centuries-old buildings around the square have been carefully restored, preserving their ornate facades. Since Jaffa was a major port in Turkish times, it's not surprising to find the Turkish Cultural Center here. ⊠ *Clock Tower Square, Yefet St., Jaffa*.

The colorful Design Museum Holon hosts changing exhibits that explore the importance of design in daily life.

↗ Design Museum Holon

Israeli-born architect Ron Arad designed this striking, much-acclaimed structure made of rounded ribbons of orange-and-red steel that rises off a drab street like a modernist mirage. Inside is a two-story space with changing exhibits on contemporary design, including fashion, jewelry, and textiles. English-language recorded tours are available for free. A good café known for tasty pastries and cakes is located at the entrance. The museum is in Holon, a suburb south of Tel Aviv that is easily reachable by taxi. ⊠ *8 Pinhas Eilon St., Holon* ☎ *073/215–1515* ⊕ *www. dmh.org.il* ✉ *NIS 35* ⊙ *Closed Sun.*

El-Mahmoudiye Mosque

RELIGIOUS SITE | Tucked behind the shops along Jaffa's Clock Tower Square is the El-Mahmoudiye Mosque, whose hexagonal minaret and pink-granite-and-marble fountain can be seen from the square. When Turkish governor Muhammed Abu Najat Aja built the fountain in the early 19th century, it had six pillars and an arched roof. The fountain's foundation is still visible in the parking lot west of the minaret. The mosque is closed to the public, though you may be able to sneak a peek through the ornate carved doors on the western side into the spacious restored courtyard. The archway on the south side formed the entrance to the hammam, or old Turkish bath. ⊠ *Yefet St., at Mifratz Shlomo St., Jaffa* ⊙ *Closed to the public.*

Ilana Goor Museum

MUSEUM | Veteran Israeli artist Ilana Goor works and resides in this restored 18th-century house with romantic stone arches and high ceilings. She's turned part of it into a museum showcasing more than 500 works of art, both from Israel and throughout the world, alongside those of Ilana Goor herself. The collection includes paintings, sculptures, video art, ethnic art, antiques, and drawings, as well as design items mostly handpicked by Goor, who also serves as the collector and curator of the museum. A gift shop occupies part of the complex. Every Friday at noon, a guided

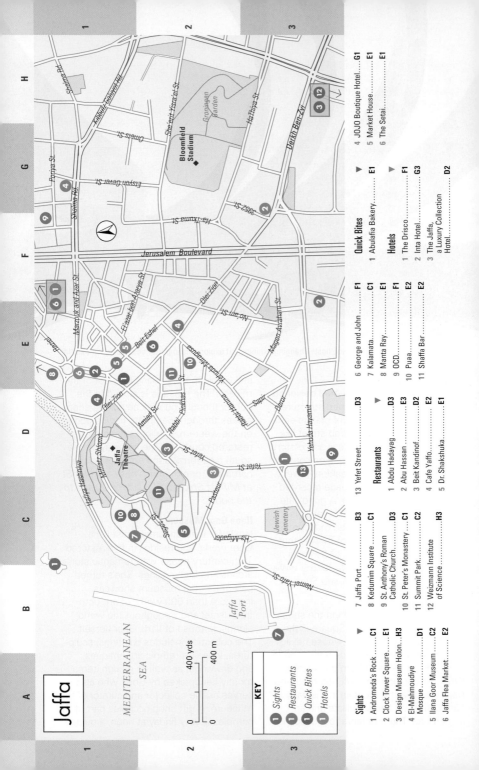

Jaffa

MEDITERRANEAN SEA

Jaffa Port

0   400 yds
0   400 m

KEY
- ① Sights
- ① Restaurants
- ① Quick Bites
- ① Hotels

Sights ▶
1 Andromeda's Rock **C1**
2 Clock Tower Square **E1**
3 Design Museum Holon .. **H3**
4 El-Mahmoudiye
   Mosque **D1**
5 Ilana Goor Museum **C2**
6 Jaffa Flea Market **E2**

7 Jaffa Port **B3**
8 Kedumim Square **C1**
9 St. Anthony's Roman
   Catholic Church **D3**
10 St. Peter's Monastery ... **C1**
11 Summit Park **C2**
12 Weizmann Institute
    of Science **H3**
13 Yefet Street **D3**

Restaurants ▶
1 Abdu Hadayag **D3**
2 Abu Hassan **E3**
3 Beit Kandinof **D2**
4 Cafe Yaffo **E2**
5 Dr. Shakshuka **E1**

6 George and John **F1**
7 Kalamata **C1**
8 Manta Ray **E1**
9 OCD **F1**
10 Puaa **E2**
11 Shaffa Bar **E2**

Quick Bites ▶
1 Abulafia Bakery **E1**

Hotels ▶
1 The Drisco **F1**
2 Inta Hotel **G3**
3 The Jaffa,
   a Luxury Collection
   Hotel **D2**

4 JOJO Boutique Hotel **G1**
5 Market House **E1**
6 The Setai **E1**

Bloomfield Stadium

Jaffa Theatre

Jaffa Port

Jewish Cemetery

Groupman Garden

Jerusalem Boulevard

Sderot Yefet St.
Sderot Eilat
Ha-Migdal
Nemal Yafo St.
Mazal Dagim
Pasteur
Amiad St.
Rabbi Pinhas
Rabbi Yohanan
Olei Zion
Beit Eshel
Netiv Ha-Mazalot
Elrad ben Artzaya St.
No'am St.
Mifratz Shlomo
Hatserot Hashuk
Sapir
Derur
Yehuda Hayamit
Magen Avraham St.
Olei Zion
5865 St.
Ha-Tkuma St.
Shalma Rd.
Shalma Rd.
Elyson Gever St.
Poriya St.
Omets St.
Sheerit Yisrael St.
Hatikva St.
Sheerit Yisrael St.
Hatsiyonut ha-Datit Rd.
Shalma Rd.
Marzouk and Azar St.
Derkh Ben-Zvi

tour is available to all visitors, covered by the museum admission fee. ⊠ *4 Mazal Dagim St., Jaffa* ☎ *03/683–7676* ⊕ *www. ilanagoormuseum.org* ⊠ *NIS 30.*

Jaffa Flea Market

MARKET | One of many small bazaars surrounding the clock tower in the mid-19th century, the Jaffa Flea Market is the only survivor of that era. Along the cobblestone streets you can find everything from European antiques to Israeli memorabilia. As some antiques sellers close their doors with no family to continue the business, chic design boutiques are arriving and shifting the Flea Market neighborhood to an upscale vibe. The market's main street is Olei Zion, but there are a number of smaller streets and arcades to explore. Watch the locals bargain, and do what they do: *never* agree to the first price a seller demands. Combine the Flea Market's shopping and cafés with the Old City of Jaffa for a relaxed half-day stroll. ⊠ *Olei Zion St., Jaffa* ⊙ *Closed Sat.*

★ Jaffa Port

MARINA | This small, intimate-feeling marina (one of the most ancient ports in the world) is home to bobbing wooden fishing boats and a waterfront of restaurants, cafés, and a small number of art galleries. Some of its warehouses have been converted into public spaces for rotating art exhibits. From here, enjoy a fish lunch or a snack from one of the food stalls, and then hop on a boat for a cruise along the city's coastline. ⊠ *Retsef Aliyah Ha'Shniyah, Jaffa.*

Kedumim Square

ARCHAEOLOGICAL SITE | The focus of Kedumim Square is an archaeological site that exposes 3rd-century BC catacombs; the site has been converted into a free underground visitor center with large, vivid, illustrated descriptions of Jaffa's history. A labyrinthine network of tiny alleys snakes in all directions from Kedumim Square down to the fishing port; a good selection of galleries and

jewelry stores can be found south of the square around Mazal Dagim Street. ⊠ *Kedumim Square St., Jaffa* ⊠ *Free.*

St. Anthony's Roman Catholic Church

RELIGIOUS SITE | Although the white bricks of St. Anthony's (also known as San Antonio's) look new, this church actually dates from 1932, when it was built to accommodate the growing needs of Jaffa's Roman Catholic community. The church is named for St. Anthony of Padua, friend and disciple of St. Francis of Assisi. ⊠ *51 Yefet St., Jaffa* ☎ *03/513–3800* ⊠ *Free.*

St. Peter's Monastery

RELIGIOUS SITE | Jaffa is famous as a meeting point of East and West, and as soon as you step into this century-old Franciscan church you'll find yourself steeped in a European atmosphere. St. Peter's was built over the ruins of a citadel dating from the Seventh Crusade, led by King Louis IX of France in the mid-13th century. A monument to Louis stands at the entrance to the friary. Napoléon is rumored to have stayed here during his Jaffa campaign of 1799. To enter, ring the bell on the right side of the door; you will probably be greeted by one of the custodians, most of whom speak Spanish and some English. ⊠ *Kedumim Sq., Jaffa* ☎ *03/682–2871* ⊠ *Free.*

Summit Park

ARCHAEOLOGICAL SITE | Seven archaeological layers have been unearthed in a part of this park called Ramses II Garden. The oldest sections of wall (20 feet thick) have been identified as part of a Hyksos city dating from the 17th century BC. Other remains include part of a 13th-century BC city gate inscribed with the name of Ramses II; a Canaanite city; a Jewish city from the time of Ezra and Nehemiah; Hasmonean ruins from the 2nd century BC; and traces of Roman occupation. At the summit is a stone sculpture called *Faith,* in the shape of a gateway, which depicts biblical stories. ⊠ *Kedumim Square St., Jaffa* ⊠ *Free.*

If you visit Jaffa, sit at the old port and watch the sun dip down into the Mediterranean.

↗ Weizmann Institute of Science

On the grounds of one of Israel's finest science research centers, the Weizmann Institute's indoor Levinson Visitors Center and the open-air Clore Garden of Science are educational and fun for kids of all ages. Experience how it feels to walk on the moon and climb on or through dozens of other interactive exhibits that explain various scientific phenomena. Also worth a visit is the glass-and-steel Eco-Sphere, which houses educational exhibits on the environment. Call ahead for reservations and guided tours. By car, the institute is about 40 minutes from Tel Aviv. Bus routes 174, 201, 301, and 274 take about an hour from central Tel Aviv. The train takes about 35 minutes; it's a 15-minute walk from the train station. ⌧ *234 Herzl St., Rehovot* ☎ *08/934–4500* ⊕ *www.weizmann.ac.il* ⌧ *NIS 30 for guided group tours* ⊙ *Closed Fri. and Sat.*

Yefet Street

NEIGHBORHOOD | Think of Yefet as a sort of thread between eras: beneath it is the old market area, while all around you stand schools and churches of the 19th and 20th centuries. Several deserve mention. At No. 21 is the Tabitha School, established by the Presbyterian Church of Scotland in 1863. Behind the school is a small cemetery where some fairly prominent figures are buried, including Dr. Thomas Hodgkin, the first to define Hodgkin's disease. No. 23 was once a French Catholic school, and it still carries the sign "Collège des Frères." At No. 25, the fortresslike Urim School was set up as a girls' school in 1882. ⌧ *Jaffa.*

🏖 Beaches

Alma Beach (Manta Ray Beach)

BEACH—SIGHT | Commonly known as Manta Ray Beach (for the outstanding restaurant that sits right on the beachfront), Alma Beach is one of those under-the-radar spots that attracts more locals than tourists. Smaller than the sprawling beaches in the city center, Alma Beach is within easy walking distance of the charming Neve Tzedek and Jaffa neighborhoods, enticing residents to pop down for a quick swim before or after work. For those with more time to spare, all mod cons are available, from sun loungers to umbrellas and public toilets. If you get peckish, Manta Ray's deliciously fresh seafood dishes are literally steps away. **Amenities:** food and drink; toilets; lifeguards; parking (fee); showers; water sports. **Best for:** sunset; surfing; swimming; walking. ✉ *7 Kaufmann St., Jaffa* ✥ *In front of Manta Ray restaurant.*

🍴 Restaurants

This ancient fishing port is great for sampling local fish and other authentic local delights. The Flea Market has new and trendy eateries opening each week, so wander around and find a place that's filled with locals, a sure sign that it's a hot spot.

Abdu Hadayag

$$ | **SEAFOOD** | Neighborhood lore says that this eatery's namesake was a fisherman in his early years (*hadayag* is Hebrew for "the fisherman"). His simple establishment has long been a fixture of Jaffa's main street. **Known for:** huge selection of fried or grilled fish; free mezes included with every main; old-school vibe in historic Jaffa. [$] *Average main: NIS 75* ✉ *37 Yefet St., Jaffa* ☎ *03/518–2595.*

Abu Hassan

$ | **MIDDLE EASTERN** | This shop serves what is often called the country's best hummus, which is not an easy task with so many places serving this addictive chickpea dish. For something quite different, order the *masabacha* with chunks of chickpeas served in warm hummus, or the hummus *ful*, made from Egyptian fava beans. **Known for:** the best hummus in Israel; one of the oldest Palestinian restaurants in Tel Aviv; very informal and always busy. [$] *Average main: NIS 25* ✉ *1 Dolphin St., Jaffa* ☎ *03/682–0387* ▭ *No credit cards* ⏲ *Closed Sat.*

Beit Kandinof

$$ | **MEDITERRANEAN** | Set in a historic building on one of the prettiest streets in Old Jaffa, Beit Kandinof is both contemporary art center and restaurant. Home to five galleries with ever-changing exhibitions from Tel Aviv's dynamic modern art scene, Beit Kandinof also houses artists of its own: chefs Yogev Yaros and Shami Golomb, masterminds behind an impressive menu that combines Mediterranean cuisine with Arabic Jaffa touches. **Known for:** changing menu and art exhibits; slow-cooked lamb spare ribs; malabi for dessert. [$] *Average main: NIS 70* ✉ *14 HaTsorfim St., Jaffa* ☎ *03/650–2938* 🌐 *www.beitkandinof.co.il* ⏲ *Closed Sun., no lunch Mon.–Thurs.*

Cafe Yaffo

$$$ | **ITALIAN** | **FAMILY** | The Italian-style ice creams and sorbets prepared daily by chef Ronnie Rivlin are the highlight of this light, airy corner café in the middle of the Jaffa Flea Market. Apple pie and berry frozen yogurt are among the most popular choices. **Known for:** Italian specialties; charming setting near Jaffa Flea Market; popular lunch buffet on Friday. [$] *Average main: NIS 84* ✉ *11 Olei Tzion St., Jaffa* ☎ *03/518–1988* 🌐 *www.caffeyaffo.com* ⏲ *No breakfast or lunch Sat.*

Dr. Shakshuka

$ | **ISRAELI** | This Jaffa institution has been serving *shakshuka*, a mouther-watering Israeli breakfast specialty, for decades, but it soared to fame in 2018 after appearing on the Tel Aviv episode of "Somebody Feed Phil." The show tells the story of how the "Doctor" did time in prison, where he perfected the art of cooking shakshuka for the other inmates. A free man again, he opened a restaurant in Jaffa, gave it his prison nickname, and the rest is history. **Known for:** best shakshuka in Tel Aviv; varieties including merguez sausage; service can be iffy but the food is worth it. [$] *Average main: NIS 49* ✉ *3 Beit Eshel St., Jaffa*

Did You Know?

The bountiful spread that is the traditional Israeli breakfast can include everything from salads to omelets to baked goods. But not all are served alfresco!

☎ *03/682–2842* 🌐 *www.doctorshakshuka.co.il* 🕑 *No dinner Fri., no lunch Sat.* 💳 *No credit cards.*

★ George and John

$$$$ | MEDITERRANEAN | Expertly hidden inside one of Tel Aviv's loveliest boutique hotels, The Drisco, George and John has a friendly atmosphere that makes you feel right at home. The menu is modern Israeli, that is, Mediterranean with a Middle Eastern twist. **Known for:** creative dishes like egg noodles with blue crab; extensive wine list; outstanding service. [$] *Average main: NIS 130* ✉ *The Drisco, 6 Auerbach St., Jaffa* ☎ *03/741–0000* 🌐 *www.gandj.co.il.*

Kalamata

$$$ | MEDITERRANEAN | With an unbeatable view of the Mediterranean Sea on one side and the Old City on the other, this Greek-influenced eatery will add a romantic touch to your visit to Jaffa. Sip ouzo or arak (a locally produced anise-flavored liqueur) alongside fresh-baked kalamata olive bread and colorful small dishes like grilled artichokes over lentils or fish kabobs with cilantro-mint salad. **Known for:** ideal spot to enjoy the Tel Aviv sunset; killer views of the Med; Greek flavors. [$] *Average main: NIS 82* ✉ *10 Kedumim Sq., Jaffa* ☎ *03/681–9998* 🌐 *www.kalamata.co.il* 🕑 *No lunch Sun.–Thurs.*

★ Manta Ray

$$$$ | SEAFOOD | FAMILY | A Tel Aviv institution, this lively restaurant wows with spectacular beach views and both indoor and outdoor dining options. Busy from breakfast to dinner, Manta Ray appeals to everyone from families to couples looking for romance, and attracts a loyal clientele. **Known for:** fresh seafood; unrivaled beachside location; lovely selection of mezes (or appetizers). [$] *Average main: NIS 115* ✉ *4 Nahum Goldmann St., Alma Beach, near the Dolphinarium, Jaffa* ☎ *03/517–4773* 🌐 *www.mantaray.co.il.*

★ OCD

$$$$ | MODERN ISRAELI | There is no Michelin guide for Israel yet but, if there was, OCD would likely be on the list. The name (an acronym for obsessive-compulsive disorder) refers to the meticulous care Chef Raz Rahav and his team pour into each elaborate dish in this 16- to 20-course adventure tasting menu. **Known for:** creative 16- to 20-course tasting menus; blind menu (not available online or presented on arrival); one of Tel Aviv's most unique gastronomic experiences. [$] *Average main: NIS 370* ✉ *17 Tirtsa St., Jaffa* ☎ *03/556–6774* 🌐 *www.ocdtlv.com* 🕑 *Closed weekends. No lunch.*

Puaa

$$ | CAFÉ | In the heart of the Jaffa Flea Market, Puaa's lumpy sofas and slightly battered tables and chairs make for a kick-your-shoes-off atmosphere—and some patrons oblige. It's a popular gathering place for thirtysomething Tel Avivians, as well as young families. **Known for:** laid-back living room feel; excellent vegetarian selection; popular outdoor patio that attracts a young crowd. [$] *Average main. NIS 54* ✉ *8 Rabbi Yohanan St., Jaffa* ☎ *03/682–3821* 🌐 *puaa.rol.co.il.*

Shaffa Bar

$$ | MEDITERRANEAN | This laid-back bar is in the middle of the action next to Jaffa's busy flea market. It draws easygoing locals and tourists of all ages, who come for the tasty, affordable food and drinks and the lively outdoor patio. **Known for:** totally unpretentious; affordable food; plenty of outdoor seating on the patio. [$] *Average main: NIS 55* ✉ *2 Nakhman St., Jaffa* ☎ *03/681–1205* 🌐 *www.facebook.com/shaffabar.*

☕ Coffee and Quick Bites

Abulafia Bakery

$ | BAKERY | There's always a crowd forming outside Abulafia Bakery, south of Jaffa's clock tower. For a simple snack with an exquisite flavor, order a pita topped with za'atar (a mixture of herbs, spices, and seeds), or stuffed with salty cheese, calzone style. **Known for:** no seating; hole-in-the-wall-style street food joint; sweet and savory Israeli baked goods. $ *Average main: NIS 20* ⊠ *7 Yefet St., Jaffa* ⊟ *No credit cards.*

🛏 Hotels

Tel Aviv's boutique hotel boom has made its way south to Jaffa, where some of the city's most exclusive properties—including The Setai, The Drisco, and The Jaffa—have opened, placing Jaffa firmly at the luxury end of the market.

★ The Drisco
$$ | **HOTEL** | The Drisco is everything an upscale boutique hotel should be: elegant without being stuffy, luxurious without being garish, and exclusive without any hint of snobbishness. **Pros:** personalized service; superb on-site restaurant; ideal location, close to Old Jaffa, Neve Tzedek, and Florentin. **Cons:** no pool; small fitness room; rooms on the small side for a five-star hotel. $ *Rooms from: $295* ⊠ *6 Auerbach St., Jaffa* ☎ *03/741–0000* ⊕ *www.thedrisco.com* ⇴ *22 rooms* ⑪ *Free Breakfast.*

Inta Hotel
$ | **HOTEL** | Since opening in 2019, Inta has filled the gap for a gay hotel in a city that's become one of the world's most popular LGBTQ+-travel destinations. **Pros:** affordable; warm, friendly atmosphere; rooftop is a popular local gay night spot. **Cons:** rooms are basic; limited toiletries and no minibar; no restaurant or breakfast. $ *Rooms from: $150* ⊠ *3 Derekh Ben-Zvi, Jaffa* ☎ *058/456–7340* ⊕ *www.intahotel.com* ⇴ *16 rooms* ⑪ *No meals.*

The Jaffa, a Luxury Collection Hotel
$$$$ | **HOTEL** | Ultra-exclusive (and with a price tag to match), The Jaffa is the chicest of all Tel Aviv's trendy new boutique hotels. **Pros:** Tel Aviv's most Instagrammable hotel; dreamy pool with

loungers; excellent dining and drinking options. **Cons:** easy on the eye, not so easy on the wallet; well located for Jaffa but quite far from the city center; more style than substance. $ *Rooms from: $750* ⊠ *2 Louis Pasteur St., Jaffa* ☎ *03/504–2000* ⊕ *www.marriott.com* ⇴ *120 rooms* ⑪ *No meals.*

★ JOJO Boutique Hotel
$ | **HOTEL** | If you're looking for a budget accommodation that's modern, clean, and well located, look no further than this modest, friendly hotel with eight rooms. **Pros:** super affordable and modern; friendly staff; spotlessly clean. **Cons:** the street appears sketchy (but is a lot safer than it looks); the bathroom is a cabin in the bedroom so there isn't much privacy; noisy street outside. $ *Rooms from: $110* ⊠ *13 Shalma Rd., Jaffa* ☎ *052/270–0222* ⊕ *www.jojotlv.com* ⇴ *8 rooms* ⑪ *No meals.*

★ Market House
$$$ | **HOTEL** | With its enviable location in the heart of the Jaffa Flea Market, Market House is a five-minute walk from the sea, surrounded by great restaurants and important biblical sites, and only a quick walk, bike, or cab ride from the center of Tel Aviv. **Pros:** close to everything; friendly and helpful front-desk staff; excellent breakfast and free happy hour. **Cons:** small rooms; not ideally situated for center city; hectic location. $ *Rooms from: $310* ⊠ *5 Beit Eshel St., Jaffa* ☎ *03/797–4000* ⊕ *www.atlas.co.il* ⇴ *44 rooms* ⑪ *Free Breakfast.*

The Setai
$$$$ | **HOTEL** | Hotels don't come more stylish than The Setai, which offers some of the most sought-after accommodation in Tel Aviv—and rightfully so. **Pros:** ideally located in Old Jaffa; close to the beach; stunning Ottoman-era building. **Cons:** infinity pool area tends to get busy; basic room classes are on the small side; no parking available. $ *Rooms from: $515* ⊠ *22 David Razi'el St., Jaffa* ✛ *Opposite*

There are plenty of spots to eat outside in Jaffa, the ancient fishing port.

Jaffa Clock Tower ☎ *03/601–6000* ⊕ *www.thesetaihotels.com* ⇥ *120 rooms* ⊚ *No meals.*

🍸 Nightlife

The winding stone alleyways of Jaffa make it a fun place to explore, and its perch on a hill in the southern end of Tel Aviv means there are alluring nighttime views of the twinkling coastline.

Saloona

BARS/PUBS | In the Noga neighborhood of Jaffa, this swank bar retains a hip, artistic feel that draws people to the area. Enjoy a drink under the gigantic chandeliers while you listen to live music. ⊠ *17 Tirza St., Jaffa* ☎ *03/518–1719* ⊕ *www.saloon-abar.co.il.*

🎭 Performing Arts

HaSimta Theatre

THEATER | In Old Jaffa, HaSimta Theatre features avant-garde and fringe performances in Hebrew (or sometimes without words at all). ⊠ *8 Mazal Dagim St., Jaffa* ☎ *03/681–2126* ⊕ *www.hasimta.com.*

Mayumana

MUSIC | This exciting troupe of drummers and dancers bangs in perfect synchronicity on anything from garbage pails to the floor. It also plays actual drums from cultures all over the world. ⊠ *15 Louis Pasteur St., Jaffa* ☎ *03/681–1787* ⊕ *www.mayumana.com.*

Nalaga'at Center

THEMED ENTERTAINMENT | This cultural and entertainment center features deaf and blind performers. Shows can be combined with a preperformance snack at the BlackOut Restaurant (eating in the dark) or Café Kapish (ordering in sign language). ⊠ *Retsif Haaliya Hashniya St., Jaffa* ☎ *03/633–0808* ⊕ *www.nalagaat.org.il.*

🛍️ Shopping

JEWELRY

Adina Plastelina

JEWELRY/ACCESSORIES | This gallery and jewelry studio in the heart of Old Jaffa sells handcrafted jewelry in sterling silver, gold, and vermeil, combined with polymer clay in the ancient technique called *millefiori,* which means "a thousand flowers" in Italian. The combination of metals and modern materials creates an innovative and classy look. ⊠ *23 Netiv Hamazalot St., Jaffa* ☎ *03/518–7894* ⊕ *www.adinaplastelina.com.*

JUDAICA

★ Frank Meisler

ART GALLERIES | A specialist in Jewish fine art and a pioneer in pewter pieces, Frank Meisler has a magical studio and gallery located in the heart of the artist's quarter in Old Jaffa. Here you'll find his regal Judaica as well as a display of caricature sculptures. ⊠ *25 Simtat Mazal Arie, Jaffa* ☎ *03/512–3000* ⊕ *www.frank-meisler.com.*

🏃 Activities

Sea Kayak Club

BOATING | This club offers two-hour kayaking tours of the coastline throughout the year. Beginners are welcome when conditions are calm. ⊠ *Pier 10, Jaffa Port, Jaffa* ☎ *054/775–7076* ⊕ *www.kayak4all.com* 🍽 *NIS 200.*

North Tel Aviv

While still considered Center City, from the east–west cross street of Arlozorov, North Tel Aviv flows into blocks of tranquil residential streets of small apartment houses, up to the banks of the Yarkon River and its beautiful park. At Hayarkon Park, a welcome swath of green on the Yarkon River, families picnic not far from joggers and bikers on well-paved paths. The Tel Aviv Port is a delightful area for eating, shopping, and strolling. Just north of the river are three important museums. The Eretz Israel Museum is close to Tel Aviv University, the Palmach Museum is next door to it, and the Museum of the Jewish People is farther north on the university campus.

GETTING HERE AND AROUND

Dan Bus Company's Route 4 is an easy way to reach the port. The museums are about 8 km (5 miles) from the downtown hotels; Dan Buses 7, 25, and 45 will take you to the area. Allow at least two hours to visit each museum.

TIMING

The port area can feel a bit overrun on the weekends, especially with families and young children. North Tel Aviv tends to be bustling by day, sleepy at night.

👁️ Sights

Eretz Israel Museum

MUSEUM | This large museum's eight pavilions span 3,000 years of culture and history in Israel, covering everything from ethnography and folklore to ceramics and other handicrafts. In the center is the ancient site of Tel Kassile, where archaeologists have uncovered 12 layers of settlements. There is also a daily sound-and-light show in the adjacent planetarium. ⊠ *2 Levanon St., North Tel Aviv* ☎ *03/641–5244* ⊕ *www.eretzmuseum.org.il* 🍽 *Museum NIS 52, planetarium NIS 84* ⊗ *Closed Sun.*

Ganei Yehoshua (*Hayarkon Park*)

CITY PARK | FAMILY | Tel Avivians go to this sprawling park to stretch out on the grass for a picnic or a nap in the shade. For those seeking more activity, a bike ride on one of its paths can be combined with a visit to the tropical garden and the rock garden. Or you can rent a pedal boat, rowboat, or motorboat to ride on the Yarkon Stream. There's even a pleasure boat, which takes up to 80 people for 20-minute rides. ⊠ *Rokach Blvd., North*

See art that reflects aspects of Jewish life, past and present, at the Museum of the Jewish People on the Tel Aviv University campus.

Tel Aviv ☎ *03/642–2828* ⊕ *www.park.co.il* ☜ *Free.*

Museum of the Jewish People (*Beit Hatfutsot*)

MUSEUM | Presented here is the story of 2,500 years of the diaspora (Jews who settled outside Israel). It begins with the destruction of the First Temple in Jerusalem in 586 BC and chronicles such major events as the exile to Babylon and the expulsion from Spain in 1492. Photographs and text labels provide the narrative, and films and music enhance the experience. One highlight is a replica collection of miniature synagogues throughout the world, both those destroyed and those still functioning. Another is the computerized genealogy section, where it's possible to look up Jewish family names to determine their origins. There's a music center with Jewish music from around the world and a children's gallery with interactive exhibits. The museum is on the Tel Aviv University Campus in the Ramat Aviv neighborhood. ⊠ *Tel Aviv University, Klausner St., Ramat Aviv, North Tel Aviv* ☎ *03/745–7800* ⊕ *www.bh.org.il* ☜ *NIS 49.*

Palmach Museum

MUSEUM | This museum makes you feel as if you were back in the days of the Palmach, the pre-State underground, with a group of young defenders. Visitors are led through rooms, each of which encompasses one part of the Palmach experience. There's the "forest," which has real-looking trees; a room with a falling bridge and faux explosions; and a chilling mock-up of an illegal-immigrants' ship. Visits to the museum must be booked in advance and the tour can accommodate up to 25 people. Call ahead for reservations. ⊠ *10 Levanon St., North Tel Aviv* ☎ *03/545–9800* ⊕ *www.palmach.org.il* ☜ *NIS 30* ⊗ *Closed Sat.*

Tel Aviv Port

CITY PARK | Once a cluster of decrepit warehouses, the old port is buzzing with cafés, restaurants, and, late at night, clubs. It ends where the pavement gives way to a wooden platform designed with moderate dips and curves, pleasing to

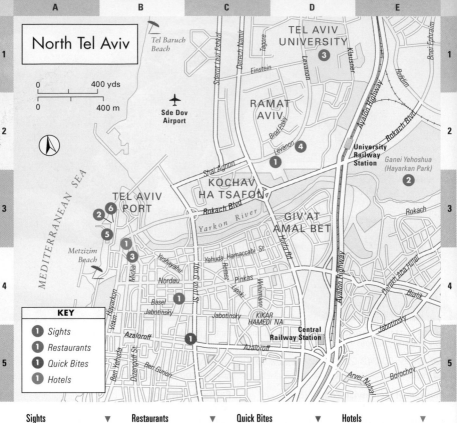

North Tel Aviv

the eye and fun for roller skaters. On weekends, restaurants are all packed by 1 pm. There's a very appealing Friday farmers' market and a small swap meet good for finding handmade jewelry, old books, and Israeli memorabilia. ⊠ *Nemal Tel Aviv St., Tel Aviv Port* 🖘 *Free.*

Tel Aviv Port Farmers' Market

MARKET | After wandering through the stalls selling organic produce, sample the fresh offerings at eateries like the in-house pasta bar or the specialty-sandwich stand. Don't miss the stand selling just-squeezed seasonal juice. Friday afternoons are particularly active with farmers and food vendors selling artisanal goodies. It's closed Sunday. ⊠ *Hangar 12, Tel Aviv Port* ⊕ *www.shukhanamal.co.il.*

Beaches

Metzizim Beach

BEACH—SIGHT | **FAMILY** | This stretch of sand near the Yarkon River attracts a younger crowd. It's an especially good choice for families because it has a long sandbar that keeps the waves gentle. Many people nurse a beer at the nearby pub and watch the sunset. Just south of Metzizim Beach is a private area for Orthodox Jews who prefer gender-separated swimming. Women come on Sunday, Tuesday, and Thursday, while men are here on Monday, Wednesday, and Friday. Everyone is welcome on Saturday, and it's one of the area's mellowest beaches. **Amenities:** food and drink; lifeguards; parking (fee); showers, toilets. **Best for:** partiers; swimming. ⊠ *Havakuk Ha'navi St., near Tel Aviv Port, North Tel Aviv* 🖘 *Free.*

Tel Baruch Beach

BEACH—SIGHT | **FAMILY** | In the northern reaches of Tel Aviv, Tel Baruch Beach is popular among families with young children because it has a breakwater that softens the waves. Because it's the farthest beach from downtown, it can often be less crowded. However family-friendly during the day, the section to the north has an unsavory reputation after dark. **Amenities:** food and drink; lifeguards; parking (fee); showers; toilets; water sports. **Best for:** swimming; walking. ⊠ *Propes St., North Tel Aviv* 🖘 *Free.*

🍴 Restaurants

Primarily a residential area, North Tel Aviv has many long-established family favorites. Most eateries are at Tel Aviv Port, where you can enjoy views of the ocean and refreshing sea breezes.

Ashtor

$$ | **CAFÉ** | **FAMILY** | This small corner café, a neighborhood favorite, is where you can catch a glimpse of the beauty of European café culture. Coffee is the main event, over which you can linger for hours along with your newspaper, computer, or friends from the neighborhood. **Known for:** upscale atmosphere; Tel Aviv classic; breakfast and coffee. 💲 *Average main: NIS 56* ⊠ *37 Basel St., North Tel Aviv* ☏ *03/546-5318* ⊕ *ashtor.business.site.*

Kitchen Market

$$$$ | **MODERN ISRAELI** | On the top floor of the farmers' market at the Tel Aviv Port, this eatery's stellar views of the sea make it an ideal rendezvous spot for a romantic lunch or dinner. Because of the location, you can bet that the ingredients are as fresh as possible. **Known for:** market-to-table cuisine; innovative Mediterranean-Israeli menu; fresh, seasonal produce from the farmers' market downstairs. 💲 *Average main: NIS 120* ⊠ *Hangar 12, Tel Aviv Port* ☏ *03/544–6669* ⊕ *www.kitchen-market.co.il* ☽ *No lunch Sun.*

Shtsupak

$$$ | **SEAFOOD** | **FAMILY** | Diners crowd the tables inside and out at this simple seafood place. They are here for the fish, which locals agree is reasonably priced, well prepared, and always fresh. **Known for:** fresh fish, affordably priced; catch of the day; great meze selection and unlimited refills. $ *Average main: NIS 99* ⊠ *256 Ben Yehuda St., North Tel Aviv* ☎ *03/544–1973* ⊕ *www.shtsupak.co.il.*

☕ Coffee and Quick Bites

Sabich Complete

$ | **MIDDLE EASTERN** | The specialty at this hole-in-the-wall eatery is *sabich*, a meal-in-a-pita popular in the region. It's considered a breakfast food (the word comes from the Arabic for "morning") because it includes a hard-boiled egg, in addition to hummus, tomatoes, peppers, and spices. **Known for:** everyone's favorite Israeli street food; apart from sabich, also meatballs, fish balls, and schnitzel; limited seating. $ *Average main: NIS 16* ⊠ *99 Ibn Gvirol St., North Tel Aviv* ☎ *03/523–1810* ▬ *No credit cards* ⊘ *No dinner.*

🛏 Hotels

With proximity to the sea, the Hayarkon Park and the Tel Aviv Port, the northern area of Tel Aviv is great for sports enthusiasts, sun seekers, and those seeking respite from the hustle of the Center City.

Yam Hotel Tel Aviv

$$ | **HOTEL** | While not directly on the sea, the Yam, meaning "beach" in Hebrew, goes to lengths to remind visitors of their location close to the water. **Pros:** abundant complimentary happy-hour spread; playful design; free bicycles. **Cons:** very small rooms; no parking facilities; quite far from Tel Aviv city center. $ *Rooms from: $220* ⊠ *16 Kaf Gimel Yordei ha-Sira St., Tel Aviv Port* ☎ *03/542–5555* ⊕ *www. atlas.co.il/yam-hotel-tel-aviv* ⤸ *42 rooms* ⦿❘ *Breakfast.*

🍸 Nightlife

Tel Aviv's hottest, loudest nightlife destination is the Tel Aviv Port, located in the city's northern reaches. With its cutting-edge music, DJ-spun music, and raucous crowds, the port has contributed in no small measure to Tel Aviv's newly acquired status as a major player in the club world.

BARS AND CLUBS

Shablul Jazz Club

MUSIC | This intimate jazz club presents everything from hip-hop to ethno jazz Monday through Saturday nights. Performers range from veteran jazz artists to up-and-coming young talents. ⊠ *Hangar 13, Tel Aviv Port* ☎ *03/546–1891* ⊕ *www. shabluljazz.com.*

Zappa Club

MUSIC | One of Tel Aviv's best venues for live music, the intimate Zappa Club is named after American music legend Frank Zappa. It is in the Ramat HaHayal neighborhood, just a short cab ride away from downtown. ⊠ *24 Raoul Wallenberg St., North Tel Aviv* ☎ *03/762–6666* ⊕ *www.zappa-club.co.il.*

🛍 Shopping

Rina Zin

CLOTHING | The European cuts of this designer's chic styles are quite sophisticated. ⊠ *280 Dizengoff St., North Tel Aviv* ☎ *03/523–5746* ⊕ *rinazin.com.*

🏃 Activities

Meymadiyon Water Park

SWIMMING | **FAMILY** | Open from June to September, Meymadiyon is a 25-acre water park featuring a swimming pool, a wave pool, a kiddie pool, waterslides, and lawns dotted with plastic chairs. ⊠ *Ganei Yehoshua, North Tel Aviv* ☎ *03/642–2777* ⊕ *www.meymadion.co.il* ▣ *NIS 122.*

Topsea

SURFING | Teaching surfing at every level, Topsea offers both private and group lessons, summer surf camps, as well as surfboard rental (by the hour or by the day) for those with previous experience. ⊠ *Kikar Atarim, 165 Hayarkon St., North Tel Aviv* ☎ *050/432–9001* ⊕ *www.topsea. co.il* ▣ *NIS 200 for 1-hr private lesson; board rental from NIS 50.*

Herzliya Pituach is a popular beach resort area north of Tel Aviv.

Herzliya Pituach

A seaside suburb north of Tel Aviv, Herzliya Pituach has a cluster of chain restaurants in the Arena Mall at the marina, with a picturesque view of the yachts at anchor. The excellent Herbert Samuel is also here.

Beaches

Herzliya Pituach Beach

BEACH—SIGHT | About 10 km (7 miles) north of Tel Aviv is this white-sand beach lined by well-manicured lawns. Nearby are restaurants, cafés, and a handful of luxury high-rise hotels. From central Tel Aviv, Dan's Bus 90 heads to this beach. **Amenities:** food and drink; lifeguards; toilets; water sports. **Best for:** snorkeling; swimming; walking. ✉ *Ramat Yam St., at Medinat Hayehudim St., Herzliya Pituach* 🎟 *Free.*

Restaurants

★ Herbert Samuel

$$$$ | **MEDITERRANEAN** | Walking through the door of this understated but elegant dining room you hear the energetic hum of good conversation. Set inside the immaculate Ritz-Carlton Herzliya hotel, Herbert Samuel boasts an upscale but accessible kosher menu, with strong Mediterranean influences that change every season. **Known for:** outstanding kosher food; open kitchen; sophisticated crowd. [$] *Average main: NIS 160* ✉ *The Ritz-Carlton Herzliya, 4 HaShunit St., Herzliya Pituach* ☎ *073/203–7596* 🌐 *www.herbertsamuel.co.il* 🕒 *Closed Fri. and Sat; no lunch.*

Hotels

Don't want to stay in a city? Herzliya Pituach is a resort area 12 km (7½ miles) up the coast from Tel Aviv. It has a number of beachfront hotels, a public square with outdoor cafés that's a short walk from the beach, and a marina and adjacent

Arena Mall with a selection of high-end shops, restaurants, and pubs. The area has a cosmopolitan air, as affluent suburbanites live here, along with diplomats and foreign journalists. A car is useful, but it's possible to get around with taxis; parking in Tel Aviv is a challenge.

Dan Accadia Herzliya

$$$$ | **HOTEL** | **FAMILY** | The three buildings of this seaside hotel are surrounded by flower-filled gardens that lead to a swimming pool overlooking the sea. **Pros:** lovely views; gorgeous grounds; right on the beach in Herzliya. **Cons:** little local atmosphere; away from the city's attractions; service on the slow side. [$] *Rooms from: $480* ✉ *22 Ramat Yam St., Herzliya Pituach* ☎ *09/959–7070* 🌐 *www.danhotels.com* 🛏 *209 rooms* 🍴 *Free Breakfast.*

The Ritz-Carlton, Herzliya

$$$$ | **HOTEL** | **FAMILY** | The exclusive Herzliya Pituach Marina is the setting for Ritz-Carlton's first hotel and residences in Israel, a striking, modern building that makes up for being 12 km (7 miles) north of central Tel Aviv with grandly plush public areas and guest rooms with large windows and balconies for viewing seaside sunsets. **Pros:** well-equipped gym and first-rate spa; superb service; large rooms and suites. **Cons:** need car or taxi to get to Tel Aviv; wind noise on the marina side can be loud; pricey on-site parking. [$] *Rooms from: $425* ✉ *4 HaShunut St., Herzliya Pituach* ☎ *09/373–5555* 🌐 *www.ritzcarlton.com* 🛏 *160 rooms* 🍴 *Free Breakfast.*

Sharon Hotel

$ | **HOTEL** | The northernmost hotel on the strip overlooking the water is a little far from the neighborhood's shopping and dining options. **Pros:** budget option in Herzliya; nice location; sense of local color. **Cons:** rooms on lower floors have uninspiring views; noisy lobby; service is hit and miss. [$] *Rooms from: $175* ✉ *5 Ramat Yam St., Herzliya Pituach* ☎ *09/952–5777* 🌐 *www.sharon.co.il* 🛏 *173 rooms* 🍴 *Free Breakfast.*

Activities

Via Maris

SAILING | At Herzliya Marina, Via Maris is the place to charter a sailboat or other vessel for a catered, private, romantic sunset cruise; a family outing; or an overnight sea stay. Options include with or without skipper. ✉ *1 Yordei Yam St., Herzliya* ☎ *09/957–8811* 🌐 *www.yamonline.co.il.*

Chapter 6

HAIFA AND THE NORTHERN COAST

WITH CAESAREA, AKKO, AND ROSH HANIKRA

Updated by
Shari Giddens

● Sights	🍴 Restaurants	🛏 Hotels	🛍 Shopping	▼ Nightlife
★★★★★	★★★★★	★★★★☆	★★★☆☆	★★★☆☆

WELCOME TO HAIFA AND THE NORTHERN COAST

TOP REASONS TO GO

★ **Baha'i Gardens:** In Haifa, this unforgettable series of gardens tumbles down from Mount Carmel into 19 terraces that enclose a gold-domed shrine.

★ **Caesarea:** Originally built by Herod the Great, these 2,000-year-old Roman ruins occupy a strategic spot on the sea. They include Byzantine bathhouses and Crusader moats.

★ **Glorious beaches:** The coast means beaches, and this is Israel's finest stretch of golden sand. Haifa's beaches are particularly beautiful. Scuba diving and paragliding are options.

★ **Great wine:** Taste and toast internationally known wines at the many wineries on the hillsides of the northern coast. Tishbi and Carmel are especially worth visiting.

★ **Underground Akko:** At this fascinating archaeological site, you can descend into Crusader knights' halls, navigate a secret tunnel toward the sea, and rest in a Turkish bathhouse.

1 Haifa. This steep-sloped port city rewards you at every turn with hillside breezes, beaches, and breathtaking vistas.

2 Nahsholim-Dor. White sandy beaches and a fantastic Carmel Mountains view await you in Nahsholim-Dor.

3 Caesarea. Ancient Roman harbor ruins and beautiful beaches aside impressive modern villas are hallmarks of beautiful Caesarea.

4 Netanya. Established in 1929 with citrus, Netanya is now a beach destination.

5 Ein Hod. This artist's village is nestled in the heart of the Carmel Forest.

6 Daliyat el Carmel and Isfiya. Enjoy a splendid drive along the uppermost rim of Carmel to these Druze villages.

7 Mukhraka. Visiting this small monastery is worth the stunning view alone.

8 Zichron Ya'akov. Quaint cafés line the main shopping street of Zichron Ya'akov, and there are top wineries nearby.

9 Benyamina. Visit the heart of Israel's wine country on the slopes of Mount Carmel.

10 Akko. Exploring Akko's atmospheric Old City, with its souk and Crusader remains, is a highlight here.

11 Nahariya. Israel's northernmost coastal city offers sun lovers an idyllic vacation spot.

12 Rosh Hanikra. The sea-battered caves here are worth the trip north.

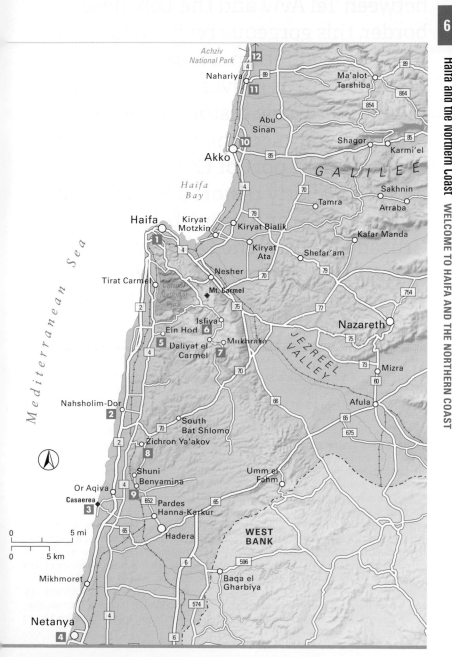

Achziv
National Park
12

Nahariya 89
11

Ma'alot-
Tarshiba 89

864
854

Abu
Sinan

Shagor 85

Karmi'el

10
Akko 85

*Haifa
Bay*

G A L I L E E

Sakhnin

4 70 Tamra Arraba

Haifa Kiryat
Motzkin 79

1 4 Kiryat Bialik

Kiryat
Ata Kafar Manda

Nesher Shefar'am

Mediterranean Sea

Tirat Carmel 70 79

*Carmel
National
Park* Mt. Carmel

75 754

Isfiya 77

Ein Hod **6**

5 Daliyat el
Carmel **7** Mukhraka

Nazareth

J E Z R E E L
V A L L E Y 75

2 4 70 73 Mizra

60

Nahsholim-Dor
2

South
Bat Shlomo 66 Afula

70 65

2 Zichron Ya'akov 675

8

Shuni
Benyamina Umm el
Fahm

Or Aqiva 4

9

Casaerea 652

3 Pardes
Hanna-Karkur 65

**WEST
BANK**

0   5 mi
0   5 km

65 Hadera

6

596

Mikhmoret

Baqa el
Gharbiya

574

Netanya
4 6

Stretched taut on a narrow coastal strip between Tel Aviv and the Lebanese border, this gorgeous region has a rare blend of Mediterranean beaches, fertile fields and citrus groves of the Sharon Plain, and seaside historical sights. Whether you succumb to the delights of the ancient port of Caesarea, with its spectacularly restored Roman ruins, the alleyways and beautifully vaulted Crusader halls of the Old City of Akko, or the vistas and gardens of modern Haifa, this lovely part of Israel doesn't disappoint.

It was in the softly contoured foothills of Mount Carmel that philanthropist Baron Edmond de Rothschild helped found the country's wine industry in the 19th century, now one of the region's most successful enterprises. The Carmel range rises dramatically to its pine-covered heights over the coast of Haifa, an amiable and thoroughly modern port city. Across the sweeping arc of Haifa Bay lies Akko, a jewel of a Crusader city that combines Romanesque ruins, Muslim minarets, and swaying palms. To the north, the resort town of Nahariya draws droves of vacationing Israelis. Just south of the Lebanese border, don't miss the amazing seaside coves of Rosh Hanikra, which have been scooped from the cliffs by the pounding surf.

As the scenery changes, so does the ethnic mix of the residents: Druze, Carmelite monks, Baha'is, Christian and Muslim Arabs, and Jews. In the caves of Nahal Me'arot on Mount Carmel, paleontologists continue to study the artifacts of the most ancient, prehistoric native people. The Baha'is, dedicated to the idea that all great religions teach the same fundamental truths about an unknowable God, dominate Haifa's mountainside. Their terraced gardens spill down the slope toward a gleaming golden-domed shrine. White Friars of the Carmelite order preside over their serene monasteries in Haifa and on Mount Carmel. The monastery in Mukhraka sits in the outskirts of Daliyat el Carmel, one of the two large Druze villages on Mount

Carmel. The Druze of the Galilee and Carmel, now numbering more than 125,000, have lived here for 1,000 years. Although they consider themselves an integral part of Israeli society, they maintain a unique cultural and religious enclave on Mount Carmel, with the esoteric rites and rituals of their faith and the distinctive handlebar moustaches and white head scarves favored by the older men. Akko's vast subterranean Crusader vaults and halls, Ottoman skyline of domes and minarets, and outdoor *shuk* (market) are enchanting.

As you drive north, enjoy long stretches of unimpeded views of the sparkling blue Mediterranean. Beautiful beaches lie beside (and in between) Netanya, Haifa, and Achziv, with soft sand, no-frills hummus joints, and seaside restaurants. You can learn to scuba dive, explore underwater shipwrecks, hike the pine-scented slopes of Mount Carmel, tread the winding lanes of Ein Hod artists' village, and taste local wines and tangy cheeses at some excellent wineries.

MAJOR REGIONS

Two seaside cities anchor this stretch of coastline. **Haifa,** a hilltop city on a peninsula jutting into the Mediterranean, offers the magnificent Baha'i Shrine and Gardens, the bustling German Colony, fine restaurants, the Carmelite Monastery, maritime museums, and more.

South of Haifa, on **the Northern Coast,** beaches abound, the sea sparkles, and skies are sunny most of the year. Archaeological sites, such as the outstanding Roman, Byzantine, and Crusader ruins at Caesarea, house beautiful restored treasures, and historical museums are fun and not fusty. Netanya and Nahsholim-Dor have plenty for seekers of sun and fun, including paragliding and other adventures.

Wine has been produced in **the Wine Country and Mount Carmel** and its fertile region for thousands of years. The Sharon Plain near the Mediterranean coast south of Haifa, including the towns of Zichron Ya'akov and Benyamina, is the largest grape-growing area in Israel.

Route 4, which runs north to south parallel to Route 2, is a more scenic drive, with Mount Carmel looming to the east beyond cultivated fields and banana plantations (though you may not see the bananas, as they're usually bagged in blue or gray plastic to protect them from bugs). The road leads through undulating countryside dotted with cypresses, palms, and vineyards.

Leave the wine region and you'll come to **Akko and the Far Northern Coast.** One of the oldest and most entrancing port cities in the world, Akko's rampart-ringed Old City encloses an 18th-century mosque, underground Crusader halls, an extraordinary tunnel, and winding lanes through a bazaar to restaurants at the water's edge. North of Akko, wide beaches, two of them within nature reserves, follow one after the other up the coast. The moshavim and kibbutzim (cooperative agricultural settlements) are unique settings for gourmet restaurants and upscale bed-and-breakfasts. Rosh Hanikra, at the top of the northern coast, has a cable car that carries you down a 210-foot cliff to caves hollowed out by wildly crashing waves.

Planning

When To Go

There's really no bad time to visit this region. Spring (April and May) and fall (October and November) are balmy and crisp, making them the most pleasant seasons for travelers. Summer (June to September) is hot, but humidity remains low, and soft sea and mountain breezes cool things down. Winter (December to March) brings cold weather (sun interspersed with rain) and chilly sea winds.

As in the rest of Israel, hotels are often booked solid on weekends. On Saturday and national holidays, Israelis hit the road, so north–south traffic out of Tel Aviv can be heavy. If you're taking a few days to explore the region, traveling Sunday to Thursday guarantees you plenty of peace and quiet. If you can only go on Friday and Saturday, make reservations well in advance, and be prepared for crowds at the beaches and tourist sights.

Planning Your Time

Haifa, the country's third-largest city, can be a useful base for exploring sights both to the south (Caesarea and the wine country) and north (the Crusader city in historic Akko and the coast up to Rosh Hanikra). Ein Hod, an artists' colony, and the Carmel Caves are also nearby. Haifa itself is notable for the Baha'i Gardens and Germany Colony. However, the coast's southern sights can also be seen easily if you're staying in Tel Aviv. Several companies run day tours to Caesarea and Akko from Jerusalem, Tel Aviv, and Netanya; this may be a useful option.

Not counting time in Haifa, you could see the area's highlights in a couple of days, starting with King Herod's port city, Caesarea, and the wine country in the Carmel Hills. Check tour information for the wineries in Benyamina and Zichron Ya'akov. The picturesque Druze villages of Daliyat el Carmel and Isfiya are well worth a visit, too. You can also spend a full day exploring Akko, to the north; the grottoes at Rosh Hanikra are lovely, but far north. Plan time for swimming or hiking; the Mediterranean coast has great beaches and scenic trails.

Getting Here and Around

AIR

Ben Gurion International Airport, the country's main gateway, is near Tel Aviv and is 105 km (65 miles) south of Haifa, about a 90-minute drive. A convenient *sherut* (shared taxi minibus) service to Haifa costs NIS 106, and runs 24 hours a day, seven days a week. For sherut service, call ☎ *04/866–2324*. Private taxi service costs NIS 545 for two passengers with two suitcases, plus a charge for extra suitcases of approximately NIS 4 per bag.

BUS

Egged serves the coastal area from Jerusalem Central Bus Station to Tel Aviv Central Station. There's service to Netanya, Hadera, Zichron Ya'akov, and Haifa from both cities. From Jerusalem, a direct bus to Haifa takes one hour and 40 minutes. Getting to Caesarea requires a change at Hadera. To get to Akko, change at Haifa. Crowds are heavy at bus stations on Thursday night and Sunday morning. Buses don't operate from Friday evening to Saturday evening; in Haifa, select buses run on Saturday.

CAR

Driving is the most comfortable and convenient way to tour this region. You can take Route 2 (the coastal road) or Route 4 (parallel to Route 2, but slightly inland) north along the coast from Tel Aviv to Haifa, continuing on Route 4 up to the Lebanese border. From Jerusalem follow Route 1 to Tel Aviv; connect via the Ayalon Highway to Herzliya and Route 2. Toll road Route 6 also connects to Route 1 and saves time.

TAXI

In towns, taxis can be hailed on the street day or night. Ask the driver to turn on the meter, or *moneh.*

TRAIN

The northern coast is one part of Israel where train travel is both practical and scenic. As always, remember that service is interrupted Friday evening to Saturday evening. Israel Railways trains from Jerusalem and Tel Aviv travel several times a day to Netanya, Benyamina, Caesarea, Haifa, Atlit, Akko, and Nahariya. You'll have to change trains in Tel Aviv when coming from Jerusalem.

The train line from Ben Gurion International Airport travels to Tel Aviv, Benyamina, Atlit, Haifa, Akko, and Nahariya. The trip from Tel Aviv to Haifa takes about one hour. Sunday to Thursday, trains depart every 20 minutes from 6 am until 10:30 pm; on Friday they run from 6 am until an hour before sundown. On Saturday there are four departures after 8:30 pm. Train travel from Jerusalem to Haifa is feasible only if you have plenty of time, as you have to change in Tel Aviv.

Restaurants

You don't have to look hard for a restaurant, whether simple or fancy, with a striking view of the Mediterranean. Fish, served with a variety of sauces, is usually grilled or baked. The most common types are *locus* (grouper), *mulit* (red mullet), *churi* (red snapper), and *farida* (sea bream). Also fresh, but from commercial ponds and the Sea of Galilee, are the ubiquitous tilapia, *buri* (gray mullet), and *iltit* (a hybrid of salmon and trout). Fresh seafood, such as shrimp and calamari, is available in abundance. Many casual restaurants serve schnitzel (breaded and fried chicken cutlets) with french fries, which kids often love.

Until recently, coastal restaurants weren't as refined as those in Tel Aviv, but no longer. Haifa now has several first-class restaurants with creative chefs. The artists' village of Ein Hod offers sumptuous Argentinean dining, and there's locally famous falafel in the Druze village of Daliyat el Carmel. Netanya boasts the area's highest concentration of kosher establishments. Dress is always informal.

Hotels

Options range from small inns to luxury hotels, though the selection and quality of accommodations doesn't equal that of, say, Tel Aviv. Gracious bed-and-breakfasts (known in Israel as *zimmers*) are tucked into coastal rural settlements, mostly north of Nahariya. The splendid spa hotel in the Carmel Forest near Haifa deserves its reputation. In some places, such as Zichron Ya'akov, pickings are slim; but because this region is so compact, you can cover many coastal sights from one base, such as Haifa. *Hotel reviews have been shortened. For more information, visit Fodors.com.*

What It Costs			
$	$$	$$$	$$$$
RESTAURANTS			
Under NIS 50	NIS 50–NIS 75	NIS 76–NIS 100	over NIS 100
HOTELS			
Under $200	$200–$300	$301–$400	over $400

Haifa

Spilling down from the pine-covered heights of Mount Carmel to Haifa Bay, Haifa is a city with a vertiginous setting that has led to comparisons with San Francisco. The most striking landmark on the mountainside is the gleaming golden dome of the Baha'i Shrine, set amid utterly beautiful garden terraces. The city is the world center for the Baha'i faith, and its members provide informative walking tours of the flower-edged

100-acre spot, a UNESCO World Heritage Site. At the top of the hill are some small but interesting museums, the larger hotels, and two major universities. At the bottom is the lovingly restored German Colony, a perfect area for strolling.

Israel's largest port and third-largest city, Haifa was ruled for four centuries by the Ottomans and gradually spread its tendrils up the mountainside, becoming a cosmopolitan city whose port served the entire Middle East. The climate is gentle, the beaches beautiful, and the locals friendly.

GETTING HERE AND AROUND

A direct bus operated by Egged leaves Tel Aviv for Haifa every 20 minutes between 5:20 am and 11 pm; travel time is one hour. Trains from Tel Aviv to Haifa also take one hour and cost NIS 28. Trains depart every half hour from 6 am until 10:30 pm; on Friday from 6 am until an hour before sundown. During the day on Saturday trains don't run, but there are four departures after 8:30 pm.

There are plenty of nice walks in the city, but to see the sights, a car or a taxi is required; another option is the local buses. The Carmel Tunnels, which bypass the most congested parts of Haifa by boring below Mount Carmel, cut a 30- to 45-minute drive down to less than 10. The toll is NIS 18 and can be paid with cash at the tollbooths. The tunnels aren't much use to visitors, but if you're just passing through, they could save you time. Coming north from Tel Aviv, the entrance is at the end of Route 2. From the north, it's off Route 4 near the Checkpoint Interchange.

You can hail a taxi in the city, or use an app like Gett to summons one. You can also call to arrange a taxi pickup.

Haifa has the six-station Carmelit subway—actually a funicular railway—that runs from Gan Ha'em Park on Hanassi Boulevard (adjacent to the Dan Panorama) in Central Carmel down to Kikar Paris in the port area in six minutes. The fare is NIS 6.60 for a single ticket (NIS 15 for a day pass), and the train operates Sunday to Thursday 6 am to midnight, Friday 6 to 3, and Saturday sundown to midnight.

The Haifa Cable Car travels from the lower station at Bat Galim to the upper station at Stella Maris, and has panoramic views of the bay. It's accessible by bus routes 41 and 42 from Bat Galim and 25, 26, 27, 30, and 31 from Stella Maris. Free parking is available at both ends.

BUS CONTACTS Egged. ☎ 03/694–8888 ⊕ www.egged.co.il.

TAXI CONTACTS Carmel. ☎ 04/838–2626, 04/838–2626. **Horev.** ✉ Horev 15 ☎ 04/888–8888.

TRAIN CONTACTS Israel Railways. ☎ *5770 ⊕ www.rail.co.il/EN.

VISITOR INFORMATION

CONTACTS Haifa Tourist Board. ✉ 48 Ben Gurion Blvd., German Colony ☎ 04/853–5606 ⊕ www.visit-haifa.org/eng.

◉ Sights

Israel's "city on the hill" is divided into three main levels, each crisscrossed by parks and gardens: the port down below; Hadar, a commercial area in the middle; and Merkaz Carmel (known as "the Merkaz"), with the posher hotels and many restaurants, on the crest of Mount Carmel.

Thanks to the beneficence of the Baha'is, you can enjoy a walking tour that takes you through the stunning terraces that lie like multicolor jewels from the crest of the city at Mount Carmel to the German Colony below.

★ Baha'i Shrine and Gardens

GARDEN | The most striking feature of the stunning gardens that form the centerpiece of Haifa is the Shrine of the Bab,

Did You Know?

The Shrine of the Bab is one of many holy sites in Israel. Perched on the slopes of Mount Carmel, the Baha'i Gardens pay homage to Baha'i's founders.

whose brilliantly gilded dome dominates the city's skyline. The renovated shrine gleams magnificently with 11,790 gold-glazed porcelain tiles.

Haifa is the world center for the Baha'i faith, founded in Iran in the 19th century. It holds as its central belief the unity of mankind. Religious truth for Baha'is consists of progressive revelations of a universal faith. Thus the Baha'is teach that great prophets have appeared throughout history to reveal divine truths, among them Moses, Zoroaster, Buddha, Jesus, Muhammad, and most recently, the founder of the Baha'i faith, Mirza Husayn Ali, known as Baha'u'llah—"the Glory of God." The Shah and then the Ottomans exiled Baha'u'llah (1817–92) from his native Persia to Akko, where he lived as a prisoner for almost 25 years. The Baha'is holiest shrine is on the grounds of Baha'u'llah's home, where he lived after his release from prison and is now buried, just north of Akko.

Here in Haifa, at the center of the shrine's pristinely manicured set of 19 garden terraces, is the mausoleum built for the Bab (literally, the "Gate"), the forerunner of this religion, who heralded the coming of a new faith to be revealed by Baha'u'llah. The Persian authorities martyred Bab in 1850. Baha'u'llah's son and successor built the gardens and shrine and had the Bab's remains reburied here in 1909. The building, made of Italian stone and rising 128 feet, gracefully combines the canons of classical European architecture with elements of Eastern design and also houses the remains of Baha'u'llah's son. The dome glistens with some 12,000 gilded tiles imported from the Netherlands. Inside, the floor is covered with rich Oriental carpets, and a filigree veils the serene inner shrine.

The magnificent gardens, with their gravel paths, groomed hedges, and 12,000 plant species, are a sight to behold: stunningly landscaped circular terraces extend from Yefe Nof Street for 1 km (½ mile) down the hillside to Ben Gurion Boulevard, at the German Colony. The terraces are a harmony of color and form—pale pink-and-gray-stone flights of stairs and carved urns overflowing with red geraniums set off the perfect cutouts of emerald green grass and floral borders, dark green trees, and wildflowers, with not a leaf out of place anywhere. The gardens, tended by 120 dedicated gardeners, are one of Israel's 11 UNESCO World Heritage Sites.

Three areas are open to the public year-round, except on Baha'i holidays: the shrine and surrounding gardens (*80 Hatzionut Avenue, near Shifra Street*); the upper terrace and observation point (*Yefe Nof Street*); and the entry at the lower terrace (*Hagefen Square, at the end of Ben Gurion Boulevard*). Free walk-in tours in English are given at noon every day except Wednesday. These depart from 45 Yefe Nof Street, near the top of the hill. Note: the Shrine of the Bab is a pilgrimage site for the worldwide Baha'i community; visitors to the shrine are asked to dress modestly (no shorts). ⊠ *80 Hatzionut Ave., Merkaz Carmel* ☏ *04/831–3131* ⊕ *www.ganbahai.org.il/en/haifa* ⊠ *Free* ◷ *Shrine closed daily after noon.*

Carmelite Monastery and Stella Maris Church

HISTORIC SITE | The imposing Stella Maris (Latin for "Star of the Sea") is graced by wall and ceiling paintings that bring to life the dramatic story of the prophet Elijah, the patron of the Carmelite order, as well as depicting King David, the Holy Family, and the four evangelists. During the Crusader period, hermits emulating Elijah's ascetic life lived in caves on this steep mountain slope. In the early 13th century, they united under the leadership of St. Berthold, who petitioned the patriarch of Jerusalem for a charter. Thus was born the Carmelite order, which spread across Europe. The Carmelite monks were forced to leave their settlements on Mount Carmel at the end of the 13th century and could not return for nearly four centuries. When they found Elijah's cave inhabited by Muslim dervishes, they set up a monastery nearby.

The church of the present monastery dates from 1836 and was built with the munificence of the French monarchy, hence the name of the surrounding neighborhood: French Carmel. A small pyramid memorial topped with an iron cross commemorates those French who were slaughtered here by the Turks in 1799 after the retreating Napoléon left his ailing troops behind at the monastery. Inside, paintings in the dome depict Elijah in the chariot of fire in which he ascended to heaven, and other biblical prophets. The small grotto a few steps down at the end of the nave is traditionally associated with Elijah and his pupil, Elisha. ⊠ *Stella Maris Rd., French Carmel* ☎ *04/833–7758* ⊡ *Free.*

Clandestine Immigration and Naval Museum

MUSEUM | The rather dull name of this museum belies the dramatic story it tells of the heroic efforts to bring Jewish immigrants to Palestine from war-torn Europe in defiance of British policy. In 1939, on the eve of World War II, the British issued the so-called White Paper, which effectively strangled Jewish immigration to Palestine. Out of 63 clandestine ships that tried to run the blockade after the war's end, all but five were intercepted, and their passengers were deported to Cyprus. The museum—full of moving stories of courage and tenacity—is centered on the *Af Al Pi Chen* (Hebrew for "Nevertheless"), a landing craft, which attempted to bring 434 Jewish refugees ashore. A photomural and model of the celebrated ship the *Exodus* recalls the story of the 4,530 refugees aboard who were forcibly transferred back to Germany in 1947, but not before

the British forces opened fire on the ship. The history of Israel's navy, told here in impressive detail, begins with the transformation of these clandestine immigration craft into warships. ⊠ *204 Allenby Rd., Kiryat Eliezer* ☎ *04/853–6249* ⊡ *NIS 15* ⊙ *Closed Fri. and Sat.*

Elijah's Cave

CAVE | Jews, Christians, and Muslims consider this site sacred; an early Byzantine tradition identified it as the cave in which Elijah found refuge from the wrath of Ahab, king of Israel from 871 to 853 BC. Graffiti from pilgrims of various faiths and centuries are scrawled on the right wall, and written prayers are often stuffed into crevices. Modest dress is required. The cave is a pretty 20-minute walk down the fairly steep path that begins across from the entrance to the Carmelite Monastery and Stella Maris Church and descends past the lighthouse and World War II fortification. It is more easily accessible by a short flight of stairs that rises from Allenby Road not far from the Bat Galim cable-car station. ⊠ *230 Allenby Rd., Ein Hayam* ☎ *04/852–7430* ⊡ *Free* ⊙ *Closed Sat.*

★ German Colony

NEIGHBORHOOD | Although it runs along a single boulevard, "The Colony" packs in history (with explanatory placards), interesting architecture, great restaurants, and wonderful spots for people-watching. Ben Gurion Boulevard was the heart of a late-19th-century colony established by the German Templer religious reform movement. Along either side are robust two-story chiseled limestone houses with red-tile roofs. Many bear German names, dates from the 1800s, biblical inscriptions on the lintels, and old wooden shutters framing narrow windows.

Neglected for years, the German Colony is now one of the city's loveliest (and flattest) strolls. It's best to start your exploration around Yaffo (Jaffa) Street so that you're walking toward the stunning

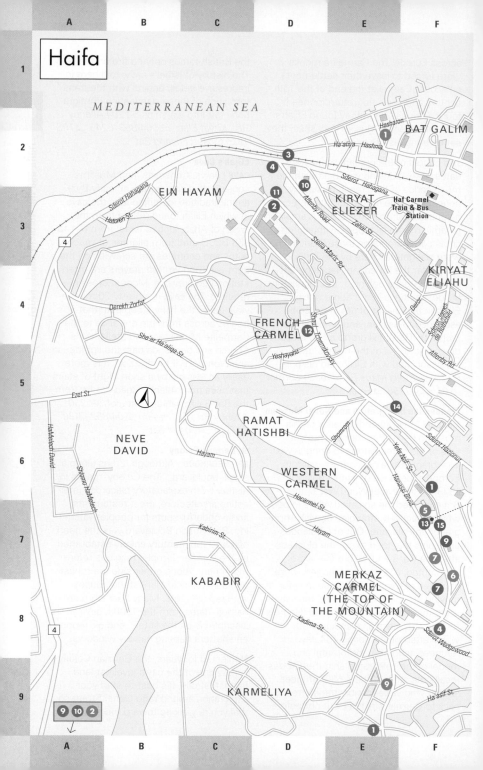

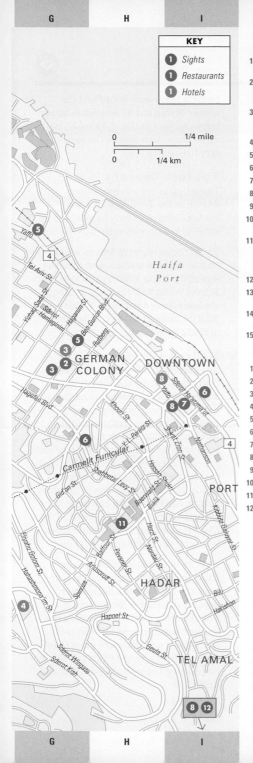

KEY

1 Sights
1 Restaurants
1 Hotels

0 ————— 1/4 mile
0 ————— 1/4 km

Sights ▼

1 Baha'i Shrine and
   Gardens................... **F6**
2 Carmelite Monastery
   and Stella Maris
   Church **D3**
3 Clandestine
   Immigration and
   Naval Museum.......... **D2**
4 Elijah's Cave **D2**
5 German Colony.......... **G5**
6 Haifa Museum of Art... **G6**
7 Haifa Zoo **F8**
8 Hecht Museum **I9**
9 Mané Katz Museum..... **F7**
10 National
   Maritime Museum...... **D2**
11 National Museum of
   Science, Technology,
   and Space
   (MadaTech) **H7**
12 Technion **I9**
13 Tikotin Museum of
   Japanese Art............. **F7**
14 Vista of Peace
   Sculpture Garden........ **E5**
15 Yefe Nof Street........... **F7**

Restaurants ▼

1 Café Louise **E9**
2 Douzan **G5**
3 Fattoush.................. **G5**
4 Giraffe.................... **F8**
5 Goldfish **G3**
6 Hanamal 24...............**I5**
7 Jacko's.....................**I5**
8 Maayan Habira **I5**
9 Minna Tomei **A9**
10 Raffaello **A9**
11 Shawatina **D3**
12 Zebra..................... **D4**

Hotels ▼

1 Bat Galim
   Boutique Hotel **E2**
2 Carmel Forest
   Spa Resort................ **A9**
3 Colony Hotel............. **G5**
4 Crowne Plaza Haifa **G8**
5 Dan Carmel............... **F7**
6 Dan Panorama Haifa.... **F7**
7 Hotel Beth Shalom....... **F7**
8 Port Inn Hostel **H5**
9 Villa Carmel............... **E9**

Haifa's History

The city's tumultuous past includes reminders of many of the events that shaped Israel and the region over the centuries. First mentioned in the Talmud, the area around Haifa had two settlements in ancient times. To the east, in what is today a congested industrial zone in the port, lay Zalmona, and 5 km (3 miles) west around the cape was Shiqmona. The city was under Byzantine rule until the Arab conquest in the 7th century, when it became a center of glass production and dye making from marine snails.

Crusaders and Ottomans

In 1099, the Crusaders conquered the city and maintained it as a fortress along the coastal road to Akko for 200 years. In the 12th century, a group of hermits established the Order of Our Lady of Mount Carmel (the Carmelite order) over Elijah's Cave. After Akko and Haifa succumbed to the Mamluk Sultan Baybars in 1265, Haifa was destroyed and left derelict. It was a sleepy fishing village for centuries.

The city reawakened under the rule of the Bedouin sheikh Dahr el-Omar, who in 1750 ordered the city to be demolished and moved about 3 km (2 miles) to the south. The new town was fortified by walls and protected by a castle, and its port began to compete with that of Akko across the bay.

From 1775 until World War I, Haifa remained under Turkish control with a brief interruption: Napoléon came to Haifa en route to ignominious defeat at Akko during his Eastern Campaign. General Bonaparte left his wounded at the Carmelite Monastery when he beat a retreat in 1799, but the French soldiers there were killed and the monks driven out by Ahmed el-Jazzar, the victorious pasha of Akko. A small memorial stands before the monastery to this day.

The 19th Century

The religious reform movement known as the Templers founded Haifa's German Colony in 1868, and in 1879 European Jews settled in the city.

Under the auspices of Sultan Abdul Hamid II, Haifa was connected to the legendary Hejaz Railway through the Jezreel Valley to Damascus. Although the line is long dormant, a Turkish-built monument to the sultan stands in Haifa to this day.

Modern Times

After World War I, Haifa was taken from the Turks by the British, and during the British Mandate period (1921–48), the city was the scene of many dramatic confrontations between the British who sought to keep Jews from entering Palestine and the clandestine efforts of the Haganah to smuggle in immigrants and survivors of the Holocaust. One of the ships used to run the British blockade, an old American craft called the *Af Al Pi Chen*, can be seen in the Clandestine Immigration and Maritime Museum.

The city became the center of the Baha'i faith in the early 20th century. With the creation of a deep-water port in 1929, Haifa's development as a modern city began. By the time the State of Israel was declared in 1948, Haifa had a population of more than 100,000. Today it's the country's third-largest city, home to 270,000 Jews and Arabs.

The blue Mediterranean, Haifa's hills, and the terraced Baha'i Gardens make for irresistible photos.

Baha'i Gardens. Along the way you can have a meal or cup of coffee, explore the shops in the City Centre Mall, and learn about the history of the Templers. Any time of day is pleasant, but evening, when the cafés and restaurants are brimming with people, is best.

The Templers' colony in Haifa was one of seven in the Holy Land. The early settlers formed a self-sufficient community; by 1883 they had built nearly 100 houses and filled them with as many families. Industrious workers, they introduced the horse-drawn wagon—unknown before their arrival—to Haifa. They also built with their own funds a pilgrimage road from Haifa to Nazareth. The Germans' labors gave rise to modern workshops and warehouses, and it was under their influence that Haifa began to resemble a modern city, with well-laid-out streets, gardens, and attractive homes.

Haifa's importance to Germany was highlighted in 1898, when Kaiser Wilhelm II sailed into the bay, on the first official visit to the Holy Land by a German emperor in more than 600 years. In the 1930s, many Templers began identifying with German nationalism and the Nazi party, and during World War II the British deported them as nationals of an enemy country. ✉ Ben Gurion Blvd.

Haifa Museum of Art
MUSEUM | FAMILY | This museum, on the southern edge of the Wadi Nisnas neighborhood, displays artwork from all over the world, dating from the mid-18th century to the present. It also serves as a special repository of contemporary Israeli art. Included are 20th-century graphics and contemporary paintings, sculptures, and photographs. The print collection is of special note, as are frequent solo exhibitions by young Israeli artists. The museum also houses an interactive children's wing. ✉ 26 Shabbetai Levy St., Hadar ☎ 04/911–5991 ⊕ www.hma.org. il 💲 NIS 45.

Haifa Zoo

ZOO | FAMILY | Amid masses of trees and lush foliage in the Gan Ha'Em park is a seemingly happy collection of roaring lions and tigers, big brown bears, chattering monkeys, stripe-tailed lemurs, a placid camel, lots of snakes and reptiles, one croc, a kangaroo, and fierce-eyed eagles and owls—plus a bat cave and a waterbird pond. It's a hilly place, but there's a tram to take visitors up the steepest terrain. A small natural history museum and petting zoo complement the regular educational exhibits. ⊠ *124 Hatishbi St., Merkaz Carmel* ☎ *04/837–2390* ⊕ *www. haifazoo.co.il* ⊠ *NIS 38* ⊗ *Closed Fri. and Sat.*

Hecht Museum

MUSEUM | It's worth the trip to Haifa University to see this museum's archaeological treasures. At the summit of Mount Carmel, in the main campus tower (called Eshkol Tower), the museum has a collection that spans the millennia from the Chalcolithic era to the Roman and Byzantine periods, concentrating on "The People of Israel in Eretz Israel." The artifacts include religious altars and lamps, Bronze Age figurines, inscribed seals from the biblical period, and a 2,400-year-old ship. Featured prominently are finds from the excavations of Jerusalem's Temple Mount. A separate art wing displays a small collection of paintings, mostly impressionist works by Monet, Soutine, and Modigliani, among others. The roof observation deck, on the 27th floor, has spectacular views. ⊠ *199 Abu Hushi St., Hadar* ☎ *04/825–7773, 04/824–0308* ⊕ *mushecht.haifa.ac.il* ⊠ *Free.*

Mané Katz Museum

MUSEUM | This whitewashed building on Panorama Road is the house and studio where the expressionist painter Emmanuel Katz (1894–1962) lived and worked for the last four years of his life. Katz spent the 1920s in Paris, where he exhibited with a group of avant-garde Jewish artists from the École de Paris. As in the canvases of fellow members Marc Chagall and Chaim Soutine, a recurring theme in his work is the village life of Eastern European Jews. Besides Katz's paintings, drawings, and sculptures are the Ukrainian-born artist's collection of rugs, 17th-century antiques from Spain and Germany, and Judaica. ⊠ *89 Yefe Nof St., Merkaz Carmel* ☎ *04/911–9372* ⊕ *mkm.org.il* ⊠ *NIS 35.*

National Maritime Museum

MUSEUM | About 5,000 years of maritime history in the Mediterranean and Red Sea are told with model ships, ancient anchors, coins minted with nautical symbols, navigational instruments, and other artifacts. There are also intriguing underwater finds from nearby excavations and shipwrecks. The ancient-art collection is one of the finest in the country, comprising mostly Greek and Roman stone and marble sculpture, Egyptian textiles, Greek pottery, and encaustic grave portraits from Fayyum, in Lower Egypt. Particularly rare are the figures of fishermen from the Hellenistic period, as well as a 1st-century wooden boat rescued in the 1980s from the muddy bottom of the Sea of Galilee. ⊠ *198 Allenby Rd., Kiryat Eliezer* ☎ *04/853–6622* ⊕ *www.nmm.org. il* ⊠ *NIS 35.*

National Museum of Science, Technology, and Space (MadaTech)

MUSEUM | FAMILY | Housed in a landmark building (designed by Alexander Baerwald, a German Jewish architect, in the early 20th century) that was the original home of the Technion, Israel's MIT, this museum features excellent interactive exhibits sure to captivate children and adults alike. Explore the mysteries of DNA, the disorientations of mirrors and visual illusions, or the promises of green energy. ⊠ *12 Balfour St., Hadar* ☎ *04/861–4444* ⊕ *www.madatech.org.il* ⊠ *NIS 89.*

Technion

COLLEGE | Israel's top university for science and technology, the 300-acre Israeli Institute of Technology is highly fertile ground for cutting-edge research in such fields as engineering, medicine, architecture, and computer science. Founded in 1912, it is the country's oldest university and a key to Israel's reputation and success as a "start-up nation" of innovators. The Coler-California Visitors Center has a virtual tour of the institute and multimedia touch-screen videos. ⊠ *Kiryat Ha-Technion, Neve Sha'anan* ☎ *04/829–3775* ⊕ *pard.technion.ac.il/ coler-visitors-center* ⊠ *Free* ⊘ *Closed Fri. and Sat.* ☞ *Reservations must be made 24 hrs in advance.*

Tikotin Museum of Japanese Art

MUSEUM | Established in 1957 by renowned collector Felix Tikotin, this graceful venue on the crest of Mount Carmel adheres to the Japanese tradition of displaying beautiful objects in harmony with the season, so exhibits change every three months. The Japanese atmosphere, created in part by sliding doors and partitions of wood and paper, enhances a display of scrolls, screens, pottery and porcelain, lacquer and metal-work, paintings from several schools, and fresh-flower arrangements. The library houses some 3,000 volumes related to Japanese art. ⊠ *89 Hanassi Blvd., Merkaz Carmel* ☎ *04/838–3554* ⊕ *www.tmja. org.il* ⊠ *NIS 35.*

Vista of Peace Sculpture Garden

GARDEN | You can contemplate one of the 29 buoyant life-size bronzes of children and animals from a bench on the winding path through this little jewel of a garden, which commands a sweeping view of Haifa Bay and beyond. Sculptor Ursula Malbin, who came to Israel as a refugee from Nazi Germany, created this oasis west of the Baha'i Shrine. It opens at sunrise and closes at 6. ⊠ *112 Hazionut Ave., Bahai* ⊠ *Free.*

Yefe Nof Street

NEIGHBORHOOD | Also known as Panorama Road, this gently curving street high above the city skirts behind Haifa's biggest hotels, providing remarkable views. Enjoy the beauty of the lushly planted Louis Promenade, with shaded benches along the way, beginning behind the Dan Carmel Hotel. On a clear day, from any of several lookouts you can see the port below, Akko across the bay, and the cliffs of Rosh Hanikra, with Lebanon in the distance. Panorama Road is spectacular during both day and night. ⊠ *Merkaz Carmel.*

🔆 Beaches

Haifa's coastline is one fine, sandy public beach after another. They span 5 km (3 miles) of coast and have lifeguard stations, changing rooms, showers, toilets, refreshment stands, sports areas, restaurants, and a winding stone promenade. In the north are the Bat Galim and Surfers Beaches. Moving south, you come across the Carmel Beach, Nirvana, Zamir, Dado, Dado South, and the Students Beach. To be on the safe side, never swim when a lifeguard isn't on duty. There's parking at every beach, and all are free. All city beaches are reachable by local buses.

Carmel Beach

BEACH—SIGHT | With its attractive boardwalk and beachside kiosks, Carmel Beach sits in front of the Leonardo Hotel at the southern entrance to Haifa. **Amenities:** food and drink; parking (fee); lifeguards; showers; toilets. **Best for:** swimming. ⊠ *Access via Andrei Sakharov St., South Haifa* ⊠ *Free.*

Dado Beach

BEACH—SIGHT | On Saturday at Dado Beach, Haifa's longest stretch of sandy beach, Israelis of all ages come and folk dance to the delight of onlookers. You can also find exercise equipment, picnic areas, and a small bathing pool for young children. The northern part of the beach is wheelchair accessible, as are the restrooms and showers. **Amenities:** food and drink; lifeguards; parking (fee); showers; toilets; water sports. **Best for:** swimming. ✉ *David Elazar St., South Haifa* 🎫 *Free.*

Hof HaShaket

BEACH—SIGHT | North of the Leonardo Hotel, and next to the Rambam Medical Center, the quiet Hof HaShaket has separate gender days: Sunday, Tuesday, and Thursday for women; Monday, Wednesday, and Friday for men; Saturday for everyone. **Amenities:** food and drink; lifeguards; parking (fee); showers. **Best for:** solitude; swimming. ✉ *Entrance from Cheyl HaYam St., South Haifa* 🎫 *Free.*

Zamir Beach

BEACH—SIGHT | Just next to Dado Beach, Zamir Beach is regarded as one of the best Haifa beaches, with fine golden sand and many amenities, including coffeehouses, restaurants, access for the disabled, and even Wi-Fi. **Amenities:** food and drink; lifeguards; parking (fee); showers; toilets. **Best for:** swimming; walking. ✉ *David Elazar St., South Haifa* 🎫 *Free.*

🍴 Restaurants

There are plenty of restaurants near the large hotels at the top of the city in Merkaz Carmel. Another popular place to eat is along Ben Gurion Boulevard in the German Colony, where the evening hours are whiled away at sidewalk terraces. The port area is being gentrified, so there are always new restaurants opening up. Dress is casual, Israeli style.

In a city known for its falafel, the universally beloved Israeli food, check out the falafel joints called Michel and Hazkenim on Wadi Street, the circular street in the Wadi Nisnas market, and George's on Yohanan Hakadosh. You get plenty of fresh, steaming chickpea balls stuffed into warm pita bread with crunchy cucumber and tomatoes.

Beach Basics

Between Tel Aviv and the Lebanese border are miles of beautiful sandy beaches, most of them public and attended by lifeguards from early May to mid-October. Many Israeli beaches are left untended off-season, but they're generally cleaned up and well maintained once warm weather returns. Beachside restaurants can make for rough-and-tumble eating because of loud music, but it's fun to eat fresh food by the beach. *Never* swim in the absence of a lifeguard, as undertows can be dangerous.

Café Louise

$$ | **VEGETARIAN** | At this nutritious vegetarian eatery, breakfast, lunch, and dinner are served in the cheerful dining room (good feng shui) or on the glass-enclosed patio. Grains are the mains here: choose from among such creative dishes as red-quinoa salad with sweet-carrot vinaigrette, whole-wheat-and-spelt quiche, and vegetable curry stew with cashews. **Known for:** vegetarian food; high-quality grains, fresh fish, organic coffee; small shop with health products. [$] *Average main: NIS 60* ✉ *58 Moriah Blvd., Merkaz Carmel* ☎ *04/834–9950* 🌐 *www.cafelouise.co.il.*

Douzan

$$$ | **MEDITERRANEAN** | Inside this old German Templer building with a pleasant outdoor terrace, a huge metal lamp studded with colored glass casts lacy designs on the walls, lending to the Middle Eastern design. The food, much of it prepared by the owner's mother, is an eclectic combination of French and local Arabic cuisines. **Known for:** Lebanese delicacies like kubbeh; attentive service; inviting atmosphere. $ *Average main: NIS 90* ✉ *35 Ben Gurion Blvd., German Colony* ☎ *04/852–5444* 🌐 *douzan.rest.co.il.*

Fattoush

$$$ | **MIDDLE EASTERN** | At this attractive restaurant-bar at the foot of the Baha'i Gardens, olive trees hung with blue and green lights set the tone for the elaborate interior, which contains several intimate rooms. One is a "cave" with Arabic script on the walls, low banquettes, wooden stools, and filigree lamps; another is modern with leather seats, embroidered cushions, and a changing art exhibit set against burnt orange walls. **Known for:** atmospheric setting; creative menu; Fattoush salad with cucumber and mint. $ *Average main: NIS 80* ✉ *38 Ben Gurion Blvd., German Colony* ☎ *04/852–4930.*

Giraffe

$$ | **ASIAN** | Here's a welcome combination of jolly atmosphere and casual pan-Asian cuisine. It's sort of a New York lounge-style hangout: stainless-steel open kitchen; black tables, chairs, bar, and stools; silver photography-studio ceiling lights; and a staff in bright white T-shirts, jeans, and long black aprons. **Known for:** delicious wok noodles; hip vibe; gluten free options. $ *Average main: NIS 55* ✉ *131 Hanassi Blvd., Merkaz Carmel* ☎ *04/810–4012* 🌐 *www.giraffe.co.il.*

Goldfish

$$ | **SEAFOOD** | Over the shabby doorway, a crooked sign announces that the fish is "fresh every day." That's all you need to know about this bare-bones, old-time favorite seafood restaurant. Take a seat at one of the 16 tables, each covered with rough white paper, and be treated to lots of what Israelis call *salatim,* or little dishes of roasted eggplant, fish roe, and homemade hummus. **Known for:** three options: shrimp, calamari, and deep-fried fish; roll-up-your-sleeves eating; strong espresso. $ *Average main: NIS 55* ✉ *26 A.L. Zissu St., Downtown* ☎ *04/855–2663* 💳 *No credit cards* 🕓 *Closed Sun.*

★ Hanamal 24

$$$$ | **MODERN ISRAELI** | Hands down, this is the finest gastronomic experience in Haifa. Tasteful renovations have transformed this old wheat-and-corn warehouse in Haifa's port into an elegant Tuscan country inn. **Known for:** excellent location; inviting ambience; reliably delicious food and house wine. $ *Average main: NIS 130* ✉ *24 Hanamal St., off Sha'ar Palmer St., Haifa Port* ☎ *04/862–8899* 🌐 *hanamal24.rest.co.il/en* 🕓 *Closed Sun.*

Jacko's

$$ | **SEAFOOD** | If ever there was a beloved eating place in Haifa, Jacko's is it. Give the name to your taxi driver; they'll nod approvingly, gun the motor, and drop you at a nondescript building with a Hebrew sign. **Known for:** seafood sautéed in butter, white wine, and garlic; attentive service; mezze presentation. $ *Average main: NIS 70* ✉ *12 Kehilat Saloniki St., Downtown* ☎ *04/866–8813* 🕓 *No dinner Sat.–Thurs.*

Maayan Habira

$$ | **EASTERN EUROPEAN** | The decor of this meat-lovers' haven is informal: beer kegs piled in a corner; the walls covered with photos of glowing restaurant reviews; and a mural of the customers painted by an art student in 1989. The Romanian family-run business has been around since 1962; today Reuven and his son Shlomi do the excellent cooking. **Known for:** hearty Romanian beer and food; generous portions; attentive service. $ *Average main: NIS 75* ✉ *4 Natanson St., Downtown* ☎ *04/862–3193* 🕓 *Closed Sat. No dinner Sun., Mon., Wed., and Fri.*

Minna Tomei

$$ | **ASIAN** | This pan-Asian gem on the top floor of the Castra mall is a bit hard to find, but worth the effort. Five kitchens (Japan, India, Korea, Vietnam, and Thailand) offer flavorful dining options in unusual juxtaposition. **Known for:** you-get-it-when-it's-ready concept; creative presentation; curry dishes that are especially good. $ *Average main: NIS 65* ⊠ *Castra Shopping Center, 8 Filman St., South Haifa* ☎ *170/050–4506* ⊕ *www. minna-tomei.co.il.*

Raffaello

$$$$ | **ITALIAN** | Pasta made on the premises with imported ingredients from Italy speaks to the close attention and high quality of this premier Italian restaurant with an open kitchen and a pleasant atmosphere. Beautiful wood furnishings and a light, bright interior provide a backdrop to innovative dishes like pizza with pear, truffle, and blue cheese, or salmon pappardelle with spinach and beets. **Known for:** advance reservations recommended; Italian fine dining and standout desserts; gracious hospitality. $ *Average main: NIS 115* ⊠ *Castra Shopping Center, 8 Filman St., South Haifa* ☎ *170/050–7107* ⊕ *raffaellocc.co.il* ⊟ *No credit cards.*

★ Shawatina

$$$ | **MIDDLE EASTERN** | No visit to Stella Maris Monastery is complete without a meal at this local favorite, where you can marvel at the eye-popping harbor view from the floor-to-ceiling windows in the exposed brick dining room while you enjoy traditional Middle Eastern fare. Start the meal with an array of salads and appetizers served family style; inventive grilled halumi cheese with crunchy peanuts and a sweet mango salad are more unusual additions to the traditional plates of eggplant, hummus, pickles, and cabbage salads. **Known for:** knockout view of Haifa Bay; seafood; attentive staff. $ *Average main: NIS 90* ⊠ *100 Stella Maris St., French Carmel* ☎ *04/833–3037.*

Zebra

$ | **AMERICAN** | One of Haifa's best-kept secrets, this intimate bar serves terrific hamburgers and salads, but the artistic vibe is what really draws you in. Owner Vicki paints, and her artwork, along with works by other locals, is featured. **Known for:** artsy bar scene; live music; hometown local vibe. $ *Average main: NIS 45* ⊠ *39 Tchernikovsky St.* ☎ *077/321–2290* ☾ *Closed Sun.*

🛏 Hotels

Haifa's best-known hotels are at the top of the hill in the Merkaz Carmel area. The Colony hotel is in the downtown area, as is the Port Inn hostel-guesthouse; both have more affordable stays. Within easy reach of the city, the Carmel Forest Resort Spa is quiet and pampering, though it's pricey.

Bat Galim Boutique Hotel

$ | **HOTEL** | This romantic boutique hotel has great views of the sea and is a five-minute walk to the beach, making it a perfect couples' getaway. **Pros:** short walk to restaurants; close to the beach; convenient to train and bus station. **Cons:** no elevator; no restaurant; small rooms. $ *Rooms from: $120* ⊠ *10 Yonatan St., Kiryat Eliezer* ☎ *04/603–7800* ⊕ *www. batgalim-boutique-hotel.co.il* ⤴ *12 rooms* ⦿ *Free Breakfast.*

★ Carmel Forest Spa Resort

$$$$ | **RESORT** | Set by itself in the Carmel Forest, this spa-resort 25 km (15 miles) south of Haifa is the ultimate escape: a top-of-the-line spa with tasteful lodgings designed to pamper guests in a calm and healthy setting (no cell phones or children under 16). **Pros:** serene setting; lovely forest walks; spa services. **Cons:** no public transportation; rather pricey; no nightlife. $ *Rooms from: $800* ⊠ *Rte. 721, Beit Oren* ✛ *About 1 mile on Rte. 721 from Hwy. 4* ☎ *04/830–7888* ⊕ *www.isrotel.com* ⤴ *126 rooms* ⦿ *Free Breakfast.*

Colony Hotel

$ | HOTEL | Step into this palm-shaded courtyard and you're in the world of the German Templers: the three-story lodging is in the center of the German Colony, amid the neighborhood's carefully restored red-roofed homes. **Pros:** uniquely charming setting; discounts at local restaurants with stay; great location in German Colony. **Cons:** no pool; no restaurant on site; small rooms. $ *Rooms from: $180* ⊠ *28 Ben Gurion Blvd., German Colony* ☎ *04/851–3344* ⊕ *www.colonyhaifa.com* ⏍ *40 rooms* ¶⊘¶ *Free Breakfast.*

Crowne Plaza Haifa

$ | HOTEL | Catering to a business crowd, this modern, well-designed chain hotel is built into a pine-shaded slope. **Pros:** indoor pool and Jacuzzi open until 9 pm; spa; free Wi-Fi in rooms and lobby. **Cons:** mediocre breakfast by Israeli standards; additional charge for business center; nicest rooms above floor 9. $ *Rooms from: $180* ⊠ *111 Yefe Nof St., Merkaz Carmel* ☎ *04/835–0801* ⊕ *www.ichotelsgroup. com/crowneplaza/hotels/us/en/haifa/ hfail/hoteldetail* ⏍ *100 rooms* ¶⊘¶ *Free Breakfast.*

Dan Carmel

$$$ | HOTEL | The Dan Carmel, beautifully situated on the heights of Merkaz Carmel, is a longtime favorite with stately charm and a devoted staff. **Pros:** superb views; attentive staff; bathroom mirrors feature built-in TV. **Cons:** pool closed in winter; buffet can get repetitive; rooms a bit dated. $ *Rooms from: $330* ⊠ *87 Hanassi Blvd., Merkaz Carmel* ☎ *04/830– 3030* ⊕ *www.danhotels.com* ⏍ *227 rooms* ¶⊘¶ *Free Breakfast.*

Dan Panorama Haifa

$$ | HOTEL | The glitzier younger sister of the Dan Carmel up the road, this 21-story hotel is popular with business executives (especially the comfortable second-floor lobby with its circular bar). **Pros:** welcoming staff; splendid views; large fitness center. **Cons:** no balconies; dated decor; slow elevators. $ *Rooms from: $220* ⊠ *107 Hanassi Blvd., Merkaz Carmel* ☎ *04/835–2222* ⊕ *www.danhotels.com* ⏍ *266 rooms* ¶⊘¶ *Free Breakfast.*

Hotel Beth Shalom

$ | B&B/INN | Plain but pleasant, this lodging has three floors of small rooms; each room has wicker furniture, beds with fluffy duvets, and good reading lights. **Pros:** central location close to Carmel Center and promenade; modest prices; clean rooms. **Cons:** no restaurant; basic decor; unreliable Wi-Fi. $ *Rooms from: $110* ⊠ *110 Hanassi Blvd., Merkaz Carmel* ☎ *04/837–7481* ⊕ *www.beth-shalom.co.il* ⏍ *30 rooms* ¶⊘¶ *Free Breakfast.*

Port Inn Hostel

$ | B&B/INN | A haven for budget travelers, this inn with a pleasant guest lounge is in a neighborhood filled with interesting shops. **Pros:** cheerful garden; small rooms good for solo travelers; well-equipped information for travelers. **Cons:** far from tourist sites; not a lot of privacy; inconsistent air conditioning. $ *Rooms from: $90* ⊠ *34 Yaffo St., Downtown* ☎ *04/852–4401* ⊕ *www.portinn.net* ⏍ *18 rooms, 10 with bath* ¶⊘¶ *Free Breakfast.*

Villa Carmel

$ | HOTEL | The facade may look ordinary, but this chic boutique hotel's interior is unlike anything else in Haifa. **Pros:** stylish atmosphere; attention to detail; on a quiet street. **Cons:** no pool; light controls and water valves confusing to operate; rooms may seem small by American standards. $ *Rooms from: $180* ⊠ *1 Heinrich Heine Sq., off 30 Moriah Blvd., Merkaz Carmel* ☎ *04/837–5777* ⊕ *www.villacarmel.co.il* ⏍ *15 rooms* ¶⊘¶ *Free Breakfast.*

⊙ Nightlife

Haifa at night may not pulse like Tel Aviv, but there are more than a few things to do after dark. In balmy weather, a stroll along the Louis Promenade and then along Panorama Road, with lovely views of nighttime Haifa, is a relaxing way to end the day.

For a festive evening, try the restaurants and cafés-cum-pubs in the German Colony. Night spots in Haifa come and go, and some open only on certain evenings, so call ahead if possible.

Colony Bar

BARS/PUBS | The Colony Bar at the hotel of the same name opens nightly to both guests and visitors. Grab a drink in the heart of the German Colony, right on the boulevard; the location can't be beat. This classy, intimate bar caters to a more mature crowd. ⊠ *Colony Hotel, 38 Ben Gurion Blvd., German Colony* ☎ *04/851–3344* ⊕ *colonyhaifa.com.*

Duke

BARS/PUBS | The lovely Duke is a civilized old-world Irish pub with good draft beers, other libations from whiskey to wine, and a menu with such standbys as fish-and-chips. Bottles on display and plenty of dark wood add to the convivial atmosphere. ⊠ *107 Moriah Blvd., Merkaz Carmel* ☎ *04/834–7282* ⊕ *www.duke-pub.co.il/en/.*

Frangelico

BARS/PUBS | With the unlikely name of Frangelico, Haifa's first sushi bar turns into an attractive pub at night—the kind of place where everyone seems to know everyone else. A side room with sofas adds to the casual ambience. ⊠ *132 Moriah Blvd., Merkaz Carmel* ☎ *04/824–8839* ⊕ *www.frangelicobar.com.*

Pundak HaDov

BARS/PUBS | One of Haifa's oldest and most reliable pubs and sports bars, the cozy Pundak HaDov (The Bear Inn) tends to fill with enthusiastic sports fans cheering on their favorite teams in front of four big screens. The menu has ample choices for snacks and full meals. ⊠ *135 Hanassi Blvd., Merkaz Carmel* ☎ *04/838–1703.*

🎭 Performing Arts

For information on performances and other special events in and around Haifa, check Friday's *Jerusalem Post* or the *Haaretz* newspaper; both publish separate weekend entertainment guides.

Haifa Symphony Orchestra

MUSIC | The orchestra performs at the Haifa Auditorium (Krieger Center) four to five times a month from October through July. For ticket and performance information, contact the box office. ⊠ *6 Eliyahu Hakim St., French Carmel* ☎ *04/833–8888 box office* ⊕ *www.haifasymphony.co.il.*

Israel Philharmonic Orchestra

MUSIC | The world-class Israel Philharmonic Orchestra gives 20 concerts at the Haifa Auditorium (Rappaport Hall) from October through July. ⊠ *138 Hanassi Blvd., Merkaz Carmel* ☎ *04/810–1558* ⊕ *www.ipo.co.il.*

🛍 Shopping

Haifa is studded with modern shopping malls with boutiques, eateries, and movie theaters, not to mention drugstores, photography stores, and money-exchange desks.

Castra Shopping Center

SHOPPING CENTERS/MALLS | Near the Hof Carmel railway station, this popular mall has three floors of jewelry stores, clothing boutiques, and art workshops. It is easily spotted by Eric Brauer's large ceramic-tile mural outside depicting Old Testament themes. ⊠ *8 Fliman St., South Haifa* ☎ *04/859–0000.*

Panorama Center

SHOPPING CENTERS/MALLS | Located in the heart of the Carmel Center next to the Dan Panorama Haifa hotel, the Panorama Center has everything from a pharmacy and newspaper stand to a wine outlet and clothing shops. ⊠ *109 Hanassi Blvd., Merkaz Carmel* ☎ *04/837–5011* ☉ *Closed Sat.*

Sara's Gift Shop

GIFTS/SOUVENIRS | This boutique in the Dan Carmel Haifa hotel is crammed with jewelry made exclusively for it, including silver inlaid with Roman glass, gold Baha'i pendants, and art-deco earrings. ⊠ *Dan Carmel Haifal, 87 Hanassi Blvd., Merkaz Carmel* ☎ *04/830–3098.*

Nahsholim-Dor

29 km (19 miles) south of Haifa.

The beautiful beach at Dor is fit for a king—not surprising since it has a royal history. Founded 3,500 years ago, biblical Dor was once the maritime capital of the Carmel coast. The storied harbor between Jaffa (near present-day Tel Aviv) and Akko, it was a target for many with imperial ambitions, from the ancient Egyptians and the "Sea Peoples" through to King Solomon and on down. It was renowned in antiquity for its precious purple dye; reserved for royalty, this hue was extracted from a mollusk that was abundant along the coast. Today, as you watch fishing boats bob in the sheltered bays, you can complement your suntanning with a swim to a small offshore island, a visit to a diving site, or a break at a pub.

GETTING HERE AND AROUND

Take Route 2, getting off at the Zichron Ya'akov exit. At the Fureidis Junction, drive north about 1 km (½ mile) until you reach the small sign for Nahsholim-Dor. There's no public transportation here.

◉ Sights

Atlit Detention Camp

JAIL | Atlit, a peninsula with the jagged remains of an important Crusader castle, also holds a more recent historical site: to the west (about 1,500 feet from the highway) is the Atlit detention camp used by the British to house refugees smuggled in during and after World War II. The reconstructed barracks, fences, and watchtowers stand as reminders of how Jewish immigration was outlawed under the British Mandate after the publication of the infamous White Paper in 1939. More than a third of the 120,000 illegal immigrants to Palestine passed through the camp from 1934 to 1948. In 1945, Yizthak Rabin, then a young officer in the Palmach, planned a raid that freed 200 detainees. The authenticity of the exhibit is striking: it was re-created from accounts of actual detainees and their contemporaries; you see the living quarters, complete with laundry hanging from the rafters. The camp is 15 km (9 miles) south of Haifa. ⊠ *Rd. 7110* ✛ *Off Rte. 2* ☎ *04/984–1980* ☒ *NIS 32* ⊙ *Closed Sat.* ☞ *Reservations required.*

Mizgaga Museum

MUSEUM | **FAMILY** | This very worthwhile museum next to Kibbutz Nahsholim and the Nahsholim Seaside Resort holds a rich trove of finds from local nautical digs and excavations at nearby Tel Dor. It's in the partly restored former glass factory opened by Baron Edmond de Rothschild in 1891 to serve the wineries of nearby Zichron Ya'akov. The sequence of peoples who settled, conquered, or passed through Dor—from the Canaanites to Phoenicians to Napoléon—can be traced through these artifacts. Of particular interest is the bronze cannon that Napoléon's vanquished troops dumped into the sea during their retreat from Akko to Egypt in May 1799. An informative film in English illuminates the history of the ancient port city of Dor. ⊠ *Kibbutz Nahsholim, Rd. 7011* ☎ *04/639–0950* ⊕ *www.mizgaga.com* ☒ *NIS 20* ⊙ *Closed Sat.*

◉ Beaches

★ Dor Beach

BEACH—SIGHT | Part of a coastal nature reserve, Dor Beach, also known as Tantura Beach, is a dreamy stretch of beige sand. Rocky islets form breakwaters

The Northern Coast

LEBANON

3

Rosh Hanikra

Shelomi

899 899 89

Betzet Beach

4

Achziv Beach

Achziv National Park

Hiram Junction

89 89

Galei Galil Beach

89

Nahariya

Byzantine Church

Ma'alot-Tarshiha

Meron

Ghetto Fighters' House Museum

70

Abu Sinan

854 864

85

Bahá'i Founder's Shrine and Gardens

Shagor

Karmi'el

Akko see detail map

85

G A L I L E E

Maghar

4

Haifa Bay

Kiryat Motzkin

79

Tamra

Sakhnin

Arraba

65

Kiryat Bialik

Eilabun

Haifa see detail map

2

Kiryat Ata

Shefar'am

Kafar Manda

Bahá'i Gardens

4

Nesher

79

Golani Junction

Lavi

Tirat Carmel

Carmel National Park

70

HaMovil Junction

77

65

Nisco Museum of Mechanical Music

75

77

754

Kafr Kamma

Janco-Dada Museum

Isfiya

Ramat Yishay

75

Nazareth

Atlit Detention Camp

Daliyat el Carmel

4

Ein Hod

Daliyat el Carmel Marketplace

73

Kelar Tavor

Nahal Me'arot Nature Reserve

Mukhraka

Carmelite Monastery

60

70

Amphorae Wines

66

J E Z R E E L   V A L L E Y

Afula

Nahsholim-Dor

First Aliya Museum

65

Mizgaga Museum

Dor Beach

70

Bat Shlomo

71

Zichron Ya'akov

Carmel Winery

669

4

Beit Aaronson

Caesarea see detail map

2

Ramat Hanadiv

667

Tishbi Estate Winery

652

Binyamina Winery

Umm el Fahm

596

66

Or Aqiva

Benyamina

65

Roman Aqueduct

Pardes Hanna-Karkur

WEST BANK

Jenin

Caesarea Beach

Hadera

57

Hof Shonit Beach

65

596

60

2

Mikhmoret Beach

6

Baqa el Gharbiya

Qabatiyah

Mikhmoret

Attil

60

Beit Yanai Beach

Ajjah

Tubas

Herzl Beach

Netanya

57

Sironit Beach

4

57

6

Tulkarem

0 ___ 5 mi

0 ___ 5 km

Mediterranean Sea

and jetties provide calm seas for happy bathers. Amenities are ample: chair and umbrella rentals, a first-aid station, a restaurant, and changing rooms. The beach, beside Kibbutz Nahsholim, gets crowded on summer weekends and holidays. **Amenities:** food and drink; lifeguards; parking; showers; toilets. **Best for:** partiers; swimming; walking. ⊠ *Off Rte. 4* ⊠ *Nature reserve NIS 35, beach entrance free.*

 ## Activities

Paradive
FLYING/SKYDIVING/SOARING | The company organizes thrilling tandem skydives 14,000 feet over the Mediterranean. No experience is required. It's about 3 km (2 miles) north of Kibbutz Nahsholim. ⊠ *Habonim Beach* ⊹ *Off Rte. 4* ☏ *04/639–1068* ⊕ *www.paradive.co.il.*

Underwater Archaeological Center
SCUBA DIVING | Kurt Raveh, a marine archaeologist and resident of Kibbutz Nahsholim, runs the Underwater Archaeological Center. Raveh conducts underwater expeditions and "dives into history" where divers (even those without experience) get to tour ancient shipwrecks (many of which he discovered) and explore reefs under his experienced eye. You can also arrange kayaking trips along the coast. ⊠ *Kibbutz Nahsholim* ☏ *052/516–2795.*

Caesarea

49 km (29½ miles) south of Haifa.

The Phoenicians discovered it, and the Romans fell in love with it: Caesarea is most famous for its intriguing Roman, Byzantine, and Crusader ruins, but also offers a stroll through artists' galleries, an underwater archaeological park, and culinary delights. This popular tourist center juxtaposes a vibrant past and bustling present. Near the archaeological site is the well-to-do community of Caesarea, a group of homes on the sea. Here you'll find the Ralli Museum and the famed Roman aqueduct.

GETTING HERE AND AROUND
A car is your best option for reaching Caesarea. It's off Route 2, about one hour by car from Tel Aviv or Haifa. You can also opt for a guided bus tour of this and other sites, departing from a number of cities, with Egged Tours or United Tours, two well-regarded companies.

⊙ Sights

★ Caesarea Maritima National Park
ARCHAEOLOGICAL SITE | **FAMILY** | By turns an ancient Roman port city, Byzantine capital, and Crusader stronghold, Caesarea is one of the country's major archaeological sites and a delightful place to spend a day of leisurely sightseeing among the fascinating ruins. You can browse in souvenir shops and art galleries, take a dip at the beach, snorkel or dive around a submerged port, and enjoy a seaside meal. Caesarea is an easy day trip from Tel Aviv and Haifa or even Jerusalem. A good strategy is to start at the Roman Theater, at the southern entrance. After exploring, you can then leave through the northern entrance. If you're short on time, enter through the northern entrance and take a quicker tour of the site. At either of the two entrances to this intriguing site, pick up the free brochure and map.

Entry to the Roman Theater is through one of the vomitoria (arched tunnels that served as entrances for the public). Herod's theaters—here as elsewhere in Israel—were the first of their kind in the ancient Near East. The theater today seats 3,600 and is a spectacular venue for summer concerts and performances. What you see today is largely a reconstruction. Only a few of the seats of the *cavea* (where the audience sat) near the

Herod's Amazing Port at Caesarea

The port's construction at Caesarea was an unprecedented challenge—there was no artificial harbor of this size anywhere in the world. But Herod wasn't one to avoid a challenge and spent 12 years, from 22 to 10 BC, building a port for the luxury-goods trade (including spices, textiles, and precious stones) that would make Caesarea the economic capital of the country and the most modern harbor in the whole Roman Empire.

During underwater research in the 1970s, archaeologists were stunned to discover concrete blocks near the breakwater offshore, indicating the sophisticated use of hydraulic concrete (which hardens underwater).

Historians knew that the Romans had developed such techniques, but before the discoveries at Caesarea, they never knew hydraulic concrete to have been used on such a massive scale. The main ingredient in the concrete,

volcanic ash, was probably imported from Italy's Mount Vesuvius, as were the wooden forms. Teams of professional divers actually did much of the trickiest work, laying the foundations hundreds of yards offshore.

Once finished, two massive breakwaters—one stretching west and then north from the Citadel restaurant some 1,800 feet and the other 600 feet long, both now submerged—sheltered an area of about 3½ acres from the waves and tides.

Two towers, each mounted by three colossal statues, marked the entrance to the port; and although neither the towers nor the statues have been found, a tiny medal bearing their image was discovered in the first underwater excavations here in 1960. The finished harbor also contained the dominating temple to Emperor Augustus and cavernous storage facilities along the shore.

orchestra are original, in addition to some of the stairs and the decorative wall at the front of the stage.

The huge Herodian Amphitheater is a horseshoe-shape stadium with sloping sides filled with rows of stone seats. It's most likely the one mentioned by 1st-century AD historian Josephus Flavius in *The Jewish War.* A crowd of 10,000 watched horse and chariot races and various sporting events here some 2,000 years ago. Up the wooden steps, you see the street's beautiful and imaginative mosaic floors in the bathhouse complex of the Roman-Byzantine administrative area.

King Louis IX of France built the walls that surround the Crusader City. The

bulk of what you see today—the moat, escarpment, citadel, and walls, which once contained 16 towers—dates from 1251, when the French monarch spent a year pitching in with his own two hands to help restore the existing fortifications. As you enter the southern wall gate of the Crusader city, you see the remains of an unfinished cathedral with three graceful apses.

At the observation point, you can gaze out over the remains of Herod's Port, once a magnificent sight that writers of the day compared to Athens' Port of Piraeus. An earthquake devastated the harbor in AD 130, which is why Crusaders utilized only a small section of it when they conquered the city in 1101.

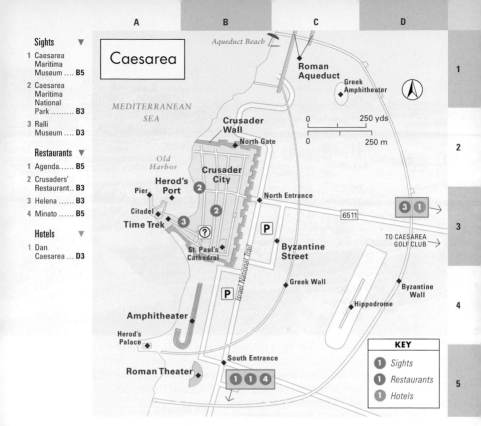

In the harbor area, don't miss the Time Trek. Inside, you meet 12 of Caesarea's fascinating historic personages—among them Herod the Great, Rabbi Akiva, and St. Paul. These realistic-looking, larger-than-life figures answer questions about their lives in Caesarea. If you climb the stairs of the nearby squarish stone tower of the re-created fortress on the pier, you can view three-dimensional animations on giant screens that explain the amazing construction of the port.

East of the northern entrance to the site, a fenced-in area encloses Caesarea's Byzantine Street. During the Byzantine period and late Roman times, Caesarea thrived as a center of Christian scholarship. In the 7th century, Caesarea boasted a famous library of some 30,000 volumes that originated with the collection of the Christian philosopher Origen (185–254), who lived here for two decades. Towering over the street are two headless marble statues, probably carted here from nearby Roman temples. The provenance of the milky-white statue is unknown; Emperor Hadrian might have commissioned the reddish figure facing it when he visited Caesarea.

A wonderful finale to your trip to Caesarea, especially at sunset, is the beachfront Roman Aqueduct. The chain of arches tumbling northward until they disappear beneath the sand is a captivating sight. During Roman times, the demand for a steady water supply was considerable, but the source was a spring about 13 km (8 miles) away in the foothills of Mount Carmel. Workers cut a channel approximately 6½ km (4 miles) long through

Ancient Caesarea, which has ruins from a variety of historical periods, is one of Israel's most popular destinations.

solid rock before the water was piped into the aqueduct. In the 2nd century, Hadrian doubled its capacity by adding a new channel. Today you can walk along the aqueduct and see marble plaques dedicated to the troops of various legions who toiled here. ⊠ *Off Rte. 2, near Kibbutz Sdot Yam* ☎ *04/626–7080* ⊕ *www. parks.org.il* ⌧ *NIS 40.*

Caesarea Maritima Museum

MUSEUM | In Kibbutz Sdot Yam just outside Caesarea, this excellent museum houses many of the remarkable artifacts found by kibbutz members as they plowed their fields in the 1940s; archaeological excavations have discovered more. The small museum has arguably the best collection of late-Roman sculpture and figurines in Israel, with impressive holdings of rare Roman and Byzantine gemstones; a large variety of coins minted in Caesarea over the ages; and oil lamps, jewelry, and urns excavated from the sea floor. ⊠ *Kibbutz Sdot Yam* ⊹ *Near southern entrance to Caesarea* ☎ *04/636–4367* ⊕ *www.*

caesareamuseum.com ⌧ *NIS 18* ⊘ *Closed Fri. and Sat.*

Ralli Museum

MUSEUM | In Caesarea's villa area, you can't miss the two Spanish colonial–style buildings of the Ralli Museum, with their red-tile roofs and terraces: one of these dazzling white buildings houses an exhibit on the ancient city's history, and the second building, in a Moorish style, examines the golden age of Spanish Jewry in the Middle Ages. It's a pleasure to wander along the walls of the courtyard and gaze at the sculptures of various dignitaries such as Maimonides and Spinoza. Inside are paintings with biblical themes by European artists of the 16th to 18th centuries. Rotating exhibitions display contemporary Latin American art. ⊠ *Rothschild Blvd., next to water tower* ☎ *04/626–1013* ⊕ *www. rallimuseums.com* ⌧ *Free* ⊘ *Mar.–Dec., closed Wed. and Sun.; Jan. and Feb., closed Sun.–Thurs.*

Caesarea: Roman City 👁

Herod the Great gave Caesarea its name, dedicating the magnificent Roman city he built to his patron, Augustus Caesar. It was the Roman emperor who had crowned Herod—born to an Idumean family that had converted to Judaism—King of the Jews around 30 BC.

Construction began in 22 BC; Herod spared nothing in his elaborate designs for the port and the city itself, which included palaces, temples, a theater, a marketplace, a hippodrome, and water and sewage systems. When Caesarea was completed 12 years later, only Jerusalem outshined it. Its population under Herod grew to around 100,000, and the city covered some 164 acres.

In AD 6, a decade after Herod died, Caesarea became the seat of the Roman procurators, one of whom was Pontius Pilate, governor of Judea when Jesus was crucified. With Jerusalem predominantly Jewish,

the Romans preferred the Hellenistic Caesarea, with its Jewish minority, as the seat of their administration.

But religious harmony did not prevail. The mixed population of Jews and Gentiles (mainly Greeks and Syrians) repeatedly clashed, with hostilities exploding during the Jewish revolt of AD 66. Vespasian, proclaimed emperor by his legions in AD 69, squelched the first Jewish rebellion. A year later, his son Titus razed Jerusalem and celebrated his suppression of the Jewish revolt.

Henceforth, Caesarea was a Roman colony and the local Roman capital of Palestine for nearly 600 years. It was here that Peter converted the Roman centurion Cornelius to Christianity—a milestone in the spread of the new faith—and Paul preached and was imprisoned for two years. In the 2nd century, Rabbi Akiva, the spiritual mentor of the Bar Kochba revolt, was tortured to death here.

🏖 Beaches

Caesarea Beach Club

BEACH—SIGHT | In a calm cove in Caesarea's ancient harbor, the Caesarea Beach Club has chairs and umbrellas. A lifeguard is on duty in season, and the restaurant sells sandwiches and other light fare. **Amenities:** food and drink; lifeguards; showers. **Best for:** sunset; swimming. ⊠ Northern entrance to archaeological site 🎫 Free.

Hof Shonit

BEACH—SIGHT | FAMILY | The largest and most popular beach in the area is the exceptionally well-kept Hof Shonit (translated as "Reef Beach"), with a refreshment stand and a restaurant, as well as

restrooms and cold showers. In addition to the beach there is a water park with extreme slides for the kids (open only on Saturdays in-season) and adult and toddler swimming pools. Parking is NIS 15. **Amenities:** food and drink; lifeguards; parking (fee); showers; toilets; water sports. **Best for:** swimming. ⊠ South of archaeological site ⊹ Off Rte. 2.

Roman Aqueduct

BEACH—SIGHT | Caesarea's Roman aqueduct frames a spacious beach with the dramatic backdrop of arches disappearing into the sand. There is no entrance fee but few amenities—no restaurants or promenade. The beach and swimming areas have been cleared of rocks and debris, but swimming outside the designated area is prohibited. Never swim unless the seasonal lifeguard is on duty. **Amenities:** lifeguards; parking (fee) **Best for:** sunset; walking. ✉ *North of archaeological site.*

🍴 Restaurants

Agenda

$$ | **ISRAELI** | **FAMILY** | If you're one of those people who could eat breakfast three times a day, Agenda is for you. Try the *shakshuka,* an Israeli dish in which eggs are poached in a sharp tomato sauce. **Known for:** friendly staff; everything from shakshuka to pizza; conveniently located off the highway. [$] *Average main: NIS 60* ✉ *Caesarea Junction, Off Rte. 2* ✣ *At Paz gas station* ☎ *04/626–2092* ⏲ *No dinner Fri. No breakfast or lunch Sat.*

Crusaders' Restaurant (*HaTzalbanim*)

$$$ | **SEAFOOD** | **FAMILY** | Sitting by the old port of Caesarea in Caesarea National Park, and with ample seating overlooking the bay, this cavernous seaside restaurant is famous for its fish. The menu features fresh seafood, caught right from the water below, as well as juicy steaks and kebabs. **Known for:** favorite place for groups; amazing harbor views; wide ranging menu. [$] *Average main: NIS 100* ✉ *Caesarea* ✣ *Northern end of port* ☎ *04/636–1679* 🌐 *pundakazalbanim.rest.co.il.*

★ **Helena**

$$$ | **MEDITERRANEAN** | Two of Israel's best-known culinary personalities, Amos Sion and Uri Yarmias, opened this restaurant to create a first-rate yet affordable dining experience. It occupies a beautifully restored stone building in the ancient harbor. **Known for:** commanding views; delicious seafood; reliable service. [$] *Average main: NIS 100* ✉ *Caesarea* ✣ *Southern end of port* ☎ *04/610–1018* 🌐 *www.hellena.co.il.*

Minato

$$ | **JAPANESE** | In a gas station (and next door to the restaurant Agenda), this place is perfect for beachgoers craving sushi. The name means "port" in Japanese, and Minato does a brisk take-out business, serving sashimi and nigiri as well as a variety of tempura dishes. **Known for:** high-quality Japanese (try the temaki); selection of up to 60 cold and hot rolls; noted foodie destination. [$] *Average main: NIS 60* ✉ *Caesarea Junction, Rte. 2* ✣ *At Paz gas station* ☎ *04/636–0812* 🌐 *www.minato.co.il* ⏲ *No dinner Fri. No lunch Sat.*

🛏 Hotels

Dan Caesarea

$$ | **HOTEL** | **FAMILY** | Equidistant from Tel Aviv and Haifa, this chain hotel suits business executives and vacationers alike, and the 15 acres of landscaped lawns, sparkling swimming pool, and 18-hole minigolf course make it great for families. **Pros:** beautiful grounds; family-friendly vibe; helpful staff. **Cons:** no public transportation; far from restaurants; pool closed during the winter. [$] *Rooms from: $300* ✉ *1 Rothschild St.* ☎ *04/626–9111* 🌐 *www.danhotels.com* 🛏 *113 rooms* 🍴 *No meals.*

🏃 Activities

GOLF

Caesarea Golf Club

GOLF | The country's only 18-hole golf course is the Caesarea Golf Club, adjacent to the Dan Caesarea. Although it was first established by the Rothschilds in the 1960s, noted golf course architect Pete Dye remodeled the course to high standards in 2009. There's a pro shop and the Albatross restaurant. ✉ *Caesarea* ✣ *Off Rte. 2* ☎ *04/610–9618* 🌐 *www.caesarea.com* 🎟 *From NIS 480* ⛳ *18 holes, 7200 yards, par 72* ☞ *Closed Mon.*

SCUBA DIVING
Old Caesarea Diving Center
SCUBA DIVING | Located inside the national park, this diving center runs a full range of courses for novices, experts, and everyone in between. Snorkelers are welcome, and divers can use a plastic map and four underwater trails marked by ropes to follow a route of numbered artifacts in the submerged port built by King Herod 2,000 years ago. Half-hour introductory dives to a depth of 6 meters range from NIS 240 to NIS 350; another option is to explore the nocturnal marine life on a night dive. You must make diving reservations in advance. ⊠ *Caesarea Harbor* ✛ *Behind Time Trek* ☎ *04/626–5898* ⊕ *www.caesarea-diving.com.*

Netanya

65 km (43 miles) south of Haifa, 30 km (18 miles) north of Tel Aviv.

The lively resort city of Netanya (literally, "gift of God") has a pretty seaside promenade along the cliffs, endless sandy beaches, a pleasant town square, and plenty of cafés and restaurants. Once a sleepy place surrounded by orange groves, the town—named after Jewish philanthropist Nathan Straus, co-owner of Macy's—has steadily grown from a few settlers in 1929 to some 210,000 residents today. Since the 1930s, it has been a center for the diamond-cutting industry. More recently, Netanya has become known for its large immigrant population, most notably from France and the former Soviet Union.

Just south of the city are several nature reserves: the Iris Reserve, where purple irises flower in February and March; the Nahal Poleg Reserve, with fauna unique to the area; and the Udim Reserve, which includes a pool with turtles, fish, and birds.

Though citrus farming is still evident on Netanya's outskirts, there are few traces of small-town charm. Tracts of residential development can be seen all along the southern approach to the city following the shoreline, with high-rise towers dotting the landscape. Vacationers from abroad have purchased many of the apartment units.

GETTING HERE AND AROUND
To get here by car from Tel Aviv or Haifa, take coastal Route 2. Trains from Haifa depart on the hour and take about 25 minutes. Egged buses from Haifa leave at least every 30 minutes and take one hour 40 minutes.

VISITOR INFORMATION
CONTACTS Netanya Tourist Information Office. ⊠ *12 Ha'atzmaut Sq.* ☎ *09/882–7286* ⊕ *www.gonetanya.com.*

◉ Sights

Ha'atzmaut Square
PLAZA | Benches sit among palm trees and surround a large fountain at this lively central square with open-air cafés and restaurants that are crowded from morning until late into the evening. Netanya attracts droves of French visitors, and in summer their lilting tones float above the café au lait and croissants. Saturday nights are often enlivened by folk dancing, and the amphitheater hosts free concerts in summer and an arts-and-crafts fair on Friday morning. ⊠ *Netanya.*

Seaside Promenade
NEIGHBORHOOD | FAMILY | Also known as "the boulevard," the seaside promenade extends north and south of the city for about 6 km (4 miles) with beautifully landscaped walkways that wind around the contours of the sandstone cliffs overlooking the sea; every angle affords a gorgeous view. It's dotted with pergola-shaded benches, wooden bridges, colorful playground areas, and waving palm trees. An elevator at the center of

Did You Know?

Fun at the coast's beaches, whether in Haifa or as shown here in Netanya, can include paragliding, windsurfing, and playing *matkot* (a popular paddle-ball game often referred to as Israel's national sport).

the promenade eases the climb up and down the seaside cliff. ✉ *Netanya.*

Beaches

Showers, restrooms and changing rooms, lifeguards, and first-aid stations are available free at all of Netanya's beaches, which cover 14 km (8½ miles) of soft, sandy coastline. Most beaches rent beach chairs and umbrellas.

Beit Yanai

BEACH—SIGHT | About 5 km (3 miles) north of Netanya is lovely Beit Yanai, named after ancient Judean king Alexander Yanai. Amenities include barbecue grills, picnic tables, restrooms with showers, and chair and umbrella rentals. There's a seafood restaurant right on the beach, and you can stroll along the Alexander Stream, shaded by eucalyptus trees. Parking is NIS 24 on weekdays and NIS 33 on Saturday. **Amenities:** food and drink; lifeguards; parking (fee); showers; toilets; water sports. **Best for:** walking; windsurfing. ✉ *Rte. 2* ☎ *09/866–6230* 🎫 *Free.*

Herzl

BEACH—SIGHT | **FAMILY** | Netanya's most popular beach, Herzl, has a broad staircase that leads down to the waterfront. For fitness nuts there's a shaded exercise area with all sorts of equipment, volleyball nets, and a paved basketball court. You can rent kayaks and windsurfing gear in the summer. The beach is wheelchair accessible. There is also a café and two lifeguard stations. **Amenities:** food and drink; lifeguards; showers; toilets; water sports; parking (fee). **Best for:** swimming; windsurfing. ✉ *Ha'atzmaut Square* 🎫 *Free.*

Mikhmoret

BEACH—SIGHT | The beach at Mikhmoret, a tiny moshav 7½ km (4½ miles) north of Netanya, is popular with swimmers as well as those who laze away the day under umbrellas. The huge dirt parking lot, which charges per car, is 1 km (½ mile) after the turnoff from Route 2. There are three lifeguard stations, a restaurant, café, and chair and umbrella rentals. This is a backpacker favorite, and the Resort Hostel is on the beach. **Amenities:** food and drink; lifeguards; parking (fee); toilets; water sports. **Best for:** sunset; swimming. ✉ *Netanya* 🎫 *Free.*

Sironit

BEACH—SIGHT | This main beach is the largest stretch of sand on the Netanya coast. An elevator takes you down the sandstone cliff to this beach. There are two cafés and two drink kiosks with seating inside and out. Fridays are filled with salsa and folk dancing. The parking lot is on the beach, just south of Ha'atzmaut Square. Handicapped accessible, the beach has a paved road that allows wheelchairs and walkers access almost to the shoreline. The lifeguard stand has ultralight wheelchairs for use that can drive right into the water. **Amenities:** food and drink; lifeguards; parking (fee); showers; toilets; water sports. **Best for:** partiers; swimming. ✉ *Gad Machness St.* 🎫 *Free.*

Restaurants

Miriam's Grill

$$ | **MEDITERRANEAN** | A stone's throw from the main approach to the beach, the well-known Shipudei Miriam has a nice location facing a bubbling fountain. Moroccan-style grilled fish and lamb dishes are served both indoors and outdoors. **Known for:** warm greetings; salads and grilled meats; generous portions. [$] *Average main: NIS 60* ✉ *11 Gad Maknes* ☎ *09/834–1376* 🌐 *http://62810590.rest.co.il* 🕒 *No dinner Fri. No lunch Sat.*

Rosemarine

$$$ | **SEAFOOD** | At this tiny seaside haven for fish lovers you can enjoy fresh and tasty fare indoors or on the terrace overlooking Netanya's famous promenade. The kitchen serves a wide range

During the Jewish holiday of Purim, revelers in Netanya and around the country dress up in costume.

of excellent fish dishes, such as tilapia, cod, and gray mullet, grilled, baked, or sautéed. **Known for:** popular with English speakers; fish such as tilapia and cod; pleasant ambience. [$] *Average main: NIS 90* ✉ *8 Nitza Blvd.* ☎ *09/832–3322* 🕑 *Closed Sat. No dinner Fri.*

Coffee and Quick Bites

Tony Ice Café

$ | **CAFÉ** | Cool off at this authentic gelateria, which scoops a huge array of flavors, all made by hand by a family of immigrants from Italy. Coffee, milk shakes, and pastries are also for sale. **Known for:** Italian ice cream; neighborhood institution; promenade location. [$] *Average main: NIS 25* ✉ *Ha'atzmaut Sq., 5 Herzl St.* ☎ *09/834–0406* 🕑 *Closed Fri. evening and Sat. until sundown.*

Hotels

Mizpe Yam

$ | **HOTEL** | Don't expect luxury at this family-owned five-story hotel; what you can count on is good value and a warm welcome. **Pros:** near the promenade and beach; nice rooftop sundeck; free Wi-Fi. **Cons:** no sea views; no-frills decor; no pool. [$] *Rooms from: $115* ✉ *1 Jabotinsky St.* ☎ *09/862–3730* 🌐 *www.mizpe-yam.co.il* 🛏 *35 rooms* 🍴 *Free Breakfast.*

Activities

HORSEBACK RIDING

The Ranch (*Hachava*)

HORSEBACK RIDING | In northern Netanya, The Ranch has horseback riding for NIS 120 per hour. It's necessary to reserve ahead for weekend trips or for sunset rides along the beach. ✉ *Havatzelet Hasharon St., Neurim Beach* ☎ *09/866–3525* 🌐 *www.the-ranch.co.il.*

PARAGLIDING

Netanya's cliffs make for exciting paragliding. Under the guidance of experienced instructors, you take off from a specially designed field along the promenade about half a mile south of the city center.

Dvir Paragliding

HANG GLIDING/PARAGLIDING/PARASAILING |
This established paragliding company leads thrilling adventures throughout the year, but the ideal time is from May to October. Make reservations at least two days in advance. The company offers different activities at two locations, both Netanya-based, depending on the time of year and the activity. ☒ *Netanya* ☎ *054/655–4466* ⊕ *dvirparagliding.co.il* ◪ *From NIS 190.*

Sky Paragliding School

HANG GLIDING/PARAGLIDING/PARASAILING |
Founded in 1998, the company arranges a onetime guided experience as well as two-day introductory courses. The one-time experience offers a 10- to 20-minute paragliding adventure in Netanya during the summer, and in northern Israel during the winter, for NIS 250–NIS 450. Call ahead to make reservations. ☒ *Netanya* ☎ *054/671–4440* ⊕ *www.paragliding. co.il.*

The Wine Country and Mount Carmel

Wine has been produced in this fertile region for thousands of years. In the biblical book of Deuteronomy, the fruit of the vine was listed as one of the seven blessed species of fruit found in the land of Israel. The Sharon Plain near the Mediterranean coast south of Haifa, including the towns of Zichron Ya'akov and Benyamina, is the largest grape-growing area in Israel. Though the Rothschilds updated viniculture around Zichron Ya'akov in the

1880s, truly world-class wines began to appear only in the 1990s. After a tour of a winery, it's delightful to sit under the grapevines and sample the vintages along with fresh salad, warm bread, and good local cheese.

The Druze villages high in the Carmel serve traditional confections like *knafeh* and baklava as well as excellent olive oil and homemade *labaneh* (yogurt cheese). A meal in one of the towns isn't only a tasty experience, but also a warmly welcoming one.

Route 4, which runs north to south parallel to Route 2, is a more scenic drive, with Mount Carmel looming to the east beyond cultivated fields and banana plantations (though you may not see the bananas, as they're usually bagged in blue or gray plastic to protect them from bugs). The road leads through undulating countryside dotted with cypresses, palms, and vineyards.

Ein Hod

15 km (10 miles) south of Haifa, 5 km (3 miles) west of Isfiya.

A charming village nestled in ancient olive groves on the western slope of Mount Carmel, Ein Hod is home to some 650 residents, most of them sculptors, painters, ceramicists, architects, jewelers, and other artists. The setting is an idyllic one, with rough-hewn stone houses built on the hillside and sweeping views down to the Mediterranean. The Dadaist painter Marcel Janco (1895–1984) wrote upon his first visit in 1950, "The beauty of the place was staggering."

Parking is across the road, opposite the entrance to the village. Climbing up the hill, you soon come to a winding street on the left that starts a lovely walk through the small village. Signs along the way indicate studios and workshops where artists paint, sculpt, and make jewelry, pottery, silkscreen prints, and clothing. You can continue straight to the town square, bordered by a restaurant and a large gallery where works by Ein Hod artists are exhibited.

GETTING HERE AND AROUND

Your best option is to get here by car via Route 4, because buses are few and far between. The village itself is small and quite walkable.

◉ Sights

Janco-Dada Museum

MUSEUM | On the village square is this museum dedicated to the art and life of one of the founders of the Dada movement. The Romanian-born Marcel Janco had already established a considerable professional reputation by the time he moved here in 1941. The museum houses a permanent collection of the artist's work in various media, reflecting Janco's 70-year output both in Europe and Israel. A 20-minute slide show chronicles the life of the artist and the Dada movement, and the DadaLab offers hands-on activities for children. Don't miss the view from the roof. ⊠ *Ein Hod ⊹ Near village square* ☎ *04/984–2350* ⊕ *www.jancodada.co.il* ▧ *NIS 24.*

★ Nahal Me'arot Nature Reserve

CAVE | **FAMILY** | The prehistoric Carmel Caves, recognized in 2012 as a UNESCO World Heritage Site, are a highlight of this nature reserve, 3 km (2 miles) south of Ein Hod. They form a key site for the study of human evolution in general and the prehistory of the Levant in particular.

The three excavated caves are up a steep flight of stairs, on a fossil reef covered by the sea 100 million years ago. The first discoveries of prehistoric remains were made when this area was being scoured for stones to build the Haifa port. In the late 1920s, Dorothy Garrod of England headed the first archaeological

expedition, receiving assistance from a British feminist group on the condition that only women carry out the dig.

In the Tannur cave, the first on the tour, the strata Garrod's team excavated are clearly marked, spanning about 150,000 years in the life of early humans. The most exciting discoveries were Homo sapiens and Neanderthal skeletons; evidence that raised fascinating questions about the relationship between the two and whether they lived side by side. A display on the daily life of early man as hunter and food gatherer occupies the Gamal cave. The last and largest cave, called the Nahal, cuts deep into the mountain and was the first discovered. A burial place with 84 skeletons was found outside the mouth of the cave along with stone tools, which suggest that people who settled here, about 12,000 years ago, were the forebears of early farmers, with a social structure more developed than that of hunters and gatherers. There is also evidence that the Crusaders once used the cave to guard the coastal road. There's a snack bar at this site. ⊠ *Off Rte. 4* ☎ *04/984–1750* ⊕ *www.parks.org. il* ▧ *NIS 22.*

Nisco Museum of Mechanical Music

MUSEUM | **FAMILY** | Nisan Cohen, a colorful and charming character who knows everything there is to know about old mechanical musical instruments, has amassed 150 music boxes, hand-operated automatic pianos, manivelles, antique gramophones on which to play his collection of old Yiddish records, and more antique musical marvels. Cohen is pleased to give you a guided tour and then treat you to a personal concert. His sense of humor and gift of the gab make for a touching and intriguing experience. Before the entrance to Ein Hod, watch for a brown wooden sign with yellow letters. ⊠ *Off Rte. 7111* ☎ *052/475–5313* ⊕ *ein-hod.info/nisco* ▧ *NIS 30.*

🍴 Restaurants

Café Ein Hod

$ | CAFÉ | Climb up the stairs beside the Doña Rosa restaurant and keep an eye out for this local favorite: a two-level collection of mismatched chairs and odd tables, complete with a cat sunning itself on a stool. Inside the old stone building, handmade clothes and handbags are for sale. **Known for:** great place to have a light meal; lovely setting in the center of Ein Hod; coffee and cold drinks. $ *Average main: NIS 35* ✉ *Near village square* ☎ *054/667–6089* ☉ *Closed Mon.*

Doña Rosa

$$$ | ARGENTINE | If you can't read the restaurant's sign in Hebrew, just follow the tantalizing aroma up the steps of this wooden building on the town square: Rosa's grandsons, Uri and Doron, import meat and special charcoal from Argentina and roast the food in the true Argentinean style. The bar is decorated with a drawing of a hefty cow that illustrates each cut of meat. **Known for:** Argentinean beef and pork; asado on Saturday; fresh sangria. $ *Average main: NIS 90* ✉ *Near village square* ☎ *04/954–3777, 057/934–5520* ☉ *Closed Sun.*

🛏 Hotels

B&B Batia & Claude

$ | B&B/INN | Batia's and Claude's bed-and-breakfast is quiet and private, hidden behind masses of hot pink bougainvillea. **Pros:** pretty, private building; fun shop; great location. **Cons:** often gets booked well in advance; breakfast not included; no nightlife. $ *Rooms from: $120* ✉ *Ein Hod* ⊕ *2nd (east) entrance to Ein Hod* ☎ *04/984–1648* ⊕ *www.eisenwasser-jan-court.co.il* ⇆ *2 rooms* ⦿ *No meals.*

Yakir Ein Hod

$ | B&B/INN | If you'd enjoy a dip in a pool ringed by olive trees while you gaze at the blue Mediterranean, consider this delightful lodging. **Pros:** quiet location; private pool; lovely sea views. **Cons:** minimum stay required on weekends. $ *Rooms from: $190* ✉ *Ein Hod* ⊕ *2nd (east) entrance to Ein Hod* ☎ *050/554–3982* ⊕ *www.yakireinhod.co.il* ⇆ *3 suites* ⦿ *No meals.*

👜 Shopping

Many of the artists living in the winding lanes of Ein Hod throw open their workshops to visitors, who are welcome to browse and buy. Between the olive trees and behind painted gates, look for signs on homes that indicate the sale of art and crafts from jewelry to artistic photography. Either start at the entrance to the village where signs point to the left or head for the village square straight ahead.

Art & Wear Gallery

ART GALLERIES | Owners Dan and Lea Ben-Arye have lived and worked in Ein Hod for more than three decades, creating and selling their art. Their gallery features paintings, sculptures, jewelry, Judaica, and wearable art. They act as village ambassadors, running an information center from their shop. Private workshops can be arranged ahead of time with Lea. ✉ *Ein Hod* ⊕ *Across from Janco-Dada Museum* ☎ *054/481–1968.*

Central Gallery

CRAFTS | The Ein Hod Central Gallery, an integral part of the artistic community here since 1953, carries a wide selection of handicrafts and art by resident artists at its space on the main square. Displayed in the front room are ceramics, enamel, and silver and gold jewelry, while through the arch into another room are paintings, sculptures, and graphic works. ✉ *Ein Hod* ☎ *04/984–2548* ⊕ *www.ein-hod.org/en/maingallery.asp* ☉ *Closed Mon.*

The Druze

The Druze are an Arabic-speaking minority whose remarkable cohesion and esoteric faith have enabled them to maintain their close-knit identity through almost a thousand years of turbulent history. In Israel, they number about 130,000 and live in 17 villages in the Carmel, the Galilee, and Golan Heights. Larger kindred communities exist in Syria and Lebanon.

So exclusive is this sect that only a fraction of the community is initiated into its religious doctrine, one tenet of which is a belief in continuous reincarnation. The Druze broke away from Islam about 1,000 years ago, incorporating other traditions and also believing in the divinity of their founder, al-Hākim bi-Amr Allāh, the Caliph of the Egyptian Fatimid dynasty from AD 996 to 1021. They don't permit gambling or the use of alcohol.

The Druze who live in the two existing villages on Mount Carmel (Daliyat el Carmel and Isfiya) serve in the Israeli army, a mark of their loyalty to Israel.

Silver Print

ART GALLERIES | This lovely little studio holds Vivienne Silver-Brody's collection of vintage works by Israel's best photographers. The emphasis is on the building of the State of Israel. There's also a wide range of 19th-century photos of the Holy Land. A digital print costs NIS 150. Call or email for hours and the address. ⊠ *Ein Hod* ☎ *04/954–1673* ✉ *vivroy@netvision. net.il* ⊕ *silverprintgallery.photoshelter. com.*

Daliyat el Carmel and Isfiya

5 km (3 miles) east of Daliyat el Carmel and Isfiya, 16 km (11 miles) south of Haifa.

Daliyat el Carmel (Vine of the Carmel) is Israel's largest Druze village, and its weekend market, oil press, and *hilweh* (house of worship) are worth exploring. Though most of the younger generation wears jeans and T-shirts, older people tend to wear traditional garb. Head coverings indicate the degree of religious belief, from the high white turban resembling a fez to the white kerchief covering the head and shoulders. Many men sport a bushy moustache, a hallmark of the Druze, and some older ones wear dark robes and black pantaloons.

Very similar to neighboring Daliyat el Carmel, Isfiya is a village of flat-roof homes built closely together into the hillside, many of them raised on pillars and cut with arched windows. It stands on the remains of a Jewish village dating back to Roman times. Hospitality is second nature to the Druze here; you may be able to visit a village home and eat pita bread with yogurt cheese and spices while hearing about Druze life. The village is about 1 km (½ mile) from Daliyat el Carmel.

GETTING HERE AND AROUND

Coming from Haifa, drive south on Route 672.

TOURS

House of Druze Hospitality

GUIDED TOURS | To really get to know Isfiya and the Druze, arrange a tour through this company. Your guide will take you to visit their place of prayer, an olive oil press, and then to a private home where the matriarch bakes pita bread in a *tabun* (oven). You'll hear about the distinctive Druze way of life. Tours are available every day except Saturday, but make reservations at least a week ahead of time. ✉ *Isfiya* ☎ *04/839–0125* 🎫 *NIS 120.*

Sights

Daliyat el Carmel Marketplace

MARKET | About 1 km (½ mile) inside town, take a right turn into the marketplace, a colorful jumble of shops lining the street. You can be assured of finding excellent falafel and fresh produce at any of the roadside stands or restaurants. ✉ *Daliyat el Carmel* 🕓 *Closed Sun.*

Restaurants

Halabi Brothers

$$ | MIDDLE EASTERN | At this storefront eatery, brothers Fouad and Ahmad Halabi greet you with a handshake and a "Hello, my cousin!" The delicious falafel and shawarma are wrapped in thin, lightly browned Druze-style pitas, a nice change from the fluffy ones served at most other places in the country. A refreshing splash of lemon tops the platter of salads. **Known for:** famous falafel; warm welcome; glass-front kitchen. [$] *Average main: NIS 50* ✉ *14 Commercial Center St., Daliyat el Carmel* ☎ *04/839–3576.*

Nof HaCarmel

$$ | MIDDLE EASTERN | People come from all over the Carmel for the fine Middle Eastern fare at this excellent Druze restaurant, especially the homemade hummus with pine nuts, olive oil, garlic, and lemon juice, and the well-seasoned kebabs on skewers. Those with a sweet tooth should sample the *sahlab* (a warm, custardlike pudding of crushed orchid bulb with thickened milk and sugar). **Known for:** every meal starts with salads served meze-style; grilled meats and fish; courteous service. [$] *Average main: NIS 70* ✉ *Rte. 672, Isfiya* ☎ *04/839–1718.*

Shopping

Along a brief stretch of the main road that winds through Daliyat el Carmel are shops selling lightweight throw rugs, handwoven baskets, brightly colored pottery, brass dishes, characteristic woven wall hangings, and embroidered skullcaps worn by men. Bargaining is expected. Some shops close on Friday; the strip is crowded on Saturday.

Mukhraka

18 km (12 miles) south of Haifa, 2 km (1 mile) west of Daliyat el Carmel.

You can't miss Mukhraka, a site on the southeastern peak of Mount Carmel that is marked by a tall white statue of Elijah the Prophet with his sword raised on high. Just beyond is the graceful Carmelite monastery with a sweeping rooftop view of the Jezreel Valley. The site has well-marked hiking trails.

GETTING HERE AND AROUND

Mukhraka is an interesting stop if you're on the way to Isfiya and Daliyat el Carmel on Route 70. It's not accessible for those without a car.

Sights

Carmelite Monastery

RELIGIOUS SITE | Past open, uncultivated fields and a goatherd's rickety shack, Mukhraka's Carmelite monastery stands on the spur of the Carmel range, at an altitude of 1,580 feet, on the site where the struggle between the prophet Elijah and the priests of Ba'al is believed to have taken place. Climb to the roof for an unforgettable panorama: to the east stretches the Jezreel Valley and the hills of Nazareth, Moreh, and Gilboa. On a clear day, you can even see Jordan's Gilead Mountains beyond the Jordan River and Mount Hermon. The stark

Continued on page 336

In a land where grapes have been grown and enjoyed since biblical times, a modern winemaking revolution has taken hold. Whether the vintage is from big producers or boutique up-and-comers, the improved quality of Israeli wine has catapulted all things oenological into the spotlight. This tiny country is now home to over 250 wineries large and small. It was Baron Edmond de Rothschild—the proprietor of France's prestigious Château Lafite winery and an early Zionist—who jump-started the modern Israeli wine industry by providing money to found wineries in the 1880s. After a few false starts, Carmel Mizrachi, which his funds helped support, flourished; to this day it is Israel's most prolific wine producer.

by Adeena Sussman

(top) Ancient floor mosaic depicting wine vase at Eretz Israel Museum, Tel Aviv. (right) Golan Heights Winery

The *Wines*

of *Israel*

WINEMAKING IN ISRAEL

(top left) Winemaking barrel shop in Zichron Ya'akov, 1890s. (bottom left) Golan Heights Winery. (right) Wine fair in Tel Aviv.

Israel manufactured mostly mediocre wines until the late 1970s, when the first *moshavim* and *kibbutzim* (living cooperatives) planted vines in the Golan Heights on the advice of scientists from California, who saw a grape-growing diamond in the rough amid the mountain ranges of this northern region. Soon thereafter Golan Heights Winery was born, and awards and accolades were uncorked almost immediately.

GROWTH AND CHALLENGE

Besides two dozen or so larger operations, more than 250 smaller wineries now operate, many less than 15 years old and some producing just a few thousand bottles per year. Five large wineries account for 75 percent of production. Winemaking is a relatively young industry, sparked by a new crop of winemakers with experience at outstanding wineries. Though top wine writers have given some Israeli wines high marks, confirming internationally that these are vintages worth seeking out, there is still room for improvement in the ongoing, so-called "quality revolution."

Per capita wine consumption in Israel has nearly doubled since the late 1990s but remains low. A culture of wine appreciation is gradually fomenting, although the lion's share of bottles are exported to the United States and Europe. Despite challenges, winemakers continue to experiment: up-and-coming regions include the Judean Hills outside Jerusalem and even the Negev desert.

KOSHER & MEVUSHAL: MESSAGE ON A BOTTLE

For a wine to be certified kosher, as many Israeli wines are, a religious supervisor must oversee the process to ensure that no nonkosher tools or ingredients are used. Only rigorously observant Jews can handle equipment. Critics agree that these regulations don't affect the quality of wine. Mevushal wines, with more stringent kosher requirements, are flash-pasteurized, and then rapidly chilled; this can affect quality. However, many top-tier Israeli wines today are non-Mevushal, or are unsupervised altogether.

WINE REGIONS AND GRAPES

Sea Horse winery

GRAPE EXPECTATIONS

After commercial vines were first planted in the 19th century, Israeli winemakers focused on a small group of grape varietals that seemed to take well to Israeli terrain. The country has no indigenous grapes. With the help of technology, experience, and trial and error, a wide range of grapes are now raised with success.

Some of Israel's red wines are world-class, notably those that blend Cabernet Sauvignon grapes with Merlot, Cabernet Franc, and Petit Verdot. Chardonnays also do well here—the warm days and cool nights of the northern region seem particularly advantageous for this varietal.

Winemakers consistently push the envelope, introducing exciting new wines into the market. Two recent examples? Viognier, which has been one of the darlings of the current Israeli wine market, and Syrah, a grape that flourishes amid the country's hot days and cool, breezy nights.

Israel's wine-growing areas are typically divided into five regions, although no official, European-style government-regulated classification system exists. Since the country is so small—about the size of New Jersey—grapes are often shared among the regions. This is especially true of the northern plains, which provide grapes to many of the country's best wineries. Still, each area is geographically unique.

GALILEE Actually two regions, this area covers a lot of geographical ground in the north. The Galilee is a rocky area, and the Golan Heights, which borders Syria, sees winter snowfall at its highest altitudes. With cool climes and rich soil, the Galilee and Golan claim bragging rights as home to many of the country's premier grapes.

SHOMRON/CARMEL The advantageous growing conditions of the lush Carmel Mountains make this coastal plain south of Haifa the most prolific grape-growing region in Israel, if not the most prestigious. The climate and soil variety make it the most traditionally Mediterranean of the regions.

SAMSON/CENTRAL COAST Situated west of Jerusalem and stretching north toward Tel Aviv and south toward Ashkelon, this region has hot, humid summers and mellow winters that make for good growing conditions. If you're in Tel Aviv, this is an easy region for accessing great wineries.

JUDEAN HILLS In 2000, barely a winery or tasting room existed here, though ancient winemaking equipment has been unearthed. Thin limey or rocky soil, sunny days, and breezy nights have helped this region's wines shine. With its winding roads, and lush, shallow mountainsides, the region west and south of Jerusalem is day-trip perfect from Jerusalem and Tel Aviv.

THE NEGEV Thanks to drip-irrigation technology and an influx of talented winemakers, grapes are thriving in the desert. Since there are relatively few wineries in the southern part of the Negev, they're best included in a trip to Eilat or Mitzpe Ramon; call to schedule a visit.

Clos de Gat Winery in the Judean Hills

WINE TOURING AND TASTING

Visiting wineries in Israel can require a different approach from touring vineyards in California, and your touring strategy may depend on the size of the winery.

Most of the **bigger players**, including Golan Heights, Carmel, and Barkan/Segal, offer tasting rooms. You can simply stop by and visit to sample and purchase wines, though generally it's good to call in advance if you want to include a winery tour. Many medium- and smaller-sized wineries are often happy to accommodate visitors, but always call ahead to ensure that English-speaking staff will be on hand and to confirm hours.

Many **boutique** wineries welcome tourists, but some of the best aren't equipped for a regular onslaught of visitors. While you can call yourself, this is where private tour guides come in handy. Often, these individuals have the connections to get you inside wineries you'd otherwise never see—not to mention the knowledge of the back roads in some of the harder-to-find locales.

Through Israel Wine Experience (☎ 972/2990-8422, | ⊕ ww.israelwinexp.com), wine expert Oded Shoham and his staff offer customized half- and full-day tours and tastings.

PICK OF THE VINEYARDS

These wineries either have open tasting rooms, or visits can be arranged with an advance phone call. Note: most kosher wineries are open only a half-day on Friday, and are closed on Saturdays and Jewish holidays. Small tastes are usually free, but expect to pay $10 or more per person for a guided tasting of three to five wines at most wineries.

Carmel Winery

GALILEE

❶ Golan Heights Winery Still the standard bearer for Israeli wines, this large producer has a welcoming visitor center and tours. Wines are made under the Yarden, Gamla, and Golan labels. Kosher. *Try: Single-vineyard Odem Organic Chardonnay; Yarden Syrah.* ⊠ Derech Ha'Yayin St., Katzrin ☎ 04/696–8435 ⊕ www.golanwines.co.il

❷ Lotem Winery One of Israel's two organic wineries offers tours and tapas near the Sea of Galilee. Call in advance. Not kosher. *Try: Rosé, Cabernet Franc-Merlot blend, Nebbiolo.* ⊠ Kibbuts Lotem, off Rte. 804, Lotem ☎ 054/791–5868 ⊕ www.lotem-winery.co.il.

WINES IN RESTAURANTS AND SHOPS

Clos de Gat

Look for vintages from these superior regional producers in restaurants or shops in Israel.

Galilee: Golan Heights, Pelter and Chateau Golan in the Golan; Dalton and Galil Mountain in the Galilee

Shomron/Carmel: Recanati, Margalit, Amphorae

Samson/Central Coast: Carmel, Barkan, Soreq

Judean Hills: Sea Horse, Domaine du Castel, Clos de Gat

The Negev: Yatir, La Terra Promessa, Rota, Kadesh Barnea

Galil Mountain

3 Galil Mountain Winery A sleek, modern low-lying stone-and-wood building offers views of the vineyards and the winemaking facilities. These are great-value wines for the money. Kosher. *Try: Fruity, mineral-tinged Sauvignon Blanc.* ⊠ Kibbutz Yiron, off Rte 899, Merom, ☏ 04/686–8748 ⊕ www.galilmountain.co.il.

4 Tabor Winery Set amid almond groves near Mount Tabor in the Galilee, this intimate visitor center offers tastings and tours, in a lovely setting. Kosher. *Robust single-vineyard limited edition Cabernet Sauvignon.* ⊠ Kfar Tavor, ☏ 04/676–0444 ⊕ www.twc.co.il/en

SHOMRON/ CARMEL
5 Tishbi Winery The visitor center at this fourth-generation winery offers a special chocolate and wine tasting. Kosher. *Try: Woodsy, berry-rich Pinot Noir.* ⊠ Rte. 652, Benyamina, Zichron Ya'akov ☏ 04/638–0434 ⊕ www.tishbi.com/en

6 Amphorae Winery This boutique winery nar Zichon Ya akov is set in a series of rustic, Tuscan-style stone buildings. Call in advance to arrange a visit. Not kosher. *Try: Balanced, full-bodied Cabernet Sauvignon.* ⊠ Makura Farm, Kerem Maharal ☏ 04/984–0702 ⊕ www.amphoraewines.com.

7 Carmel Winery The Center for Wine Culture at the country's largest winery offers a restaurant, a tour encompassing Israel's viticultural history, several tasting options, and a visit to a historic wine cellar built by founder Baron Edmond de Rothschild.

JUDEAN HILLS
8 Ella Valley Vineyards Domaine du Costel This family-run winery produces some of Israel's finest wines. Call for a tour and wime and cheese tasting. ERte. 4115, Yad Hasmona P02/534–2449 wwww.castel.co.il

9 Flam Winery Two dynamic brothers, the sons of a former chief winemaker for Carmel Mizrachi, run this well-regarded producer. Call to arrange a cheese and wine tasting. *Try: Woodsy, berry-rich Flam Reserve Merlot.*

⊠ Eshtal Junction, Ya'ar Ha'kodshim ☏ 02/992–9923 ⊕ www.flamwinery.com.

THE NEGEV
10 Yatir Winery Generating great excitement, Yatir is a desert gem with promise. Call in advance. Kosher. *Try: Yatir Forest, whose grape*

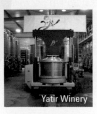

Yatir Winery

blend varies from year to year; fruity, light Viognier. ⊠ Off Rte. 80, Tel Arad ☏ 052/830–8196 ⊕ www.yatircoinery.com/en

stone monastery was built in 1883 over Byzantine ruins. There's a small gift shop in the monastery, but no place to buy drinks or snacks.

Mukhraka is the Arabic word for a place of burning, referring to the fire that consumed the offering on Elijah's altar. The conflict developed because the people of Israel had been seduced by the pagan cults introduced by King Ahab's wife, Jezebel. Elijah demanded a contest with the priests of Ba'al in which each would erect an altar with a butchered ox as an offering and see which divinity sent down fire. Elijah drenched his altar with water, yet it burst into flames. On his orders, the pagan priests were taken down to the Kishon ravine and slain, an event depicted by the impressive statue of Elijah inscribed in Hebrew, Arabic, and Latin.

⊠ *Off Rte. 672* ⊕ *www.muhraqa.org* ✆ *Free.*

Zichron Ya'akov

25 km (15 miles) southwest of Mukhraka, 35 km (22 miles) south of Haifa, 61 km (40 miles) north of Tel Aviv.

Zichron Ya'akov, the country's first moshava, or cooperative farming community, was founded in 1882 with the help of Baron Edmond de Rothschild. From the beginning, it centered on its vineyards and large winery. A visit to the charming town should start on its main street, Hameyasdim, a cobblestone pedestrian mall lined with small, restored, red-roofed, 19th-century homes. Pick up a town map in the tourist office at the entrance to the town.

GETTING HERE AND AROUND
If driving from Haifa or Tel Aviv, take Route 2 to the Zichron Ya'akov exit. Buses run from Haifa and Tel Aviv.

VISITOR INFORMATION
CONTACTS Zichron Ya'akov Tourist Office. ⊠ *HaMeyasdim St.* ✛ *Southern entrance to town, opposite cemetery* ☎ *04/639–8811.*

◉ Sights

Amphorae Wines
WINERY/DISTILLERY | The setting of one of Israel's leading boutique wineries, in a pastoral landscape overlooking the forests of the Carmel Mountains, couldn't be prettier. Call ahead to tour the winery, see the demonstration vineyard, and learn about these attention-getting wines. For your tasting, select a flight of three to five wines: the reds, including blends, are notable. Order a generous tasting platter of bread and fine cheeses (extra charge) to accompany them. ⊠ *Makura Farm, Off Rte. 7021, Kerem Maharal* ✛ *14 km (9 miles) north of Zichron Ya'akov via Rte. 4* ☎ *04/984–0702* ⊕ *www.amphoraewines.com* ✆ *Tour and tasting of 4 wines NIS 140.*

Beit Aaronson (*Aaronson House*)
HOUSE | About halfway down Hameyasdim Street is Beit Aaronson, whose late-19th-century architecture successfully combines art nouveau and Middle Eastern traditions. This museum was once the home of the agronomist Aaron Aaronson (1876–1919), who gained international fame for his discovery of an ancestor of modern wheat. The house remains as it looked after World War I, with family photographs and French and Turkish furniture, as well as Aaronson's library, diaries, and letters. Aaronson and his two sisters became local heroes as leaders of an underground group called NILI, dedicated to ousting the Turks from Palestine. A tour in English is provided; the last one takes place at 1:30. You must reserve ahead by phone or online. Credit cards aren't accepted, and children under five are not permitted in the museum. ⊠ *40 Hameyasdim St.* ☎ *04/639–0120*

⊕ *www.nili-museum.org.il* ✉ *NIS 26* ⊙ *Closed Fri. and Sat.*

Binyamin Pool

BUILDING | The name of this site is a misnomer because it's actually the town's original water tower, built in 1891. Zichron Ya'akov was the first village in Israel to have water piped to its houses; Meir Dizengoff, the first mayor of Tel Aviv, came here to see how it was done. The facade, with its inscription honoring Baron de Rothschild, resembles that of an ancient synagogue. ✉ *Hameyasdim St.* ✛ *Near Beit Aaronson.*

★ Carmel Winery

WINERY/DISTILLERY | Rare among Israel's many wineries are Carmel Winery's underground vaulted-ceiling wine cellars. Dating from 1892, the huge, old, and chilly rooms are a contrast to the state-of-the art facility above ground, where top wines are produced. Founder Baron Edmond de Rothschild, owner of France's famous Château Lafite, would be pleased at the success of his viniculture venture, now the country's largest winery. At the Center for Wine Culture, a guided 45-minute tour outlines the stages of local wine production. Included in the tour are a tasting of some four varieties and a seven-minute audiovisual presentation screened in the original wine cellar. Tours depart between 9 and 4 and must be reserved in advance. Other wine tastings and workshops are also available by reservation. ✉ *2 Yekev Way* ☎ *04/639–1788* ⊕ *www.carmelwines.co.il* ✉ *NIS 30 tour* ⊙ *Closed Sat.*

First Aliya Museum

MUSEUM | The museum is dedicated to the lives of the 30,000 immigrants who came to Palestine with the First Aliya (a period of settlement from 1882 until 1904). Life-size model displays of local immigrants (like Zachariya, the seed vendor, and Izer, the cobbler) illustrate life at that time. A film traces the struggles of a family who came from Europe in this difficult period of Israel's

modern history. Commissioned by Baron Edmond de Rothschild, the museum's three-floor building is a fine example of late-19th-century Ottoman-style architecture, built of white stone with a central pediment capped by a tile roof. During World War I, the Turks used it as a military hospital. ✉ *2 Hanadiv St.* ☎ *04/629–4777* ✉ *NIS 20* ⊙ *Closed weekends.*

Ohel Ya'akov

RELIGIOUS SITE | On a prominent corner stands the old synagogue, Ohel Ya'akov, built by Baron de Rothschild in 1886 to serve immigrants from Romania. It's only occasionally open to visitors, but worth strolling by. ✉ *Hameyasdim St. and Hanadiv St.*

Ramat Hanadiv

GARDEN | **FAMILY** | In the hills near Zichron Ya'akov, this sprawling garden is a fitting tribute to Baron Edmond de Rothschild. (*Hanadiv* means "the benefactor.") At its center is the dignified tomb where Rothschild and his wife Ada lie buried. A 20-minute film in the welcoming Visitors Pavilion tells of his legacy in Israel: the last screening on weekdays is at 3:30. Outside, curving paths framed rolling green lawns, abundant patches of flowers, carob trees, waving palms, and 42 rare plant species. Clearly marked trails lead to a 2,000-year old Roman farmhouse and a hidden spring. After all that legwork, the terraces of the on-site café beckon. A children's playground is set off to one side. ✉ *Rte. 652* ✛ *Southern end of Mount Carmel, south of Zichron Ya'akov* ☎ *04/629–8111* ⊕ *www.ramat-hanadiv.org.il* ✉ *Free.*

🍴 Restaurants

Kashtunyo Wine Cellar

$$$ | **MEDITERRANEAN** | This restaurant in a 140-year-old underground wine cellar is an auspicious place to hear about the extensive wine list from owner Amos Meroz, whose hat always rakishly tilts to one side. Eight tables covered with checkered cloths fill a small space defined by curving stone walls. **Known for:** wine and cheese pairings; charming Ottoman-era building; romantic. $ *Average main: NIS 100 ⊠ 56 Hameyasdim St.* ☎ *04/629–1244.*

Oratorio

$$$ | **MODERN ISRAELI** | Whether you're at the Elma Arts Complex for a performance or simply for the spectacular views of the Mediterranean, Oratorio satisfies with fine dining in a magnificent setting. The modern dining room provides gallery space for interesting, thought-provoking art from Israel and around the world. **Known for:** breakfast buffet; excellent service; pretheater dinner. $ *Average main: NIS 100 ⊠ Elma Arts Complex Luxury Hotel, 1 Yair St.* ☎ *04/630–0110* ⊕ *www. elma-hotel.com.*

🛏 Hotels

★ Elma Arts Complex Luxury Hotel

$$$ | **HOTEL** | You would be forgiven if you thought this hotel was newly built: with its exposed cement, clean white lines, and natural walnut furnishings, the modern design from 1973 has been renovated into a striking hotel and world-class center for the arts. **Pros:** breathtaking views; historically significant building; world-class art collection. **Cons:** standard rooms are quite small; difficult to reach without a car; a bit pricey. $ *Rooms from: $325 ⊠ 1 Yair St.* ☎ *04 /630–0123* ⊕ *elmahotel.co.il* ⇨ *95 rooms* ⍟❜ *Breakfast.*

Hotel Beit Maimon

$ | **HOTEL** | On the western slopes of Zichron Ya'akov, a 10-minute walk from the center of town, this family-run hotel has a spectacular view of the coastal valley and the sea. **Pros:** delicious Israeli breakfast is included; superb views; accommodating staff. **Cons:** lots of steps to climb; old-fashioned; outlets not conveniently placed. $ *Rooms from: $150* ⊠ *4 Zahal St.* ☎ *04/629–0390* ⊕ *www.*

maimon.com ⇨ 25 rooms ⍟❜ *Free Breakfast.*

Benyamina

5 km (3 miles) south of Zichron Ya'akov, 40 km (25 miles) south of Haifa, 55 km (34 miles) north of Tel Aviv.

Picturesque Benyamina, the youngest settlement in the area, was founded in 1922 and has several wineries. It was named after Baron Edmond de Rothschild, the head of the French branch of the famous family, who took a keen interest in the welfare of his fellow Jews in Palestine. (His Hebrew name was Benyamin.)

GETTING HERE AND AROUND

You can easily reach Benyamina by train. If you're driving, take Route 4. Either option makes for a very pretty ride. Once you're here, you need a car to get around because public transport is uneven.

👁 Sights

Binyamina Winery

WINERY/DISTILLERY | The large visitor center at the country's fourth-largest winery is housed in a former perfume factory built by Baron de Rothschild in 1925. It hasn't changed as much as you'd think, as cosmetics made from grape seeds are some of the products for sale here. You can also find olive oil, vinegar, and, yes, wine. The production facilities are next door in buildings surrounded by towering palm trees. Reservations are required for the 45-minute tour of the winery and barrel rooms, including a sampling of four or five wines. You can do your tasting while having lunch or dinner in the restaurant, once an orange-packing facility. Or, you can simply drop in for coffee and cake. ⊠ *1 HaYekev St.* ☎ *04/610–7535* ⊕ *www. binyaminawines.com* ⇨ *Tour and tasting NIS 25* ⍟ *Closed Sat.*

Akko's History

👁

History clings to the stones in the Old City of Akko, which bear the marks of the many civilizations that have inhabited and built it. The city's history began 4,000 years ago, when Akko was first mentioned in Egyptian writings that refer to the mound northeast of its walls. The Old Testament describes in Judges 1 how after the death of Joshua, the tribe of Asher was unable to drive the Canaanites from Akko, so they lived among them.

With its well-protected harbor, fertile hinterland, and strategic position, Akko has always proved worth fighting for. Alexander the Great had such regard for Akko that he set up a mint here. Akko was Phoenician for long periods, but the Hellenistic King Ptolemy II gained control in the 2nd century BC and renamed it Ptolemais.

King Baldwin I led the Crusaders who conquered Akko in 1104, and the port city was the Crusaders' principal link to home. Commerce thrived, and the European maritime powers—Genoa, Pisa, Venice, and Marseilles—developed separate quarters here. After the disastrous defeat of the Crusader armies in 1187, Akko surrendered to Saladin, but Richard the Lionheart soon recaptured the European stronghold. In its Crusader heyday, Akko had about 40 churches and monasteries and a population of 50,000.

In the 13th century, after the conquest of Jerusalem by the Muslims, Akko became the effective capital of a shrunken Latin kingdom; it fell to the Mamluks in 1291 and lay in ruins for centuries. In 1749 Dahr el-Omar, the Bedouin sheikh, moved his capital from Tiberias to Akko and rebuilt the walls of the city.

Napoléon's attempt to conquer the city in 1799 was repulsed, but the British captured it in 1918. With the founding of the State of Israel in 1948, many Arab inhabitants left Akko, though a good number remain. Akko's population now numbers about 46,000, with people living inside the Old City itself and in new developments pushing the city limits to the north.

Tishbi Estate Winery

WINERY/DISTILLERY | Set among the hills and valleys of this pastoral area is one of the country's most esteemed wineries and premier labels, Tishbi Estate: the Sauvignon Blanc and Chardonnay are among the best in Israel. The vines were planted here 120 years ago. At the country-style visitor center, you can pair a French Valrhona chocolate with a Tishbi wine, or enjoy breakfast, brunch, or lunch under the grapevines in the courtyard. Apart from wine, you can purchase local cheeses, olive oil, honey, and wine jellies at the shop. Call ahead to arrange a one-hour tour, which includes tastings and a visit to the old alembic distillery, where their prized brandy is made. It's about 3 km (1½ miles) north of Benyamina. ✉ *Rte. 652, Benyamina Industrial Area* ☎ *04/638–0434* ⊕ *www.tishbi.com* 🎫 *Tour and tasting NIS 15* ☻ *Closed Sat.*

Akko

22 km (13½ miles) north of Haifa.

The Old City of Akko, a UNESCO World Heritage Site, is an enchanting mix of mosques, markets, and vaulted Crusader ruins (many of them underground). A walk through the cobbled alleys and outdoor market stalls brings you to a small port filled with fishing boats. Views from the surrounding ramparts are some of the country's best. On the way, sample fresh halvah, nougat-filled pralines, whole-wheat pita, or homemade *kibbeh* (a ground lamb and bulgur wheat dish), a specialty of the city's small Greek Orthodox community.

To reach the historic parts of Akko, you'll be driving through a modern city: a bustling metropolis of about 46,000. It's rather plain, so reserve judgment until you've seen the Old City.

GETTING HERE AND AROUND

From Haifa, you can get here via Route 4. A much slower but far prettier inland route takes you north on Route 70, passing through rolling hills and avoiding the drab satellite towns north of Haifa. There are direct buses from Haifa, and trains from Jerusalem and Tel Aviv (you may have to change trains). Once you're here, a car is the best way to get around.

TIMING AND PRECAUTIONS

Plan on spending the better part of a day if you want to see everything, including the excellent presentation in the Turkish bathhouse. Women should exercise caution walking around alone at night.

VISITOR INFORMATION

CONTACTS Akko Visitor Center. ⊠ *1 Weizmann St.* ✛ *At town entrance, just inside stone arch* ☎ *04/995–6706* ⊕ *www.akko. org.il/en/.*

Old City

Start your tour at the Akko Visitor Center, just inside the main entrance to the Old City. This is where you purchase tickets. A combination ticket that includes all sights in the Old City is NIS 40. A combination ticket that includes all the sights along with the Turkish bath is NIS 62.

Once you've bought your ticket, take the time to get a map of the area and see the seven-minute film on the history of the region. Before you enter the Old City, you might want to walk along the ramparts and visit the Ethnography Center. To get there, ascend the steps at the opening in the city walls. The Al-Jazzar Mosque, south of the main entrance, also makes a good stop. Deeper in the Old City is the fascinating Hospitaller Fortress, as well as many other sights. You end up at the seaside walls of the Pisan Harbor.

◉ Sights

The walled city of Old Akko is relatively small and the well-marked sights are close to one another, making it easy to tour. You approach the Old City on Weizmann Street (watch for signs that say Old Akko), proceeding through a breach in the walls. If driving, park in the large lot.

Al-Basha Turkish Bathhouse

HOT SPRINGS | FAMILY | Built for Pasha al-Jazzar in 1781, Akko's remarkable Turkish bathhouse (*Hamam al-Basha*, in Arabic) was in use until 1947. Don't miss the sound-and-light show called *The Story of the Last Bath Attendant*, set in the beautiful bathhouse itself. You follow the story, with visual and audio effects, from the dressing room decorated with Turkish tiles and topped with a cupola, through the rooms with colored-glass bubbles protruding from the roof domes. The glass bubbles send a filtered green light to the steam rooms below. ⊠ *Al-Jazzar St.* ☎ *04/995–6707* ⊕ *www.akko.org.il* 🎟 *Combination ticket NIS 46.*

★ Al-Jazzar Mosque

RELIGIOUS SITE | This house of worship, the largest mosque in the country outside of Jerusalem, is also considered one of the most beautiful in Israel. Ahmed el-Jazzar, who succeeded Dahr el-Omar after having him assassinated, ruled Akko from 1775 to 1804. During his reign he built this mosque along with other public structures. His cruelty was so legendary that he earned the epithet "the Butcher."

Now a museum, the 18th-century Turkish bathhouse in Akko is illuminated through a dome with glass bubbles.

(He is buried next to his adopted son in a small white building to the right of the mosque.)

Just beyond the entrance is a pedestal engraved with graceful calligraphy; it re-creates the seal of a 19th-century Ottoman sultan. Some of the marble and granite columns in the mosque and courtyard were plundered from the ruins of Caesarea. In front is an ornate fountain used by the faithful for ritual washings of hands and feet before prayer. Inside the mosque, enshrined in the gallery reserved for women, is a reliquary containing a hair believed to be from the beard of the prophet Muhammad; it is removed only once a year, on the 27th day of Ramadan.

The mosque closes five times a day for prayers, so you might have a short wait. On Friday, the prayer duration is longer, as it is the holiest day of the week for Muslims. Although the mosque is open, visitors are advised to plan their trip accordingly. Dress modestly. ⊠ *Off Al-Jazzar St.* ☎ *04/991–3039* ✉ *NIS 10.*

★ **Hospitaller Fortress (Knights' Halls)**
ARCHAEOLOGICAL SITE | This remarkable 12th-century Crusader fortress was once known as the Crypt of St. John—before excavation, it was erroneously thought to have been an underground chamber. The dimensions of the colossal pillars that support the roof (girded with metal bands for extra strength) make this one of Israel's most monumental examples of Crusader architecture. It's also one of the oldest Gothic structures in the world. In the right-hand corner opposite the entrance is a fleur-de-lis carved in stone, the crest of the French house of Bourbon, which has led some scholars to suggest that this was the chamber in which Louis VII convened the knights of the realm.

Just outside this room is an entrance to an extremely narrow subterranean passageway. Cut from stone, this was a secret tunnel that the Crusaders probably used to reach the harbor when besieged by Muslim forces. (Those who are claustrophobic can take an alternate route,

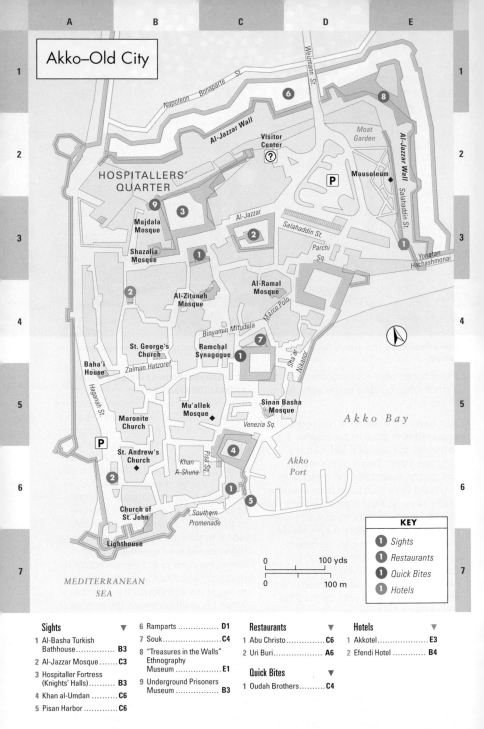

Akko–Old City

HOSPITALLERS' QUARTER

Visitor Center

Majdala Mosque

Shazalia Mosque

Al-Jazzar

Al-Jazzar Wall

Napoleon Bonaparte St.

Weizmann St.

Moat Garden

Al-Jazzar Wall

Mausoleum

Salahaddin St.

Salahaddin St.

Parchi Sq.

Yonatan Hachashmonai

Al-Zituneh Mosque

Al-Ramal Mosque

Marco Polo

Binyamin Mitudela

Baha'i House

St. George's Church

Zalman Hatzoref

Ramchal Synagogue

Sha'ar Hanikanor

Maronite Church

Mu'allek Mosque

Sinan Basha Mosque

Venezia Sq.

Akko Bay

Haganah St.

St. Andrew's Church

Khan A-Shuna

Pisa Sq.

Akko Port

Church of St. John

Southern Promenade

Lighthouse

MEDITERRANEAN SEA

0   100 yds
0   100 m

KEY

1 Sights
1 Restaurants
1 Quick Bites
1 Hotels

Sights ▼

1 Al-Basha Turkish Bathhouse.............. **B3**
2 Al-Jazzar Mosque....... **C3**
3 Hospitaller Fortress (Knights' Halls).......... **B3**
4 Khan al-Umdan **C6**
5 Pisan Harbor **C6**

6 Ramparts **D1**
7 Souk...................... **C4**
8 "Treasures in the Walls" Ethnography Museum **E1**
9 Underground Prisoners Museum **B3**

Restaurants ▼

1 Abu Christo............... **C6**
2 Uri Buri.................... **A6**

Quick Bites ▼

1 Oudah Brothers.......... **C4**

Hotels ▼

1 Akkotel.................... **E3**
2 Efendi Hotel **B4**

which goes back to the entrance of the Turkish bathhouse and continues from there.) Emerge in the cavernous vaulted halls of the fortress guard post, with a 13th-century marble Crusader tombstone at the exit.

Here, a series of six barrel-vaulted rooms known as the Knights' Halls has been discovered. Arrows point the way through vast rooms filled with ongoing reconstruction work, huge marble columns, and archaeological pieces from the past. Above this part of the Crusader city stands the Ottoman citadel, which you can glimpse from the courtyard. Built by Dahr el-Omar in the 18th century on the rubble-filled Crusader ruins, the citadel was the highest structure in Akko.

The different factions within Akko's walls probably sowed the seeds of the Crusaders' downfall here. By the mid-13th century, open fighting had broken out between the Venetians and Genoese. When the Mamluks attacked with a vengeance in 1291, the Crusaders' resistance crumbled, and the city's devastation was complete. It remained a subdued place for centuries, and even today Akko retains a medieval cast. ⊠ 1 Weizmann St. ☎ 04/995–6706 ⊕ www.akko.org.il ⊠ Combination ticket NIS 40.

Khan al-Umdan

BUILDING | In Venezia Square, in front of the port, is the two-tiered Inn of the Pillars. Before you visit this Ottoman khan—the largest of the four in Akko—and the Pisan Quarter beyond, take a stroll around the port, with its small flotilla of fishing boats, yachts, and sailboats. Then walk through the khan's gate beneath a square clock tower, built at the turn of the 20th century. The khan served vast numbers of merchants and travelers during Akko's golden age of commerce, in the late 18th century. The 32 pink-and-gray granite pillars that give it its name are compliments of Ahmed el-Jazzar's raids on Roman Caesarea. There was

once a market at the center of the colonnaded courtyard. ⊠ Venezia Sq.

Pisan Harbor

MARINA | Climbing the stone steps at the water's edge, you can walk along the sea walls at the Pisan Harbor, so named after an Italian commune here in Crusader times. Start at the café perched on high—a great lookout—and head west in the direction of the 18th-century Church of St. John. You end up at the southwestern extremity of Akko, next to the lighthouse. Head north along Haganah Street, which runs parallel to the crenellated western sea wall. After five minutes you reach the whitewashed, blue-trimmed Baha'i house (not open to the public), where the prophet of the Baha'i religion, Baha'u'llah, spent 12 years of his exile. His burial site is just north of Akko at the Baha'i Founder's Shrine and Gardens. ⊠ Akko ✛ At southern tip of Old Akko.

Ramparts

MILITARY SITE | As you enter the Old City, climb the blue-railing stairway on your right for a stroll along the city walls. Walking to the right, you can see the stunted remains of the 12th-century walls built by the Crusaders, under whose brief rule—just less than two centuries—Akko flourished as never before or since. The indelible signs of the Crusaders, who made Akko the main port of their Christian empire, are much more evident inside the Old City.

The wall girding the northern part of the town was built by Ahmed el-Jazzar, the Pasha of Akko, who added these fortifications following his victory over Napoléon's army in 1799. With the help of the British fleet, el-Jazzar turned Napoléon's attempted conquest into a humiliating rout. Napoléon had dreamed of founding a new Eastern empire, thrusting northward from Akko to Turkey and then seizing India from Great Britain. His defeat at Akko hastened his retreat to France, thus changing the course of history. Walk around to the guard towers and up an incline just opposite; there's a view of the moat below and Haifa across the bay. Turn around and let your gaze settle on the exotic skyline of Old Akko, the sea green dome of the great mosque its dominating feature. Walk down the ramp, crossing the rather messy Moat Garden at the base of the walls; straight ahead is the Al-Jazzar Mosque. ⊠ *Akko* 🎫 *Free.*

Souk

MARKET | At this outdoor market, stalls heaped with fresh produce and seafood alternate with specialty stores: a pastry shop with exotic Middle Eastern delicacies; a spice shop filled with Eastern flavors and aromas; a bakery with steaming fresh pita. You often see fishermen sitting on doorsteps, intently repairing their lines and nets to the sounds of Arabic music blaring from the open windows above. The loosely defined area twists and turns through the center of the Old City, but Marco Polo Street is a good place to begin your exploration. ⊠ *Akko.*

"Treasures in the Walls" Ethnography Museum

MUSEUM | There are two sections to this small but charming museum: one re-creates a 19th-century marketplace, with craftsmen's workshops such as a hatmaker and a blacksmith, filled with every tool needed to make hats and horseshoes; the other room displays a traditional Damascene living room, complete with astounding furniture and accoutrements. To get here once you're up the steps to the Ramparts, keep an eye out for the short flight of stairs heading down to the left. ⊠ *Eastern Wall, 2 Weizmann St.* 🕿 *04/991–1004* 🎫 *NIS 15.*

Underground Prisoners Museum

MUSEUM | Located at the sea's edge, this museum run by the Ministry of Defense is housed in several wings of the citadel built by Dahr el-Omar and then modified by Ahmed el-Jazzar in 1785. It served as a major prison during the British Mandate. On the way in, you pass

Need a Break? 🍴

In the plaza outside the Al-Jazzar Mosque are **outdoor restaurants,** where you can enjoy a falafel, fresh-squeezed orange or pomegranate juice, and coffee while watching the world go by.

the citadel's outer wall; the difference between the large Crusader building stones and the smaller Turkish ones above is easy to spot. The original cells and their meager contents, along with photographs and documents reconstructing the history of the Jewish resistance to British rule in the '30s and '40s, illustrate prison life. During the Mandate, the citadel became a high-security prison whose inmates included top members of Jewish resistance organizations, among them Ze'ev Jabotinsky and, later, Moshe Dayan. ⊠ *10 Hahagana St.* 🕿 *04/991– 1375* 🎫 *NIS 15* ⊘ *Closed Fri. and Sat.*

🍴 Restaurants

Abu Christo

$$$ | **SEAFOOD** | In the Old City, this popular waterfront fish restaurant stands at one of the original 18th-century gates built by Pasha Ahmed el-Jazzar when he fortified the city after his victory over Napoléon. It's a Greek family business that's been passed from father to son since 1948. **Known for:** seaside location with covered patio; outstanding service; daily catch (often grouper, red snapper, or sea bass). 🖇 *Average main: NIS 80* ⊠ *Crusader Port, Leofeld HaSheni St.* 🕿 *04/991–0065.*

★ Uri Buri

$$$$ | **SEAFOOD** | Justly known far and wide for its excellent fish and seafood, this Akko institution is housed in an old Turkish building near the lighthouse. One

Despite modern boats, the old harbor in Akko retains echoes of past eras.

room is furnished with sofas, copper dishes, and *nargillas* (water pipes). **Known for:** knowledgeable, attentive waitstaff; gorgeous dining room; flavorful seasonal fish dishes. $ *Average main: NIS 110* ✉ *11 Ha-haganah St.* ✛ *On promenade near lighthouse* ☎ *04/955–2212* ⊕ *www.2eat.co.il/uriburi.*

☕ Coffee and Quick Bites

Oudah Brothers

$ | **MEDITERRANEAN** | In the souk, duck into this café and enjoy a coffee, some hummus, or a kebab in the courtyard of the 16th-century Khan al-Faranj, or Franks' Inn. Note the 18th-century Franciscan monastery and tower to your left. **Known for:** excellent service; wide menu including hummus and kebabs; lovely location. $ *Average main: NIS 40* ✉ *Khan Ha-Frankim St.* ☎ *04/991–2013.*

🛏 Hotels

Akkotel

$$ | **HOTEL** | This three-story hostelry, a former Turkish police station, is built into the city wall. **Pros:** family run; unusual lodging built into the Old City walls; warm service. **Cons:** no pool; small rooms; roof deck could use updating. $ *Rooms from: $240* ✉ *1 Salahaddin St.* ☎ *04/987–7100* ⊕ *www.akkotel.com* ➷ *18 rooms* ⦿ *Free Breakfast.*

★ Efendi Hotel

$$$ | **HOTEL** | Two notable Ottoman-era palaces overlooking the Mediterranean from the Israeli town of Akko have been united to form this uniquely charming boutique hotel. **Pros:** historic palace-home setting; design flair with local flavor; superb staff; perfect Old City location. **Cons:** not a lively nighttime neighborhood; early reservations required; spa services not always available. $ *Rooms from: $320* ✉ *Louis IX St.* ☎ *074/729–9799* ⊕ *www.efendi-hotel.com* ➷ *12 rooms* ⦿ *Free Breakfast.*

Near the City

👁 Sights

Baha'i Founder's Shrine and Gardens
GARDEN | For the Baha'is, this is the holiest place on earth, the site of the tomb of the faith's prophet and founder, Baha'u'llah. The gardens' west gate is only open to Baha'is, so enter from the north (main) gate. Baha'u'llah lived in the red-tile mansion here after released from jail in Akko and was buried in the small building next door, now the Shrine of Baha'u'llah. It's best to go on weekend mornings (Friday to Monday), when the inner gardens and shrine are open. Going through the black-iron gate, follow a white gravel path in the exquisitely landscaped gardens, with a fern-covered fountain and an observation point along the way, until you reach the shrine. Visitors are asked to dress modestly. The shrine is on Route 4, about 1 km (½ mile) north of the gas station at Akko's northern edge. ✉ *Rte. 4* ☎ *04/835–8845* 🌐 *www.ganbahai.org.il/en/haifa* 🎟 *Free.*

Ghetto Fighters' House Museum (*Beit Lochamei Hageta'ot*)
MUSEUM | Founded in 1949 by survivors of the German, Polish, and Lithuanian Jewish ghettos set up by the Nazis, kibbutz Lochamei Hageta'ot commemorates their compatriots who perished in the Holocaust at this museum. Exhibits include photographs documenting the Warsaw Ghetto and the uprising, and halls are devoted to different themes, among them Jewish communities before their destruction in the Holocaust; death camps; and deportations at the hands of the Nazis.

The adjacent Yad LaYeled (Children's Memorial) is dedicated to the memory of the 1½ million children who perished in the Holocaust. It's designed for young visitors, who can begin to comprehend the events of the Holocaust through a series of tableaux and images accompanied by recorded voices, allowing them to identify with individual victims without seeing shocking details. There is a small cafeteria on the premises. ✉ *Kibbutz Lochamei Hageta'ot, Rte. 4* ☎ *04/995–8080* 🌐 *www.gfh.org.il/eng* 🎟 *30 NIS* 🕒 *Closed Fri. and Sat.*

🛏 Hotels

Nes Ammim Hotel
$ | HOTEL | FAMILY | Founded in 1963, this ecumenical Christian settlement between Akko and Nahariya focuses on mutual respect and tolerance; it also runs a hotel. **Pros:** good for families; outdoor swimming pool in summertime; beautiful pastoral setting. **Cons:** basic rooms; few activities; modest furnishing. [$] *Rooms from: $115* ✉ *Rd. 8611, off Rte. 4* ☎ *04/995–0000* 🌐 *www.nesammim.com* 🛏 *48 rooms* 🍴 *Free Breakfast.*

Rimonim Palm Beach Hotel
$ | HOTEL | FAMILY | A private beach with exceptional views and a country club with state-of-the-art facilities make this hotel a great deal, especially for families. **Pros:** attentive staff; private beach; tennis and squash courts. **Cons:** small rooms; far from Old City sights; maintenance is wanting. [$] *Rooms from: $175* ✉ *Rte. 4* ☎ *04/987–7777* 🌐 *www.rimonimhotels.com* 🛏 *125 rooms* 🍴 *Free Breakfast.*

Nahariya

8 km (5 miles) north of Akko.

This seaside recreation spot, Israel's northernmost coastal town, was built along the banks of a river lined with eucalyptus trees. (The town's name comes from *nahar,* Hebrew for "river.") Nahariya is popular with vacationing Israelis who throng the small shops and cafés along the main street, Haga'aton Boulevard. It's a good place to stop for lunch if you're traveling along the coast. One of the region's most beautiful stretches of sand is just at the end of the main street. Achziv Beach, just 4 km (2 ½ miles) north of town, is one of the country's finest.

GETTING HERE AND AROUND
There are direct buses from Haifa. Trains from Tel Aviv travel several times a day to Nahariya. By car, take Route 4 north of Akko.

Sights

Byzantine Church
RELIGIOUS SITE | This church dedicated to St. Lazarus features an elaborate, 17-color mosaic floor, discovered in 1964, that depicts peacocks, other birds, hunting scenes, and plants. It was part of what experts consider one of the largest and most beautiful Byzantine churches in the Western Galilee, where Christianity spread from the 4th to the 7th century. ⊠ *Bielefeld St.* 🔁 *Free.*

Beaches

★ Achziv Beach
BEACH—SIGHT | **FAMILY** | This beautifully maintained stretch of sand in the Achziv National Park is north of Nahariya, on the road to Rosh Hanikra. Beside the ruins of the ancient settlement of Achziv are two huge lagoons along the shore, one shallow, the other deep. There are also watchful lifeguards and playground facilities. In July and August, turtles lay their eggs on the beach. You can picnic on the grassy slopes or make use of the restaurant. Enter at the second sign for Achziv Beach, not the first. For NIS 63 per person, you can camp here overnight. **Amenities:** food and drink; lifeguards; parking (fee); showers; toilets. **Best for:** swimming; walking. ⊠ *Rte. 2* 🕿 *04/982–3263* 🔁 *NIS 35.*

Betzet Beach
BEACH—SIGHT | A bit farther north of Achziv Beach is this nature reserve with abundant vegetation, shade-giving trees, and the ruins of an ancient olive press. In season, a lifeguard is on duty on the

beach, but otherwise there are few frills. **Amenities:** food and drink; lifeguard. **Best for:** solitude, walking. ⊠ *Rte. 2* 🔁 *Free.*

Galei Galil Beach
BEACH—SIGHT | **FAMILY** | Nahariya's public bathing facilities at Galei Galil Beach are ideal for families. Apart from the lovely beach, facilities include an Olympic-size outdoor pool, heated indoor pool, wading pool, playground for children, and clean changing rooms. The pool area is closed in winter. In peak season, the beach has exercise classes early in the morning. **Amenities:** food and drink; lifeguards; parking (fee); showers; toilets. **Best for:** swimming. ⊠ *North of Haga'aton Blvd.* 🔁 *Beach free; pool area NIS 45.*

Restaurants

★ Adelina
$$$$ | **MEDITERRANEAN** | When dining at this stellar restaurant, you may wonder how you got so lucky: there's the knockout view of the Mediterranean from the stone terrace, olive-tree-shaded setting, and wonderful Catalonian-accented dishes prepared by Adelina. Cooking is done in the huge silver tabun oven as Spanish music drifts across the dark wooden tables. **Known for:** excellent paella, sirloin, and cannelloni; lovely kibbutz atmosphere; gorgeous views. Ⓢ *Average main: NIS 110* ⊠ *Kibbutz Kabri, Rte. 89* 🕿 *04/952–3707* ⊕ *www.adelina.org.il* ⊙ *Closed Sun.*

Penguin
$$ | **ECLECTIC** | Stop into this legendary institution, opened in 1940, for coffee and cake, or a meal of spinach blintzes with melted cheese, hamburgers, or Chinese dishes. Three generations of the Oppenheimer family work here, and the walls carry enlarged photographs of how the place looked when just a hut. **Known for:** institution for more than 75 years; Israeli breakfasts; seaside location. Ⓢ *Average main: NIS 70* ⊠ *31 Haga'aton Blvd.* 🕿 *04/992–8855* ⊕ *www.penguin-rest.co.il.*

Rosh Hanikra

*7 km (4½ miles) north of Nahariya, 38 km
(24 miles) north of Haifa.*

GETTING HERE AND AROUND

It's a short drive from Nahariya to Rosh
Hanikra, the last destination on the country's northern coast. You need your own
car, as there's no public transportation.

Sights

Rosh Hanikra

CAVE | The dramatic white cliffs on the
coast signal both Israel's border with
Lebanon and the sea grottoes of Rosh
Hanikra. Before you get in line for the
steep two-minute ride down on the
Austrian-made cable car, take a moment
to absorb the stunning view back down
the coast. Bring binoculars. Still clearly
visible is the route of the railway line,
now mostly a dirt road, built by the British through the hillside in 1943 to extend
the Cairo–Tel Aviv–Haifa line to Beirut.
(You are now much closer to Beirut than
to Jerusalem.) After the descent, you can
see the 12-minute audiovisual presentation called *The Sea and the Cliff.*

The incredible caves beneath the cliff
have been carved out by relentless
waves pounding away at the white
chalky rock for millennia. Footpaths
inside the cliff lead from one huge cave
to another, while the sound of waves—
and the squealing of fruit bats—echoes
off the water-sprayed walls. Huge bursts
of seawater plunge into pools at your feet
(behind protective rails). It's slippery, so
hang on. ⊠ *Rosh Hanikra* ⊕ *End of Rte.
4* ☎ *073/271–0100* ⊕ *www.rosh-hanikra.
com* ⊠ *NIS 45.*

Chapter 7

LOWER GALILEE

WITH NAZARETH, TIBERIAS, AND
THE SEA OF GALILEE

Updated by
Shari Giddens

◉ **Sights**
★★★★☆

🍴 **Restaurants**
★★★☆☆

🛏 **Hotels**
★★☆☆☆

🛍 **Shopping**
★☆☆☆☆

🍸 **Nightlife**
★☆☆☆☆

WELCOME TO LOWER GALILEE

TOP REASONS TO GO

★ **A spiritual source:** Tune your ear to the Galilee's spiritual reverberations. Listen as pilgrims chant a Mass at the Mount of Beatitudes or sit meditatively on Tabgha's shore.

★ **Mount Gilboa:** This little-visited region offers natural beauty and grand views for the independent traveler who has a bit of time and no checklist of must-see famous sites.

★ **Nazareth:** Tradition and modernity collide in the town where Jesus grew up. Today it's a city of baklava and BMWs, new politics and ancient passions. Talk to a local as you sample Middle Eastern delicacies.

★ **Sunset on the Sea of Galilee:** The lake at sundown is always evocative, often beautiful, and occasionally spectacular. Walk a beach, sip a drink, or take a sail as dusk slowly settles.

★ **Zippori:** The distant past is palpable at this archaeological site, once a worldly Jewish and Hellenistic city. Set amid woods, it has the loveliest ancient mosaics in the land.

1 **Beit She'arim National Park.** Ancient Roman city.

2 **Tel Megiddo National Park.** "Armageddon."

3 **Mount Gilboa.** Home to scenic routes.

4 **Beit She'an.** Ruins.

5 **Belvoir.** Fortress.

6 **Nazareth.** Town of Jesus's boyhood.

7 **Zippori National Park.** Hilltop with mosaics.

8 **Cana.** Where Jesus turned water into wine.

9 **Mount Tabor.** Biblical site with hiking trails.

10 **Tiberias.** Famous for its hot springs.

11 **Arbel National Park and Nature Reserve.** Breathtaking views.

12 **Kibbutz Ginosar.** Peaceful town.

13 **Tabgha.** Green oasis.

14 **Mount of Beatitudes.** Where Jesus delivered the Sermon on the Mount.

15 **Korazim.** Byzantine town ruins.

16 **Capernaum.** Great views for hikers.

17 **Kursi National Park.** Major pilgrimage spot.

18 **Hammat Gader.** Roman-era thermal baths.

19 **Degania, Kinneret, and Yardenit.** Kibbutzim.

The Lower Galilee is a historic region where scores of events in the Hebrew Bible and the New Testament took place. Blessed with forested hills, fertile valleys, gushing springs, and the Sea of Galilee, it has strong appeal. The graves of Jewish, Christian, Muslim, and Druze holy men attract those seeking spiritual solace, but the region is also the scene of earthly delights, including fine restaurants and great spas.

To most Israelis, the Galilee is synonymous with "the North," a land of nature reserves and national parks. In short, they claim, it's a great place to visit but not a place to live: it's provincial and remote. Still, the Lower Galilee has its own quiet beauty and varied landscape. Whatever your agenda is—spiritual, historical, recreational, or restful—savor your time here. Follow a hiking trail above the Sea of Galilee. Wade through fields of irises in the spring. Bathe in a warm mineral spa. Buy some good goat cheese. Nazareth, the region's administrative center, has character and deserves some time.

Farming and tourism form the economic base. The region's kibbutzim and a smaller number of moshavim (Jewish family-farm villages) are concentrated in the Jezreel and Jordan valleys and around the Sea of Galilee. The rockier hill country is predominantly Arab (Israeli Arab; this isn't disputed territory) and Israeli Druze. For the last half century, the communities—Jewish, Druze, and Arab—have been attempting neighborly relations despite the ethnic tensions that swirl around them. By and large, they've succeeded.

Culture and entertainment aren't this region's strong suits. A number of annual festivals and events are the highlights. Tiberias's pubs and restaurants probably come closest to providing lively nightlife, but there are worse ways to spend an evening than sitting by a moonlit lake washing down a good St. Peter's fish or a lamb kebab with an excellent Israeli wine.

MAJOR REGIONS
The Hebrew word *gal* means "wave," and the Lower Galilee is indeed a hilly country, with deep valleys framed by mountain ridges. Not much more than a creek, the Jordan River cuts through the topography on the eastern border, first draining into the freshwater Sea of Galilee and then flowing south toward the Dead Sea.

On a topographical map, **the Jezreel Valley** appears as an equilateral triangle with sides about 40 km (25 miles) long, edged by low mountains and with a narrow extension east to Beit She'an in the Jordan Rift. Farther east, **the Jordan Valley** stretches like a ribbon north to the Sea of Galilee. They frame the area.

To the north are **Nazareth and the Galilee Hills**; remove the modern roads and power lines, and the landscape becomes a biblical illustration. There are several New Testament settings here—Nazareth, where Jesus grew up; the Cana wedding feast; and Mount Tabor, identified with the Transfiguration—but Jewish history resonates strongly, too. Tabor and Yodefat were fortifications in the Great Revolt against the Romans; Shefar'am, Beit She'arim (in a nearby valley), and Zippori were in turn the national centers of Jewish life (2nd–4th centuries AD); and latter-day Jewish pioneers, attracted to the region's untamed scenery, put down roots where their ancestors had farmed.

To the northeast lies the **Sea of Galilee,** which is, in fact, a freshwater lake, measuring 21 km (13 miles) from north to south and 11 km (7 miles) east to west. Almost completely ringed by cliffs and steep hills, the lake lies in a hollow about 700 feet below sea level, which accounts for its warm climate and subtropical vegetation. This is Israel's Riviera-on-a-lake, replete with beaches and outdoor recreation facilities. Its shores are also dotted with sites hallowed by Christian tradition (note that several of these sites demand modest dress) as well as some important ancient synagogues. Tiberias itself is one of Judaism's four holy cities, along with Jerusalem, Hebron, and Tzfat.

The city of **Tiberias** is the logical starting base for exploration. One sightseeing strategy is to circle the Sea of Galilee clockwise from Tiberias (via Routes 90, 87, 92, and 98).

Planning

When to Go

The Galilee is prettiest in the spring months of March and April when it's covered with wildflowers, and its hills are draped in green. Summer can be torrid. Avoid the Sea of Galilee during Passover (March and April) and the High Holidays and Sukkot (September and October): although the weather is great at these times, half the country vacations here and rates soar.

Some hotels charge high-season rates during July and August; this is also true the week of Christmas. Weekends in general (Thursday night through Saturday night) are more crowded; some hotels hike rates substantially.

Planning Your Time

It's possible to get a feeling for this region in a few days, but you can expand your trip to include some highlights of the Upper Galilee and the Golan including Tzfat (Safed). Tiberias, with its many accommodations, and the Sea of Galilee region are good bases for exploring archaeological sites—Beit She'an is impressive—as well as sites associated with the ministry of Jesus. Nazareth is worth a trip, either from Tiberias or en route to other areas. The Galilee is a low-key area with some lovely national parks and natural sites, including Mount Tabor, if you choose to linger.

Ein Gev, on the eastern shore of the Sea of Galilee, has an Israeli-music festival in the spring. Beit She'an revives its ancient Roman theater for a short series of events in October. In May and December, Jacob's Ladder, the twice-annual folk festival held in Nof Ginosar on the Sea of Galilee, presents traditional folk and country music of the British Isles and North America.

Getting Here and Around

BUS

The Egged bus cooperative provides regular service from Jerusalem, Tel Aviv, and Haifa to Nazareth, Beit She'an, Afula, and Tiberias. There's no direct service from Ben Gurion International Airport; change in Tel Aviv or Haifa. There are several buses an hour from Tel Aviv to Afula (2 hours). Egged Bus 825 (*yashir,* or "direct") is quickest. Express bus 821 stops at major stations en route. Super-Bus 354 from Afula Central Bus Station to Nazareth (20 minutes) runs once an hour. The Egged 442 and 541 buses leave frequently, every 20 minutes, and continue from Afula to Tiberias (about an hour). The Kavim lines 411 and 412 link Afula to Beit She'an (every 30 minutes).

To get from Haifa to Tiberias, take Egged Bus 430 (about an hour), which leaves hourly from Merkazit Hamifratz. From the same Haifa station, the slow SuperBus buses leave two or three times an hour for Afula. Buses from Jerusalem to Beit She'an and Tiberias (Egged Buses 961, 966 to Beit She'an; 961, 962 to Tiberias) depart a few times a day; change in Beit She'an for Afula, where you change again for Nazareth. The ride to Beit She'an is about two hours, to Tiberias another 25 minutes. Nazareth Transport and Tourism runs Bus 431, which connects Nazareth and Tiberias about once every hour.

CAR

Driving is the best way to explore the Lower Galilee. Driving time from Tel Aviv or Jerusalem to Tiberias is two hours. Some newer four-lane highways are excellent, but some secondary roads may be in need of repair.

Signposting is clear (and usually in English), with route numbers clearly marked. Brown signs indicate most sights. The Lower Galilee is served by a number of highways. Route 90, going up the Jordan Valley to Tiberias and on to Metulla on the Lebanese border, is the most convenient road from Jerusalem. Although Route 90 is the quickest route, it traverses occupied territories and you may pass a military checkpoint. Routes 2 and 4, both multilane expressways, lead north from Tel Aviv. Turn east onto Route 65, then north onto Route 60 to get to Nazareth. Stay on Route 65 and turn east on Route 77 to reach Tiberias. While Route 6 is a modern superhighway, it's also an electronic toll road. If driving a rental car, you are charged for using it.

Restaurants

Tiberias in particular and the Sea of Galilee in general have far livelier culinary options than other parts of Lower Galilee. Some places in the countryside are worth going out of your way for. Restaurant attire is casual. The local specialty is the native St. Peter's fish (tilapia), though most restaurants serve the (still excellent) pond-bred variety. Meat dishes tend to be Middle Eastern: *shashlik* and kebabs (ground meat grilled on skewers) accompanied by hummus, pickles, and french fries. Most economical are shawarma (slices of spit-grilled turkey meat served in pita bread) and falafel. The cheapest eats are always at the stands.

Hotels

Tiberias, the region's tourist center, has hotels for budgets from deluxe to economy. Within a 20- to 30-minute drive are excellent guesthouses, some run by kibbutz residents and some on the Sea of Galilee. Nazareth has a couple of deluxe hotels and several older inexpensive ones that cater primarily to Christian pilgrim groups but also attract individual travelers and Israelis. Also in Nazareth, and to a lesser extent around Tiberias, are hospices run by Christian orders.

Bed-and-breakfasts have sprung up in profusion. Many are in or adjacent to private homes in rural farming communities; others are within kibbutzim. These are a good value, especially for families. Many "guesthouses," as upgraded youth hostels are now called, are suitable for families; these are generally the cheapest deals.

Hotel reviews have been shortened. For more information, visit Fodors.com.

What It Costs

	$	$$	$$$	$$$$
RESTAURANTS				
	Under NIS 50	NIS 50–NIS 75	NIS 76–NIS 100	over NIS 100
HOTELS				
	Under $200	$200–$300	$301–$400	over $400

Tours

Both Egged Tours and United Tours have one-day tours around the region from Jerusalem and Tel Aviv that take in Nazareth, the Sea of Galilee, and other highlights. Current prices vary, but are in the neighborhood of NIS 335 from Tel Aviv, NIS 355 from Jerusalem.

CONTACTS Egged Tours. ☎ 03/920–3992 ⊕ www.eggedtours.com. **United Tours.** ☎ 03/617–3315 ⊕ www.unitedtours.co.il.

Beit She'arim National Park

20 km (12½ miles) southeast of Haifa, 25 km (15½ miles) west of Nazareth.

GETTING HERE AND AROUND
Driving from Tel Aviv, take Route 4 (the old Tel Aviv–Haifa Highway) to Furadis Junction, then turn east on Route 70. Continue to Yokneam Junction, then take Route 722 to Hashomrim Junction. Take the first left, and continue about 10 minutes until you reach the national park.

⊙ Sights

Beit She'arim National Park
ARCHAEOLOGICAL SITE | Chalk slopes are honeycombed with catacombs around this attractively landscaped ancient site. Orthodox Jews pilgrimage here to the early-3rd-century Tomb of Judah ha-Nasi, chief editor and redactor of the Mishnah, the seminal text of rabbinic Judaism, but you don't need to be religious to appreciate the role this vast necropolis has played in the development of modern Judaism. The landscape is soothing, there are pleasant walking paths, and some of the caves have an *Indiana Jones*–style intrigue. Equipped with a flashlight, a free park brochure, and a map, discover ornately carved sarcophagi that attest to the complex intercultural relations in the Roman world.

A Jewish town flourished here after the eclipse of Jerusalem brought about by Titus's legions in AD 70 and its reconstruction as a pagan town by Hadrian in AD 135. For generations, Jews were denied access to their holy city and its venerated burial ground on the Mount of Olives, so the center of Jewish life and religious authority shifted first to Yavne, in the southern coastal plain, and then northward to the Lower Galilee.

By around AD 200 Beit She'arim had become the unofficial Jewish capital, owing its brief preeminence to the enormous stature of a native son. Rabbi Yehuda (or Judah) "ha-Nasi" (the Patriarch: a title conferred on the nominal leader of the Jewish community) was responsible for the city's inner workings and relations with its Roman masters. Alone among his contemporaries, ha-Nasi combined worldly diplomatic skills with scholarly authority and spiritual leadership.

The rabbi eventually moved east to Zippori because of its more salubrious climate, and there gathered the great Jewish sages of his day and compiled the Mishnah, which remains the definitive interpretation of biblical precepts for religious Jews. Nonetheless, it was in his hometown of Beit She'arim that ha-Nasi was laid to rest. If Beit She'arim was a magnet for scholars and petitioners in his lifetime, it became a virtual shrine after his death. With Jerusalem still off-limits, the town became the most prestigious burial site in the Jewish world for almost 150 years.

Two major expeditions in the 1930s and '50s uncovered a series of 20 catacombs. The largest of these is open to the public, with 24 chambers containing more than 200 sarcophagi. A wide range of carved Jewish and Roman symbols and more than 250 funerary inscriptions in Greek, Hebrew, Aramaic, and Palmyrene testify to the great distances people traveled—from Yemen and Mesopotamia, for instance—to be buried here. Without exception, the sarcophagi were plundered over the centuries by grave robbers seeking the possessions with which the dead were often interred. ✉ *Off Rte. 75 or 722, Beit She'arim National Park* ✥ *Take a left turn at HaShomrim Junction on Rte. 722* ☎ *04/983–1643* 🌐 *www.parks.org.il* 🎫 *NIS 22.*

🍴 Restaurants

Kamah Coffee Shop and Gallery

$ | **ISRAELI** | You can have a tasty meal and shop, too, at this showcase for the creative work produced by members of the local special-needs community. Visiting the coffee shop should include a peek at the workshops based on anthroposophy (a system for nurturing the individual's healthy core), where community members work in the organic vegetable garden and the bakery, as well as in handweaving, ceramics, and paper-products workshops. **Known for:** community artwork; Galilee-style breakfast; vegetable garden and bakery. [$] *Average main: NIS 35* ✉ *Kibbutz Harduf, Off Rte. 7626* ☎ *04/905–9338* 🌐 *www.eng.kamah.org.il.*

Tel Megiddo National Park

This ancient city was built on foundations dating back to the biblical era. Today called Tel Megiddo National Park, it's one of the region's most impressive ruins.

GETTING HERE AND AROUND

A car is the best way to get here, as the site is poorly served by public transportation. You can reach the site by taxi from Afula. Taxi-stand published price for trip: NIS 78.

TAXI CONTACT Yizre'el. ☎ *04/652–3111.*

👁 Sights

★ Tel Megiddo National Park

ARCHAEOLOGICAL SITE | Megiddo's centuries of settlement, from prehistoric times through the Canaanite and early Israelite periods, have left fascinating layers of remains at this UNESCO World Heritage Site. Most people are fascinated by the site's ancient water system. In a masterful stroke, King Ahab's engineers

The archaeological layers at Megiddo include prehistoric remains and a biblical-era water system.

dug a deep shaft and a horizontal tunnel through solid rock to reach the vital subterranean spring outside the city walls. With access secure, the spring's original opening was permanently blocked. There is nothing more than a trickle today, though, the flow perhaps choked by subsequent earthquakes. As you descend 180 steps through the shaft, traverse the 65-yard-long tunnel under the ancient city wall, and climb up 83 steps at the other end, look for the ancient chisel marks and hewn steps. A visit to the water system at noon provides a reprieve from the summer heat.

Apart from the ancient water system, don't miss the partially restored Late Bronze Age gate, perhaps the very one stormed by Egyptian troops circa 1468 BC, as described in the victory stela of Pharaoh Thutmose III. A larger gate farther up the mound was long identified with King Solomon (10th century BC)—Megiddo was one of his regional military centers—but has been redated by some

scholars to the time of Ahab, a half century later. There is consensus, however, on the ruined stables at the summit of the tell: they were certainly built by Ahab, whose large chariot army is recorded in an Assyrian inscription.

Evidence indicates prehistoric habitation here as well, but among the earliest remains of the *city* of Megiddo are a round altar dating from the Early Bronze Age and the outlines of several Early Bronze Age temples, almost 5,000 years old, visible in the trench between the two fine lookout points.

A tiny museum at the site's entrance has good visual aids, including maps, a video, and a model of the tell. A small gift shop alongside the museum sells handsome silver and gold jewelry, some incorporating pieces of ancient Roman glass. There is also a restaurant. ⊠ *Rte. 66* ☎ *04/659–0316* ⊕ *www.parks.org.il* 🎟 *NIS 28.*

History in the Jezreel and Jordan Valleys 👁

"Highways of the world cross Galilee in all directions," wrote the eminent Victorian scholar George Adam Smith in 1898. The great international highway of antiquity, the Via Maris (Way of the Sea), swept up the Mediterranean coast from Egypt and broke inland along three separate passes through the hills to emerge in the Jezreel Valley before continuing northeast to Damascus and Mesopotamia. It made the Jezreel Valley a convenient and frequent battleground. In fact, the Jezreel Valley heard the clash of arms so often that the very name of its most commanding tell Har Megiddo (Mount Megiddo), or Armageddon—became a New Testament synonym for the final apocalyptic battle of all time. Today, this and other ancient sites such as Beit She'an remain highlights here. Your first impression is one of lush farmland as far as the eye can see, and eating places in this rustic area are confined to roadside cafeterias. A road trip to the Jezreel and Jordan valleys will take you back in time (almost).

Mount Gilboa

24 km (15 miles) southeast of Tel Megiddo National Park via Rtes. 675 and 667, 10 km (7 miles) southeast of Afula.

Visit Mount Gilboa in February or March, and find yourself surrounded by people enraptured with the delicate purple iris native to these slopes. The views of the valley below and the hills of Galilee beyond are great year-round, but on a clear winter or spring day they're amazing, reaching as far as the snowcapped Mount Hermon, far to the north. Afternoon is the best time to come.

Mount Gilboa—actually a steep mountain range rather than a single peak—is geographically a spur of the far greater Samaria Range (the biblical Mount Ephraim, today the West Bank) to the southwest. Half the mountain has been reforested with evergreens, while the other half has been left in pristine rockiness. Environmentalists prefer the latter, as it protects the wildflowers that splatter the slopes with color every spring. From the gravel parking area off Route 667, easy and well-marked trails wind through the natural habitat of the rare black (actually deep purple) iris, which draws hordes of Israelis every spring.

Three thousand years ago, the Philistines routed the Israelites on Mount Gilboa. Saul, the nation's first king, was wounded and took his own life on the battlefield. The next day, the Bible relates, when the Philistines came to plunder their fallen foes, they discovered the bodies of Saul and his sons. Seeking trophies, "they cut off his head and stripped off his armor, and they fastened his body to the wall of [Beit She'an]" (I Samuel 31). In his eulogy for Saul and his son Jonathan, king-to-be David cursed the battlefield where "thy glory, O Israel" was slain: "Let there be no dew or rain upon you" (II Samuel 1).

GETTING HERE AND AROUND
Driving from Afula, follow Route 71 east, turn right on Route 675, then left on Route 667. There's no reliable public transportation.

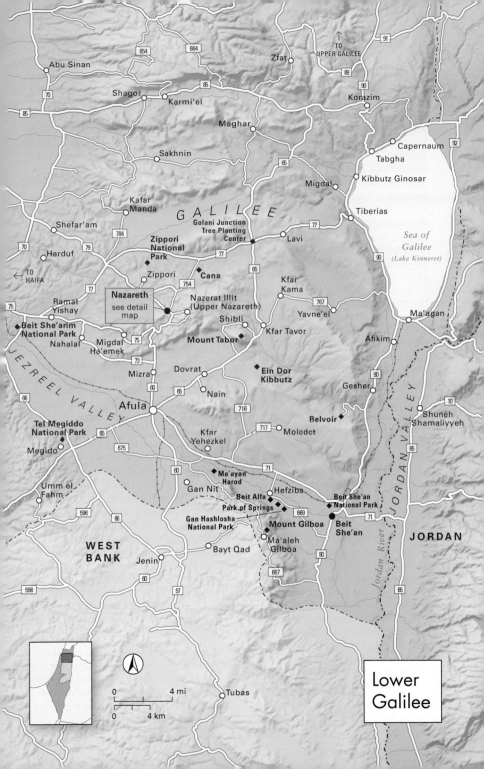

Lower Galilee

◉ Sights

Beit Alfa

ARCHAEOLOGICAL SITE | In 1928, members of Kibbutz Hefziba were digging an irrigation trench when they discovered this ancient synagogue, now part of Beit Alfa Synagogue National Park. Their tools hit a hard surface, and excavation uncovered a multicolored mosaic floor, almost entirely preserved. The art is somewhat stylized and childlike, but that, too, is part of its charm. An Aramaic inscription dates the building to the reign of Byzantine emperor Justinian in the second quarter of the 6th century AD; a Greek inscription credits the workmanship to one Marianos and his son, Aninas. In keeping with Jewish tradition, the synagogue faces Jerusalem, with an apse at the far end to hold the ark. The building faithfully copies the architecture of the Byzantine basilicas of the day, with a nave and two side aisles, and the doors lead to a small narthex and a onetime outdoor atrium. Stairs indicate there was once an upper story.

Classic Jewish symbols in the top mosaic panel leave no doubt that the building was a synagogue: a holy ark flanked by lions, a menorah, and a *shofar* (ram's horn). The middle panel, however, is the most intriguing: it's filled with human figures depicting the seasons, the zodiac, and—even more incredible for a Jewish house of worship—the Greek sun god, Helios, driving his chariot across the sky. These images indicate more liberal times theologically, when the prohibition against making graven images was perhaps not applied to two-dimensional art. The last panel tells the story of Abraham's near-sacrifice of his son Isaac, captioned in Hebrew. Take time to watch the lighthearted but informative film. Allocate 45 minutes for a visit here. ⊠ *Kibbutz Hefziba, Rte. 669* ☎ *04/653–2004* ⊕ *www.parks.org.il* 🖘 *NIS 22.*

Gan Hashlosha National Park

NATIONAL/STATE PARK | **FAMILY** | This beautiful oasis is a national treasure, popular with picnickers and swimmers alike. Lush palm trees and green lawns draw swarms of people who come for the day to relax. The spring water maintains a constant, year-round water temperature of 28°C, or 82°F. As the stream ambles around the property, it has been widened into pools in some areas; there are also some artificial waterfalls. Lifeguards are on duty. Facilities include changing rooms for bathers, two snack bars, and a restaurant. ⊠ *Off Rte. 669* ☎ *04/658–6219* ⊕ *www.parks.org.il* 🖘 *NIS 39.*

Ma'ayan Harod (*Spring of Harod*)

NATIONAL/STATE PARK | **FAMILY** | At the foot of Mount Gilboa is this small national park with huge eucalyptus trees and a big swimming pool fed by a spring. Today it's a bucolic picnic spot, but almost 3,200 years ago, Gideon, the reluctant hero of the biblical book of Judges, organized his troops to fight a Midianite army that had invaded from the desert. At God's command—in order to emphasize the miraculous nature of the coming victory—Gideon dismissed more than two-thirds of the warriors and then, to reduce the force still more, selected only those who lapped water from the spring. Equipped with swords, ram's horns, and flaming torches concealed in clay jars, this tiny army of 300 divided into three companies and surrounded the Midianite camp across the valley in the middle of the night. At a prearranged signal, the attackers shouted, blew their horns, and smashed the jars, revealing the flaming torches, whereupon the Midianites panicked and fled, resulting in an Israelite victory.

The spring has seen other armies in other ages. It was here in 1260 that the Egypt-based Mamluks stopped the invasion of the hitherto invincible Mongols. In the 1930s, the woods above the spring

The remains of the wealthy late Roman and Byzantine city of Beit She'an include a large public bathhouse.

hid Jewish self-defense squads training in defiance of British military law. ✉ *Off Rte. 71* ☎ *04/653–2211* 🌐 *www.parks.org.il* 🎫 *NIS 28.*

Park of Springs

NATURE PRESERVE | Three beautiful springs and a stream are the attractions at this nature park. Electric carts and bicycles are available to rent but not necessary to enjoy a swim or hike. You can also watch the birds of many varieties that make this nature preserve their home and a migration waypoint. ✉ *Rte. 669, at entrance to Gan Hashlosha* ☎ *04/688–1427* 🎫 *Free.*

🍴 Restaurants

Herb Farm on Mount Gilboa

$$$ | **MODERN ISRAELI** | The sweeping panorama from the wooden deck and picture windows is attraction enough at this family restaurant operated by Yossi Mass, his wife Penina, and son Oren. Known for its greens and imaginative salads, it also impresses with homemade bread and tarts of shallot, forest mushroom, and goat cheese, not to mention a colorful pie of beef, lamb, goose, tomatoes, pine nuts, and basil. **Known for:** organic fare; seasonal greens; homemade food. [$] *Average main: NIS 100* ✉ *Rte. 667, 3 km (2 miles) off Rte. 675, Gan Nir* ✥ *At entrance to Mount Gilboa* ☎ *04/653–1093* 🌐 *www.herb-farm.co.il* ⏲ *Closed Sun.*

☕ Coffee and Quick Bites

Barkanit Dairy

$ | **ISRAELI** | At Michal and Avinoam Barkin's goat farm, you can sample excellent cheeses over wine or coffee in the wooden reception room or enjoy a light meal of salads, toasted sandwiches, or hot stuffed pastries. The farm is open Friday 10–2 and Saturday 10–4. **Known for:** excellent cheeses; organic food; rural atmosphere. [$] *Average main: NIS 49* ✉ *Rtes. 71 and 675, 1 km (½ mile) east of Navot Junction, Kfar Yehezkel* ☎ *04/653–1431* 💳 *No credit cards* ⏲ *Closed Sun.–Thurs. No dinner.*

Hotels

Ein Harod Country Suites and Guest Houses
$ | B&B/INN | FAMILY | Set in a lovely landscape, this 95-year-old kibbutz has beautiful cabins and suites to meet every need. **Pros:** serene atmosphere; pretty views; options for both families and couples. **Cons:** luxury suites are pricey on weekends; no nightlife; restaurant selection limited. [$] *Rooms from: $150* ✉ *Kibbutz Ein Harod* ☎ *04/648–6083* 🌐 *www.ein-harod.co.il/en* 🛏 *42 units* 🍴 *Free Breakfast.*

Activities

Big Walks
HIKING/WALKING | Two annual *Tza'adot* (Big Walks) take place in March or April: one along the shore of the Sea of Galilee (2½ km [1½ miles] and 9 km [5½ miles]), the other along the trails of Mount Gilboa (routes range from 6 km [4 miles] to 40 km [25 miles] over two days). These mass rambles attract folks from all over the country and abroad. For information, contact Israeli Sports for All Association. ☎ *03/562–1441* 🌐 *www.isfa.co.il.*

Beit She'an

23 km (14 miles) southeast of Afula, 39 km (24 miles) south of Tiberias.

At the intersection of the Jordan and Jezreel valleys, the modern town of Beit She'an has little to offer visitors, but the past beckons at a national park nearby. Unlike some archaeological sites that appear to be just piles of rocks, ancient Beit She'an is a gloriously rich ruin, complete with bathhouses, pagan temples, and public theaters.

GETTING HERE AND AROUND

The national park is northeast of modern Beit She'an. From Route 90, turn west on Sha'ul Hamelech Street, and right after Bank Leumi.

Sights

★ Beit She'an National Park
ARCHAEOLOGICAL SITE | The extensive remains of lavish ancient structures at this archaeological treasure trove make it one of Israel's most notable sites. A Roman theater was excavated in the 1960s, but the rest of Scythopolis, as this Late Roman and Byzantine (2nd–6th centuries AD) city was known, came to light only in more recent excavations. The enormous haul of marble statuary and friezes says much about the opulence in its heyday—especially when you remember that there are no marble quarries in Israel, and all stone was imported from what is today Turkey, Greece, or Italy.

A free site map available at the visitor center gives a good layout. In summer, it's best to arrive early in the morning, as the heat quickly becomes insufferable. Better yet, consider returning in the evening for the engaging sound-and-light spectacle, presented Monday through Thursday at sundown. Reserve tickets in advance and check times.

Scythopolis's downtown area, now exposed, has masterfully engineered, colonnaded main streets converging on a central plaza that once boasted a pagan temple, decorative fountain, and monument. An elaborate Byzantine bathhouse covered more than 1¼ acres. On the main thoroughfare are the remains of Scythopolis's amphitheater, where gladiatorial combats were once the order of the day.

The high tell dominating the site to the north was the location of Old Testament Canaanite-Israelite Beit She'an 2,500 to 3,500 years ago. Climb to the top not for the meager archaeological remains, but rather the fine panoramic view of the surrounding valleys and the superb bird's-eye view of the main excavations.

The semicircular Roman theater was built of contrasting black basalt and white limestone blocks around AD 200, when Scythopolis was at its height. Although the upper *cavea,* or tier, has not survived, the theater is the largest and best preserved in Israel, with an estimated original capacity of 7,000 to 10,000 people. The large stage and part of the *scaena frons* (backdrop) behind it have been restored, allowing outdoor sound-and-light performances March to November. ✉ *Off Sha'ul Hamelech St., Beit Shean* ☎ *04/658–7189* 🌐 *www.parks.org.il* 🎟 *NIS 28; NIS 55 for sound-and-light show.*

🍴 Restaurants

Shipudei HaKikar

$$$ | **ISRAELI** | You can't miss the imposing restaurant commanding the corner as you enter Beit She'an. Inside, friendly service in a sparkling clean dining room is a pleasant surprise. **Known for:** grilled meats; fresh and interesting salads; kosher food. [$] *Average main: NIS 80* ✉ *35 Sha'ul HaMelech St., Beit Shean* ☎ *04/606–0198* 🕓 *No dinner Fri. No lunch Sat.*

🛏 Hotels

Beit She'an Hostel

$ | **HOTEL** | A cross between a guesthouse and a hostel, this modern limestone and basalt building is wrapped around a courtyard shaded by palm trees. **Pros:** convenient to the national park; pretty pool area; lovely, rural setting. **Cons:** sometimes noisy with teenage groups; no evening entertainment; not many meal options outside of hotel. [$] *Rooms from: $117* ✉ *129 Menachem Begin Blvd., Beit Shean* ☎ *02/594–5644* 🛏 *80 rooms* 🍽 *Free Breakfast.*

🎟 Performing Arts

Roman Theater

THEATER | This marvelous theater hosts concerts, mostly by Israeli artists, every October. ✉ *Sha'ul HaMelech St., Beit Shean* ☎ *04/658–7189.*

Belvoir

20 km (12½ miles) north of Beit She'an.

The Crusaders chose the site for this fortress well: the Hebrew name *Kochav Hayarden* (the Star of the Jordan) and the Arabic *Kaukab el Hauwa* (the Star of the Wind) underscore Belvoir's splendid isolation. You don't need to be a military historian to marvel at the never-breached concentric walls.

GETTING HERE AND AROUND

Driving north on Route 90 from Beit She'an, turn west on Route 717. While any bus traversing Route 90 lets off at the road, the fortress is high above the valley. It's a long hike of 5 km (3 miles), and don't count on getting a ride. The road from Ein Harod via Moledet is passable in dry weather but in very bad condition in places.

👁 Sights

Belvoir

CASTLE/PALACE | The Hospitallers (the Knights of St. John) completed the mighty castle in 1173; they called it Belvoir—"beautiful view"—and it was the most invincible fortress in the land. In the summer of 1187, the Arabs under Saladin crushed the Crusader armies at the Horns of Hittin, west of Tiberias, bringing an end to the Latin Kingdom of Jerusalem with one decisive battle. The Crusaders' remnants struggled on to Tyre (in modern Lebanon), but Belvoir alone refused to yield; 18 months of siege got the Muslims no farther than undermining the outer eastern rampart. The Crusaders, for their part, sallied out from time to time to battle the enemy, but their lone resistance had become pointless. They struck a deal with Saladin and surrendered the stronghold in exchange for free passage, flags flying, to Tyre. Today Belvoir is part of Kochav Hayarden National Park.

Don't follow the arrows from the parking lot; instead, take the wide gravel path to the right of the fortress. This brings you to the panoramic view of the Jordan River Valley and southern Sea of Galilee, some 1,800 feet below (the view is best in the afternoon). It's also the best spot from which to appreciate the strength of the stronghold, with its deep, dry moat, massive rock and cut-stone ramparts, and gates. Once inside the main courtyard, you're unexpectedly faced with a fortress within a fortress, a scaled-down replica of the outer defenses. Not much remains of the upper stories; in 1220, the Muslims systematically dismantled Belvoir, fearing another crusade. Once you've explored the modest buildings, exit over the western bridge (once a drawbridge) and spy on the postern gates, the protected and sometimes secret back doors of medieval castles. ⊠ Rte. 717, Belvoir National Park ✛ 5 km (3 miles) west of Rte. 90 ☎ 04/658–1766 ⊕ www.parks.org.il ☎ NIS 22.

Nazareth

25 km (15½ miles) east of Beit She'arim, 56 km (35 miles) east of Haifa, 15 km (9½ miles) north of Afula.

The Nazareth where Jesus grew up was an insignificant village in a hollow in the Galilean hills, but today's city of 75,000 pulses with energy. Apart from the occasional donkey plying traffic-clogged Paulus VI Street, there's little that evokes the Bible in contemporary Nazareth, unless you know where to look—and indeed, droves of Christian pilgrims come to pray at the awe-inspiring Basilica of the Annunciation or seek quiet contemplation at one of Nazareth's many smaller churches.

For nonbelievers, Nazareth is a fascinating day or half-day stop; the Christian devout want to spend a full day, if not two. If your goal is to experience Nazareth as Jesus did, plan a tour at Nazareth Village. The calmest days to visit the town are Wednesday, when many businesses close for a midweek sabbatical, and Sunday, the day of rest for the Christians who make up a third of the town. If you're looking for local color (and traffic jams), come on Saturday, when Arab villagers come to the big city to sell produce and buy goods.

GETTING HERE AND AROUND
If you're driving from Beit She'arim or Haifa on Route 75, Route 77 breaks off to the north—to Zippori, the Golani Junction, and Tiberias. Route 75 continues to skirt the north side of the picturesque Jezreel Valley as it climbs into the hills toward Nazareth; at the crest of the hill, Route 60 from Afula joins it. A turn to the left takes you down to Paulus VI, Nazareth's main drag. If you pick up Route 77 from the opposite side, from Tiberias and points north, a left turn onto Route 764 takes you into Nazareth's Paulus VI Street. Nazareth's Central Bus Station is downtown on Paulus VI Street, near the Basilica of the Annunciation.

Nazareth itself is mired in traffic, but the historic and religious sites are all close together, so it's best to park and walk.

TAXI CONTACTS Abu el-Assal. ☎ 04/655–4745. **Diana.** ☎ 04/655–5554.

TOURS
Both Egged Tours and United Tours run one-day tours that take in Nazareth, Capernaum, Tabgha, the Sea of Galilee,

Tiberias, and the Jordan River. Current prices are NIS 330 from Tel Aviv, NIS 350 from Jerusalem.

Nazareth is the starting point of two walking trails that trace a path between sites relating to the life of Jesus; both trails are long, but it's possible to walk just a section of either. The **Jesus Trail** (⊕ jesustrail.com) is 65 km (40 miles) and goes from Nazareth to Capernaum on the Sea of Galilee. The 60 km (37 miles) of the **Gospel Trail** (⊕ www.goisrael.com) go from Nazareth to sites along the Sea of Galilee; it can be done by foot or on bike.

Fauzi Azar Tour

GUIDED TOURS | The Old City tour that begins at the Fauzi Azar Inn is unique in that it skips religious sites almost entirely and focuses instead on the sights, sounds, and smells of daily life in Nazareth. You are taken to the souk, where shop owners let you view and taste their wares; unique gift shops far from city center; and various coffee shops, whose managers answer questions about Nazareth life. Tours are offered every day except Sunday at 9.30 am and cost NIS 20 per person (free for inn guests). ⊠ Fauzi Azar Inn, 2606 St. ⊹ Off the souk ☎ 04/602–0469 ⊕ abrahamhostels.com ➲ NIS 20.

VISITOR INFORMATION

CONTACTS Nazareth Tourist Information Office. ⊠ Casa Nova St. ☎ 04/657–0555.

Sights

Ancient Bathhouse in Nazareth

ARCHAEOLOGICAL SITE | In 1993, Elias and Martina Shama-Sostar were renovating their crafts shop when they discovered ancient steam pipes under the store. Further excavation revealed a huge, wonderfully preserved Roman-style bathhouse. Israel's Antiquities Authority has not made any official announcements about the site, but several historians

speculate that it might date from the 1st century AD. A one-hour tour takes you to the hot room, heating tunnels, and furnace. Coffee is served in the arched hall where wood and ashes were once kept. ⊠ Mary's Well Sq. ☎ 04/657–8539 ⊕ www.nazarethbathhouse.org ➲ NIS 120 for up to 4 visitors ⊙ Closed Sun.

★ Basilica of the Annunciation

RELIGIOUS SITE | The Roman Catholic Basilica of the Annunciation, the largest church in the Middle East, was consecrated in 1969; it enshrines a small ancient cave dwelling or grotto, identified by many Catholics as the home of Mary. Here, they believe, the angel Gabriel appeared to her and announced she would conceive and "bear a son" and "call his name Jesus" (Luke 1). Pilgrim devotions suffuse the site throughout the day. Crusader-era walls and some restored Byzantine mosaics near the grotto bear witness to the antiquity of the tradition. The grotto is in the so-called lower church. Look up through the "well," or opening over the grotto, that connects with the upper church to the grand cupola, soaring 195 feet above you.

A spiral staircase leads to the vast upper church, the parish church of Nazareth's Roman Catholic community. Italian ceramic reliefs on the huge concrete pillars represent the Stations of the Cross, captioned in the Arabic vernacular. You now have a closer view of the cupola, its ribs representing the petals of an upside-down lily—a symbol of Mary's purity—rooted in heaven.

The large panels on the walls of the upper church, touching on the theme of mother and child, include a vivid offering from the United States, a fine Canadian terra-cotta, and mosaics from England and Australia. Particularly interesting are the gifts from Japan (with gold leaf and pearls), Venezuela (a carved-wood statue), and Cameroon (a stylized painting in black, white, and red).

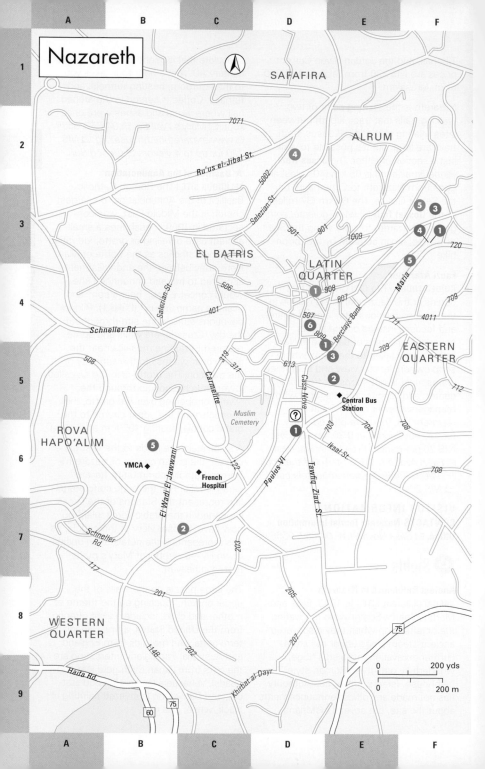

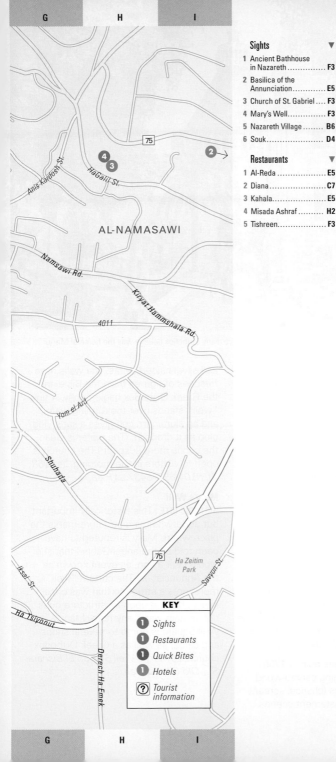

G   **H**   **I**

AL-NAMASAWI

Anis Kardosh St.

HaGalil St.

75

Namsawi Rd.

Kiryat Hammshala Rd.

4011

Yom el Ard

Shibada

75

Ha Zeitim
Park

Savyon St.

Iksal St.

Ha Tsiyonut

Derech Ha Emek

KEY

1 Sights
1 Restaurants
1 Quick Bites
1 Hotels
? Tourist
information

G   **H**   **I**

The Basilica of the Annunciation has a venerable cave many Catholics believe was the home of Mary.

In the exit courtyard, a glass-enclosed baptistery is built over what is thought to have been an ancient *mikvah,* a Jewish ritual bath. The adjacent small Church of St. Joseph, just past Terra Sancta College, is built over a complex of rock-hewn chambers traditionally identified as the workshop of Joseph the Carpenter. Note that parking is hard to find; try Paulus VI Street or the side streets below it. ⊠ *Casa Nova St.* ☎ *04/657–2501* ✉ *Free* ⊘ *Basilica closed for touring Sun. morning.*

Church of St. Gabriel
RELIGIOUS SITE | This Greek Orthodox church is built over Nazareth's only natural water source, a spring dubbed Mary's Well. The Greek Orthodox, citing the noncanonical Gospel of St. James, believe it to be the place where the angel Gabriel appeared to Mary to announce the coming birth of Jesus.

The ornate church was built in 1750 and contains a stunning carved-wood pulpit and iconostasis (chancel screen) with painted New Testament scenes

and silver-haloed saints. The walls have frescoes of figures from the Bible and the Greek Orthodox hagiography. A tiny "well" stands over the running water, and an aluminum cup gives a satisfying plop as it drops in. (The water is clean; the cup is more suspect.) The church is open to visitors in the morning. ⊠ *6053 St.* ☎ *04/657–6437* ✉ *Free.*

Mary's Well
HISTORIC SITE | This historically important but underwhelming structure marks the place where Mary is reputed to have been told by the angel Gabriel that she would bear a son, an event known as the Annunciation. The current "well" represents a structure that was once in use, but the open-air structure does not contain water anymore. Mary's Well Square is home to several shops and cafés, as well as a Greek Orthodox church. ⊠ *Mary's Well Sq., 55 El Bishara St., Old City* ✉ *Free.*

Nazareth Village

MUSEUM VILLAGE | FAMILY | The shepherds, weavers, and other characters in this reconstructed Jesus-era community delight children and adults alike. Using information gained from archaeological work done in the area, this attraction aims to re-create Jewish rural life as Jesus would have known it more than 2,000 years ago. Workshops, farms, and houses have been built with techniques that would have been used at the time. Interpreters in period costume cook and work at wine presses and looms, giving a sense of daily life. Reservations are required for guided tours, which meet on the second floor of the Nazareth YMCA. ✉ *Nazareth YMCA, 5105 St., 2nd fl.* ☎ *04/645–6042* 🌐 *www.nazarethvillage.com* 🎟 *NIS 50* 🕒 *Closed Sun.*

Souk

MARKET | Bathed in the aromas of herbs and spices, this market in the Old City has something for everyone, from coffee sets to antiques to freshly baked pastries. The old lanes are narrow and shops tiny, with goods spilling into the street, but this souk is more orderly than those in many other Israeli cities. When it gets overwhelming, take a coffee break. ✉ *6129 St.* 🎟 *Free* 🕒 *Closed Sun.*

🍴 Restaurants

After a full day of visiting Nazareth's shrines, you can quench your thirst with the locals at one of the little Arab restaurants along Paulus VI Street. Dinner here usually means hummus, shish kebab, baklava, and the like. Decor is incidental, atmosphere a function of the clientele of the moment, and dinnertime early. Needless to say, reservations aren't necessary, and dress is casual. If looking for more upscale dining, several high-end restaurants have opened in the past few years, serving traditional Arab and fusion fare.

Al-Reda

$$$ | MIDDLE EASTERN | In a magnificent 19th-century mansion with a *Thousand and One Nights* atmosphere, this eatery matches its magical setting with excellent Arab cuisine, including interesting salads and kebabs, as well as dishes with Indian and European influences. Pesto and grilled vegetables stuffed in a chicken breast is a good choice, as are the vegetarian dishes. **Known for:** beautiful dining room; modern Arab cuisine; eggplant with cheese salad. [$] *Average main: NIS 76* ✉ *23 Al Bishara St.* ✣ *Next to Basilica of the Annunciation* ☎ *04/608–4404.*

Diana

$$$$ | MIDDLE EASTERN | Ranked among the region's best Arab restaurants, Diana doesn't fail to impress. Owner Duhul Safadi is most famous for his kebabs and lamb chops, but the fish and seafood dishes are all equally wonderful. **Known for:** plant-filled terrace; upscale dining room; delicious kebabs. [$] *Average main: NIS 101* ✉ *51 Paulus VI St.* ☎ *053/944–1630* 🌐 *dianaa.rest.co.il* 🕒 *Closed Sat.*

Kahala

$ | CAFÉ | Recharge in an elegant setting in the Old City, sampling delicious pastries and coffee or perhaps a glass of wine. This small café, set in a 200-year-old building, is run by local architect Razan Zoubi, whose professional studio is upstairs. **Known for:** historic building; homemade, delicious pastries; comfortable, architect-designed interior. [$] *Average main: NIS 25* ✉ *23 Al Bishara St.* 🕒 *No dinner* 💳 *No credit cards.*

Misada Ashraf

$$ | FAST FOOD | Stop in for a plate of creamy and delicious hummus with various toppings: whole chickpeas, tahini, lamb meat, or pine nuts. Shawarma, schnitzels, and kebabs round out the menu, as do the especially delicious fresh salads. **Known for:** hummus, kebabs, and salads; midday meal; budget-friendly menu. $ *Average main: NIS 60* ⊠ *86 HaGalil St.* ☎ *04/655–5579.*

Tishreen

$$ | **MIDDLE EASTERN** | The tile floors, stone walls, and dim lighting at this restaurant and bar named after a month on the Muslim calendar are the perfect setting for the Middle Eastern menu. Known for the wood-burning oven from which fresh breads emerge, this restaurant is big on kebabs and eggplant stuffed with pesto and cheese. **Known for:** friendly service; delicious Middle Eastern menu; inviting dining room. $ *Average main: NIS 75* ⊠ *HaBsora St., near Mary's Well St.* ☎ *04/608–4666.*

☕ Coffee and Quick Bites

Mahroum Sweets

$ | **MIDDLE EASTERN** | Try the unbeatable Arab pastries at this bakeshop. The place serves wonderful *bourma* (cylindrical pastries filled with whole pistachio nuts), cashew baklava, and great halvah. **Known for:** halvah; baklava; bourma. $ *Average main: NIS 30* ⊠ *Casal St., at Paulus VI St.* ☎ *04/655–4470* ⊕ *www.mahroum-baklawa.com.*

Hotels

Fauzi Azar Inn

$ | **B&B/INN** | A 200-year-old mansion in the heart of the Old City, this inn has rooms with soaring ceilings that are perfect for couples or families, especially since some rooms are spacious (some are dorm style). **Pros:** historic building; reasonable rates; friendly staff. **Cons:** no elevator; not much parking; hard to find. $ *Rooms from: $100* ⊠ *2606 St., Old City* ⊹ *Off the souk* ☎ *04/602–0469* ⊕ *abrahamhostels.com* ⇆ *14 rooms* ❛❍❜ *Free Breakfast.*

Nazareth Plaza Hotel

$ | **HOTEL** | The imposing stone facade of the Nazareth Plaza is the first hint that the city has finally acquired an upscale hotel. **Pros:** sweeping views; pretty swimming pool; air-conditioned rooms. **Cons:** no evening entertainment; far from Nazareth's shrines. $ *Rooms from: $150* ⊠ *2 Hermon St., Upper Nazareth* ☎ *04/602–8200* ⇆ *182 rooms* ❛❍❜ *Free Breakfast.*

Rimonim Hotel Nazareth

$ | **HOTEL** | Most of the action here is underground, where the adjoining bar, lounge, and dining room add a bit of buzz. **Pros:** convenient to the sights; air-conditioned rooms; fourth floor has balconies. **Cons:** street noise; no evening entertainment. $ *Rooms from: $130* ⊠ *1 Paulus VI St.* ☎ *04/650–0000* ⊕ *www. rimonim.com* ⇆ *226 rooms* ❛❍❜ *Free Breakfast.*

St. Gabriel

$ | **HOTEL** | High on the ridge that overlooks Nazareth, this hotel began life as a convent—hence the charming neo-Gothic church still in use on the property today. **Pros:** near the shrines; memorable views; plenty of character. **Cons:** no evening entertainment. $ *Rooms from: $130* ⊠ *50 Reus El Jibal St.* ☎ *04/657–2133, 04/645–4448* ⊕ *www.stgabrielhotel.com* ⇆ *60 rooms* ❛❍❜ *Free Breakfast.*

Villa Nazareth

$ | **HOTEL** | A restored schoolhouse, this charming boutique hotel in Mary's Well Square is a perfect place to base your Nazareth visit. **Pros:** great location; attentive staff; reliable Wi-Fi. **Cons:** bathrooms a bit small by American standards. $ *Rooms from: $130* ⊠ *Mary's Well Sq., 6053 St.* ☎ *04/600–0569* ⊕ *www. villa-nazareth.co.il* ⇆ *18 rooms* ❛❍❜ *Free Breakfast.*

Zippori National Park

Village 5 km (3 miles) northwest of Nazareth off Rte. 79, site 3 km (2 miles) from village via bypass; 47 km (29 miles) east of Haifa.

Lush beauty and fantastic archaeological finds make this place worth a visit, especially if you have an interest in Roman culture or Talmudic thought. Like many places during the Roman era, Zippori—known in the classical world as Sepphoris—was a prosperous city where Jews and gentiles coexisted fairly peaceably. The ancient city, situated on a high ridge with commanding views, can be visited in two hours. The key sites are relatively close together.

GETTING HERE AND AROUND

Driving to this national park from Nazareth, follow Route 79 west and turn north at the signs. No buses service this route. If you don't have a car, take a taxi from Nazareth (agree on the price in advance, and consider asking the driver to wait).

⊙ Sights

★ Zippori National Park

ARCHAEOLOGICAL SITE | The multiple narratives of Zippori, today an impressive, popular archaeological site known for Israel's finest Roman-era mosaics, begin with a Jewish town that stood here from at least the 1st century BC, and Christian tradition reveres the town as the birthplace of the Virgin Mary. Zippori's refusal to join the Great Revolt of the Jews against the Romans (AD 66–73) left a serious gap in the rebel defenses in the Galilee, angering its compatriots but sparing the town the usual Roman vengeance when the uprising failed. The real significance of Zippori for Jewish tradition, however, is that in the late 2nd or early 3rd century AD, the legendary sage Rabbi Yehuda ha-Nasi, head of

the country's Jewish community at the time, moved here from Beit She'arim, whereupon the Sanhedrin (the Jewish high court) soon followed. Rabbi Yehuda summoned the greatest rabbis in the land to pool their experiences. The result was the encyclopedic work known as the Mishnah. Further commentary was added in later centuries to produce the Talmud, the primary guide to Orthodox Jewish practice to this day.

By the 3rd century AD, Zippori had acquired a mixed population of Jews, pagans, and Christians. The most celebrated find is the mosaic floor of a Roman villa, perhaps the governor's residence, depicting Dionysian drinking scenes. Its most stunning detail is the exquisite face of a woman, which the media dubbed "the Mona Lisa of the Galilee." The restored mosaics are housed in an air-conditioned structure with helpful explanations. In other parts of the park, the so-called Nile Mosaic displays Egyptian motifs, and a mosaic synagogue floor (below the parking lot) is decorated with the signs of the zodiac, like those found in Beit Alfa and Hammat Tiberias.

If the mosaic floors reveal the opulence of Roman Sepphoris, the relatively small Roman theater is evidence of the cultural life the wealth could support. Take a few minutes to climb the watchtower of Dahr el-Omar's 18th-century castle for the panoramic view and the museum of archaeological artifacts. About 1 km (½ mile) east of the main site—near the park entrance—is a huge section of ancient Zippori's water system, once fed by springs north of Nazareth. The ancient aqueduct-reservoir is in fact a deep, man-made plastered canyon, and the effect is extraordinary. ⊠ *Off Rte. 79, Nazareth* ☎ *04/656–8272* ⊕ *www.parks. org.il* ☑ *NIS 28.*

Continued on page 379

Jesus *in the* Galilee

Galilee beckons shyly. As in days of old, there is little of the frenetic pace and charged emotions of Jerusalem. For many Christians, the evocative, soft landscapes breathe new life into old familiar stories, and brush black-and-white scriptures with color. But curious visitors with less religious motivation will be drawn into Galilee's gentle charm. This tour of selected sights will speak to both.

"And passing along by the Sea of Galilee, he saw Simon and Andrew the brother of Simon casting a net into the sea, for they were fishermen. And Jesus said to them,

'Follow me and I will make you become fishers of men.'

(Mark 1: 16–17)

Jesus was born in Bethlehem and died in Jerusalem, but it was in the Galilee that his ministry was forged. Over time, archaeologists and historians have unearthed many sites referred to in the New Testament. Today you can walk the hillsides, sail the Sea of Galilee, explore the ruins, and touch the churches of this beautiful region. Or you can sit under a tree and read scripture in the place where its narrative unfolded. If you have an eye for the contours of the land and an ear for echoes of the past, the experience can be unforgettable.

The activity and teachings of Jesus gain meaning and resonance from the landscape and social setting in which they emerged. Understand their context, and you will enhance your understanding of the events that have so shaped Western civilization.

By Mike Rogoff

RESTLESS SOCIETY, TURBULENT TIMES

Christ in the Storm on the Sea of Galilee by Jan Brueghel the Elder

The Romans came for the weekend in 63 BC and stayed for four centuries. Herod (later "the Great"), scion of a powerful political family, began his brutal reign as King of the Jews, courtesy of Rome, in 37 BC. He died in 4 BC, only a short time after the birth of Jesus (Matt. 2:1).

Herod's kingdom was divided among his three surviving sons: Archelaus, Herod Antipas (who got Galilee, and Perea beyond the Jordan River), and Philip. It was Herod Antipas who executed John the Baptist (Matt. 14:10), and was in Jerusalem at the time of the crucifixion (Luke 23:7).

RIVAL THEOLOGIES

Jewish society in the land of Israel was anything but unified and placid 2,000 years ago. Two ideological streams dominated: the Sadducees were the establishment, many of them wealthy, led by the priestly class that controlled the Temple-based cult of Yahweh, the One God, in Jerusalem. They took religious texts literally, and rejected the idea of resurrection and an afterlife (Acts 23:6–9).

The Pharisees, on the other hand, drew their strength from the common people, offering a comforting belief in resurrection and an afterlife in a better world.

Their rabbis, or teachers, would interpret biblical law, a practice that laid the groundwork for post-Temple Judaism as practiced until today.

Jesus himself came from the Pharisaic tradition, and "taught in their synagogues" (Luke 4:15). He was critical of the Pharisees' behavior, but not of their theology: They "sit on Moses' seat," he told his followers, "so practice and observe whatever they tell you" (Matt. 23:2).

SECTS AND CATACLYSM

Theological differences and domestic politics gave rise to numerous Jewish sects with strong religious agendas: the followers of Jesus, and of John the Baptist before him, were just two. One of the best known at the time were the Essenes, widely identified today as the monastic Jewish community that wrote the Dead Sea Scrolls.

There were other, less spiritual types like the Zealots—extreme nationalists who spearheaded the Great Revolt against Rome in AD 66. The cataclysm was not long in coming: Jerusalem and the Temple were razed in AD 70, four decades after Jesus's prediction that "there will not be left here one stone upon another" (Matt. 24:2).

Marriage Feast at Cana by Hieronymus Bosch

FACT, FAITH, AND TRADITION

The church on the Mount of Beatitudes has sweeping views of the Sea of Galilee.

Finding evidence of events or personalities in the distant past, the New Testament era included, is a kind of treasure hunt; and there is rarely an "X" to mark the spot. But when you do strike gold, through archaeological discoveries or ancient writings, for example, it thrills scholars and laypeople alike.

POPULATING ANCIENT MAPS

There are Galilean towns, like Nazareth and Tiberias, that have survived the centuries and are obviously genuine. Others, like Cana, are still debated. A lot of rocks have been turned over in the last three-quarters of a century, however, and archaeologists have exposed and identified Capernaum, Bethsaida, Chorazin (Korazim), Caesarea Philippi (Banias) in the Upper Galilee, and, to the satisfaction of many, Gennasaret (Ginosar) and Nain as well.

"TRADITIONAL" SITES: WHERE MEMORIES ENDURE

Other sites have been linked to events over time, though no real evidence exists. Scriptural descriptions don't exactly offer geographical coordinates, and some locations that are still much visited by pilgrims are conjecture that has jelled into tradition. Visitors in the distant past often took local hearsay for hard fact when tour guides and other opportunists pointed out the very rock or glade or spring where this or that happened. It's not surprising that many traditional holy places are found so close to each other. Guides were often paid by the site—why should they journey unnecessary distances?

Events like the Sermon on the Mount, the Transfiguration, the feeding of the multitudes, the "feed my sheep" encounter of John 21, and the swine of the Gadarenes are all in this category. But for the faithful, the personal spiritual experience is more than a search for "the very stone" on which a particular event actually took place. Centuries of prayers and tears will sanctify a site, making it a remembrance place in the region where it all began.

TOURING THE CRADLE OF CHRISTIANITY

An astonishing three-quarters of the activity of Jesus recorded in the New Testament took place on, around, or within sight of the "Sea" of Galilee. The lake provided the largely Jewish towns and villages on its shores with a source of fresh water, a fishing industry, and a means of transportation.

Base yourself in Tiberias and head north, or clockwise, around the lake. The sights are close enough to see in a day. To visit Nazareth, Cana, and Mount Tabor, 25 miles west of Tiberias, allot another day or be selective. Below are key places associated with Jesus, and scriptural references to them.

❶ TIBERIAS *"... boats from Tiberias came near the place..." (John 6:23).* Herod Antipas, son of Herod the Great, built the city as the capital of the Galilee in AD 20. The town never lost its importance, and is today the region's urban center.

❷ GINOSAR/GENNESARET Eight kms (5 miles) north of Tiberias, modern Ginosar is a kibbutz, with a museum that houses the extraordinary 1st-century-AD wooden boat found nearby. *"... they came to land at Gennesaret... immediately the people recognized him... and as many as touched [the fringe of his garment] were made well" (Mark 6:53–56).*

❸ MOUNT OF BEATITUDES *"Seeing the crowds, he went up on the mountain, and when he sat down his disciples came to him... 'Blessed are the poor in spirit...'" (Matt. 5–7).* The traditional site of Jesus's Sermon on the Mount is set in hilltop gardens, with a church and a superb view of the lake.

❹ TABGHA Two events in the life of Jesus are recalled in two churches here. The Multiplication was one: a famous 5th-century mosaic records the event. Crowds followed Jesus and evening came. What about food? *" 'You give them something to eat'... 'We have only five loaves here and two fish'... 'Bring them...' He looked up to heaven, and blessed... And they all ate and were satisfied... about 5,000 men, besides women and children" (Matt. 14: 15–21).*

The primacy of Peter is another. The beach and an attractively simple chapel recall the appearance of Jesus on the shore: *" 'Have you any fish?'... 'No'... 'Cast the net'... 'It is the Lord!'... 'Simon [Peter]... Do you love me?... Feed my sheep' " (John 21:1–19).*

❺ CAPERNAUM Jesus made this thriving Jewish town, now an archaeological site, the center of his ministry: *"He went and dwelt in Capernaum..." (Matt. 4:13).* Here he preached— *"... and immediately on the sabbath he entered the synagogue and taught" (Mark 1:21).*

Greek Orthodox church, Cana

Basilica of the Annunciation, Nazareth

Golani Junction

Lavi

❾ Cana

Zippori

754

65

Kfar Kama

Nazerat Illit (Upper Nazareth)

Nazareth ❿

Migdal Ha'emek

79

Kfar Tavor

Shibli
Mount Tabor
❶❶

Mount Tabor

716

6 BETHSAIDA This was the hometown of the disciples Philip, Andrew, and Peter (John 1:44), and the place where Jesus cured a blind man (Mark 8:22–25). The town was left stranded when its lagoon dried out, and eluded identification until recently. It's in th Jordan River Park.

7 KURSI Jesus cured two madmen on the Golan Heights slopes, *"the country of the Gadarenes": "...a herd of swine was feeding... [the demons]* came out [of the demoniacs] and went into the swine..." (Matt. 8:28–34).

8 JORDAN RIVER Today people come to be baptized in the Jordan at Yardenitin this northern region, but the New

Synagogue at Capernaum

Testament story almost certainly refers to the river's southern reaches, near Jericho: *"Then Jesus came from the Galilee to the Jordan to John, to be baptized by him" (Matt. 3:13).*

9 CANA When the wine ran out at a wedding feast, Jesus (after some persuasion) turned six stone jars-full of water into superior wine. *"This, the first of his signs, Jesus did in Cana of Galilee..." (John 2:1–11).*

10 NAZARETH Here, the New Testament relates, an angel appeared to Mary to announce the coming birth of Jesus (Luke 1:26–38). It was here he

Byzantine church at Kursi

Mount of Beatitudes
Bethsaida
Capernaum
Tabgha
Ginosar
Kursi
Sea of Galilee (Lake Kinneret)
Tiberias
Fin Gev

Ancient boat at Ginosar.
Kinneret
Jordan River
Yavne'el
Degania Alef
Baptism in the Jordan River

0 4 mi
0 4 km

grew up (his so-called "hidden years") and to Nazareth he returned as a teacher: *"... he went to the synagogue... on the sabbath... he stood up to read... the prophet Isaiah..."(Luke 4:16–30).*

11 MOUNT TABOR In the event called "the Transfiguration," Jesus took three of his disciples *"up a high mountain apart,"* where they had a vision of him as a radiant white figure flanked by Moses and Elijah (Mark 9:2–8). Mount Tabor has long been identified as the place, though some prefer Mount Hermon in the far north.

TIPS FOR EXPLORING THE GALILEE

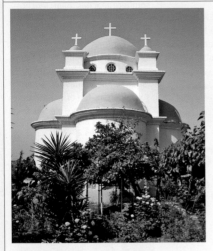

Greek Orthodox church at Capernaum

only 2% of its citizens are Christian. In the Galilee, the exception is Nazareth, with its lights and Christmas trees, and a traditional procession downtown at 3 pm on Christmas Eve. Many denominations are represented here, but Nazareth has no scheduled services in English.

In Tiberias, English-speakers can attend Catholic mass in St. Peter's Church (daily at 6:30 pm Sundays at 8:30 am) and occasional Protestant services at YMCA Penuel (just north of town) and St. Andrew's (opposite the Scots Hotel).

VISITING SUGGESTIONS

Christian sites demand respectful behavior and conservative dress (no shorts, short skirts, or sleeveless tops). Photography is usually permitted, but professionals may require prior permission. Pay attention to advertised opening times and allow time for unexpected delays in getting there.

GETTING AROUND

Buses may be the cheapest way to see Israel, but they are not time-effective in the Galilee. Nazareth and Tiberias are easy to get to (and are 45 minutes apart), and a few less-frequent lines stop at Cana, Ginosar, and near Tabgha. Other Christian sites in the area are a fair hike from the highway or only doable by car.

HIKING THE LANDSCAPE

Hikers can consider the Jesus Trail (www.jesustrail.com). Its primary route is 65 kms (40 miles) long from Nazareth to Capernum, but you can select sections for a shorter hike.

You can also walk or cycle along the footpaths of the 60-km (37-mile) Gospel Trail (www.goisrael.com), which traces the path that Jesus took along the Sea of Galilee.

HOLIDAYS, SERVICES, AND MORE

The Christmas and Easter celebrations that are so much part of the culture in many places are absent in Israel, where

CREATING SPECIAL MOMENTS IN THE GALILEE

■ Carry a Bible and a good map.

■ In fine weather, the Mount of Beatitudes is best in the afternoon, when the light is gentler on the lake and the hills.

■ If you are unencumbered by luggage, and don't have a car to retrieve, stroll the easy trail from Mount of Beatitudes down to Tabgha (cross the highway with care), visit the two sites there, and then walk the 2-mile

promenade that follows the highway east to Capernaum.

■ The little beach of volcanic pebbles at Tabgha (the Primacy site) can be magical.

■ Bethsaida in Jordan River Park is evocative—pure 1st century: no Byzantine, Crusader, or modern structures. It's never crowded, and offers a great place to sit with a view of the lake and read your favorite verses.

Cana

8 km (5 miles) north of Nazareth on Rte. 754, 1 km (½ mile) south of junction of Rtes. 77 and 754, 50 km (31 miles) east of Haifa.

Near the large, modern Arab village of Kfar Kanna is the site of the ancient Jewish village of Cana, mentioned in the New Testament. Here Jesus performed his first miracle, turning water into wine at a wedding feast, thereby emerging from his "hidden years" to begin a three-year ministry in the Galilee.

Within the village, red signs lead to rival churches—one Roman Catholic, the other Greek Orthodox—that enshrine the scriptural tradition. (The alley to these churches is just wide enough for cars, and you can sometimes park in the courtyard of a souvenir store. If the street is blocked, park on the main road.)

The plaza of the Greek Orthodox St. George Convent is a peaceful spot. The First Miracle Church, on the grounds, is rarely open to visitors, but you can wander the landscape freely. On a lower plaza is a handsome statue of Jesus (surrounded, perhaps predictably, by souvenir shops).

GETTING HERE AND AROUND
Part of the sprawling suburbs of Nazareth, Kfar Kanna sits astride Route 754, linking Route 77 to the north and Route 79 to the south.

Sights

Cana Wedding Church
RELIGIOUS SITE | This quaint church on a hill was built in 1881 where Catholics believe Jesus performed his first miracle (John 2:1–11). The basement has stones and mosaics that bear witness to the ancient building that once stood on this site. ⊠ *Off Rte. 754* ☎ *04/651–7011* 🎫 *Free* ⊘ *Closed Sun.*

Golani Junction Tree Planting Center
GARDEN | Around the Golani Junction are groves of evergreens planted by visitors as part of the Plant a Tree With Your Own Hands project of the Jewish National Fund. Since the early 1900s, more than 250 million trees have been restored to barren hillsides across Israel. At the Golani Junction Tree Planting Center, you can choose a sapling, dedicate it to someone, and plant it yourself; the cost is $18 for adults and $10 for children. Email ahead of time to coordinate your tree planting. ⊠ *Off Rte. 77, Givat Avni* ⊹ *East of Golani Junction* ☎ *02/658–3349* 🖎 *tovad@kkl.org.il* ⊕ *www.jnf.org* ⊘ *Closed Fri. afternoon and Sat.*

Mount Tabor

16 km (10 miles) south of the Golani Junction, off Rtes. 65 and 7266, 17 km (10½ miles) northeast of Afula.

Now covered with pine trees, Mount Tabor has a serene look that belies its strategic and historical importance. Here you find the Church of the Transfiguration, which marks the place where tradition says Jesus began to radiate light and was seen conversing with Moses and Elijah. Christian pilgrims have venerated this site for centuries: Napoléon brought 3,000 French soldiers here to battle the Ottomans in 1799. Today Mount Tabor is popular with hang-gliding enthusiasts, and there's a marathon around the mountain in April.

GETTING HERE AND AROUND
If you're driving, take Route 7266 through Shibli, a village of Bedouins who abandoned their nomadic life a few generations ago. A narrow switchback road starts in a clearing between Shibli and the next village, Dabouriya. Nazareth-based taxis often wait at the bottom of the mountain to provide shuttle service to the top. Watch out for them if

driving your own car up; they come down in overdrive like the lords of the mountain they almost are.

◉ Sights

Church of the Transfiguration

RELIGIOUS SITE | As far back as the Byzantine period, Christian tradition identified Mount Tabor as the "high mountain apart" that Jesus ascended with his disciples Peter, James, and John. There, report the Gospels, "he was transfigured before them" (Matthew 17:2) as a radiant white figure, flanked by Moses and Elijah. The altar of the present imposing church, which was consecrated in 1924, represents the tabernacle of Jesus that Peter suggested they build; those of Moses and Elijah appear as small chapels at the back of the church. Step up to the terrace to the right of the church doors for a great view of the Jezreel Valley to the west and south. From a platform on the Byzantine and Crusader ruins to the left of the modern church (watch your step), there is a panorama east and north over the Galilean hills. A nearby Franciscan pilgrim rest stop has refreshments and restrooms. ✉ Off Rte. 7266, Kfar Tavor ☎ 04/662–0720 ☞ Free.

Marzipan Museum

MUSEUM | FAMILY | In the same compound as the Tabor Winery, this charming museum contains explanations about almonds and delectable products made from locally grown almonds. If you have kids in tow, don't think twice about signing up for the fun marzipan-making workshop. (There's also a chocolate workshop.) Best of all, you take your creations home. ✉ Kfar Tabor Visitor Center, Keren Kayemet L'Yisrael Ave., Kfar Tavor ☎ 04/677–2111 ⊕ www.shakedtavor.co.il ☞ Museum free, workshop NIS 64 for children.

En Route ◉

If heading to the Sea of Galilee, take Route 767, which breaks off Route 65 at Kfar Tavor. It's a beautiful drive of about 25 minutes. The first village, **Kfar Kama**, is one of two in Israel of the Cherkessi (Circassian) community, Sunni Muslim non-Arabs from Russia's Caucasus Mountains who settled here in 1876. The unusually decorative minaret of the mosque is just one element of the tradition the community vigorously continues to preserve. On the descent to the Sea of Galilee, there's a parking area precisely at sea level. The lake is still more than 700 feet below, and the view is superb, especially in the afternoon.

Mount Tabor

MOUNTAIN—SIGHT | The domelike mountain, the region's highest, looms over one of the prettiest stretches of the Lower Galilee. Quilts of farmland kaleidoscope through the seasons as different crops grow, ripen, and are harvested. Modern woods of evergreens cover the hillsides, making this a lovely place for a walk or a hike. To get here from Route 7266, take the narrow switchback road that starts in a clearing between Shibli and the next village, Dabouriya.

Apart from the natural beauty, Mount Tabor and its immediate surroundings have considerable biblical history. About 32 centuries ago, Israelite warriors of the prophetess-judge Deborah and her general, Barak, routed a Canaanite chariot army that had gotten bogged down in the mud. The modern kibbutz of Ein Dor, south of the mountain, is the site of ancient Endor, where King Saul unsuccessfully beseeched the spirit of the prophet Samuel for help before his

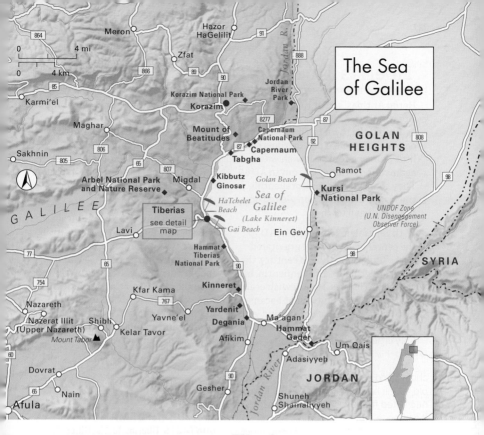

fateful (and fatal) battle against the Philistines (I Samuel 28:3–25). ✉ *Rte. 7266, Kfar Tavor* ⊕ *www.parks.org.il* ✉ *Free.*

Tabor Winery

WINERY/DISTILLERY | An excellent time-out from historical sights, this winery was founded in 1999, and the quality of its wines has risen steeply since 2005. Chill out with a cheese platter while tasting the winery's finest vintages. Tours are available for groups of more than 10 participants. ✉ *Kfar Tavor Visitor Center, Keren Kayemet L'Yisrael Ave., Kfar Tavor* ☎ *04/676–0444* ✉ *Free* ⊙ *Closed Sat.*

Tiberias

38 km (23½ miles) north of Beit She'an, 36 km (23 miles) east of Nazareth, 70 km (43 miles) east of Haifa.

As the only city on the Sea of Galilee, Tiberias, with a population of more than 40,000, has become the region's hub. The city spreads up a steep hillside, from 700 feet below sea level at the lake, to about 80 feet above sea level in its highest neighborhoods—a differential big enough to create significant variations in comfort levels during midsummer.

The splendid panoramic views of both the lake and the Golan Heights on the far shore deserved a better sort of development. Tiberias has little beauty and less

Tiberias Through Time

Herod Antipas, son of Herod the Great, founded Tiberias in AD 18 and dedicated the town to Tiberius, then emperor of Rome. The Tiberians had little stomach for the Jewish war against Rome that broke out in AD 66. They soon surrendered, preventing the vengeful destruction visited on other Galilean towns.

With Jerusalem laid waste in AD 70, the center of Jewish life gravitated to the Galilee. By the 4th century, the Jewish high court, the Sanhedrin, had settled in Tiberias. Here Jewish oral law was compiled into what became known as the Jerusalem Talmud, and Tiberias's status as one of Judaism's holy cities was assured.

Tiberias knew hard times under the Byzantines, and further declined under the hostile Crusaders in the Middle Ages. Starting in the 1700s, newcomers from Turkey and Eastern Europe swelled the Jewish population, but an 1837 earthquake left Tiberias in ruins.

Relations between Jews and Arabs were generally cordial until the Arab riots of 1936, when some 30 Jews were massacred. During the 1948 War of Independence, an attack by local Arabs brought a counterattack from Jewish forces, and the Arabs abandoned the town. Today the citizenry is entirely Jewish, and abandoned mosques stand as silent monuments.

charm, and although almost 2,000 years old, it still has the atmosphere of a place neglected for decades, if not centuries. It's at once brash and sleepy, with a reputation as a resort town based more on its location than its attractions. Travelers tend to see little of the town itself, sticking to the restaurants and hotels along the lake, and the boardwalk, which comes alive at night with vendors hawking clothes, jewelry, and knickknacks. Those traveling by car often skip the town altogether, opting for the numerous bed-and-breakfasts that dot the region.

GETTING HERE AND AROUND
The city sits astride the junction of Routes 90 and 77. Egged buses regularly serve Tiberias from Haifa, Nazareth, Tel Aviv, and Jerusalem. Haifa is one hour away, while Tel Aviv and Jerusalem are both two hours distant. Tiberias is small enough to walk to most locations, though given the punishing summer heat you may wish to have a taxi take you for even short jaunts.

TAXI CONTACTS HaEmek. ☎ *04/604–4888.* **Udi Taxi.** ☎ *072/221–4701.*

VISITOR INFORMATION
CONTACTS Tiberias Tourist Office. ✉ *9 Habanim St.* ☎ *04/672–5666.*

◉ Sights

Hammat Tiberias National Park
ARCHAEOLOGICAL SITE | This is where Israel's hottest spring gushes from the earth at 60°C (140°F) due to cracks in the earth's crust along the Syrian-African Rift. Alas, this is an archaeological site known for its superb mosaics, so you don't get to dip your toes into the waters here. (You can do that at the more impressive hot springs at Hammat Gader.)

By the end of the Second Temple period (the 1st century AD), when settlement in the Sea of Galilee region was at its height, a Jewish town called Hammat (Hot Springs) stood here. With time, Hammat was overshadowed by its newer neighbor, Tiberias. The benefits of the mineral hot springs were already legendary: a coin minted in Tiberias during the rule of Emperor Trajan, around AD 100, shows Hygeia, the goddess of health, sitting on a rock with a spring gushing out beneath it.

Parts of ancient Hammat have been uncovered, bringing to light a number of ruined synagogues. The most dramatic dates from the 4th century AD, with an elaborate mosaic floor that uses motifs almost identical to those at Beit Alfa: classical Jewish symbols, human figures representing the four seasons and the signs of the zodiac, and the Greek god Helios at the center. They are among the finest ever found in Israel.

As for how the spring was created, legend says that Solomon, the great king of Israel, wanted a hot bath and used his awesome authority to force some young devils below ground to heat the water. Seeing that the springs brought great happiness to his subjects, Solomon worried about what would happen when he died and the devils stopped their labors. Solomon made the hapless devils deaf, so to this day they continue to heat the water for fear of his wrath. ⊠ *Rechov HaMerchatzaot, Rte. 90 ✛ 2 km (1 mile) south of Tiberias* ☎ *04/672–5287* ⊕ *www. parks.org.il* ☜ *NIS 14.*

Promenade

HIKING/WALKING | A promenade ideal for walking or running follows the lakeshore for about 5 km (3 miles) south of Tiberias, with nice views of the lake and Golan Heights. As you leave the hotels behind, you appreciate the Sea of Galilee's mystic beauty. The path is lighted. ⊠ *Tiberias* ☜ *Free.*

Tiberias Hot Springs

HOT SPRINGS | In addition to sophisticated therapeutic services and facilities, this modern spa has a large, warm indoor mineral pool (35°C [95°F]) and a small

outdoor one right near the lake's edge. A restaurant serves lunch. ⊠ *Eliezer Kaplan Blvd. (Rte. 90)* ☎ *04/612–3600* ☜ *NIS 88.*

Tomb of Moses Maimonides

MEMORIAL | Foremost among Tiberias's many venerated resting places is this tomb. Born in Córdoba, Spain, Moses Maimonides (1135–1204)—widely known by his Hebrew acronym, the "Rambam" (for Rabbi Moshe Ben Maimon)—was the greatest Jewish scholar and spiritual authority of the Middle Ages. To his profound knowledge of the Talmud, Maimonides brought an incisive intellect honed by his study of Aristotelian philosophy and the physical sciences. The result was a rationalism unusual in Jewish scholarship and a lucidity of analysis and style admired by Jewish and non-Jewish scholars alike.

Maimonides never lived in Tiberias, but after his death in Egypt, his remains were brought to this Jewish holy city for interment. His whitewashed tomb, topped by a soaring spire of red steel girders, has become a shrine, dripping with candle wax and tears. ⊠ *Ben Zakkai St.* ☜ *Free* ☾ *Closed Sat.*

☺ Beaches

The Sea of Galilee—a freshwater lake—is a refreshing but rocky place for a swim. You can recline on pleasant commercial beaches with amenities ranging from cafeterias to water parks, or on free beaches with minimal facilities. Note that after several years of drought conditions in the region, the water level remains low.

September's Kinneret Swim, a tradition since 1953, has amateur (3½ km [2 miles] and 1½ km [1 mile]) categories.

Gai Beach

BEACH—SIGHT | Open May to October, Gai Beach has a private bathing beach and one of the country's most attractive water parks. **Amenities:** food and drink;

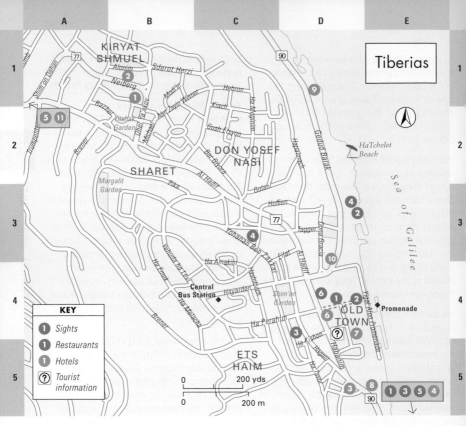

Tiberias

KEY
- 🔵 Sights
- 🔵 Restaurants
- 🔵 Hotels
- ❓ Tourist information

0 ————— 200 yds
0 ————— 200 m

Sights ▼

1 Hammat Tiberias National Park............ **E5**
2 Promenade.............. **D4**
3 Tiberias Hot Springs..... **E5**
4 Tomb of Maimonides....**C3**

Restaurants ▼

1 Big Ben Pub............. **D4**
2 Decks.................... **D3**
3 Guy...................... **D4**
4 Pagoda.................. **D3**
5 Rene..................... **E5**
6 Yali's Coffee Shop and Restaurant......... **D4**

Hotels ▼

1 Astoria................... **B1**
2 Beit Berger.............. **B1**
3 Emily's Boutique Hotel..................... **D5**
4 Gai Beach Hotel......... **E5**
5 Lavi Kibbutz Hotel....... **A2**
6 Leonardo Club Hotel Tiberias........... **D4**
7 Leonardo Plaza Hotel Tiberias........... **D4**
8 Rimonim Galei Kinnereth................. **E5**
9 Ron Beach Hotel........ **D1**
10 Scots Hotel.............. **D3**
11 Shavit's Arbel Guest House............. **A2**

lifeguards; parking (fee); showers; toilets; water sports. **Best for:** swimming. ✉ *Rte. 90* ☎ *04/670–0713* 🎟 *NIS 99.*

HaTchelet Beach

BEACH—SIGHT | Near the northern entrance to Tiberias, this well-kept private beach is open May to October. Picnic areas and raft rentals are available. **Amenities:** food and drink; lifeguards; parking (fee); showers; toilets; water sports. **Best for:** swimming. ✉ *Rte. 90* ☎ *04/672–0105* 🎟 *NIS 50.*

🍴 Restaurants

At a right angle to the waterside promenade, the *midrachov* (pedestrian mall) has a wide range of affordable dining options. If you're into local color, look for the tiny, modest restaurants (where English really *is* a foreign language) on Hagalil Street and in the little streets that connect it to Habanim Street, like the pedestrian-only Kishon Street.

Big Ben Pub (*Big Ben BBQ Restaurant*)

$$ | BRITISH | FAMILY | You can't miss Big Ben, just at the top of the boardwalk; this casual spot is practically a landmark. An outdoor terrace with seating overlooks the promenade, and inside, a beautiful antique wooden bar features eight beers on tap. **Known for:** casual dining; easy to find; easy access to boardwalk. [$] *Average main: NIS 70* ✉ *Tiberias Promenade* ✣ *On waterfront near Caesar Hotel* ☎ *53/944–0764* 🌐 *bigben.rest.co.il* 💳 *No credit cards.*

Decks

$$$ | MODERN ISRAELI | Built on a pier extending into the Sea of Galilee, this family-run restaurant has breathtaking views from seats indoors and outside. This airy, casual spot with wooden tables and metal chairs is something of an institution, and locals keep coming back for the delicious meats—sizzling steaks, succulent goose liver, or long skewers of veal and vegetables, grilled slowly over hickory wood. **Known for:** homemade fare; grilled meats; casual dining. [$] *Average main: NIS 100* ✉ *11 HaGdud Barak St.* ☎ *04/671–0800* 🌐 *www.decks.co.il* ⏲ *No dinner Fri. No lunch Sat.*

Guy

$ | MIDDLE EASTERN | Stuffed vegetables are the calling card at this kosher eatery, whose name means "ravine" in Hebrew. The cook-matriarch Geula comes from a Tiberias family, but her Moroccan ancestry shines through in delicious dishes like eggplant stuffed with seasoned ground beef. **Known for:** homemade Moroccan food; stuffed vegetables; lovely views. [$] *Average main: NIS 48* ✉ *52 Hagalil St.* ☎ *04/672–3036* 💳 *No credit cards* ⏲ *Closed Sat. No dinner Fri.*

Pagoda

$$ | ASIAN | This faux-Chinese temple has an outdoor patio overlooking the lake, and across the road is a maze of more intimate rooms entered through a garden. The kosher menu of various Asian cuisines and some international favorites is identical at both places, so pick your favorite and try the Thai soups (such as the tasty hot-and-sour soup), the lamb spareribs, or strips of beef with peanut sauce. **Known for:** pan-Asian menu; sushi bar; kosher restaurant. [$] *Average main: NIS 75* ✉ *Gedud Barak St.* ☎ *04/671–0800* ⏲ *Closed Sat. No dinner Fri.*

Rene

$$ | CAFÉ | An impressive brick building and a terrace with lovely views of the Sea of Galilee are great draws. The dairy and salad menu of this bistro, bar, and café has a fine selection of breakfast dishes, salads, pasta, calzones, sandwiches, quiche, and desserts. **Known for:** beautiful views of the sea; dairy menu with cheese blintzes; casual dining. [$] *Average main: NIS 70* ✉ *Eliezar Kaplan Blvd.* ✣ *Across from Tiberias Hot Springs*

☎ 04/646–2323 🌐 renebistrobarcafe.co.il 🕒 Closed Fri. No lunch Sat.

Yali's Coffee Shop and Restaurant

$$ | **ISRAELI** | This quiet, modern café is a good place for a meal anytime. The menu features pasta, pizza, and salads as well as breakfast items. **Known for:** upgraded café fare; people-watching; all-day menu. *[$] Average main: NIS 60 ✉ 4 HaBanim St. ☎ 04/999–7996 🕒 Closed Fri. afternoon, Sat. 💳 No credit cards.*

Hotels

Astoria

$ | **HOTEL** | One of Tiberias's better moderately priced hotels, the Astoria is set away from the lake, but don't worry; there are still views from some of the guest rooms. **Pros:** good value; some rooms with water views; family friendly. **Cons:** too far to walk downtown; basic decor; no nightlife. *[$] Rooms from: $160 ✉ 13 Bruria St. ☎ 04/672–2351 🌐 www.astoria.co.il 🛏 100 rooms 🍴 Free Breakfast.*

Beit Berger

$ | **HOTEL** | This family-run hotel has spacious rooms, most with balconies. **Pros:** reasonable rates; hillside views; handy kitchens. **Cons:** too far to walk downtown; no swimming pool; no nightlife. *[$] Rooms from: $120 ✉ 27 Neiberg St. ☎ 04/671–5151 🌐 www.bergerhotel.co.il 🛏 43 rooms 🍴 Free Breakfast.*

★ Emily's Boutique Hotel

$$ | **HOTEL** | On-site parking and a central location attracts young and budget-watching tourists to this small, family-owned boutique hotel, one of Tiberias's newer hotels. **Pros:** friendly staff; reasonably priced; easy access to attractions. **Cons:** on main road; no parking; room may seem small for American standards. *[$] Rooms from: $220 ✉ 66 HaGalil St. ☎ 04/664–7500 🌐 emilys_hotel.xwx.co.il 🛏 48 rooms 🍴 Free Breakfast.*

Gai Beach Hotel

$$$ | **RESORT** | **FAMILY** | The rare lakeshore location is a big plus, and for some, so is the distance from the noisy downtown promenade. **Pros:** on the lake; gorgeous spa; far from the hubbub. **Cons:** a bit isolated; crowded on weekends; water park attracts rambunctious kids. *[$] Rooms from: $400 ✉ Rte. 90 ☎ 04/670–0700 🌐 www.gaibeach.co.il 🛏 198 rooms 🍴 Free Breakfast.*

Lavi Kibbutz Hotel

$$ | **HOTEL** | With a peaceful rural location, high on a mountain, the relaxed kibbutz atmosphere of this hotel mainly caters to Jewish religious travelers and family groups. **Pros:** opportunity to experience kibbutz life; central location; good children's programs. **Cons:** no evening entertainment; the kibbutz is religious so no checking in or out Friday evening and Saturday; public area furnishings need freshening up. *[$] Rooms from: $250 ✉ Rte. 77, Lavi ✥ 11 km (7 miles) west of Tiberias ☎ 77/997–5501 🌐 hotel.lavi.co.il 🛏 184 rooms 🍴 Free Breakfast.*

Leonardo Club Hotel Tiberias

$$ | **HOTEL** | **FAMILY** | Cascading down a hillside, this all-inclusive, all-suites hotel boasts an unimpeded view of the lake. **Pros:** spectacular views; spacious rooms; resort feel. **Cons:** crowded on weekends; away from downtown; can get loud. *[$] Rooms from: $300 ✉ HaBanim St. ☎ 04/671–4444 🌐 www.leonardo-hotels.com 🛏 400 rooms 🍴 All-inclusive.*

Leonardo Plaza Hotel Tiberias

$$$ | **HOTEL** | With lake views, comfortable rooms, relaxing common areas, and a variety of spa services, the Leonardo Plaza is a welcoming spot. **Pros:** convenient to Tiberias; lake views from most rooms; most luxurious of the city's Leonardo hotels. **Cons:** no beach. *[$] Rooms from: $310 ✉ 1 Habanim St. ☎ 04/671–3333 🌐 www.leonardo-hotels.com 🛏 262 rooms 🍴 Free Breakfast.*

The god Helios occupies the center of a spectacular 4th-century mosaic of the zodiac at Hammat Tiberias.

Rimonim Galei Kinnereth

$$$ | **HOTEL** | It's easy to understand why this resort was a personal favorite of Israel's founding prime minister, David Ben-Gurion: its location on the lake with its own private beach is unbeatable. **Pros:** convenient to Tiberias; lakeside swimming pool; quiet atmosphere. **Cons:** can be crowded on weekends and in summer; lunch included on weekends only. [$] *Rooms from: $350* ✉ *1 Eliezer Kaplan St.* ☎ *04/672–8888* 🌐 *www.rimonim.com* 🛏 *120 rooms* 🍴 *Some meals.*

Ron Beach Hotel

$$ | **HOTEL** | The family-run establishment is the northernmost hotel in Tiberias and has rare private lake frontage, though no beach. **Pros:** lakeside location; pretty pool; good value. **Cons:** too far to walk to downtown; no beach. [$] *Rooms from: $244* ✉ *Gedud Barak St.* ☎ *04/679–1350* 🌐 *www.ronbeachhotel.com* 🛏 *127 rooms* 🍴 *Free Breakfast.*

★ Scots Hotel

$$$$ | **HOTEL** | This upscale hotel, with a contemporary structure linking two older, superbly refurbished Ottoman-style ones, has a pleasingly asymmetrical design filled with pleasant surprises, such as a roof terrace, where you can enjoy a drink or light meal. **Pros:** boutique-hotel feel; historic setting; central location; private beach. **Cons:** no nightly entertainment. [$] *Rooms from: $450* ✉ *1 Gedud Barak St., at Hayarden St.* ☎ *04/671–0710* 🌐 *www.scotshotels.co.il* 🛏 *69 rooms* 🍴 *Free Breakfast.*

Shavit's Arbel Guest House

$$ | **B&B/INN** | A riot of greenery, including an inviting *bustan* (a local-style garden redolent with fragrant herbs), surrounds this inn, which has whirlpools and wooden balconies. **Pros:** warm host is a licensed tour guide and chef; delicious food; pretty grounds. **Cons:** far from downtown Tiberias. [$] *Rooms from: $200* ✉ *Rte. 7717, off Rte. 77, Arbel Village* ☎ *04/679–4919* 🌐 *www.4shavit.com* 🛏 *5 suites* 🍴 *Free Breakfast.*

🎭 Performing Arts

Much of the entertainment, especially in the larger hotels in Tiberias, is of the live lounge-music variety: piano bars, one-man dance bands, and crooners. Generally speaking, the younger set wouldn't be caught dead here, preferring to hang out at one of the few pubs, where the recorded rock music is good and loud and the beer is on tap.

Bet Gabriel

ARTS CENTERS | This cultural center is located on the southern shore of the Sea of Galilee, a 10-minute drive from Tiberias. Its fine architecture, beautiful garden setting, movie theater, galleries for changing art exhibits, and concert facilities have established its popularity in the area. ⊠ Rte. 92 ✛ East of Tzemach Junction ☎ 04/675–1175 ⊕ www.betgabriel.co.il.

👜 Shopping

Tiberias relies heavily on tourism yet has little particularly interesting in the way of shopping. The exception is jewelry. There are a few jewelry stores near the intersection of Habanim and Hayarden streets and in some of the better hotels.

Big Center Tiberias

SHOPPING CENTERS/MALLS | Take a break from the hot, sticky weather in the city's newest mall, just five minutes on foot from the Central Bus Station. Home to 150 stores, restaurants, and coffee shops, this is where the locals go for a shawarma or slice of pizza and to escape the punishing heat. ⊠ 1 Yehuda HaLevi St. ☎ 072/360–0477 ⊕ www.bigcenters. co.il ۞ Closed Fri. evening and Sat.

🏃 Activities

WATER SPORTS

At several locations around the Sea of Galilee, you can hire pedal boats, rowboats, and motorboats and arrange to water-ski. Serious kayakers convene for an annual international competition in March.

Holyland Sailing

BOATING | This company has seven wooden boats that are replicas of those in use during the time of Jesus. The 45-minute cruises include historical commentary and concerts of traditional music. Sunset cruises are especially popular. Groups of 20 people can order a cruise for $150, while smaller groups can take sunset sails or call ahead and see if they can join an existing group for $15 per person. Private charters are available too. ⊠ Tiberias Marina ☎ 04/672–3006 ⊕ jesusboats. com.

Arbel National Park and Nature Reserve

8 km (5 miles) northwest of Tiberias.

Jesus is said to have preached and performed miracles at the foot of Mount Arbel, which is now a popular nature reserve. The reserve has few trees, but, depending on the season, there are flowers and small fauna.

GETTING HERE AND AROUND

To get here from the Tiberias-Golani junction road (Route 77), turn at the Kfar Hittim junction to Route 7717. Turn right at the turnoff for Moshav Arbel, then turn left.

Kibbutz Life Then and Now

Israel's founding fathers and mothers would probably be bewildered by life on a 21st-century kibbutz (a collective settlement, but literally translated as "a gathering"). Many of the country's founders came from Russia in the early 20th century, inspired by Zionist ideals of returning to their ancestral homeland and a work ethic that regarded manual labor as an almost spiritual value. They were socialists who believed "from each according to his ability, to each according to his need."

Early Days

Degania, the first kibbutz, was founded in 1909 on the shores of the Sea of Galilee, where 10 men and 2 women began to work the land. The utopian ideology, in which individual desires were subordinated to the needs of the community, was wedded to the need for a close-knit communal structure, in order to cope with forbidding terrain and a hostile neighborhood. Life was arduous, but their numbers grew.

Kibbutzim played a considerable role in molding the fledgling state, absorbing immigrants, and developing agriculture. By 1950, two years after Israel's independence, there were more than 200 kibbutzim. Their egalitarian ethos meant that all shared chores and responsibility—but also ownership of the means of production. The kibbutz movement became the world's largest communitarian movement.

Growth and Challenge

With time, many kibbutzim introduced light industry or tourism enterprises, and some became successful businesses. The standard of living improved, and kibbutzim took advantage of easy bank loans. When Israel's hyperinflation reached 454% during the mid-1980s, many communities found themselves bankrupt. Change became inevitable, and the movement peaked around 1990, when the almost 270 kibbutzim across the country reached 130,000 members. (An individual kibbutz can range from fewer than 100 to more than 1,000 members.)

The Kibbutz Today

In today's Israel, many young "kibbutzniks," after compulsory military service or university studies, have found the kibbutz ethos stifling and have opted for the individualism and material attractions of city life. Despite the changes, city folk, volunteers, and tourists are still drawn to this rural environment, which has a slower pace.

Only some 15% of kibbutz members now work in agriculture, though they account for a significant proportion of the national production. Industry, services, and tourism—including kibbutz guesthouses and hotels—are the real sources of income. Differential wage systems have been introduced, and foreign laborers often provide menial labor in fields and factories. All kibbutzim have abandoned children's dormitories, instead allowing parents to raise their children in a family home.

Many members of the older generation have become distressed by what they see as the contamination of pioneering principles. But reality bites hard, and ironically, only those kibbutzim that succeed economically can afford to remain socialist.

◉ Sights

Arbel National Park and Nature Reserve
MOUNTAIN—SIGHT | This 2,600-acre park sits on a plateau that slopes from the Arbel Valley to a towering cliff at the top of Mount Arbel, with panoramic views of the Sea of Galilee, the Golan Heights, and Mount Hermon beyond. Ancient texts indicate that the Seleucid Greeks conquered the Biblical-era Jews of Arbel while making their way to Jerusalem. Roman historian Flavius Josephus describes a battle here in 37 BC between the Jews and Marc Antony, who had been sent to suppress the Jewish rebellion. According to Josephus, the Jews were "lurking in caves... opening up onto mountain precipices that were inaccessible from any quarter except by torturous and narrow paths." Antony eventually crushed the rebels by lowering his soldiers into the caves from above. Today, hikers can take trails to that fortress of natural caves, and see other evidence of ancient settlements, including the ruins of an ancient synagogue. ⊠ *Rte. 7717, Tiberias* ☎ *04/673–2904* ⊕ *www.parks. org.il* ⊠ *NIS 22.*

Kibbutz Ginosar

10 km (6 miles) north of Tiberias.

Many Israelis know Ginosar, a kibbutz founded in 1937, as the home of the late Yigal Allon (1918–80), commander of the crack Palmach battalions in the War of Independence and deputy prime minister of Israel in the 1970s under Golda Meir and Yitzhak Rabin. Travelers, however, come here to see the ancient fishing boat.

GETTING HERE AND AROUND
Egged buses frequently make the short trip here from the Tiberias Central Bus Station. Ask the driver to tell you where to get off.

Kibbutz Music 🎵

Nof Ginosar hosts the twice-annual **Jacob's Ladder Festival** (⊕ *www. jlfestival.com*), a perennial favorite for folk-music fans. The music is eclectic, with international artists performing anything from Celtic to country classics. The crowd is equally diverse, coming from the United States, Canada, Britain, and around the world.

◉ Sights

Yigal Alon Museum
ARCHAEOLOGICAL SITE | Kibbutz Ginosar's premier tourist attraction is a wooden fishing boat from the 1st century AD, found on the shore by two amateur archaeologists in 1986. Today it is beautifully exhibited in all its modest but evocative glory in a specially built pavilion in the Yigal Alon Museum: a short video tells the story. Three years of drought had lowered the level of Lake Kinneret and exposed bits of the ancient wood in the mud. Excavated in a frenetic 11 days, the 28-foot-long boat became an instant media sensation. Given the frequency of New Testament references to Jesus and his disciples boating on the Sea of Galilee—including coming ashore at Gennesaret, perhaps today's Ginosar—the press immediately dubbed it the "Jesus Boat."

On the other hand, the vivid relic might have been a victim of the Roman naval victory over the rebellious Jewish townspeople of nearby Magdala in AD 67, as described by the historian Flavius Josephus. Whatever its unknown history, it is the most complete boat this old ever found in an inland waterway anywhere in the world. ⊠ *Nof Ginosar, Off Rte. 90* ☎ *04/672–7700* ⊕ *bet-alon.co.il* ⊠ *NIS 20.*

Churches are among the sights along the peaceful shores of the Sea of Galilee.

Restaurants

★ Magdalena Chef Restaurant

$$$$ | INTERNATIONAL | Located in the "holy triangle," an area north of the Sea of Galilee considered to be one of the most important pilgrimage sites in the world, Magdalena upgrades Galilee-style Arabic food into contemporary gourmet. Using mostly local ingredients, Magdelena's menu includes Christian-Arab cuisine with influences of Lebanese and Mediterranean traditions. **Known for:** new Arab cuisine; fish dishes; stunning hillside and lake views. $ *Average main: NIS 150 ⊠ Migdal Junction compound, Rte. 90, Migdal* ☎ *04/673–0064* ⊕ *www. magdalena.co.il.*

Tanureen Authentic Lebanese Restaurant

$$$ | LEBANESE | No fewer than 20 fresh salads of seasonal produce and traditional recipes arrive at your table in this large and efficient dining room. Catering to busloads of tourists, the dining room is surprisingly quiet, and small groups do not feel outnumbered. **Known for:** delicious salads; grilled fish; big groups. $ *Average main: NIS 85 ⊠ Sonol Gas Station, Rte. 90, Tiberias-Migdal Rd., Migdal* ☎ *053/809-6629* ⊕ *tanureen.rest. co.il.*

🛏 Hotels

Ginosar Village

$$ | B&B/INN | Its grand location—with a private beach right on the Sea of Galilee—makes this kibbutz guesthouse near Tiberias especially popular. **Pros:** convenient location; opportunity to experience kibbutz life; beautiful gardens. **Cons:** too far to walk to town; no evening entertainment. $ *Rooms from: $275 ⊠ Rte. 90* ☎ *04/670–0300* ⊕ *www.ginosar.co.il* ⤳ *243 rooms* ⦿❙ *Free Breakfast.*

Tabgha

4 km (2½ miles) north of Ginosar, 14 km (8 miles) north of Tiberias, at Capernaum Junction (Rtes. 90 and 87).

With a name that's an Arabic corruption of the Greek *Heptaegon* (Seven Springs), Tabgha is a cluster of serene holy places associated with Jesus's ministry in the Galilee. A promenade and hiking trails connect the shrines.

GETTING HERE AND AROUND

Tabgha is located off Route 87, a few hundred meters from the junction with Route 90. A promenade connects the Church of the Multiplication with the Church of the Primacy of St. Peter. A trail leads up to the Mount of Beatitudes, but the hike is best enjoyed going downhill, with the glorious views of the lake in front of you.

◉ Sights

Church of the Multiplication

RELIGIOUS SITE | The German Benedictines dedicated this large, orange-roofed Roman Catholic church in 1936 on the scanty remains of earlier shrines. The site has long been venerated as the "deserted place" (Mark 6:30–6:34) where Jesus miraculously multiplied two fishes and five loaves of bread to feed the crowds. The present airy limestone building with the wooden-truss ceiling was built in the style of a Byzantine basilica to give a fitting context to the beautifully wrought 5th-century mosaic floor depicting the loaves and fishes in front of the altar. The nave is covered with geometric designs, but the front of the aisles is filled with flora and birds and, curiously, a nilometer, a graded column once used to measure the flood level of the Nile for the purpose of assessing that year's collectible taxes. ⊠ *Rte. 87, Ginosar* ☎ *04/667–8100* 🎫 *Free.*

Church of the Primacy of St. Peter

RELIGIOUS SITE | The austere, black basalt church, just east of the Church of the Multiplication, is built on the water's edge, over a flat rock known as *Mensa Christi* (the Table of Christ). After his resurrection, the New Testament relates, Jesus appeared to his disciples by the Sea of Galilee and presented them a miraculous catch of fish. Three times Jesus asked his disciple Peter if he loved him, and after his reply of "You know that I love you," Jesus commanded him to "feed my sheep" (John 21:17). Some scholars see this affirmation as Peter's atonement for having thrice denied Jesus in Jerusalem. The episode is seen as establishing Peter's "primacy." ⊠ *Rte. 87, Ginosar* ☎ *04/672–4767* 🎫 *Free.*

Mount of Beatitudes

8 km (5 miles) north of Ginosar, 3 km (2 miles) north of Capernaum Junction.

Tradition identifies this tranquil hillside as the site of Jesus's most comprehensive teaching, recorded in the New Testament as the Sermon on the Mount: "And seeing the multitudes, he went up into a mountain; and when he was set, his disciples came unto him. And he opened his mouth, and taught them, saying: 'Blessed are the poor in spirit, for theirs is the kingdom of Heaven'" (Matthew 5:3).

GETTING HERE AND AROUND

It's best to drive here. Lots of tourist buses make the journey, but there's no public transportation. It's on a spur road off the main lake road, atop a hill.

◉ Sights

Church of the Beatitudes

RELIGIOUS SITE | This domed Roman Catholic church, run by the Franciscan Sisters, was designed by the famous architect and monk Antonio Barluzzi. Commissioned by Fascist leader Benito Mussolini while he was dictator of Italy, the church was completed in 1937. The windows are inscribed with the opening words of the Sermon on the Mount. The terrace surrounding the church has a superb view of the Sea of Galilee, best enjoyed in the afternoon when the diffused western sun softens the light and heightens colors. Keep in mind this is a pilgrimage site, so dress modestly and respect the silence. The gardens on the Mount of Beatitudes and the church open daily at 8 am, but they close from noon until 2:30 pm. ✉ *Rte. 8177, off Rte. 90, Ginosar* ☎ *04/672–6712* 🎟 *NIS 10 per vehicle.*

Korazim

Rte. 8277 at Rte. 90, 6 km (4 miles) north of Capernaum Junction.

Built on a basalt bluff a few miles north of the Sea of Galilee, the town of Korazim has long been renowned for its high-quality wheat. It's famous as the home of Korazim National Park.

GETTING HERE AND AROUND

Scenic Route 8277 has some breathtaking views of the Sea of Galilee far below, but you need a car to enjoy them. There's no public transit to Korazim. Consider saddling up a horse from the stables at Vered Hagalil and riding here.

Sights

Korazim National Park

ARCHAEOLOGICAL SITE | These extensive and often remarkable ruins, dating from the 4th or 5th century AD, are on the site of the ancient Jewish village that Jesus condemned for rejecting him (Matthew 11:21). The monumental basalt synagogue is decorated with the stone carvings of plants and animals. One remarkable artifact, a decorated and inscribed stone "armchair" dubbed the Throne of Moses, is thought to have been used by the worthies of the community during the reading of the Torah. The views of the Sea of Galilee are also impressive. ✉ *Rte. 8277* ☎ *04/693–4982* 🌐 *www.parks.org.il* 🎟 *NIS 22.*

Hotels

The Frenkels Bed-and-Breakfast

$ | **B&B/INN** | Americans Etha and Irwin Frenkel retired to this rustic village on the border between the Lower and Upper Galilee and have made gracious hospitality a second career. **Pros:** convenient to national parks; charming rooms; pleasant hosts. **Cons:** no evening entertainment; no telephones in rooms; some may consider it too quiet. [$] *Rooms from: $160* ✉ *Rte. 8277* ☎ *04/680–1686* 🌐 *www.thefrenkels.com* 💳 *No credit cards* 🛏 *3 suites* 🍴 *Free Breakfast.*

Vered Hagalil Guest Farm

$$ | **RESORT** | Yehuda Avni and his Jerusalem-born wife Yonah have created something special in Israel: a ranch where guests can ride horses during the day and retire to cozy rooms at night. **Pros:** best stables in the area; convenient to national parks; panoramic views. **Cons:** no evening entertainment; quite a far drive to other sites; limited food options. [$] *Rooms from: $220* ✉ *Rtes. 8277 and 90* ☎ *04/693–5785* 🌐 *veredhagalil.com* 🛏 *30 rooms* 🍴 *Free Breakfast.*

Capernaum

3 km (2 miles) east of Tabgha and the Capernaum Junction, 17 km (10½ miles) northeast of Tiberias.

A must-see destination for many Christian travelers, Capernaum is one of the places most often associated with Jesus. Many of the sites mentioned in the Gospels are found in and around Capernaum National Park.

Anyone raised on spirituals extolling the Jordan River's width and depth will be

Capernaum was the base of Jesus's Galilean ministry, but the synagogue remains date from a later era.

surprised to find how small a stream it really is. The Jordan enters the Sea of Galilee near Capernaum.

GETTING HERE AND AROUND

Capernaum is on Route 87, east of the intersection with Route 90. Since buses leave you a few miles from the site, it's best to drive.

◉ Sights

★ Capernaum National Park

ARCHAEOLOGICAL SITE | For Christians, this park is among the most moving places in Israel, because it's where Jesus established his base for three years and recruited some of his disciples ("Follow me, and I will make you fishers of men" [Matthew 4:19]). It is also the site of the House of St. Peter, the ruins of an actual home where Jesus is believed to have lodged. Astride the ruins is an ultramodern Franciscan church, looking a bit like a spaceship.

Capernaum is also a site of interest to Jews, and the prosperity of the ancient Jewish community (it is *Kfar Nahum* in Hebrew) is immediately apparent from the remains of its synagogue, which dominates the complex. Once thought to date to the 2nd or 3rd century AD, the synagogue is now regarded by many scholars as belonging to the later Byzantine period (4th–5th centuries AD).

Limestone reliefs on the synagogue exterior represent a typical range of Jewish artistic motifs: the native fruits of the land, the biblical Ark of the Covenant, a seven-branched menorah, a shofar, and an incense shovel (to preserve the memory of the Temple in Jerusalem, where they were used prior to the city's destruction in AD 70). A small 1st-century mosaic from Magdala shows a contemporary boat, complete with oars and sails—a dramatic illustration of the many New Testament and Jewish references to fishing on the lake.

Jesus eventually cursed the people of Capernaum for failing to heed his message, saying "And you, Capernaum, will you be lifted up to the skies? No, you will go down to the depths" (Matthew 11:23–24). When visiting Capernaum, dress appropriately: you aren't allowed in shorts or a sleeveless shirt. ⊠ *Rte. 87* ☎ *04/679–3865* ⊕ *www.parks.org.il* 🎫 *Free.*

Jordan River Park

ARCHAEOLOGICAL SITE | Jordan River Park extends over an area of approximately 250 acres where the Jordan River meets the Sea of Galilee. There are several notable ancient sites in the park, including Tabgha, Katzrin Archeological Park, and Bethsaida. Well-marked sites, footpaths, and hiking routes make it easy to navigate the treasures of this national park. In the southeast section, archaeologists have partially excavated an ancient fishing village. It includes the remains (now rubble) of several homes that provide an idea of how communal life once occurred here. Now, as then, the village has a view of the Sea of Galilee (though the shoreline moved drastically in an earthquake in AD 363). A shaded and serene sitting area includes arrows pointing to other Christian sites around the lake. Other than sitting area, shade is limited here, so bring a hat and plenty of water. Several well-marked hiking trails lead to sites of historical and religious importance. Jordan River Park is 9 km (5½ miles) northeast of Capernaum. ⊠ *Rte. 888, Bethsaida* ☎ *04/692–3422* ⊕ *www.kkl-jnf.org* 🎫 *NIS 60 per car.*

🏃 Activities

Abukayak

WATER SPORTS | Northeast of Capernaum, this outfitter's so-called kayaks are really inflated rubber canoes, used for serene one-hour paddles down the lower Jordan River; a truck picks you up at the end. Life jackets are provided, and the trip is appropriate for young children. ⊠ *Jordan River Park, Rte. 888, Bethsaida* ☎ *04/692–1078* ⊕ *www.abukayak.co.il* 🎫 *NIS 90* ⤙ *Closed Sat. and Dec.–Feb.*

Kursi National Park

Kursi is 17 km (10½ miles) southeast of Capernaum on Rte. 92, 5 km (3 miles) north of Ein Gev.

Kursi, where Jesus healed two men possessed by demons (Matthew 8:28–32), is today a park incorporating the ruins of a Byzantine monastery. The eastern shore of the Sea of Galilee is far less developed, retaining more of its relatively rural character than the western and northern sides.

GETTING HERE AND AROUND

Route 92 follows the eastern shore of the Sea of Galilee, while Route 87 circles to the north of the lake. You can reach Kursi either by driving north or south from Tiberias. Whether you circle the lake clockwise or counterclockwise, the views are often breathtaking.

👁 Sights

Kursi National Park

ARCHAEOLOGICAL SITE | Huddling under the imposing cliffs of Golan Heights, where Route 789 climbs away from 92, this place is linked with the New Testament story of a man possessed by demons. Jesus exorcised the spirits, causing them to enter a herd of swine grazing nearby, which then "rushed down the steep bank into the lake, and perished in the waters" (Matthew 8:32). Fifth-century Byzantine Christians identified the event with this spot and built a monastery. It was an era in which earnest pilgrims inundated the holy places, and the monastery prospered from their gifts. The partly restored ruins of a fine Byzantine church are a classic example of the basilica style common at the time; the ruined monastery is higher up the hillside. ⊠ *Rte. 92, Kursi* ☎ *04/673–1983* ⊕ *www.parks.org.il* ◱ *NIS 14.*

🏖 Beaches

The shoreline of the Sea of Galilee has receded somewhat with the low level of the water, and the bottom now drops precipitously. Keep a close eye on children.

Golan Beach

BEACH—SIGHT | The best-known beach on the lake's northeastern shore has powerboat, rowboat, kayak, and pedal-boat rentals, as well as waterskiing and other water sports. It's also home of LunaGal water park. **Amenities:** food and drink; lifeguards; parking (fee); showers; toilets; water sports. **Best for:** swimming. ⊠ *Rte. 92, Kursi* ⊕ *7 km (4½ miles) north of Ein Gev* ☎ *04/667–8010* ◱ *NIS 6 for 3 hrs of parking.*

Kursi–Lavnun–Halukim Beach

BEACH—SIGHT | Each of the three beaches has its own personality: the Lavnun (named after an indigenous fish) and Halukim ("pebbles") beaches have vast lawns with abundant shade. You must wear shoes on Halukim Beach, because it is, indeed, filled with pebbles. Young people with grills and music find Kursi (named after the nearby Byzantine Church) and Lavnun more attractive, while families and those seeking a quieter experience find the Halukim Beach more to their liking. **Amenities:** food and drink; lifeguards; parking (fee); showers; toilets. **Best for:** swimming. ⊠ *Rte. 92, located 3 km (2 miles) north of Ein Gev, Kursi* ◱ *NIS 6 for 3 hrs of parking.*

🍴 Restaurants

Ein Gev Fish Restaurant

$$$ | **MIDDLE EASTERN** | At lunchtime this popular establishment on the eastern shore bustles with tour groups, but it's a fine dinner option, too. Famous for St. Peter's fish, it has added sea bream, trout, and gray mullet to the menu, as well as entrées such as quiche, pizza, pasta, and salads. **Known for:** fish specialties; lovely views; local favorite. $ *Average main: NIS 80* ⊠ *Kibbutz Ein Gev, Rte. 92, Ein Gev* ☎ *053/944–4101* ⊕ *www.eingev.co.il.*

Marinado

$$$$ | **BARBECUE** | Marinado started as a cattle ranch and is still a butcher and gourmet food shop. It is the only restaurant in Israel that produces its own meat, wine, and olive oil. **Known for:** artisan meats, wine, and olive oil; beef dishes; lovely sea views. $ *Average main: NIS 150* ⊠ *Kibbutz Ein Gev, Off Rte. 92, Ein Gev* ☎ *04/665–8555* ⊕ *marinado.rest. co.il.*

🏨 Hotels

Ein Gev Holiday Resort

$ | **RESORT** | **FAMILY** | Located on the palm-shaded eastern shore of the Sea of Galilee, this complex has everything from waterfront units with sunset-watching patios to spacious apartments with room for the whole family. **Pros:** private beach; convenient to national parks; convenient for family groups. **Cons:** no evening entertainment; cook your own food; need a car to get around. $ *Rooms from: $180* ⊠ *Rte. 92, Ein Gev* ⊕ *12 km (7½ miles) north of Tzemach Junction* ☎ *04/665–9800* ⊕ *www.eingev.com* ⤢ *178 rooms* ⦿I *Free Breakfast.*

Activities

Ein Gev Spring Festival

MUSIC FESTIVALS | This festival's focus is Israeli vocal music, from traditional to contemporary. It is held on Kibbutz Ein Gev during Passover each spring. ⊠ *Kibbutz Ein Gev, Off Rte. 92, Ein Gev* ☎ *04/675–1195.*

Hammat Gader

10 km (6 miles) east of Tzemach Junction on Rte. 98, 22 km (14 miles) southeast of Tiberias, 36 km (22½ miles) northeast of Beit She'an.

Built around three hot springs, the impressive complex of baths and pools at Hammat Gader attests to its opulence during the time of the Romans. The large number of ancient clay oil lamps found in one small pool is proof of nighttime bathing.

GETTING HERE AND AROUND

Whether you're driving via Tiberias (Route 90) or the Golan Heights (Route 98), this highway is one of the most captivating in Israel, with expansive views across the Yarmuk River into Jordan. Don't leave the roadway. The minefield signs mean exactly what they say.

Sights

Hammat Gader

AMUSEMENT PARK/WATER PARK | FAMILY | Popular with Israelis—who come for the freshwater and mineral pools, giant waterslide, alligator farm, performing parrots, petting zoo, and restaurants—this place has history, too: in its heyday, it was the second-largest spa in the Roman Empire (after Baiae, near Naples). There's a hotel, a spa, and restaurants here, too. ✉ *Rte. 98* ☎ *04/665–9999* 🌐 *www.hamat-gader.com* 🎫 *NIS 105.*

Hotels

Spa Village at Hammat Gader

$$$ | RESORT | In a Thai-style complex that's a world apart from anything else in this region, these recently renovated suites have hot tubs that use thermal mineral water from the nearby springs. **Pros:** sybaritic experience; tropical gardens; pampering staff. **Cons:** no evening entertainment; no room service; no Wi-Fi in rooms. [$] *Rooms from: $400* ✉ *Rte. 98, Tiberias* ☎ *04/665–5555* 🌐 *www.spa-village.co.il* 🛏 *29 suites* 🍴 *Some meals.*

Degania, Kinneret, and Yardenit

Degania Alef: 10 km (6 miles) south of Tiberias; Kinneret: 2 km (1 mile) northwest of Degania Alef.

Degania and Kinneret, two historic kibbutzim founded in the early 20th century, contain museums and historic graveyards worth a visit. Also nearby is Yardenit, a baptism site for Christians.

GETTING HERE AND AROUND

Both Degania Alef and Kinneret are south of Tiberias along Route 90. If you take a bus, ask the driver in advance about stopping.

Sights

Galita Chocolate Farm

FARM/RANCH | FAMILY | At Kibbutz Degania Bet, a short drive from Degania Alef, you can smell the chocolate long before you get to the farm. In addition to the "bar" serving hot and cold chocolate drinks, and a tempting gift shop, Galita has eight different chocolate-making workshops. Reservations can be made on the website; there are workshops in English. ✉ *Kibbutz Degania Bet, Off Rte. 90, Degania Aleph* ☎ *04/675–5608* 🌐 *www.galita.co.il* 🎫 *Free; workshops from NIS 55.*

Kibbutz Kinneret

CEMETERY | Across the Jordan River from Degania, Kinneret was founded in 1911 as the country's second kibbutz, taking its name from the Hebrew word for the Sea of Galilee. The serene Kibbutz Kinneret Cemetery includes the grave of Rachel Bluwstein, better known as Rachel HaMeshoreret (Rachel the

Poetess), a secular shrine for many Israelis. The pebbles left on her grave by visitors (a token of respect in the Jewish tradition) are a tribute to her renown and the romantic hold she has on the national imagination. Born in Russia in 1890, she became a poet of national stature in the Hebrew language; she died in 1931. The cemetery has a superb view of the lake, Golan Heights, and majestic Mount Hermon. ✉ *Off Rte. 90, Degania Aleph* ✣ *South of junction with Rte. 767* ☎ *04/675–9500.*

Yardenit

RELIGIOUS SITE | On a picturesque bend of the Jordan River, where huge eucalyptus trees droop into the quiet water, this spot was developed as a baptism site by Kibbutz Kinneret for Christian pilgrims. The baptism of Jesus by John the Baptist (John 1:28) is traditionally identified with the southern reaches of the Jordan River, near Jericho. But when the area became a hostile frontier between Israel and Jordan, pilgrims began to seek out accessible spots beyond the conflict zone. You often see groups of pilgrims being immersed in the river amid prayers and hymns and expressions of joy. The white robes required to enter the water become transparent when wet, so bring a bathing suit or large towel. Snacks and souvenirs are available. ✉ *Off Rte. 90, Degania Aleph* ☎ *04/675–9111* 🌐 *www.yardenit.com* 🎟 *Free.*

Hotels

Ma'agan Holiday Village

$$ | **RESORT** | **FAMILY** | At the southern tip of the Sea of Galilee, this kibbutz has arguably the most enchanting view of all the properties around the lake. **Pros:** pretty beach; gorgeous lake views; convenient location. **Cons:** no evening entertainment; limited dining options; basic furnishings in room and common areas. [$] *Rooms from: $250* ✉ *Rte. 92, 1 km (½ mile) east of Tzemach Junction, Ma'agan* ☎ *04/665–4411* 🌐 *www.maagan.co.il* 🛏 *148 rooms* 🍴 *Free Breakfast.*

Chapter 8

UPPER GALILEE AND THE GOLAN

WITH TZFAT (SAFED)

8

Updated by
Inbal Baum

👁 **Sights**
★★★★★

🍴 **Restaurants**
★★★★☆

🛏 **Hotels**
★★★☆☆

🛍 **Shopping**
★★☆☆☆

🍸 **Nightlife**
★★☆☆☆

WELCOME TO UPPER GALILEE AND THE GOLAN

TOP REASONS TO GO

★ **Gamla Nature Reserve:** This is the site of the Jews' heroic last stand following a siege by the Romans in AD 67. It also offers a challenging hike or an easy amble, all with glimpses of wildlife.

★ **Hermon Stream Nature Reserve:** Hike to the Banias Waterfall and the Crusader ruins, and pick up a freshly baked pita from the Druze mill along the way.

★ **Hula Lake Nature Reserve:** The Hula reserve provides shelter for birds, some 500 million of which fly over the Hula Valley twice a year on migrations between Europe and Africa.

★ **Kayaking on the Jordan River:** A cool ride downriver can be a strenuous adventure or a tame family float; either way, it adds an interesting accent to a trip to the northern Galilee.

★ **Old City of Tzfat:** While the tiny historic synagogues offer a rare taste of Jewish houses of worship from bygone days, the galleries are saturated with contemporary colors and shapes.

1 Tzfat (Safed). The center of Kabbalah.

2 Mount Meron. One of Israel's highest peaks.

3 Bar'am National Park. A well-preserved 3rd-century synagogue is tucked into green mountain landscape.

4 Rosh Pina. A historic farming community turned artist colony.

5 Tel Hatzor National Park. Israel's largest Bronze Age fortified city.

6 Hula Lake Nature Reserve. A bird-watcher's heaven.

7 Kiryat Shmona. The north's urban center has a scenic cable car.

8 Metulla. This tranquil town is just meters from Lebanon.

9 Tel Dan Nature Reserve. This nature sanctuary has biblical-era ruins and hiking trails.

10 Hermon Stream (Banias) Nature Reserve. Israel's most powerful waterfall is surrounded by lush green vegetation.

11 Nimrod's Fortress National Park. Israel's largest surviving Middle Age fortress.

12 Mount Hermon. The country's highest point and only mountain for winter skiing.

13 Majdal Shams. Druze village and gateway to Mount Hermon.

14 Merom Golan. Historic kibbutz that lies at the foothills of the Bental volcano's crater.

15 Katzrin. Unofficial Golan Heights "capital" with exquisite wines.

16 Gamla Nature Reserve. Rugged terrain with a waterfall and wildlife.

LEBANON

Bar'am National Park   Jish

Mount Meron

Meron

899

866

85

806

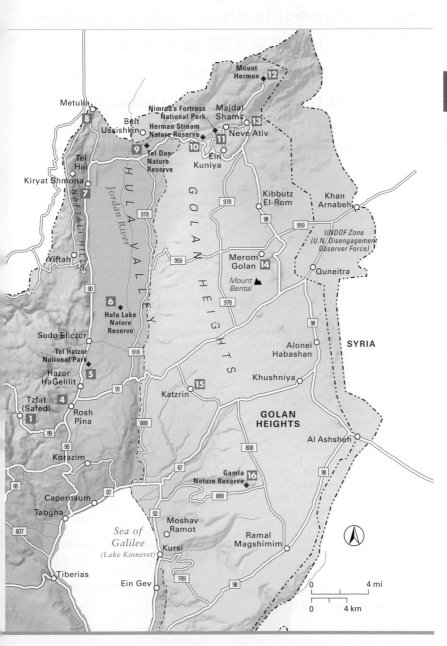

"Israel's Little Tuscany" has long been a nickname for the Upper Galilee. The green countryside, the growing numbers of both large-scale and boutique wineries, and the laid-back atmosphere have attracted urbanites on weekend jaunts as well as adventurous travelers.

The mountain air is redolent with the fragrance of spice plants; visitors can hike, cycle, or ride horses along trails that range from easy to challenging; and opportunities for kayaking, bird-watching, and other outdoor pursuits abound. These are the best vacation treats, all in a fascinating historical setting.

The main geographical feature of this region is towering Mount Hermon, known as Israel's "sponge." Huge volumes of water from winter snow and rainfall soak into its limestone, emerging at the base of the mountain in an abundance of springs that feed the Jordan River and its tributaries and provide a significant amount of Israel's water supply. The water also sustains lush vegetation that thrives year-round and is home to wildcats, hyraxes, gazelles, and hundreds of species of birds.

This water and the strategic vantage points of the Galilee mountaintops and the Golan Heights have made the region a source of political contention since time immemorial. Over the centuries, Egyptians, Canaanites, Israelites, Romans, Byzantines, Muslims, Crusaders, and Ottomans locked horns here; in the 20th century alone, the borders have been changed by Britain, France, and, of course, Israel, Lebanon, and Syria.

Borders aren't the only things that have shifted here. A geological fault line, the Syrian–African Rift, cuts straight through the 30-km (19-mile) Hula Valley; in 1837 an earthquake razed Tzfat and Tiberias, though no significant rumbles have been heard since. Extinct volcanic cones give the Golan its unusual topographic profile.

With all this water and fertile soil, the region has long been an agricultural center and is today studded with apple and cherry orchards, fishponds, and vineyards. The pastoral beauty and variety of outdoor activities attract visitors from elsewhere in Israel and the world, supplying the region's other main industry: tourism.

Proximity to Lebanon and Syria doesn't ordinarily deter people from visiting the Upper Galilee and the Golan. On the contrary, the combination of an exciting past with a gorgeous natural setting is precisely the draw here.

Over the last century, both Jews and non-Jews have faced hardships and hurdles in this region. Yet the tenacious Galileans will say there's no better place to live. Although the area is only a three-hour drive from Tel Aviv and Jerusalem, visitors find this is a world away in personality.

MAJOR REGIONS

The undulating hills of **Western Galilee** push upward into sharp limestone and basalt formations, bordered on the north by Lebanon and on the east by the volcanic, mountainous **Golan Heights,** beyond which lies Syria. The major cities—**Tzfat** in the rugged Galilee mountains and Katzrin in the Golan Heights—are a study in contrasts. The former is immersed in Jewish mysticism, and the latter is the result of a hardheaded determination to secure Israel's border with Syria by establishing a modern town in what was once a battlefield.

Golan Heights' main geographic feature is the Sea of Galilee, the country's primary water reservoir. This is the northernmost part of the country, and from Mount Hermon you can gaze out over Lebanon and Syria. The Golan Heights draws visitors to its relaxing countryside, inventive restaurants, and leading wineries.

Situated between the Golan Heights, Naftali Ridge, and the Beqaa Valley, the **Upper Hula Valley** is best known for the Tel Dan Nature Reserve. Spread out over 800 acres, it's a prime spot for hiking, cycling, or picnicking. Kiryat Shmona and sleepy Metulla are the region's largest communities.

Planning

When to Go

Unlike other parts of the country, there's no best time of the year to tour the Upper Galilee and the Golan. The range of colors is wonderful in spring, when hillsides are covered with wildflowers. Summer brings families traveling with children, as well as music and culinary festivals. Days can be hot, but the low humidity makes summer manageable. Nights can be cold year-round. Wine fans

appreciate the area in autumn during harvest time at the vineyards. In winter, more precipitation means gushing streams and gray skies, and a bit of skiing for a few weeks of the year.

Planning Your Time

A day trip to the Golan Heights from Tiberias is doable, but there's something about the lush foliage and the mountain air that makes you want to linger. Three or four days is ideal to explore the region, including visiting Tzfat, doing some wine tasting, hiking a piece of wilderness, kayaking, or just kicking back in a room with a stunning view. The ideal way to see this area is by car, though local buses will get you almost anywhere you want to go if you have time.

Getting Here and Around

Flights are no longer taking off from Sde Dov, so there are no longer flights to Rosh Pina. To get here, you can take a local bus or drive.

BUS

Local Egged buses stop at all major sights in this region (there's always a kibbutz or some other residential settlement nearby). Avoid buses if you're on a tight schedule, as they tend to be infrequent.

CONTACTS Egged. ☏ *2800 ⊕ www. egged.co.il.*

CAR

The Upper Galilee and the Golan are a 1½-hour, 60-km (37-mile) drive from both Akko and Nahariya; a three-hour, 180-km (112-mile) drive from Tel Aviv; and three hours from Jerusalem, which is 200 km (124 miles) to the south.

The state of Israel's roads is generally fair to good, but in the Upper Galilee some roads are still two-lane. Drive cautiously. Try to avoid driving during peak hours (usually late Thursday and Saturday afternoons), when city folk crowd the roads back to Jerusalem and Tel Aviv after a day out in the country.

Hotels

There are few grand hotels here; instead, the area has an ample selection of guesthouses and inns ranging from ranch to home-style. As the tourist industry has developed, luxury-level bed-and-breakfasts are often the most enjoyable options, and for budget-minded travelers many kibbutzim and moshavim have added hotels (or guest wings attached to homes); some also arrange tours, from rafting to Jeep excursions. Rooms in kibbutz guesthouses can be reserved directly or through the Kibbutz Hotels and Guest Houses chain (⊕ *en.kibbutz. co.il*), a central reservation service based in Tel Aviv, although not all the kibbutzim are represented. *Hotel reviews have been shortened. For more information, visit Fodors.com.*

Restaurants

The Upper Galilee and the Golan's crisp, appetite-whetting air is an exquisite backdrop for some excellent restaurants. Fresh grilled Dan River trout, Middle Eastern fare prepared by Druze villagers, or home-style Jewish cooking in Tzfat are all regional treats. Excellent wines enhance any meal—be sure to ask for local boutique wines, as most restaurants carry at least a handful. In a few places (such as Tzfat), it can be hard to find a restaurant open on Shabbat (sundown Friday to sundown Saturday).

What It Costs			
$	$$	$$$	$$$$
RESTAURANTS			
Under NIS 50	NIS 50–NIS 75	NIS 76–NIS 100	over NIS 100
HOTELS			
Under $200	$200–$300	$301–$400	over $400

Visitor Information

Beit Ussishkin Nature Museum near Tel Dan Nature Reserve has information about area nature reserves, natural history, and bird-watching. The Israel Nature and Parks Authority website (⊕ *www. parks.org.il*) has detailed information about national parks in this area and around the country; you can also buy money-saving multipark tickets. The Tourist Information Center–Upper Galilee can also provide information.

CONTACTS Tourist Information Center–Upper Galilee. ⊠ *Gome Junction, Rte. 90 and Rte. 977, Kiryat Shmona* ☎ *04/955–2426* ⊕ *go.galil.gov.il.*

Tzfat

33 km (20 miles) north of Tiberias, 72 km (45 miles) northeast of Haifa.

This magical town on a hill attracts artists searching for inspiration, travelers charmed by its cobblestone alleys, and religious people in search of meaning—a rare example of harmony between the secular and the spiritual. The city is known for its spiritual, even sacred, vibe and its breathtaking views.

It doesn't take long to walk all of Tzfat's Old City, but allow plenty of time to poke around the little stone passages, remnants of the Crusader and Ottoman eras, that seem to lead nowhere. You can linger over some minute architectural

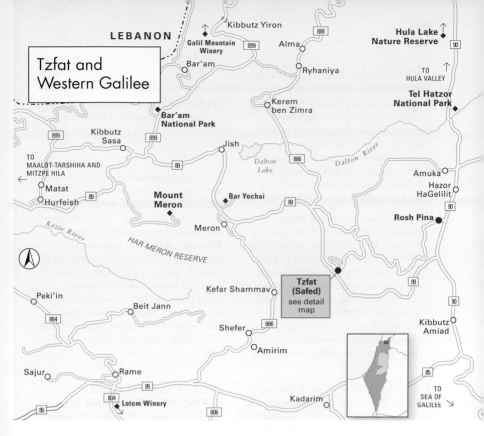

Tzfat (Safed) see detail map

detail on a building from another time, or browse through shops filled to overflowing with locally made art. It's almost impossible to get lost; Yerushalayim (Jerusalem) Street is a good orientation point—it runs through the heart of the Old City, encircles the Citadel, and from there, steps lead down to the two main areas of interest, the Old Jewish Quarter and the adjacent Artists' Colony. There's no way to avoid the hilly topography, so remember to wear comfortable walking shoes. As the town is largely Jewish Orthodox, modest dress is recommended when visiting synagogues. For women, this means a below-the-knee skirt or long pants and at least a short-sleeve top; for men, long pants are appropriate. In the hot summer days, dress lightly and carry around a shawl or cover up for visiting holy places.

Tzfat hibernates from October through June, when the city's artists move to their galleries in warmer parts of the country. This doesn't mean you should leave Tzfat out of your itinerary during those months; there's enough to occupy the curious wanderer for at least a few hours, and much of it is free. In summer, especially during July and August, Tzfat is abuzz with activity: galleries and shops stay open late, *klezmer* music (Eastern European Jewish "soul music") dances around corners, and the city extends a warm welcome to everyone.

GETTING HERE AND AROUND

If you're driving to Tzfat from Jerusalem, take Route 6 north. If you're starting in Tel Aviv, head north on Route 2. Either way, you'll want to turn east on Route 65, then north on Route 90, then west on Route 89 to Tzfat. If your journey starts in

What Is Kabbalah?

Kabbalah, which means "receiving," is an ancient study of Jewish mysticism that gained popularity in the 13th century. Tzfat has been the main center for Kabbalah scholarship since the 16th century, making it one of Judaism's four holiest cities (along with Jerusalem, Tiberias, and Hebron).

Kabbalah, as opposed to formal rabbinical Judaism, is about reading between, behind, and all around the lines. Each letter and accent of every word in the holy books has a numerical value with particular significance, offering added meaning to the literal word. One of the most popular Kabbalistic concepts is that of *tikkun olam*, or "fixing the world." According to Jewish mystics, the universe was "broken" by God in order to make room for the physical realm. Thus the quest of humankind is to repair the universe through good works and service to God.

Although classical Kabbalah studies are intertwined with those of the Bible and the Talmud, not all religious Jews study Kabbalah. In fact, tradition holds that a person studying Kabbalah must be at least 40 years old and have a thorough knowledge of other Jewish texts. Outside of Hasidic Judaism, which has incorporated some Kabbalah into its worldview, many mainstream Orthodox Jews don't study Kabbalah at all, preferring to focus on matters of the perceivable world.

Haifa, head north on Route 4, then east on Route 89 to Tzfat. Egged runs at least two buses daily to Tzfat from Tel Aviv, at least seven from Jerusalem, and at least 30 from Haifa.

Both of Israel's major bus companies, Egged Tours and United Tours, offer one- and two-day guided tours of the region, departing from Tel Aviv and Jerusalem. In Tzfat, the private company Nateev Express runs 13 local routes. Buses from Tzfat's central station, at the entrance to the city, head to most towns in the region.

Within the Old City, the many streets closed to traffic make it difficult to drive. You may have to drive around the perimeter of the city rather than through it. The best way to get around is on foot.

BUS CONTACTS Nateev Express. ☎ *3553 ⊕ www.nateevexpress.com.

VISITOR INFORMATION

CONTACTS Tzfat Visitor Center. ⊠ 17 Alkabets St. ☎ 04/692–4427 ⊕ www. safed-home.com.

 Sights

Abuhav Synagogue

RELIGIOUS SITE | This spacious Sephardic synagogue is named for a 14th-century Spanish scribe whose Torah scrolls found their way here with the Spanish Jewish exiles 200 years later. A look around reveals several differences between this synagogue and its Ashkenazi counterparts: for example, the walls are painted the lively blue typical of Sephardic tradition, and the benches run along the walls instead of in rows (so that no man turns his back on his neighbor).

Every detail is loaded with significance. There are three arks—for the three forefathers, Abraham, Isaac, and Jacob (the one on the right is said to be the Abuhav original)—and 10 windows in the dome, referring to the Commandments. The charmingly naive illustrations on the squinches (supports) include a depiction of the Dome of the Rock (referring to the destruction of the Second Temple) and pomegranate trees, whose seed-filled fruit symbolizes the 613 Torah Commandments. The original building was destroyed in the 1837 earthquake, but locals swear that the southern wall—in which the Abuhav Torah scroll is set—was spared. ⊠ *Abuhav St.* ☎ *52/370–5012* ☎ *Free* ⊘ *Closed Sat. to visitors.*

Artists' Colony

NEIGHBORHOOD | Set in the city's old Arab Quarter, the Artists' Colony was established in 1951 by six Israeli artists who saw the promise hidden in Tzfat's war-torn condition. For them, the old buildings, the fertile landscape, and the cool mountain air fused into the magic ingredients of creativity. Others soon followed until, at its peak, the colony was home to more than 50 artists, some of whom exhibit internationally. Many galleries host workshops as well as exhibits, and many are open only in the spring and summer, from about 10 am to 6 pm. ⊠ *Old City* ☎ *Free.*

Caro Synagogue

RELIGIOUS SITE | Tucked among art galleries, the charming Caro Synagogue appears quite run-down, but it is considered one of the Old City's most interesting destinations by those who feel a deep spiritual connection to the great scholar who lent it his name. Rabbi Yosef Caro arrived in Tzfat in 1535 and led its Jewish community for many years. He is the author of Shulchan Aruch, the code of law that remains a foundation of Jewish religious interpretation to the present day, and this synagogue is said to have been his private study hall. It was destroyed in the great earthquake of 1837 and rebuilt in the mid-19th century. If you ask, the attendant might open the ark containing the Torah scrolls, one of which is at least 400 years old.

A glass-faced cabinet at the back of the synagogue is the *geniza*, where damaged scrolls or prayer books are stored (because they carry the name of God, they cannot be destroyed). The turquoise paint here—considered the "color of heaven"—is believed to help keep away the evil eye. ⊠ *Alkabets St.* ☎ *052/370–5012* ☎ *Free* ⊘ *Closed Sat. to visitors.*

Citadel Park

ARCHAEOLOGICAL SITE | In Talmudic times, hilltop bonfires here served as a beacon to surrounding communities, heralding the beginning of the lunar month, the basis for the Jewish calendar. In the 12th century, the Crusaders grasped the strategic value of this setting and built the Citadel. The Muslim sultan Baybars conquered it in 1266, leaving only the scattered pieces you see today.

The Jewish settlement outside the Citadel's walls grew and prospered during and after the Crusader era, becoming a center of Kabbalah studies. When the departing British Mandate forces left the town's strategic positions to the Arab forces, the remains of the Citadel again became a battleground between Jews and Arabs. ⊠ *Derech Hativat Yiftach* ☎ *Free.*

General Exhibition

MUSEUM | An important stop in a tour of the Artists' Colony, the works inside this large space are a representative sample of the work of Tzfat's artists, ranging from oils and watercolors to silkscreens and sculptures, in traditional and avant-garde styles. The permission of the Muslim authorities was required to organize the exhibition, as it is housed in the old mosque, easily identified from afar by its minaret. The Artists' Colony has recognized the growing presence of artists from the former Soviet Union, and the adjacent building holds the **Immigrant Artists' Exhibition.** In either facility, if any works catch your fancy, just ask directions to the artist's gallery for a more in-depth look at his or her work. ⊠ *Leon*

Tzfat (Safed)

0   150 yds

0   150 m

← TO MOUNT MERON

KEY

❶ Sights
❶ Restaurants
❶ Hotels

Isakov and Zvi Levanon Sts. ☎ *052/370–5012* ✉ *Free.*

Hameiri House

MUSEUM | This centuries-old three-story stone building, at the northern end of Keren Ha'yesod Street, houses a historical museum that offers great insight into the daily life of Jews in Tzfat over the past 200 years. Textiles, tableware, and Judaica-like ornate menorahs are displayed with notations in Hebrew and English. Guided tours are available by appointment. ✉ *158 Keren Ha'yesod St.* ☎ *04/697–1307* ✉ *NIS 20* ⊙ *Closed Sat.*

Ha'Ari Synagogue

RELIGIOUS SITE | This Ashkenazi synagogue has associations going back to the 16th century. It's named for a rabbi who left an indelible mark on Judaism: Isaac Luria, known to all as the Ari, Hebrew for "lion" and an acronym for Adoneinu Rabbeinu Itzhak ("our master and teacher Isaac"). In his mere three years in Tzfat, he evolved his own system of the Kabbalah, which drew a huge following that would influence Jewish teaching the world over. Even more astounding is that he died in his thirties; it is generally said that one should not even consider study of the Kabbalah before the age of 40, when one reaches the requisite level of intellectual and emotional maturity.

The pale colors of this tiny Ashkenazi synagogue contrast sharply with its olive-wood Holy Ark, a dazzlingly carved tour de force with two tiers of spiral columns and vibrant plant reliefs. The Sephardic Ari Synagogue, where the rabbi prayed, is farther down the quarter, by the cemetery. The oldest of Tzfat's synagogues, this 16th-century structure has especially fine carved wooden doors. ✉ *Najara St.* ✉ *Free* ⊙ *Closed Sat. to visitors.*

Kikar Hameginim

PLAZA | In the Old Jewish Quarter, "Defenders' Square" was once its social and economic heart. A sign points to a two-story house that served as the command post of the neighborhood's defense in 1948—hence the plaza's name. ✉ *Bar Yochai St., at Ma'alot Gore Ha'Ari* ✉ *Free.*

Ma'alot Olei Hagardom

NEIGHBORHOOD | Part of Tzfat's charm is its setting, on the slope of a hill. This *ma'alot,* or stairway, which extends from Yerushalayim Street to Keren HaYesod Street, forms the boundary between the Old Jewish Quarter and the Artists' Colony. It is named for Tzfat freedom fighters executed by the British during the Mandate. ✉ *Off Yerushalayim St.* ✉ *Free.*

Memorial Museum of Hungarian-Speaking Jewry

MUSEUM | The founders of this museum are Tzfat residents and Holocaust survivors Hava and Yosef Lustig. The exhibits in the museum's three small rooms, including letters, children's books, drawings, items of clothing, and more, tell of the everyday life of communities and individuals in the Hungarian-speaking Jewish pre-Holocaust world. The computer database has information about 1,700 Jewish communities in Hungary, Transylvania, Slovakia, and other countries. Guided tours can be arranged in advance. ✉ *Old Ottoman Government Center, Independence Sq.* ☎ *04/692–5881* ⊕ *www.hjm.org.il* ✉ *NIS 15* ⊙ *Closed Sat.*

Old Jewish Cemetery

CEMETERY | Old and new cemeteries are set into the hillside below the Old Jewish Quarter. The old plots resonate with the names and fame of the Kabbalists of yore, as their graves are identifiable by sky-blue markers. It is said that if the legs of the devout suddenly get tired here, it is because they are walking over hidden graves. The new cemetery holds the graves of members of the pre-State underground Stern Gang and Irgun forces, who were executed by the British in Akko's prison. In a separate plot, bordered by cypresses, lie the 21 Tzfat teenagers killed by terrorists in 1974—they were taken hostage while on a field trip

8

Upper Galilee and the Golan TZFAT

in the northern Galilee town of Ma'alot. ✉ *Below Keren Hayesod St.* 🎟 *Free.*

🍴 Restaurants

★ Ein Camonim

$$$ | ISRAELI | FAMILY | The Galilee Hills make a perfect pasture for livestock—in this case, goats—and here you can taste the fresh output of Ein Camonim's dairy, one of the best in Israel. The all-you-can-eat menu includes a platter of about three dozen goat cheeses, a selection of home-baked breads, a variety of fresh salads, and house wine. **Known for:** goats on-site; artisanal cheeses; homemade goodies. [$] *Average main: NIS 88* ✉ *Rte. 85* ☎ *04/698–9894.*

Gan Eden

$$ | ECLECTIC | The setting, a charming stone house with both indoor and outdoor seating, lends great atmosphere to this family-run eatery set above the Old City and taking in the view of Mount Meron (the restaurant's name means "paradise"). Gan Eden is best known for its fish, especially fillets of sea bass and sea bream. **Known for:** Mount Meron views; fish and calzone dumplings stuffed with Tzfat cheese; kosher. [$] *Average main: NIS 70* ✉ *Mount Canaan Promenade, 33 HaGedud Hashlishi St.* ☎ *052/434–9755* ⏲ *Closed Sat.*

Lachuch Original

$ | MIDDLE EASTERN | This popular Old City eatery's upstairs dining room has benches and tables inlaid with Middle Eastern designs, walls painted the soft shade of blue found inside local synagogues, and colorful carpets from all over the region. The strikingly dressed owner and chef, Ronen Jarufi, makes each meal to order. **Known for:** Yemenite food; casual atmosphere; memorable owner. [$] *Average main: NIS 40* ✉ *18 Alkabets St.* ☎ *050/225–4148* ⏲ *Closed Sat. No dinner Fri.*

🛏 Hotels

Canaan Spa

$$$ | HOTEL | The focus of this hotel on the outskirts of Tzfat is on the spa treatments, including aromatic massages with olive oil and honey or hot-stone treatments using warmed pieces of basalt. **Pros:** pool; brunch and dinner included; tennis and basketball facilities. **Cons:** remote location; outdated room furnishings; not for families with young kids. [$] *Rooms from: $396* ✉ *Mount Canaan Promenade, 106 Ha-Gdud Ha-shlishi St.* ☎ *04/699–3000* 🌐 *www.canaan-spa.com* 🔑 *124 rooms* 🍴 *Free Breakfast.*

Joseph's Well Country Inn

$ | B&B/INN | FAMILY | Each room at this friendly kibbutz lodging is like a cozy studio apartment, with pine furnishings and chintz curtains. **Pros:** informal vibe; terrific for families; a peek into kibbutz life. **Cons:** plain decor; basic breakfast; inadequate air conditioning. [$] *Rooms from: $199* ✉ *Kibbutz Amiad, Off Rte. 90* ✣ *10 km (6 miles) south of Tzfat* ☎ *073/759–9747* 🌐 *www.amiad-inn.com* 🔑 *27 rooms* 🍴 *Free Breakfast.*

Ruth Rimonim

$$ | HOTEL | Built 200 years ago for a Turkish sultan, this spectacular castle has been transformed into a hotel with a reputation for charming rooms. **Pros:** romantic retreat; nice pool; central location. **Cons:** some older rooms are on the small side; crowded pool in summertime; outdated furnishings. [$] *Rooms from: $273* ✉ *45 HaNasi St., off Tet Zayin St.* ☎ *04/699–4666* 🌐 *www.rimonim.com* 🔑 *77 rooms* 🍴 *Free Breakfast.*

Safed Inn

$ | B&B/INN | On the outskirts of Tzfat, the budget-minded Safed Inn caters especially well to families. **Pros:** good value; family-friendly atmosphere; shared rooms available. **Cons:** owner can be a bit brusque; no kids in deluxe rooms; breakfast not included. [$] *Rooms from:*

Tzfat is an artsy village known for being a historic center of Kabbalah (Jewish mysticism).

$87 ⊠ *Mount Canaan Promenade, Off HaGdud Hashlishi St.* ☎ *04/697–1007* ⊕ *www.safedinn.com* ⮑ *20 rooms* ⦿ *No meals.*

 Performing Arts

Klezmer Festival

FESTIVALS | Every July or August Tzfat hosts the Klezmer Festival, and there could be no better setting for three days of "Jewish soul music" than this mystical community. Many events are street performances and therefore free. Tzfat practically bursts at the seams at this time, with revelers both religious and secular. ⊠ *Tzfat* ☎ *04/697–4403* ⊕ *klezmerim.info.*

🛍 Shopping

Safed Candles

CRAFTS | This place has grown from a one-room workshop to a huge space filled with the pleasant aroma of beeswax and the bright colors of hand-decorated Sabbath, Havdalah, and Hanukkah candles. ⊠ *62 HaAri St.* ☎ *04/682–2068.*

Safed Craft Pottery

CERAMICS/GLASSWARE | Creative stoneware, porcelain, and ceramics can be found in Daniel Flatauer's studio and shop in the Old City. His salt-fire glazes are especially worth noting. The artist, who came to Tzfat from England, is welcoming and helpful. ⊠ *63 Yud Alef St.* ☎ *04/697–4970 .*

Sheva Haya Glassblowing Gallery

ART GALLERIES | Colorado-born Sheva Haya's blown-glass sculptures and vibrant watercolors are meant to evoke the beauty of the land and its people. The artist offers demonstrations of her work and explains how it relates to Kabbalah, but you can also just poke around her studio. ⊠ *7 Tet Vav St.* ☎ *050/430–5107* ⊕ *www.shevachaya.com.*

⚡ Activities

Bat Ya'ar Ranch

HORSEBACK RIDING | FAMILY | In the Birya Forest near Tzfat, Bat Ya'ar Ranch offers outdoor fun for the whole family including pony rides through the fields, rope bridges swinging between the trees, and outdoor bowling with wooden lanes and balls. The wooded-mountaintop setting enhances the timbered restaurant's delicious food. A meaty bowl of bean stew, eaten by the fireplace, is a pleasure any time of year. Bat Ya'ar is 5 km (3 miles) north of Tzfat. It's best to call for directions. ⊠ *Off Rte. 90, Amuka* ☎ *04/692–1788* ⊕ *www.batyaar.co.il.*

Mount Meron

29 km (18 miles) northwest of Tzfat.

For many centuries, Mount Meron has drawn thousands upon thousands of Orthodox Jews to pay homage to the great rabbis of the Roman era who are buried at the eastern foot of the mount. It's also a nature reserve. Around the area are a number of other sights.

GETTING HERE AND AROUND

From Tzfat, take Route 89 west, following signs to "Tomb of Rashbi," which is an abbreviation for the Tomb of Rabbi Shimon Bar Yochai.

👁 Sights

Erez Komarovsky

$$$$ | RESTAURANT—SIGHT | |RESTAURANT— SIGHT | Chef Erez Komarovsky's cooking workshops are held in his home in Matat, which is surrounded by gardens of fresh herbs and vegetables. An unforgettable day of fine food, great wine, and breathtaking views will give you plenty of inspiration as you can learn recipes to bring home with you. The dishes are all seasonal and focus on local ingredients: think red snapper tartare with avocado, fish steamed in banana leaves, lamb stuffed with pistachios, and fennel sautéed in saffron-infused clarified butter. At lunch you enjoy everything you've prepared, along with slabs of crusty bread. Matat is 14 km (9 miles) west of Mount Meron. ⊠ *North of Rte. 89, off Rte. 899, Matat* ☎ *03/977–2929* ⊕ *www. erez-komarovsky.co.il* ⊠ *NIS 260* ⌖ *Reservations essential.*

★ Lotem Winery

WINERY/DISTILLERY | Come for the wine, stay for the delicious tapas, and find yourself hours later still at Lotem for the good company, live music, and valley views. At this organic winery (one of Israel's two of this kind), a tour and tasting includes learning about organic grapes in Israel and about why the winery plays music to the barrels and bottles 24/7. The winemaker, Jonathan, can also whip up some of the region's tastiest ceviche, fish kebabs, and salads to balance the elegant red blends. The restaurant is open on the weekends and tasting tours are possible throughout the week with advance reservations. The winery is 45 minutes by car south of Mount Meron. ⊠ *Kibbutz Lotem, Off Rte. 804, Amirim* ⌖ *Go south on Rte. 804 from Rte. 85 and enter through kibbutz gate, following winery signs* ☎ *054/791–5868* ⊕ *lotem-winery.co.il* ⊠ *35 NIS for tasting and tour.*

Mount Meron

MOUNTAIN—SIGHT | The most important site on lovely Mount Meron—and one of the holiest places in Israel—is the **Tomb of Rabbi Shimon Bar Yochai,** survivor of the Bar Kochba Revolt of almost 2,000 years ago. The simple building that houses the tomb is a place for quiet reflection and prayer, though you may encounter a bar mitzvah or other festive event in the courtyard outside. Women and men have separate prayer areas, and all are expected to dress modestly (coverups are available for those who don't have them). ■**TIP→ Signs point to the Tomb of**

Rashbi, which is the Hebrew acronym of the rabbi's name.

Bar Yochai is said to have fled from the Romans with his son Elazar after the fall of Jerusalem to a cave at Peki'in, not far from here, where he remained for 13 years. The faithful, beginning with the 16th-century mystics who settled in Tzfat, believe that from his cave-hideout Bar Yochai penned the *Zohar* (*The Book of Splendor*), his commentary on the first five books of the Hebrew Bible. Others claim that the Zohar dates from 13th-century Spain. Nevertheless, the constant flow of visitors is evidence of the pilgrims' devotion to the great rabbi and rebel.

The pilgrimage is still celebrated en masse on Lag Ba'Omer, the festive 33rd day of the seven solemn weeks that begin with Passover. At this time Mount Meron comes alive as a grand procession arrives on foot from Tzfat, with many participants carrying Torah scrolls and singing fervently. Bonfires are lighted, with celebrations lasting days.

Mount Meron is the highest peak in Israel after Mount Hermon, and parts of it are a nature reserve (🌐 *www.parks.org.il*) with hiking trails. ✉ *Off Rte. 89* 🎫 *Free* 🕓 *Closed Sat.*

🍴 Restaurants

Aluma Bistro

$$$$ | MODERN ISRAELI | The town of Maalot-Tarshisha is home to Jewish, Christian, and Muslim families, and they rub elbows while dining at Aluma Bistro. Decorated with artifacts from Provence, the burgundy-toned dining room buzzes with locals in search of an extraordinary meal. **Known for:** foraged vegetables; Galilean cuisine; co-existence. [$] *Average main: NIS 116* ✉ *Tarshisha Rd., Maalot-Tarshisha* ✥ *21 km (13 miles) west of Mount Meron via Rte. 89* ☎ *04/957–4477* 🌐 *www.alumabistro.co.il.*

Bread Men (Anshey HaLechem)

$ | BAKERY | Fresh-baked sourdough breads, oil- and preservative-free pastries, and healthy whole wheat challah are the cornerstone of this bakery in the rural heart of the Galilee. Grab a seat on Friday morning in the backyard outdoor garden with the locals to taste stone-oven-baked Turkish-style cheese *burekas,* artichoke carpaccio with olives and sun-dried tomatoes, or a light dish of homemade granola and locally produced yogurt. **Known for:** fresh breads and cheese burekas; backyard outdoor garden; family-owned. [$] *Average main: NIS 40* ✉ *Kibbutz Moran, HaZayit St.* ✥ *South of Rte. 85* ☎ *04/698–8992* 🌐 *www.breadmen.co.il* 🕓 *Closed Sat. No dinner.*

Maarag

$$ | CAFÉ | FAMILY | This kosher restaurant's colorful dishes highlight Galilean delicacies, in particular the rich Israeli breakfast with homemade jams or grilled baby eggplant with tahini. For a light lunch try the plentiful salads, especially the halloumi cheese and sautéed mushrooms served over romaine lettuce. **Known for:** plentiful breakfasts; homemade jams; ceramics shop. [$] *Average main: NIS 58* ✉ *1 Meron Rd., Kfar Vradim* ✥ *Kfar Vradim is south of Maalot-Tarshisha, 21 km (13 miles) west of Mount Meron* ☎ *04/997–1369* 🌐 *www.maarag.org* 🕓 *No dinner.*

🛏 Hotels

Hacienda Forest View

$$ | HOTEL | FAMILY | Families with active kids will enjoy the enclosed green grounds of this hotel surrounded by forest. **Pros:** kosher meals, including Friday night traditional dinner; kid-friendly activities; various meal plans available. **Cons:** grounds are dated; isolated location; loud dining experience. [$] *Rooms from: $250* ✉ *Yafeh Nof, Maalot-Tarshisha* ✥ *21 km (13 miles) west of Mount Meron* ☎ *04/957–9000* 🌐 *www.c-hotels.co.il/en* 🛏 *142 rooms* 🍴 *Some meals.*

Tamar v'Gefen
$$$ | B&B/INN | In the Western Galilee, Tamar and Yaron Cohen created three lovely suites off their home, where they focus on their love of wine. **Pros:** hot tub in a stunning garden; complimentary use of bikes; delicious breakfast. **Cons:** away from the usual tourist attractions; no family options; in a residential neighborhood. [$] *Rooms from: $320* ✉ *Off Rte. 89, Mitzpe Hila* ✣ *25 km (15 miles) west of Mount Meron* ☎ *050/997–8911* 🌐 *www.tamar-gefen.co.il* 🛏 *3 rooms* 🍴 *Free Breakfast.*

Bar'am National Park

15 km (9 miles) northwest of Meron, 22 km (14 miles) northwest of Tzfat.

In an otherwise deserted spot lie the ruins of Bar'am, one of the best-preserved ancient synagogues anywhere. Like most other synagogues uncovered in this area, this structure dating from the 3rd century faces south toward Jerusalem; unlike any other, however, this one has lavish architectural elements, such as an entrance with a segmental pediment and freestanding columns in front.

GETTING HERE AND AROUND

From Mount Meron or Tzfat, head west on Route 89, then north on Route 899. After 2 km (1 mile), turn right onto a dirt road. There's no bus service to Bar'am. Near the park, you can check out one of the area's wineries as well as an ice-cream factory.

Sights

Bar'am National Park
ARCHAEOLOGICAL SITE | The interior of this ancient house of worship, which resembles that of other Galilean synagogues of the Talmudic period (3rd to 8th centuries AD), is less well preserved than the impressive exterior. Rows of pillars in the prayer hall apparently served as supports for the ceiling, and the building may have had a second story. A section of the facade's lintel, now in the Louvre in Paris, contains the Hebrew inscription "May there be peace in this place, and in all the places of Israel. This lintel was made by Jose the Levite. Blessings upon his works. Shalom." Allow at least an hour to wander around or bring a picnic and enjoy it on one of the tables. ✉ *Off Rt. 899, 3 km (2 miles) east of Khiram Junction, Tzivon* ☎ *04/698–9301* 🌐 *www.parks.org.il* 🎟 *NIS 15.*

Buza Ice Cream Factory
FACTORY | FAMILY | Artisanal ice-cream-making workshops are offered at the factory of the budding Buza Ice Cream chain. During the hour-long session, participants earn about the ice-cream-making process and taste the results of their hard work. Although the workshop is geared toward kids, adults can participate; everyone can savor tastings from the adjacent shop, including cardamom- or chocolate-flavored specialty cones filled with seasonal sorbets and ice creams. Reservations are required for the workshop. ✉ *Kibbutz Sasa, Off Rte. 89* ✣ *Enter kibbutz and follow signs to right toward Buza* ☎ *04/691–8880* 🌐 *buzaisrael.co.il* 🎟 *Workshop NIS 50.*

Galil Mountain Winery
WINERY/DISTILLERY | Producing more than 15 blends and varietals in a yearly production of 1 million bottles, this is one of Israel's largest wineries. The tour in the modern, well-designed visitor center begins with an overview map of the six Upper Galilee vineyards, continues with a look at the modern press and stainless-steel storage tanks, and then moves to the tasting room for a sampling of whites, a rosé, and reds. End the tour on the balcony with its panoramic view of vineyards and hills. ✉ *Kibbutz Yiron, Off Rte. 899* ✣ *Enter through kibbutz gate and follow signs to winery* ☎ *04/686–8748* 🌐 *www.galilmountain.co.il* 🎟 *Tour NIS 20* ⏲ *Closed Sat.*

Rosh Pina

31 km (19 miles) east of Bar'am National Park, 10 km (6 miles) east of Tzfat, 25 km (15½ miles) north of Tiberias.

The restored village of Rosh Pina is a gift-shop-and-gallery-browser's delight, and the dilapidated wooden doors and stonework of some still-abandoned premises are part of the charm.

Rosh Pina—literally "cornerstone"—gets its name from Psalm 118:22: "The stone that the builders rejected has become the chief cornerstone." This verse inspired the Galilee's first Zionist pioneers, who came from Romania in 1882, determined to build a village in the malaria-infested area. They bought this land, at the foot of the mountain ridge east of Tzfat, from the neighboring Arab villagers of Ja'uni.

The pioneers, who had little experience in agriculture, struggled to survive until Jewish philanthropist Baron Edmond de Rothschild bought the land. He provided them with tools, workers, and a new industry: the production of silk by silkworms. By the turn of the 20th century, Rosh Pina had grown into the country's fourth-largest Jewish farming community. Today it's a vacation destination and a year-round residence for 3,100 people.

GETTING HERE AND AROUND

There are daily buses from Tel Aviv, Tzfat, Tiberias, and Haifa. The most practical way is driving. If arriving from Tzfat, head east on Route 89, then north on Route 90.

TAXI CONTACTS Meir Taxi. ☎ *04/693–5735.*

Sights

HaBaron Garden

CITY PARK | Unveiled in 1886, this public park was created at the request of philanthropist Baron Edmond de Rothschild. Olive and almond trees and fragrant herbs like rosemary are planted in terraces on the hillside so that you can enjoy shade and a tree-framed view of the valley below. ✉ *HaChalutzim St.* 🎟 *Free.*

Professor Mer House

HOUSE | This office and house belonged to Professor Gideon Mer, a leading expert on malaria in the 1930s. Legend has it that Mer used to inject his wife and children with experimental remedies in his efforts to combat malaria in this region. (Happily, all survived.) The British were so impressed with Mer's work that they sent him to Burma to fight malaria epidemics there. Implements and household items from the early days of Rosh Pina are on display. Next door, a colorful audiovisual presentation showcases the founding of this pioneering community. ✉ *HaRishonim St.* ☎ *04/693–6603* 🎟 *NIS 15.*

Synagogue

RELIGIOUS SITE | The old synagogue's interior remains pretty much as it was when it was built in the mid-1880s. The dark pews, made of the timber brought from Romania, have aged gracefully. The painted ceiling has depictions of palm trees and biblical motifs. The building is usually locked, but ask around and you might find someone to open it for you. ✉ *HaRishonim St.*

Restaurants

★ Auberge Shulamit

$$$$ | **EUROPEAN** | This charming inn takes its name from the original Hotel Shulamit, where the 1948 Armistice Treaty was signed. The home-smoked meats and fish are unique and worth trying, as are the seasonal soups, seafood dishes, and the elegant array of desserts. **Known for:** seafood and smoked meats; French country-style guest rooms; scenic views. [$] *Average main: NIS 160* ✉ *34 David Shuv St.* ☎ *04/693–1485* 🌐 *www.shulamit.co.il.*

Visit Rosh Pina for its charming streets, shops, and galleries.

Chocolata

$$ | **CAFÉ** | **FAMILY** | The original arched stone basement of the old synagogue is the setting of this chocolate shop and café. True to its name, the kitchen serves a host of chocolate delights (drinks, cakes, and more), including 37 different kinds of pralines made by the house chocolatier. **Known for:** chocolate; art gallery; chocolate making workshops. [$] *Average main: NIS 60* ✉ *HaRishonim St., lower entrance to synagogue* ☎ *04/686–0219* 🌐 *www.chocolatte.co.il.*

Meat-balim

$$$$ | **STEAKHOUSE** | Go easy on the appetizers here, as you'll want to save room for this sleek, modern kosher eatery's savory meat dishes. Those in the know recommend the generous veal entrecôte and the lamb chops in a flavorful sauce of caramel, oranges, mint, and ginger. **Known for:** kosher; meat-forward menu; extensive wine list. [$] *Average main: NIS 130* ✉ *Derech Hagalil St.* ☎ *04/686–0107* 🕑 *Closed Apr.–Sept., no dinner Fri., no lunch Sat.; Oct.–Mar., closed Fri. and Sat.*

Hotels

Rosh Pina is a budding center of tourism for this region, and many residents are now opening their homes as B&Bs, some of whose breakfasts alone are worth the stay.

Ahuzat Hameiri

$$$ | **B&B/INN** | This stunning mansion has been in the Hameiri family since it was built in the late 1880s. **Pros:** breathtaking views; nice grounds; family-friendly atmosphere. **Cons:** no pool; many steps to rooms; breakfast down the street. [$] *Rooms from: $325* ✉ *1 HaChalutzim St.* ☎ *04/693–8707* 🌐 *www.hrp.co.il* 🛏 *9 rooms* 🍴 *Free Breakfast.*

★ Mitzpe Hayamim

$$$$ | **HOTEL** | With a splendid view of the Sea of Galilee, this colonial-style hotel south of Rosh Pina specializes in pampering its clients. **Pros:** great food and spa; enchanting walking paths; pretty pool. **Cons:** need a car to get around; not a place for kids. [$] *Rooms from: $580* ✉ *Off Rte. 8900* ☎ *04/699–4555* 🌐 *www.*

mizpe-hayamim.com 🛏 *100 rooms* 🍴 *Some meals.*

★ Pina BaLev
$$$ | B&B/INN | Each of these distinctively designed suites offers all of the amenities you could want in a Rosh Pina retreat. **Pros:** welcoming owner; soothing spa treatments; luxurious amenities. **Cons:** limited number of suites; no fitness room; no dinner option. [$] *Rooms from: $395* ✉ *31 HaChalutzim St.* ☎ *04/693–0970* 🌐 *www.pinabalev.com* 🛏 *5 suites* 🍴 *Free Breakfast.*

Pina Barosh
$$ | HOTEL | The stained-glass windows, wood furniture, and handwoven rugs make it hard to guess that this charming small boutique hotel used to house livestock. **Pros:** romantic restaurant; relaxing atmosphere; great place for couples. **Cons:** no view from rooms; not for families; stone rooms can get chilly. [$] *Rooms from: $210* ✉ *8 HaChalutzim St.* ☎ *04/693–6582* 🌐 *www.pinabarosh.com* 🛏 *7 rooms* 🍴 *Free Breakfast.*

Villa Tehila
$$ | B&B/INN | FAMILY | Amichai and Tehila Yisraeli bought this 19th-century farm and converted the former stables, storehouse, and dairy into a charming guesthouse. **Pros:** family-friendly vibe; convivial owners; pool open year-round. **Cons:** some rooms very small; courtyard dimly lit at night; not for those with animal allergies. [$] *Rooms from: $220* ✉ *7 HaChalutzim St.* ☎ *04/693–7788* 🌐 *www.villa-tehila.co.il* 🛏 *11 rooms* 🍴 *Free Breakfast.*

Nightlife

Shiri's Bistro
WINE BARS—NIGHTLIFE | A must for wine lovers, this pleasant spot is not only a good place to sample local varietals but also a great source of information about the wine industry. The bar stocks local wines from both well-known and up-and-coming vineyards, all at reasonable prices. Enjoy the wine alongside creative smaller plates like the sweet potato and onion fritters, or more substantial homemade pasta dishes. ✉ *8 HaChalutzim St.* ☎ *04/693–6582* 🌐 *www.pinabarosh.com/engBistro.htm.*

Shopping

The Well
FOOD/CANDY | Sigal Eshet-Shafat and her husband, Inbar, used to sell typical handicrafts, but it turned out that their jams, sauces, and liqueurs were what attracted customers. The on-site shop lets you sample the store's many unique delights. The onion jam is a favorite for both dairy and meat dishes. ✉ *HaRishonim St.* ☎ *04/693–0020.*

Tel Hatzor National Park

8 km (5 miles) north of Rosh Pina, 14 km (9 miles) east of Tzfat.

On the Via Maris—the major trade route linking Egypt and Mesopotamia—Hatzor is referred to several times in documents from ancient archives in both lands, and scholars believe a huge archive may someday be found here.

GETTING HERE AND AROUND

From Rosh Pina, head north on Route 90; from Tzfat, head east on Route 89, then north on Route 90.

Sights

Tel Hatzor National Park
ARCHAEOLOGICAL SITE | This site on the Via Maris, an ancient trade route, is a good stop for archaeology buffs—its massive mound is made up of the remnants of 21 cities. The excavation and restoration of some of these antiquities have produced fascinating results.

The book of Joshua (11:13) notes that Joshua destroyed Canaanite Hatzor in the 13th century BC, and Israelites resettled it. Its next heyday came three centuries later, when King Solomon decided it would serve him well as a regional military and administrative center, like Megiddo and Gezer. In 732 BC, Hatzor met its end when invading Assyrian king Tiglath Pileser III conquered the Galilee and forced its Israelite inhabitants off the land in chains and into exile.

The huge site is divided into two areas: the **Upper City,** where you can explore the remains of some ancient settlements, and the **Lower City,** first settled in the 18th century BC. Only the Upper City, covering less than a fifth of the total excavation site, is open to the public. The **Hatzor Museum** (on the grounds of Kibbutz Ayelet Hashachar, across the highway) houses figurines, weapons, stone pots, and other artifacts unearthed in the two areas; others are at the Israel Museum in Jerusalem. It's open by appointment: check ahead. ✉ *Rte. 90, Yesod Hama'ala* ☎ *04/693–7290* 🌐 *www.parks.org.il* 🎫 *NIS 18.*

Hula Lake Nature Reserve

14 km (8½ miles) north of Tel Hatzor, 35 km (22 miles) northeast of Tzfat.

These wetlands were drained during the 1950s after a malaria outbreak, which drove away the unique wildlife. In recent years, the lake was reflooded and birds, especially cranes, once again make it their winter home. About a half-million birds pass through each year.

GETTING HERE AND AROUND

From Tzfat, head east on Route 89 and north on Route 90.

Sights

Ahuzat Dobrovin

HOUSE | For a bit of history head to Ahuzat Dobrovin, near the entrance to the Hula Lake Nature Reserve. The Dobrovin family, Russian immigrants who moved here in 1909, once owned this reconstructed farmhouse. The property was eventually donated to the Jewish National Fund and opened to the public in 1986. An exhibit in the former family home highlights the old days of the Hula Valley, and a short video provides context. A pleasant garden surrounds the property. ✉ *East of Rte. 90, Yesod Hama'ala* ☎ *04/693–7371* 🎫 *NIS 10* 🕒 *Closed Sat.*

Hula Lake Nature Reserve

NATURE PRESERVE | More than 390 avian species flock to the Hula Lake during the migration season (fall and spring), and some remain here for the winter or to nest, which makes this nature preserve a prime spot for bird-watching. The park offers an 8.5-km (5.2-mile) trail with bird-watching huts along the way. Bicycles and golf carts are available for rent. The tractor-drawn safari wagon allows visitors to see otherwise restricted sections of the park. Sunrise and night tours are available for 85 shekels, as are private guides for 350 shekels. Note that this is different from the Hula Nature Reserve (🌐 *www.parks.org.il*). ✉ *Off Rte. 90, Yesod Hama'ala* ☎ *04/681–7137* 🌐 *www.agamon-hula.co.il* 🎫 *NIS 55.*

Hotels

Hotel Galilion

$$$ | **HOTEL** | At the entrance to the Hula Lake Nature Reserve, the Hotel Galilion is a luxurious haven for bird-watchers. **Pros:** convenient location for exploring the north; scenic views; variety of meal plan options. **Cons:** pool area may be noisy if there is a conference or event; lacks character; no heated pool in winter. [$] *Rooms from: $301* ✉ *Rte. 90, Yesod*

Hama'ala ✥ Near entrance to Hula Lake Nature Reserve ☎ 04/697–8008 ⊕ www.galilion.co.il/en/ ✈ 120 rooms ⦿ Some meals; Free Breakfast.

Kiryat Shmona

55 km (34 miles) north of Tiberias, 42 km (26 miles) north of Tzfat.

The major urban center in the Upper Hula Valley, Kiryat Shmona is known for the scenic cable car up Manara Cliff and as a practical base for exploring the most northern sections of the country. Adventure seekers and families can enjoy kayaking and sports in the many surrounding nature parks. For years, the instability in neighboring Lebanon profoundly affected life in the town, and by 1982 the spate of terrorist attacks had reached such proportions that Israel responded by invading Lebanon, the first stage of what would become the First Lebanon War. In 2006, Hezbollah again lobbed rockets into northern Israel, sparking the 34-day Second Lebanon War.

GETTING HERE AND AROUND
From Tzfat, head east on Route 89, then north on Route 90; from Tiberias, head north on Route 90. There are at least 20 buses daily from Tel Aviv, at least 19 from Haifa, and three from Jerusalem.

TAXI CONTACTS Hatzafon Taxi.
☎ 04/694–2333.

⦿ Sights

Manara Cliff
SPORTS VENUE | FAMILY | The Kiryat Shmona–Kibbutz Manara cable car at Manara Cliff gives you a bird's-eye view of the Hula Valley. It has one station midway on the 1,890-yard trip, where the adventurous can step out and do some rappelling and dry sliding (a roller-coaster-like activity) or try the climbing wall. Another option is to ride a mountain bike down or

experience the thrill of a 600-foot zipline. If you opt to remain in the cable car, the trip takes eight minutes each way, overlooking cliffs and green hills. At the bottom are a trampoline and other attractions for kids. There is wheelchair access to the cable car and upper station. ✉ *Kibbutz Manara, Rte. 90 ☎ 04/690–5830 ⊕ www.cliff.co.il ✉ From NIS 59.*

Tel Hai
HISTORIC SITE | Perched on the northern edge of Kiryat Shmona is Tel Hai, meaning "Hill of Life," a site that played an important role in Israel's history. In the aftermath of World War I, while Britain and France bickered over control of the Upper Hula Valley, bands of Arabs often harassed the Jewish farms, and finally overran Tel Hai in 1920. Only Kibbutz Kfar Giladi was successful in defending itself.

Following this incident, Tel Hai resident Josef Trumpeldor and seven comrades were called on to protect the place. Trumpeldor already had a reputation as a leader in the czar's army in his native Russia. Fired by Zionist ideals, he had moved to Palestine in 1912 at the age of 32. During the final battle in 1920, Trumpeldor and his comrades were killed, and it is for them that Kiryat Shmona—City of the Eight—is named. It is said that Trumpeldor's last words were: "It is good to die for our country." He is buried up the road from the Tel Hai Courtyard Museum, beneath the statue of a lion.

The heroic last stand at Tel Hai was important not only because it was the first modern instance of Jewish armed self-defense, but also because the survival of at least two of the Jewish settlements meant that when the final borders were drawn by the League of Nations in 1922, these settlements were included in the British-mandated territory of Palestine and thus, after 1948, in the State of Israel. ✉ *Off Rte. 90, Kfar Giladi.*

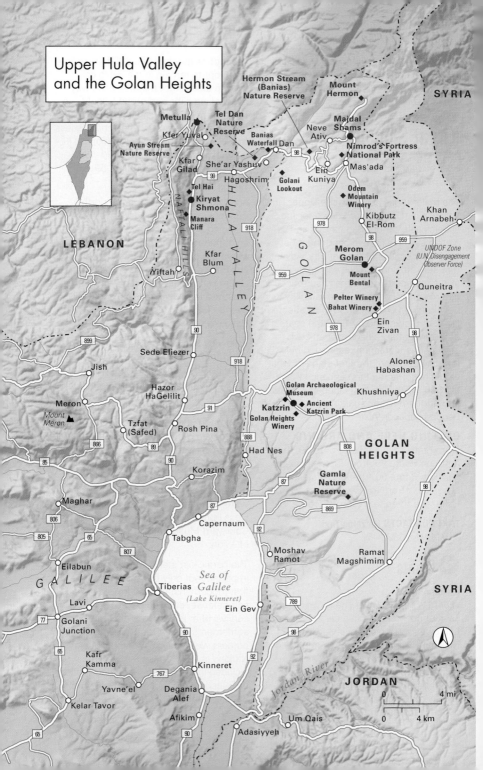

Tel Hai Courtyard Museum

MUSEUM | This museum displays agricultural tools used in the early 20th century when Josef Trumpeldor lived here. A moving audiovisual show highlights the history of the place. Call ahead for reservations. ⊠ *Off Rte. 886, Kfar Giladi* ☎ *04/695–1333.*

 Restaurants

Dag al Hadan

$$$$ | **SEAFOOD** | This forested area beside the gurgling Dan River draws enthusiastic crowds, especially on the weekends for fresh river trout. This was the first restaurant in the region to specialize in the abundant fish from the river; you can also take a look at the trout ponds in a small installation on the grounds. **Known for:** river-to-table trout; salads; fun for kids. $ *Average main: NIS 101* ⊠ *Off Rte. 99, Hagoshrim* ☎ *04/695–0225* ⊕ *www. dagaldan.co.il.*

★ Focaccia Gan Hatzfon

$$$$ | **ECLECTIC** | Ask any local about their favorite place to eat and they will direct you toward this family restaurant tucked into a small shopping center. The menu has a hearty selection of pastas, pizzas, seafood, and meat dishes, all with a contemporary Middle Eastern touch. **Known for:** diverse menu; local favorite; pasta. $ *Average main: NIS 105* ⊠ *Gan Hatzfon, Off Rte. 99, Hagoshrim* ☎ *04/690–4474.*

The Witch's Cauldron and the Milkman

$$$$ | **ECLECTIC** | **FAMILY** | This whimsically decorated restaurant specializes in warming casseroles, such as salmon cooked with coconut milk, ginger, and oranges. Another tasty dish is the lamb simmered in white wine and served with root vegetables. **Known for:** enchanting decor; cauldron casseroles; witch dolls on the walls. $ *Average main: NIS 108* ⊠ *Hagoshrim* ☎ *04/687–0049* ⊕ *the-witch.co.il.*

🛏 Hotels

Grand Vista Boutique Hotel

$$$ | **B&B/INN** | Orchards surround this small hotel, so the heady aromas of the peaches and nectarines will bring you closer to nature as soon as you arrive. **Pros:** mountain views from the pool; cozy environment; whirlpool tub in each room. **Cons:** in a residential neighborhood; decor is a bit outdated; minimal number of rooms. $ *Rooms from: $375* ⊠ *31 Kfar Yuval, Kfar Yuval* ☎ *052/638–8783* ⊕ *www.grandvista.co.il* ⌁ *5 rooms* ⏍ *Free Breakfast.*

Hagoshrim Kibbutz and Resort Hotel

$$$ | **HOTEL** | The waters of the Hermon Stream flow through a glass-covered channel in the lobby of this laid-back lodging. **Pros:** pools and spa; kid-friendly vibe; good selection of tours. **Cons:** basic decor; can get loud in summer; can feel crowded during Israeli holidays. $ *Rooms from: $309* ⊠ *Rte. 99, Hagoshrim* ☎ *04/681–6000* ⊕ *www.hagoshrim-hotel. co.il* ⌁ *164 rooms* ⏍ *Free Breakfast.*

Pastoral Kfar Blum Hotel

$ | **HOTEL** | **FAMILY** | Part of Kibbutz Kfar Blum, this hotel in the Upper Hula Valley has spacious and elegantly appointed rooms. **Pros:** excellent amenities; lovely spa; variety of programs for children. **Cons:** not all rooms are close to the amenities; dated furnishings; few activities in off-season. $ *Rooms from: $154* ⊠ *Off Rte. 90, Kfar Blum* ☎ *04/683–6611* ⊕ *www.kfarblum-hotel.co.il* ⌁ *120 rooms* ⏍ *Free Breakfast.*

🎭 Performing Arts

Chamber Music Days

MUSIC | Each year in late July and early August, the Upper Galilee Regional Council hosts Chamber Music Days, a nationally renowned festival of chamber music in a pastoral setting. ⊠ *Off Rte. 90, Kfar Blum* ☎ *04/681–6640.*

Bird watchers will enjoy the Tel Dan Nature Reserve and the Hermon Stream (Banias) Nature Reserve.

🏃 Activities

A plethora of outfits organize water-sports trips in this region, and almost all hotels can make reservations for you. The minimum age for kayaks and other water "vehicles" is usually six.

KAYAKING
Hagoshrim Kayaks
KAYAKING | This outfit offers a 5-km (3-mile) family course that takes about 90 minutes and a 6-km (4-mile) "stormy" course that lasts almost two hours. ☒ *Off Rte. 99, Hagoshrim* ☎ *077/271–7500* ⊕ *www.kayak.co.il* ✉ *From NIS 89.*

Kibbutz Kfar Blum
KAYAKING | **FAMILY** | Kibbutz Kfar Blum rents two-person rubber kayaks for 1½-hour or two-hour runs. Open March to October, the cost is NIS 97 per person for the short course and NIS 129 per person for the long course. The same site has a climbing wall, a zipline across the water, and archery. ☒ *Kibbutz Kfar Blum, off Rte. 9778* ☎ *072/395–1180* ⊕ *kayaks.co.il.*

OFF-ROAD VEHICLES
Easy Track
LOCAL SPORTS | Based in the northern Hula Valley, Easy Track offers wind-in-your-hair ways to explore the countryside, including self-drive dune buggies and 1½-hour guided Jeep trips. ☒ *Near Rte. 99, She'ar Yashuv* ☎ *04/690–4440* ⊕ *www.mbez. co.il* ✉ *NIS 150 per family for 1½-hr guided Jeep trip.*

Royi Rimon Jeep Tours
FOUR-WHEELING | Set your alarm clock to the crack of dawn and head out with expert guide Royi Rimon for a sunrise Jeep tour through the wilderness, usually including part of the Golan Heights and a ride by a river. He'll drive you up through terrain you would not otherwise be able to visit without a 4x4 vehicle, stopping along the way to explain the surroundings and to brew coffee and tea. Daytime and sunset rides are also fun options. ☒ *Off Rte. 99, Kfar Blum* ☎ *052/297–6312* ✉ *From $190.*

Metulla

9 km (6 miles) north of Kiryat Shmona, 50 km (31 miles) north of Tzfat.

Israel's northernmost town, Metulla, is so picturesque that it's hard to believe this tranquil spot is just a stone's throw from a contentious border. The tensions of the Middle East dissipate here in the charm of the European-style limestone buildings that line Metulla's quaint main street, and the city itself seems to have changed little since its founding as a farming settlement in 1896. The signs offering *zimmer* (German for "room") for rent enhance the Continental atmosphere. Even the weather is un-Mediterranean, with refreshingly cool mountain breezes carrying whiffs of cypress and spice plants in summer, and snow in winter.

GETTING HERE AND AROUND

From Tzfat, head east on Route 89, then north on Route 90.

Sights

Ayun Stream Nature Reserve

NATURE PRESERVE | In summer, the stream that gives this nature reserve its name slows to a trickle because the water is channeled away to irrigate crops. In winter, though, the water gushes, becoming a beautiful backdrop for hiking trips. Two trails meander through the reserve; the shorter one, taking about half an hour, begins and ends in the lower parking lot and goes to Tanur (Oven) Falls, the most famous of the reserve's four waterfalls. The longer one, taking 1½ hours, begins in the upper parking lot and leads downstream. ✉ *East of Rte. 90* ☎ *04/695–1519* 🌐 *www.parks.org.il* 🎟 *NIS 29.*

🍴 Restaurants

HaTachana

$$$$ | **STEAKHOUSE** | This ranch-style restaurant, whose name means "The Mill," uses only the best beef from local cattle for its T-bones. The kitchen also grills up tasty sausages, lamb chops, and hamburgers. **Known for:** farmstead; local meat; veal. [$] *Average main: NIS 140* ✉ *1 Harishonim St.* ☎ *04/694–4810* 🌐 *www.hatachana-m.co.il.*

Tel Dan Nature Reserve

15 km (9½ miles) southeast of Metulla, 10 km (6 miles) northeast of Kiryat Shmona, 50 km (31 miles) northeast of Tzfat.

Full of biblical-era ruins, the nature sanctuary of Tel Dan has three trails running through about 120 protected acres dotted with laurel trees.

GETTING HERE AND AROUND

From Tzfat, head east on Route 89, then turn north on Route 90. Once you pass Kiryat Shmona, turn east on Route 99. The reserve is near Kibbutz Dan.

Sights

Beit Ussishkin Museum

MUSEUM | **FAMILY** | Adjacent to the Tel Dan Nature Reserve, the Beit Ussishkin Museum has interesting exhibits about the flora, fauna, and geology of the Hula Valley, the Golan Heights, and the Jordan River. The audiovisual presentations are concise and informative. The museum is open daily, but you must make an appointment to visit on Friday and Saturday. ✉ *Off Rte. 99, Dan* ☎ *04/694–1704* 🎟 *NIS 18.*

★ Tel Dan Nature Reserve

NATURE PRESERVE | This wildlife sanctuary is hard to beat for sheer natural beauty, and it also contains Tel Dan, an important archaeological site; allow an hour or two for a visit. A river, the Dan Stream, surges through it, and lacy trees provide shade. A host of small mammals lives here—many partial to water, such as the otter and the mongoose—as well as the biblical coney, also known as the hyrax. Tel Dan is home to Israel's largest rodent, the nocturnal Indian crested porcupine, and its smallest predator, the marbled polecat. The reserve has several hiking trails, and a raised wooden walkway is wheelchair accessible.

Dan was a majestic city in biblical times. According to Genesis, Abraham came here to rescue his nephew Lot and, five centuries later, Joshua led the Israelites through the area to victory. Fine ruins from several epochs lie here. Among them are the 9th-century BC city gate and the cultic site where King Jeroboam set up a golden calf to rival the Jerusalem Temple. Just inside the city gate is the platform for a throne, where the city's king pronounced judgment. One of the site's most extraordinary finds is an arched gateway dating from the 18th-century BC Canaanite period, more than a millennium earlier than scholars had previously thought. ⊠ *North of Rte. 99, Dan* ☎ *04/695–1579* ⊕ *www.parks. org.il* ⊠ *NIS 28.*

Hermon Stream (Banias) Nature Reserve

20 km (12½ miles) east of Kiryat Shmona, 50 km (31 miles) northeast of Tzfat.

The country's most impressive waterfall is fed from the spring at the foot of Mount Hermon, which flows powerfully through a canyon before cascading over the rocks.

GETTING HERE AND AROUND
From Tzfat, head east on Route 89, then turn north on Route 90. Once you pass Kiryat Shmona, go east on Route 99.

◉ Sights

★ **Hermon Stream (Banias) Nature Reserve**
NATURE PRESERVE | One of the most stunning parts of Israel, this reserve contains gushing waterfalls, dense foliage along riverbanks, and the remains of a temple dedicated to the god Pan. There are two entrances, each with a parking lot: the sign for the first reads "Banias Waterfall," and the other is 1 km (½ mile) farther along the same road and is marked "Banias."

The **Banias Spring** emerges at the foot of mostly limestone Mount Hermon, just where it meets the basalt layers of the Golan Heights. The most popular short route in the reserve is up to the **Banias Cave,** via the path that crosses the spring. Excavations have revealed the five niches hewed out of the rock to the right of the cave; these are what remain of Hellenistic and Roman temples, depicted in interesting artist renderings. Three of the niches bear inscriptions in Greek, mentioning Pan, the lover of tunes, Echo, the mountain nymph, and Galerius, one of Pan's priests. All early references to the cave identify it as the source of the spring, but earthquakes over the years have changed the landscape, and the water now emerges at the foot of the cave rather than from within it.

The reserve offers three interconnected hiking trails—ask for the English-language trail map and advice at the cashier's booth. One, which passes a Crusader gate, walls, and moat, takes about 45 minutes. The second, also about 45 minutes, explores the magnificent 1,613-square-foot palace complex dating to the 1st century AD and the reign of Herod's grandson, Agrippa II, on top of which are the ruins of what is thought to have been the marketplace of the day: a string of single chambers along a well-preserved section of wall might well have been shops. The third is a 90-minute trail leading past the **Officers' Pool,**

Banias, the City of Pan

The name *Banias* is an Arabic corruption of the Greek *Panias* (Arabic has no *p*), the original name given to the area that, in the early 4th century BC, was dedicated to the colorful Greek god Pan, the half-goat, half-human deity of herdsmen, music, and wild nature—and of homosexuals and nymphs. The Banias Nature Reserve encompasses the ruins of this ancient city.

Herod the Great ruled the city in the 1st century BC; his son Philip inherited it and changed the city's name to Caesarea Philippi, to distinguish it from the Caesarea his father had founded on the Mediterranean coast. The city continued to flourish until after the Muslim conquest in the 7th century AD, when it declined into little more than a village. In the 10th century AD, Muslim immigration brought renewed settlement and Jews also came to Banias (as it became known sometime during the 7th century).

In the early 12th century, Crusaders held Banias, who saw it as a natural border between their kingdom and the neighboring Muslim realm, whose center was Damascus. The Muslims recaptured Banias in 1132, but the city declined in importance and was taken over by Bedouin chieftains. It became a small village, which it remained until the Israel Defense Forces (IDF) conquered the area in the 1967 Six-Day War.

built by the Syrians, and a water-operated flour mill, to the thundering 33-meter-high **Banias Waterfall.** The trails are spiced with the pungent aroma of mint and figs, and studded with blackberry bushes. If time is short, you may prefer to take a brief walk to the falls, return to your car, then drive on to the second entrance to see the caves and the spring where the Hermon Stream originates. The cost of admission covers entry to both sites.

If you're ready for a real hiking challenge and can have a car waiting at the other end, a long, very steep trail leads from the parking lot at the Banias Nature Reserve through the oak and thorny broom forest up to Nimrod's Fortress, a 40- to 60-minute climb. ✉ *Off Rte. 99, Snir* ☎ *04/695–0272, 04/690–2577* 🌐 *www.parks.org.il* 🎫 *NIS 28.*

↗ Golani Lookout

The large number of monuments to fallen soldiers in the Golan is a reminder of the region's strategic importance—and the price paid to secure it. Among the easily accessible sites, where pre-1967 Syrian bunkers give a gunner's-eye view of the valley below, is the Golani Lookout, known in Arabic as Tel Faher, in the northern Golan. Here you can explore the trenches and bunkers that now stand silent. ✉ *Off Rte. 99, Snir.*

Coffee and Quick Bites

Druze Pita Stand

$ | **ISRAELI** | A few minutes' walk along the trail leading to the Banias Waterfall is the ancient flour mill and a stall where Druze villagers make their traditional pita bread (bigger and flatter than the commercial version). It's not only baked on the premises but also milled here. **Known for:** Druze pita; labaneh (yogurt cheese); Turkish coffee. [$] *Average main: NIS 20* ✉ *Hermon Stream (Banias) Nature Preserve, Off Rte. 99, Snir* 💳 *No credit cards.*

Nimrod's Fortress National Park

5 km (3 miles) east of Hermon Stream (Banias) Nature Reserve, 58 km (36 miles) northeast of Tzfat.

Don't pass up a chance to explore the medieval castle called Nimrod's Fortress, which sits near Mount Hermon. Set in a strategic spot, it was sought after by both Christians and Muslims for centuries.

GETTING HERE AND AROUND

From Tzfat, head east on Route 89, then turn north on Route 90. Once you pass Kiryat Shmona, go east on Route 99. Once you pass the Hermon Stream Nature Reserve, turn north on Route 989. The fortress is on the left.

◉ Sights

★ Nimrod's Fortress National Park

MILITARY SITE | FAMILY | The dramatic views of this towering, burly 13th-century fortress, appearing and disappearing behind each curve of the narrow road that leads to it, are part of the treat of a visit to Nimrod's Fortress (Kal'at Namrud), the largest surviving Middle Ages fortress in Israel. The Mamluk warlord al-Malik al-Aziz Othman built it in 1218 to guard the vital route against a possible Crusader reconquest after their 1187 defeat. It changed hands between Muslims and Christians in the succeeding centuries, as both vied for control of the region.

The fortress commands superb vistas of the Golan and the Upper Galilee, especially through the frames of its arched windows and the narrow archers' slits in its walls. Nimrod's Fortress is a highlight for kids, with a ladder down to a vaulted cistern, a shadowy spiral staircase, and unexpected nooks and crannies. A path leads up to the fortress's central tower,

or keep, where the feudal lord would have lived.

⊠ *Rte. 989, Mount Hermon* ☎ *04/694-9277* ⊕ *www.parks.org.il* ⊠ *NIS 22.*

Mount Hermon

16 km (10 miles) north of Nimrod's Fortress National Park, 25 km (15½ miles) northeast of Kiryat Shmona, 66 km (41 miles) northeast of Tzfat.

Israel's highest point is not to be missed for the pleasures the mountain provides, including flower-lined hiking trails in the summer and ski slopes that open with the winter's snow.

GETTING HERE AND AROUND

From Tzfat, head east on Route 89, then turn north on Route 90. Once you pass Kiryat Shmona, go east on Route 99. At Mahanayim Junction turn east on Route 91, then north on Route 98.

◉ Sights

Mount Hermon

MOUNTAIN—SIGHT | The summit of Mount Hermon—famous as Israel's highest mountain, at 9,230 feet above sea level—is actually in Syrian territory. Its lower slopes attract winter visitors to the country's only ski resort, though summer is arguably the most interesting time on the Hermon. After the winter snows melt, hikers can discover chasms and hidden valleys here, the long-term result of extremes in temperature. A powerful array of colors and scents emerges from the earth as the summer sun draws out cockscomb, chamomile, and scores of other flowers and wild herbs. Approaching from Nimrod's Fortress, you'll pass **Moshav Neve Ativ,** designed to look like a little piece of the Alps in the Middle East, complete with A-frame chalet-style houses, a handful of which have guest rooms. A detour through the old Druze village of **Majdal Shams** offers a number of good eateries. **Ein Kiniya**, another Druze village, appears across a valley on your left as you head east into the Golan on Route 99, is the most picturesque in the area. The houses are built from the black basalt typical of the Golan. ✉ *Rte. 98.*

Majdal Shams

25 km (15½ miles) east of Kiryat Shmona, 35 km (22 miles) north of Katzrin.

Majdal Shams may not look like much, but the Druze town is a hub for skiers in the winter and berry pickers in the fall. The area is a year-round destination for wine lovers because of the local vineyards, and for foodies, as Druze cuisine is renowned in the region.

Unlike their counterparts in the Galilee, the Druze of the Golan Heights do not, for the most part, consider themselves Israeli citizens. They do, however, consider themselves an important part of the country's cultural landscape.

GETTING HERE AND AROUND

From Kiryat Shmona, head east on Route 99, then turn north at Mas'ada onto Route 98, which will take you into Majdal Shams. The streets aren't signed in English, so call ahead for directions to your hotel.

Sights

Odem Mountain Winery

WINERY/DISTILLERY | This family-owned boutique kosher winery, located between Majdal Shams and Merom Golan, produces 80,000 bottles a year, mostly dry reds nurtured by the area's volcanic soil, but also a crisp Chardonnay. There are lovely fortified wines and cherry wines as well. Drop in for an impromptu tasting, where local cheeses are also for sale. Half-hour tours of the vineyards are available by appointment. ✉ *Moshav Odem, Off Rte. 978* ☎ *04/687–1122* 🌐 *www.harodem.co.il* 🎫 *Free* 🕒 *Closed Sat.*

Restaurants

Abu Zaid

$ | MIDDLE EASTERN | For a delicious dessert, stop by Abu Zaid on Majdal Shams' main street, which sells a type of orange-hued pastry called *knafeh*. Similar to baklava, it has delicious layers of gooey goat cheese covered in a flaky crust and peppered with pistachios. Ask for a slice from the large tray—one serving could be easily enjoyed by two. **Known for:** knafeh; pastries big enough to share; warm to-go snacks. [$] *Average main: NIS 15* ✉ *Northern end of main street* ☎ *052/698–3190* 💳 *No credit cards.*

Merom Golan

20 km (12½ miles) south of Mount Hermon, 46 km (28 miles) northeast of Tzfat.

Kibbutz Merom Golan was the first settlement built in the Golan after the Six-Day War. Its fields and orchards are typical of local kibbutzim. Apples and cherries are especially good in these parts. Another popular attraction is the nearby Mount Bental lookout.

GETTING HERE AND AROUND

From Tzfat, head east on Route 89, then north on Route 90. At Mahanayim Junction, turn east on Route 91, then north on Route 98. Merom Golan is on the left.

Sights

Bahat Winery

WINERY/DISTILLERY | This winery sells 5,000 bottles of its kosher wine, made using traditional methods, each year. The grapes—mostly Cabernet Sauvignon, Pinot Noir, and Chardonnay—are grown in basalt soil 3,280 feet above sea level. The wines' distinctive flavor comes from being aged in French oak barrels. Owner Ofer Bahat is happy to divulge information and offer tastings. ✉ *Off Rte. 91, Ein*

Zivan ☎ *050/877–1770* 🌐 *bahatwinery.co.il* 🕒 *Closed Sat.*

De Karina Chocolate Boutique
STORE/MALL | Selling treats for the young and young at heart, De Karina was founded by a third-generation chocolatier from Argentina. Try the Mount Hermon—milk-chocolate cones topped by white-chocolate "snow." Call in advance for factory tours and chocolate-making workshops. ✉ *Off Rte. 91, Ein Zivan* ☎ *04/699–3622* 🌐 *www.de-karina.co.il* 🎫 *Tour NIS 22, workshop NIS 65* 🕒 *Closed Sat.*

Mount Bental
VIEWPOINT | From the top of this volcanic cone, at an open-air lookout that was once a military outpost, you can see Mount Hermon rising majestically to the north and the Syrian side of the Golan stretching eastward. Opposite is the ruined town of Kuneitra, captured by Israel in 1967, lost and regained in the 1973 Yom Kippur War, and returned to Syria in the subsequent disengagement agreement—it is now a demilitarized zone. Modern Kuneitra is in the distance. The cluster of white buildings south of old Kuneitra houses the United Nations Disengagement Observer Force. A pine-cabin shop serving coffees, herbal teas, and a nice selection of snacks is the perfect place to get out of the wind that often sweeps this peak. The lookout is near Kibbutz Merom Golan; signs along the rural roads point the way. It's open all the time. ✉ *Off Rte. 98 and Rte. 959, Mount Bental* 🎫 *Free.*

★ **Pelter Winery**
WINERY/DISTILLERY | An Australian-trained winemaker named Tal Pelter aspired to bring his modern oenology training and methodology to the Israeli market. Starting with a yearly release of 4,000 bottles and rapidly increasing production to more than 100,000 bottles, Pelter is now one of Israel's most beloved wineries. In addition Pelter makes cognac, arak, and brandy, which he offers as part of the intimate winery tours; both wine and cognac pair nicely with his wife's homemade goat cheese—also available for purchase. ✉ *Off Rte. 91, Ein Zivan* ☎ *052/866–6384* 🌐 *pelter.co.il/en* 🎫 *NIS 50 for tour and wine tasting.*

🍴 Restaurants

Cowboys' Restaurant
$$$$ | **STEAKHOUSE** | This is the best corral this side of the Israel-Syria disengagement zone. Saddle-shape stools at the bar and cattle hides on the walls contribute to the frontier atmosphere. **Known for:** kosher meats; Friday night buffet; rack of lamb. [$] *Average main: NIS 125* ✉ *Off Rte. 959* ☎ *04/696–0206.*

Mattarello
$ | **CAFÉ** | **FAMILY** | Professional photographer turned baker Adi Peretz shares his passion for doughs by churning out daily batches of savory breads, sweet brioches, and classics like iced carrot cake with walnuts and raisins. Pack your coffee and breads to go or eat a delicious egg-filled croissant sandwich before heading to one of the neighboring wineries. **Known for:** baked goods; breakfast croissants; good coffee. [$] *Average main: NIS 48* ✉ *In the Kibbutz, Off Rte. 91, Ein Zivan* ☎ *054/246–8019.*

Katzrin

20 km (12½ miles) south of Merom Golan, 38 km (23½ miles) northeast of Tiberias, 35 km (22 miles) northeast of Tzfat.

Katzrin, founded in 1977 near the site of a 3rd-century town of the same name, has a suburban feel, despite its strategic location. The water here, which comes straight from the basalt bedrock, is delicious and makes your skin feel like silk.

GETTING HERE AND AROUND

From Tzfat, head east on Route 89, then north on Route 90. At Mahanayim Junction turn east on Route 91, then south on Route 9088.

Sights

Ancient Katzrin Park

ARCHAEOLOGICAL SITE | FAMILY | About 2 km (1 mile) east of downtown Katzrin, this attraction is a partially restored 3rd-century Jewish village. The Katzrin synagogue has decorative architectural details, such as a wreath of pomegranates and amphorae in relief on the lintel above the entrance. The complexity of its ornamentation reflects the importance of the city. Built of basalt, the synagogue was used for 400 years until it was partly destroyed, possibly by an earthquake, in AD 749. Two reconstructed buildings, the so-called House of Uzi and House of Rabbi Abun, are attractively decorated with rope baskets, weavings, baking vessels, and pottery (based on remnants of the originals), and lighted with little clay oil lamps. ✉ *Rte. 87* ☎ *04/696–2412* 🎟 *NIS 28, includes Golan Archaeological Museum.*

Golan Archaeological Museum

MUSEUM | This museum has a fascinating collection of animal bones, stones, and artifacts that put the region into historical and geographical perspective. Among the exhibits is a Bronze Age dwelling reconstructed from materials excavated nearby. Don't miss the moving film on the last stand at Gamla, the "Masada of the North," during the Jews' Great Revolt against Rome in AD 66. The museum reveals how it was rediscovered by archaeologists 1,900 years later. ✉ *Near corner of Sion and Daliyot Sts.* ☎ *04/696–1350* 🎟 *NIS 28, includes Ancient Katzrin Park* 🕒 *Closed Sat.*

Golan Heights Winery

WINERY/DISTILLERY | This winery caught the world's attention with its award-winning Yarden, Gamla, and Golan labels. The area's volcanic soil, cold winters, and cool summers, together with state-of-the-art wine making, have proven a recipe for success. The shop sells the full line of wines, including the Katzrin Chardonnay, the Yarden Gewürztraminer, and the Yarden Cabernet Sauvignon, as well as sophisticated accessories for the oenophile. Call in advance about a tour of the winery and a tasting; the winery offers a number of options. ✉ *Derekh-ha-Yayin St., near southern entrance to town* ☎ *04/696–8435* 🌐 *www.golanwines.co.il* 🎟 *NIS 20 1-hr tour and tasting* 🕒 *Closed Sat.*

Restaurants

The commercial center of Katzrin, the "capital" of the Golan Heights, has a number of falafel stands, a couple of restaurants, and a pizzeria, making it a convenient midday stop for travelers.

Hotels

★ Assaf Cabins and Winery

$$$ | B&B/INN | A family business in every sense, the Kedem family's "wine village" includes a full-range culinary experience from the welcoming lunch and made-to-order breakfast from daughter Adi's on-property café to wine tastings at the family's award-winning winery and complimentary homemade snacks and wine in the luxurious cabins designed by son Shahar. **Pros:** warm and welcoming hosts; spacious cabins; complimentary bottles of wine in the room. **Cons:** no pool; breakfast can be crowded on weekends; often booked up. [$] *Rooms from: $350* ✉ *Katzrin* ☎ *054/391–5552* 🌐 *www.assafwinery.com* 🛏 *3 rooms* 🍴 *Free Breakfast.*

Gamla Nature Reserve

20 km (12 miles) southeast of Katzrin.

Aside from the inspiring history of the "Masada of the North," the beauty of Gamla's rugged terrain, softened in spring by greenery and wildflowers, is truly breathtaking. Griffon vultures soar above, and you can often see gazelles bounding through the grasses.

GETTING HERE AND AROUND

From Tzfat, head east on Route 89, then south on Route 90. Turn east on Route 87, then south on Route 808. Watch for the Gamla signpost.

Sights

Gamla Nature Reserve

ARCHAEOLOGICAL SITE | **FAMILY** | Tour the ruins of an ancient town, look out to the cliffs at Gamla Stream canyon, and see Israel's tallest waterfall (51 m) from an accessible lookout station at this national park and reserve. There are picturesque streams for nature walks, and varied wildlife to spot, including gazelles and nesting bird colonies.

The main story of the camel-shape Gamla (the name comes from *gamal,* the Hebrew word for "camel") goes back to the year AD 67, when at the beginning of the Great Revolt, Vespasian launched a bloody attack here that ended seven months later, when the 9,000 surviving Jews flung themselves to their deaths in the abyss below the town. The vivid descriptions of the battle, as written by Flavius Josephus in *The Jewish War,* are engraved in stones along the trail site: "Built against the almost vertical flank, the town seemed to be hung in the air"—exactly the impression visitors still have as they approach the site. Because Gamla was never rebuilt, the relics of the battlefield still eerily match the ancient sources, among them the fortifications, 2,000 "missile stones," and a large number of arrowheads. From a much earlier period (probably the 2nd millennium BC), there are about 200 **dolmens** scattered in the area—strange basalt structures shaped like the Greek letter *pi,* probably used for burial. There is an excellent film on the story of Gamla at the Golan Archaeological Museum in Katzrin. The raptor observation station is fun for kids. ✉ *Off Rte. 869, Gamla* ☎ *04/682–2282* 🌐 *www.parks.org.il* 🎫 *NIS 28.*

Restaurants

HaBikta

$$$$ | **ISRAELI** | With a name that literally means "the cabin," HaBikta evokes the smoked meats for which it's best known. The chicken and steaks, smoked over cherrywood and grapevines, come with access to the generous salad buffet. **Known for:** smoked meats; kosher; great salads. [$] *Average main: NIS 130* ✉ *East of Rte.92* ✥ *Follow directions (there are no street names in the area) when you get to Moshav Ramot* ☎ *04/679–4016* 🌐 *www.ha-bikta.co.il* 🕒 *Closed Fri. and Sat.*

Moshbutz

$$$$ | **STEAKHOUSE** | The local spirit at play in this restaurant's name—a combination of moshav and kibbutz, two types of Israeli agricultural communities—also shapes the menu at Moshbutz. This eatery's farm-fresh philosophy is integral, as the chef sources all of the ingredients from Golan Heights. **Known for:** farm-to-table dining; aged lamb and beef; Sea of Galilee views. [$] *Average main: NIS 130* ✉ *Nof Kinneret St.* ☎ *04/679–5095* 🌐 *www.moshbutz.co.il.*

🛏 Hotels

Beit Ram Sheraf

$$ | **B&B/INN** | **FAMILY** | The four suites owned by Judit Sheraf and Avi Ram are the perfect place for a family weekend: each cottage has a double bedroom, living room that sleeps three, kitchenette, heated outdoor Jacuzzi, and very large private yard with grill and hammock or swing set. **Pros:** heated pool; child-friendly atmosphere; helpful owners. **Cons:** relatively expensive; mosquitoes in summer; beds could use more modern coverings. Ⓢ *Rooms from: $250* ✉ *32 Zevitan St.* ☎ *052/284–4013* ⊕ *www.beit-ram.co.il* ⤵ *5 cottages* ⦿ *No meals.*

★ Cnaan Village

$$$ | **B&B/INN** | If relaxation is what you're after, look no further than this homey getaway, a good base for exploring the sights in the Golan Heights. **Pros:** unique pool; extraordinary breakfast; lovely owner. **Cons:** signage is hard to see; in a residential area; no dinner option. Ⓢ *Rooms from: $345* ✉ *Had Nes 13, Had Nes* ☎ *04/682–2128* ⊕ *www.cnaan-village.co.il* ⤵ *5 rooms* ⦿ *Free Breakfast.*

Ramot Resort Hotel

$$ | **HOTEL** | High in the foothills of Golan Heights, this hotel is only a few minutes from good beaches and a water park. **Pros:** convenient to national parks; cooler temperatures than at the lake; beautiful vistas. **Cons:** no evening entertainment; not all rooms have Jacuzzi; only some rooms renovated. Ⓢ *Rooms from: $221* ✉ *East of Rte. 92* ☎ *04/673–2636* ⊕ *www.ramot-nofesh.co.il* ⤵ *123 rooms* ⦿ *Free Breakfast.*

Chapter 9

EILAT AND
THE NEGEV

Updated by
Shari Giddens

◉ Sights	🍴 Restaurants	🛏 Hotels	🛍 Shopping	🍸 Nightlife
★★★★★	★★★★☆	★★★★☆	★★★☆☆	★★☆☆☆

WELCOME TO EILAT AND THE NEGEV

TOP REASONS TO GO

★ **Coral Beach Nature Reserve:** Put on a snorkel and marvel at the brilliantly colored fish and entrancing corals at one of the world's finest protected coral reefs.

★ **Hiking the Negev:** Explore the splendid scenery, deep wadis, rugged heights, and steep cliff faces of the Negev. The mountains of Eilat and the desert craters offer spectacular hikes.

★ **Makhtesh Ramon:** This giant crater is an utterly unique geological phenomenon, with hundreds of rock formations and multihue cliffs.

★ **Timna Park:** A half-hour from Eilat, trek across the lunarlike landscape, making sure to see this desert park's famous red-hue Solomon's Pillars and its 20-foot mushroom-shape rock formation.

★ **Yotvata Hai-Bar Nature Reserve:** Come face-to-face with fearsome birds of prey in the Predator Center of this thrilling nature preserve north of Eilat.

Three basic areas in the inverted triangle of the Negev, Israel's southern desert, make up the southern part of the country. The first, and farthest south, is carefree Eilat, with the Underwater Observatory Marine Park at Coral Beach, and Timna Park. Next is the Negev's heart, with sites such as Ben-Gurion's desert home and grave, the ancient Nabatean-Roman-Byzantine ruins at Avdat, and the amazing Makhtesh Ramon (Ramon Crater). The third, in the north, includes the regional capital city of Beersheva.

1 Eilat. Sun-drenched Eilat, a resort town on the shores of the Red Sea, brims with hotels, restaurants, duty-free shopping, and the lion's share of the Negev's nightlife.

2 Timna Park. With a majestic desert setting, Timna Park is home to the world's first copper mines.

3 Red Canyon. Just northwest of Eilat you can hike a beautiful, narrow canyon that may remind you of the American Southwest.

4 Yotvata Hai-Bar Nature Reserve. Endangered animals are bred here for possible reintroduction to the Negev desert.

5 Mitzpe Ramon and Makhtesh Ramon. Impressive natural wonders with great meals nearby.

6 Avdat National Park. A critical stop on the Incense Route, Avdat National Park is home to the remains of a ruined city.

7 Ein Avdat National Park and Vicinity. This accessible and striking national park allows for easy desert hiking.

8 Beersheva. Israel's fourth-largest city, Beersheva makes a great jumping-off point for trips around the Negev. Tel Beersheva, with the remains of a biblical-era city, is a World Heritage Site.

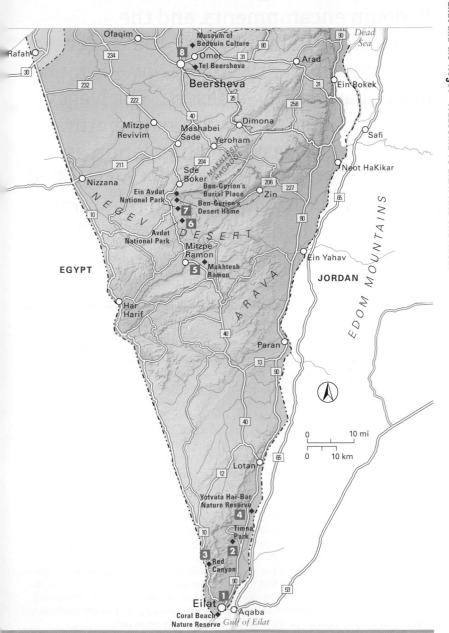

Ofaqim

Museum of
Bedouin Culture

Rafah

234

30

80

90

Dead
Sea

8 Omer
31
Tel Beersheva

Arad

31 Ein Bokek

Beersheva

232

222

25

258

40

Mitzpe
Revivim

Mashabei
Sade
Yeroham

Dimona

Safi

211

204

Sde
Boker

MAKHTESH
HAGADOL

Neot HaKikar

Nizzana

NEGEV

10

Ein Avdat
National Park

Ben-Gurion's
Burial Place

7

6 Ben-Gurion's
Desert Home

206
Zin

227

65

90

Avdat
National Park

DESERT

Mitzpe
Ramon

Ein Yahav

EGYPT

5 Makhtesh
Ramon

JORDAN

EDOM MOUNTAINS

ARAVA

Har
Harif

40

Paran

13

90

0   10 mi

0   10 km

40

Lotan

65

12

Yotvata Hai-Bar
Nature Reserve

4

Timna
Park

10

2

3 Red
Canyon

90

1

Eilat

53

Coral Beach
Nature Reserve Gulf of Eilat

Aqaba

With its stark mountains, dramatic wadis, archaeological treasures, colorful Bedouin encampments, and the spectacular Ramon Crater, the Negev—a word meaning "dry" in Hebrew—is much more than simply "a desert." The Negev contains Israel's most dramatic natural scenery, with its rugged highlands, as well as Eilat, a resort town set on the Red Sea, with luxury hotels, good restaurants and bars, and duty-free shopping. There's even a growing winery scene here that will intrigue oenophiles.

The region can satisfy both history buffs and adventure lovers. You can visit the kibbutz home and grave of Israel's founding father and first prime minister—David Ben-Gurion, the man who first dreamed of settling the desert—and on the same day, you can tour the millennia-old ruins at Tel Beersheva, visited by the biblical patriarch Abraham. For those seeking adventure, the Negev is the place to take camel treks and Jeep tours, spend the afternoon hiking, or scuba dive in the Red Sea.

The Negev makes up about half the country's land area, yet is home to only about 8% of its population. The ancient Israelites had fortifications here, as did the merchant Nabateans and the Romans after them. The region's first kibbutzim were established in the early 1940s, with new immigrants sent south after the War of Independence, in 1948.

Two years later, people started trickling into Eilat, which was nothing but a few rickety huts. The desert itself was made to bloom, and the semiarid areas between Tel Aviv and Beersheva became fertile farmland. Today, agricultural settlements throughout the Negev make use of advanced irrigation to raise tomatoes, melons, olives, and dates that are exported to winter markets in Europe.

MAJOR REGIONS

In **Eilat and Southern Israel,** the Arava Plain comes to an abrupt end where it meets the Bay of Eilat, home to Israel's southernmost town: the sun-drenched resort of Eilat. The Gulf of Eilat gives way to the Red Sea, which lies between the Sinai Mountains to the west and Jordan's Edom Mountains to the east. The Jordanian port of Aqaba is directly across the bay, so close you can see the distinctive flag flapping on its pole.

Most travelers fly down to Eilat to flop down on its beaches and snorkel or scuba dive among its tropical reefs. But if you have time, explore the vast desert landscape to the north of Eilat. You'll find cliffs, canyons, and unique geological formations at Timna Park and indigenous animals at Yotvata Hai-Bar Nature Reserve. Both make good side trips from Eilat.

In **the Heart of Negev,** the very center of the upside-down triangle that makes up the Negev, you'll find several of the region's top sites, including the immense Makhtesh Ramon (Ramon Crater) and Ben-Gurion's desert home and grave, as well as the remains of the ancient Nabatean city of Avdat, an icy desert pool at Ein Avdat. You'll also have the opportunity to meet the Negev's indigenous people, the Bedouin.

Israel's fourth-largest city, **Beersheva** makes a great jumping-off point for trips around the Negev. Tel Beersheva, with the remains of a biblical-era city, is a World Heritage Site.

Planning

When to Go

October through May is the best time to explore the Negev. In early March, scarlet, bright yellow, and hot pink desert flowers burst out against the brown desert earth; March is also when Eilat's International Bird-watchers' Festival takes place. In January and February, it's dry and cold, especially at night. Scorching-hot conditions prevail in the summer, from June through September, though it's very dry, and locals claim this is the "sleeper season" to be here: no humidity, cool nights, fewer crowds, and easier availability at desirable hotels, restaurants, and venues.

Desert Precautions

To remain comfortable and safe, respect certain rules of the desert. Drink 2 quarts of water a day in winter and 1 quart per hour in summer. Keep a jerrican (which holds 5 gallons) of water in your car, plus extra bottles. Water fountains along the way don't always work. Flash floods pose an occasional danger from September through March, especially after rainfall farther north. If even a small amount of water is flowing across the road, wait for it to stop (it can take a while); it can be a sign of imminent flooding. Driving at night isn't recommended; plan to reach your destination by 5 pm in winter and by 8 pm in summer. Make sure to have a car charger for your cell phone; service is spotty, and phones seeking available networks eat up battery life.

Planning Your Time

The main attraction in Israel's south is the resort town of Eilat, the country's beach playground. Its attractions are sand, sun, and surf, and it's the place for a few days of scuba, snorkeling, and sunbathing. Some desert excursions like Timna Park are nearby, and it's also easy to arrange a day trip to Petra, in Jordan, from Eilat.

However, if you don't care for the beach, or if you love the desert landscape, consider a couple of days in Mitzpe Ramon instead. About an hour's drive south of Beersheva, and perched on the edge of a vast crater 40 km (25 miles) long, Mitzpe Ramon offers abundant outdoor activities. Ecotours, mountain biking, and Jeep trekking, as well as guide-led hiking to take in the history and science of the area, are among the options. You can explore nearby sites including Sde Boker, the desert home of David Ben-Gurion, Israel's first prime minister, and the remains of the ancient Nabatean city of Avdat, a UNESCO World Heritage

Site. Israel's wine industry has put down some roots in the Negev, and you can visit wineries such as Carmey Avdat.

Most Negev sites open at 8:30 am and close by 4 pm in winter and 5 pm in summer. Keep in mind that outside Eilat, restaurants close early on Friday for the Jewish Sabbath, and since the main meal of the day is served at noon in the desert, lunch may be history if you arrive after 1:30; roadside diners close at around 1:30 pm.

Getting Here and Around

AIR
Flights to Eilat take off from Ben Gurion Airport (about halfway between Jerusalem and Tel Aviv), Sde Dov Airport in north Tel Aviv, and Haifa Airport. Two domestic airlines serve Eilat: Arkia and Israir. Fares vary wildly, often cheapest for crack-of-dawn flights or off-hours. The new regional and international airport, **Ramon Airport** (⊕ www.ramon-airport. com), is 18 km (11 miles) north of Eilat; shuttles take travelers to Eilat.

BUS
Egged, the national bus company, runs frequent service to Beersheva from Tel Aviv and Jerusalem; each takes about 1½ hours. Buses to Eilat from the same cities take 4½ to 5 hours. You can reserve tickets up to two weeks in advance, which is recommended for weekend travel. Within Eilat, Bus 15 starts at the Central Bus Station (near the entrance to town) and runs through the hotel area before heading south to the Taba border with Egypt. Bus 16 follows the same route, only in reverse.

CAR
The only way to see the Negev Desert is to drive (air-conditioning is a must, especially in the summer). Beersheva is 113 km (70 miles) southeast of Tel Aviv and 83 km (52 miles) south of Jerusalem. To

get to Eilat from Tel Aviv, the most direct way is Route 40 south to Beersheva, which takes about five hours.

TRAIN
Israel Railways runs between Tel Aviv and Beersheva. There's frequent service (except on Saturday, when there are only two trains, both late in the evening). High-speed trains have shaved a lot of time off the trip, allowing you to get from Tel Aviv to Beersheva in 50 minutes.

Hotels

Hotels in sunny Eilat run from family-style inns to huge, lush, and luxurious lodgings. Luxurious spas with a wide range of treatments can be found at every large hotel. Even many of the smaller hotels have installed spas to catch the attention of travelers in search of pampering. In Eilat, a few hotels operate on an all-inclusive basis. Rooms are hardest to come by, and most expensive, around Hanukkah and Christmas, Passover and Easter, and July and August. Eilat is Israel's number one destination for families, so expect lots of kids at the pool.

Hotel reviews have been shortened. For more information, visit Fodors.com.

Restaurants

Although Eilat is nestled at the southern tip of a desert, there are all sorts of cuisines to choose from when you're dining out: Italian, Indian, French, Argentinean, Yemenite, and Thai among them. There's excellent fish, including delicacies such as *denis* (sea bream). In the past few years, Beersheva has added a host of tasty options to its dining scene. In the rest of the Negev, meals often reflect the cook's ethnic heritage. Visitors who keep kosher should note that while most hotels serve kosher meals, few of the restaurants in Eilat are kosher, including chains with kosher branches elsewhere.

What It Costs

$	$$	$$$	$$$$
RESTAURANTS			
Under NIS 50	NIS 50–NIS 75	NIS 76–NIS 100	over NIS 100
HOTELS			
Under $200	$200–$300	$301–$400	over $400

Eilat

307 km (190 miles) south of Jerusalem, 356 km (221 miles) south of Tel Aviv.

A legend says that after the Creation, the angels painted the earth and when they got tired, they spilled their paints: the blue became the waters of Eilat, and the other colors became its fish and coral. Combine Eilat's year-round warm weather, its superb natural surroundings of sculptural red-orange mountains, and its prime location on the sparkling Red Sea—whose coral reefs attract divers from all over the world—and you've got a first-rate resort.

Eilat, a city of about 50,000, is now Israel's prototypical "sun-and-fun" destination. But its strategic location as a crossroads between Asia and Africa has long given it a place in history. Because of its position on a main trade and travel route, Eilat was conquered by every major power: the Romans, Byzantines, Arabs, Crusaders, Mamluks, Ottoman Turks, and, most recently, the British, whose isolated police station, called Umm Rash Rash (headquarters of their camel corps), was the first building in modern-day Eilat.

Most travelers agree that Eilat's natural assets more than make up for its undistinguished architecture and overdevelopment. For wherever you are in Eilat, a glance eastward presents you with the dramatic sight of the granite mountain range of Edom, whose shades of red intensify toward evening, culminating in a crimson sunset blaze over the Red Sea.

GETTING HERE AND AROUND

The most direct way to Eilat from both Tel Aviv and Jerusalem is via Beersheva. By car, the trip takes about five hours. For bus travel between Eilat, Tel Aviv, Jerusalem, and points in between, the national bus company, Egged, provides widespread service.

In Eilat, the preferred way of hopping from one place to another is by taxi. Rides don't usually cost much more than NIS 35, and you can hail a cab on the street.

CONTACTS Eilat Central Bus Station. ⊠ *12 Ha-Tmarim Blvd., next to Shalom Mall.*

VISITOR INFORMATION

The Eilat Tourist Information Office packs lots of information into a tiny space. Inside, you'll find a wall of helpful flyers about attractions and cultural events. Accommodating employees will happily connect you with guides and outfitters, writing down numbers and even making calls when they can.

CONTACTS Eilat Tourist Information Office. ⊠ *8 Beit HaGesher St.* ☎ *08/630–9111* ⊕ *eilat.city/en.*

◉ Sights

Botanical Garden of Eilat

GARDEN | FAMILY | This former military base is now home to plants from all over the world, as well as some grown from seeds thousands of years old. The small, family-friendly park is a green oasis in the middle of the desert. An easy walk takes you to a waterfall and an artificial rain forest that mists every few minutes. You can explore the whole garden in under an

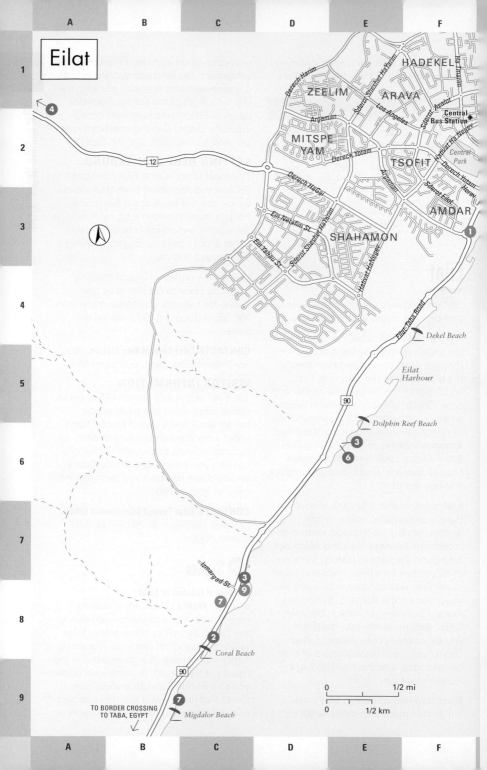

Eilat

HADEKEL

ZEELIM

ARAVA

Derech Harim

Sderot Shesher Ha'arim

Los Angeles

Argaman

Sderot Ayalot

Central Bus Station

MITSPE YAM

Derech Yotam

TSOFIT

Central Park

Derech HaGai

Argaman

Sderot Eilat

Sderot Yotam

Derech Yotam Horev

AMDAR

①

Ein Netafim St.

Sderot Shesher Ha'arim

SHAHAMON

Ein Yahav St.

Ha'arri Ha'avara

Eilat Taba Road

Dekel Beach

Eilat Harbour

90

Dolphin Reef Beach

③

⑥

Jarragad St.

③

⑨

⑦

②

90

Coral Beach

⑦

Migdalor Beach

TO BORDER CROSSING
TO TABA, EGYPT

0		1/2 mi
0		1/2 km

④

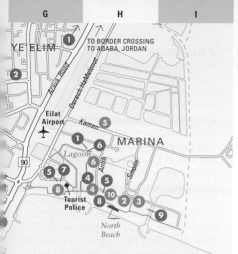

Sights ▼

1 Botanical Garden of Eilat **G1**
2 Coral Beach Nature Reserve **C8**
3 Dolphin Reef **E6**
4 Mount Yoash **A1**
5 Promenade **H3**
6 The Relaxation Pools at Dolphin Reef **E6**
7 Underwater Observatory Marine Park **B9**

Restaurants ▼

1 Agadir **H2**
2 Lalo **G1**
3 Last Refuge **C7**
4 Les Sardines **H3**
5 Olla **G3**
6 Pago Pago Restaurant **H2**
7 Pastory **G3**
8 Ranch House **H3**
9 Whale **H3**

Hotels ▼

1 Aria Hotel **F3**
2 Dan Eilat Hotel **H3**
3 Herods Palace Hotel ... **H3**
4 Hilton Eilat Queen of Sheba **H3**
5 Isrotel Agamim **H2**
6 Isrotel King Solomon ... **H2**
7 Isrotel Yam Suf **C8**
8 Leonardo Plaza Hotel Eilat **G3**
9 The Reef Hotel by Herbert Samuel **C8**
10 Royal Beach Eilat **H3**

hour. The refreshment area serves coffee and ice cream. ⊠ *HaCarmel St.* ⊕ *Behind gas station* ☎ *08/631–8788* ⊕ *www. botanicgarden.co.il* ⊠ *NIS 25* ⊗ *Closed after 3 pm on Fri. and Sat.*

★ Coral Beach Nature Reserve

NATURE PRESERVE | Less than 1 km (½ mile) south of Eilat, this is one of the finest and most densely populated coral reefs in the world. Close to the shoreline, the reef is 1¼ km (¾ mile) long and is zealously guarded by the Israel Nature and Parks Authority. The northernmost reef in the world, it contains more than 100 types of coral and 650 species of fish. In the lagoon, divers and snorkelers take two bridges or a trail marked by buoys to get to the reef wall. Stunning multicolored fish and soft and hard corals are your rich reward. There are hot showers, a snack bar, and snorkel rentals. Kids should be at least five to snorkel. ⊠ *Rte. 90 (Eilat–Taba Rd.), opposite Eilat Field School* ☎ *08/632–6422* ⊕ *www.parks. org.il* ⊠ *NIS 35.*

Dolphin Reef

BEACH—SIGHT | **FAMILY** | Very popular with families, this observation point has a high admission charge, but the perks make it worthwhile. The highlight is the opportunity to walk on wooden paths extending into the water. You may see a dolphin leaping, but more likely you'll see groups snorkeling with dolphins. If you feel like trying it yourself, it costs about NIS 290 per person. In addition to a spacious sandy beach punctuated with billowing palms and bright tropical flowers, chairs and umbrellas are available (but get there early to avoid crowds). There's an indoor café-bar to escape the sun, a great gift shop, and even a video you can watch to learn about dolphins. ⊠ *Rte. 90 (Eilat– Taba Rd.), South Beach* ☎ *08/630–0111* ⊕ *dolphinreef.co.il* ⊠ *NIS 72.*

↗ Mount Yoash

This lookout point along the border road with Egypt is an easy trip from Eilat. Head west along Route 12 into the Eilat Mountains Nature Reserve. After 12 km (7½ miles), turn left at the orange sign for Mount Yoash and continue 1 km (½ mile) up a rough and winding stone road. Park and take in knockout views of the alternating light and dark ridges of the Eilat Mountains, the mountains of Edom rising behind the Jordanian city of Aqaba, and the Nahal Geshron gorge emptying into the Red Sea at Taba, in Egypt. A beautiful two-hour hiking trail begins in the parking lot. The Jordanian army operated a strategic post here until 1949, when Israeli forces took it during the last campaign of the War of Independence. The raising of a makeshift Israeli flag here marked the end of the war. ⊠ *Rte. 12.*

Promenade

PROMENADE | Start at the quieter, northernmost end of Eilat's waterfront *tayelet,* or promenade, which begins near the Jordanian border. The 3-km (2-mile) stretch is also known as the Peace Walk, because it is hoped that one day it will continue to Aqaba, Jordan. As you head south, purple and pink bougainvillea pour down from the Royal Beach Hotel's terrace above. Add to your enjoyment by stopping for an ice cream from one of the stands. If you're here at sunset, savor the show-stopping view of the Red Sea turning deeper and deeper shades of red against the backdrop of the Edom Mountains to the east and the rugged Eilat Mountains to the west. On a clear day, you can see as far as Saudi Arabia and Egypt.

A stroll past swanky hotels on one side and palm-lined beaches on the other brings you to the Dutch Bridge, which opens for tall-masted vessels. The lagoon is where yachts are anchored and various small craft are for hire; on the other side is the marina, where cruise boats of all types wait to sally forth. The promenade winds past more beaches covered with sunbathers. The scene includes artists doing quick portraits, vendors selling all sorts of knickknacks, and meandering street performers.

At the roundabout at Durban and Arava Streets you can continue along the waterfront—with the Mul Yam shopping mall on your right—until you reach a small palm-filled plaza with a tiny, cement-block-shaped building with a statue of four fighters raising a comrade aloft. This is Umm Rash Rash, where the Israelis first took control of the Gulf of Eilat in March 1949, as determined by the United Nations' partition plan. The small building—the only one that existed at that point—is a far cry from today's luxury resorts. The promenade effectively ends right before U Suites hotel. ⊠ *Eilat* ⊠ *Free.*

★ **The Relaxation Pools at Dolphin Reef**
HOT SPRINGS | A planked walkway leads to a hideaway consisting of a warren of open spaces designed for pure relaxation. Blink and you might miss it—and trust us, you won't want to. This place offers a true one-of-a-kind experience. Three pools—a deep seawater pool, a soft rainwater pool, and a saltwater pool that'll have you floating Dead Sea–style—offer hours of rest and relaxation. Before you change and shower, help yourself to a glass of wine or the delicious selection of cookies and dried fruits, or slice and squeeze your own fresh orange juice from a juicer set up on a rustic tree stump. Admission to the pools is strictly capped, ensuring a lack of overcrowding; you must reserve in advance by booking online or by phone. During the day, the pools offer stunning views of the water through tented-plastic windows; at night, candles and heaters enhance the atmosphere. For an additional fee, an instructor will float you around the pool in a 30-minute "relaxation technique," a

Need a Break? 🍴

On the promenade underneath the Royal Beach hotel sits Aldo, one of Israel's better ice-cream chains. Queue up for a luscious cup or cone topped with a generous lashing of halvah or seasonal fruit.

series of undulating exercises that further enhance the experience. Once you're done floating, you can spend the rest of the day walking along the boardwalk to look at the dolphins or ordering drinks from the small bar in the front room. For the price of admission, you get to stay as long as you want. ⊠ *Rte. 90 (Eilat–Taba Rd.)* ☎ *08/630–0111* ⊕ *dolphinreef.co.il* ⊠ *Weekdays NIS 190, weekends and holidays NIS 220.*

★ **Underwater Observatory Marine Park**
ZOO | **FAMILY** | One of Eilat's star attractions can be recognized by its tall, space-needle-like structure punctuating the waves just offshore. A short drive from Eilat, this is the largest aquarium complex in the Middle East. Plan to spend several hours here (there's a cafeteria for lunch on the premises). The **Aquarium's** 12 windows provide views of rare fish so magnificent and so Day-Glo colorful that it's hard to believe they're real; there's an unlighted room where phosphorescent fish and other sea creatures glow in the dark. And there are turtle and stingray pools, too. Don't miss feeding time (11 am daily) in the 650,000-liter **Shark Pool.** The anaconda snakes, poisonous frogs, and piranha are fed in the **Amazonas** exhibit at 3 pm. Captain Jaws takes you on a sea journey during an audiovisual show presented in a simulated-motion theater with moving seats at the **Oceanarium.**

The Red Sea, just off the coast of Eilat, offers spectacular snorkeling and scuba diving.

A 300-foot wooden bridge leads to the **Underwater Observatory.** Head down the spiral staircase and into the sea—you are now 15 feet underwater, where two round, glass-windowed halls, connected by a tunnel, offer stunning views of the surrounding coral reef, home to exotic tropical fish. The **Observatory Tower**—reached by stairs—gives coastal views of Israel's neighboring countries. There's a café up here. You can also take a ride on the *Coral 200* glass-bottom boat. Bus 16 runs to, and Bus 15 runs from, downtown Eilat every half hour. ⊠ *Rte. 90 (Eilat–Taba Rd.)* ⊕ *8 km (5 miles) south of Eilat* ☎ *08/636–4200* ⊠ *NIS 99; Oceanarium NIS 10, glass-bottom boat NIS 35.*

⚓ Beaches

Families and luxury travelers favor North Beach, which fronts most of Eilat's high-end hotels and generally has a sleeker, more organized look and feel. Young people tend to hang out at the southernmost beaches, near the dive centers (south of

the port, along the Eilat–Taba road). In recent years Eilat has made a number of beaches wheelchair accessible. The best is opposite the Neptune Hotel, where a wheelchair path leads from the promenade to the water's edge.

★ North Beach

BEACH—SIGHT | Running northeast from the intersection of Durban and Arava streets, North Beach is what comes to mind when most people think about Eilat. This part of the beach is convenient if food and drink are on your agenda. Here you'll find kiosks selling drinks, ice cream, and other snacks, and along the Promenade are many more options for fuller meals. Adventurous types can go paragliding or rent a paddleboat. Across the bridge—opposite the Queen of Sheba, Royal Beach, Dan, and Herods hotels—lies a beautifully landscaped series of beaches.

Walking south, you'll pass several mellow beaches, including Kochav Hayam and HaZahav, before you come to Royal

Beach, where white-shirted attendants rent space on private platforms. Very expensive drinks can be ordered from the nearby Royal Beach Hotel and vendors sell popsicles and sodas. Head past the marina, where you can enjoy a ride in a glass-bottom boat, and you'll encounter family-friendly beaches with names like Tarshish, Leonardo, Rimonim, and HaPnina, where hard-core sunbathers oil themselves for maximum exposure. North Beach comes to a natural end by Le Meridien Hotel, whose beach is the only private one. **Amenities:** food and drink; lifeguards; showers; water sports. **Best for:** partiers; sunset; swimming; walking.

South Beach

BEACH—SIGHT | Attracting a younger crowd, South Beach retains a bit of a funky vibe. Stretching for 11 km (7 miles), South Beach is actually much longer than North Beach, but Eilat Port (look for the gaudy gambling boats moored there) cuts it in two pieces. North of the port sits Dekel Beach, with a shaded Bedouin tent, tanning raft, snorkeling station, and beach bar. It's great for families during the day, and often hosts private parties in the evening. Past Dolphin Reef sits Almog Beach, a relaxation haven with a full bar and restaurant, low-slung tables, and ample parking. Farther down the shore, Aquasport Beach is a standout; local scuba divers and water-sports enthusiasts know this is the laid-back alternative to better-trodden coves, and the vibe is free-spirited and decidedly chilled-out. There's a scuba school suitable for all levels of skill and experience. **Amenities:** food and drink; showers; water sports. **Best for:** swimming, snorkeling. ✉ *Off Rte. 90 (Eilat–Taba Rd.).*

🍴 Restaurants

Eilat has so many restaurants that you can easily dine on a different cuisine each night over a long holiday. Savor fine local seafood and fresh fish, charcoal-grilled meats of every kind, or Chinese, Indian, Yemenite, and Italian cuisine that represent Israel's many waves of immigration. Many restaurants offer outdoor seating, often amid pots of pink bougainvillea or within sight of the sea. Outdoor cafés serve *hafuch* (strong coffee with a frothy, hot-milk topping) and light meals.

Agadir

$$ | BURGER | FAMILY | The Eilat offshoot of the Tel Aviv chain is known for juicy burgers and a copious selection of beers on tap. In a small complex of bars and restaurants, Agadir's slightly off-the-beaten-track locale makes it feel more intimate than your average burger joint. **Known for:** burgers; relaxed atmosphere; generous portions. [$] *Average main: NIS 55* ✉ *10 Kamen St.* ☎ *08/633–3777* 🌐 *www.agadir.co.il.*

Lalo

$ | MOROCCAN | A longtime favorite in Eilat, this kosher lunch place is a top-drawer example of Moroccan-Israeli cooking, all of it by an accomplished mother-and-son team. When you arrive at this simple dining room, five different salads (including cauliflower, tahini, eggplant, and hot peppers) are quickly placed in front of you. **Known for:** homemade food; Moroccan delicacies like beef

The Red Sea 👁

This incongruous name for a body of water that's brilliantly turquoise along the shore is the result of a 17th-century typographical error by an English printer: in setting the type for an English translation of a Latin version of the Bible, the printer left out an *e* and thus *Reed Sea* became *Red Sea.* The name was easily accepted because of the sea's red appearance at sunset.

cooked with hummus; lunch menu only. $ *Average main: NIS 50* ✉ *259 Horev St.* ☎ *08/633–0578* ⊘ *Closed Fri. and Sat. No dinner.*

Last Refuge

$$$ | **SEAFOOD** | Locals hold this fish and seafood restaurant (known in Hebrew as Hamiflat Ha'acharon) in high regard and take their guests from "up north" here as a real treat. The dining room, with dark paneling and nautical motifs like ships' wheels, spills out onto a spacious balcony where diners eat beside the water, looking at Jordan across the way. **Known for:** fish dishes; knockout scenery; stir-fried sea crabs. $ *Average main: NIS 100* ✉ *Rte. 90* ⊹ *Across from Isrotel Yam Suf Hotel* ☎ *08/637–3627.*

Les Sardines

$$$ | **SEAFOOD** | This chic bar and upscale fish restaurant overlooks the harbor at the Eilat promenade, offering white-tablecloth dining indoors and out. Recommended starters are gravlax and seafood carpaccio. **Known for:** great views; fresh fish; location at the edge of the marina. $ *Average main: NIS 90* ✉ *3 HaMayim St.* ⊹ *Under Laguna Hotel* ☎ *08/676–7488* ⊕ *les-sardines.net.*

★ Olla

$$$ | **TAPAS** | One of the best tapas bars in Eilat, Olla has a relaxing atmosphere, thanks to leather-backed booths and tastefully subdued lighting. The bar, quite lively on weekends, offers some of the most accomplished bartenders in the city. **Known for:** stylish decor; attentive service; Spanish-inspired menu. $ *Average main: NIS 95* ✉ *Bell Hotel, 7 Tarshish St.* ☎ *08/632–5566* ⊕ *www.olla-tapas. co.il* ⊘ *No dinner Fri. No lunch Sat.*

Pago Pago Restaurant

$$$ | **SEAFOOD** | This longtime crowd-pleaser began serving in 1986 from its present location on a boat in the marina, but today Pago Pago occupies a striking, nautical-looking building (it resembles a ship) with walls of windows overlooking the water. The fusion of South American, Asian, and Mediterranean influences creates interesting menu options. **Known for:** dramatic dining on a "boat"; sophisticated presentation of seafood and pasta; great views. $ *Average main: NIS 100* ✉ *99 HaMayim Rd.* ☎ *08/637–6660* ⊕ *www.pagopagorest.com/en.*

★ Pastory

$$$$ | **ITALIAN** | At this authentic Italian restaurant, the flavors of Tuscany star on a menu offering fish, meat, seafood, and handmade pasta. The casual dining room and outdoor patio fill up fast, so it's best to call ahead for a table. **Known for:** pasta dishes like spaghetti de mer; friendly service; innovative takes on old favorites. $ *Average main: NIS 110* ✉ *7 Tarshish St.* ☎ *08/634–5111* ⊕ *pastory.co.il* ⊘ *Closed Fri. 5–6 pm.*

Ranch House

$$$$ | **STEAKHOUSE** | Accessed directly from the Promenade, this kosher steak house distinguishes itself from the pack with service as solicitous as its steaks are juicy. Wooden tables and comfy chairs set the stage for a meal that will have you begging for a doggy bag. **Known for:** attentive service; rib eye; seaside terrace dining. $ *Average main: NIS 110* ✉ *Royal Beach Hotel, 3 Shvil Hayam* ☎ *08/636–8989* ⊕ *www.ranchhouse.co.il* ⊘ *No lunch. No dinner Fri.*

Whale

$$$$ | **SEAFOOD** | The husband-and-wife chef-owners of Whale draw foodies from all over the country to what has become one of Israel's top seafood restaurants. Browse the cookbooks on the shelves while you wait for your order. **Known for:** creative seafood dishes; the shrimpburger; elegant, sophisticated atmosphere. $ *Average main: NIS 120* ✉ *Herods Hotel, 6 HaYam St., North Beach* ☎ *08/920–9393* ⊕ *whale-eilat.com* ⊘ *Closed Sat.*

Kids in the Negev

Think of the Negev as a huge sandbox for kids. There's lots to do and enjoy: beaches, alpaca rides, camel trips, Jeep excursions, snorkeling, and boat rides on the Red Sea. And children like the kind of food prevalent in the Negev, such as french fries, schnitzel (fried, breaded chicken cutlets), and ice cream. Even fancy restaurants have these on their menus to please the young ones, and it's not unusual to see baby strollers parked beside candlelit tables. Many hotels in Eilat go out of their way to cater to kids, trying to outdo one another with their children's programs and playrooms. These are separate facilities on the hotel grounds, filled with every imaginable distraction, from toys and crafts to PlayStations, and qualified supervisors are on hand. Many hotels employ staff trained to keep kids entertained, allowing parents some much-needed R&R.

Hotels

Aria Hotel

$$$ | HOTEL | FAMILY | The first thing you'll see when you enter this all-suite hotel is its breathtaking view of the shimmering sea and the mountains beyond. **Pros:** lovely views; short walk from shopping area; feels separated from the boardwalk hubbub. **Cons:** pool can be cold in winter months; late-night music may disturb some guests; not much of a beachfront. [$] *Rooms from: $320* ✉ *Arava Rd.* ☎ *08/638–3333* 🌐 *www.fattal-hotels.com* 🛏 *246 suites* 🍴 *Free Breakfast.*

★ Dan Eilat Hotel

$$$ | RESORT | FAMILY | The design of the glitzy Dan Eilat, by internationally acclaimed Israeli architect Adam Tihani, effectively combines high style with creature comforts. **Pros:** great location on the beach; excellent breakfasts; fun for kids. **Cons:** sometimes noisy; crowded dining room; must reserve lounge chairs early in the day. [$] *Rooms from: $325* ✉ *North Beach Promenade* ☎ *08/636–2222* 🌐 *www.danhotels.com* 🛏 *423 rooms* 🍴 *Free Breakfast.*

Herods Palace Hotel

$$$$ | HOTEL | Designed with the legendary king in mind, this massive hotel is all about over-the-top opulence and Vegas-style pizzazz. **Pros:** on the quietest beach in Eilat; wide choice of accommodations; largest hotel in the area. **Cons:** public areas could use a refresh; furniture worn in some rooms; lots of walking due to the hotel's massive scale. [$] *Rooms from: $405* ✉ *North Beach, 6 Hayam St.* ☎ *08/638–0000* 🌐 *www.herods-hotels.com* 🛏 *297 rooms* 🍴 *Free Breakfast.*

Hilton Eilat Queen of Sheba

$$$$ | HOTEL | The palatial entrance of this grand hotel is certainly fit for a queen, capped with a pillared dome rising between two turrets. **Pros:** elegant rooms; prime location near the waterfront; stunning views of the Eilat Bay. **Cons:** late-night music can be heard on lower floors; lines for the dining room at dinner are sometimes long; property is huge. [$] *Rooms from: $405* ✉ *8 Antib Rd.* ☎ *08/630–6666* 🌐 *www3.hilton.com* 🛏 *501 rooms* 🍴 *Free Breakfast.*

Isrotel Agamim

$$ | HOTEL | The name means "lakes," so it's no surprise that this cluster of four-floor buildings is set amid palm trees, emerald grass, and tropical plants, around a lagoon-shaped pool with hammocks and swing chairs. **Pros:** laid-back atmosphere; great pool area; excellent breakfast buffet. **Cons:** a 10- to 15-minute walk to the beach; must drive to promenade area. $ *Rooms from: $295* ✉ *Campne St., North Beach* ☎ *08/630–0300* ⊕ *www.isrotel.co.il* ⤴ *288 rooms* ⦿ *Free Breakfast.*

Isrotel King Solomon

$$$$ | **HOTEL** | **FAMILY** | Solomon's entire court could easily have been accommodated at this huge and comfortably furnished family hotel. **Pros:** Eilat's most child-friendly hotel; lots of activities for the whole family; rooftop lounge with free Internet access. **Cons:** not on beach; food is uninspired; not recommended for couples. $ *Rooms from: $415* ✉ *Piestany St., North Beach* ☎ *08/636–3444* ⊕ *www.isrotel.com* ⤴ *419 rooms* ⦿ *Free Breakfast.*

Isrotel Yam Suf

$$$ | **HOTEL** | Across from Coral Beach, this charming property has a six-story wing where most of the rooms have balconies facing the sea, as well as a couple of three-story buildings set amid private gardens. **Pros:** great beach for snorkeling; daily activities for kids; close to the aquarium. **Cons:** bland food in dining room; not within walking distance of downtown; decor could use an update. $ *Rooms from: $350* ✉ *Rte. 90 (Eilat–Taba Rd.), South Beach* ☎ *08/638–2222* ⊕ *www.isrotel.com* ⤴ *261 rooms* ⦿ *Free Breakfast.*

Leonardo Plaza Hotel Eilat

$$$ | **HOTEL** | Sitting along the Promenade, this hotel near the beach and the marina puts everything within walking distance. **Pros:** excellent beachfront location, in the middle of the action; extensive children's activities; noteworthy spa. **Cons:** within earshot of the beachfront discos; expensive online access; large, noisy groups come through occasionally. $ *Rooms from: $350* ✉ *North Beach Promenade* ☎ *08/636–1111* ⊕ *www.leonardo-hotels.com* ⤴ *308 rooms* ⦿ *Free Breakfast.*

★ The Reef Hotel by Herbert Samuel

$$$ | **RESORT** | **FAMILY** | This boutique beachcombing property is one of South Beach's favorites because it's one of the few with direct ocean access. **Pros:** lots of complimentary amenities; great beach proximity; free Internet access. **Cons:** limited dining options; not close to downtown; you'll need a car to get around. $ *Rooms from: $315* ✉ *Rte. 90 (Eilat–Taba Rd.), Almog Beach* ☎ *08/636–4444* ⊕ *www.herbertsamuel.com/En/Reef-Eilat-Hotel* ⤴ *79 rooms* ⦿ *Free Breakfast.*

Royal Beach Eilat

$$$$ | **HOTEL** | One of the most sprawling hotels on the Red Sea, this hotel, part of the Isrotel chain, blends comfort, glamour, and sophistication. **Pros:** pleasant pool area graced by waterfalls; excellent seaside location; lots of dining options nearby. **Cons:** standard rooms can be small; some in-room fixtures could use a refresh; public areas need new furnishings. $ *Rooms from: $650* ✉ *North Beach Promenade* ☎ *08/636–8888* ⊕ *www.isrotel.com* ⤴ *383 rooms* ⦿ *Free Breakfast.*

ⓨ Nightlife

Most hotels in Eilat have a bar, and many have dance clubs. Other nightlife options include beach parties, where bronzed bodies groove all night to recorded music (often local favorites like trance or house). Keep an eye out in town for English-language posters listing times and places. Admission is free.

Fifth Avenue

BARS/PUBS | If you're looking to avoid the more touristy spots, this restaurant and bar in the park is the closest you'll get in Eilat. This New York–style joint has tables lit with flickering candles, a wide-ranging menu, and a dance floor where locals venture late at night. Low ceilings make this a louder-than-necessary experience, particularly on Friday when the DJs spin

After a day at the beach, secure a seat with a waterside view at one of Eilat's many restaurants.

electronic music. It's closed Sunday. ✉ *Shofron St.* ☎ *08/633–3303.*

Mike's Place

BARS/PUBS | This lively sports bar and live-music destination offers a friendly oasis with an American vibe. Families as well as nightlife seekers will feel equally at home with the menu of more than 70 sandwiches and salads, burgers, and burritos. ✉ *King Solomon Promenade* ✣ *Facing harbor* ☎ *08/864–9550* ⊕ *www. mikesplacebars.com* ☞ *Closed Fri.*

Paddy's Irish Pub

BARS/PUBS | Looking for all the world like an American sports bar, Paddy's Irish Pub stocks more than 50 kinds of international beers, including 16 on draft. Everything here is big: the food menu, wooden patio, and the bar, said to be the largest in Eilat. On game nights you have your choice of nine different screens, or you can pass the time upstairs on one of the four pool tables. Bands play twice a week on summer nights. ✉ *Derekh Yotam St.* ☎ *08/637–0921* ⊕ *paddys.co.il/en.*

Three Monkeys Pub

BARS/PUBS | Live music is the claim to fame at this very popular pub, where the shows kick off most nights at around 10:30 pm. The crowd includes people of all ages, and they hang out around the bar or dance until last call. ✉ *Royal Beach Promenade* ☎ *08/636–8888.*

🎭 Performing Arts

For an overview of local events, pick up a copy of the detailed leaflet "Events and Places of Interest" at the tourist information office. Check out Friday's *Jerusalem Post* magazine, or the *Herald Tribune*'s *Haaretz Guide,* both of which carry listings for Eilat.

★ Red Sea Jazz Festival

FESTIVALS | Many Israelis and foreign visitors plan their trips to coincide with this annual three-day event, which draws top-notch musicians from all over the world. The main festival is typically held the third week in August and generally attracts Israeli, European, and American artists. A second winter festival, usually held in February, highlights Israeli talent, and is centered in Tel-Aviv. Now that the festival is sponsored by Isrotel, many of the winter performances take place at one of the hotels in the chain. Summer concerts are held in large outdoor stage areas at the port created with shipping containers ✉ *Eilat* ⊕ *redseajazz.co.il.*

WOW

THEATER | **FAMILY** | This 90-minute circus-style show combines magic, juggling, and gravity-defying acrobatics—all in a 3–D video-art setting. New shows, produced by a top Israeli choreographer, debut every year or two. Call ahead to reserve tickets. There are no shows on Sunday. ✉ *Isrotel Royal Garden, Antibes St., North Beach* ☎ *08/638–6701* ✉ *NIS 150.*

🛍 Shopping

Eilat is a duty-free zone, meaning that shoppers from all over Israel make the journey here to take advantage of tax-free shopping. You'll find that most of the prices are lower here than the rest of the country.

Along the beachside Promenade, on the ground level of each hotel, you'll pass one designer boutique after another. If you'd rather hit the beach during the day, you'll still have plenty of time to shop after dark—these places are open until 9 pm or later every night except Friday.

ART AND CRAFTS

Cardo

GIFTS/SOUVENIRS | This intriguing series of shops carries unusual paintings, sculptures, Judaica, old-style objets d'art, Moroccan furnishings, painted and inlaid mirrors, boxes and frames, gifts, and wall hangings. ✉ *Herods Vitalis Hotel, North Beach Promenade, North Beach* ☎ *08/638–0000.*

BEAUTY

Laline

PERFUME/COSMETICS | Israeli-made soaps, shampoos, and candles are the specialty of this chain. The salt scrubs, infused with mineral oils, are especially luxurious, and the verbena-coconut body lotion is a perfect salve for sunburned skin. ✉ *North Beach Promenade* ✛ *Near Hilton Eilat Queen of Sheba* ☎ *054/334–5024* ⊕ *www.laline.co.il.*

CLOTHING

Designer Gallery

CLOTHING | A cluster of boutiques offers an excellent variety of high-end Israeli designer women's clothing and accessories. Some of the most internationally renowned Israeli designers—including Ronen Chen, Daniela Lehavi, and Naama Bezalel—display their airy knit dresses, classy leather bags, and sassy shoes in adjacent showrooms, which make for a great local shopping experience that's a far cry from the ubiquitous large shopping malls found in Eilat. Once or twice a year, the shops put on a fashion show on the promenade out front. ✉ *King Solomon Promenade, North Beach.*

JEWELRY AND ACCESSORIES

H. Stern

JEWELRY/ACCESSORIES | With two locations in Eilat, this shop has an excellent reputation for high-quality gold and diamond pieces. The location at the Royal Beach Hotel has an especially good selection. ✉ *Royal Beach Hotel, North Beach Promenade* ☎ *08/633–0674* ⊕ *www.hstern.net.*

Padani

JEWELRY/ACCESSORIES | Look for Breitling and Cartier timepieces at this shop, considered one of Israel's premier sources for watches. Both locations are at the Royal Beach—one inside the hotel and one on the promenade below. ✉ *Royal Beach Hotel, North Beach Promenade* ☎ *08/631–5038* ⊕ *padani.co.il.*

MALLS AND SHOPPING CENTERS
Adom Mall and Shalom Plaza
SHOPPING CENTERS/MALLS | The two sections of this shopping center are connected by a passage filled with cafés where you can stop and take stock of all the bargains you've found. On a smaller scale than Mul HaYam Mall, it nevertheless has a wide variety of stores. There's a notable absence of tacky souvenir shops. ⊠ *2 HaTamarim St.* ✛ *Near entrance to Eilat Airport.*

Mull HaYam Mall
SHOPPING CENTERS/MALLS | One of Eilat's prime shopping destinations, Mull HaYam Mall is noted for its made-in-Israel products. Here you can stroll along with the chattering crowd, pick up a lottery ticket, or enjoy a glass of freshly squeezed orange or carrot juice. Then check out such stores as **Intima** for soft and sexy lingerie, **Gottex** for famous swimwear, **Honigman** for women's casual wear, and **Fox** for cheeky clothing for adults and children. The more than 90 stores also include a bookstore and drugstore, and there are several coffee shops. ⊠ *Arava Rd. and Yotam St.*

🏃 Activities

At its heart, Eilat is one long oceanfront resort, and the town takes pride in its beaches. It's not unusual to hear locals bragging about the clarity of the water and the quality of the snorkeling, scuba diving, and other water sports. Beach managers ensure the cleanliness of their sections, which everyone refers to as North and South Beaches. Look for beaches with large white signs indicating that swimming is authorized. Here you'll find lifeguards that are usually on duty until 4 or 5 in the afternoon. Many beaches turn into clubs after sunset, with plenty of music and dancing.

Many outdoor activities can be arranged through your hotel. Several tour operators maintain desks in the lobbies of larger hotels.

BIRD-WATCHING
International Birding and Research Center of Eilat
BIRD WATCHING | More than a billion birds migrate annually through these skies between Africa and Eurasia, and bird-watching enthusiasts increasingly come for the spectacle between late February and mid-May and early September to late November. Spring is by far the larger of the two migrations. This nonprofit birding center seeks to create a safe haven for the species whose natural habitats in and around Eilat have degraded due to pollution, overdevelopment, and other environmental factors. The center offers guided tours of the sanctuary where birds like imperial eagles, desert eagle owls, and long-legged buzzards can be seen in a majestically preserved habitat. Tours must be arranged in advance. Binoculars are provided. ⊠ *Rte. 90* ✛ *10 km (6 miles) north of center of Eilat* ☎ *050/767–1290* ⊕ *www.birds.org. il* ✉ *Free.*

DESERT TOURS
Camel Ranch Eilat
GAME RESERVE/SAFARI | **FAMILY** | A 10-minute drive from Eilat, this family-friendly venue lets kids get up close and personal with camels. You can explore the surrounding hills on a 90-minute trek, a half-day excursion, or a sunset tour. Longer trips end in Bedouin style with food and drink. There are plenty of other activities, including a ropes course designed for climbers of all ages. Reserve the camel excursions in advance. ⊠ *Nahal Shlomo St., South Beach* ☎ *08/637–0022* ⊕ *www.camel-ranch.co.il/en* ✉ *Free; rides from NIS 170.*

Glitch
CAMPING—SPORTS-OUTDOORS | This multisport company, which specializes in desert tourism, runs customized Jeep tours and rappelling (known in Israel as

snappelling) trips for both novices and more seasoned adventurers. It also offers desert archery courses. Call ahead to reserve. ⊠ *Eilat* ☎ *053/739–9557* ⊕ *www. glitch.co.il.*

SNORKELING AND DIVING

Snorkeling and scuba diving are extremely popular activities in Eilat, and no wonder: Eilat Bay is located at the northern tip of a coral reef that extends from the equator. Here you'll find everything from beginner's courses to expert certification courses.

★ Aqua-Sport

DIVING/SNORKELING | For more than 50 years, this dive center has been operating PADI-certified diving courses in Eilat, as well as snorkeling and diving trips to the most magnificent sections of the reef. There are special Bubblemaker introductory courses for kids and courses ranging from a few hours to several days to help you get accreditation. Prices vary according to courses, excursions, and your experience level. ⊠ *Coral Beach, Rte. 90 (Eilat–Taba Rd.), South Beach* ☎ *08/633–4404* ⊕ *www.aqua-sport.com.*

★ Manta Diving Center

SCUBA DIVING | Known for its incredibly supportive staff, Manta offers the full range of equipment and courses for scuba divers and snorkelers of all levels. Courses are available in English for groups or four and more. ⊠ *Isrotel Yam Suf Hotel, Rte. 90 (Eilat–Taba Rd.), South Beach* ☎ *08/633–3666* ⊕ *www.divemanta.com* ⌚ *1-hr snorkeling from $60 up to 3 people.*

Red Sea Lucky Divers

SCUBA DIVING | In business for decades, Eilat's only PADI Gold Palm five-star diving center offers all manner of dive courses, from two-hour introductory dives to a five-day, open-water certification course. ⊠ *Rte. 90 (Eilat–Taba Rd.), Coral Beach* ✛ *Near The Reef by Herbert Samuel Hotel* ☎ *08/632–3466* ⊕ *www. luckydivers.com.*

Snuba Eilat

SCUBA DIVING | **FAMILY** | Kids ages eight and older have fun exploring Caves Reef, one of the most popular diving spots in the Coral Beach Nature Reserve. Snuba, a snorkeling-diving hybrid, lets you breathe through tubes connected to tanks carried in an inflatable raft on the surface. The price includes instruction, a practice session, and a guided underwater tour that goes no deeper than 20 feet. Snorkels and wet suits are also available for rental. Reserve in advance. ⊠ *Rte. 90 (Eilat–Taba Rd.), South Beach* ✛ *Between Underwater Observatory and Princess Hotel* ☎ *08/637–2722* ⊕ *www.snuba.co.il* ⌚ *NIS 35.*

Timna Park

25 km (15 miles) north of Eilat, 15 km (9 miles) south of Yotvata Hai-Bar Nature Reserve.

A lunarlike desert landscape interspersed with amazing geological shapes and ancient archaeological sites, Timna Park is surrounded by beautiful cliffs ranging from sandy beige to rich red and dusky black.

GETTING HERE AND AROUND

From Route 90 (Dead Sea–Eilat Road), turn left at the sign for Timna Park and Timna Lake. A 3-km (2-mile) access road (which passes Kibbutz Elifaz) leads to the entrance booth.

◉ Sights

★ Timna Park

NATURE SITE | The granite Timna Mountains (whose highest peak is 2,550 feet) are just the beginning of this park's spectacular collection of rock formations and canyons. Millions of years of erosion have sculpted shapes of amazing beauty, such as the red-hue Solomon's Pillars (sandstone columns created by rare patterns of erosion, not by the biblical king) and

the 20-foot-high freestanding Mushroom. Late afternoon provides the best light for spectators and photographers alike.

People have also left their mark here. South of the pillars are the remains of a small **temple** built in white sandstone by Egyptians who worked the mines 3,400 years ago, during the Egyptian New Kingdom (the time of Moses). The temple was dedicated to the cow-eared goddess Hathor. This "Lady of the Rock" was the patroness of miners, as you can discover at the multimedia presentation called *Mines of Time*. Inside the temple, archaeologists have discovered a snake made of copper (*nehushtan* in Hebrew)—according to Numbers 21:4–9, Moses made a serpent in the wilderness to heal people suffering from snake bites, and the snake remains a symbol of healing to this day. Near the temple, a path and

stairway lead up to the observation platform overlooking the valley. Above the platform is a rock-cut inscription whose hieroglyph you can see clearly with the aid of a telescope. It shows Ramses III offering a sacrifice to Hathor. You can also explore a life-size replica of the biblical tabernacle the Israelites carried through the desert.

When you arrive, ask for the explanatory pamphlet, which shows the driving route in red. The park measures 60 square km (23 square miles), so we suggest driving from sight to sight and exploring each on foot. A small building just inside the entrance screens a multimedia video (with a revolving stage and 360-degree screen) detailing humanity's 6,000-year-old relationship with the Timna area. Wall panels explain the valley's fascinating geological makeup.

One of many unique rock formations in Timna Park

Experienced hikers can pick up a map detailing various serious hikes that take from 7 to 10 hours to complete. They're best done in winter, as summer daytime temperatures exceed 100 degrees. Watch out for old mine shafts, take adequate water, and be sure to let the staff at the gate know you are going and when you plan to return. You can also rent bikes and paddleboats near the small lake, where you'll find a restaurant serving charred bread cooked in a *taboon* (traditional oven), along with goodies and refreshing drinks. ✉ *Rte. 90 (Dead Sea–Eilat Rd.), Yotvata* ☎ *08/631–6756* 🌐 *www.parktimna.co.il* 🎫 *NIS 49; night entrance for concerts and special events NIS 59.*

☕ Coffee and Quick Bites

Yotvata Inn

$ | **ISRAELI** | If you're looking for fantastic kibbutz-made ice cream, stop by this inn, an Israeli institution next to a gas station on Route 90 between the Yotvata Hai-Bar Nature Reserve and Timna Park, 40 km (25 miles) north of Eilat. The kibbutz of the same name is across the way, and its dairy products are much loved by locals. **Known for:** unique ice cream flavors like tmarim (date); welcome rest stop on way to or from Eilat; souvenirs. [$] *Average main: NIS 35* ✉ *Rte. 90 (Dead Sea–Eilat Rd.), Yotvata* ☎ *08/635–7449.*

Red Canyon

23 km (14 miles) northwest of Eilat.

A 5-km (3-mile) hike marked by stunning red rock formations in the desert, the Red Canyon is a good half-day (or less) trip from nearby Eilat. Hiking difficulty varies as some sections are narrow and winding.

GETTING HERE AND AROUND

From Eilat, the canyon is about 20 minutes north off Route 12. You can use Bus 392 to get there, but we suggest using a professional guide like Desert Eco Tours (see Activities below). Allow for an hour or two to get through the canyon.

Sights

Red Canyon (Wadi Shani)

CANYON | The Red Canyon is a short section of Wadi Shani that begins in the Sinai Desert and continues through the stunning Eilat Mountains. At some point, the wadi carves its way into deep, rich red sandstone, creating a superb little gorge and a narrow and impressive canyon. The exquisite red color, a reaction to oxidized minerals and sunlight, changes with the daylight. There are several hikes of varying difficulties and time requirements. The most popular is a short circular trail that may take up to an hour and a half to complete. It's a relatively easy hike as you descend and ascend canyon walls, sometimes using fortified handholds in the rock. The scenery is breathtaking. The main benefit of this scenic trail is that it offers a dose of desert hiking without having to sweat too much. Make sure you take a good supply of water and wear suitable footwear. It is advisable to begin your hike early in the day, as midday temperatures can become unbearably hot. Don't forget water and a hat. You can only visit during daylight hours. Note that the entrance to the canyon is at the parking lot. There is no visitor center, food, Internet, or restrooms on-site. ■ TIP→ **Check with your hotel concierge to make sure there are no road closures or security threats before heading out. We recommend using a tour guide for any excursion to the Eilat Mountains.** ✉ *Eilat* ✛ *Parking lot is 20 minutes north of Eilat, off Rte. 12. Enter "Red Canyon" into Waze app for best directions.*

 Activities

Desert Eco Tours

Jeep tours are a wonderful way to see dramatic off-road routes to and through the Eilat Mountains. Desert Eco Tours offers a popular four-hour morning trip from Eilat to the Red Canyon in open topped Land Rover jeeps, an unforgettable tour of astonishing beauty. ✉ *Tzofit Center Office Bldg., Eilat* ☎ *08/632–6477* ⊕ *desertecotours.com/English/eilat-tours/red-canyon-tours-eilat* ☞ *$65 per adult.*

Yotvata Hai-Bar Nature Reserve

35 km (21½ miles) north of Eilat on Rte. 90, between Kibbutz Yotvata and Kibbutz Samar, 15 km (9 miles) north of Timna Park.

In the southern Arava Valley, this nature preserve makes a good day trip from Eilat and can be combined with a visit to the Timna Park. It was created not only as a refuge for animals that were almost extinct in the region, but also as a breeding ground for animals that will be set free in the Negev.

GETTING HERE AND AROUND

The reserve is located on Route 90 (Dead Sea–Eilat Road), between Kibbutzim Yotvata and Samar. Look for the sign for Yotvata Hai-Bar Nature Reserve, opposite the entrance to Kibbutz Samar. Drive 1½ km (1 mile) to the entrance. The reserve is also accessible via Egged Bus 390 from Tel Aviv, Bus 397 from Beersheva, or Bus 444 from Jerusalem.

 Sights

★ Yotvata Hai-Bar Nature Reserve

NATURE PRESERVE | **FAMILY** | This popular nature preserve is a natural habitat for biblical-era animals and birds. Roaming around are stripe-legged Africa wild asses, Dorcas gazelles, Arabian oryx, and other desert herbivores. Try to be here in the morning, when animals are most active. You need a car in order to enter the safari-like nature reserve. There are audio players available for rent if you want a 45-minute "guided tour." A second section, the Desert Night Exhibition

Hall, is a darkened room where you can observe the habits of nocturnal animals such as bats and barn owls. An upgraded ticket allows you into the Predator Center, where feeding time is a highlight. Carnivores, including feral wolves, foxes, leopards, jackals, birds of prey, and striped hyenas are kept in enclosures. ⊠ *Rte. 90 (Dead Sea–Eilat Rd.), Yotvata* 🕾 *08/637–6018* ⊕ *www.parks.org.il* 🎫 *NIS 29; combination ticket including Predator Center NIS 46.*

Mitzpe Ramon and Makhtesh Ramon

21 km (13 miles) south of Avdat National Park, 80 km (50 miles) south of Beersheva, 150 km (93 miles) north of Eilat.

Israel's most spectacular natural sight, and one of the largest craters in the world, the Makhtesh Ramon (Ramon Crater) in the heart of the Negev is a place of unparalleled serenity and breathtaking views. The crater's walls are made from layers of different-color rock beds containing fossils of shells, plants, and trees. Once under the sea, the makhtesh floor is today covered with heaps of black basalt, the peaks of ancient volcanoes, jagged chunks of quartzite, natural prism rock, and beds of multicolor clays.

Mitzpe Ramon, a town of 5,200 people on the northern edge of the crater, makes a great base for exploring the area. Slowly but surely, commerce and culture are beginning to catch up with the area's unparalleled scenic and adventure offerings. A promenade winds along the edge of the crater, and a huge sculpture park sits on its rim. Outdoors enthusiasts will enjoy exploring the stunning scenery by foot, mountain bike, or four-wheel-drive vehicle. The winter weather here is cool and pleasant.

GETTING HERE AND AROUND

On Route 40, Mitzpe Ramon sits between Beersheva and Eilat. Egged Buses 392, 382, and 395, as well as Metropoline Bus 160, run about once an hour until 5 pm from Beersheva (a 1¾-hour drive); there are no direct buses from Jerusalem. There are no gas stations between Mitzpe Ramon and Yotvata, near Eilat, a distance of more than 100 km (62 miles).

⊙ Sights

Alpaca Farm

FARM/RANCH | FAMILY | Just west of Mitzpe Ramon you'll find this farm and its herd of 200 sweet-faced alpacas and llamas. Young and old get a kick out of feeding the animals, even if they receive the occasional spit in the face from these long-lashed creatures. Children weighing less than about 55 pounds can take a llama ride, and grown-ups can enjoy horseback rides. You can also weave wool on a loom, purchase items at the local factory, and enjoy a picnic on the grounds. The shearing festival, which takes place around Passover, is worth catching if you're here. ⊠ *Extension of Ben Gurion Blvd., 4 km (2 miles) west of downtown, Mitzpe Ramon* ⊹ *Turn off main road onto Ben Gurion Blvd., opposite gas station at town's main roundabout* 🕾 *08/658–8047* ⊕ *www.alpaca.co.il* 🎫 *NIS 40.*

★ Makhtesh Ramon (*Ramon Crater*)

NATURE SITE | Words simply cannot do this natural wonder justice. This immense depression is 40 km (25 miles) long, 10 km (6 miles) wide, and at its deepest, it measures 2,400 feet. Because it's a phenomenon known only in this country (there are two others in the Negev), the Hebrew term *makhtesh* is now accepted usage. By definition, a makhtesh is an erosion valley walled with steep cliffs on all sides and drained by a single watercourse.

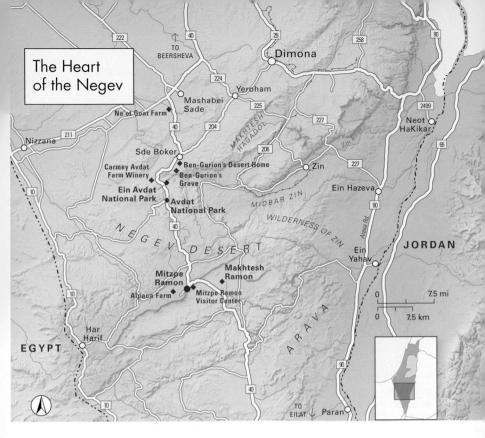

The Heart
of the Negev

You can take a 1-km (½-mile) walk along the Albert Promenade, which winds westward along the edge of the crater from the Mitzpe Ramon Visitor Center to a cantilevered observation platform hanging over the rim. This is not the time to forget the camera—the view is overwhelming. The promenade is fashioned from local stone, as is the huge sculpture by Israel Hadani, the back of which faces the town and represents the crater's geological layers.

With the crater as a magnificent backdrop, the Desert Sculpture Park exhibits a collection of 19 huge contemporary sculptures. The park took shape in 1962 with the work of a group of prominent national and international sculptors under the direction of Negev artist Ezra Orion. Their idea was to add to the natural stone formations with geometric sculptures

of similar design. Ibex often wander through the area. To get to the sculpture park, turn off the main road (Route 40) near the gas station at the sign marked Ma'ale Noah.

For a look at one of Makhtesh Ramon's geological wonders, drive down into the crater to see the Carpentry Shop, a hill of black rocks that appears to have neatly sawed edges. Long ago, the sandstone was warmed by volcanic steam and split into the shapes seen today. A wooden walkway protects this fascinating area from travelers' feet.

Another of nature's works is the Ammonite Wall, on the right as you finish the descent into the crater. The rock face, actually part of the crater wall, contains hundreds of ammonite fossils, which look like spiraled rams' horns. From here

Makhtesh Ramon (Ramon Crater), shown in the valley below, is one of the Negev's top sites.

there's a 5-km (3-mile) hiking trail, suitable for more experienced hikers. ⊠ *Rte. 40, Mitzpe Ramon* ⊕ *parks.org.il* ✉ *Free*.

Mitzpe Ramon Visitor Center

INFO CENTER | This visitor center—dedicated to Israeli astronaut Ilan Ramon, who perished in the 2003 Space Shuttle *Columbia* disaster—is perched at the very edge of the crater. Interesting 3-D models and other information about the history and formation of the crater makes it a good place to start your journey. The museum's panoramic view of the crater is breathtaking. There is also a restaurant and a branch of the popular Faran beauty products store. ⊠ *1 Maale Ben Tor, Mitzpe Ramon* ☎ *08/658–8691, 08/658–8698* ⊕ *www.goisrael.com* ✉ *NIS 28*.

🍴 Restaurants

HaHavit

$$ | **BURGER** | At this pub-restaurant frequented by all ages, you can choose juicy homemade burgers, tasty onion soup, and stuffed mushrooms, among other dishes. HaHavit is an established institution around here known for original and delicious food. **Known for:** interesting menu; kitschy, fun interior; expansive selection of draught beer. $ *Average main: NIS 60* ⊠ *Chachmov Center, 10 Nakhal Tsikhor, Mitzpe Ramon* ☎ *08/658–8226*.

🛏 Hotels

★ Beresheet Hotel

$$$$ | **RESORT** | For sheer natural magnificence, few venues can top the splendor of the most luxurious lodging in Mitzpe Ramon. **Pros:** unmatched setting; access to natural wonders; gorgeous pools. **Cons:** extremely pricey; amenities could be spiffier for a five-star hotel; isolated environment. $ *Rooms from: $450* ⊠ *1 Derech Beresheet, Mitzpe Ramon* ☎ *08/638–7797* ⊕ *www.isrotel.com* ⇥ *111 rooms* ℟ *Free Breakfast*.

Desert Home

$$ | **B&B/INN** | Here's a little piece of heaven on the outskirts of Mitzpe Ramon: a laid-back lodging with five lovely guest rooms with covered terraces facing the surrounding desert hills. **Pros:** lots of privacy; well-stocked kitchenette; lovely vistas. **Cons:** remote location; not for families with kids; very quiet, no nightlife. *[$] Rooms from: $225 ✉ 70 Ein Shaviv St., Mitzpe Ramon ☎ 052/322–9496 🌐 www.baitbamidbar.com 💳 No credit cards 🛏 5 rooms 🍴 Free Breakfast.*

InnSense

$$ | **HOTEL** | Set in the slowly developing industrial zone, this unpretentious boutique restaurant-hotel has half a dozen high-ceilinged suites outfitted with modern furnishings, local beauty products, and cozy fireplaces—some even have private jetted tubs. **Pros:** ideal for couples looking for privacy; sweet spot to stay a few nights in the desert; quite possible to find live music in pubs nearby. **Cons:** no views; no bathtubs; can feel a bit remote. *[$] Rooms from: $250 ✉ 8 Har Hardon St., Spice Quarter ☎ 08/653–9595 🌐 www.innsense.co.il 🛏 6 suites 🍴 Free Breakfast.*

Isrotel Ramon Inn

$$ | **HOTEL** | There's nothing rugged about a stay at this charming desert hotel, which has an open fireplace in the lobby for chilly winter nights. **Pros:** ideal for mountain bikers looking to take advantage of nearby trails; tasty meals; feels private. **Cons:** no elevator; not much to do nearby at night; limited interaction with other guests. *[$] Rooms from: $230 ✉ 1 Ein Akev St., Mitzpe Ramon ☎ 08/658–8822 🌐 www.isrotel.com 🛏 96 rooms 🍴 Free Breakfast.*

Succah in the Desert

$ | **B&B/INN** | Down an unpaved road, this out-of-the-ordinary cluster of stone-and-wood huts sits on a rocky hillside; for the rugged traveler seeking the starkness and purity of the desert, it's an appealing example of ecotourism. **Pros:** homemade vegetarian breakfasts included in price; great for stargazing; dinner may be included in price on weekends. **Cons:** can be cold at nights; difficult to reach without a car; shared bathrooms. *[$] Rooms from: $130 ✉ Off Rte. 171, Mitzpe Ramon ✣ 7 km (4½ miles) west of Mitzpe Ramon ☎ 08/658–6280 🌐 www.succah.co.il 🛏 9 rooms 🍴 Free Breakfast.*

Shopping

Faran

PERFUME/COSMETICS | For all-natural, deliciously scented cosmetics, soaps, and skin-care products, visit this shop. The products use local herbs and goat and camel milk, making them great souvenirs of the region. Groups of eight or more can arrange a tour of the factory and workshop area. *✉ 12 Har Ardon St., Spice Quarter ☎ 08/653–9333 🌐 www.faran-cosmetic.com 🕒 Closed Sat.*

Activities

ARCHERY

Desert Archery

TOUR—SPORTS | This outfit offers excursions where you hike through a desert course while shooting arrows at targets—a kind of cross between archery and golf. The company works with groups, and you need to call ahead to arrange an activity. *✉ Derech Mitzpe Kohavim, Mitzpe Ramon ☎ 050/534–4598 🌐 www.desertarchery.co.il.*

HIKING

Adam Sela Tours

TOUR—SPORTS | Camel-supported hikes, four-wheel-vehicle excursions, and mountain-bike trips are run by Adam Sela Tours, which also offers ecological tours and visits to Bedouin villages. *✉ Mitzpe Ramon ☎ 050/530–8272 🌐 www.adamsela.com 🎟 $200 for up to 8 people for 2-hr guided Jeep tour.*

★ **Negev Jeep**

CAMPING—SPORTS-OUTDOORS | Though the name refers to the wonderful Jeep tours—you'll get a firsthand education on the flora, fauna, animal life, and anthropological history of the region—there's so much more. Owner Haim Berger, a longtime area resident and excellent English speaker, is a behavioral scientist by training but also an expert in everything about Mitzpe Ramon and the environs. He and his friendly staff can coordinate many activities, from tours highlighting prehistoric rock art to hikes to the top of Mount Karkom, which some believe to be biblical Mount Sinai. ⊠ *Mitzpe Ramon* ☎ *054/534–3797* ⊕ *negevjeep.co.il* ⊟ *$200 for up to 8 people for 2-hr guided Jeep tour.*

STARGAZING

★ **Astronomy Israel**

STARGAZING | Mitzpe Ramon turns pitch-black at night—one of the factors Astronomy Israel guide Ira Machefsky claims makes the city a stargazer's paradise. American transplant Machefsky will either pick you up from your hotel or lead you in a two-car caravan to a secret desert plateau where his telescopes have been expertly situated for maximum viewing pleasure (if you've never seen the surface of the Moon up close, you're in for a treat). Machefsky's easygoing charm allows him to impart his vast knowledge in terms even inexperienced stargazers can understand, from pointing out constellations to explaining the basic science behind astronomy. What's more, to counteract Mitzpe Ramon's chilly nights, he supplies blankets, hot-water bottles, and a double dose of good cheer. ⊠ *Mitzpe Ramon* ☎ *052/544–9789* ⊕ *www.astronomyisrael.com* ⊟ *NIS 150.*

Avdat National Park

21 km (13 miles) north of Mitzpe Ramon, 101 km (63 miles) south of Beersheva.

The name Avdat is the Hebrew version of Oboda (30 BC–9 BC), a deified Nabatean king who may have been buried here. The prominent local dynasty intermarried with the family of Herod the Great, and in AD 106 the Romans finally abolished the Nabatean kingdom. The Nabatean temple on Avdat's acropolis left almost no remains, but its magnificence can be imagined from its restored gateway.

GETTING HERE AND AROUND

On Route 40 (Beersheva–Mitzpe Ramon Road), Avdat is a 15-minute drive south of Sde Boker.

◉ Sights

★ **Avdat National Park**

ARCHAEOLOGICAL SITE | The remains of the Nabatean city of Avdat loom on a hilltop over part of the old Incense Route between Petra and Gaza, a reminder of how valuable incense, spices, and perfumes from Arabia were in ancient times. The Nabateans were seminomadic people who came here from northern Arabia in the 3rd century BC. With their prosperous caravan routes connecting the desert hinterland to the port city of Gaza, they soon rose to glory with a vast kingdom whose capital was Petra, in present-day Jordan. Strongholds to protect the caravans were established along these routes, usually a day's journey apart. Most of the remains on the acropolis date from the 3rd, 4th, and 5th centuries—the Christian Byzantine period. The city continued to flourish until it was sacked by the Persians in AD 620; it was rediscovered only in the 20th century.

Start at the **visitor center,** where you can learn about the Nabateans in a 10-minute

These ruins in the ancient Nabatean city of Avdat are perched more than 2,000 feet above sea level.

video, see examples of what these ancient traders actually transported across the desert, and examine archaeological artifacts found in the excavations. Drive up the road (save your energy for walking around the site), stopping first at the sign for the **Roman burial cave,** which is well worth a quick peek. The 21 double catacombs cut into the rock date from the 3rd century BC.

Back in your car, drive up to the lookout point at the restored Roman building (note the watchtower with an inscription dating to the late 3rd century). The cultivated fields below were re-created in 1959 in order to see if the ancient Nabatean and Byzantine methods of conserving the meager rainfall would still work. The proof is in the lush greenery before you.

Using the Israel Nature and Parks Authority's excellent map, you can trace the lifestyle of the original inhabitants at sites that include a reconstructed three-story Roman tower, a rare Nabatean pottery workshop, a Byzantine-era winepress, two Byzantine churches, and a large baptismal font built to accommodate the converted. Near the baptismal font, you can walk down the steps to see 6th-century Byzantine dwellings, each consisting of a cave (possibly used as a wine cellar) behind a stone house. At the bottom of the hill, north of the gas station, is a Byzantine bathhouse. There is a rest area with food and drinks near the visitor center. ⊠ Rte. 40, Avdat ☎ 08/655–1511 ⊕ www.parks.org.il ⊠ NIS 28.

Ein Avdat National Park and Vicinity

14 km (9 miles) north of Avdat National Park on Rte. 40.

Ein Avdat (Avdat Spring) lies at the foot of the narrow canyon dividing the plateau between the ancient Nabatean city of Avdat and Kibbutz Sde Boker, in Ein Avdat National Park. This oasis is a lovely place to explore. Also worth visiting is Sde Boker, where David Ben-Gurion, Israel's first prime minister and a man dedicated to the dream of making the Negev flourish, lived and is now buried. Nearby are other attractions including goat farms.

GETTING HERE AND AROUND
Ein Avdat National Park is located off the Beersheva–Mitzpe Ramon road (Route 40). To get to the lower entrance, head down the curving road from Ben-Gurion's grave. The upper entrance is about 5 km (3 miles) to the south.

Ben-Gurion's home and grave are also along Route 40; driving north, you'll see the sign for Ben-Gurion's home directing you to turn right immediately after Kibbutz Sde (pronounced se-day) Boker. Egged Bus 392 runs to Sde Boker from Beersheva five times a day, and Metropoline Bus 60 runs seven times a day (a 45-minute ride).

◉ Sights

Ben-Gurion's Desert Home
HOUSE | Thousands of people make their way to this pilgrimage site every year. David Ben-Gurion (1886–1973), Israel's first prime minister, was one of the 20th-century's great statesmen. He regarded the Negev as Israel's frontier and hoped that tens of thousands would settle there. When Ben-Gurion resigned from government in 1953 (later to return), he and his wife, Paula, moved to Kibbutz Sde Boker to provide an example for others. "Neither money nor propaganda builds a country," he announced. "Only the man who lives and creates in the country can build it." And so, the George Washington of Israel took up his new role in the kibbutz sheepfold. In February 1955, he became prime minister once more, but he returned here to live when he retired in 1963.

Set amid the waving eucalyptus trees is Paula and David Ben-Gurion's simple dwelling, a testament to their typically Israeli brand of modesty and frugality. Ben-Gurion's small Negev home is commonly known as "the hut," owing to its humble appearance. It's a one-story wooden home with a small kitchen, an eating corner with a table and two chairs, and simple furniture throughout. Visitors such as United Nations Secretary-General Dag Hammarskjöld drank tea with Ben-Gurion in the modest living room. Ben-Gurion's library shelves contain 5,000 books (there are 20,000 more in his Tel Aviv home, on Ben Gurion Boulevard). His bedroom, with its single picture of Mahatma Gandhi, holds the iron cot on which he slept (often only three hours a night) and his slippers on the floor beside it. The house is exactly as he left it.

Next door, in three adjacent painted-wood buildings, are exhibitions with original documents whose themes are the story of Ben-Gurion's extraordinary life in Sde Boker, his youth, leadership, and army service, and the leader's vision for the Negev. A film showing the footage of kibbutz members actually voting on his acceptance into their community is shown in the **visitor center**; the shop here sells gifts, jewelry, and books about the "Old Man," as he was known locally. ✉ Off Rte. 40, Sde Boker ☎ 08/656–0469 ⊕ www.bgh.org.il ▨ NIS 20 ⌖ Last admission 1 hr before closing.

Ben-Gurion's Grave
MEMORIAL | The revered prime minister's grave, just 3 km (2 miles) south of his desert home in Kibbutz Sde Boker, is often visited at the same time. Walk through the beautiful garden until you reach the quiet, windswept plaza; in the center are the simple raised stone slabs marking the graves of David and Paula Ben-Gurion (she died five years before her husband). The couple's final resting place commands a view of Zin Valley's geological finery: a vast, undulating drape of stone that changes hue as the

daylight shifts. The cluster of greenery and palm trees to the right on the valley floor marks Ein Avdat (Avdat Spring). ⊠ *Off Rte. 40, Sde Boker* ☎ *08/655–5684* 🖳 *Free.*

★ Carmey Avdat Farm Winery

ARCHAEOLOGICAL SITE | Set on an ancient riverbed and vineyard, this winery-guesthouse–gift shop complex is the labor of love of Hannah and Eyal Israel, who moved here in 1998. Pick up a handy map of the property, which includes ancient stone terraces and rock drawings, a small olive grove, and assorted fruit trees and herb bushes. Then ask Eyal to show you around the winery, where he'll share the story of how he came to plant new vines on an ancient terrace with a 1,500-year legacy. You can sample the delicious kosher wines and learn about Eyal's fascinating journey to wine making—even create your own customized wine label (NIS 90). At the farm store you can buy wines, local fruit, and local pottery. You need to call ahead for scheduling and pricing information. ⊠ *Rte. 40, south of Tziporim Junction, Midreshet Ben Gurion* ☎ *08/653–5177* ⊕ *www.carmeyavdat.com* 🖳 *NIS 30.*

Ein Avdat National Park

NATIONAL/STATE PARK | **FAMILY** | Water flowing from Ein Avdat (Avdat Spring) has cut a beautiful, narrow canyon through the area's soft white chalk, forming a marvelous oasis that offers the ideal respite from your desert travels. Walk toward the thickets of rushes and look for ibex tracks, made with pointed hoofs that enable these agile creatures to climb sheer rock faces. It's not easy to spot an ibex—their coats have striped markings that resemble the rock's strata. Rock pigeons, sooty falcons, and Egyptian vultures (black-and-white feathers, bright yellow beak, and long, pinkish legs) nest in the natural holes in the soft rock and in cliff ledges.

The big surprise at Ein Avdat is the Ein Marif pools of ice-cold, spring-fed water, complete with a splashing waterfall. To reach this cool oasis, shaded by the surrounding cliffs, walk carefully along the spring and across the dam toward the waterfall. Swimming and drinking the water are not allowed (you'll not be *sorely* tempted, though—the water is swarming with tadpoles), but enjoying the sight and sound of water in the arid Negev certainly is. The trail leads through stands of Euphrates poplars, and by caves inhabited by monks during Byzantine days, and then continues up the cliff side (using ladders and stone steps), but you can't follow it unless your party has two cars and leaves one at the destination. The easier and more common option is to walk along the streambed from the lower entrance to the Ein Marif pools at the foot of the waterfall and then return along the same path. Ask for the explanatory leaflet when you pay. Lock your car, taking valuables with you. ⊠ *Rte. 40, Avdat* ☎ *08/655–5684* ⊕ *www. parks.org.il* 🖳 *NIS 28.*

Na'ot Goat Farm

FARM/RANCH | Make sure to sample the local goat cheeses that have become cult favorites around the country. At this farm, Gadi and Lea Nachimov craft soft and hard cheeses, yogurt, and other products from a herd of 150 goats who clamber over their land. Sign up for 45-minute tours of the facility. ⊠ *Rte. 40, Mashabbe Sade* ⊕ *www.naotfarm.co.il* 🖳 *NIS 22.*

🍴 Restaurants

Kornmehl Goat Cheese Farm

$$ | **ISRAELI** | After you watch the adorable goats on the farm, sample the superb (and often quite pungent) cheeses at this charming restaurant. Perched on a beautiful desert hillside, the wooden restaurant offers indoor or outdoor seating and a menu that includes goat-cheese pizza, bruschetta, and calzones—there's even a tender goat-cheese cheesecake lavished in fruit sauce. **Known for:** rustic setting; high quality handcrafted cheeses; inventive menu options. $ *Average main: NIS 51* ✉ *Rte. 40, Mashabbe Sade* ⊕ *www.kornmehl.co.il* ☉ *Closed Mon.*

Pola's Café

$ | CAFÉ | This café and gift shop is a pleasant, clean place for a break before or after a tour of the Ben-Gurion Desert Home complex. It's convenient for coffee and pastries or a soft drink and a slice of pizza. **Known for:** convenience; pastries; often hosts local vendors. $ *Average main: NIS 35* ✉ *Ben-Gurion Desert Home Complex, Sde Boker* ☎ *08/656–0479.*

☕ Coffee and Quick Bites

Menta

$ | CAFÉ | Just off Route 40 at a gas station, south of the entrance to Ben-Gurion's Desert Home in Kibbutz Sde Boker, is a small café called Menta. It's conveniently open around the clock and offers tasty cappuccino, espresso, muffins, and sandwiches. **Known for:** pitstop on the way; fresh pastries with your coffee; stretch your legs. $ *Average main: NIS 20* ✉ *Rte. 40, Sde Boker* ☎ *08/657–9938* ▭ *No credit cards.*

🛏 Hotels

Carmey Avdat Farm

$$ | B&B/INN | These six cabins are designed for anyone craving an authentic Negev experience. **Pros:** unique experience; quiet setting; private feel. **Cons:** two-night minimum stay on weekends and holidays; paths to rooms could be better lit; no nightlife. $ *Rooms from: $220* ✉ *Rte. 40, south of Tziporim Junction, Midreshet Ben Gurion* ☎ *08/653–5177* ⊕ *www.carmeyavdat.com* ➟ *6 rooms* ❑ *Free Breakfast.*

Beersheva

Although Beersheva has often been overlooked by visitors, in recent years Israel's fourth-largest city (population 205,000) has managed to raise its profile by introducing or renewing public spaces, museums, and attractions and encouraging investment in infrastructure and the arts. Beersheva houses a major university, named after David Ben-Gurion, a sparkling performance hall, and a regional hospital serving Bedouin shepherds, kibbutzniks, and other desert dwellers.

The Old City, anchored by Smilansky Street and dotted with handsome stone structures and the lion's share of Beersheva's better restaurants, continues to evolve. The Ottomans had controlled the Beersheva area since the 16th century, but it wasn't until the early 1900s that they quarried stone from a nearby canyon to build the distinctive buildings that form the nucleus of the Old City. These historic buildings are gradually being repurposed as restaurant, gallery, and nightlife spaces, pumping fresh, much-needed energy into the area. The famed Bedouin market, once a source of some of Israel's best ethnic handicrafts, has been hit hard by modern times (especially the competition of cheap imports from the Far East), and isn't what it used to be. But it now has a permanent location, and you might still find something authentic. Most intriguing are the Bedouin themselves, sitting cross-legged with their goods spread out on the ground.

Tel Beersheva, just outside the city, is the site of biblical Beersheva and could easily be the site of Abraham's well. An expression from the book of Judges, "from Dan to Beersheva," once indicated the northern and southern boundaries of the land of Israel. UNESCO declared Tel Beersheva a World Heritage Site in 2005.

Today this unpretentious city serves as a northern jumping-off point for Negev travel—main roads branch out from here; buses serving the Negev depart from here; and trains from the north end up in Beersheva. If your schedule permits, stay overnight in Beersheva for a glimpse of a growing desert city with an interesting citizenry and a gentrifying population.

GETTING HERE AND AROUND
Beersheva is 113 km (70 miles) southeast of Tel Aviv and 120 km (75 miles) southwest of Jerusalem. The drive from either Tel Aviv or Jerusalem takes about 1½ hours. To get to Beersheva from Tel Aviv, take Route 2 (the Ayalon Highway) south until the turnoff marked "Beersheva–Ashdod." After this you'll be on Route 41, which runs into Route 40 after 6 km (4 miles). Continue on Route 40 to Beersheva; there are clear signs all the way.

To reach Beersheva from Jerusalem, take Route 1 west to the Route 6 turnoff. Follow Route 6 southbound; after Kiryat Gat it turns into Route 40 south, which leads into Beersheva.

The Israel Air Force Museum is 7 km (4½ miles) west of Beersheva on a narrow desert road that pushes past the city's drab outskirts.

◉ Sights

Israel Air Force Museum
MILITARY SITE | FAMILY | For plane lovers, this is a field of dreams. Housed on the Hatzerim Air Force Base, this open-air museum has more than a hundred airplanes and helicopters parked in rows. The fighter, transport, and training (plus a few enemy) aircraft tell the story of Israel's aeronautic history, from the Messerschmitt—obtained in 1948 from Czechoslovakia, and one of four such planes to help halt the Egyptian advance in the War of Independence—to the Kfir, the first fighter plane built in Israel. Young Air Force personnel lead tours (included in the price) that take about 90 minutes and include a movie shown in an air-conditioned Boeing 707 used in the 1977 rescue of Israeli passengers held hostage in a hijacked Air France plane in Entebbe, Uganda. Another attention-getting display is a shiny, black Supermarine Spitfire with a red lightning bolt on its side, flown by Ezer Weizmann, the IAF's first pilot and later president of Israel. The museum also houses an antiaircraft exhibit and a rare collection of historical and instructive films. Tours are available in English, French, and Russian. ✉ *Hatzerim Air Force Base, Rte. 2357* ✛ *7 km (4½ miles) west of Beersheva on a desert road* ☎ *08/990–6888* 💲 *NIS 30* ☾ *Closed Fri. and Sat.*

★ Museum of Bedouin Culture
MUSEUM | FAMILY | This one-of-a-kind museum focuses on the Bedouin people, who have long populated the Negev and whose traditional way of life is changing in the 21st century. The study center (marked with an orange sign) is named for the late Colonel Joe Alon, a pilot who took a great interest in this area and its people. Housed in a circular building designed by Israeli architect Tzvi Lissar, the museum tells the story of the Bedouin's rapid change from a nomadic to a modern lifestyle through tableaux of life-size mannequins. They are grouped by subject: wool spinning and carpet weaving, bread baking, wedding finery (including a camel elaborately decorated for the event), donkeys and camels at work, and toys made from found objects such as pieces of wire and wood. The tools and artifacts—most handmade, and many already out of use in modern Bedouin life—form an outstanding collection. Another wing of the museum explores the Bar Kochba revolt of the Jews against Romans in the 2nd century AD. Admission includes a cup of thick coffee in a real Bedouin tent, where the sheikh performs the coffee ceremony over an open fire. ✉ *Rte. 325* ✛ *Next to*

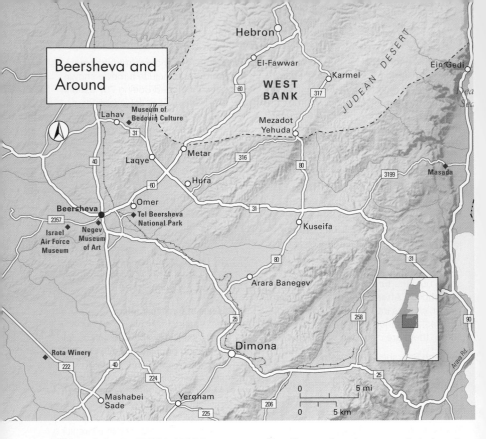

Kibbutz Lahav ☎ *08/991–3322* ⊕ *www. joealon.org.il* 🎟 *NIS 25* ⊘ *Closed Fri. and Sat.*

Negev Museum of Art

MUSEUM | This handsomely renovated structure—once home to a Ottoman Mandate–era governor—houses a rotating exhibit of classic and modern Israeli art. Located in Beersheva's Old City, the museum displays art from national and international artists. During the summer it hosts live concerts in its sculpture-laden courtyard. In the same area is the Museum of Islamic and Near Eastern Cultures, in a 1906 mosque. ⊠ *60 HaAtzma'ut St.* ☎ *08/699–3535* ⊕ *www.negev-museum.org.il* 🎟 *Free* ⊘ *Closed Sun.*

Rota Winery

WINERY/DISTILLERY | One of the pioneers of the Negev wine-making scene, Erez Rota lives and works on a secluded ranch that's worth a stop. Since Rota began to make wines over a decade ago, his vintages have gained recognition for their complexity and sophistication—and they're all made in an incredibly rustic, mildly hippie-dippie setting. Call in advance to arrange a tasting (try the Yael, a nuanced Cabernet-Merlot fusion) accompanied by a selection of local Negev cheeses. An accomplished artist, Rota has created a free-form sculpture garden around the property, punctuated by his metal creations. He'll tour you around the property and tell you the story of how a Tel Aviv artist became one of the Negev's winemakers to watch. ⊠ *Rte. 222, Revivim* ✛ *40 km (25 miles) south of Beersheva* ☎ *054/496–8703* ⊕ *www.rotawinery.co.il* 🎟 *NIS 35 with minimum group of 10* ⊘ *Closed Fri. and Sat.*

Tel Beersheva National Park
ARCHAEOLOGICAL SITE | Traditionally associated with the biblical patriarch Abraham, Tel Beersheva is a mound of ruins created by nine successive settlements. Archaeologists have uncovered two-thirds of a city dating from the early Israelite period (10th century BC). Because of the site's significance for the study of biblical-period urban planning, UNESCO has recognized Tel Beersheva as a World Heritage Site. At the top of the tell is the only planned Israelite city uncovered in its entirety; the site includes sophisticated waterworks and a fascinating reconstructed horned altar. A fine example of a circular layout typical of the Iron Age, the city is believed to have been destroyed around 706 BC by Sennacherib of Assyria. At the northeastern end, outside the 3,000-year-old city gate, is a huge well (the deepest in Israel), which apparently once reached groundwater 90 feet below. This ancient well served the city from its earliest times, and scholars speculate that it could be the well that is documented in the Bible as Abraham's Well (Genesis 21:22–32). The observation tower is rather ugly, but it does afford beautiful views. ✉ *Off Rte. 60* ☎ *08/646-7286* 🌐 *www.parks.org.il* 🎫 *NIS 28.*

🍴 Restaurants

★ Cafe Lola
$ | MODERN ISRAELI | This whimsically decorated café in the Old City is a breath of fresh air in every respect. Eclectic, funky decor with wooden tables and splashes of color are the backdrop for a menu serving tasty dishes at breakfast, lunch, and dinner. **Known for:** lovely outdoor café; Israeli breakfast, haloumi salad at lunch, tapas at dinner; interesting neighborhood. [$] *Average main: NIS 45* ✉ *13 Smilansky St., Old City* ☎ *08/628-8937.*

Kapara
$$ | EUROPEAN | On a tree-lined stretch with old-fashioned streetlights, this is the perfect place for a laid-back meal. Located in a renovated Ottoman-era building in Beersheva's Old City, the rustic restaurant and tapas bar has high ceilings, arabesque tilework, an inner courtyard for alfresco dining, and an atmospheric balcony. **Known for:** shakshuka; creative tapas-style dishes; fun atmosphere. [$] *Average main: NIS 60* ✉ *23 Smilansky St., Old City* ☎ *08/665-4854* 🌐 *www.rol.co.il/sites/kapara.*

Saba Gepetto
$ | MODERN ISRAELI | If you need a break from traditional Middle Eastern food, head to Grandpa Gepetto, tucked into an alleyway off a small shopping mall. The dark, cavelike room features gourmet sandwiches served on fresh focaccia bread, with fillings ranging from stir-fried goose breast to chicken breast with pesto. **Known for:** sandwiches; being a hidden gem; beer on tap at the unmarked bar. [$] *Average main: NIS 45* ✉ *109 Rasco St., near Leonardo Hotel Negev* ☎ *08/627-2829* 🕒 *No lunch Sat.*

Yakota
$$$$ | MOROCCAN | On a sleepy corner in the Old City sits this classic Moroccan restaurant, run by the same family since the 1960s. Though Yakota—decorated sumptuously in Moroccan textiles, hammered metal, and ornate tilework—often seems empty, the food is exceedingly fresh, creative, and delicious. Just say the word and chef Bebe will order for you, starting with a course of delicious house-made salads featuring seasonal ingredients like fennel, dates, and candied oranges, followed by simmering *tagines* of tender meat and vegetables (even local specialties like *kmehin*, a tuberlike desert root). **Known for:** neighborhood institution; Moroccan tagine and mint tea; Bebe, the host with the most. [$] *Average main: NIS 120* ✉ *27 Mordai Hagettaíot St., Old City* ☎ *08/623-2689* 🕒 *No lunch Sat.*

Hotels

Leonardo Hotel Negev

$$ | **HOTEL** | The biggest and most well-known chain hotel in town, the Leonardo is a business-oriented hotel that has some amenities with appeal for many travelers. **Pros:** decent rates for what you get; well-equipped gym; convenient city-center location. **Cons:** listless service; Internet costs extra; frill-free, thrill-free. [$] *Rooms from: $245* ✉ *4 Henrietta Szold St., near City Hall* ☎ *08/640–5444* 🌐 *www.leonardo-hotels.com* 🛏 *300 rooms* 🍴 *Free Breakfast.*

Trumpeldor Ba'Atika

$ | **B&B/INN** | The Ottoman Empire's expansion plans in the early 20th century envisaged Beersheva as a regional capital, and the Turks built handsome stone structures in what is now the Old City; this special boutique lodging occupies what could have been an office complex surrounding a central courtyard. **Pros:** historic and charming setting; close to restaurants; Ottoman-era carved wooden furniture in guest room. **Cons:** can be loud, so ask for room far from main street; some challenges for those with mobility issues; mattresses may need updating. [$] *Rooms from: $140* ✉ *21 Trumpeldor St., Old City* ☎ *54/761–1933 for reservations, ask for Oshrat* 🛏 *4 rooms* 🍴 *No meals.*

Nightlife

BARS

Atica Beersheva Bar

BARS/PUBS | You can choose from 15 beers on tap and five local brews in bottles at this bar in a finely preserved former home with much of its original tilework. This laid-back spot attracts a more mature crowd in the evening. Old-timers may remember a similarly named Attica, but don't be put off; this is a different place. ✉ *28 Histadrut St., corner of Smilansky St., Old City* ☎ *54/558–7202.*

Coca Bar

BARS/PUBS | Join Ben-Gurion University students for a beer, pizza, and burgers at Coca Bar, behind the student dorms. ✉ *50 Arlozorov St.* ☎ *050/773–7772.*

MUSIC

Israel Sinfonietta Beer Sheva

MUSIC | This well-regarded symphony orchestra was founded in 1973 as an outlet for immigrant musicians; the concert season includes classical music from around the world as well as some family-focused performances. The orchestra's concert hall seats more than 400 and has state-of-the-art acoustics. ✉ *Center for Performing Arts, 41 Rager Blvd.* ☎ *08/626–6422.*

Shopping

Bedouin Market

OUTDOOR/FLEA/GREEN MARKETS | Although the Negev is still home to the Bedouin people, many of today's Bedouin women are less inclined to stay home weaving. But if you have an eagle eye and a saint's patience, Beersheva's Bedouin Market might yield goods made by elder generations. The market starts at daybreak each Thursday and lasts until early afternoon, but it's best to get there early. Walk to the back, passing coffee and tea sellers. For sale, if you can find them, are embroidered dresses, woven camel bags, bales of wool, coin headbands (used as dowry gifts), and *finjans* (Bedouin coffeepots). ✉ *Derech Eilat and Derech Hevron Sts.*

Chapter 10

SIDE TRIP TO PETRA

Updated by
Sunny Fitzgerald

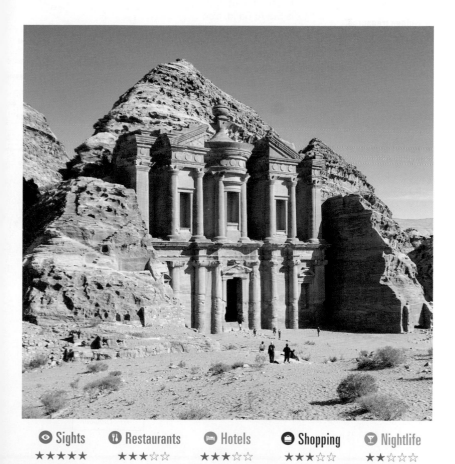

👁 Sights	🍴 Restaurants	🛏 Hotels	💼 Shopping	🍸 Nightlife
★★★★★	★★★☆☆	★★★☆☆	★★★☆☆	★★☆☆☆

WELCOME TO SIDE TRIP TO PETRA

TOP REASONS TO GO

★ **Choose your own adventure.** With so much to see, Petra offers many choices: walk the Siq to the Treasury, hike hundreds of stairs to the Monastery, or take a guided trek to Jabal Haroun.

★ **Hidden treasures.** Archaeologists believe that much of the Lost City of Petra is yet to be uncovered. If you enlist the help of a knowledgeable guide, you'll discover hidden paths, caves, and carvings with stories of their own.

★ **Lunar landscapes.** Trekking the ancient pink-and orange-hue trails of Petra gives you the feeling that you've been transported to another planet.

★ **The Siq.** Learn about the historical significance of Petra as you stroll between the dramatic canyon walls, pausing to study carvings, sculptures, and water channels along the way.

★ **The Treasury.** Stand in awe of the impressive architecture of the iconic facade that attracts nearly one million visitors each year.

The Red Rose City of Petra lies in the southern region of Jordan, about two hours from the Red Sea city of Aqaba. Visitors to Petra will find accommodations, shops, and eateries in the neighboring village of Wadi Musa. Fifteen minutes away is Siq Al Barid, also known as Little Petra, a smaller archaeological site with carvings and views to enjoy. Nearby in the Al Beidha area, tented Bedouin camps offer a rustic cultural experience.

1 Petra. Ancient architecture, rugged mountains, and an air of mystery beckon hikers and history buffs to Petra, a UNESCO World Heritage Site and New Wonder of the World.

2 Wadi Musa. The closest town to Petra is likely where you will stay and eat during your trip.

KEY

········ Footpath

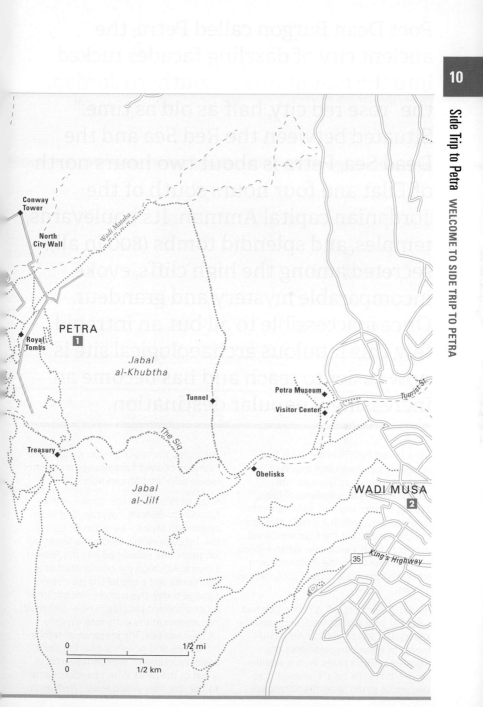

Poet Dean Burgon called Petra, the ancient city of dazzling facades tucked into the mountains of southern Jordan, the "rose red city, half as old as time." Situated between the Red Sea and the Dead Sea, Petra is about two hours north of Eilat and four hours south of the Jordanian capital Amman. Its boulevards, temples, and splendid tombs (800 in all), secreted among the high cliffs, evoke incomparable mystery and grandeur. Once inaccessible to all but an intrepid few, this fabulous archaeological site is now easier to reach and has become an increasingly popular destination.

Petra (called Rekem in the Dead Sea Scrolls) lies in the biblical region of Edom. According to Genesis, the Edomites were descendants of Esau, Jacob's brother and rival. Edom's fertile land was a magnet that desert dwellers couldn't ignore, but the Edomites were careful to keep it exclusive. When Moses led the Israelites to the Promised Land and asked to pass through Edom, he was denied.

By the 7th century BC, a new group had swept in from Arabia: the Nabateans. The spectacular tombs and carved monuments of these intrepid traders draw travelers to Petra today. With a wealthy empire that at its height reached from Damascus to the Sinai, the Nabateans controlled the region's trade routes, their caravans bearing frankincense and myrrh, Indian silks, and African ivory.

Most of Petra's famous tombs—which fuse Greco-Roman, Egyptian, and Mesopotamian styles—were carved during the 1st century AD, before the Nabatean kingdom was subsumed into the Roman Empire. Although the combination of a necropolis and a capital city may seem strange today, this custom was common among ancient peoples, who established cemeteries at the entrances to many of their capitals. The presence of tombs of the rich and powerful near the city's major monuments was perhaps part of a cult of the dead. When travelers came to the city, they would leave offerings at the tombs to honor the success of their journeys.

Gradually, Christianity replaced the old religion, and churches were built in Petra. Around the same time, the rise of sea trade began to precipitate Petra's decline, as ancient traders learned that they could use prevailing winds to hasten ships across the sea. Some Arabian goods began to come to Egypt and its Mediterranean ports via the Red Sea. It didn't help that a series of earthquakes left a ruinous mark on the city.

After Petra's takeover by the Muslims in 633, alliances and crossroads changed and the rest of the world lost interest in the area. The Crusaders built fortifications among the ruins in the 11th century, but after their 1189 surrender to the Muslim warrior Saladin, the city sank into oblivion. Only the local Bedouin knew its treasures. It wasn't until 1812 that Swiss explorer Johann Ludwig Burckhardt rediscovered Petra, providing the Western world with its first contemporary description of the marvels of this Nabatean caravan-city. It's now justly recognized as a UNESCO World Heritage Site.

Planning

When to Go

Summer (May through mid-September) temperatures can creep above 100 degrees, while winter (mid-November through mid-March) weather tends to be quite cold and wet. Winter rains bring a risk of flash floods and occasionally even snow that can lead to a temporary closure of roads and the Petra archeological site. Spring (mid-March and April) and autumn (September and October) offer ideal weather for trekking with more moderate temperatures and less rain. In all seasons, sturdy shoes are essential for negotiating the rocky, uneven terrain.

If traveling during the Muslim holy month of Ramadan (the ninth month of the Islamic calendar—the start and end date shift each year, so do check the Ramadan dates for the year you are traveling), be aware that some services and sites throughout the country may operate at reduced hours; however, the Petra archaeological site remains open for regular business. As things in Jordan can change quickly, always consult with the tourist office or tour operator for the most up-to-date information before you travel.

Planning Your Time

An overnight trip to Petra is optimal. Be prepared for a lot of walking: it's about 4 km (2½ miles) from the entrance to the Basin restaurant. To reach the Monastery, you'll need to continue on for another 1.6 km (1 mile) up the infamous 800 plus steps just beyond the Basin.

After you pass the ticket checkpoint at the entrance to the Petra site you'll begin the nearly 2 km (1 mile) walk through the winding Siq to the Treasury, Petra's most iconic facade. Continue along what was once the Rose City's main street, lined with monuments from Petra's glory days. From here, you can choose your own adventure, depending on your pace and which sights you want to see. Hike up to the High Place of Sacrifice for a spectacular view or take the stairs past the tombs and trek up to the Treasury lookout. Or, opt to stroll along the flat trail of the colonnaded street to the Basin for lunch before making the climb up the steps to the Monastery. Enjoy a Turkish coffee or *shai bil nana* (tea with mint) at the top. The route back down is the same, but the sun striking the rocks at different angles reveals new dimensions of the site's beauty; note that the walk back through the Siq is slightly uphill. You will see camels, donkeys, and horse-drawn carriages transporting visitors in,

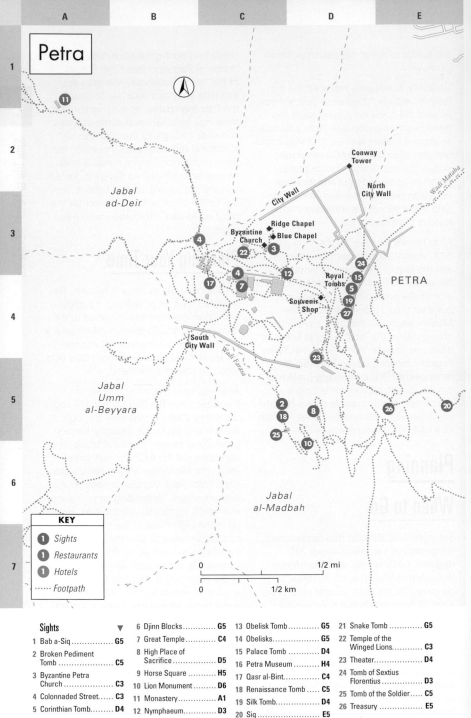

Petra

KEY

- ● Sights
- ● Restaurants
- ● Hotels
- ⋯⋯ Footpath

0   1/2 mi

0   1/2 km

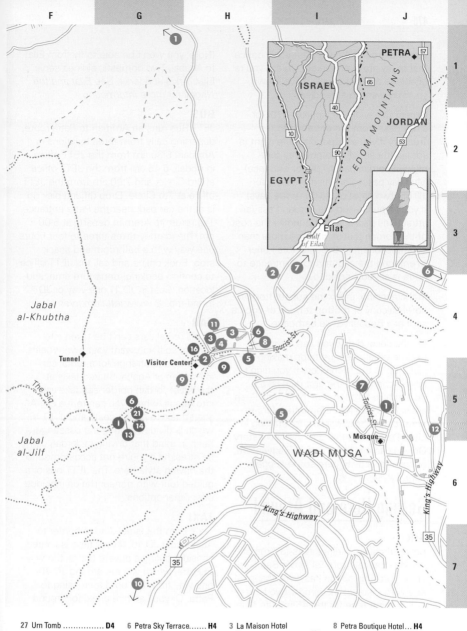

out, and around the site, but you'll notice that many are overworked. Unless you're unable to make the walk on your own, you may want to steer clear.

Expect to pay JD 50 (approx. $70) for a day pass from the entrance to the Treasury if you are spending the night in Jordan (those who do not stay overnight in Jordan pay JD 90 for entrance). Multiday passes are also available for JD 55 (two days) or JD 60 (three days). If you've purchased the Jordan Pass (an attractions package that bundles the cost of the Jordan tourist visa and more than 40 attractions for 70–80 JD total) prior to entering the country, your entrance to Petra is already included.

In the evening, enjoy the sunset from a hotel balcony or rooftop terrace or book a spot at a Bedouin-style barbecue.

On the second day, you can return to explore other sites, perhaps making the climb up to the Monastery if you didn't have a chance on the first day; take a guided hike through the "backdoor"—an alternative way for intrepid travelers to enter the archaeological site, starting in Little Petra and arriving at the Monastery. Or, you can arrange a cultural, adventure, or spiritual activity (*see some suggestions below*).

Getting Here and Around

AIR

Royal Jordanian Airlines flies to Amman, Jordan's capital, from Tel Aviv's Ben Gurion Airport. This option has limited appeal, as you must be at the airport two hours before flight time for the 45-minute flight, then drive three hours from Amman to Petra.

Many people traveling in Israel use Eilat, the resort city at the southern tip of Israel, as a base for visiting Petra, which is about two hours away by car. There are frequent, one-hour flights to Eilat's Ramon Airport from Tel Aviv and Haifa.

(Note: you won't be able to fly from Eilat to Aqaba.) Two domestic airlines serve Eilat: Arkia and Israir. *See Eilat and the Negev for more information.*

BUS

JETT Bus runs an Amman to Petra route, departing daily from three locations in Amman: 6:30 am from the JETT office in Abdali, 6:45 am from the JETT office at 3rd Circle, and 7:00 am from the JETT office at 7th Circle. Drop off and pick up is at the car park near the Petra entrance. The return to Amman departs at 5:00 pm. The journey takes three to four hours one way with a bathroom and snack stop. Book online and call the JETT office to confirm booking, departure time, and location. Cost is JD 11 one-way or JD 17 round-trip. ⊕ *www.jett.com.jo/en*

CAR

Israeli rental cars can't be taken into Jordan, so if you want your own wheels you'll have to arrange for a rental car in Amman or Aqaba. Shared taxis at the Israel-Jordan border can take you into Aqaba, where you can rent a car. A shared taxi to Aqaba costs about JD 10, which is divided among the passengers. Keep in mind that driving in Jordan can be stressful if you're not accustomed to the driving style here. The JETT bus or a guided tour with transportation included offer other options.

TAXI

Taxis from the Israel-Jordan border to Aqaba cost JD 10. If your time is limited, consider taking a private taxi all the way to Petra, which will run around JD 70 one way from the border crossing to Petra. Or you can hire a taxi for around JD 10 from the border to Aqaba center and then hire a separate one from there to Petra for about 30 JD. Be prepared to negotiate.

Crossing the Border

The closest border crossing to Petra is just north of Eilat at what's called the Arava Crossing. Cross the border early in the morning to avoid waiting in line behind large tour groups and so that you can arrive in Petra before noon. It's about a two-hour ride from Aqaba to Petra. Expect to pay NIS 173 to exit Israel. When crossing back from Jordan to Israel, bring JD 10 for the Jordanian exit tax.

Americans need a visa to enter Jordan. Individuals can no longer purchase visas on the spot at the Arava Crossing, so you will need to arrange your visa ahead of time. If you are traveling on a group tour, ask your tour operator; they generally arrange the visas for their guests.

Two other border crossings might be convenient if you don't plan to visit Eilat, but both of these options require you to arrange for a visa in advance. The Allenby Bridge Crossing (known in Jordan as the King Hussein Crossing) is about 45 minutes from Jerusalem. From the border it's a nearly four-hour drive to Petra. The northern Beit She'an Crossing (also called the Jordan River or Sheikh Hussein Border Crossing in Jordan) is approximately 40 minutes from Tiberias. Once you're across it's a five-hour drive to Petra. Note that you cannot get a visa at these borders, so arrange one in advance at the Jordanian consulate. The exit tax to leave from these crossings is NIS 176.

Regardless of where or how you cross the border, the rules can change, often without any advance notice. For this reason, we strongly advise anyone planning a trip to Petra to use a knowledgeable and experienced tour operator.

Money Matters

The Jordanian unit of currency is the dinar, abbreviated JD. The exchange rate at this writing was approximately JD 0.71 to the U.S. dollar. You can change money at the Mövenpick Resort Petra, next to the entrance to Petra or simply withdraw dinar from an ATM. Local and international ATM fees vary by bank. Be sure to consult your bank prior to traveling and let them know your travel dates and countries to prevent any issues.

What It Costs			
$	$$	$$$	$$$$
RESTAURANTS			
Under JD 9	JD 9–JD 12	JD 13–JD 17	over JD 17
HOTELS			
Under $75	$75–$129	$130–$200	over $200

Health and Safety

In general, Jordan is a safe, friendly, and welcoming country. However, there are a few important things to bear in mind.

It is not uncommon for locals to invite visitors into their home for tea or a meal; Jordanians are known for their hospitality and breaking bread with locals can be a very meaningful and memorable experience. Most invitations are well-intentioned but there have been reports of some solo travelers caught in uncomfortable or dangerous situations after accepting invitations to caves or tents in the Petra area. So it's best to either meet up in a public place (rather than a private home, tent, or cave) or go in a group. You can also arrange to have a meal with a local family through a company like Engaging Cultures (see Tours below).

The weather can impact your health and outdoor activities. Be sure to bring sun protection, stay hydrated, and always check the weather forecast. If you are traveling to Petra in the summer, try to plan your outdoor activities for the early morning and late afternoon so you can skip the midday sun. If you'll be visiting in the wintertime, don't forget warm layers and rain gear, and keep in mind that heavy rains can cause flash flooding. The Petra site may close for inclement weather.

Drivers in Jordan do not always follow the rules, so if you are planning to rent a car and drive here, be prepared to be alert and drive aggressively. Some stretches of highway are very dark and there is not always cell phone service, so try to drive during daylight hours, if possible. And if you are spending a full day hiking in Petra, you will likely be tired so it's best to spend the night rather than make the drive when you're exhausted.

Like most touristic places around the world, Petra has plenty of folks hawking souvenirs and offering to play guide. There's no harm in haggling for a fair price for goods and you can feel free to say "no, thank you" or just simply say "*shukran*," meaning "thanks," if you're not interested. But hiring an unlicensed guide in Petra can be a risk. Guides in Petra are required to be licensed, so if you follow an unlicensed one, you may be scolded by the authorities or led astray by the guide, who might be more interested in leading you to a café or shop they own rather than whatever trail or site you are seeking. Avoid the hassle and book a guide through a trusted operator instead (*see Tours below*).

Tours

A number of operators run tours to Petra that you can reserve in advance from Eilat. They're an excellent option to see the highlights without worrying about what can be rather complex logistics.

Arkia
GUIDED TOURS | Several times a week, Arkia Israeli Airlines offers one-day guided tours to Petra from Tel Aviv via Eilat. They pick you up directly from Eilat's Ramon Airport early in the morning,

drive you to the Arava Border crossing where you'll meet a Jordanian guide, and then transfer in an air-conditioned bus to Petra. As this tour brings you back to Eilat the same evening, you'll only have a few hours in the Petra archaeological site and will spend a fair amount of time in transit, so it's best suited to travelers looking for a quick—rather than in-depth or overnight—visit. ☎ *03/690–2255* ⊕ *www.arkia.com/petra-day-tours-c182* ✉ *From $409 per person for 1-day tour to Petra from Tel Aviv (via Ramon Airport), including lunch, guides, transport, and round-trip Tel Aviv to Eilat.*

Desert Eco Tours
GUIDED TOURS | With consistently friendly and professional service, Desert Eco Tours remains a popular choice for Petra tours. In addition to Petra, the company can arrange other tours in Jordan, as well as more extensive travel to Egypt and the Sinai Desert. ✉ *Eilat* ☎ *08/632–6477* ⊕ *www.desertecotours.com* ✉ *From $249 for 1-day tour to Petra from Eilat.*

Discover Jordan
ADVENTURE TOURS | This Jordan-based operator organizes private small group trips throughout Jordan, including border crossings from Israel and Palestine. They recommend at least a three-day stay in Jordan for your Petra side trip, in order to include an overnight adventure in Wadi Rum or a relaxing spa day at the Dead Sea. Tours are tailored to guest interests and budget, so rates vary. ✉ *Khalda Cir.* ☎ *06/541–1550* ⊕ *discoverjordan.com* ✉ *Four-day tours with premium accommodations, private driver, entrance and visa fees, most meals, camel ride, and a jeep tour in Wadi Rum from $995 per person for 2 people.*

★ Engaging Cultures
GUIDED TOURS | FAMILY | This Jordan-based operator is ideal for travelers seeking historic and religious context, cultural experiences, and knowledgeable, personable guides to complement their adventure activities in Petra. Engaging

Cultures handles border crossings and arranges private tours throughout Israel, Palestine, and Jordan (as well as Tunisia and Egypt for those seeking multicountry programs). They can include activities such as homestay experiences, cooking lessons with locals, and hiking with Bedouin, in addition to classic tour options, active adventures, and the full range of accommodation options, from goat hair Bedouin tents located in the Petra Reserve to five-star hotels found just outside the Petra entrance. ⊠ *Senad Complex #9 2nd fl., 8th Cir.* ☏ *07/9511–8105* ⊕ *engagingcultures.com* ✉ *Two-day private tours including accommodations, guides, driver, border assistance, and most meals from $400 per person for 2 people.*

★ Experience Jordan

ADVENTURE TOURS | This fun and friendly Jordan-based tour company is highly experienced in designing and leading customized adventure tours. They have the local knowledge and contacts to make your visit safe, enjoyable, and unforgettable. Experience Jordan can prepare all pieces of your Petra side trip—from navigating border crossings and pairing you with an expert guide to hiking the "backdoor" and arranging special private events and add-on activities such as cycling and canyoning. They operate throughout Jordan so if you're planning to stay a few days, don't hesitate to inquire about other sites and cities as well. Tours are customized so rates vary depending on your specific needs. ⊠ *44 Ali Nasouh Al Taher St.* ☏ *06/582–4159* ⊕ *www.experiencejordan.com* ✉ *Tours from $200 per person per day (based on a group of 2–4 people) including border assistance, private transportation, guides, accommodations, activities, and some meals.*

In2Jordan

ADVENTURE TOURS | **FAMILY** | With team members based in Petra, Aqaba, and Amman, In2Jordan can help you no matter where you cross into Jordan.

They arrange fully customized one-day and multiday tours that include border assistance, private driver, and expert guides with optional add-ons for activities such as canyoning, bird-watching, yoga and meditation, visiting religious sites, and diving. All tours are customized, so exact cost depends on your needs and interests. ⊠ *21 Mahmoud Musa Obeidat St.* ☏ *07/911–02629* ⊕ *in2jordan.com* ✉ *A day trip from Eilat to Petra, including transfers and a guide in Petra for a classic tour, starts at $195 per person for 2 people.*

Intrepid Travel

ADVENTURE TOURS | Although Intrepid does not run Petra-only tours, they do include Petra on their Jordan itineraries. If you are looking to join an organized group trip to Jordan with a reliable, certified B Corp company and a set departure date, this is an excellent option. You can choose a program that includes Israel or plan to join the group in Jordan after you cross the border. Intrepid offers special interest trips to Jordan, such as their "Jordan: Real Food Adventure" culinary-focused tour or their female-only "Jordan: Women's Expedition" that brings female travelers up close and personal with local women and the culture in a way that is simply not possible otherwise. ☏ *800/970–7299* ⊕ *www.intrepidtravel.com/us/jordan.*

Visitor Information

Petra Visitor Center

The visitor center, next to the main entrance, is stocked with maps and brochures and can help you arrange local guides for a tour to the Treasury for a fee of JD 50 (add JD 20 for a tour all the way to the basin or an additional JD 50 if you want to go up the Monastery). If the weather is particularly hot, or if you're simply interested in the long and fascinating history of the place, check out the museumlike exhibition. It's a compact overview of Petra and will not take more than 15 minutes, but the site miniatures are helpful in getting your bearings before your visit. Or, if you've got the time, head over to the newly built Petra Museum for a more interactive experience. A one-day pass to Petra costs JD 50, a two-day pass JD 55, and three days JD 60. If you don't stay overnight in Jordan, a one-day pass costs JD 90. ⊠ *Tourism St., Wadi Musa* ☎ *03/215–7093* ⊕ *international. visitjordan.com.*

◉ Sights

Bab a-Siq

ARCHAEOLOGICAL SITE | Just after passing through the ticket kiosk at the main entrance to the Petra site, you'll walk a dirt footpath nearing the main Siq, the canyon-lined passageway leading to Petra's main sights. Here you'll find massive rounded rocks and orange-color cliffs flanking the trail—this area is Bab a-Siq, meaning "Gate to the Siq." From here you can spot the remains of a Nabatean tunnel, built to divert flood waters from coursing through the narrow cleft and flooding the city. A dam, constructed for the same purpose in the second half of the 1st century AD, was restored by the Jordanians in the 1960s and again in 1991. As you approach Bab a-Siq, you can also see three large, carved "djinn (spirit) blocks," so named as it's believed they were designed as a place for spirits to stand watch over the water supply. Nearby you'll find the Obelisk Tomb. Many visitors may skip over Bab a-Siq in their excitement to reach the Treasury, but if you have the chance, you can spend some time exploring the caves, tombs, and shrines around here. ⊠ *Petra* ⊕ *visitpetra.jo.*

Broken Pediment Tomb

ARCHAEOLOGICAL SITE | One of a series of facades carved into the western face of Jabal Madhbah, or the Mount of the Altar, this tomb is characterized by the broken-off gable of its roof, supported by four pilasters topped with Nabatean capitals. ⊠ *Petra* ⊕ *visitpetra.jo.*

Byzantine Petra Church

ARCHAEOLOGICAL SITE | Decorated with mosaics in the characteristic style of the period, this church (rediscovered by the American archaeologist Kenneth Russell, and excavated in the 1990s) appears to have been burned soon after its construction in the 5th century, and perhaps further destroyed by earthquakes in the 6th century. The remains, including a spectacular mosaic floor, have undergone only partial conservation; papyrus scrolls were found here. ⊠ *Petra* ⊕ *visitpetra.jo.*

Colonnaded Street

ARCHAEOLOGICAL SITE | This column-lined street was the city's major thoroughfare, suitable for both commerce and grand ceremonial processions. After the Roman annexation of the Nabatean kingdom, it's believed that the street was restored. In AD 363, an earthquake devastated Petra and the surrounding region. Little is left of the markets, and the street never returned to its former glory but marble paving stones, partial columns, and the remains of statues of deities, including those depicting Hermes (messenger of the gods) and Tyche (goddess of fortune), still stand as a reminder of the ancient past. ⊠ *Petra* ⊕ *visitpetra.jo.*

Corinthian Tomb

ARCHAEOLOGICAL SITE | Set among some of Petra's finest tombs is one named for its large number of Corinthian capitals—now badly deteriorated—that once decorated its facade. The water basins on the front are believed to have been used for cleansing rituals. ⊠ *Petra* ⊕ *visitpetra.jo.*

Djinn Blocks

ARCHAEOLOGICAL SITE | The function of these three large, square-carved blocks of stone near Bab a-Siq is unclear; they may have been connected to Nabatean worship, perhaps believed by Nabateans to be carved by spirits or to act as a resting place for spirits watching

Did You Know?

The Siq, a canyon-lined passageway, opens suddenly to reveal the Khazneh (Treasury), Petra's most famous monument. Sadly, it does not contain the Holy Grail.

Did You Know?

The Monastery, one of Petra's most famous facades, is well worth the long walk from the ancient city's other monuments.

over waterways. Another possibility is that the blocks may have been funerary monuments. There are other Djinn blocks inside the site—25 in total—but these three are most often seen due to their . proximity to the entrance and main trail. In Arabic, *djinn* refers to malevolent spirits, a common theme in Arab folklore. You may recognize the term by the anglicized name, "genies." ⊠ *Petra* ⊕ *visitpetra.jo.*

Great Temple

ARCHAEOLOGICAL SITE | No one can say for sure which god was worshipped at this temple, or whether it was the seat of the city's government. But the dozens of columns that adorn its courtyards, beautifully restored by archaeologists from Brown University, attest to its ancient grandeur. The building even boasted its own theater, which some scholars believe may have been a meeting hall for Petra's rulers. ⊠ *Petra* ⊕ *visitpetra.jo.*

High Place of Sacrifice

ARCHAEOLOGICAL SITE | An ancient flight of stairs cut into the rock—and restored by the Jordanian Department of Antiquities—leads to the summit of Jabal Madhbah, or the Mount of the Altar. Two large obelisks (on your left as you near the top) indicate you're on the right path. Its peak, besides offering spectacular views of Petra below, contains a rectangular court surrounded on three sides by benches in the triclinium style of the Roman dining room. The details of what happened here are uncertain. In the center of the court is a raised block of stone, upon which the priest may have stood. To the west are two altars accessed by steps, as well as a channel into which it's believed the blood of sacrificial animals drained. ⊠ *Petra* ⊕ *visitpetra.jo.*

Horse Square

PLAZA | The Petra admission price includes a horseback ride along the first 800 yards of the path to the Siq, but keep in mind that some horses are overworked and, if you are able, it may be best to skip this activity and walk the trail at your own pace. If you do take the horseback ride, offer a tip of about JD 3–JD 5. ⊠ *Petra* ⊕ *visitpetra.jo.*

Lion Monument

ARCHAEOLOGICAL SITE | Surface runoff fed this rock-carved fountain along the path to the High Place of Sacrifice via a channel leading to the lion's mouth. ⊠ *Petra* ⊕ *visitpetra.jo.*

★ Monastery *(Al-Deir)*

ARCHAEOLOGICAL SITE | Although the Treasury may receive more visitors due to its proximity to the Siq, this remarkable structure carved into a mountaintop cliff is equally impressive—or perhaps even more so. It takes 1½ to 2 hours to reach by a winding 4 km (2 miles) trail with more than 800 steps at the end, so plan your time accordingly.

To reach it, trek the Main Trail through the Siq to the Treasury, passing the Roman Theater and Royal Tombs en route, then wind your way to the Basin through the Colonnaded Street. Just beyond the Basin, you'll climb the more than 800 steps to reach the Monastery. It may be less decorated than the Treasury, but at about 165 feet wide and 150 feet tall, it's larger, and there's much more space up here to spread out.

Cross etchings inside likely earned this monument its nickname. An inscription discovered nearby refers to "the symposium of Obodas, the God." From this inscription, archaeologists deduced that the Monastery was built around the 1st century BC as a meeting place for worshippers of Obodas. Either tomb or temple, it holds a spacious chamber cut deep into the mountainside, and offers sweeping views of the adjacent gorges. ⊠ *Petra* ⊕ *visitpetra.jo.*

Nymphaeum

ARCHAEOLOGICAL SITE | Dedicated to water nymphs, this public fountain was fed by waters flowing from the Siq and used for both refreshment and worship. Very little of the original is left today, so it may be a challenge to find. Look for the oversize pistachio tree near the start of the Colonnaded Street, and you'll see the foundation of the fountain there. ⊠ *Petra* ⊕ *visitpetra.jo.*

Obelisks

ARCHAEOLOGICAL SITE | On a terrace on the path to the High Place of Sacrifice stand two 23-foot (7 meters) obelisks hewed from the bedrock, examples of a common method of representing deities in the ancient Near East. Some scholars believe them to be representations of Dushara and al-Uzza; others believe they are simply the remains of quarries. Either way, their creation appears to have required removal of the mountain around them to leave the towering rock sculptures standing—an impressive feat indeed. ⊠ *Petra* ⊕ *visitpetra.jo.*

Obelisk Tomb

ARCHAEOLOGICAL SITE | This top level of a two-story tomb is named for the four obelisk-shape pillars that decorate its facade. They are likely *nefeshes*, which would have been used as funerary markers. The obelisks and the relief of a robed man at the center are believed to represent the people buried there. The lower level, the Triclinium Tomb, was so named because three walls of the empty room are lined with *triclinia*, a Latin term for a dining table with three benches or sofas. Sacred memorial feasts to honor the dead were held here. ⊠ *Petra* ⊕ *visitpetra.jo.*

Palace Tomb

ARCHAEOLOGICAL SITE | This tomb is named for its Roman palacelike appearance. It's the largest of the Royal Tombs and one of the few in Petra not carved entirely out of solid rock; some of the 18 columns on the third story where built rather than carved. Many of the tomb's constructed segments have fallen away, so it's hard to ascertain its original dimensions. ⊠ *Petra* ⊕ *visitpetra.jo.*

Petra Museum

MUSEUM | Opened in 2019, the Petra Museum provides an informative introduction to the history of the archaeological site and the Nabataens who inhabited it. Whereas many museums in Jordan have relied on foreign scholars, the displays here were curated and designed primarily by Jordanians. The interior space is large, accessible, and lined with ancient artifacts and interactive touchscreens. It's also climate-controlled, offering reprieve from the desert sun. Do a loop around the "Active Nabataens" hall to learn more about Nabataen life through the sculptures and multimedia devices. If you're interested in Bedouin traditions and the timeline of the rediscovery of Petra and the archaeological projects that followed, be sure to visit the "Revitilization of Petra" room. The museum is located next to the bus parking lot, just outside the Petra entrance, so if you arrive in Wadi Musa in the afternoon and won't have a chance to enter the Petra archaeological site until the following morning, you can get acquainted with the region's history and whet your appetite for your Petra adventure here. ⊠ *Tourism St., Wadi Musa* ⊕ *Next to main bus parking lot.*

Qasr al-Bint

ARCHAEOLOGICAL SITE | Located on the left side of the western end of the Colonnaded Street, Qasr al-Bint is shrouded in mystery and lore. The structure's full name, Qasr al-Bint Far'un, translates as the "Palace of the Daughter of Pharaoh" and is based on a legend that the pharaoh's daughter promised she would marry the man who could channel water to the city where she lived. When she had to choose between two winners, she asked each how he had managed his appointed task. The one whose answer she preferred won her hand. Another legend says that the pharaoh of the Exodus tired of pursuing Israelites and settled here. The structure was once the most important temple in Petra, believed to have been built in the 1st century BC. As is the case with the Temple of the Winged Lions, the identity of the deities worshipped here isn't known for certain, but Roman inscriptions indicate that one of them may be al-Uzza, one of the most significant Nabatean deities. The bits of paint and stucco that remain suggest it was once plastered and painted in bright colors. ⊠ *Petra* ⊕ *visitpetra.jo.*

Renaissance Tomb

ARCHAEOLOGICAL SITE | This tomb gets its name from its resemblance to Italian architecture, seen in the urn atop the archivolt. It also resembles another tomb, the Tomb of Sextius Florentinus, in the main part of the city. They may have been built around the same time during the 2nd century AD. ⊠ *Petra* ⊕ *visitpetra.jo.*

Silk Tomb

ARCHAEOLOGICAL SITE | The striations of natural color in the Silk Tomb's facade make it one of Petra's finest (and certainly one of the easiest to spot). The ribbons of rock flow across the facade like a multicolored silk scarf blowing in the wind. ⊠ *Petra* ⊕ *visitpetra.jo.*

Siq

ARCHAEOLOGICAL SITE | The main entrance to Petra, in ancient times as well as today, winds through the Siq (meaning "cleft"), a long, narrow canyon between towering walls of astonishing red, beige, orange, and purple-hue stone. Water channels and bands of Nabatean paving stones are still visible along the way. Votive niches, some of which contain inscriptions dating from the 2nd and 3rd centuries AD, show that this road served as much as a ceremonial path as a passageway. Your first glimpse of the magnificent Treasury, after you've walked 1.2 km (0.75 miles) or so through the Siq, will take your breath away. Film buffs may recall Harrison Ford galloping through this area in *Indiana Jones and the Last Crusade.* ⊠ *Petra* ⊕ *visitpetra.jo.*

Snake Tomb

ARCHAEOLOGICAL SITE | No outward decoration marks this tomb, but 12 burial niches are carved into the floor inside. The name comes from a rough wall relief that shows two snakes attacking a four-legged creature, which may be symbolic of grave guards. Notice also the horse relief above it, which appears to be carrying a *baetyl*, a type of sacred stone or idol. ⊠ *Petra* ⊕ *visitpetra.jo.*

Temple of the Winged Lions

ARCHAEOLOGICAL SITE | This impressive building overlooking the Colonnaded Street takes its name from the sculptures that serve as capitals for its columns. The identity of the deity (or deities) worshipped within is unknown, but an inscribed plaque with a female face suggests that it may have been al-Uzza, one of the most significant Nabatean deities, while votive figurines indicate it could be Isis, Egyptian goddess of the heavens and patroness of fertility. An inscription dates the construction of the temple to around AD 27, during the reign of Aretas IV ⊠ *Petra* ⊕ *visitpetra.jo.*

Theater

ARCHAEOLOGICAL SITE | This semicircular amphitheater is believed to have been built by Nabateans before the Romans entered the city, and then renovated by the Romans after annexation. The seating area was cut from rock while the stage in front was constructed. It seems the Nabateans had no qualms about building a theater in a cemetery; their stonemasons destroyed some of the existing tombs (the remains of which you can see at the back of the theater) to do so. The capacity of the theater has been estimated at 4,000. You cannot enter the auditorium area but it's still worth a look when you pass by on the main trail. ⊠ *Petra* ⊕ *visitpetra.jo.*

Tomb of Sextius Florentinus

ARCHAEOLOGICAL SITE | This is one of the few Petra monuments that can be dated with certainty; the name of this Roman governor of Arabia who died in office in AD 128 appears in the Latin inscription over the tomb's doorway. Take a look inside to find eight graves carved into the rock. ✉ *Petra* 🌐 *visitpetra.jo.*

Tomb of the Soldier

ARCHAEOLOGICAL SITE | The headless figure in the niche of this unusual tomb's facade is dressed in typical Roman military garb, while the friezes and floral capitals appear more typical of Nabatean architecture before the Roman annexation. Directly opposite the Roman Soldier's Tomb is a triclinium; it's possible that the rubble in between was once a colonnaded courtyard connecting the two edifices. ✉ *Petra* 🌐 *visitpetra.jo.*

★ **Treasury** (*Al-Khazneh*)

ARCHAEOLOGICAL SITE | The Siq opens suddenly onto Petra's most famous monument, known locally as Al-Khazneh. This 130-foot-tall structure displays a splendid frontage graced by a number of mythological figures adopted by the Nabateans from Greek and Roman worship. Castor and Pollux (who after their deaths became the two brightest stars in the constellation Gemini), Amazons, eagles, and other creatures march across the Khazneh's rosy facade. Between the columns of the *tholos* (the rounded section above the tympanum) are the remains of a female deity holding a cornucopia; she is believed to be al-Uzza, the patroness of Petra and the Nabatean version of Aphrodite, goddess of love.

The full Arabic name for this monument is Al-Khazneh Far'un, or "Pharaoh's Treasury." It was assumed by archaeologists to be a temple, royal tomb, or simply a site for storage. Legends of treasures have drawn grave robbers to this place for centuries. The urn carved at the top of the tholos was thought to be the hiding place for the hoard. The Bedouin have been taking potshots at it for generations in the hopes of dislodging its contents, a practice whose results are still visible. ✉ *Petra* 🌐 *visitpetra.jo.*

Urn Tomb (*The Royal Tomb of Malchus*)

ARCHAEOLOGICAL SITE | Named for the vaselike decoration at the top of its pediment, this royal tomb is supported by a series of vaults at its lower level, dubbed *al makhamah* (the law court) by the locals for some long-lost reason; the upper level was called *a-sijn* (the prison). Although originally carved around AD 70, according to an inscription within, it may have been turned into a church around AD 446. ✉ *Petra* 🌐 *visitpetra.jo.*

🍴 Restaurants

Finding a quality meal in Wadi Musa—the town closest to the antiquities site of Petra—can be a challenge. There are dozens of restaurants but only a handful that serve up true Jordanian hospitality and fresh, flavorful food at fair prices. Beware of fake online reviews—if something sounds too good to be true, it probably is. When you arrive at a restaurant, ask to see a menu and then spend a moment observing the staff and guests, as well as the dishes that come out of the kitchen before you commit. Don't be put off by the simplistic style of the eateries; some of the best meals are found at such unostentatious restaurants. And if it's a more elevated experience you're looking for, you can find that, too, at rooftop restaurants and four- and five-star establishments.

Al-Arabi Restaurant

$ | **MIDDLE EASTERN** | This simple but bright eatery is a reliable place for a quick, inexpensive lunch. You can expect a substantial meal with options that include hummus, shawarma, and a tasty mixed grill (the house specialty). **Known for:** shawarma; mixed grill; quick and friendly service. [$] *Average main: JD7* ✉ *Main St., Wadi Musa* ⊕ *Near Martyr Cir.* ☎ *03/215–7661.*

Al Iwan Restaurant

$$$ | **MEDITERRANEAN** | This tastefully decorated and candlelit restaurant is the place

Bedouin Camps and Barbecues 🍴

Looking for an enriching cultural experience in Petra? Consider staying overnight in a Bedouin camp, where you'll stay in traditional-style tents that allow you to experience Petra in a more rustic (but generally comfortable) atmosphere. Whether or not you opt to overnight in a Bedouin camp, you can still get a taste of the local culture and cuisine at a Bedouin barbecue. Several centrally located Wadi Musa hotels such as Mövenpick and Petra Moon host rooftop barbeques in the summer. The Petra Marriott Hotel also hosts summertime barbecues on their lawn, in a Bedouin tent overlooking the Sharah Mountains. And Bedouin camps like Ammarin invite visitors to experience traditional dishes prepared by locals (and sometimes cooked in the ground, as is the case with *zarb*, made of rice, chicken or lamb, and vegetables) before gathering around the campfire to enjoy stories, music, and that famous sweet tea with mint.

for a romantic dinner or extra special celebration. Jordanian and Mediterranean fare, including seared tuna and other seafood, is on the menu, and alcohol is available. Reservations are recommended and this restaurant is open only in the winter, so do call ahead. **Known for:** fresh seafood; elegant and intimate setting; open only in winter. $ *Average main: JD15* ✉ *Mövenpick Resort Petra, Tourism St., Wadi Musa* ☎ *07/982–00253* 🌐 *www.movenpick.com* 🕒 *Closed spring, summer, and fall.*

Al Multaqa Lounge

$$ | EUROPEAN | If you've had your fill of casual falafel and are searching for a more stylish (but not stuffy) setting to try Arabic cuisine, Al Multaqa Lounge is the answer. You can order traditional Arabic dishes such as *mansaf* or international favorites like steak, seafood, pizzas, and pastas in the brightly lit, artfully decorated atrium. **Known for:** daily chocolate hour at 4 pm; accommodating; inviting open space design. $ *Average main: JD12* ✉ *Mövenpick Resort Petra, Tourism St., Wadi Musa* ☎ *07/982–00253* 🌐 *www.movenpick.com.*

The Basin

$$$ | MIDDLE EASTERN | FAMILY | Located inside the archaeological site at the end of the Colonnaded Street, this restaurant serves a hearty buffet lunch with a variety of offerings. Run by Petra Guest House Hotel, the dining room caters to large tour groups and is ready for a crowd. **Known for:** leafy outdoor terrace; fresh food, AC and restrooms; cool lemon mint beverage. $ *Average main: JD17* ✉ *Petra* ☎ *07/972–03384* 🌐 *www.guesthouse-petra.com/dining.htm.*

★ Petra Kitchen

$$$$ | MIDDLE EASTERN | FAMILY | If you're looking for an interactive experience, Petra Kitchen's cooking class is an enticing choice. Meet other travelers and learn from local chefs as you chop, slice, and cook traditional Jordanian dishes like *maqluba*, a layered meat-and-rice dish, and *fattoush*, an Arabic salad topped with fried bread. **Known for:** cooking lessons with local chefs; fresh, locally sourced ingredients; fun for families. $ *Average main: JD35* ✉ *Petra Boutique Hotel, Main St., Wadi Musa* ☎ *03/215–5900* 🌐 *www.petrakitchen.com.*

Petra Sky Terrace

$$$ | MIDDLE EASTERN | One of the area's newest restaurants serves up fresh, Jordanian flavors and sweeping views over the village and mountains. Snack on meze (start with some fresh hummus and *galayet bandora*) and cool off with an icy lemon mint drink or warm up with a Bedouin-style tea while you watch the sunset. **Known for:** sunset views; open-air terrace year round (weather permitting); fresh ingredients. [$] *Average main: JD15* ✉ *Petra Boutique Hotel, Tourism St., Wadi Musa.*

★ Reem Beladi Restaurant

$ | **MIDDLE EASTERN** | This cozy and casual space serves authentic and delicious local dishes, like *shish taouk* and *mansaf*, at a fair price. It can get busy at dinnertime, so try to dine here earlier in the day if your schedule allows. **Known for:** barbecue chicken; shish taouk; friendly service. [$] *Average main: JD7* ✉ *Tourism St., Wadi Musa* ☎ *07/773–12455.*

Hotels

Petra has a variety of lodging options, from Bedouin tents and B&Bs to five-star resorts. And, as the number of construction sites sprinkled around the town indicates, many more hotels are on the way to accommodate the increasing number of visitors. Hotels closest to the site obviously provide the most convenient access to Petra and save you taxi fare, but a number of good hotels are a short car drive away, with some on the ridge above Wadi Musa. The Old Village Resort is about a 10-minute drive from the site, but its uniquely authentic flavor is worth the ride.

Keep in mind that star rankings and luxury designations in Petra hotels are not always on par with international expectations. This is not an intentionally deceptive practice, just a difference in standards. For example, a hotel with a four-star ranking in Petra might be classified as three-star in the U.S.

It's also worth nothing that there may be discrepancies between what you see on the Internet and what you find in reality. For example, a three-star hotel in Petra may advertise "luxury" accommodations, but when you arrive, you may find basic rooms. They may be clean and comfortable, but certainly not luxury. There's also a growing number of properties and restaurants posting fake reviews on sites like TripAdvisor to increase their ranking, so if you are relying on reviews, be sure to search for reviews written by active accounts (travelers that regularly post reviews) rather than trusting the one-offs.

★ Ammarin Bedouin Camp

$ | **B&B/INN** | Owned and run by the local Ammarin tribe, this camp offers the chance to spend a night under the stars in a Bedouin-style goat hair tent. **Pros:** Bedouin camping experience; home-cooked meals; 10-minute walk to Little Petra archaeological site. **Cons:** shared bathrooms with hot water available at set times; 15-minute drive to Petra entrance; tents can be cold in winter, hot in summer. [$] *Rooms from: US$39* ✉ *Tourism St.* ✥ *Al Baidha (Little Petra)* ☎ *07/997–55551* 🌐 *www.ammarinbedouincamp.com* 🛏 *34 tents* 🍴 *No meals.*

B&B Petra Fig Tree Villa

$ | **B&B/INN** | **FAMILY** | This clean and comfortable four-bedroom villa sits above the main tourist area of Wadi Musa, in a quiet residential area with views of the Petra mountains. **Pros:** chair massages available on-site; sunset views and serene setting; garden with fresh herbs, fruits, and flowers. **Cons:** 35-minute walk or 5-minute car ride from Petra entrance; cats on-site; not suitable for people with animal allergies; shared bathrooms. [$] *Rooms from: US$56* ✉ *Wadi Musa* ☎ *07/790–92675* 🌐 *www.petrafigtreevilla.com* 🛏 *4 rooms* 🍴 *Free Breakfast.*

La Maison Hotel Petra

$$ | **HOTEL** | This hotel's fair rates and close proximity to the Petra entrance make it a favorite among budget-conscious travelers. **Pros:** five-minute walk to Petra entrance; omelet and pancake station at breakfast; rooftop terrace. **Cons:** small rooms; poorly designed bathrooms; no alcohol available. [$] *Rooms from: US$80*

✉ *Tourism St., Wadi Musa* ✣ *Behind Mövenpick Hotel* ☎ *03/215–6401* 🌐 *www.lamaisonhotel.com.jo* 🛏 *76 rooms* 🍴 *Free Breakfast.*

★ Mövenpick Resort Petra

$$$$ | HOTEL | FAMILY | Just steps from the entrance to Petra, this Swiss-run hotel blends Middle Eastern decor and five-star amenities. **Pros:** rooftop garden, pool, spa, and seven on-site dining options; closest five-star resort to the Petra entrance; excellent breakfast buffet. **Cons:** extreme rate fluctuations; often hosts large groups. [$] *Rooms from: US$300* ✉ *Tourism St., Wadi Musa* ☎ *03/215–7111* 🌐 *www.movenpick.com* 🛏 *183 rooms* 🍴 *No meals.*

Nomads Hotel Petra

$ | HOTEL | With fair rates and a friendly vibe, this hotel with minimalist design and local art offers both dorms and private rooms that are a good choice for travelers on a budget. **Pros:** bright, clean, and welcoming; good value; removed from the noise and crowds but still walking distance to Petra. **Cons:** 15 minutes walking to Petra entrance; dorm rooms do not include breakfast; instant coffee. [$] *Rooms from: US$14* ✉ *Tourism St., Wadi Musa* ✣ *Next to Civil Defense station* ☎ *03/215–7171* 🌐 *nomadsjo.com* 🛏 *48 rooms* 🍴 *No meals.*

★ The Old Village Resort

$$$ | RESORT | FAMILY | True to its name, this five-star resort was once a village settled by the Nawafleh tribe; now, the interior has been renovated while preserving much of the stone structure, including lovely archways in the bedrooms. **Pros:** unique sense of place; exceptional food and amenities; Jordanian history and hospitality. **Cons:** 10-minute drive to Petra entrance (not walking distance); no alcohol served (though guests are allowed to bring their own). [$] *Rooms from: US$183* ✉ *Kings Hwy., Wadi Musa* ☎ *03/215–9555* 🌐 *www.oldvillageresort.com* 🛏 *157 rooms* 🍴 *Free Breakfast.*

Petra Bed and Breakfast

$ | B&B/INN | An adorable house on the hill in the Garara area of Wadi Musa, this bed-and-breakfast is a cozy, affordable spot for travelers to call home-away-from-home. **Pros:** sunset views from rooftop terrace; horses on-site; guided rides can be booked; friendly hosts. **Cons:** not suited for travelers with animal allergies (cat and horses on-site); five-minute car ride to Petra entrance; minimum two-night stay required. [$] *Rooms from: US$42* ✉ *Wadi Musa* ✣ *Garara area* ☎ *07/772–20825* 🌐 *www.petrabedandbreakfast.com* 🛏 *4 rooms* 🍴 *Free Breakfast.*

Petra Boutique Hotel

$$$$ | HOTEL | Modern technology meets classic Jordanian hospitality in this conveniently located "smart" hotel. **Pros:** centrally located, within walking distance to Petra; thoughtful tech touches; year-round rooftop dining. **Cons:** small rooms (except for suites). [$] *Rooms from: US$212* ✉ *Tourism St., Wadi Musa* ☎ *03/215–4444* 🛏 *24 rooms* 🍴 *Free Breakfast.*

Petra Guest House Hotel

$$ | HOTEL | This recently renovated hotel with clean, serviceable rooms is the closest lodging to the Petra entrance. **Pros:** prime location; dining and alcohol options on-site; recently renovated. **Cons:** overpriced; decor lacks a sense of place; its four-star rating may not be four-star to all. [$] *Rooms from: US$127* ✉ *Tourism St., Wadi Musa* ☎ *03/215–6266* 🌐 *www.guesthouse-petra.com* 🛏 *72 rooms* 🍴 *Free Breakfast.*

★ Petra Marriott Hotel

$$$$ | HOTEL | FAMILY | This five-star hotel sits on the ridge above Petra, so most rooms offer spectacular views of the Sharah Mountains. **Pros:** sunset views; removed from the crowds and noise of Wadi Musa center; accommodating chefs. **Cons:** 5- to 10-minute drive to Petra entrance; does not change Israeli currency; spa could use an update. [$] *Rooms from: US$335* ✉ *Queen Rania Al Abdallah*

St., Wadi Musa ☎ *03/215–6407* 🌐 *www.marriott.com* 🛏 *100 rooms* 🍴 *Free Breakfast.*

★ Petra Moon Hotel

$$ | HOTEL | FAMILY | This perfectly located hotel, just 350 meters (1,200 feet) from the main entrance to Petra, is a popular choice and has a rooftop swimming pool. **Pros:** convenient location; flavorful, fresh meals; rooftop Bedouin BBQ during summer months. **Cons:** undergoing renovations so some rooms are updated while others are outdated. [$] *Rooms from: US$120* ✉ *Tourism St., Wadi Musa* ☎ *03/215–6220* 🌐 *www.petramoonhotel.com* 🛏 *93 rooms* 🍴 *Free Breakfast.*

Petra Princes Hotel

$ | HOTEL | FAMILY | A family-run hotel on the hill above Wadi Musa center, Petra Princes Hotel (also called Petra Guests Hotel and Petra Smile Hotel) offers clean rooms, a tasty local breakfast with beautiful views, and options for shared accommodations suited to budget and solo travelers as well as private and family rooms with en suite bathrooms. **Pros:** shared and private room options; affordable rate; family-run. **Cons:** decor lacks a sense of place; not walking distance to Petra entrance; hotel's several names can be confusing. [$] *Rooms from: US$49* ✉ *Kings Hwy., Wadi Musa* ☎ *07/700–55442* 🛏 *24 rooms* 🍴 *Free Breakfast.*

🍸 Nightlife

Because the majority of the residents here are Muslim, alcohol is not served in most establishments. Nightlife, in the Western sense of bars and clubs, is nearly nonexistent. Jordanian and international brews, wines, and spirits are typically found in four- and five-star hotels, and some hotels do allow you to bring your own alcohol to enjoy on your balcony. Be sure to ask ahead; some properties such as the Bedouin camps do not allow any alcohol on-site.

Al Maqa'ad Bar

BARS/PUBS | The tasteful decor of this bar sets a casual yet chic tone, inviting exhausted hikers and suited-up business people alike to take a seat. Natural light streams in through hand-carved wooden screens, glinting off golden accents on the walls and ceiling, a reminder of the region's rich history. Al Maqa'ad serves international and local beverages (try a local Saint George wine or a lemon mint slushie) and snacks such as sandwiches, salads, and soups as well as main dishes that include *mansaf*, *maqluba*, shrimp, and steak. Those in need of a caffeine kick, you're in luck: this is also one of the only places in Petra you'll find coffee and espresso drinks. ✉ *Mövenpick Resort Petra, Tourism St., Wadi Musa* ☎ *03/215–7111* 🌐 *www.movenpick.com.*

The Cave Bar

BARS/PUBS | The proximity of the so-called oldest bar in the world to the Petra entrance makes it an easy place to land after a long day trekking the ruins of the Lost City. Kick back on Bedouin cushions on the terrace and sample shisha as well as regional and international spirits. If you are unsure what to choose, Arak, a popular anise-flavored distilled spirit that turns milky-white when water is added, is a great place to start. You can also drink and dine inside, but it may get smoky. The Cave Bar has a daily happy hour 3–4 pm (50% off drinks) and live music from 8 pm. ✉ *Tourism St.* ✥ *Next to Petra Guest House Hotel* ☎ *03/215–6266* 🌐 *www.guesthouse-petra.com.*

Petra by Night

SOUND/LIGHT SHOW | Strolling through the Siq by candlelight as shadows play on the canyon walls allows you to appreciate another side of the magnificent carved city. During this two-hour event offered on Monday, Wednesday, and Thursday starting at 8:30 pm, music is briefly played on traditional instruments such as the *rababa* and lights are projected onto the Treasury facade. The walk from the visitor center through the Siq to the Treasury is about 2.4 km (1½ mile)—downhill on the way in, uphill on the way back. Keep in mind that you won't be alone; this activity has become increasingly popular and an unlimited number of tickets are available, so it can be crowded and not as charming as it once was. There are no carriages at night and you must have a valid daylight ticket in addition to the Petra by Night ticket. Purchase your Petra by Night ticket during the day to avoid the long queues in the evening, and consider leaving the Treasury before the end of the show to allow for some quiet time in the Siq before it's flooded with folks exiting at the end of the event. ⊠ *Petra Visitor Center, Tourism St.* ☎ *03/215–7093* ⊕ *www.visitpetra.jo* 🖃 *JD 17.*

🛍 Shopping

There are ample opportunities to buy souvenirs—including the quintessential red-and-white checkered scarf called the *shemagh, keffiyeh,* or *hattah*—inside the Red Rose City as well as in the shops around Wadi Musa town. Souvenir stalls line the main trail of Petra and even the stairs leading up to the Monastery. As is the case with popular tourist sites around the world, goods may be overpriced. Go with a price in mind and have fun haggling with the local shopkeepers. Petra is a protected UNESCO World Heritage Site, so be mindful not to purchase products that appear to be made of stones or other artifacts from the site.

Katy's Shop Near the Top
GIFTS/SOUVENIRS | As you might guess from the name, Katy's Shop is near the top of the stairs leading up to the Monastery. Like many of the kiosks in Petra, you will find embroidered scarves, trinkets, and other souvenirs on display, but what makes this shop a standout is the owner, Raedh: she offers fair prices and an engaging demeanor. Haggle for the best

prices, always with a smile and a sense of humor. ⊠ *Monastery* ☎ *07/776–75005.*

Nabataean Ladies Cooperative
JEWELRY/ACCESSORIES | You'll find silver jewelry handcrafted by local women at this shop. You can also arrange jewelry-making lessons in advance (subject to availability) through B&B Petra Fig Villa. The Ladies Cooperative works to perpetuate the Nabataean jewelry-making tradition while creating economic opportunities to empower women. ⊠ *Wadi Musa* ✛ *Opposite Shaqilath Hotel* ☎ *07/724–46413* ☉ *Closed after 3 pm.*

Petra Pottery Association
CERAMICS/GLASSWARE | After you've seen the traditional clay pots in the Petra Museum, you might want to take home one of your own. The Taybeh Village Women's Society handcrafts artisan pottery pieces in the same style as the Nabataens did in AD 50. The bowls, vases, mugs, and more are sold at the Petra Pottery Association in Taybeh Village (about 20 minutes from Petra). Workshops can also be arranged in advance. ⊠ *Kings Hwy., Taybeh* ☎ *03/215–0280.*

Souk Zara
ANTIQUES/COLLECTIBLES | This boutique located in the Mövenpick Resort Petra sells antiques alongside handmade gifts such as ceramics, jewelry, and accessories. This is the flagship Souk Zara store—the other four are located in Grand Hyatt Amman Hotel, Mövenpick Resort & Spa Dead Sea Hotel, Mövenpick Resort Aqaba Hotel, and Mövenpick Resort Tala Bay Aqaba Hotel. ⊠ *Mövenpick Resort Petra, Tourism St., Wadi Musa* ☎ *06/465–5385.*

🏃 Activities

Although you can easily fill your days exploring the Petra archaeological site, there are other activities in the area that afford opportunities to connect with the land, people, and culture of this ancient place.

BIRD-WATCHING
B&B Petra Fig Tree Villa
BIRD WATCHING | FAMILY | Rise early to spot birds in the sky over Wadi Musa with B&B Petra Fig Tree Villa, who can arrange bird-watching tours with a local guide. Keep your eyes to the sky and you may see the Egyptian vulture, short-toed eagle, black kite, steppe buzzard, European bee-eater, Palestine sunbird, Sinai rosefinch, Alpine swift, and more. ⌧ Wadi Musa ✛ Garara area ☎ 07/790–92675 ⊕ www.petrafigtreevilla.com.

CAMEL TREKKING
Engaging Cultures
ADVENTURE TOURS | Engaging Cultures arranges multiple special interest tours. You can take a camel to Jabal Garoon and enjoy a picnic of Bedouin tea and *arbood* bread (baked the traditional way, in the ground) while watching the sunset over Wadi Araba. The journey is approximately four to five hours, arranged on request. The company also arranges lunches with a local family at their home in Al Beidha. As a guest, you'll have a chance to learn about the culture and cuisine while sampling a home-cooked meal. All Engaging Cultures itineraries are customized, so cost varies, depending on group size and activity preferences. ⌧ Senad Complex #9 2nd fl., 8th Cir. ☎ 07/951–18105 ⊕ engagingcultures.com.

CYCLING
Cruise along dirt roads and climb stretches of the Kings Highway when you ride the Shobak to Petra section of the **Jordan Bike Trail.** More experienced cyclists can opt for multiday trips and pedal off-road tracks and desert mudflats on a Petra to Wadi Rum tour. Several operators including **Wadi Araba Cycling, Terhaal Adventures,** and **Cycling Jordan** can assist with arranging bike rentals, guides, and support for groups. The Jordan Bike Trail website provides downloadable route maps and tips for those setting out on their own. ⊕ jordanbiketrail.com

HIKING
Avid hikers looking for a full-day adventure can leave the crowds behind and trek to Jabal Haroun where Aaron's tomb awaits. The hike is about 14 miles (22 km) round-trip from Qasr al Bint in Petra. You'll want to get an early start and pack plenty of water and snacks as the midday sun can be intense and the trip takes about five- to six hours. To arrange a guided trip to Jabal Haroun or another hike in the area, contact outfitters like TREKS (⊕ treks.jo) whose owners are fun and experienced in hiking tours, or Engaging Cultures (see listing under Camel Trekking).

HORSEBACK RIDING
Horse Riding Tours Jordan
HORSEBACK RIDING | FAMILY | Petra local Eid Alhasanat of Horse Riding Tours Jordan will lead you through the mountains near Petra for a few hours or for a full day. More experienced riders can opt for two-day excursions in Little Petra or six-day treks to Wadi Rum. Eid and his wife also own B&B Petra Fig Tree Villa; the stables are located next to the B&B. ⌧ Tourism St., Wadi Musa ✛ Next to B&B Petra Fig Tree Villa ☎ 07/772–20825 ✉ petrabedandbreakfast@gmail.com.

YOGA
★ Pink Spirit Jordan
AEROBICS/YOGA | Slow down and connect with the stillness and magic of this ancient place through a yoga and meditation session. Pink Spirit Jordan arranges private experiences on the sandstone rocks of Petra, in the wadi (valley) near your camp, or on the terrace of your hotel, for groups with a minimum of four participants. They also offer multiday retreats in Petra and Wadi Rum complete with campfires, stargazing, and "horse soul sessions," guided meditation experiences alongside horses, also known as equine therapy. Yoga mats are provided. ⌧ Petra ☎ 07/771–05647 ⊕ www.pinkspiritjordan.com.

Index

494

Photo Credits

Front Cover: Nick Brundle Photography [Description: The Red Canyon in the Eilat Mountains. It is one of Israel's most beautiful yet accessible hiking trails.]. **Back cover, from left to right:** vvvita/Shutterstock, Sean Pavone/Shutterstock, Xantana /Dreamstime. **Spine:** Cezary Wojtkowski/Shutterstock. **Interior, from left to right:** Botond Horvath/iStockphoto (1). vblinov/Shutterstock (2). **Chapter 1: Experience Israel:** john norman / Alamy (6-7). vvvita/Shutterstock (8). kavram/Shutterstock (9). Afik Gabay (9). Sivan Askayo (10). Manta ray (10). Golan Heights Winery (10). Bahá´í International Community (10). Perekotypole/Shutterstock (11). Miroslav Orinčák/iStockphoto (11). Courtesy of Yad Vashem (12). Try Media/Shutterstock (12). Roniuru/Shutterstock (12). Shuki Kook (12). silverjohn/iStockphoto (13). BobWC/ iStockphoto (14). Israel Tourism (14). Danielcgold/Dreamstime (14). Denis Kabanov/Shutterstock (14). StockStudio Aerials/Shutterstock (15). Angelina Borowska/iStockphoto (15). Alexey Stiop/Shutterstock (16). Yalla Basta, en.machne.co.il (16). Mano Grinshpan, Israel Nature and Parks Authority (16). tenkl/Shutterstock (17). Dr. Asaf Zevuloni, Israel Nature and Parks Authority (17). vvvita/Shutterstock (20). kavram/ Shutterstock (20). vvvita/Shutterstock (20). Mano Grinshpan, Israel Nature and Parks Authority (21). efesenko/iStockphoto (21). Robert Hoetink/Shutterstock (22). kaetana/Shutterstock (22). Noam Chen/Israeli Ministry of Tourism (22). ColorMaker/Shutterstock (22). Noam Chen/ Israeli Ministry of Tourism (22). Itamar Grinberg/Israeli Ministry of Tourism (23). Noam Chen/Israeli Ministry of Tourism (23). oasisisgood/ Shutterstock (23). kavram/Shutterstock (23). majeczka/Shutterstock (23). TeodoraDjordjevic/iStockphoto (24). gkrphoto/shutterstock (25). Haifa Museums P.R (26). Magic W/Shutterstock (26). Vadim Mikhailov (26). The Israel Museum, Jerusalem, by Elie Posner (27). Richie Chan/ Dreamstime (27). Lucky-photographer/Shutterstock (37). Lebrecht Music and Arts Photo Library / Alamy (38). Wikipedia.org (38). Wikipedia. org (38). Mikhail Levit/Shutterstock (39). Israel Ministry of Tourism (39). The London Art Archive / Alamy (39). Wikipedia.org (39). The Print Collector / Alamy (40). North Wind Picture Archives / Alamy (40). Israel images / Alamy (41). Wikipedia.org (41). Wikipedia.org (41). Robert Judges / Alamy (42). INTERFOTO Pressebildagentur / Alamy (42). Wikipedia.org (42). **Chapter 3: Jerusalem:** nicole_pappas, Fodors.com member (75). Rostislav Glinsky / Shutterstock (91). Chadica/Flickr (95). moris kushelevitch / Alamy (98). Israel Ministry of Tourism (102). Israel Ministry of Tourism (103). Elan Fleisher / age fotostock (103) Mikhail Levit/Shutterstock (104). Jason Moore / Alamy (104). Israel images / Alamy (104). North Wind Picture Archives / Alamy (105). Mikhail Levit/Shutterstock (106). Mikhail Levit/Shutterstock (107). Israel Ministry of Tourism (107). Israel images / Alamy (108). Mikhail Levit/Shutterstock (109). TNT Magazine / Alamy (109). wikipedia.org (109). Joel Carillet/ iStockphoto (110). mikhail/Shutterstock (111). DZarzycka/iStockphoto (111). Israel Ministry of Tourism (113). Mikhail Levit/Shutterstock (113). ARCO/J Erichsen / age fotostock (114). Joshua Haviv/iStockphoto (115). Itpow/Dreamstime (115). Terry J Alcorn/iStockphoto (116). Robin Laurance / age fotostock (117). Robert Hoetink / Alamy (123). Rostislavv/Dreamstime (129). ARCO/J Erichsen / age fotostock (130). Israel Ministry of Tourism (139). Eitan Simanor / Alamy (141). Alexeys/Dreamstime (148). **Chapter 4: Around Jerusalem and the Dead Sea With Masada and Bethlehem:** markdewd (173). Alexirina27000/Dreamstime (183). Images&Stories / Alamy (185). Yvette Cardozo/age fotostock (185). R. Matina (189). ARCO/J Erichsen (192). Israel images / Alamy (196). Gisella Caroti (197). Israel images / Alamy (198). Roger Cracknell 18/Israel / Alamy (198). Ppja (199). PhotoStock-Israel / Alamy (199). Israel images / Alamy (199). Israel images / Alamy (199). Han-an Isachar / Alamy (199). Israel images / Alamy (200). David Shankbone (200). kavram (215). Israel images / Alamy (218). Jon Arnold Images Ltd / Alamy (224). **Chapter 5: Tel Aviv:** Anna Bryukhanova (227). Arkadiy Yarmolenko/Shutterstock (230). Paul Cowan/Shutterstock (231). Andrea Skjold/Shutterstock (231). Elan Fleisher / age fotostock (232). Israel Ministry of Tourism (233). Ted Eytan/Flickr, [CC BY-SA 4.0] (241). Lucidwaters/Dreamstime.com (242). dtokar (247). Lucidwaters/Dreamstime.com (248). Itzhaki/Dreamstime.com (253). Colman Lerner Gerardo / Shutterstock (259). Alan M. Kolnik/iStockphoto (263). Israel Ministry of Tourism (264). Benjamin Balint (264). Israel images / Alamy (264). Avi Ganor (265). Avi Ganor (265). Mann Auditorium (265). Lior Alon (266). PhotoStock-Israel / Alamy (266). Eddie Gerald / Alamy (266). Israel Tourism/Flickr, [CC BY 2.0] (275). Israel Ministry of Tourism (278). LOOK Die Bildagentur der Fotografen GmbH / Alamy (280). Dnaveh/Dreamstime.com (283). Eddie Gerald / Alamy (285). Anna Bryukhanova (289). **Chapter 6: Haifa and the Northern Coast With Caesarea, Akko, and Rosh Hanikra:** Karol Kozlowski / Shutterstock (291). GeneZ (299). Rafael Ben-Ari / Alamy (305). Solovki/Dreamstime.com (318). Israel images / Alamy (322). Vitaliy Berkovych/Shutterstock (324). Eddie Gerald / Alamy (330). Rina Nagila (330-331). Golan Heights Winery (332). Eddie Gerald / Alamy (332). Bernard Edelstein (332). Sea Horse Winery (333). Clos de Gat (333). Clos de Gat (334). Carmel Winery (334). Daniel P. Acevedo/agefotostock (334). Carmel Winery (335). TK (335). Acre/Akko (341). R. Matina (345). **Chapter 7: Lower Galilee With Nazareth, Tiberias, and the Sea of Galilee:** Yoavsinai/Dreamstime (349). Jon Arnold Images Ltd / Alamy (357). Israel Ministry of Tourism (361). Alexandre Grigoriev/Shutterstock (368). itpow/istockphoto (372-373). Israel Ministry of Tourism (372). www.wga.hu (374). www.wga.hu (374). Israel Ministry of Tourism (375). Israel images / Alamy (376). Israel images / Alamy (376). Israel Ministry of Tourism (376). Tomasz Parys/Shutterstock (377). Israel images / Alamy (377). Israel Ministry of Tourism (377). Israel images / Alamy (377). paul prescott/ Shutterstock (378). Israel images / Alamy (387). Johnny Stockshooter (391). Tomasz Parys/Shutterstock (394). **Chapter 8: Upper Galilee and the Golan with Tzfat (Safed):** Israel images / Alamy (399). Rndmst/Dreamstime.com (411). Itamar Grinberg/IMOT (416). Niall Benvie / Alamy (422). Keith_Marks (428). **Chapter 9: Eilat and the Negev:** Keith_Marks (433). Elisei Shafer/Shutterstock (444). Benjamin Balint (449). Buurserstraat386/Dreamstime (454). Eddie Gerald / Alamy (458). Israel Ministry of Tourism (461). **Chapter 10: Side Trip to Petra:** Felix Lipov / Shutterstock (469). Josefuente/Dreamstime.com (481). RIEGER Bertrand (482). **About Our Writers:** All photos are courtesy of the writers.

Every effort has been made to trace the copyright holders, and we apologize in advance for any accidental errors. We would be happy to apply the corrections in the following edition of this publication.

Notes

Notes

Notes

Notes

Notes

Notes

Notes

Notes

Fodor's ESSENTIAL ISRAEL

Publisher: Stephen Horowitz, *General Manager*

Editorial: Douglas Stallings, *Editorial Director*; Jill Fergus, Jacinta O'Halloran, Amanda Sadlowski, *Senior Editors*; Kayla Becker, Alexis Kelly, Rachael Roth, *Editors*

Design: Tina Malaney, *Director of Design and Production*; Jessica Gonzalez, *Graphic Designer*; Mariana Tabares, *Design and Production Intern*

Production: Jennifer DePrima, *Editorial Production Manager*; Elyse Rozelle, *Senior Production Editor*; Monica White, *Production Editor*

Maps: Rebecca Baer, *Senior Map Editor*; David Lindroth, Mark Stroud and Henry Colomb (Moon Street Cartography), *Cartographers*

Photography: Viviane Teles, *Senior Photo Editor*; Namrata Aggarwal, Ashok Kumar, Carl Yu, *Photo Editors*; Rebecca Rimmer, *Photo Intern*

Business and Operations: Chuck Hoover, *Chief Marketing Officer*; Robert Ames, *Group General Manager*; Devin Duckworth, *Director of Print Publishing*; Victor Bernal, *Business Analyst*

Public Relations and Marketing: Joe Ewaskiw, *Senior Director Communications and Public Relations*; Esther Su, *Senior Marketing Manager*

Fodors.com: Jeremy Tarr, *Editorial Director*; Rachael Levitt, *Managing Editor*

Technology: Jon Atkinson, *Director of Technology*; Rudresh Teotia, *Lead Developer*; Jacob Ashpis, *Content Operations Manager*

Writers: Elianna Bar-El, Inbal Baum, Sunny Fitzgerald, Shari Giddens, Isabelle Kliger, Shira Rubin, Sara Toth Stub

Editor: Kayla Becker

Production Editor: Carrie Parker, Monica White

2nd Edition

ISBN 978-1-64097-270-4

ISSN 2475–1243

All details in this book are based on information supplied to us at press time. Always confirm information when it matters, especially if you're making a detour to visit a specific place. Fodor's expressly disclaims any liability, loss, or risk, personal or otherwise, that is incurred as a consequence of the use of any of the contents of this book.

SPECIAL SALES

This book is available at special discounts for bulk purchases for sales promotions or premiums. For more information, e-mail SpecialMarkets@fodors.com.

PRINTED IN CHINA

10 9 8 7 6 5 4 3 2 1

About Our Writers

Elianna Bar-El is a southern California expat who has been living in Tel Aviv for the past 10 years, where she is the editor of *Time Out Israel*. She loves to travel, read, eat, and shop (sometimes all at once). Elianna updated the Jerusalem chapter.

Inbal Baum, who updated the Upper Galilee chapter, founded Delicious Israel, the country's leading culinary tour company that reveals local and insider aspects of Israel. Passionate about lifestyle and culture, Inbal left her career as an attorney and immigrated to Israel in 2009. Based in Tel Aviv, she spends her time as a travel writer, amateur chef, and yogi. Contact Inbal at ⊕ *www.deliciousisrael.com* and inbal@deliciousisrael.com.

Sunny Fitzgerald spent the past 15 years traveling and living around the world with extended stints in Japan, Thailand, Costa Rica, Hawai`i, and, most recently, Jordan. Sunny is a Professional Member of the American Society of Journalists and Authors (ASJA) and a Media Member of the Adventure Travel Trade Association (ATTA). She has a BA from Middlebury College, an MA in cultural sustainability, and certification in sustainable tourism. In addition to *Fodor's,* her work appears in *National Geographic, The Washington Post, The New York Times,* BBC, *Forbes Travel Guide,* and elsewhere. She updated the Side Trip to Petra chapter.

Shari Giddens updated the Haifa and the Northern Coast, Lower Galilee, Eilat and the Negev, Travel Smart, and Experience Israel chapters. Contact her at shari.giddens@gmail.com.

Isabelle Kliger is a freelance travel and lifestyle writer based in Barcelona. Having grown up in Sweden, she lived in the U.K. and Ireland before moving to Spain in 2010. Isabelle loves spicy food, sunshine, and red wine, and is happiest when she's out exploring a new city. Her favorite destinations include Italy, Tel Aviv, and Southeast Asia. Isabelle updated the Tel Aviv chapter for this edition. Follow her on Instagram @ ikliger.

Shira Rubin, a Tel Aviv–based journalist, is a lover of travel and living abroad. She has called Israel home since 2010. Shira updated parts of the Experience chapter. Contact her at shirarrubin@gmail.com.

Sara Toth Stub is an American journalist living in Jerusalem. She writes about many topics, including travel, business, and archaeology. Her work has been published in *The Wall Street Journal, The New York Times, US News & World Report, The Atlantic,* and other outlets. She is a graduate of Northwestern University and the Hebrew University of Jerusalem. When not writing, she likes to run, swim, and spend time with her husband and three young children. She updated Around Jerusalem and the Dead Sea for this edition.